First Chicago Guide

A Scholl Corporate Guide® 1995-96

Major publicly held corporations and financial institutions
headquartered in Illinois

Published by:
Scholl Communications Incorporated
P.O. Box 560
Deerfield, Ilinois 60015

Telephone 708.945.1891

After January 20, 1996: 847.945.1891

Also from Scholl Corporate Guides ®

First Chicago Guide / Electronic Edition

The computer database version of the *First Chicago Guide* is available for personal computers.

ISBN: 0-912519-17-7
Library of Congress Catalog Card Number 86-640098

Printed in U.S.A.

FIRST CHICAGO
The First National Bank of Chicago

One First National Plaza
Chicago, Illinois 60670-0518

Richard L. Thomas
Chairman and Chief Executive Officer

To Our Customers and Friends:

We are pleased to sponsor this new edition of the *First Chicago Guide*, a concise reference to the major publicly held corporations and financial institutions headquartered in Illinois. We believe you will find the *Guide* a valuable source of up-to-date company profiles, financial and investment data, and personnel information.

At First Chicago, we consider Illinois a great state in which to do business. And we are not alone. Of the Fortune 1000 companies, 83 are head-quartered here, thereby ranking the state second in the nation. In all, 18,985 manufacturing businesses and 261,718 nonmanufacturing firms call Illinois their home.

Among the state's many advantages are:

- ❏ An outstanding transportation system and a location that provides easy access to one-half of all the goods and services produced nationwide—all within 500 miles of the Illinois state line.
- ❏ A superior technology resource base and programs that foster international trade.
- ❏ A well-trained work force with a diversity of skills.
- ❏ Natural, historic, educational and cultural attractions that are among the finest in the world.
- ❏ World-class financial resources.

As the largest bank holding company in Illinois, First Chicago is proud to be a major resource in meeting the financial needs of individuals, small and mid-sized businesses, and corporations. In the pages immediately following you will find a brief overview of our corporate philosophy, our key businesses, and the quality products and services we provide. We invite you to contact the officers listed for additional information on the areas of special interest to you.

Yours sincerely,

First Chicago Corporation

First Chicago Corporation, a multibank holding company, offers a broad range of banking, fiduciary, financial and other services domestically and overseas. Our principal subsidiary, The First National Bank of Chicago, was founded in 1863 and is the oldest, largest national bank still operating under its original name and charter.

The mission of First Chicago Corporation is to be a world-class financial services company with a reputation for customer excellence.

To fulfill this mission, we commit to:

❏ **Focus on our customers.**
We will anticipate and meet our customers' needs by providing quality products, technology and service.

❏ **Invest in our employees.**
We will respect and value our work force and will offer competitive opportunities for professional growth and financial reward.

❏ **Reward our shareholders.**
We will produce attractive returns on equity and long-term earnings growth based on a strong financial position and prudent risk management practices.

❏ **Support our communities.**
We will be responsible corporate citizens and participate in enriching the quality of community life.

❏ **Take personal responsibility for the success of First Chicago.**
We will each demonstrate the highest level of professionalism and integrity in all that we do.

We commit to being FIRST in all we do.

Office of the Chairman

Richard L. Thomas
Chairman, President &
Chief Executive Officer
First Chicago Corporation
Chicago, Illinois 60670-0518
(312) 732-6480

David J. Vitale
Vice Chairman &
Sr. Risk Management Officer
First Chicago Corporation
Chicago, Illinois 60670-0458
(312) 732-8913

First Card

First Chicago's credit card business, First Card, develops and markets card services to individuals nationwide using direct response, telemarketing and other techniques that do not require a local physical presence. With more than 12 million customers nationwide, First Card ranks among the industry leaders in receivables and transaction volume, and is the world's largest issuer of Gold Cards.

Visa® and MasterCard® accounts are the primary products sold by First Card. Other services include check-accessed lines of credit and certificates of deposit.

Most of First Chicago's credit card accounts are owned and administered by FCC National Bank, headquartered in Wilmington, Delaware. First Card operations centers are located in Wilmington; Elgin, Illinois; and Uniondale (Long Island), New York.

Scott P. Marks, Jr.
Executive Vice President
First Chicago Corporation
Chicago, Illinois 60670-0681
(312) 732-2014

Community Banking

Community Banking develops and markets diversified financial services to individuals and small businesses located in the Chicago metropolitan area. These services include deposits and loans, investment advisory and trust, brokerage, mutual funds, annuities and mortgage loans. Specialized financial services are offered to high net worth individuals through the Private Banking and Trust Department, and to small companies through the Business Banking Department.

Community Banking services are distributed through more than 80 branch locations and over 500 automatic teller machines (ATMs) in the Chicago area, and through Bank-by-Mail, Bank-at-Work, and telephone and computer home-banking programs. Including Chicago-area credit card customers, nearly half of Chicagoland's 2.7 million households have relationships with First Chicago.

Beginning in 1995, a new "direct banking" department, using 24-hour telephone support and nationwide debit card access to ATMs and merchants, will focus on sales and service to consumers beyond Chicagoland.

W. G. Jurgensen
Executive Vice President
First Chicago Corporation
Chicago, Illinois 60670-0560
(312) 732-8877

First Chicago Investment Management Company

Organized in early 1995 with more than $25 billion in assets under management, First Chicago Investment Management Company (FCIMCO) provides investment advisory, management and administrative services to a variety of clients, including individuals, businesses and institutions. Key products and services are retail mutual funds, personal investment advice, 401(k) plans, pension programs and institutional cash portfolios.

FCIMCO acts as investment manager for the Prairie Funds family of 14 retail mutual funds and four institutional funds. These offerings cover the full spectrum of investment needs, including domestic and international equity and bond funds and several money market mutual fund alternatives.

FCIMCO is a registered broker-dealer and a member of the National Association of Securities Dealers.

J. Stephen Baine
President
First Chicago Investment
Management Company
Chicago, Illinois 60670-0840
(312) 732-7357

Corporate and Institutional Banking

Corporate and Institutional Banking (C&IB) encompasses a broad range of commercial and investment banking products and services that First Chicago, along with key subsidiaries, provides to domestic and foreign customers. The principal focus of these activities is the delivery of operating products and financial services, including the extension of credit, to commercial, financial and governmental customers.

In corporate banking relationships, First Chicago is a leader in Chicago and the Midwest and ranks among the foremost banks nationwide. With headquarters in Chicago and offices throughout the U.S. and in selected markets overseas, C&IB serves the global financial needs of large corporations and institutions. Industries served include: light and heavy manufacturing, retailing, commodities, banking, finance, insurance, transportation, securities, real estate, mortgage banking, communications, utilities, and petroleum and mining, as well as health, education and service organizations and municipalities.

In the global financial marketplace, C&IB is responsible for First Chicago's activities in U.S. government and municipal securities, federal agency securities, money markets, corporate fixed income securities, federal agency securities, foreign exchange and the futures markets. It also provides risk insurance products, such as foreign exchange options, interest rate options, and interest rate and currency swaps.

In addition, C&IB is a leading provider of money transfer, collection, disbursement, documentary, remittance, trade finance, international securities clearing, custody, corporate trust and shareholder services to corporate customers in the United Sates and abroad.

C&IB - INTERNATIONAL

John W. Ballantine
Executive Vice President
First Chicago Corporation
Chicago, Illinois 60670-0560
(312) 732-4640

C&IB - DOMESTIC

Thomas H. Hodges
Executive Vice President
First Chicago Corporation
Chicago, Illinois 60670-0095
(312) 732-4004

First Chicago Capital Markets

First Chicago Capital Markets, Inc. (FCCM) is a wholly owned securities subsidiary of First Chicago Corporation. FCCM facilitates the marketing and delivery of the broad range of banking services First Chicago offers to large corporations, selected specialized industry groups, municipalities and not-for-profit corporations.

FCCM is a primary government bond dealer and is also active in underwriting corporate and municipal fixed income securities. Operations include large corporate and public banking, trading, sales, underwriting and research.

FCCM is a separately incorporated, registered broker-dealer and a member of the National Association of Securities Dealers.

John E. Gilchrist, Chairman
Robert J. Patterson, President
First Chicago Capital Markets, Inc.
Chicago, Illinois 60670-0826
(312) 732-4848

Middle Market Banking

Middle Market Banking is conducted primarily through First Chicago's American National Corporation (ANC) subsidiary, which offers a wide range of banking and financial products and services principally to middle market corporate customers through its 20 locations in the Chicago area and Wisconsin. ANC has the largest middle market share in Chicagoland.

Services for commercial as well as correspondent bank customers include commercial loans, demand and time deposit accounts, and cash management services. Separate divisions target small businesses, commercial real estate, associations and not-for-profits, and asset-based lending opportunities.

In addition, ANC offers a number of ancillary products and services targeted mainly to its commercial middle market customer base. These include corporate finance; international trade banking and foreign exchange; treasury and investment products; personal banking, personal trust and investment services; and corporate trust services.

Alan F. Delp
Chairman, President & Chief Executive Officer
American National Corporation
Chicago, Illinois 60690-1205
(312) 661-3566

Foreword

This is the 31st annual edition of the *Guide*, which is sponsored by First Chicago Corporation and published by Scholl Communications Incorporated.

Originally published by A.G. Becker & Co. Incorporated in 1965 as *The A.G. Becker Guide*, the book was acquired in 1984 by Scholl Communications Incorporated and has enjoyed the sponsorship of First Chicago Corporation for the past 11 years. Editorial management has been unchanged through the 31 editions.

The 1995-96 *First Chicago Guide* provides information on 279 publicly held corporations headquartered in Illinois as well as 33 of the Chicago area's largest banks and savings institutions.

These organizations were selected principally because of their size in terms of total revenues, total assets, and trading activity. The information presented is intended to be of general interest.

Directory Organization
Companies are listed in alphabetical order, with a separate listing for commercial banks and savings institutions beginning on page 283. Beginning on page 319 is a listing of companies classified according to Standard Industrial Classification (S.I.C.) business code numbers prepared by the Office of Management and Budget of the Executive Office of the President. The S.I.C. codes listed in this edition are based on the revised classification manual published in 1987.

An ordinal ranking of industrial, retail, transportation, utility, insurance and diversified financial companies with respect to total revenues and total assets begins on page 335. Bank and thrift holding companies, commercial banks and savings institutions are ranked separately. For comparative purposes, these lists include rankings from the 1994-95 edition.

Changes From Prior Year
Company changes from last year's edition are found on page 342. These include companies whose names have changed during the year as well as a summary of companies that have been added to or deleted from the book.

Statement of Financial Accounting Standards principally referred to in this edition are FAS 106 – "Employers' Accounting for Postretirement Benefits Other Than Pensions"; FAS 109 – "Accounting for Income Taxes"; and FAS 112 – "Employers' Accounting for Postemployment Benefits."

Sources of Information

The information contained in this book was obtained principally from the companies included and from annual reports, proxy statements, prospectuses and 10Ks. Unless otherwise noted, earnings per share are reported on a primary basis.

While such information has been collected from sources believed to be reliable, and due care and caution have been exercised in preparing and producing this book, its accuracy and completeness are not guaranteed, and liability cannot be assumed for correctness of the data herein.

The descriptions are not to be construed as an offer to sell or the solicitation of an offer to buy any of the securities of these companies. Because of the abbreviated nature of the data, the *Guide* is designed as a general source of reference rather than as the basis for investment decisions.

Businesses in Illinois are constantly changing. Therefore, some of the data, particularly lists of directors and officers, may have changed since compilation.

> Readers who find this publication useful may be interested in the **First Chicago Guide/Electronic Edition**, a self-contained computer database version of the book. For information about the Electronic Edition, please contact the publisher at the address or phone on the back cover of this book.

Contents

Industrial, Commercial and Financial Corporations

_____

_____

_____

_____

_____

_____

_____

_____

_____

_____

_____

_____

_____

_____

_____

_____

_____

_____

AAR CORP.

1111 Nicholas Boulevard, Elk Grove Village, Illinois 60007
Telephone: (708) 439-3939

AAR CORP. and its worldwide network of companies, located in the U.S., Europe and the Asia/Pacific, provide products and services to the aviation industry. Principal products and services include the purchase, sale and lease of turbine aircraft engines and engine parts to airlines and independent overhaul facilities; supply of aircraft aftermarket parts and equipment; and distribution of high-strength hardware. Additionally, the company's technical service capabilities include the overhaul, repair and exchange of aviation components and systems such as avionics, instrumentation, electronics, accessories, and landing gear; restoration of turbine engine components; and maintenance, modification and refurbishment of aircraft for airframe manufacturers, airlines and corporate operators. Manufacturing expertise encompasses air cargo handling equipment; air cargo pallets and containers; aerospace and aircraft structures; bonded composite panels; nuclear shielding products and floor maintenance equipment. The company also provides financial services, primarily the leasing of commercial aircraft. Incorporated in Illinois in 1955; reincorporated in Delaware in 1966.

Directors   (In addition to indicated officers)

A. Robert Abboud	Erwin E. Schulze
Howard B. Bernick	Joel D. Spungin
Edgar D. Jannotta	Lee B. Stern
Robert D. Judson	Richard D. Tabery

Officers   (Directors*)

*Ira A. Eichner, Chm. & C.E.O.
*David P. Storch, Pres. & C.O.O.
 Ann T. Baldwin, V.P.—Corp. Comm.
 Michael K. Carr, V.P.—Tax
 A. Lee Hall, V.P.—Strategic Planning
 Douglas S. Hara, V.P.—Facilities & Procurement

John C. Mache, V.P.—Mgt. Info. Systems
Howard A. Pulsifer, V.P., Gen. Coun. & Secy.
Timothy J. Romenesko, V.P., C.F.O., Cont. & Treas.
Philip C. Slapke, V.P.

Consolidated Balance Sheet   As of November 30, 1994 (000 omitted) Unaudited

Assets		Liabilities & Stockholders' Equity	
Current assets	$310,681	Current liabilities	$ 69,590
Net property, plant & equipment	55,009	Long-term debt	115,469
Other assets	47,839	Deferred items	32,520
		Other liabilities	5,370
		*Stockholders' equity	190,580
Total	$413,529	Total	$413,529

*15,916,000 shares common stock outstanding.

Consolidated Income Statement

Years Ended May 31	Thousands — — — — Net Sales	Net Income	Per Share — — — Earnings	Cash Dividends	Common Stock Price Range Fiscal Year
1994	$407,754	$ 9,494	$ .60	$ .48	17-3/8 — 12-5/8
1993	382,780	283[a]	.02[a]	.48	14-5/8 — 11
1992	422,657	10,020[b]	.63[b]	.48	16-7/8 — 10-5/8
1991	466,542	14,801[c]	.93[c]	.48	24-1/4 — 9-1/8
1990	444,875	25,655	1.60	.47	37-1/4 — 20-5/8

[a]Includes $7,200,000 of aftertax expenses primarily related to the writedown of certain inventories to reflect the impact of market conditions and a reduction in income tax expense of $1,200,000.
[b]Includes $3,800,000 ($.24 per share) of aftertax expenses related to the company's restructuring of its Oklahoma City maintenance subsidiary and a reduction of income tax expense of $700,000 ($.04 per share).
[c]Includes $2,150,000 ($.13 per share) of aftertax expenses related to restructuring of the Oklahoma City subsidiary.

Transfer Agent & Registrar: First Chicago Trust Co. of New York; The First National Bank of Chicago

Special Counsel:	Schiff, Hardin & Waite	Auditors:	KPMG Peat Marwick LLP
Investor Relations:	Ann T. Baldwin, V.P.	Traded (Symbol):	NYSE (AIR)
Human Resources:	Robert J. Naughton	Stockholders:	14,500
		Employees:	1,939
Mgt. Info. Svcs.:	John C. Mache, V.P.	Annual Meeting:	In October

Aasche Transportation Services, Inc.

10214 North Mt. Vernon Road, Shannon, Illinois 61078-9415
Telephone: (815) 864-2421

Aasche Transportation Services, Inc., through its wholly owned subsidiary, Asche Transfer, Inc., is a non-union truckload carrier that operates exclusively in the temperature-controlled segment of the transportation services industry. The company transports a variety of foods, including processed foods, frozen foods, and products which require temperature-sensitive service and "just-in-time" delivery. In September 1994, Aasche Transportation Services completed an initial public offering of 1,150,000 shares of common stock. In May 1995, the company completed the purchase of AG Carriers, Inc., a Tavares, Florida-based carrier specializing in transporting temperature-controlled foodstuffs and juice concentrates. Incorporated in Delaware in 1994.

Directors   (In addition to indicated officers)

Richard Baugh
Steven R. Green

Paul G. Taylor

Officers   (Directors*)

*Larry L. Asche, Chm. & C.O.O.
*Kevin M. Clark, Pres. & C.E.O.

*Diane L. Asche, V.P. & Secy.
Brian Gast, Treas. & C.F.O.

Consolidated Balance Sheet   As of December 31, 1994 (000 omitted)

Assets		Liabilities & Stockholders' Equity	
Current assets	$ 6,676	Current liabilities	$ 5,900
Net property, plant & equipment	18,437	Long-term debt	11,009
		Other liabilities	567
		*Stockholders' equity	7,637
Total	$25,113	Total	$25,113

*2,425,000 shares common stock outstanding.

Consolidated Income Statement

Years Ended Dec. 31	Thousands — — — —		Per Share — — — —		Common Stock Price Range[a] Calendar Year
	Revenues	Net Income	Earnings	Cash Dividends	
1994	$26,319	$698	$ .44[b]	$ .00	8-7/8 — 7-1/4
1993	19,335	332	.26[b]		
1992	16,999	488			

[a]Initial public offering in September 1994.
[b]Pro forma.

Transfer Agent & Registrar: Continental Stock Transfer & Trust Co.

General Counsel:	Sachnoff & Weaver, Ltd.	Auditors:	Ernst & Young LLP
Investor Relations:	Kevin M. Clark, Pres.	Traded (Symbol):	NASDAQ (ASHE)
		Stockholders:	975
Human Resources:	Ron Asche	Employees:	273
Mgt. Info. Svcs.:	Mike Ossi	Annual Meeting:	In July

Abbott Laboratories

100 Abbott Park Road, Abbott Park, Illinois 60064-3500
Telephone: (708) 937-6100

Abbott Laboratories' principal business is the discovery, development, manufacture, and sale of a broad and diversified line of human health care products and services. Pharmaceutical and nutritional products account for 54 percent of total sales and include a broad line of adult and pediatric pharmaceuticals, nutritionals, and vitamins. These products are sold primarily on the prescription or recommendation of physicians or other health care professionals. Hospital and laboratory products account for 46 percent of total sales and include diagnostic systems for blood banks, hospital and commercial laboratories, and alternate care and testing sites; and intravenous and irrigation fluids, and related administration equipment, drugs and drug delivery systems, anesthetics, critical care products, and other medical specialty products for hospitals, commercial laboratories, and alternate care sites. The company also develops, manufactures, and sells other lines of personal care, agricultural and chemical products, and bulk pharmaceuticals. Products are marketed in about 130 countries through affiliates and distributors. Principal domestic manufacturing facilities are located in Arizona, California, Illinois, Michigan, North Carolina, Ohio, Texas, Utah, Virginia and Puerto Rico. Incorporated in Illinois in 1900.

Directors (In addition to indicated officers)

K. Frank Austen, M.D.	David A. Jones	William D. Smithburg
H. Laurance Fuller	Boone Powell, Jr.	John R. Walter
Bernard J. Hayhoe	Addison Barry Rand	William L. Weiss
Allen F. Jacobson	W. Ann Reynolds, Ph.D.	

Officers (Directors*)

*Duane L. Burnham, Chm. & C.E.O.
*Thomas R. Hodgson, Pres. & C.O.O.
Joy A. Amundson, Sr. V.P.—Chem./Agri. Prods.
Paul N. Clark, Sr. V.P.—Pharm. Oper.
Gary P. Coughlan, Sr. V.P.—Fin. & C.F.O.
José M. de Lasa, Sr. V.P., Secy. & Gen. Coun.
John G. Kringel, Sr. V.P.—Hosp. Prods.
Thomas M. McNally, Sr. V.P.—Ross Prods.
David V. Milligan, Ph.D., Sr. V.P. & Chf. Scientific Off.
Robert L. Parkinson, Jr., Sr. V.P.—Int'l. Oper.
Ellen M. Walvoord, Sr. V.P.—Hum. Res.
Miles D. White, Sr. V.P.—Diagnostic Oper.
Catherine V. Babington, V.P.—Inv. Rel. & Pub. Aff.
Christopher B. Begley, V.P.—Hosp. Prods. Bus.
Thomas D. Brown, V.P.—Diag. Commerc. Oper.

Gary R. Byers, V.P.—Int. Audit
Kenneth W. Farmer, V.P.—M.I.S.
Thomas C. Freyman, V.P. & Treas.
David B. Goffredo, V.P.—Pharm. Prods. Mktg. & Sales
Richard A. Gonzales, V.P.—Health Syst.
Jay B. Johnston, V.P.—Diag. Assays & Oper.
James J. Koziarz, Ph.D., V.P.—Diag. Prods. R&D
John F. Lussen, V.P.—Taxes
Richard H. Morehead, V.P.—Corp. Plan. & Devel.
Theodore A. Olson, V.P. & Cont.
Andre G. Pernet, Ph.D., V.P.—Pharm. Prods. R&D
Carl A. Spalding, V.P.—Ross Pediatric Prods.
William H. Stadtlander, V.P.—Ross Med. Nut. Prods.
Daniel O. Struble, V.P.—Eng.
Josef Wendler, V.P.—Eur. Oper.
Don G. Wright, V.P.—Corp. Qual. Assur. & Reg. Affairs

Consolidated Balance Sheet As of December 31, 1994 (000 omitted)

Assets		Liabilities & Stockholders' Equity	
Current assets	$3,876,328	Current liabilities	$3,475,866
Net property, plant & equipment	3,920,850	Long-term debt	287,091
Other assets	726,546	Deferred items	55,597
		Other liabilities	655,770
		*Stockholders' equity	4,049,400
Total	$8,523,724	Total	$8,523,724

*803,279,722 shares common stock outstanding.

Consolidated Income Statement

Years Ended Dec. 31	Thousands — — — — Net Sales	Net Income	Per Share[a] — — — — Earnings	Cash Dividends	Common Stock Price Range[a] Calendar Year
1994	$9,156,009	$1,516,683	$1.87	$ .74	34 — 25-3/8
1993	8,407,843	1,399,126	1.69	.66	30-7/8 — 22-5/8
1992	7,851,912	1,239,057	1.47	.56[b]	34-1/8 — 26-1/8
1991	6,876,588	1,088,745	1.27	.48	34-3/4 — 19-5/8
1990	6,158,682	965,774	1.11	.41	23-1/8 — 15-5/8

[a]Adjusted to reflect 2-for-1 stock splits in May 1992 and May 1990.
[b]Includes one-time payment of $.0025 per share for rights redemption in August 1992.

Transfer Agent & Registrar: The First National Bank of Boston

General Counsel:	José M. de Lasa, Sr. V.P.
Investor Relations:	Catherine V. Babington, V.P.
Human Resources:	Ellen M. Walvoord, Sr. V.P.
Mgt. Info. Svcs.:	Kenneth W. Farmer, V.P.
Auditors:	Arthur Andersen LLP

Traded (Symbol):
NYSE,CSE,PSE,PHL,BOS,CIN,LON,SWISS (ABT)

Stockholders:	86,324
Employees:	49,464
Annual Meeting:	In April

ABC Rail Products Corporation

200 South Michigan Avenue, #1300, Chicago, Illinois 60604-2402
Telephone: (312) 322-0360

ABC Rail Products Corporation (formerly ABC Rail Corporation) is in the engineering, manufacturing and marketing of replacement products and original equipment for the freight railroad and rail transit industries. The company's products include specialty trackwork, such as rail crossings and switches, and mechanical products, such as railcar, locomotive and idler wheels, and composition and metal brake shoes. In December 1993, the company completed an initial public offering of 3,000,000 shares of common stock. Incorporated in Delaware in 1987; current name adopted in 1993.

Directors (In addition to indicated officers)

Marion H. Antonini
Donald R. Gant
Clarence E. Johnson
Robert R. Kiley

James A. Kohlberg
Christopher Lacovara
George W. Peck IV

Officers (Directors*)

*Donald W. Grinter, Chm. & C.E.O.
 Ben R. Yorks, Pres. & C.O.O.
*D. Chisholm MacDonald, Sr. V.P. & C.F.O.

David G. Kleeschulte, V.P. & Gen. Mgr.—Int'l. Div.
Robert C. Roberts, V.P. & Gen. Mgr.—Mech. Div.
Eugene S. Ziemba, V.P.—Trackwork Div.

Consolidated Balance Sheet As of July 31, 1994 (000 omitted)

Assets		Liabilities & Stockholders' Equity	
Current assets	$56,622	Current liabilities	$26,937
Net property, plant & equipment	31,553	Long-term debt	27,914
Other assets	7,599	Other long-term liabilities	1,819
		Deferred income taxes	4,186
		*Stockholders' equity	34,918
Total	$95,774	Total	$95,774

*7,663,887 shares common stock outstanding.

Consolidated Income Statement

Years Ended July 31	Thousands — — — — Net Sales	Net Income	Per Share[a] — — — Earnings	Cash Dividends	Common Stock Price Range[ab] Calendar Year
1994[c]	$187,176	$ 5,197	$ .79	$ .00	23-1/4 — 14-1/8
1993	148,676	3,555	.81	.00	15 — 12
1992[d]	143,412	(79)	(.02)		
1991	150,275	(2,049)	(.90)		
1990	160,553	1,067	.49		

[a]Adjusted to reflect a 2,000-for-1 stock split in September 1993.
[b]Initial public offering in December 1993.
[c]Includes an extraordinary charge of $1,690,000 ($.26 per share).
[d]Includes the cumulative gain of an accounting change of $1,079,000 ($.27 per share).

Transfer Agent & Registrar: American Stock Transfer & Trust Co.

General Counsel:
 Jones, Day, Reavis & Pogue

Investor Relations:
 D. Chisholm MacDonald, Sr. V.P.

Human Resources: Joseph A. Parsons, V.P.

Mgt. Info. Svcs.: Dominic D. Violante, V.P.

Auditors: Arthur Andersen LLP

Traded (Symbol): NASDAQ (ABCR)

Stockholders: 65

Employees: 1,402

Annual Meeting: In November

First Chicago Guide

Acme Metals Incorporated

13500 South Perry Avenue, Riverdale, Illinois 60627-1182
Telephone: (708) 849-2500

Acme Metals Incorporated (formerly Acme Steel Company), a holding company for four subsidiaries, is an integrated manufacturer of steel and steel products, including steel strapping products, sheet and strip products, semi-finished steel, iron products, welded steel tube, and auto and truck jacks. Acme Steel Company sells flat-rolled steel strip and related products primarily to the following markets: industrial equipment, processor, automotive, agricultural, and pipe and tube converter. Acme Packaging Corporation markets strapping products, consisting mainly of steel strapping, strapping tools, seals and stitching wire, to industrial customers. Universal Tool & Stamping Company, Inc., is a manufacturer and distributor of automotive and truck jacks and related equipment. Acme Metals supplies Universal's products to U.S. and foreign automobile producers in the U.S. Alpha Tube Corporation is a major producer of high-quality welded carbon steel tubing for a variety of consumer and industrial markets. Incorporated in Delaware in 1992.

Directors   (In addition to indicated officers)

C.J. Gauthier	Julien L. McCall
Edward G. Jordan	Carol O'Cleireacain
Andrew R. Laidlaw	William P. Sovey
Frank A. LePage	L. Frederick Sutherland
Reynold C. MacDonald	William R. Wilson

Officers   (Directors*)

*Brian W.H. Marsden, Chm. & C.E.O.
*Stephen D. Bennett, Pres. & C.O.O.
Gerald G. Shope, V.P.—Hum. Res.
Edward P. Weber, Jr., V.P., Gen. Coun. & Secy.

Jerry F. Williams, V.P.—Fin. & Admin.
James W. Hoekwater, Treas.
Gregory J. Pritz, Cont.

Consolidated Balance Sheet   As of December 25, 1994 (000 omitted)

Assets		Liabilities & Stockholders' Equity	
Current assets	$273,842	Current liabilities	$ 81,391
Net property, plant & equipment	148,829	Long-term debt	265,055
Investments & other assets	259,659	Other liabilities	112,606
		*Stockholders' equity	223,278
Total	$682,330	Total	$682,330

*11,637,299 shares common stock outstanding.

Consolidated Income Statement

Years Ended Abt. Dec. 31	Thousands — — — —		Per Share — — —		Common Stock Price Range Calendar Year
	Net Sales	Net Income	Earnings	Cash Dividends	
1994	$522,880	$ 16,971[a]	$ 2.16[a]	$ .00	27-1/4 — 15
1993	457,406	6,259	1.15	.00	20-3/4 — 12-1/4
1992[b]	391,562	(53,172)[c]	(9.85)[c]	.00	19-3/4 — 11
1991	376,951	(2,318)	(.43)	.00	15-3/4 — 10-1/4
1990	446,042	5,633	1.05	.00	18-1/2 — 13

[a]Includes an extraordinary charge of $1,787,000 ($.22 per share).
[b]Reclassified to conform to the current year's presentation.
[c]Includes FAS 106 and FAS 109, resulting in a one-time, non-cash charge of $50,323,000 ($9.32 per share).

Transfer Agent & Registrar: First Chicago Trust Co. of New York; Montreal Trust Co.

General Counsel:	Edward P. Weber, Jr., V.P.	Auditors:	Price Waterhouse LLP
Investor Relations:	Charles A. Nekvasil, Dir.	Traded (Symbol):	NASDAQ (ACME); TOR (AMK)
		Stockholders:	6,500
Human Resources:	Gerald G. Shope, V.P.	Employees:	2,750
Mgt. Info. Svcs.:	Gregory J. Pritz, Cont.	Annual Meeting:	In April

Advance Ross Corporation

233 South Wacker Drive, Suite 9700, Chicago, Illinois 60606-6502
Telephone: (312) 382-1100

Advance Ross Corporation administers value added tax (VAT) refunds to foreign tourists in Europe. This business is conducted through the company's wholly owned Swedish subsidiary, Europe Tax-free Shopping AB (ETS), and operates under the trade name "Tax-free for Tourists." Advance Ross entered into the business of providing VAT refunds and operating a duty-free perfume/cosmetic shop through the purchase of all the capital stock of ETS, completed in November 1992. Advance Ross also is involved in manufacturing and installing electrostatic precipitators for pollution control purposes, through its subsidiary, PPC Industries, located in Longview, Texas. The company also designs and installs patented biofiltration pollution control installations. Advance Ross, through its wholly owned subsidiary, Uintah Basin, Inc., is the general partner and 25 percent owner of Uintah Basin Limited Partnership. Incorporated in Delaware in 1993.

Directors   (In addition to indicated officers)

Roger E. Anderson
Harold E. Guenther
Duane R. Kullberg

Thomas J. Peterson
Herbert S. Wander

Officers   (Directors*)

*Harve A. Ferrill, Chm. & C.E.O.
*Paul G. Yovovich, Pres. & C.O.O.

Randy M. Joseph, V.P., C.F.O. & Treas.
Constance Schirmer, Secy. & Asst. Treas.

Consolidated Balance Sheet   As of December 31, 1994 (000 omitted)

Assets		Liabilities & Stockholders' Equity	
Current assets	$42,900	Current liabilities	$22,502
Net property, plant & equipment	1,996	Long-term debt	6,707
Other assets	19,224	Other liabilities	1,380
		*Stockholders' equity	33,531
Total	$64,120	Total	$64,120

*3,447,520 shares common stock outstanding.

Consolidated Income Statement

Years Ended Dec. 31	Thousands — — — — Net Sales	Net Income[a]	Per Share[b] — — — Earnings	Cash Dividends	Common Stock Price Range[b] Calendar Year
1994	$66,503	$8,346	$1.93	$ .00	30-1/4 — 14-3/4
1993	50,288	5,087	1.29	.00	18-5/8 — 6-1/2
1992	11,041	669	.18	.00	8-1/8 — 4-3/8
1991	5,870	7,270	1.97	.00	6 — 4-1/4
1990	3,314	2,662	.68	.00	5-7/8 — 4-1/8

[a]1991 includes a pretax gain of $11,727,000 from sale of stock.
[b]Adjusted to reflect a 2-for-1 stock split in January 1994.

Transfer Agent & Registrar: Mellon Securities Trust Co.

General Counsel: Katten Muchin & Zavis

Investor Relations: Randy M. Joseph, V.P.

Auditors: Deloitte & Touche LLP

Traded (Symbol):   NASDAQ (AROS)

Stockholders: 3,267

Employees: 327

Annual Meeting: In June

Alberto-Culver Company

2525 Armitage Avenue, Melrose Park, Illinois 60160-1163
Telephone: (708) 450-3000

Alberto-Culver Company and its subsidiaries manufacture and distribute a varied line of food products and mass-marketed personal use products for men and women, including the Alberto VO5® line of hair care products, as well as the Alberto VO5 Hot Oil Hair Therapy, Bold Hold, Consort, TRESemmé, TCB, and Indola lines of hair care products. Alberto-Culver's institutional and industrial products segment produces more than 400 food products for institutional customers and professional hair care products for barbershop and beauty salon suppliers. The household/grocery products division produces Baker's Joy®; SugarTwin®; Kleen Guard® household products; Static Guard®; Mrs. Dash® low-sodium products; and Molly McButter® products. Main plant and warehouse facilities are located in Melrose Park, Illinois. Subsidiaries include Sally Beauty Company, Inc., a wholesale distributor of beauty salon and barbershop supplies and equipment, Alberto-Culver USA, Inc., Alberto-Culver International, Inc., and Draper Daniels Media Services, Inc. Alberto-Culver's products are manufactured in seven countries and distributed to more than 100. Incorporated in Delaware in 1961.

Directors (In addition to indicated officers)

A. Robert Abboud
Robert P. Gwinn
Lee W. Jennings

Harold M. Visotsky
William W. Wirtz

Officers (Directors*)

*Leonard H. Lavin, Chm.
*Howard B. Bernick, Pres. & C.E.O.
*Bernice E. Lavin, V. Chm., Secy. & Treas.
*Carol L. Bernick, Exec. V.P. & Pres.—Alberto-Culver USA
William J. Cernugel, Sr. V.P.—Fin. & Cont.
Frederick C. Broda, V.P.—Corp. Dev.
James J. Chickarello, V.P.—Logistics
Raymond W. Gass, V.P. & Gen. Coun.
Michael L. Goldberg, V.P.—Cont.
Allan R. Linderman, V.P.—Adv. Svcs.
Raymond A. Maslanka, V.P.—Oper.
Douglas E. Meneely, V.P.—Hum. Res.

Janice J. Miller, V.P.—Market Research
Thomas J. Pallone, V.P.—R&D
Richard N. Paulsen, V.P.—Info. Sys.
Daniel B. Stone, V.P.—Comm.
John G. Horsman, Jr., Pres.—Int'l. Grp.
Michael H. Renzulli, Pres.—Sally Beauty Co., Inc.
John T. Boone, Grp. V.P.—Domestic Cons. Prods.
David D. DeTomaso, Sr. V.P.—Prof. Domestic Div.
Leah S. Bailey, V.P.—Toiletries Div.
Anthony J. Borgese, V.P.—Sales, Toiletries Div.
Ronald M. Kirshbaum, V.P.—Food Serv. Div.
Kristin B. Muntean, V.P.—Household/Groc. Prod. Div.

Consolidated Balance Sheet   As of September 30, 1994 (000 omitted)

Assets		Liabilities & Stockholders' Equity	
Current assets	$401,757	Current liabilities	$216,010
Net property, plant & equipment	132,881	Long-term debt	42,976
Other assets	75,570	Deferred income taxes	14,780
		Other liabilities	9,472
		*Stockholders' equity	326,970
Total	$610,208	Total	$610,208

*10,913,198 shares Class A common and 16,767,240 shares Class B common stock outstanding.

Consolidated Income Statement

Years Ended Sept. 30	Thousands — — — — Net Sales	Net Income[b]	Per Share[a] — — — — Earnings[b]	Cash Dividends[c]	Common Stock Price Range[ad] Calendar Year
1994	$1,216,119	$44,068	$1.57	$ .27	27-3/8 — 19-3/8
1993	1,147,990	41,272	1.44	.27[e]	28-1/4 — 20-1/4
1992	1,091,286	38,616	1.36	.24	32 — 21-1/4
1991	873,719	30,116	1.06	.22	34-1/4 — 20-1/2
1990	795,825	35,010	1.30	.20	33-1/4 — 19-1/8

[a]Adjusted to reflect a 2-for-1 stock split in January 1990.
[b]From continuing operations.
[c]Class A common stock dividends per share are equal to those of Class B common stock.
[d]Class B common stock.
[e]Includes a one-time extraordinary dividend of $.02 per share in recognition of the company surpassing $1,000,000,000 in sales for the fiscal year ending September 30, 1992.

Transfer Agent & Registrar: The First National Bank of Boston

General Counsel:	Raymond W. Gass, V.P.	Traded (Symbol):	NYSE (ACVA, Class A; ACV, Class B common stock)
Investor Relations:	Daniel B. Stone, V.P.		
Human Resources:	Douglas E. Meneely, V.P.	Stockholders:	2,520
Mgt. Info. Svcs.:	Richard N. Paulsen, V.P.	Employees:	8,600
Auditors:	KPMG Peat Marwick LLP	Annual Meeting:	In January

Allied Products Corporation

10 South Riverside Plaza, Suite 400, Chicago, Illinois 60606
Telephone: (312) 454-1020

Allied Products Corporation manufactures and markets agricultural equipment and industrial products. Agricultural equipment includes farm implements and related equipment. Industrial products include metal forming presses and custom compounding of thermoplastic resins. The original predecessor of the business was a partnership known as Richard Brothers Die Works, founded in 1915 to manufacture automotive dies. Major divisions include Bush Hog, Verson, and Coz. Incorporated in 1928; reincorporated in Delaware in 1967.

Directors (In addition to indicated officers)

Lloyd A. Drexler
William D. Fischer
Stanley J. Goldring
John E. Jones

John W. Puth
Mitchell I. Quain
Saul S. Sherman

Officers (Directors*)

*Richard A. Drexler, Chm., Pres. & C.E.O.
*Kenneth B. Light, Exec. V.P., C.F.O. & C.A.O.
 Martin A. German, Sr. V.P.

Bobby M. Middlebrooks, Sr. V.P.
Robert J. Fleck, V.P.—Acct. & Chf. Acct. Off.
Patrick J. Riley, V.P. & Treas.

Consolidated Balance Sheet   As of December 31, 1994 (000 omitted)

Assets		Liabilities & Stockholders' Equity	
Current assets	$ 96,832	Current liabilities	$ 63,301
Net property, plant & equipment	30,561	Long-term debt	630
Other assets	23,162	Deferred items	2,622
		Other liabilities	11,500
		*Stockholders' equity	72,502
Total	$150,555	Total	$150,555

*9,104,482 shares common stock outstanding.

Consolidated Income Statement

Years Ended Dec. 31	Thousands — — — —		Per Share — — — —		Common Stock Price Range Calendar Year
	Net Sales	Net Income	Earnings	Cash Dividends	
1994	$215,529	$ 14,333	$ 1.37	$ .00	17-3/8 — 12
1993	217,988	15,284	1.47	.00	15-7/8 — 2-3/4
1992	195,341	(24,954)	(3.32)	.00	4 — 1-1/2
1991	159,023	(34,043)	(5.62)	.00	6-3/4 — 2-1/4
1990	172,506	(5,768)	(1.68)	.00	9-3/8 — 3

Transfer Agent & Registrar: LaSalle National Trust, N.A.

General Counsel: David B. Corwine

Investor Relations: Kenneth B. Light, Exec. V.P.

Human Resources: Kenneth B. Light, Exec. V.P.

Mgt. Info. Svcs.:   Kenneth B. Light, Exec. V.P.

Auditors: Coopers & Lybrand L.L.P.
Traded (Symbol):   NYSE(ADP), PSE(ADPP)
Stockholders: 2,600
Employees: 1,600
Annual Meeting: In May

First Chicago Guide

The Allstate Corporation

Allstate Plaza, 2775 Sanders Road, Northbrook, Illinois 60062-6127
Telephone: (708) 402-5000

The Allstate Corporation, through its Allstate Insurance Company subsidiary, is a leading U.S. property-liability and life insurer. Allstate has more than 20 million customers, and its name and the "You're in Good Hands" mark are widely recognized. Allstate's primary business is the sale of private passenger automobile and homeowners insurance, and it maintains national market shares in each of those lines of approximately 12.1 percent and 11.8 percent, respectively. The company also sells life insurance, annuity and group pension products, and selected commercial property and casualty coverages. In 1995, Sears Roebuck and Co. spun off the 80 percent of the company that it owned to Sears stockholders; and Allstate sold 70 percent of The PMI Group Inc., a residential mortgage guaranty insurance subsidiary. Allstate was established in 1931. Incorporated in Delaware in 1992.

Directors (In addition to indicated officer)

James G. Andress	Christopher F. Edley
Warren L. Batts	William E. LaMothe
Edward A. Brennan	Nancy C. Reynolds
James M. Denny	Donald H. Rumsfeld

Officers (Director*)

*Jerry D. Choate, Chm. & C.E.O.	Robert W. Pike, V.P., Secy. & Gen. Coun.
Edward M. Liddy, Pres. & C.O.O.	Myron J. Resnick, V.P. & Treas.
Norbert A. Florek, V.P. & C.F.O.	Thomas J. Wilson, V.P.—Fin.

Consolidated Balance Sheet As of December 31, 1994 (000 omitted)

Assets		Liabilities & Stockholders' Equity	
Total investments	$48,178,700	Insurance reserves	$22,157,200
Net property, plant & equipment	787,900	Long-term debt	869,200
Deferred policy acquisition costs	2,073,900	Unearned premiums	5,907,800
Premium installment receivables	2,316,100	Contract holder funds	17,974,100
Other assets	8,012,800	Other liabilities	6,035,100
		*Stockholders' equity	8,426,000
Total	$61,369,400	Total	$61,369,400

*449,362,200 shares common stock outstanding.

Consolidated Income Statement

Years Ended Dec. 31	Thousands — — — — Total Revenues	Net Income	Per Share — — — Earnings	Cash Dividends	Common Stock Price Range[a] Calendar Year
1994	$21,464,300	$ 483,800	$ 1.08	$ .72	29-7/8 — 22-5/8
1993	20,946,300	1,301,500	2.99[b]	.36[c]	34-1/4 — 27-1/8
1992	20,228,100	(825,200)[d]	(1.91)[bd]		
1991	19,350,200	722,500			
1990	18,199,100	701,300			

[a]Initial public offering in June 1993.
[b]Pro forma.
[c]Represents dividends per share since becoming a public company in June 1993.
[d]Includes FAS 106 and FAS 112, resulting in a charge to net earnings of $325,600,000 ($.75 per share).

Transfer Agent & Registrar:	Harris Trust and Savings Bank		
General Counsel:	Robert W. Pike, V.P.	Auditors:	Deloitte & Touche LLP
Investor Relations:	Martin Przygoda	Traded (Symbol):	CSE, NYSE (ALL)
Human Resources:	Joan Crockett, V.P.	Stockholders:	5,779
		Employees:	46,300
Mgt. Info. Svcs.:	Frank Pollard, V.P.	Annual Meeting:	In May

First Chicago Guide

Alternative Resources Corporation

75 Tri-State International, Suite 100, Lincolnshire, Illinois 60069
Telephone: (708) 317-1000

Alternative Resources Corporation (ARC) is a leading provider of technical personnel specializing in information services operations. ARC technical employees are skilled in mainframe and mid-range computer operations, personal computer and client-server support, voice and data communications (including local and wide area networks), and help desk support. In May 1994, the company completed an initial public offering of 1,340,325 shares of common stock. Incorporated in Delaware in 1988.

Directors   (In addition to indicated officer)

JoAnne Brandes
Robert L. Cummings

Raymond R. Hipp
Bruce R. Smith

Officers   (Director*)

*Larry I. Kane, Chm., Pres. & C.E.O.
 Lisa A. DesCoteaux, V.P.—Oper.

Michael E. Harris, V.P.—Fin., C.F.O., Treas. & Secy.
Silvia U. Masini, V.P.—Hum. Res.

Consolidated Balance Sheet   As of December 31, 1994 (000 omitted)

Assets		Liabilities & Stockholders' Equity	
Current assets	$25,155	Current liabilities	$ 5,948
Net property, plant & equipment	1,249	Deferred items	662
Other assets	177	*Stockholders' equity	19,971
Total	$26,581	Total	$26,581

*7,390,676 shares common stock outstanding.

Consolidated Income Statement

Years Ended Dec. 31	Thousands — — — —		Per Share[a] — — —		Common Stock Price Range[ab] Calendar Year
	Revenues	Net Income	Earnings	Cash Dividends	
1994	$94,478	$ 6,190	$ .51	$ .00	15-7/8 — 8-1/8
1993	53,061	3,226	.66		
1992	27,948	1,601[c]	.32[c]		
1991	13,889	26	(.03)		
1990	7,607	(792)	(.24)		

[a]Adjusted to reflect a 2-for-1 stock split in May 1995 and a 7-for-1 stock split in February 1994.
[b]Initial public offering in May 1994.
[c]Includes an extraordinary item, utilization of net operating loss carryforward of $479,731 ($.11 per share).

Transfer Agent & Registrar: Harris Trust and Savings Bank

General Counsel: McDermott, Will & Emery

Investor Relations: Michael E. Harris, V.P.

Human Resources: Silvia U. Masini, V.P.

Mgt. Info. Svcs.:   Robin Anderson

Auditors: KPMG Peat Marwick LLP
Traded (Symbol):   NASDAQ (ALRC)
Stockholders: 100
Employees: 4,608
Annual Meeting: In April

AM International, Inc.

9399 Higgins Road, Suite 900, Rosemont, Illinois 60018
Telephone: (708) 282-0600

AM International, Inc., provides equipment, supplies and services to the worldwide graphics market. The company conducts its business through two divisions — AM Multigraphics and AM Graphics. AM International manufactures and sells a wide range of printing and print production equipment, newspaper mailroom systems and bindery systems, and provides services and supplies to the worldwide graphics industry. These products and services are marketed to publishers, commercial printers, independent print shops, in-plant print shops, and governmental and educational institutions. The company serves more than 52,000 customers in more than 82 countries through its sales and service organization. In addition, the AM Multigraphics division is a value-added distributor of high-quality, high-performance supplies and equipment manufactured by third parties for use in commercial and in-plant print shops, including master and plate imaging equipment, and collating, sorting and bindery equipment. In May 1993, the company filed for Chapter 11 bankruptcy relief and was discharged from bankruptcy on October 13, 1993. Incorporated in Delaware in 1924 as Addressograph-Multigraph Corporation, an outgrowth of a business originally started in 1893; present name adopted in 1979.

Directors   (In addition to indicated officer)

Robert E. Anderson III
Jeffrey D. Benjamin
Robert N. Dangremond

William E. Hogan II
A. Carl Mudd
Asher O. Pacholder

Officers   (Director*)

*Jerome D. Brady, Chm., Pres. & C.E.O.
 Steven R. Andrews, V.P., Gen. Coun. & Secy.
 Richard J. Bonnie, V.P. & Pres.—AM
  Graphics

David A. Roberts, V.P. & Pres.—AM Multigraphics
Thomas D. Rooney, V.P. & C.F.O.

Consolidated Balance Sheet   As of October 29, 1994 (000 omitted) Unaudited

Assets		Liabilities & Stockholders' Equity	
Current assets	$210,938	Current liabilities	$184,212
Net property, plant & equipment	33,822	Long-term debt	25,893
Other assets	50,578	Other liabilities	39,584
		*Stockholders' equity	45,649
Total	$295,338	Total	$295,338

*6,998,833 shares common stock outstanding.

Consolidated Income Statement

Years Ended July 31	Thousands — — — —		Per Share[c] — — — —		Common Stock Price Range Calendar Year
	Revenues	Net Income	Earnings	Cash Dividends	
1994[a]	$421,625	$ 6,652	$ .95	$ .00	12-1/4 — 8-1/2
1993[b]	69,214	52,689			
1993[b]	534,738	(125,678)			
1992[b]	618,746	(124,778)			

[a]From September 30, 1993, through July 31, 1994. Due to reorganization and fresh start reporting, financial statements for the new reorganized company are not comparable to those of predecessor.
[b]Predecessor company from August 1 to September 29, 1993, and prior fiscal years.
[c]Due to restructuring and fresh start reporting, prior periods per share information is not meaningful.

Transfer Agent & Registrar: First Chicago Trust Co. of New York

General Counsel:	Steven R. Andrews, V.P.	Traded (Symbol):	AMEX (AM)
Investor Relations:	Thomas D. Rooney, V.P.	Stockholders:	8,500
Human Resources:	Marianne Gruber, Dir.	Employees:	3,400
Auditors:	Arthur Andersen LLP	Annual Meeting:	In December

AMCOL International Corporation

One North Arlington, 1500 West Shure Drive, Suite 500, Arlington Heights, Illinois 60004-7803
Telephone: (708) 392-4600

AMCOL International Corporation (formerly American Colloid Company) and its subsidiaries operate in three major industry segments: minerals, absorbent polymers, and environmental. The company is one of the principal world producers of bentonite, a non-metallic clay primarily composed of a mineral called montmorillonite. The minerals division (American Colloid Company) mines, processes and distributes bentonite and products with similar applications to various industrial and consumer markets, including metalcasting, well drilling, cat box fillers and agriculture. The company has redirected its emphasis from bulk commodities of bentonite to special blends tailored to specific customer needs. The absorbent polymers division (Chemdal) produces and distributes water absorbent polymers primarily to consumer markets. The environmental division (CETCO) produces and distributes products relating to wastewater treatment, groundwater monitoring/drilling, soil sealing/landfill liners, and engineered building materials. The company also operates a trucking and freight business, which provides services to both the company's plants and outside customers. AMCOL operates 20 processing plants in the U.S., nine of which include mining operations, as well as processing plants in Canada, Australia and England. Subsidiaries include Ameri-co Carriers, Inc.; Nationwide Freight Services, Inc.; Chemdal Corporation; Colloid Environmental Technologies Company; Chemdal, Ltd. (England); American Colloid Company, Ltd. (Canada); Volclay, Ltd. (England); Volclay De Mexico; Colloid Australia PTY.LTD.; and Volclay Standard PTY.LTD. (Australia). Incorporated in South Dakota in 1924 as Bentonite Mining & Manufacturing Co.; reincorporated in Delaware in 1959; present name adopted in 1995.

Directors   (In addition to indicated officers)

C. Eugene Ray, Chm.	Raymond A. Foos	Clarence O. Redman, Secy.
Arthur Brown	Robert C. Humphrey	Paul C. Weaver
Robert E. Driscoll III		

Officers   (Directors*)

*John Hughes, Pres. & C.E.O.
 Roger P. Palmer, Sr. V.P. & Pres.—CETCO
*Paul G. Shelton, Sr. V.P. & C.F.O.
 Robert C. Steele, Sr. V.P. & Pres.—American Colloid Co.

Lawrence E. Washow, Sr. V.P. & Pres.—Chemdal
Peter L. Maul, V.P.

Consolidated Balance Sheet   As of December 31, 1994 (000 omitted)

Assets		Liabilities & Stockholders' Equity	
Current assets	$105,839	Current liabilities	$ 36,617
Net property, plant & equipment	141,420	Long-term debt	71,458
Other assets	13,788	Deferred items	4,376
		Other liabilities	7,277
		*Stockholders' equity	141,319
Total	$261,047	Total	$261,047

*19,014,342 shares common stock outstanding.

Consolidated Income Statement

Years Ended Dec. 31	Thousands — — — —		Per Share[a] — — — —		Common Stock Price Range[a] Calendar Year
	Net Sales	Net Income[b]	Earnings[b]	Cash Dividends	
1994	$265,443	$15,283	$ .78	$ .24	25-1/4 — 10-1/2
1993	219,151	13,120	.76	.20	33 — 9-1/8
1992	182,669	8,506	.52	.16	9-3/8 — 3-7/8
1991	148,790	4,152	.26	.15	4-1/4 — 2-3/8
1990	131,665	2,513	.16	.15	4-3/8 — 2-7/8

[a]Adjusted to reflect a 2-for-1 stock split paid in June 1993 and a 3-for-2 stock split paid in January 1993.
[b]Restated to reflect FAS 109.

Transfer Agent & Registrar:	Harris Trust and Savings Bank		
General Counsel:	Keck, Mahin & Cate	Auditors:	KPMG Peat Marwick LLP
Investor Relations:	Paul G. Shelton, Sr. V.P.	Traded (Symbol):	NASDAQ (ACOL)
		Stockholders:	2,344
Human Resources:	Steve Alexander, Mgr.	Employees:	1,328
Mgt. Info. Svcs.:	Russ Petrik, Mgr.	Annual Meeting:	In May

First Chicago Guide

AMCORE Financial, Inc.

501 Seventh Street, Rockford, Illinois 61104
Telephone: (815) 968-2241

AMCORE Financial, Inc., is a multi-bank holding company for AMCORE Bank N.A., Rockford; AMCORE Bank N.A., Northwest; and AMCORE Bank N.A. Rock River Valley. Other subsidiaries are AMCORE Bank Princeton, AMCORE Bank Ashton-Rochelle, AMCORE Bank Gridley, and AMCORE Bank Aledo. Personal banking services include savings and checking accounts; and consumer, small business and mortgage loans. Commercial banking provides services to commercial and governmental organizations. AMCORE Financial Life Insurance Company reinsures credit life, accident and health insurance. AMCORE Mortgage, Inc., provides a full range of mortgage-banking services. AMCORE Consumer Finance, Inc. is a consumer finance entity specializing in consumer lending. AMCORE Trust Co. provides personal trust service, employee benefit plan and estate administration, and various other services to corporations and individuals. AMCORE Investment Services, Inc., is a broker/dealer providing a full line of retail brokerage products and services. AMCORE Capital Management, Inc., is an investment advisory affiliate that manages AMCORE Vintage mutual funds and AMCORE Trust Co., and bank affiliate investment portfolios. AMCORE Investment Banking, Inc., provides assistance with the acquisition and sale of companies, mergers, valuations, debt and debt placement for bank customers and other clients. AMCORE Insurance Group, Inc., is a full-service insurance agency offering both personal and commercial insurance products. AMCORE Financial operates in the northern one-half of Illinois, excluding Cook County. Incorporated in Nevada in 1982.

Directors   (In addition to indicated officer)

Milton R. Brown	Theresa P. Gilbert	Robert J. Smuland
Richard C. Dell	Lawrence E. Gloyd	Jack D. Ward
Robert A. Doyle	Robert A. Henry, M.D.	Gary L. Watson
Frank A. Fiorenza	Ted Ross	

Officers   (Director*)[a]

*Carl J. Dargene, Chm., Pres. & C.E.O.
F. Taylor Carlin, Exec. V.P. & C.O.O.—Diversified Fin. Svcs. Grp.
Robert J. Meuleman, Exec. V.P. & C.O.O.—Bank Subsidiaries
James S. Waddell, Exec. V.P., C.A.O. & Corp. Secy.

Kenneth E. Edge, Grp. V.P.
Gerald W. Lister, Grp. V.P.
James J. Brown, Sr. V.P.—Mergers & Acquis.
John R. Hecht, Sr. V.P. & C.F.O.
William T. Hippensteel, Sr. V.P.—Corp. Mktg.

[a]Dargene will retire as Pres. & C.E.O. on December 31, 1995; Meuleman will assume those positions.

Consolidated Balance Sheet   As of December 31, 1994 (000 omitted)

Assets		Liabilities & Stockholders' Equity	
Current assets	$ 102,603	Total deposits	$1,565,032
Total securities	710,117	Borrowings	231,595
Net loans & leases	1,067,552	Other liabilities	21,954
Net property, plant & equipment	47,192	*Stockholders' equity	166,048
Other assets	57,165		
Total	$1,984,629	Total	$1,984,629

*12,400,720 shares common stock outstanding.

Consolidated Income Statement[a]

Years Ended Dec. 31	Thousands — — — —		Per Share[b] — — — —		Common Stock
	Total Income	Net Income	Earnings	Cash Dividends	Price Range[b] Calendar Year
1994	$158,136	$19,600	$1.58	$ .56	22-3/4 — 15-3/4
1993	154,260	19,052	1.54	.41	20 — 13-1/2
1992	148,077	16,225	1.35	.34	14-5/8 — 7-7/8
1991	137,995	12,988	1.09	.30	10-1/8 — 6-5/8
1990	136,405	11,014	.88	.26	10-1/8 — 6-1/2

[a]Restated to reflect the August 1994 merger with First State Bancorp of Princeton, Illinois, and the December 1994 merger with NBA Holding Company of Aledo, Illinois.
[b]Adjusted to reflect a 3-for-2 stock split in November 1993 and a 10% stock dividend in May 1992.

Transfer Agent & Registrar: First Wisconsin

General Counsel:	Maggio & Fox	Auditors:	McGladrey & Pullen, LLP
Investor Relations:	F. Taylor Carlin, Exec. V.P.	Traded (Symbol):	NASDAQ (AMFI)
Human Resources:	James S. Waddell, Exec. V.P.	Stockholders:	4,500
		Employees:	1,130
Mgt. Info. Svcs.:	Ronald M. Zarnick, Sr. V.P.	Annual Meeting:	In May

American Classic Voyages Co.

Two North Riverside Plaza, Suite 600, Chicago, Illinois 60606-2639
Telephone: (312) 258-1890

American Classic Voyages Co. (formerly The Delta Queen Steamboat Co.) and its subsidiaries are the leading providers of overnight passenger cruises on inland waterways in the continental U.S. and among the Hawaiian islands. The company operates two cruise lines — The Delta Queen Steamboat Co. and American Hawaii Cruises. Delta Queen currently operates two vessels having 588 total passenger berths. American Hawaii operates two vessels having 1,590 total passenger berths. Incorporated in Delaware in 1985; present name adopted in 1994.

Directors (In addition to indicated officers)

Corinne C. Boggs
Arthur A. Greenberg
Jerry R. Jacob

Jon E.M. Jacoby
Ann Lurie
Sheli Z. Rosenberg

Officers (Directors*)

*Samuel Zell, Chm.
*Philip C. Calian, Pres. & C.E.O.
Steven M. Isaacson, Exec. V.P., C.F.O. & Treas.
Albert Luthmers, Sr. V.P.—Dev.
Jordan B. Allen, V.P. & Gen. Coun.
William J. Binnie, V.P.—Dev.
Brian J. Higgins, V.P.—Marine Opers.

David W. Kish, V.P. & Secy.
Doreen J. Lubeck, V.P.—Corp. & Investor Rel.
Cornel J. Martin, V.P.—Corp. Affairs
Ray Yee, V.P.—MIS
Michael Kilbridge, Cont.—Dev.
Susan S. Obuchowski, Secy.
Randa R. Saleh, Cont.

Consolidated Balance Sheet   As of December 31, 1994 (000 omitted)

Assets		Liabilities & Stockholders' Equity	
Current assets	$ 22,559	Current liabilities	$ 71,315
Net property, plant & equipment	175,966	Long-term debt	65,000
Goodwill	29,273	Deferred income taxes	2,544
		Minority interest	6,834
		*Stockholders' equity	82,105
Total	$227,798	Total	$227,798

*13,760,757 shares common stock outstanding.

Consolidated Income Statement

Years Ended Dec. 31	Thousands — — — — — Revenues	Net Income	Per Share — — — — Earnings	Cash Dividends	Common Stock Price Range Calendar Year
1994[a]	$195,197	$ (983)	$ (.07)	$ .16	19-1/4— 12
1993[b]	121,689	4,220	.36	.16	22-1/4— 11-3/8
1993[c]	66,725	9,181	.81	.04	
1992[cd]	61,686	4,245	.37	.00	15-3/4— 9-5/8[e]
1991[cd]	51,167	3,467	.31	.00	

[a]Includes one-time charges of $5,700,000 ($.20 per share).
[b]Includes the results of American Hawaii Cruises since its acquisition in August 1993, and the impact of the Mississippi River flood.
[c]Fiscal year ended March 31.
[d]Pro forma.
[e]Initial public offering in March 1992.

Transfer Agent & Registrar:	Bank of Boston		
General Counsel:	Jordan B. Allen, V.P.	Auditors:	KPMG Peat Marwick LLP
Investor Relations:	Doreen J. Lubeck, V.P.	Traded (Symbol):	NASDAQ (AMCV)
Human Resources:	Amy Klein-Alter	Stockholders:	800
		Employees:	2,248
Mgt. Info. Svcs.:	Ray Yee, V.P.	Annual Meeting:	In June

American Publishing Company

111-115 South Emma Street, West Frankford, Illinois 62896
Telephone: (618) 937-6411

American Publishing Company is a leading newspaper publishing group in the U.S., where it publishes a total of 391 newspapers and related publications. Internationally, the company publishes *The Jerusalem Post*. Major subsidiaries are The Sun-Times Company, Daily Southtown Inc., and The Palestine Post Limited. In May 1994, the company completed an initial public offering of 7,300,000 Class A shares of common stock. Incorporated in California in 1979; reincorporated in Delaware in 1991.

Directors (In addition to indicated officers)

F. David Radler, Chm.
Conrad M. Black, Dep. Chm.
Dixon S. Chant, V. Chm.
George R. Sample, V. Chm.
Richard Burt

Daniel W. Colson
Sam S. McKeel
Richard N. Perle
Leonard P. Shaykin
James R. Thompson

Officers (Directors*)

*Larry J. Perrotto, Pres. & C.E.O.
*Kenneth W. Cope, Exec. V.P.
*J. David Dodd, Exec. V.P. & C.F.O.
*John H. Satterwhite, Exec. V.P.
Joseph C. Piccirillo, Sr. V.P.
Jerry J. Stradler, Sr. V.P.

*J.A. Boultbee, V.P.
*Charles G. Cowan, V.P.
Gene A. Hall, V.P.
Roland L. McBride, Grp. Cont.
Kenneth L. Serota, Secy.
Linda Loye, Asst. Secy.

Consolidated Balance Sheet As of December 31, 1994 (000 omitted)

Assets		Liabilities & Stockholders' Equity	
Current assets	$ 91,779	Current liabilities	$ 91,313
Net property, plant & equipment	152,671	Long-term debt	311,814
Intangible assets, net of accum.	386,079	Deferred income taxes	20,419
depreciation		Other liabilities	16,197
Other assets	5,591	*Stockholders' equity	196,377
Total	$636,120	Total	$636,120

*8,355,000 shares Class A common and 14,990,000 shares Class B common stock outstanding.

Consolidated Income Statement

Years Ended Dec. 31	Thousands — — — —		Per Share — — — —		Common Stock Price Range[a] Calendar Year
	Net Sales	Net Income	Earnings	Cash Dividends	
1994[b]	$422,594	$ 12,869	$ .63	$ .05	14-1/2 — 10
1993	185,044	(1,479)			
1992	173,219	(7,468)			
1991	157,397	(13,683)			
1990	139,874	(11,503)			

[a]Initial public offering in May 1994.
[b]Includes the results of Chicago Sun-Times since March 31, 1994, the date of acquisition.

Transfer Agent & Registrar:	First Chicago Trust Co. of New York		
General Counsel:	Kirkpatrick & Lockhart	Traded (Symbol):	NASDAQ (AMPC)
Investor Relations:	J. David Dodd, Exec. V.P.	Stockholders:	204
		Employees:	5,000
Auditors:	KPMG Peat Marwick LLP	Annual Meeting:	In May

Amerihost Properties, Inc.

2400 East Devon Avenue, Suite 280, Des Plaines, Illinois 60018
Telephone: (708) 298-4500

Amerihost Properties, Inc., and its subsidiaries are engaged in the development, construction, acquisition, renovation, operation and management of limited service and mid-market hotels. The company provides a complete product, from site evaluation and selection stages through the operating stages. As of December 1994, the company operated 53 hotels in 12 states. Amerihost conducts its business through four departments: Hotel Development; Hotel Operations; Hotel Management; and Employee Leasing. The company builds, manages and owns AmeriHost Inns and intends to expand the chain extensively over the next several years. Amerihost also owns and manages hotels with national franchise affiliations. Amerihost Properties' wholly owned subsidiaries include: Amerihost Lodging Group, Inc.; Amerihost Development, Inc.; Amerihost Renovations, Inc.; Amerihost Management, Inc.; and Amerihost Staffing, Inc. (ASI), which was formed in January 1992. The company mainly concentrates in secondary and tertiary markets in the midwestern and southeastern United States. Incorporated in Delaware in 1984.

Directors   (In addition to indicated officers)

Robert L. Barney
Reno J. Bernardo

David J. Brail
Marshall S. Geller

Officers   (Directors*)

*H. Andrew Torchia, Chm.
*Michael P. Holtz, Pres. & C.E.O.

*Richard A. D'Onofrio, Exec. V.P.—Corp. Dev.
*Russell J. Cerqua, Sr. V.P., C.F.O., Treas. & Secy.

Consolidated Balance Sheet   As of December 31, 1994 (000 omitted)

Assets		Liabilities & Stockholders' Equity	
Current assets	$ 9,693	Current liabilities	$ 5,512
Net property, plant & equipment	16,466	Long-term debt	12,975
Other assets	8,244	Deferred items	1,051
		Other liabilities	1,193
		*Stockholders' equity	13,672
Total	$34,403	Total	$34,403

*5,570,013 shares common stock outstanding.

Consolidated Income Statement

Years Ended Dec. 31	Thousands — — — — Revenues	Net Income	Per Share — — — Earnings	Cash Dividends	Common Stock Price Range Calendar Year
1994	$43,347	$ 571	$ .10	$ .00	6-3/4 — 3-1/2
1993	34,274	(761)	(.15)	.00	12-1/4 — 4
1992	29,411	511	.22	.00	8 — 3
1991	6,524	280	.17	.00	3-3/8 — 2
1990	6,906	116	.07	.00	4-1/4 — 2-1/4

Transfer Agent & Registrar: Affiliated Stock Transfer Co.

Legal Counsel: McDermott, Will & Emery

Investor Relations:
  Richard A. D'Onofrio, Exec. V.P.

Human Resources: William Roclaw

Mgt. Info. Svcs.:   Gary Brookshier

Auditors: BDO Seidman

Traded (Symbol):   NASDAQ (HOST)

Stockholders: 1,664

Employees: 1,900

Annual Meeting: In July

Ameritech Corporation

30 South Wacker Drive, Chicago, Illinois 60606
Telephone: (312) 750-5000

Ameritech Corporation provides full-service communications to 13 million customers, primarily in the Midwest, helping them communicate and manage information. Ameritech also has operations in Hungary, New Zealand, Norway, Poland and other international areas. The company has restructured its five geographically based operating companies into 15 customer-specific business units supported by a single regionally coordinated network unit. The company is now marketing services under the single brand name "Ameritech." Business units include Consumer Services, Custom Business Services, Enhanced Business Services, Small Business Services, Long Distance Industry Services, Information Industry Services, Telephone Industry Services, Pay Phone Services, Cellular Services, Advertising Services, Leasing Services, International, Long Distance, New Media Enterprises, and Network Services. Incorporated in Delaware in 1983.

Directors (In addition to indicated officers)

Donald C. Clark	Sheldon B. Lubar	John D. Ong
Melvin R. Goodes	Lynn M. Martin	Addison Barry Rand
Hanna Holborn Gray, Ph.D.	Arthur C. Martinez	James A. Unruh
James A. Henderson	John B. McCoy	

Officers (Directors*)

*Richard C. Notebaert, Chm. & C.E.O.
*Richard H. Brown, V. Chm.
W. Patrick Campbell, Exec. V.P.—Corp. Strategy
Walter S. Catlow, Exec. V.P.—Int'l. Bus. Dev.
Thomas P. Hester, Exec. V.P. & Gen. Coun.
Oren G. Shaffer, Exec. V.P. & C.F.O.
Walter M. Oliver, Sr. V.P.—Hum. Res.
Thomas J. Reiman, Sr. V.P.—State & Govt. Aff.

Rita P. Wilson, Sr. V.P.—Corp. Comm.
Betty F. Elliott, V.P. & Comptroller
Joel S. Engel, V.P.—Tech.
Gary R. Lytle, V.P.—Fed. Reg.
Sari L. Macrie, V.P.—Investor Rel.
Richard W. Pehlke, V.P. & Treas.
Lawrence E. Strickling, V.P.—Public Policy
Kelly R. Welsh, V.P. & Assoc. Gen. Coun.
Bruce B. Howat, Secy.

Consolidated Balance Sheet As of December 31, 1994 (000 omitted)

Assets		Liabilities & Stockholders' Equity	
Current assets	$ 2,890,600	Current liabilities	$ 5,156,100
Net property, plant & equipment	13,454,500	Long-term debt	4,447,900
Other assets	3,601,700	Deferred items	4,287,700
		*Stockholders' equity	6,055,100
Total	$19,946,800	Total	$19,946,800

*551,462,000 shares common stock outstanding.

Consolidated Income Statement

Years Ended Dec. 31	Thousands — — — —		Per Share[a] — — —		Common Stock
	Net Sales[b]	Net Income	Earnings	Cash Dividends	Price Range[a] Calendar Year
1994	$12,569,500	$(1,063,600)[c]	$(1.94)[c]	$1.92	43-1/8 — 36-1/4
1993	11,864,700	1,512,800	2.78	1.84	45-1/2 — 35
1992	11,284,700	(400,400)[d]	(.75)[d]	1.76	37 — 28-1/8
1991	10,983,000	1,165,300	2.19	1.70	34-7/8 — 27-7/8
1990	10,773,000	1,253,100	2.37	1.58	34-7/8 — 26-1/4

[a]Adjusted to reflect a 2-for-1 stock split in December 1993.
[b]Prior years have been reclassified to conform with the 1994 presentation.
[c]Includes an extraordinary loss of $2,234,000,000 ($4.07 per share).
[d]Includes a charge to reflect FAS 106 and FAS 112, resulting in a cumulative effect of $1,746,400,000 ($3.26 per share).

Transfer Agent & Registrar: First Chicago Trust Co. of New York

General Counsel: Thomas P. Hester, Exec. V.P.		Traded (Symbol):	NYSE, BSE, CSE, PSE, PHSE, Lond., Tokyo, Basel, Geneva, Zurich, Amsterdam (AIT)
Investor Relations:	Sari L. Macrie, V.P.		
Human Resources:	Walter M. Oliver, Sr. V.P.	Stockholders:	922,432
Mgt. Info. Svcs.:	Betty F. Elliott, V.P.	Employees:	63,594
Auditors:	Arthur Andersen LLP	Annual Meeting:	In April

Amoco Corporation

200 East Randolph Drive, Chicago, Illinois 60601
Telephone: (312) 856-6111

Amoco Corporation and its consolidated subsidiaries form one of the largest petroleum and chemical companies in the nation. The company engages in exploration, production, and transportation of crude oil and natural gas, and in manufacturing, transporting, and marketing of petroleum and chemical products. There are three principal wholly owned subsidiaries: Amoco Production Company carries out exploration and production activities; Amoco Oil Company is responsible for manufacturing, transporting, and marketing petroleum products; and Amoco Chemical Company conducts chemical operations. U.S. refineries process approximately 1,079,000 barrels of crude oil and natural gas liquids per day. Products are sold through about 3,000 company-owned or leased retail outlets, in addition to about 6,600 other retail outlets. Incorporated in Indiana in 1889.

Directors (In addition to indicated officers)

Donald R. Beall	Richard J. Ferris	Martha R. Seger
Ruth S. Block	Floris A. Maljers	Michael H. Wilson
John H. Bryan	Robert H. Malott	Richard D. Wood
Erroll B. Davis, Jr.	Walter E. Massey	

Officers (Directors*)

*H. Laurance Fuller, Chm., Pres. & C.E.O.
*Lawrason D. Thomas, V. Chm.
John L. Carl, Exec. V.P. & C.F.O.
James E. Fligg, Exec. V.P.—Chemicals Sector
W. Douglas Ford, Exec. V.P.—Petroleum Products Sector
William G. Lowrie, Exec. V.P.—Exploration & Prod. Sector
R. Wayne Anderson, Sr. V.P.—Hum. Res.
L. Richard Flury, Sr. V.P.—Shared Services
Rady A. Johnson, Sr. V.P.—Govt. Rel.
Gary P. Mihaichuk, Sr. V.P. (China)

George S. Spindler, Sr. V.P.—Law & Corp. Affairs
Robert C. Carr, V.P.—Chem. Dev. & Diversification
Roxanne J. Decyk, V.P.—Plan.
Stephen F. Gates, V.P. & Gen. Coun.
William R. Hutchinson, V.P.—Fin. Oper.
Larry D. McVay, V.P.—Progress
Daniel R. Mitchell, V.P. & Gen. Tax Coun.
Walter R. Quanstrom, V.P.—Env., Health & Safety
John R. Reid, V.P. & Cont.
Carl C. Williams, V.P.—Info. Tech.
Patricia A. Brandin, Corp. Secy.
Marsha C. Williams, Treas.

Consolidated Balance Sheet As of December 31, 1994 (000 omitted)

Assets		Liabilities & Stockholders' Equity	
Current assets	$ 6,642,000	Current liabilities	$ 5,024,000
Net property, plant & equipment	21,543,000	Long-term obligations	4,387,000
Other assets	1,131,000	Deferred items	5,508,000
		Minority interest	15,000
		*Stockholders' equity	14,382,000
Total	$29,316,000	Total	$29,316,000

*496,393,067 shares common stock outstanding.

Consolidated Income Statement

Years Ended Dec. 31	Thousands — — — —		Per Share — — —		Common Stock Price Range Calendar Year
	Total Revenues[a]	Net Income	Earnings	Cash Dividends	
1994	$30,362,000	$ 1,789,000	$ 3.60	$2.20	64-1/8 — 50-7/8
1993	28,617,000	1,820,000	3.66	2.20	59-1/4 — 48-1/8
1992	28,219,000	(74,000)[b]	(.15)[b]	2.20	53-3/4 — 41-3/4
1991	28,296,000	1,484,000[b]	2.98[b]	2.20	55 — 45-5/8
1990	31,581,000	1,913,000	3.77	2.04	60-3/8 — 49-1/4

[a]Includes consumer excise taxes.
[b]Includes FAS 106 and 109, resulting in cumulative charges of $924,000,000 ($1.86 per share) in 1992; and FAS 96, resulting in a cumulative benefit of $311,000,000 ($.62 per share) in 1991.

Transfer Agent & Registrar: First Chicago Trust Co. of New York; The R-M Trust Co., Toronto; Amoco Corp. Shareholder Services

General Counsel:	George S. Spindler, Sr. V.P.	Auditors:	Price Waterhouse LLP
Investor Relations:	Chuck K. Koepke, Mgr.	Traded (Symbol):	NYSE, CSE, PSE, Toronto, 4 Swiss SE (AN)
Human Resources:	R. Wayne Anderson, Sr. V.P.	Stockholders:	134,776
		Employees:	43,205
Mgt. Info. Svcs.:	Carl C. Williams, V.P.	Annual Meeting:	In April

Ampace Corporation

Three First National Plaza, Suite 1400, Chicago, Illinois 60602
Telephone: (312) 214-6133

Ampace Corporation is a national non-union full-truckload transportation services company. The company is presently a "core carrier" for Dow Chemical, International Paper, and a division of General Motors Corporation. Core carrier relationships involve alliances between volume shippers and their distribution partners. In February 1995, Ampace Corporation completed an initial public offering of 1,200,000 shares of common stock; and concurrent with the closing of the offering, completed the acquisition of the stock of Merchants Dutch Express, Inc., a company that provides dry-van truckload transportation services. Incorporated in Delaware in 1994.

Directors (In addition to indicated officers)

Richard A. Murphy, Ph.D.
John J. Terry

Officers (Directors*)

*Bruce W. Jones, Chm. & C.E.O.
*Jay N. Taylor, Pres. & C.O.O.
*David C. Freeman, Exec. V.P.—Oper.

*Stephen G. Fleischer, V.P., C.F.O. & Treas.
*Steven R. Green, V.P.—Corp. Dev. & Secy.

Consolidated Balance Sheet[a] As of December 31, 1994 (000 omitted)

Assets		Liabilities & Stockholders' Equity	
Current assets	$ 7,003	Current liabilities	$ 5,038
Net property, plant & equipment	14,615	Long-term debt	10,527
Other assets	872	Deferred items	21
		*Stockholders' equity	6,904
Total	$22,490	Total	$22,490

[a]Pro forma.
*1,950,000 shares common stock outstanding.

Consolidated Income Statement

Years Ended Dec. 31	Thousands — — — — Operating Revenues	Net Income	Per Share — — — Earnings	Cash Dividends	Common Stock Price Range[a] Calendar Year
1994	$21,553	$598[b]	$ .31[b]		
1993	17,450	338			

[a]Initial public offering in February 1995.
[b]Pro forma.

Transfer Agent & Registrar: Continental Stock Transfer & Trust Co.

General Counsel:
  Siegan Barbakoff Gomberg & Kane, Ltd.

Investor Relations: Steven R. Green, V.P.

Human Resources: Bruce W. Jones, Chm.

Mgt. Info. Svcs.:
  David C. Freeman, Exec. V.P.

Auditors: KPMG Peat Marwick LLP

Traded (Symbol): NASDAQ (PACE)

Stockholders: 750

Employees: 239

Annual Meeting: As set by Directors

Andrew Corporation

10500 West 153rd Street, Orland Park, Illinois 60462
Telephone: (708) 349-3300

Andrew Corporation is a multinational supplier of communications products and systems to worldwide commercial, industrial, governmental and military customers. The Commercial Products Group supplies complete packages of transmission products and services, including terrestrial microwave, broadcast and earth station antennas and systems, coaxial cables, waveguide, towers and shelters. The Government Products Group offers electronic radar and communications reconnaissance receiving systems, position finding systems, positioners, cable, waveguide and high frequency and other antenna systems. The Network Products Group provides protocol converters and gateway devices, coaxial multiplexers and channel interfaces. Field sales offices are located in Atlanta, Dallas, Orland Park, Washington, D.C., Tokyo, Zurich and other cities around the world. The company has 11 plants in five countries: the U.S., Canada, Switzerland, Australia and Great Britain. Subsidiaries include Andrew Data Corp., Andrew Kintec Corp., Andrew KMW Systems Inc., Emerald Technology Inc., Andrew SciComm Inc., and Andrew VSAT Systems Inc. Incorporated in Illinois in 1947 as a successor to a partnership formed in 1937; reincorporated in Delaware in 1987.

Directors (In addition to indicated officer)

John G. Bollinger
Jon L. Boyes, Ph.D.
George N. Butzow
Kenneth J. Douglas

Donald N. Frey
Carole M. Howard
Ormand J. Wade

Officers (Director*)

*Floyd L. English, M.D., Chm., Pres. & C.E.O.
Joan P. Bowman, V.P.—Hum. Res.
William R. Currer, V.P.—Antenna Systems
John R. Dickson, V.P.—Corp. Mkt.
Richard A. Guipe, V.P.—HELIAX Prods.
Barry J. Houlihan, V.P.—Antenna Prods.
Anthony J. Lacopulos, V.P.—Comm. Support Equip.

Gregory F. Maruszak, V.P. & Cont.
Charles R. Nicholas, V.P.—Fin. & Adm., & C.F.O.
Edward C. Nield, V.P.—Mgmt. Info. Systems
Thomas E. Charlton, Grp. V.P.—Comm. Prods.
Alan Rossi, Grp. V.P.—Telecom Networks
William L. Shockley, Grp. V.P.—Comm. Syst.
M. Jeffrey Gittelman, Treas.
James F. Petelle, Secy.

Consolidated Balance Sheet As of September 30, 1994 (000 omitted)

Assets		Liabilities & Stockholders' Equity	
Current assets	$260,649	Current liabilities	$ 91,628
Net property, plant & equipment	74,966	Long-term debt	45,455
Other assets	79,548	Deferred items	5,226
		*Stockholders' equity	272,854
Total	$415,163	Total	$415,163

*25,544,722 shares common stock outstanding.

Consolidated Income Statement

Years Ended Sept. 30	Thousands — — — — Net Sales	Net Income	Per Share[a] — — — Earnings	Cash Dividends	Common Stock Price Range[a] Calendar Year
1994	$558,457	$44,395	$1.13	$ .00	35-7/8 — 16
1993	430,820	27,862	.73	.00	19-3/8 — 8-5/8
1992	442,008	24,987	.58	.00	10-7/8 — 4-7/8
1991	416,229	22,178	.51	.00	8-1/4 — 4-3/8
1990	365,990	18,161	.40	.00	5-3/4 — 3-3/8

[a]Adjusted to reflect 3-for-2 stock splits declared in February 1995 and 1994, and a 2-for-1 stock split declared in February 1993.

Transfer Agent & Registrar: Harris Trust and Savings Bank

General Counsel: Gardner, Carton & Douglas

Investor Relations: Charles R. Nicholas, V.P.

Human Resources: Joan P. Bowman, V.P.

Mgt. Info. Svcs.: Edward C. Nield, V.P.

Auditors: Ernst & Young LLP

Traded (Symbol): NASDAQ (ANDW)

Stockholders: 1,482

Employees: 3,096

Annual Meeting: In February

Anicom, Inc.

6133 North River Road, Suite 410, Rosemont, Illinois 60018
Telephone: (708) 518-8700

Anicom, Inc., specializes in the sale and distribution of communications-related wire, cable, fiber optics, and computer network and connectivity products. The products offered by the company generally fall into four categories: voice and data communications and fiber optics; sound, security, fire, alarm, and energy management systems; electronic cable; and industrial cable. In February 1995, the company completed an initial public offering of 1,380,000 shares of common stock. Incorporated in Delaware in 1995.

Directors (In addition to indicated officers)

William R. Anixter   Michael Segal
Ira J. Kaufman   Lee B. Stern

Officers (Directors*)

*Alan B. Anixter, Chm.   Robert L. Swanson, Exec. V.P.
*Scott C. Anixter, Co-Chm. & C.E.O.   *Donald C. Welchko, V.P. & C.F.O.
*Carl E. Putnam, Pres. & C.O.O.

Consolidated Balance Sheet   As of December 31, 1994 (000 omitted)

Assets		Liabilities & Stockholders' Equity	
Current assets	$5,799	Current liabilities	$3,123
Net property, plant & equipment	228	Long-term debt	2,730
Other assets	13	Other liabilities	30
		*Stockholders' equity	157
Total	$6,040	Total	$6,040

*1,200,000 shares common stock outstanding.

Consolidated Income Statement[a]

Years Ended Dec. 31	Thousands — — — — Net Sales	Net Income	Per Share — — — Earnings	Cash Dividends	Common Stock Price Range[b] Calendar Year
1994[c]	$17,866	$ 351	$ .15		
1994[d]	14,257	241	.20		
1993[d]	8,503	(391)	(.33)		

[a]The company was formed in July 1993 as a result of the division of a predecessor corporation into two separate corporations.
[b]Initial public offering in February 1995.
[c]Pro forma.
[d]Nine months ending December 31.

Transfer Agent & Registrar:	Harris Trust and Savings Bank		
General Counsel:	Katten Muchin & Zavis	Auditors:	Coopers & Lybrand L.L.P.
Investor Relations:	Donald C. Welchko, V.P.	Traded (Symbol):	NASDAQ (ANIC)
		Stockholders:	100
Human Resources:	Lee Smela	Employees:	50
Mgt. Info. Svcs.:	Linda Buchanan	Annual Meeting:	In May

ANTEC Corporation

2850 West Golf Road, Rolling Meadows, Illinois 60008
Telephone: (708) 439-4444

ANTEC Corporation is a leading developer, manufacturer, and supplier of optical transmission, construction, rebuild, and maintenance equipment for the broadband communications industry, having served this industry since 1969. The company is developing products and integrated systems that will enable cable operators to transform their networks from one-way, video-only coaxial cable systems to interactive, broadband fiber optic, video, voice, and data delivery networks. ANTEC was originally a wholly owned subsidiary of Anixter, Inc., which is a wholly owned subsidiary of Itel Corporation. During 1994, ANTEC made five strategic acquisitions: Electronic Systems Products, Inc., Engineering Technologies Group, Inc., Power Guard, Inc., Keptel, Inc., and Comunicaciones Broadband. Incorporated in Delaware in 1993.

Directors (In addition to indicated officers)

Bernard F. Brennan
Rod F. Dammeyer
John R. Petty

Samuel K. Skinner
Mary Agnes Wilderotter

Officers (Directors*)

*Bruce Van Wagner, Chm.
*John M. Egan, Pres. & C.E.O.
James L. Faust, Exec. V.P.—Int'l.
Gordon E. Halverson, Exec. V.P.—Sales
Martin C. Ingram, Exec. V.P. &
  Pres.—Comunicaciones Broadband

Richard K. Laird, Exec. V.P.—Opers. & Mfg.
Lawrence A. Margolis, Exec. V.P. & Secy.
Stephen K. Necessary, Exec. V.P.—Prod. Grp.
Andrew W. Paff, Exec. V.P.—Strat. Plan. & Tech.
James A. Bauer, Sr. V.P.—Comm. & Adm.
Daniel J. Distel, V.P. & Cont.

Consolidated Balance Sheet As of December 31, 1994 (000 omitted)

Assets		Liabilities & Stockholders' Equity	
Current assets	$234,178	Current liabilities	$ 83,074
Net property, plant & equipment	22,437	Long-term debt	125,197
Other assets	181,402	*Stockholders' equity	229,746
Total	$438,017	Total	$438,017

*22,100,000 shares common stock outstanding.

Consolidated Income Statement

Years Ended Dec. 31	Thousands — — — — Net Sales	Net Income[ab]	Per Share — — — Earnings[a]	Cash Dividends	Common Stock Price Range Calendar Year
1994	$553,510	$18,888	$ .89	$ .00	38-1/2 — 15
1993	427,601	11,545	.56	.00	30-1/4 — 21[c]
1992	300,974	6,210	.31		
1991	258,337	341			
1990	328,198	6,094			

[a]Pro forma for 1993 and 1992.
[b]Includes FAS 109.
[c]Initial public offering in September 1993.

Transfer Agent & Registrar: The Bank of New York

General Counsel:	Mayer, Brown & Platt	Traded (Symbol):	NASDAQ (ANTC)
Investor Relations:	James A. Bauer, Sr. V.P.	Stockholders:	500
Human Resources:	James A. Bauer, Sr. V.P.	Employees:	2,000
Auditors:	Ernst & Young LLP	Annual Meeting:	In May

Aon Corporation

123 North Wacker Drive, Chicago, Illinois 60606
Telephone: (312) 701-3000

Aon Corporation is a holding company, the subsidiaries of which provide insurance and financial services to individuals and corporate clients. Aon offers a broad range of innovative and specialized insurance services and products, including insurance brokerage and consulting, accident and health, extended warranty, traditional life, and capital accumulation. Operating through its subsidiaries in the U.S., Canada, Europe, and the Pacific, Aon markets its products and services through a wide variety of distribution channels: consultants, advisors, brokers, career agents, banks, and stockbrokers. The principal subsidiaries of Aon Corporation are Rollins Hudig Hall Group, Inc.; Combined Insurance Company of America; The Life Insurance Company of Virginia; Ryan Insurance Group, Inc.; and Union Fidelity Life Insurance Company. Incorporated in Delaware in 1979.

Directors (In addition to indicated officers)

Daniel T. Carroll	Peer Pedersen
Franklin A. Cole	Donald S. Perkins
Edgar D. Jannotta	John W. Rogers, Jr.
Perry J. Lewis	George A. Schaefer
Joan D. Manley	Fred L. Turner
Andrew J. McKenna	Arnold R. Weber
Newton N. Minow	

Officers (Directors*)

*Patrick G. Ryan, Chm., Pres. & C.E.O.	Arthur F. Quern, Sr. V.P. & Corp. Secy.
Daniel T. Cox, Exec. V.P.	Jerome I. Baer, V.P.—Taxes
Harvey N. Medvin, Exec. V.P., C.F.O. & Treas.	Thomas A. Curatolo, V.P.—Internal Auditor
	John A. Reschke, V.P.—Compensation & Benefits
*Raymond I. Skilling, Exec. V.P. & Chf. Coun.	Joan E. Steel, V.P.—Fin. Rel.
Michael A. Conway, Sr. V.P. & Sr. Invest. Off.	Stephen C. Taylor, V.P.—Prof. Dev.
Richard F. Ferruci, Sr. V.P.	James D. White, V.P. & Cont.

Consolidated Balance Sheet   As of December 31, 1994 (000 omitted)

Assets		Liabilities & Stockholders' Equity	
Investments	$ 9,782,500	Policy liabilities	$ 9,310,400
Cash	508,800	General liabilities	6,304,100
Deferred policy acquisition costs	1,186,600	Redeemable preferred stock	50,000
Total receivables	2,653,200	*Stockholders' equity	2,257,400
Other assets	3,790,800		
Total	$17,921,900	Total	$17,921,900

*107,696,000 shares common stock outstanding.

Consolidated Income Statement

Years Ended Dec. 31	Thousands — — — — Total Revenues	Net Income[ab]	Per Share[c] — — — Earnings[ab]	Cash Dividends	Common Stock Price Range[c] Calendar Year
1994	$4,157,000	$360,000	$3.14	$1.26	35-3/4 — 29-1/4
1993	3,845,000	324,000	2.81	1.18	39 — 30-7/8
1992	3,337,000	206,000	1.93	1.11	36 — 26-1/8
1991	2,931,000	242,000	2.47	1.05	27-7/8 — 19-7/8
1990	2,626,000	239,000	2.41	.99	28-3/8 — 17-7/8

[a]Before cumulative effect of FAS 106 and 109 in 1992.
[b]After realized investment gains.
[c]Adjusted to reflect a 3-for-2 stock split in May 1994.

Transfer Agent & Registrar: First Chicago Trust Co. of New York

Chief Counsel:
  Raymond I. Skilling, Exec. V.P.

Investor Relations: Joan E. Steel, V.P.

Auditors: Ernst & Young LLP

Traded (Symbol):   NYSE, CSE, London (AOC)

Stockholders: 14,000

Employees: 27,000

Annual Meeting: In April

First Chicago Guide

AptarGroup, Inc.

475 West Terra Cotta Avenue, Suite E, Crystal Lake, Illinois 60014-9695
Telephone: (815) 477-0424

AptarGroup, Inc., produces three broad categories of dispensing packaging components — pumps, aerosol valves and dispensing closures — which are sold to the personal care, fragrance/cosmetics, pharmaceutical, household products and food industries. In April 1993, Pittway Corporation completed the spinoff of AptarGroup (a wholly owned subsidiary of Pittway formed to hold Pittway's Seaquist Group packaging components businesses). The spinoff distribution consisted of one share of AptarGroup common stock for each share of Pittway stock outstanding. Immediately after the spinoff, AptarGroup completed an exchange of its stock for the 65 percent of The Pfeiffer Group, a privately held Germany-based manufacturer of pumps, that it did not already own. AptarGroup also completed an exchange of its stock for the minority interest in its European operations held by a private French investment company. Incorporated in Delaware in 1992.

Directors   (In addition to indicated officers)

Eugene L. Barnett	King Harris
Ralph Gruska	William W. Harris
Leo A. Guthart	Alfred Pilz

Officers   (Directors*)[a]

*Ervin J. LeCoque, Chm. & C.E.O.	Francois Boutan, Fin. Dir.—Eur. Oper.
*Peter Pfeiffer, V. Chm.	Pierre Cheru, Gen. Dir.—Valois S.A.
*Carl A. Siebel, Pres. & C.O.O.	Francesco Mascitelli, Gen. Mgr.—SAR SpA
Stephen J. Hagge, Exec. V.P., Secy. & Treas.	James R. Reed, Pres.—Seaquist Dispensing Div.
Lawrence Lowrimore, V.P.—Hum. Res.	Eric S. Ruskoski, Pres.—Seaquist Closures Div.
Ralph Poltermann, V.P.—Risk Mgt.	Hans-Josef Schutz, Man. Dir.—Pfeiffer Grp.
Jacques Blanie, Man. Dir.—Perfect-Valois Ventil GmbH	Alain Vichot, Gen. Dir. Adj.—Valois S.A.

[a]LeCoque will retire on December 31, 1995, but remain a director; Siebel will become C.E.O.; and King Harris, a director, will become Chairman in a nonexecutive capacity.

Consolidated Balance Sheet   As of December 31, 1994 (000 omitted)

Assets		Liabilities & Stockholders' Equity	
Current assets	$184,394	Current liabilities	$106,272
Net property, plant & equipment	216,347	Long-term debt	53,763
Other assets	64,654	Deferred items	34,750
		*Stockholders' equity	270,610
Total	$465,395	Total	$465,395

*17,900,000 shares common stock outstanding.

Consolidated Income Statement

Years Ended Dec. 31	Thousands — — — — Net Sales	Net Income	Per Share — — — — Earnings	Cash Dividends	Common Stock Price Range[a] Calendar Year	
1994	$474,266	$27,258	$1.65	$ .23	29	— 20-1/8
1993[b]	411,525	21,563[c]	1.34[c]	.10	22	— 16[d]
1992	370,293	19,479				
1991	314,310	13,708				
1990	299,163	9,794				

[a]Pittway Corporation spun off AptarGroup, Inc., in April 1993.
[b]Includes the effects of The Pfeiffer Group and minority interest since acquisition on April 22, 1993.
[c]Before cumulative effect of accounting change for FAS 109, which positively impacted net income by $1,400,000 ($.09 per share).
[d]Trading commenced on April 23, 1993, on the New York Stock Exchange.

Transfer Agent & Registrar:	Chemical Bank		
General Counsel:	Sidley & Austin	Auditors:	Price Waterhouse LLP
Investment Relations: Stephen J. Hagge, Exec. V.P.		Traded (Symbol):	NYSE (ATR)
		Stockholders:	1,120
Human Resources:	Lawrence Lowrimore, V.P.	Employees:	3,300
Mgt. Info. Svcs.:	Ruth Freer	Annual Meeting:	In May

Archer-Daniels-Midland Company

4666 Faries Parkway, Decatur, Illinois 62526-5666
Telephone: (217) 424-5200

Archer-Daniels-Midland Company (ADM) is in the business of procuring, transporting, storing, processing and merchandising agricultural products. The Oilseed Processing Division operates extraction plants that produce a broad line of vegetable oils including soy, corn, sunflower, peanut, conola and cottonseed. The ADM Corn Processing Division manufactures and distributes sweeteners, starches, beverage alcohol and ethanol. Dextrose from corn is being used to produce such bioproducts as amino acids for animal feed, and food and beverage additives for human consumption. The Protein Specialties Division produces soy flours, protein isolates and textured vegetable protein used in processed meat products, convenience foods and pet food. ADM Milling Co. produces wheat flour used in bakery products, cereals, processed foods and pasta products. Its grain division handles grain acquisition and merchandising. The Supreme Sugar Company, Inc., includes a sugar refinery and a sugar cane grinding mill. The Southern Cotton Oil Company processes cottonseed. American River Transportation Company assists the company as a carrier of drybulk and liquid commodities. ADM conducts operations throughout the U.S. and in the United Kingdom, Canada, Germany, Spain, the Netherlands, Ireland, France and Portugal. Other major subsidiaries include: ADM/Growmark; The British Arkady Co., Ltd.; Fleischmann Malting Co., Inc.; Gooch Foods, Inc.; Hickory Point Bank & Trust; Smoot Grain Company; Tabor Grain Co.; and ADM International Ltd. Incorporated in Delaware in 1923.

Directors (In addition to indicated officers)

Lowell W. Andreas	Ray A. Goldberg, Ph.D.	Mrs. Nelson A. Rockefeller
Shreve M. Archer, Jr.	H.D. Hale	Robert S. Strauss
Ralph Bruce	F. Ross Johnson	John K. Vanier
John H. Daniels	M. Brian Mulroney	O. Glenn Webb

Officers (Directors*)

*Dwayne O. Andreas, Chm. & C.E.O.	Raymond V. Preiksaitis, V.P.—MIS
*Michael D. Andreas, V. Chm. & Exec. V.P.	John G. Reed, Jr., V.P.
*James R. Randall, Pres.	Richard P. Reising, V.P., Secy. & Gen. Coun.
*Martin L. Andreas, Sr. V.P. & Exec. Asst. to C.E.O.	John D. Rice, V.P.
G. Allen Andreas, V.P. & Coun. to Exec. Comm.	Douglas J. Schmalz, V.P., Cont. & C.F.O.
Charles T. Bayless, V.P.	Mark E. Whitacre, V.P.
Dale F. Benson, V.P.	Charles P. Archer, Treas.
William H. Camp, V.P.	Steven R. Mills, Cont.
Larry H. Cunningham, V.P.	Howard E. Buoy, Grp. V.P.
Thomas A. Duffield, V.P.	Craig L. Hamlin, Grp. V.P.
Edward A. Harjehausen, V.P.	Burnell D. Kraft, Grp. V.P.
Paul L. Krug, Jr., V.P.	Terrance S. Wilson, Grp. V.P.
Jack McDonald, V.P.	

Consolidated Balance Sheet   As of June 30, 1994 (000 omitted)

Assets		Liabilities & Stockholders' Equity	
Current assets	$3,910,795	Current liabilities	$1,126,978
Net property, plant & equipment	3,538,575	Long-term debt	2,021,417
Other assets	1,297,483	Deferred items	553,037
		*Stockholders' equity	5,045,421
Total	$8,746,853	Total	$8,746,853

*343,639,000 shares common stock outstanding.

Consolidated Income Statement

Years Ended June 30	Thousands — — — —		Per Share[a] — — —		Common Stock
	Net Sales	Net Income	Earnings	Cash Dividends	Price Range[a] Calendar Year
1994	$11,374,372	$484,069	$ .93	$ .05	21-1/8 — 14-1/4
1993	9,811,362	567,527[b]	1.05[b]	.05	17-1/2 — 13-1/4
1992	9,231,502	503,757	.93	.05	18-7/8 — 12-7/8
1991	8,468,198	466,678	.86	.05	19-1/8 — 10-5/8
1990	7,751,341	483,522	.89	.04	14-1/8 — 9-3/8

[a]Adjusted for annual 5% stock dividends through September 1994 and a 3-for-2 stock split in December 1994.
[b]Includes a gain to reflect FAS 106 and FAS 109, resulting in a cumulative effect of $33,018,000 ($.06 per share).

Transfer Agent & Registrar: Harris Trust and Savings Bank

General Counsel:	Richard P. Reising, V.P.	Traded (Symbol):	
Investor Relations:	Charles P. Archer, Treas.	NYSE,CSE,Tokyo,Frankfurt,2 Switzerland SE(ADM)	
Human Resources:	Dale F. Benson, V.P.	Stockholders:	33,940
Mgt. Info. Svcs.:	Raymond V. Preiksaitis, V.P.	Employees:	16,013
Auditors:	Ernst & Young LLP, Minneapolis	Annual Meeting:	In October

Argosy Gaming Company

219 Piasa Street, Alton, Illinois 62002-6232
Telephone: (618) 474-7500

Argosy Gaming Company, through its subsidiaries, owns and operates riverboat casinos in Alton, Illinois, Riverside, Missouri, Baton Rouge, Louisiana, and Sioux City, Iowa, including the *Alton Belle* riverboat casino, which commenced operations in September 1991 as the first riverboat in the state of Illinois. The *Alton Belle II*, which commenced operations on May 29, 1993, is a contemporary styled cruise liner which operates on the Mississippi River in Alton, Illinois, approximately 20 miles northeast of downtown St. Louis. The *Alton Belle Casino II* is a tri-level casino which accommodates 1,300 passengers, features 650 slot machines and 41 gaming tables. The *Argosy IV*, the largest of the Argosy fleet, serves the Kansas City operation, while the *Belle* serves the Baton Rouge market. The *Belle of Sioux City* commenced operation in October 1994. Subsidiaries are Alton Gaming Company, The Missouri Gaming Company, Argosy of Louisiana, Inc., Iowa Gaming Company—Sioux City, The Indiana Gaming Company, and Argosy of Iowa Inc.—Osceola. Incorporated in Delaware in 1992.

Directors (In addition to indicated officer)

William F. Cellini, Chm.
Edward F. Brennan
George L. Bristol
F. Lance Callis

Jimmy F. Gallagher
William McEnery
John B. Pratt, Sr.

Officers (Director*)

*J. Thomas Long, V. Chm. & C.E.O.
H. Steven Norton, Pres. & C.O.O.
Daniel E. Evans, V.P.—Opers.
Walter I. Rogers, V.P.—Casino Dev.

Joseph G. Uram, V.P., C.F.O. & Treas.
Dale Black, Cont.
Patsy S. Hubbard, Corp. Secy.

Consolidated Balance Sheet   As of December 31, 1994 (000 omitted)

Assets		Liabilities & Stockholders' Equity	
Current assets	$ 29,334	Current liabilities	$ 22,506
Net property, plant & equipment	167,548	Long-term debt	115,000
Other assets	35,949	Deferred items	1,750
		Other liabilities	2,988
		*Stockholders' equity	90,587
Total	$232,831	Total	$232,831

*24,333,333 shares common stock outstanding.

Consolidated Income Statement

Years Ended Dec. 31	Thousands — — — — Net Revenues	Net Income	Per Share — — — Earnings[a]	Cash Dividends	Common Stock Price Range Calendar Year
1994	$153,045	$ 9,635	$ .40	$ .00	27 — 10
1993	67,525	10,825	.38	.00	36-3/4— 15-1/4[b]
1992	58,019	15,214	.36	.00	
1991[c]	14,119	659			

[a]Pro forma for 1993 and 1992.
[b]Initial public offering in February 1993.
[c]Financial information includes all preopening expenses, totaling $1,569,000, associated with the developmental stage of the company through September 10, 1991, the date the company was granted its operating license from the Illinois Gaming Board. The company received no operating revenues prior to September 10, 1991.

Transfer Agent & Registrar: Harris Trust and Savings Bank

General Counsel: Winston & Strawn

Investor Relations: G. Dan Marshall, Dir.

Human Resources: Dan Bolin

Mgt. Info. Svcs.: Robert Pekel

Auditors: Ernst & Young LLP
Traded (Symbol): NASDAQ (ARGY)
Stockholders: 801
Employees: 3,068
Annual Meeting: In April

ARTRA GROUP Incorporated

500 Central Avenue, Northfield, Illinois 60093
Telephone: (708) 441-6650

ARTRA GROUP Incorporated, through its subsidiaries, operates in two businesses: as a manufacturer of flexible packaging; and as a creator and distributor of fashion jewelry and accessories. Subsidiaries include: Bagcraft Corporation of America, which supplies specialty wraps and bags to the food industry; and Lori Corporation, a 64 percent-owned subsidiary, which creates and distributes jewelry and accessories through two wholly owned subsidiaries: Rosecraft, Inc., and Lawrence Jewelry Corporation. Lori's fashion/costume jewelry products and accessories are sold in retail outlets nationwide. Incorporated in Pennsylvania in 1933.

Director (In addition to indicated officers)

Gerard M. Kenny

Officers (Directors*)

* John Harvey, Chm. & C.E.O.
* Peter R. Harvey, Pres. & C.O.O.
John G. Hamm, Exec. V.P.
John Conroy, V.P.—Corp. Admin.

James D. Doering, V.P., Treas. & C.F.O.
Robert S. Gruber, V.P.—Corp. Rel.
Lawrence D. Levin, Cont.
Edwin G. Rymek, Secy.

Consolidated Balance Sheet As of December 29, 1994 (000 omitted)

Assets		Liabilities & Stockholders' Equity	
Current assets	$38,517	Current liabilities	$ 98,989
Net property, plant & equipment	31,040	Long-term debt	19,673
Other assets	23,872	Other liabilities	32,527
		* [a]Stockholders' equity	(57,760)
Total	$93,429	Total	$ 93,429

*6,678,243 shares common stock outstanding.
[a]ARTRA GROUP Incorporated is involved in pending litigation to recover its investment in Emerald Acquisition Corp. common stock and Emerald junior debentures. For further information, please refer to ARTRA's Form 10-K.

Consolidated Income Statement

| Years Ended Dec. 31 | Thousands — — — — — | | Per Share — — — — | | Common Stock Price Range Calendar Year |
	Net Sales	Net Income	Earnings	Cash Dividends	
1994[a]	$152,115	$(20,470)[b]	$(3.73)[b]	$ .00	7-3/4 — 3-3/4
1993	159,638	13,514[b]	2.61[b]	.00	8-3/8 — 3
1992[c]	196,568	(37,972)	(8.90)	.00	11-1/4 — 3-3/8
1991	230,740	(13,161)	(3.36)	.00	13-1/8 — 5-3/4
1990[d]	231,526	(4,237)	(1.30)	.00	13-1/4 — 5

[a]Includes the operations of Arcar Graphics, Inc., since its acquisition on April 9, 1994.
[b]Includes extraordinary credit of $8,965,000 ($1.57 per share) in 1994; and a non-recurring gain of $22,057,000 ($4.49 per share) from extinguished debt at Lori Corporation subsidiary in 1993.
[c]Includes non-recurring charges of $18,150,000.
[d]Unaudited pro forma results of operations as if ARTRA had acquired Bagcraft on January 1, 1989.

Transfer Agent & Registrar: Mellon Securities Transfer Services

General Counsel:
Kwiatt, Silverman & Ruben Ltd.

Investor Relations:
Robert S. Gruber, V.P.—(212) 628-2554

Human Resources: John Conroy, V.P.

Auditors: Coopers & Lybrand L.L.P.
Traded (Symbol): NYSE, PSE (ATA)
Stockholders: 2,500
Employees: 1,600
Annual Meeting: As set by Directors

AutoFinance Group, Inc.

601 Oakmont Lane, Suite 110, Westmont, Illinois 60559-5549
Telephone: (708) 655-7100

AutoFinance Group, Inc., is engaged in the business of acquiring and servicing non-prime retail automotive installment sales contracts. The non-prime market segment is comprised of individuals who are deemed to be greater credit risks due to the manner in which they have handled their previous credit; the absence, or limited nature, of their previous credit; and/or their limited income and/or financial resources. The company has expanded its contract acquisition activities to include the bulk purchase of automotive installment sales contracts and secured promissory notes from financial institutions and independent finance companies. The company also has commenced offering to service third party receivables and providing consulting and other services to organizations in the automotive financing business. Subsidiaries are AFG Receivables Corporation and Patlex Corporation. In March 1995, AutoFinance Group announced that it would be acquired by KeyCorp of Cleveland, Ohio. Incorporated in California in 1980 as Vitalmetrics, Inc.; present named adopted in 1990.

Directors (In addition to indicated officers)

Frank Borman, Chm.	Kenneth G. Langone
Ronald M. Brill	W. Robert Lappin
Gary E. Erlbaum	Allen T. Newman
Peter S. Gold	Russell L. Ray, Jr.
Steven D. Holzman	

Officers (Directors*)

*A.E. Steinhaus, V. Chm., Pres. & C.E.O.   Jack D. Ward, Chf. Acct. Officer & Asst. Secy.
*Blair T. Nance, C.F.O. & Secy.

Consolidated Balance Sheet As of June 30, 1994 (000 omitted)

Assets		Liabilities & Stockholders' Equity	
Current assets	$ 4,804	Current liabilities	$ 26,505
Net property, plant & equipment	955	Long-term debt	2,313
Other assets	102,737	Deferred items	3,464
		*Stockholders' equity	76,214
Total	$108,496	Total	$108,496

*18,449,699 shares common stock outstanding.

Consolidated Income Statement

Years Ended June 30	Thousands — — — — Net Sales	Net Income	Per Share[a] — — — Earnings	Cash Dividends	Common Stock Price Range[a] Fiscal Year
1994	$29,031	$ 7,136	$ .42	$ .00	13-1/2 — 8-1/2
1993	15,340	3,033	.24	.00	10-5/8 — 3-1/2
1992	9,264	1,268	.17	.00	9-1/8 — 3-3/4
1991	4,676	(2,279)	(.38)	.00	6-1/2 — 2-1/4
1990	1,737	(3,207)	(.86)	.00	

[a]Adjusted to reflect a 1-for-5 reverse stock split in August 1990.

Transfer Agent & Registrar: LaSalle National Trust, N.A.

General Counsel:	Kindel & Anderson	Traded (Symbol):	NASDAQ (AUFN)
Investor Relations:	Blair T. Nance, C.F.O.	Stockholders:	800
Mgt. Info. Svcs.:	Lloyd K. Zellner	Employees:	106
Auditors:	Ernst & Young LLP	Annual Meeting:	In December

Avondale Financial Corp.

20 North Clark Street, Chicago, Illinois 60602-5085
Telephone: (312) 782-6200

Avondale Financial Corp. is the holding company for Avondale Federal Savings Bank, a federally chartered stock savings bank currently serving the Chicago metropolitan area through its six retail banking offices in Chicago, Niles and Lake Forest. The principal business of Avondale consists of attracting retail deposits from the general public and investing those funds primarily in mortgage-backed securities and first and second mortgages, including equity lines of credit, on owner-occupied and non-owner-occupied, one-to-four-family residences. In April 1995, Avondale Financial Corp. completed an initial public offering of 3,680,000 shares of common stock. Incorporated in Delaware in 1993.

Directors   (In addition to indicated officers)

Jameson A. Baxter
Arthur L. Knight, Jr.
Peter G. Krivkovich

Hipolito (Paul) Roldan
Robert A. Wislow

Officers   (Directors*)

*R. Thomas Eiff, Chm.
*Robert S. Engelman, Jr., Pres., C.E.O. & Treas.

Craig D. Johnston, V.P.
Doria L. Koros, Secy.

Consolidated Balance Sheet   As of March 31, 1995 (000 omitted)

Assets		Liabilities & Stockholder's Equity	
Total assets	$539,703	*Total liabilities & stockholder's equity	$539,703
Total	$539,703	Total	$539,703

*3,978,080 shares common stock outstanding (as of April 3, 1995, upon completion of public offering and conversion).

Consolidated Income Statement[a]

Years Ended March 31	Thousands — — — — Total Income	Net Income	Per Share — — — Earnings	Cash Dividends	Common Stock Price Range[b] Calendar Year
1995	$27,569	$(1,400)			
1994	33,854	2,707			
1993	39,488	(3,991)			
1992	.45,987	1,467			
1991	47,485	1,224			

[a]1995-90 data are for Avondale Federal Savings Bank.
[b]Initial public offering in April 1995.

Transfer Agent & Registrar: LaSalle National Trust, N.A.

General Counsel:
  Silver, Freedman & Taff L.L.P.

Investor Relations: Craig D. Johnston, V.P.

Auditors: Arthur Andersen LLP

Traded (Symbol):   NASDAQ (AVND)
Stockholders: 1,087
Employees: 101
Annual Meeting: In October

Baker, Fentress & Company

200 West Madison Street, Suite 3510, Chicago, Illinois 60606
Telephone: (312) 236-9190

Baker, Fentress & Company is a non-diversified closed-end investment company which invests primarily for capital appreciation. The company is internally managed by its officers under the supervision of its Board of Directors. Until 1960, the company conducted business as an investment banker and a dealer and broker in securities. In 1960, it became a private investment firm. Since 1970, Baker, Fentress & Company has been registered as an investment company under the Investment Company Act of 1940. The company invests primarily in common stocks and other equity-type securities. In addition, Baker, Fentress invests in preferred stocks, bonds, debentures and notes, and short-term obligations. Major investments include: Consolidated-Tomoka Land Co., MCI Communications Corp., Barnett Banks, Inc., and United HealthCare/Complete Health. Incorporated in Delaware in 1954.

Directors   (In addition to indicated officers)

Frederick S. Addy
Bob D. Allen
J. Barton Goodwin
David D. Grumhaus

Richard M. Jones
Burton G. Malkiel
William H. Springer

Officers   (Directors*)

*James P. Gorter, Chm.
*David D. Peterson, Pres. & C.E.O.
 Steven C. Carhart, V.P.
 George V. Carracio, Jr., V.P.

James P. Koeneman, V.P., C.F.O. & Secy.
Scott E. Smith, V.P.
Janet Sandona Jones, Treas. & Asst. Secy.

Consolidated Balance Sheet   As of December 31, 1994 (000 omitted)

Assets		Liabilities & Stockholders' Equity	
Current assets	$462,107	Current liabilities	$ 609
Other assets	433	*Stockholders' equity	461,931
Total	$462,540	Total	$462,540

*26,441,682 shares common stock outstanding.

Consolidated Income Statement

Years Ended Dec. 31	Thousands Net Investment Income	Per Share Cash Dividend	Capital Gain Distr.	Net Asset Value	Common Stock Price Range Calendar Year
1994	$ 6,933	$0.35	$1.46	$17.47	17-7/8 — 13-3/8
1993	7,116	0.48	1.76	20.42	19-7/8 — 16-3/8
1992	8,430	0.39	1.42	20.82	19-1/8 — 16-5/8
1991	9,880	0.58	1.15	21.49	18-1/4 — 14-3/8
1990	12,287	0.70	1.25	18.66	21-5/8 — 14-1/4

Transfer Agent & Registrar: Harris Trust and Savings Bank

General Counsel:	Bell, Boyd & Lloyd	Traded (Symbol):	NYSE (BKF)
Investor Relations:	James P. Koeneman, V.P.	Stockholders:	14,000
Human Relations:	Lana Spence, Mgr.	Employees:	15
Auditors:	Ernst & Young LLP	Annual Meeting:	In April

Bally Entertainment Corporation

8700 West Bryn Mawr Avenue, Chicago, Illinois 60631-3547
Telephone: (312) 399-1300

Bally Entertainment Corporation is a leading operator of casino/hotel resorts and fitness centers. The company is organized within two operating segments. The Casino segment includes the ownership and operation (through subsidiaries) of Bally's Park Place casino hotel and tower, and The Grand casino hotel in Atlantic City, New Jersey. In addition, the company (with subsidiaries) has an approximate 80 percent equity interest in Bally's Grand, Inc., which owns and operates Bally's Las Vegas casino resort in Nevada. The company (through a subsidiary) manages that same casino. The company (through a subsidiary) owns and operates Bally's Saloon & Gambling Hall, a dockside casino in Tunica, Mississippi. This casino ceased operations in February 1995. Bally Entertainment has entered into a joint venture agreement with Lady Luck Gaming Corp. to relocate the Tunica casino to Robinsonville, Mississippi. Another subsidiary of the company owns an equity interest of approximately 50 percent in Bally's New Orleans, which is expected to operate a riverboat casino facility in New Orleans in 1995. The subsidiary also will manage the casino. The Fitness Centers segment (treated as a discontinued operation) includes the operation of 332 fitness centers. Subsidiaries include: Bally's Grand, Inc., Bally's Park Place, Inc., GNAC, Corp., Bally's Casino Holdings, Inc., Bally's Tunica, Inc., Bally's Louisiana, Inc., Bally's Health & Tennis Corporation, and Health & Tennis Corporation of America. During 1994, Bally Entertainment changed its name from Bally Manufacturing Corp., announced plans to spin off its health club operation, and increased its equity ownership in Bally's Grand, Inc. Incorporated in Delaware in 1968.

Directors (In addition to indicated officer)

George N. Aronoff	J. Kenneth Looloian	Patrick L. O'Malley
Barrie K. Brunet	Rocco J. Marano	James M. Rochford
Edwin M. Halkyard		

Officers (Director*)

*Arthur M. Goldberg, Chm., Pres. & C.E.O.
Lee S. Hillman, Exec. V.P., C.F.O. & Treas.
James Montana, Sr. V.P. & Gen. Coun.
Robert G. Conover, V.P.—MIS & Chf. Info. Officer
John W. Dwyer, V.P. & Corp. Cont.

Harold Morgan, V.P.—Hum. Res.
Bernard J. Murphy, V.P.—Corp. Affairs & Govt. Rel.
Jerry W. Thornburg, V.P.—Audit
Carol Stone DePaul, Secy.

Consolidated Balance Sheet   As of December 31, 1994 (000 omitted)

Assets		Liabilities & Stockholders' Equity	
Current assets	$ 248,693	Current liabilities	$ 177,642
Net property, plant & equipment	1,186,868	Long-term debt	1,258,990
Other assets	500,600	Deferred items	152,851
		Other liabilities & minority interests	53,066
		*Stockholders' equity	293,612
Total	$1,936,161	Total	$1,936,161

*46,991,542 shares common stock outstanding.

Consolidated Income Statement

Years Ended Dec. 31	Thousands — — — —		Per Share — — —		Common Stock Price Range Calendar Year
	Revenues[a]	Net Income	Earnings	Cash Dividends	
1994	$942,255	$(68,389)	$(1.52)	$ .00	9-5/8 — 5-1/4
1993	628,205	(46,498)[b]	(1.06)[b]	.00	12-3/4 — 6
1992	555,996	11,774	.22	.00	8-1/8 — 4-1/8
1991	544,500	21,528	.55	.00	6-1/2 — 1-7/8
1990	564,800	(280,343)	(10.15)	.23	15-5/8 — 2-1/8

[a]Restated to reflect Bally's Health & Tennis Corp. as a discontinued operation due to planned spinoff.
[b]Includes a loss to reflect FAS 109, resulting in a cumulative effect of $28,197,000 ($.61 per share).

Transfer Agent & Registrar:	Chemical Bank		
General Counsel:	James Montana, Sr. V.P.	Auditors:	Ernst & Young LLP
Investor Relations:	Lee S. Hillman, Exec. V.P.	Traded (Symbol):	CSE, NYSE (BLY)
Human Resources:	Harold Morgan, V.P.	Stockholders:	16,249
		Employees:	12,900
Mgt. Info. Svcs.:	Robert G. Conover, V.P.	Annual Meeting:	In May

Bankers Life Holding Corporation

222 Merchandise Mart Plaza, Chicago, Illinois 60654-2076
Telephone: (312) 396-6000

Bankers Life Holding Corporation is an insurance holding company for Bankers Life and Casualty Company, Certified Life Insurance Company, and Bankers Life Insurance Company of Illinois. Founded in 1880, Bankers Life and Casualty is one of the nation's largest writers of individual health insurance products based on premiums collected. Bankers Life and Casualty has offered health insurance policies for more than 50 years and Medicare supplement policies since the creation of the federal Medicare program in 1966. It focuses on the senior citizen marketplace and maintains a strong presence in this individual health insurance niche market primarily by emphasizing Medicare supplement and long-term care policies. Incorporated in Delaware in 1992.

Directors (In addition to indicated officers)

Kevin Cogan
Ngaire E. Cuneo
Rollin M. Dick

Donald F. Gongaware
James E. Rogers, Jr.

Officers (Directors*)

*Stephen C. Hilbert, Chm.
*Barth T. Murphy, Pres. & C.E.O.
*Fred E. Crosley, Exec. V.P. & C.F.O.
Eric J. Bedel, Sr. V.P.—Brokerage
Robert G. Clancy, Sr. V.P.—Data Proc.
Systems

Thomas E. Dunphy, Sr. V.P.—Group
Laurence Good, Sr. V.P.—Oper.
*Paul W. Janus, Sr. V.P.—Actuarial
Leroy J. Kunselman, Sr. V.P.—Mktg.

Consolidated Balance Sheet As of December 31, 1994 (000 omitted)

Assets		Liabilities & Stockholders' Equity	
Total investments	$2,868,900	Total liabilities	$3,450,600
Accounts receivable & uncollected premiums	46,200	*Stockholders' equity	478,200
Other assets	1,013,700		
Total	$3,928,800	Total	$3,928,800

*52,782,700 shares common stock outstanding.

Consolidated Income Statement[a]

Years Ended Dec. 31	Thousands — — — — Total Revenues	Net Income[c]	Per Share[b] — — — — Earnings	Cash Dividends	Common Stock Price Range[b] Calendar Year
1994	$1,437,900	$133,600	$2.49	$ .47	25-3/4 — 16-1/2
1993[d]	1,459,100	136,100	2.49	.04	28-1/4 — 17
1992[e]	222,500	9,400			
1992[f]	1,013,800	62,500			
1991	1,185,000	80,400			

[a]Restated to reflect adoption of FAS 109, effective January 1, 1991.
[b]Adjusted to reflect a 350-for-1 stock split in March 1993. IPO in March 1993.
[c]Includes equity in losses of First Executive Corporation, income (loss) from discontinued operations, and cumulative effect of change in accounting method. Net income for the two months ended December 31, 1992, reflects adoption of FAS 106.
[d]Pro forma as if IPO and recapitalization occurred January 1, 1993.
[e]Two months ending December 31, 1992, for Bankers Life Holding Corporation.
[f]10 months ending October 31, 1992, for Bankers Life and Casualty Company. 1991 financial information is for Bankers Life and Casualty Company.

Transfer Agent & Registrar: First Union National Bank, North Carolina			
General Counsel: Lawrence W. Inlow		**Auditors:**	Coopers & Lybrand L.L.P.
Investor Relations: Patrick J. Mitchell		**Traded (Symbol):**	NYSE (BLH)
		Stockholders:	6,050
Human Resources: Thomas M. Skahen, V.P.		**Employees:**	1,950
Mgt. Info. Svcs.: Robert G. Clancy, Sr. V.P.		**Annual Meeting:**	As set by Directors

Baxter International Inc.

One Baxter Parkway, Deerfield, Illinois 60015
Telephone: (708) 948-2000

Baxter International Inc. engages in the worldwide development, manufacture and distribution of a diversified line of products, systems and services used in hospitals and other health-care settings. Products are manufactured in 21 countries and sold in about 100. Health care is concerned with the preservation of health and with the diagnosis, cure, mitigation, and treatment of disease and body defects and deficiencies. The company's more than 200,000 products are used primarily by hospitals, clinical and medical research laboratories, blood and dialysis centers, rehabilitation centers, nursing homes, doctors' offices and at home under physician supervision. The company also distributes and manufactures a wide range of products for research and development facilities and manufacturing facilities. The company concentrates research-and-development programs in biotechnology, cardiovascular medicine, renal therapy, and related medical fields. Baxter subsidiaries include Baxter World Trade Corp. and Baxter Healthcare Corp. Incorporated in Delaware in 1931.

Directors (In addition to indicated officers)

Silas S. Cathcart	Frank R. Frame	Georges St. Laurent, Jr.
John W. Colloton	David W. Grainger	Monroe E. Trout, M.D.
Susan Crown	Martha R. Ingram	Fred L. Turner
Mary Johnston Evans	Arnold J. Levine, Ph.D.	

Officers (Directors*)

*William B. Graham, Sr. Chm.
*Vernon R. Loucks, Jr., Chm. & C.E.O.
Lester B. Knight, Exec. V.P.
Tony L. White, Exec. V.P.
Harry M. Jansen Kraemer, Jr., Sr. V.P. & C.F.O.
Arthur F. Staubitz, Sr. V.P. & Gen. Coun.
Herbert E. Walker, Sr. V.P.—Hum. Res.

Dale A. Smith, Grp. V.P.—R&D
David J. Aho, V.P.
John F. Gaither, Jr., V.P.—Corp. Dev. & Strategy
Roberto Perez, V.P.—Manuf. Strategy
Brian P. Anderson, Cont.
Lawrence D. Damron, Treas.
A. Gerard Sieck, Secy.

Consolidated Balance Sheet As of December 31, 1994 (000 omitted)

Assets		Liabilities & Stockholders' Equity	
Current assets	$ 4,340,000	Current liabilities	$ 2,766,000
Net property, plant & equipment	2,562,000	Long-term debt	2,341,000
Other assets	3,100,000	Deferred items	167,000
		Other liabilities	1,008,000
		*Stockholders' equity	3,720,000
Total	$10,002,000	Total	$10,002,000

*282,310,155 shares common stock outstanding.

Consolidated Income Statement

Years Ended Dec. 31	Thousands — — — — Net Sales[a]	Net Income	Per Share — — — Earnings	Cash Dividends	Common Stock Price Range Calendar Year
1994	$9,324,000	$ 596,000	$ 2.13	$1.02	28-7/8 — 21-5/8
1993	8,879,000	(198,000)[b]	(.72)[b]	1.00	32-3/4 — 20
1992	8,471,000	441,000[c]	1.56[c]	.86	40-1/2 — 30-1/2
1991	7,799,000	591,000	2.03	.74	40-7/8 — 25-5/8
1990[d]	7,234,000	40,000	(.05)	.64	29-3/8 — 20-1/2

[a]Restated to exclude operations discontinued in 1992.
[b]Includes a provision for restructuring charges of a pretax amount of $700,000,000 and a provision for litigation charges of a pretax amount of $330,000,000; and includes a gain to reflect FAS 109 and FAS 112, resulting in a cumulative effect of $70,000,000 ($.25 per share).
[c]Includes a charge to reflect FAS 106, resulting in a cumulative effect of $165,000,000 ($.59 per share).
[d]Results include a provision for restructuring program costs of a pretax amount of $562,000,000.

Transfer Agent & Registrar: First Chicago Trust Co. of New York

General Counsel:	Arthur F. Staubitz, Sr. V.P.	Traded (Symbol):	CSE, NYSE, PSE, LON, SWISS (BAX)
Investor Relations:	Neville Jeharajah, V.P.	Stockholders:	78,400
Human Resources:	Herbert E. Walker, Sr. V.P.	Employees:	53,500
Auditors:	Price Waterhouse LLP	Annual Meeting:	In May

Bell & Howell Holdings Company

5215 Old Orchard Road, Skokie, Illinois 60077-1076
Telephone: (708) 470-7660

Bell & Howell Holdings Company is a leading provider of systems and services for information access and dissemination. The company consists of two business segments, Information Access and Mail-Processing Systems. Information Access develops and markets imaging and information services and systems that provide its customers with access solutions to targeted segments of complex public and private information databases. Mail-Processing Systems develops and markets a complete range of high volume mail-processing systems, which increasingly utilize the company's proprietary software to expand the capabilities and improve the efficiencies and effectiveness of customers' mailing operations. In May 1995, the company completed an initial public offering of 5,000,000 shares of common stock. Incorporated in Delaware in 1993.

Directors   (In addition to indicated officers)

David Bonderman
David Brown
J. Taylor Crandall
Daniel L. Doctoroff

William E. Oberndorf
Gary L. Roubos
John H. Scully

Officers   (Directors*)

*William J. White, Chm. & C.E.O.
*James P. Roemer, Pres. & C.O.O.
*Nils A. Johansson, Exec. V.P. & C.F.O.
 Richard S. Austin, V.P.
 Patrick J. Graver, V.P. & Treas.
 Stuart T. Lieberman, V.P., Cont. & Chf. Acct.
  Officer

Robert A. Nero, V.P.
Maria T. Rubly, V.P.
Robert T. Stirling, V.P.
Dieter E.A. Tannenberg, V.P.
Gary S. Salit, Corp. Coun. & Secy.

Consolidated Balance Sheet   As of December 31, 1994 (000 omitted)

Assets		Liabilities & Stockholders' Equity	
Current assets	$254,502	Current liabilities	$ 317,689
Net property, plant & equipment	131,524	Long-term liabilities	564,784
Other assets	217,719	*Stockholders' equity	(278,728)
Total	$603,745	Total	$ 603,745

*3,129,904 shares common stock outstanding.

Consolidated Income Statement

Years Ended Dec. 31	Thousands — — — — Net Sales	Net Income[a]	Per Share[b] — — — Earnings	Cash Dividends	Common Stock Price Range[bc] Calendar Year
1994[d]	$720,340	$ (9,460)	$ (.52)		
1993[e]	675,553	(188,047)			
1992	670,039	(22,335)			
1991	624,961	(24,142)			
1990	612,140	(30,695)			

[a]Applicable to common stock.
[b]Adjusted to reflect a 4.26-for-1 stock split in May 1995.
[c]Initial public offering in May 1995.
[d]Unaudited pro forma; Includes extraordinary losses of $9,193,000.
[e]Includes extraordinary losses of $6,625,000, and a charge to reflect FAS 106, resulting in a cumulative effect of $4,759,000.

Transfer Agent & Registrar: The First National Bank of Boston

General Counsel: Gary S. Salit, Secy.

Investor Relations:
 Henry A. D'Ambrosio, V.P.—Adm.

Human Resources: Maria T. Rubly, V.P.

Auditors: KPMG Peat Marwick LLP

Traded (Symbol): NYSE (BHW)

Stockholders: 2,000

Employees: 5,791

Annual Meeting: In May

First Chicago Guide

Bell Bancorp, Inc.

79 West Monroe Street, Chicago, Illinois 60603-4988
Telephone: (312) 346-1000

Bell Bancorp, Inc., is a holding company organized for the purpose of acquiring all of the capital stock of Bell Federal Savings and Loan Association. Bell Federal was originally organized by employees of Illinois Bell Telephone Company in 1925 as an Illinois-chartered building and loan association under the name Bell Savings, Building and Loan Association. In 1969, Bell Federal converted to a federal savings association under its current name. The savings and loan currently operates out of 14 locations, four in Chicago, five in suburban Cook County, three in DuPage County, one in Lake County and one in Winnebago County. Bell Federal's home office is located in the Chicago financial district. Bell Federal has been and continues to be a traditional thrift institution offering a variety of deposit and mortgage loan products. Incorporated in Delaware in 1991.

Directors (In addition to indicated officers)

Richard T. Garrigan, Ph.D.
Fred I. Gillick
Richard W. Hanzel

Louis A. Holland
John L. Vitale

Officers (Directors*)

*Edmond M. Shanahan, Chm.
*Robert G. Rowen, Pres. & C.E.O.

*John C. Savio, Sr. V.P., C.F.O. & Treas.
Robert E. Ulbricht, Sr. V.P., Gen. Coun. & Secy.

Consolidated Balance Sheet   As of March 31, 1995 (000 omitted)

Assets		Liabilities & Stockholders' Equity	
Cash & due from banks	$ 10,647	Deposits	$1,519,220
Interest-earning deposits	7,503	Borrowed funds	79,600
Loans receivable, net	1,338,414	Advance payment by borrowers	7,736
Investment securities	44,266	for taxes	
Mortgage-backed securities, net	480,564	Other liabilities	7,939
Premises & equipment	5,840	*Stockholders' equity	292,964
Accrued interest receivable	10,988		
Foreclosed real estate, net	4,256		
Prepaid expenses & other assets	4,981		
Total	$1,907,459	Total	$1,907,459

*9,103,348 shares common stock outstanding.

Consolidated Income Statement[a]

Years Ended March 31	Thousands — — — — Total Income	Net Income	Per Share[b] — — — Earnings	Cash Dividends	Common Stock Price Range[b] Fiscal Year
1995	$117,961	$13,367	$1.32	$ .22	29-1/2 — 21-1/2
1994	122,383	15,413[c]	1.39[c]	.00	28-7/8 — 19
1993	143,162	22,917	1.92	.00	22-5/8 — 15-1/8
1992[d]	168,749	14,714	N/M		15-5/8 — 13[e]
1991	172,461	18,261			

[a]1991 financial data are for Bell Federal Savings and Loan Association, the wholly owned subsidiary of Bell Bancorp, Inc.
[b]Adjusted to reflect a 2-for-1 stock split in September 1994.
[c]Includes a charge to reflect FAS 109, resulting in a cumulative effect of $3,001,000 ($.27 per share).
[d]Includes an additional provision of $6,100,000 to the general loan loss reserve.
[e]Initial public offering in December 1991.

Transfer Agent & Registrar: Harris Trust and Savings Bank

General Counsel: Muldoon, Murphy & Faucette

Investor Relations: Robert E. Ulbricht, Sr. V.P.

Human Resources:
  Kathryn C. Banky, V.P.—Bell Federal

Mgt. Info. Svcs.:
  Peter J. Grealish, Sr. V.P.—Bell Federal

Auditors: KPMG Peat Marwick LLP

Traded (Symbol): NASDAQ (BELL)

Stockholders: 2,298

Employees: 350

Annual Meeting: In July

Binks Manufacturing Company

9201 West Belmont Avenue, Franklin Park, Illinois 60131-2887
Telephone: (708) 671-3000

Binks Manufacturing Company and its subsidiaries design, manufacture, and distribute spray finishing and coating application equipment. The company divides its products into two general groups: standard equipment and industrial equipment. The standard equipment line consists of more than 50 models of spray guns, a wide variety of air and fluid nozzles, a complete line of high and low pressure material handling pumps, pressure tanks, portable and stationary air compressors, and accessories such as siphon cups, pressure cups, oil and water extractors, air and fluid regulators, ball valves, hose connections and fittings, air and fluid hoses, paint heaters and replacement parts. The industrial equipment line includes spray booths, paint circulating systems, air replacement systems, automatic spray coating machines, electrocoating systems, electrostatic application equipment, spray painting robots, and complete industrial finishing systems involving custom design and engineering services. Binks also manufactures a small number of water cooling towers used in connection with air conditioning and water treatment systems. In the U.S., the company operates 12 branch offices with warehouse facilities, 26 sales offices and a network of more than 5,200 distributors. Foreign subsidiaries are located in Australia, Belgium, Canada, the United Kingdom, France, Italy, Japan, Mexico, Sweden and Germany. Major subsidiaries are: Binks R&D, Sames Electrostatic, Binks Manufacturing Co. of Canada, Binks International, S.A. (Belgium), Binks-Bullows, Ltd. (England), Sames, S.A. (France), Binks Japan, Ltd., and Binks Deutschland GmbH. Incorporated in Delaware in 1929.

Directors   (In addition to indicated officers)

Jacques DeFreitas	William W. Roche	John J. Schornack

Officers   (Directors*)

*Burke B. Roche, Pres. & C.E.O.
*Doran J. Unschuld, Sr. V.P. & Secy.
 Stephen R. Kennedy, V.P.
 Ernest F. Watts, V.P.—Mktg.

Jeffrey W. Lemajeur, Treas.
Terence P. Roche, Asst. Secy. & Asst. Treas.
Carl M. Springer, Asst. Secy. & Asst. Treas.

Consolidated Balance Sheet   As of November 30, 1994 (000 omitted)

Assets		Liabilities & Stockholders' Equity	
Current assets	$155,997	Current liabilities	$ 56,758
Net property, plant & equipment	27,384	Long-term debt	38,114
Other assets	9,983	Deferred items	8,264
		*Stockholders' equity	90,228
Total	$193,364	Total	$193,364

*3,088,837 shares common stock outstanding.

Consolidated Income Statement

Years Ended Nov. 30	Thousands — — — —		Per Share[a] — — — —		Common Stock Price Range[a] Calendar Year
	Net Sales	Net Income	Earnings	Cash Dividends	
1994	$243,599	$3,415	$1.11	$ .30	23-1/4 — 18-1/2
1993	210,405	1,331	.44	.36	26-1/8 — 21-3/4
1992	223,680	1,609[b]	.55[b]	1.00	25-3/4 — 20-1/2
1991	222,171	1,214	.41	1.10	31-1/4 — 21
1990	279,297	6,716[c]	2.28[c]	1.15	46-1/4 — 24-3/8

[a]Adjusted to reflect a 2% stock dividend paid in August 1993 and a 3% stock dividend paid in June 1993.
[b]Includes a gain to reflect FAS 109, resulting in a cumulative effect of $194,956 ($.07 per share).
[c]Includes a gain to reflect a change in the company's accounting method of applying overhead to inventory, resulting in a cumulative effect of $930,000 ($.31 per share) in 1990.

Transfer Agent & Registrar: Harris Trust and Savings Bank

General Counsel:
 Skadden, Arps, Slate, Meagher & Flom

Patent Counsel:
 Juettner, Pyle, Lloyd & Verbeck

Investor Relations: Doran J. Unschuld, Sr. V.P.

Human Resources: James Lindquist

Mgt. Info. Svcs.:   Burke B. Roche, Pres./C.E.O.
Auditors: KPMG Peat Marwick LLP
Traded (Symbol):   AMEX, CSE (BIN)
Stockholders: 1,371
Employees: 1,682
Annual Meeting: In April

Bio-logic Systems Corp.

One Bio-logic Plaza, Mundelein, Illinois 60060-3700
Telephone: (708) 949-5200

Bio-logic Systems Corp. designs, develops, assembles, and markets computerized systems for use by medical practitioners, hospitals, and clinics to perform various electro-diagnostic tests and brain mapping. Electro-diagnostic tests done by the company's systems are typically used by physicians, primarily neurologists, otolaryngologists, anesthesiologists, audiologists, and psychiatrists, as an aid in diagnosis of neurological and sensory disorders, brain disorders, and tumors by collecting, measuring, and analyzing electrical signals generated by the brain. Incorporated in Delaware in 1981.

Directors (In addition to indicated officers)

Irving Kupferberg
Albert Milstein

Craig Moore

Officers (Directors*)

*Gabriel Raviv, Pres. & C.E.O.
 Thomas S. Lacy, V.P.—Sales & Mktg.
*Charles Z. Weingarten, V.P. & Treas.

*Gil Raviv, Secy.
 William K. Roenitz, Cont. & Asst. Treas.

Consolidated Balance Sheet As of February 28, 1995 (000 omitted)

Assets		Liabilities & Stockholders' Equity	
Current assets	$ 9,047	Current liabilities	$ 2,122
Net property, plant & equipment	2,012	Long-term debt	809
Marketing securities	1,728	Deferred items	200
Other assets	713	*Stockholders' equity	10,369
Total	$13,500	Total	$13,500

*4,227,823 shares common stock outstanding.

Consolidated Income Statement

Years Ended Abt. Feb. 28	Thousands — — — —		Per Share[b] — — —		Common Stock Price Range[bc] Calendar Year
	Revenue[a]	Net Income	Earnings	Cash Dividends	
1995	$12,073	$740	$ .18	$ .00	3-3/4 — 1-3/4
1994	10,749	540	.13	.00	5 — 2-3/4
1993	10,985	100	.02	.00	5-7/8 — 2-3/4
1992	10,108	365	.08	.00	6-3/8 — 3-1/2
1991	10,955	276	.07	.00	8 — 2

[a]1991 restated.
[b]Adjusted to reflect a 3-for-2 stock split payable in the form of a 50% stock distribution on May 28, 1991.
[c]1995-94 fiscal year price range.

Transfer Agent & Registrar: American Stock Transfer & Trust Co.

General Counsel:
  Bachner, Tally, Polevoy, Misher & Brinberg

Investor Relations: Gabriel Raviv, Pres.

Human Resources: Faith I. Curtis, Mgr.

Mgt. Info. Svcs.: William K. Roenitz, Cont.

Auditors: Deloitte & Touche LLP
Traded (Symbol): NASDAQ (BLSC)
Stockholders: 320
Employees: 82
Annual Meeting: In August

First Chicago Guide

Bliss & Laughlin Industries Inc.

281 East 155th Street, Harvey, Illinois 60426-3797
Telephone: (312) 264-1800

Bliss & Laughlin Industries Inc. operates through two subsidiaries, Bliss & Laughlin Steel Company (BLSC) and Canadian Drawn Steel Co. Inc. (CDSC). It manufactures and markets cold finished steel bars which are used by various manufacturers for shafting requirements or parts that will be machined for electrical, industrial, automotive and agricultural equipment, machinery and appliances. The company offers cold finished steel bars in a wide range of grades, sizes, and shapes. The company sells its products to about 800 primary customers, including steel service centers. Manufacturing facilities are located in Harvey and Batavia, Illinois; Medina, Ohio; Cartersville, Georgia; and Hamilton, Ontario. Incorporated in Delaware in 1988.

Directors (In addition to indicated officers)

George Binnie
Roger G. Fein
Charles P. McLarnon

Karl H. Reitz
Dennis W. Sheehan

Officers (Directors*)

*Gregory H. Parker, Chm., Pres. & C.E.O.
*Anthony J. Romanovich, Sr. V.P.
George W. Fleck, V.P.—Fin., Secy. & Treas.
Nancy J. Horvath, Asst. Secy.
Michael P. Houlihan, Asst. Treas.
R. James Barnett, Pres.—CDSC

Richard M. Bogdon, V.P.—Hum. Res., BLSC
Gerald E. Brady, V.P., BLSC
Michael A. DeBias, V.P.—Purch., BLSC
Kenneth P. Morris, V.P.—Cartersville Opers., BLSC
Chester J. Pucilowski, V.P.—Medina Oper., BLSC

Consolidated Balance Sheet As of September 30, 1994 (000 omitted)

Assets		Liabilities & Stockholders' Equity	
Current assets	$47,484	Current liabilities	$37,047
Net property, plant & equipment	16,843	Long-term debt	3,600
Other assets	3,412	Deferred items	411
		Other liabilities	1,959
		*Stockholders' equity	24,722
Total	$67,739	Total	$67,739

*3,969,518 shares common stock outstanding.

Consolidated Income Statement

Years Ended Sept. 30	Thousands — — — — Net Sales	Net Income	Per Share — — — Earnings	Cash Dividends	Common Stock Price Range Calendar Year
1994	$152,435	$ 3,578[a]	$ .90[a]	$ .00	7-1/4 — 2-3/4
1993	136,923	(4,219)[b]	(1.06)[b]	.00	3-3/4 — 2-1/4
1992	121,677	297	.07	.00	3-1/2 — 2
1991	114,528	(2,397)	(.60)	.00	4-3/4 — 1
1990	116,648	(225)	(.07)	.00	6-1/2 — 3-1/2

[a]Includes a gain to reflect FAS 109, resulting in a cumulative effect of $813,000 ($.20 per share).
[b]Includes a non-cash charge to reflect FAS 106, resulting in a cumulative effect of $1,789,000 ($.45 per share).

Transfer Agent & Registrar: LaSalle National Trust, N.A.

General Counsel:
  Wildman, Harrold, Allen & Dixon

Investor Relations: George W. Fleck, V.P.

Human Resources: Richard M. Bogdon, V.P.

Mgt. Info. Svcs.: Doremus & Co.

Auditors: Arthur Andersen LLP

Traded (Symbol): NASDAQ (BLIS)

Stockholders: 475

Employees: 437

Annual Meeting: In February

Boise Cascade Office Products Corporation

800 West Bryn Mawr Road, Itasca, Illinois 60143
Telephone: (708) 773-5000

Boise Cascade Office Products Corporation is one of the largest direct suppliers of office products to businesses in the U.S. The company distributes a broad line of 11,200 branded and private label products for use in the office, including consumable supplies, furniture, and other products. The company's product line is offered through its annual full-line catalog and a variety of specialized catalogs, and sold by the company's direct sales force. Boise Cascade Corporation owns 82.7 percent of the company's outstanding common stock. In April 1995, Boise Cascade Office Products completed an initial public offering of 5,318,750 shares of common stock. Incorporated in Delaware in 1995.

Directors (In addition to indicated officer)

George J. Harad, Chm.
John B. Carley
James G. Connelly III

Theodore Crumley
A. William Reynolds

Officers (Director*)

*Peter G. Danis, Jr., Pres. & C.E.O.
Christopher C. Milliken, Sr. V.P.—Oper.
Carol B. Moerdyk, Sr. V.P. & C.F.O.
Lawrence E. Beeson, V.P.—Mktg.
Julie M. Cade, V.P. & Region Mgr.

Darrell R. Elfeldt, V.P. & Cont.
John W. Holleran, V.P. & Gen. Coun.
John A. Love, V.P.—Hum. Res.
Stephen M. Thompson, V.P. & Region Mgr.
Richard L. Black, Pres.—The Reliable Corp.

Consolidated Balance Sheet[a] As of December 31, 1994 (000 omitted)

Assets		Liabilities & Stockholders' Equity	
Current assets	$218,633	Current liabilities	$ 73,144
Net property, plant & equipment	73,258	Accrued liabilities	31,467
Other assets	60,850	Other liabilities	5,511
		*Stockholders' equity	242,619
Total	$352,741	Total	$352,741

[a]Unaudited pro forma.
*30,000,000 shares common stock outstanding.

Consolidated Income Statement

Years Ended Dec. 31	Thousands — — — — Net Sales	Net Income	Per Share — — — Earnings	Cash Dividends	Common Stock Price Range[a] Calendar Year
1994[b]	$962,045	$28,434	$ .95		
1993	682,819	18,046			
1992	625,860	6,321[c]			
1991	614,035	15,631			
1990	613,411	21,033			

[a]Initial public offering in April 1995.
[b]Unaudited pro forma.
[c]Includes a charge to reflect FAS 106, resulting in a cumulative effect of $2,444,000.

Transfer Agent & Registrar:	Mellon Securities Trust Co.; Boise Cascade Shareholder Services; West One Bank		
General Counsel:	John W. Holleran, V.P.	Auditors:	Arthur Andersen LLP
Investor Relations:	Carol B. Moerdyk, Sr. V.P.	Traded (Symbol):	NYSE (BOP)
		Stockholders:	1,900
Human Resources:	John A. Love, V.P.	Employees:	3,976
Mgt. Info. Svcs.:	Carol B. Moerdyk, Sr. V.P.	Annual Meeting:	In April

Borg-Warner Automotive, Inc.

200 South Michigan Avenue, Chicago, Illinois 60604
Telephone: (312) 322-8500

Borg-Warner Automotive, Inc., develops, manufactures, and markets highly engineered components primarily for automotive powertrain applications. These products are produced and sold worldwide, primarily to original equipment manufacturers of passenger cars, light trucks and sport-utility vehicles. The company's products fall into four categories: Powertrain Systems, Automatic Transmission Systems, Morse TEC, and Control Systems. Borg-Warner Automotive was a wholly owned subsidiary of Borg-Warner Security Corporation until January 27, 1993, at which time it was distributed to the stockholders of BW-Security in a tax-free distribution, or spinoff. In August 1993, Borg-Warner Automotive completed an initial public offering of 3,500,000 shares of common stock. In April 1995, the company completed the purchase of the Precision-Forged Products Division (PFPD) of Federal-Mogul Corp. Incorporated in Delaware in 1987.

Directors   (In addition to indicated officer)

J. Gordon Amedee, Chm.
Robert F. End
Albert J. Fitzgibbons III
Paul E. Glaske

James J. Kerley
Alexis P. Michas
Donald C. Trauscht

Officers   (Director*)

* John F. Fiedler, Pres. & C.E.O.
Gary P. Fukayama, Exec. V.P.
Fred M. Kovalik, Exec. V.P.
Ronald M. Ruzic, Exec. V.P.
Robin J. Adams, V.P. & Treas.

William C. Cline, V.P. & Cont.
Christopher A. Gebelein, V.P.—Bus. Dev.
Laurene H. Horiszny, V.P., Gen. Coun. & Secy.
Geraldine Kinsella, V.P.—Hum. Res.

Consolidated Balance Sheet   As of December 31, 1994 (000 omitted)

Assets		Liabilities & Stockholders' Equity	
Current assets	$ 215,800	Current liabilities	$ 247,800
Net property, plant & equipment	462,300	Long-term debt	86,800
Other assets	562,200	Deferred items	367,600
		Other liabilities	3,200
		* Stockholders' equity	534,900
Total	$1,240,300	Total	$1,240,300

*21,704,588 shares common stock outstanding.

Consolidated Income Statement[a]

Years Ended Dec. 31	Thousands		Per Share		Common Stock
	Net Sales	Net Income	Earnings	Cash Dividends	Price Range[b] Calendar Year
1994	$1,223,400	$ 64,400	$ 2.75	$ .60	34 — 21-5/8
1993	985,400	(98,000)[c]	(4.21)[c]	.00	28 — 20-1/2
1992	926,000	(12,100)	(.53)		
1991	820,300	(31,000)[d]	(1.59)[d]		
1990	925,800	(13,000)	(.67)		

[a]For all periods prior to 1993, the financial statements reflect the company as a subsidiary of Borg-Warner Security Corporation subject to certain allocations.
[b]Initial public offering in August 1993.
[c]Includes a charge to reflect FAS 106, resulting in a cumulative effect of $130,800,000 ($5.62 per share).
[d]Includes a gain to reflect FAS 109, resulting in a cumulative effect of $4,800,000 ($.25 per share).

Transfer Agent & Registrar: Chemical Bank	
General Counsel: Laurene H. Horiszny, V.P.	Traded (Symbol): NYSE (BWA)
Investor Relations: Leslie Cleveland Hague, Dir.	Stockholders: 151
Human Resources: Geraldine Kinsella, V.P.	Employees: 8,500
Auditors: Deloitte & Touche LLP	Annual Meeting: In April

First Chicago Guide

Borg-Warner Security Corporation

200 South Michigan Avenue, Chicago, Illinois 60604
Telephone: (312) 322-8500

Borg-Warner Security Corporation (formerly Borg-Warner Corporation) provides a broad line of protective services, including guard, alarm, armored transport, and courier services. The company entered the protective services industry in 1977 through the acquisition of Baker Industries, Inc. Borg-Warner's guard services units provide a variety of guard and related security services to more than 13,000 government and business customers throughout the U.S. and in Canada, Colombia, and the United Kingdom under the Wells Fargo®, Burns®, and Globe service marks. The company's alarm services unit designs, installs, monitors, and services electronic detection systems located at the premises of approximately 120,000 commercial and residential customers in the U.S. and Canada under the Wells Fargo® and Pony Express® service marks. The company's armored transport services unit is a security-related cash service business that provides armored transport services, automated teller-machine (ATM) servicing, and cash management services in the U.S. under the Wells Fargo® service mark. Borg-Warner's courier services unit transports time-sensitive non-negotiable financial documents and small packages for Federal Reserve banks, financial institutions, and commercial business entities under the Pony Express® service mark. Incorporated in Delaware in 1987.

Directors (In addition to indicated officers)

James J. Burke, Jr.	Robert A. McCabe
Albert J. Fitzgibbons III	Alexis P. Michas
Dale W. Lang	H. Norman Schwarzkopf

Officers (Directors*)

*Donald C. Trauscht, Chm. & C.E.O.	Edwin L. Lewis, V.P.—Law & Corp. Secy.
*J. Joe Adorjan, Pres. & C.O.O.	Timothy M. Wood, V.P.—Fin.
*Neal F. Farrell, Exec. V.P.	Diana W. Bligh, Asst. Secy.
John D. O'Brien, Sr. V.P.	Scott R. Veldman, Asst. Treas.

Consolidated Balance Sheet As of December 31, 1994 (000 omitted)

Assets		Liabilities & Stockholders' Equity	
Current assets	$159,500	Current liabilities	$196,300
Net property, plant & equipment	295,100	Long-term debt	454,000
Other assets	375,700	Other long-term liabilities	136,200
		*Stockholders' equity	43,800
Total	$830,300	Total	$830,300

*21,758,400 shares common stock outstanding.

Consolidated Income Statement

Years Ended Dec. 31	Thousands — — — — Net Service Revenues	Net Income[a]	Per Share — — — Earnings[a]	Cash Dividends	Common Stock Price Range Calendar Year
1994	$1,792,900	$13,100	$ .56	$ .00	22 — 8-1/4
1993	1,764,600	34,900[b]	1.50[b]	.00	22-7/8 — 18[c]
1992	1,620,600	30,500[b]	1.30[b]		
1991	1,555,400	25,100[b]	1.07[b]		
1990	1,413,800	20,300	1.02		

[a]Continuing operations.
[b]Pro forma.
[c]Initial public offering in January 1993.

Transfer Agent & Registrar: The Bank of New York

General Counsel: Wachtell, Lipton, Rosen & Katz		Auditors:	Deloitte & Touche LLP
		Traded (Symbol):	NYSE (BOR)
Investor Relations:	Timothy M. Wood, V.P.	Stockholders:	174
Human Resources:	John D. O'Brien, Sr. V.P.	Employees:	92,000
Mgt. Info. Svcs.:	John D. O'Brien, Sr. V.P.	Annual Meeting:	In April

Brunswick Corporation

1 North Field Court, Lake Forest, Illinois 60045-4811
Telephone: (708) 735-4700

Brunswick Corporation serves worldwide markets in the marine power, pleasure boating, and recreation fields through seven operating divisions. The Marine segment consists of the Mercury Marine Division, which produces Mercury, Mariner and Force outboard motors, and MerCruiser stern drives and inboard engines; US Marine Division, which produces Bayliner, Maxum, Trophy and Robalo fiberglass boats; Sea Ray Division, which manufactures Sea Ray fiberglass boats; and Fishing Boat Division, which builds Starcraft, Spectrum, MonArk and Fisher aluminum fishing boats, and ProCraft and Astro-Craft fiberglass fishing boats. The Recreation segment consists of the Zebco Division, which produces fishing reels, reel/rod combinations, and MotorGuide trolling motors; Brunswick Division, which produces bowling capital equipment, and consumer products, billiards tables, and golf club shafts; and Brunswick Recreation Centers Division, which operates a chain of 126 bowling centers in North America and Europe. Incorporated in Delaware in 1907.

Directors (In addition to indicated officers)

Michael J. Callahan	Bernd K. Koken	Robert N. Rasmus
John P. Diesel	Jay W. Lorsch	Roger W. Schipke
George D. Kennedy	Bettye Martin Musham	

Officers (Directors*)[a]

* Jack F. Reichert, Chm.
* Peter N. Larson, Pres. & C.E.O.
  John M. Charvat, Exec. V.P.
  Jim W. Dawson, V.P.
  Frederick J. Florjancic, Jr., V.P.
  David D. Jones, V.P.
  William R. McManaman, V.P.—Fin.

Dianne M. Yaconetti, V.P.—Admin. & Secy.
James C. Hubbard, Asst. V.P.
Judith P. Zelisko, Asst. V.P.
Thomas K. Erwin, Cont.
Robert T. McNaney, Gen. Coun.
Richard S. O'Brien, Treas.
Michael D. Schmitz, Asst. Secy.

[a]Reichert will retire as Chairman on October 1, 1995.

Consolidated Balance Sheet As of December 31, 1994 (000 omitted)

Assets		Liabilities & Stockholders' Equity	
Current assets	$1,057,500	Current liabilities	$ 621,300
Net property, plant & equipment	565,400	Long-term debt	318,800
Other assets	499,400	Deferred items	271,500
		* Stockholders' equity	910,700
Total	$2,122,300	Total	$2,122,300

*95,451,136 shares common stock outstanding.

Consolidated Income Statement

Years Ended Dec. 31	Thousands — — — — Net Sales[a]	Net Income	Per Share — — — Earnings	Cash Dividends	Common Stock Price Range Calendar Year
1994	$2,700,100	$ 129,000	$ 1.35	$ .44	25-3/8 — 17
1993[b]	2,206,800	23,100	.24	.44	18-1/2 — 12-1/2
1992[c]	2,059,400	(26,300)	(.28)	.44	17-3/4 — 12-1/4
1991[d]	1,841,000	(23,700)	(.27)	.44	16-1/8 — 8-3/4
1990[e]	2,106,900	70,900	.80	.44	16 — 6-5/8

[a]From continuing operations.
[b]Includes FAS 112, resulting in an aftertax provision of $14,600,000. The company also recorded an aftertax provision of $12,200,000 for its divestiture of the Technical segment plus an aftertax provision of $4,600,000 for redemption of $100 million in sinking fund debentures.
[c]Includes FAS 106, resulting in aftertax provisions of $2,800,000 in 1992 and $38,300,000 for the cumulative prior years' effect. The company also recorded an aftertax provision of $26,000,000 for its divestiture of the Technical segment.
[d]Includes aftertax provisions of $23,600,000 for litigation matters. The income tax provision on the pretax loss resulted primarily from the inability to utilize $9,300,000 of foreign tax credits in the calculation of the consolidated tax provision.
[e]Net earnings include an aftertax charge of $10,000,000 for the consolidation of operations in the Marine segment, and aftertax gain of $46,700,000 from the disposition of businesses of the Technical segment.

Transfer Agent & Registrar: Brunswick Corporation

Corporate Counsel: Mayer, Brown & Platt

Investor Relations: Ross H. Stemer, Dir.

Human Resources: Mary Kay Bottorff, Dir.

Mgt. Info. Svcs.: Howard Gielow, Dir.

Auditors: Arthur Andersen LLP

Traded (Symbol):
  NYSE, CSE, PSE, London, Tokyo SE (BC)

Stockholders: 25,800

Employees: 20,800

Annual Meeting: Last Wednesday in April

Calumet Bancorp, Inc.

1350 East Sibley Boulevard, Dolton, Illinois 60419
Telephone: (708) 841-9010

Calumet Bancorp, Inc., is the holding company for Calumet Federal Savings and Loan Association of Chicago, a federally chartered stock savings and loan association. The Association attracts retail deposits from the Chicago area with its greatest emphasis on the south Chicago suburban communities and the northwest Indiana communities that it serves. The Association's home office is located in Chicago, its main administrative office is in Dolton, and its five full-service branch offices are located in Chicago, Lansing and Sauk Village. It also operates through several service corporation subsidiaries, including Calumet Savings Service Corporation, Calumet Residential Corporation and Calumet Mortgage Corporation. Incorporated in Delaware in 1991.

Directors (In addition to indicated officers)

Louise Czarobski
Sylvester Lulinski

William A. McCann
Henry J. Urban, D.D.S.

Officers (Directors*)

*Thaddeus Walczak, Chm. & C.E.O.
*Carole J. Lewis, Pres.
 John L. Garlanger, Sr. V.P. & Treas.

Jean A. Adams, V.P.
Susan M. Linkus, V.P. & Secy.

Consolidated Balance Sheet As of December 31, 1994 (000 omitted)

Assets		Liabilities & Stockholders' Equity	
Cash & cash equivalents	$ 9,350	Deposits	$346,668
Loans receivable, net	360,578	Borrowings	70,335
Investment securities	104,549	Other liabilities	8,737
Other assets	29,549	*Stockholders' equity	78,286
Total	$504,026	Total	$504,026

*2,791,632 shares common stock outstanding.

Consolidated Income Statement[a]

Years Ended Dec. 31	Thousands — — — —		Per Share[b] — — —		Common Stock
	Total Income	Net Income	Earnings	Cash Dividends	Price Range[bc] Calendar Year
1994	$39,202	$ 7,419	$2.47	$ .00	25-1/2 — 19-1/2
1993	40,571	10,532[d]	3.22[d]	.00	24 — 15-5/8
1992	39,143	6,697	1.91	.00	16-3/8 — 10-3/8
1991	42,259	2,059			
1990	39,142	2,739			

[a]1991-90 financial data are for Calumet Federal Savings and Loan Association, the wholly owned subsidiary of Calumet Bancorp, Inc.
[b]Adjusted to reflect a 3-for-2 stock split in the form of a 50% common stock dividend in November 1994.
[c]Initial public offering on February 20, 1992.
[d]Includes a gain to reflect FAS 109, resulting in a cumulative effect of $1,500,000 ($.46 per share).

Transfer Agent & Registrar: Harris Trust and Savings Bank

General Counsel:
 Kemp, Grzelakowski & Lorenzini, Ltd.

Investor Relations: John L. Garlanger, Sr. V.P.

Human Resources: Nancy Layne, Asst. V.P.

Auditors: Ernst & Young LLP

Traded (Symbol): NASDAQ (CBCI)

Stockholders: 392

Employees: 158

Annual Meeting: In April

Capsure Holdings Corp.

Two North Riverside Plaza, Chicago, Illinois 60606
Telephone: (312) 879-1900

Capsure Holdings Corp. (formerly Nucorp, Inc.) is a holding company whose principal subsidiaries, United Capitol Insurance Company, Universal Surety of America, and Western Surety Company, are specialty property and casualty insurers. Through these subsidiaries, the company writes commercial general liability, property, and small contract surety business principally in the excess and surplus lines market, and provides miscellaneous surety and fidelity bonds in all 50 states through a network of 120,000 independent agents. Incorporated in Delaware in 1988; present name adopted in 1993.

Directors (In addition to indicated officers)

Rod F. Dammeyer
Herbert A. Denton
Bradbury Dyer III
Talton R. Embry
Dan L. Kirby

Joe P. Kirby
Donald W. Phillips
L.G. Schafran
Richard I. Weingarten

Officers (Directors*)

*Samuel Zell, Chm. & C.E.O.
*Bruce A. Esselborn, Pres.
Arthur A. Greenberg, Sr. V.P. & Treas.
Mary Jane Robertson, Sr. V.P. & C.F.O.
Ronald D. Bobman, V.P.—M&A

*Sheli Z. Rosenberg, V.P. & Asst. Secy.
Kelly L. Stonebraker, V.P. & Gen. Coun.
John M. Zoeller, V.P.—Taxes
John S. Heneghan, Cont.
Susan S. Obuchowski, Secy.

Consolidated Balance Sheet As of December 31, 1994 (000 omitted)

Assets		Liabilities & Stockholders' Equity	
Current assets	$ 39,582	Reserves	$225,671
Invested assets & cash	305,898	Long-term debt	71,000
Other assets	207,890	Other liabilities	31,834
		*Stockholders' equity	224,865
Total	$553,370	Total	$553,370

*15,394,149 shares common stock outstanding.

Consolidated Income Statement

Years Ended Dec. 31	Thousands — — — — Total Revenues	Net Income	Per Share — — — Earnings[a]	Cash Dividends	Common Stock Price Range[b] Calendar Year
1994[c]	$112,662	$14,378	$ .95	$ .00	16 — 12-1/8
1993	108,445	16,284	1.08	.00	19-3/8 — 12-1/4
1992[de]	59,519	10,695	.88	.00	14-3/8 — 6-7/8
1991	34,890	7,208	.79	.00	9 — 4-1/4
1990[f]	39,034	5,273	.62	.00	9-3/8 — 4-5/8

[a]Fully diluted.
[b]Traded on NASDAQ prior to June 16, 1993.
[c]Includes the results of Universal Surety of America since the date of acquisition in September 1994.
[d]Includes the results of Surewest Financial Corp. since the date of acquisition in August 1992.
[e]Restated to reflect FAS 109.
[f]Includes the results of United Capitol Holding Co. since the date of acquisition in February 1990.

Transfer Agent & Registrar:	Bank of Boston		
General Counsel:	Kelly L. Stonebraker, V.P.	Traded (Symbol):	NYSE (CSH)
Investor Relations:	Doreen J. Lubeck, V.P.	Stockholders:	2,400
		Employees:	600
Auditors:	Coopers & Lybrand L.L.P.	Annual Meeting:	In May

Caremark International Inc.

2215 Sanders Road, Northbrook, Illinois 60062
Telephone: (708) 559-4700

Caremark International Inc. is a leading provider of patient services through health care networks dedicated to delivering quality health care in four major business segments. Physician Practice Management involves the management of large multi-specialty physician practices. Pharmaceutical Services is the largest independent pharmacy benefit manager in the nation, combining drug distribution, formulary management, clinical case management, and reimbursement consulting. Disease State Management networks are an innovative and comprehensive approach to helping people with chronic, high-cost diseases by seeing to all or part of their health care needs. International extends Caremark's health care businesses overseas, where it is often a partner in helping to create the first managed care systems in many countries. Incorporated in Delaware in 1992.

Directors (In addition to indicated officers)

Nancy G. Brinker	Raymond D. Oddi
Vincent A. Calarco	Phillip B. Rooney
J. Ira Harris	Peter F. Whitington, M.D.
Roger L. Headrick	Blaine J. Yarrington
Ralph W. Muller	

Officers (Directors*)

*C.A. Lance Piccolo, Chm. & C.E.O.	Michele J. Hooper, V.P.—Int'l. Bus.
*James G. Connelly III, Pres. & C.O.O.	K.J. Michael McDonald, V.P.—Therapeutic/Spec.
*Thomas W. Hodson, Sr. V.P. & C.F.O.	Pharm. Svcs.
Donna C.E. Williamson, Sr. V.P.—Integrated	Diane L. Munson, V.P.—Physician Svcs.
Svcs.	John M. Pellettiere, V.P. & Cont.
Kent J. De Lucenay, V.P.—Hum. Res.	Thomas R. Schuman, V.P., Gen. Coun. & Secy.
Kris Gibney, V.P.—Pharmaceutical Svcs.	Dennis R. Owczarski, Treas.

Consolidated Balance Sheet   As of December 31, 1994 (000 omitted)

Assets		Liabilities & Stockholders' Equity	
Current assets	$ 665,900	Current liabilities	$ 459,600
Net property, plant & equipment	217,200	Long-term debt & lease	236,900
Other assets	392,100	obligations	
		Deferred items	42,700
		Minority interests	12,400
		Other liabilities	36,900
		*Stockholders' equity	486,700
Total	$1,275,200	Total	$1,275,200

*71,638,866 shares common stock outstanding.

Consolidated Income Statement

Years Ended Dec. 31	Thousands — — — — Net Revenues	Net Income	Per Share — — — Earnings	Cash Dividends	Common Stock Price Range[a] Calendar Year
1994	$2,426,000	$80,400[b]	$1.08	$ .04	26-3/4 — 15-3/4
1993	1,783,200	77,700	1.06	.04	20-3/4 — 11-7/8
1992	1,461,200	27,300[c]	.39	.00	15 — 12
1991	1,194,200	69,000			
1990	927,800	52,000			

[a]Caremark International Inc. was spun off by Baxter International Inc. in November 1992.
[b]Includes a pretax charge of $25,000,000 related to the integration of Critical Care America.
[c]Includes pretax charges of $67,600,000 related to restructuring.

Transfer Agent & Registrar:	First Chicago Trust Co. of New York		
General Counsel:	Thomas R. Schuman, V.P.	Traded (Symbol):	NYSE (CK)
Investor Relations:	Nancy V. Westcott, V.P.	Stockholders:	54,849
Human Resources:	Kent J. De Lucenay, V.P.	Employees:	9,150
Auditors:	Price Waterhouse LLP	Annual Meeting:	In May

A.M. Castle & Co.

3400 North Wolf Road, Franklin Park, Illinois 60131
Telephone: (708) 455-7111

A.M. Castle & Co. is a North American industrial distributor of specialty metals such as carbon, alloy, and stainless steels; aluminum; nickel alloys; titanium; and copper and brass. The metals that A.M. Castle distributes are used by more than 30,000 customers in a highly diversified range of end-use industries — from pollution control equipment to machine tools; agricultural, construction, and mining machinery to electric and power generation equipment; oil and oil-field services to chemical and petroleum refineries; and the space shuttle to commercial aircraft. In the U.S., the company maintains a coast-to-coast metals service center network consisting of 26 locations with more than two-million square feet of capacity. In Canada, A.M. Castle serves customers from three service centers in the provinces of Manitoba, Ontario, and Quebec. Incorporated in Illinois in 1904; reincorporated in Delaware in 1967.

Directors   (In addition to indicated officers)

Daniel T. Carroll	John W. McCarter, Jr.
William K. Hall	William J. McDermott
Robert S. Hamada	John W. Puth
John P. Keller	Richard A. Virzi

Officers   (Directors*)

*Michael Simpson, Chm.	Richard G. Phifer, V.P.—East Region
*Richard G. Mork, Pres. & C.E.O.	Thomas D. Prendergast, V.P.—Hum. Res.
*Edward F. Culliton, V.P.—Fin.	Alan D. Raney, V.P.—Advanced Materials Grp.
Sven G. Ericsson, V.P.—Plate & Carbon Prod. Grp.	Gise Van Baren, V.P.—Alloy Prod. Grp.
M. Bruce Herron, V.P.—West. Region	Jerry M. Aufox, Secy. & Legal Coun.
Stephen V. Hooks, V.P.—Midwest Region	James A. Podojil, Treas. & Cont.

Consolidated Balance Sheet   As of December 31, 1994 (000 omitted)

Assets		Liabilities & Stockholders' Equity	
Current assets	$158,083	Current liabilities	$ 82,138
Net property, plant & equipment	41,190	Long-term debt	38,531
Other assets	13,854	Deferred items	7,772
		Other liabilities	2,525
		*Stockholders' equity	82,161
Total	$213,127	Total	$213,127

*11,079,645 shares common stock outstanding.

Consolidated Income Statement

Years Ended Dec. 31	Thousands — — — — Net Sales	Net Income	Per Share[a] — — — Earnings	Cash Dividends	Common Stock Price Range[a] Calendar Year
1994	$536,568	$15,410	$1.40	$ .33	16-3/8 — 11-1/8
1993	474,108	6,899	.63	.27	11-5/8 — 7-1/2
1992	423,913	3,614	.33	.27	8-5/8 — 7
1991	436,441	201	.02	.36	9-1/2 — 6-1/2
1990	478,856	3,128	.29	.45	9-3/8 — 6-5/8

[a]Adjusted to reflect a 50% stock dividend in 1994.

Transfer Agent & Registrar: American Stock Transfer & Trust Co.

General Counsel: Mayer, Brown & Platt

Investor Relations:
Financial Relations Board Co.

Human Resources:
Thomas D. Prendergast, V.P.

Mgt. Info. Svcs.: Paul T. Jara, Dir.

Auditors: Arthur Andersen LLP

Traded (Symbol): AMEX, CSE (CAS)

Stockholders: 1,639

Employees: 1,185

Annual Meeting: Fourth Thursday in April

Caterpillar Inc.

100 N.E. Adams Street, Peoria, Illinois 61629-5310
Telephone: (309) 675-1000

Caterpillar Inc., together with its consolidated subsidiaries, operates in three principal categories: the design, manufacture, and marketing of earthmoving, construction, and materials handling machinery and equipment; the design, manufacture, and marketing of engines; and the offering of a wide range of financial services. Machinery manufactured includes: track-type tractors; bulldozers; rippers; track and wheel loaders; lift trucks; pipelayers; motor graders; wheel tractors; compactors; wheel tractor-scrapers; track and wheel excavators; skidders; automated guided vehicles; asphalt and soil compactors; backhoe loaders; log loaders; tree harvesters; off-highway trucks; asphalt and concrete paving machines; and related parts and equipment. Diesel and natural gas engines are designed for earthmoving and construction machines; on-highway trucks; marine, petroleum, agricultural, and industrial applications; and electric power generation systems. Caterpillar Financial Services Corporation assists customers in acquiring Caterpillar and noncompetitive related equipment. In addition to 23 manufacturing facilities in the U.S., Caterpillar maintains manufacturing locations in Australia, Belgium, Brazil, Canada, England, France, Hungary, and Mexico. Incorporated in California in 1925; reincorporated in Delaware in 1986.

Directors (In addition to indicated officer)

Lilyan H. Affinito	Jerry R. Junkins	Joshua I. Smith
John W. Fondahl	Peter A. Magowan	Clayton K. Yeutter
David R. Goode	Gordon R. Parker	
James P. Gorter	George A. Schaefer	

Officers (Director*)

*Donald V. Fites, Chm. & C.E.O.	Ronald P. Bonati, V.P.	Siegfried R. Ramseyer, V.P.
Glen A. Barton, Grp. Pres.	James E. Despain, V.P.	Alan J. Rassi, V.P.
Gerald S. Flaherty, Grp. Pres.	Roger E. Fischbach, V.P.	Gerald L. Shaheen, V.P.
James W. Owens, Grp. Pres.	Michael A. Flexsenhar, V.P.	Gary A. Stroup, V.P.
Richard L. Thompson, Grp. Pres.	Donald M. Ings, V.P.	Sherril K. West, V.P.
R. Rennie Atterbury III, V.P., Secy. & Gen. Coun.	Duane H. Livingston, V.P.	Donald G. Western, V.P.
	Douglas R. Oberhelman, V.P. & C.F.O.	Wayne M. Zimmerman, V.P.
James W. Baldwin, V.P.		Robert R. Gallagher, Cont.
Vito H. Baumgartner, V.P.	Gerald Palmer, V.P.	Rudolf W. Wuttke, Treas.
James S. Beard, V.P.	Robert C. Petterson, V.P.	Robin D. Beran, Asst. Treas.
Richard A. Benson, V.P.	John E. Pfeffer, V.P.	

Consolidated Balance Sheet As of December 31, 1994 (000 omitted)

Assets		Liabilities & Stockholders' Equity	
Current assets	$ 7,409,000	Current liabilities	$ 5,498,000
Net property & equipment	3,776,000	Long-term debt	4,270,000
Other assets	5,065,000	Deferred items	23,000
		Other liabilities	3,548,000
		*Stockholders' equity	2,911,000
Total	$16,250,000	Total	$16,250,000

*200,442,087 shares common stock outstanding.

Consolidated Income Statement

Years Ended Dec. 31	Thousands — — — —		Per Share[a] — — — —		Common Stock Price Range[a]
	Sales	Net Income	Earnings	Cash Dividends	Calendar Year
1994	$13,863,000	$ 955,000	$ 4.70	$ .63	60-3/4 — 44-1/2
1993	11,235,000	652,000[b]	3.21[b]	.30	46-1/2 — 27
1992	9,840,000	(2,435,000)[c]	(12.06)[c]	.30	31-1/8 — 20-5/8
1991	9,838,000	(404,000)	(2.00)	.53	28-7/8 — 18-7/8
1990	11,103,000	210,000	1.04	.60	34-1/4 — 19-1/8

[a]Adjusted to reflect a 2-for-1 stock split in November 1994.
[b]Includes extraordinary loss on early retirement of debt of $29,000,000 ($.15 per share).
[c]Includes FAS 106, FAS 109 and FAS 112, resulting in an additional loss aftertax of $2,217,000,000 ($10.98 per share).

Transfer Agent & Registrar: First Chicago Trust Co. of New York

General Counsel: R. Rennie Atterbury III, V.P.

Investor Relations: James F. Masterson, Dir.

Human Resources: Wayne M. Zimmerman, V.P.

Mgt. Info. Svcs.: Robert Hinds

Auditors: Price Waterhouse LLP

Traded (Symbol):
NYSE, BSE, CSE, PHSE, PSE, Belgium, France, Great Britain, Switzerland, Germany (CAT)

Stockholders: 29,363

Employees: 53,986

Annual Meeting: In April

CBI Industries, Inc.
800 Jorie Boulevard, Oak Brook, Illinois 60521-2268
Telephone: (708) 572-7000

CBI Industries, Inc., has subsidiaries operating in the industrial gas industry, in the construction of metal plate structures and other contracting services, oil blending and storage, and in other investments. Industrial Gases is organized under Liquid Carbonic Industries Corporation, which supplies carbon dioxide in its various forms, produces and markets other gases for industrial, medical and specialty applications, and assembles and sells related equipment. Carbon dioxide is used in the refrigeration, freezing, processing and preservation of food, beverage carbonation, water treatment, and chemical production. Other gases are used in a variety of industrial, medical and specialty applications. Liquid Carbonic currently has operations in the U.S., Canada and 23 other countries. Contracting Services is organized under Chicago Bridge & Iron Company as a worldwide construction group that provides, through separate subsidiaries, a broad range of services. These include design, engineering, fabrication, project management, general contracting and specialty construction services, including non-destructive inspection and post-weld heat treatment, primarily associated with metal plate vessels as well as water and wastewater treatment structures. CBI's Investments include interests in Statia Terminals, which provides trans-shipment, storage, bunkering, and blending services for hydrocarbon products in the Caribbean and Nova Scotia, Canada, and operates a special products terminal in Brownsville, Texas; and other financial investments. Incorporated in Illinois in 1889 as Chicago Bridge and Iron Company; reincorporated in Delaware in 1979 as CBI Industries, Inc.

Directors (In addition to indicated officers)

Wiley N. Caldwell	Gary E. MacDougal	John F. Riordan
E.H. Clark, Jr.	Stephanie Pace Marshall	Robert T. Stewart
Robert J. Day	Edward J. Mooney, Jr.	Robert G. Wallace
John T. Horton		

Officers (Directors*)

* John E. Jones, Chm., Pres. & C.E.O.
* Lewis E. Akin, Exec. V.P.
* Robert J. Daniels, Exec. V.P.
* George L. Schueppert, Exec. V.P.—Fin. & C.F.O.
  Charles O. Ziemer, Sr. V.P. & Gen. Coun.

Buel T. Adams, V.P. & Treas.
Stephen M. Duffy, V.P.—Hum. Res.
Alan J. Schneider, V.P. & Cont.
Charlotte C. Toerber, Secy.

Consolidated Balance Sheet   As of December 31, 1994 (000 omitted)

Assets		Liabilities & Stockholders' Equity	
Current assets	$ 517,854	Current liabilities	$ 379,052
Net property, plant & equipment	1,246,930	Long-term debt	666,730
Other assets	243,928	Deferred items	41,687
		Other liabilities	205,407
		* Stockholders' equity	715,836
Total	$2,008,712	Total	$2,008,712

*38,096,964 shares common stock outstanding.

Consolidated Income Statement

Years Ended Dec. 31	Thousands — — — — Revenues	Net Income	Per Share[a] — — — — Earnings	Cash Dividends	Common Stock Price Range[a] Calendar Year
1994	$1,890,907	$ 51,484	$ 1.20	$ .48	35 — 20-1/8
1993	1,671,744	(34,013)[b]	(1.07)[b]	.48	32 — 21-7/8
1992	1,672,774	63,963[c]	1.59[c]	.48	37-1/8 — 25-7/8
1991	1,614,901	61,076	1.54	.44	36-3/4 — 23-7/8
1990	1,565,409	55,135[d]	1.58[d]	.40	29-1/4 — 20-3/4

[a]Adjusted to reflect a 3-for-2 stock split in May 1991.
[b]Includes an aftertax special charge of $68,400,000 ($1.84 per share).
[c]Includes FAS 106 and FAS 109, resulting in a net charge of $7,170,000 ($.20 per share).
[d]Includes special credit from sale of equity interest in Australian Submarine Corporation of $6,580,000 ($.23 per share).

Transfer Agent & Registrar:	CBI Industries, Inc.		
General Counsel:	Charles O. Ziemer, Sr. V.P.	Traded (Symbol):	NYSE (CBI)
Investor Relations:	George L. Schueppert, Exec. V.P.	Stockholders:	7,700
Human Resources:	Stephen M. Duffy, V.P.	Employees:	14,600
Auditors:	Arthur Andersen LLP	Annual Meeting:	In May

CCH Incorporated

2700 Lake Cook Road, Riverwoods, Illinois 60015-3888
Telephone: (708) 940-4600

CCH Incorporated (formerly Commerce Clearing House, Inc.) and its subsidiaries are leading providers of tax and business law information, software and services. Principal users of this information are accountants, businesses, financial institutions, government agencies, lawyers, libraries and schools. CCH's business can be separated into three primary segments. The publishing segment is dominated by the sale of loose-leaf current news reports, sold on an annual subscription basis. These reports are designed to be included in organized, indexed publications housed in ring binders. Increasingly, CCH publishing is migrating toward electronic delivery, including the CD-ROM format. The computer processing segment provides software and computer services for the processing of tax returns. In response to the changing market, CCH has repositioned itself as a software provider while maintaining on a smaller basis its role as a service bureau for return processing. The Legal Information Services segment offers a variety of services to assist attorneys in handling corporate, securities, credit, and intellectual property matters. This segment operates through the following wholly owned subsidiaries: CT Corporation System and Washington Service Bureau. CCH provides information on foreign laws and current news as well. Global coverage is achieved through CCH's foreign subsidiaries: CCH Australia Limited, CCH Canadian Limited, CCH Editions Limited, CCH Japan Limited, CCH Europe, Inc., CCH New Zealand Limited, Les Publications CCH/FM Lte'e, and CCH Asia Limited. Incorporated in Delaware in 1927.

Directors (In addition to indicated officers)

John C. Burton
William C. Egan III
Edward L. Massie

Robert H. Mundheim
Daniel K. Thorne

Officers (Directors*)

*Oakleigh B. Thorne, Chm.
*Oakleigh Thorne, Pres. & C.E.O.
*Ralph C. Whitley, Member, Exec. Comm.
John I. Abernethy, Exec. Comm., Finance (C.F.O.)
Christopher Ainsley, Exec. Comm., Int'l.
Jonathan Copulsky, Exec. Comm., Customer Management/Oper.

John J. Lynch, Jr., Exec. Comm., Service Products/Strategy
Nancy McKinstry, Exec. Comm., Product Management
Hugh J. Yarrington, Exec. Comm., Knowledge

Consolidated Balance Sheet As of December 31, 1994 (000 omitted)

Assets		Liabilities & Stockholders' Equity	
Current assets	$355,099	Current liabilities	$363,814
Net property, plant & equipment	124,003	Long-term obligations	269
Other assets	102,054	Other liabilities	125,259
		*Stockholders' equity	91,814
Total	$581,156	Total	$581,156

*17,123,812 shares Class A common and 16,910,822 shares Class B common stock outstanding.

Consolidated Income Statement

Years Ended Dec. 31	Thousands — — — —		Per Share[b] — — — —		Common Stock Price Range[bc] Calendar Year
	Total Revenue[a]	Net Income	Earnings	Cash Dividends	
1994	$578,776	$ 18,929	$ .55	$ .70	21 — 15
1993	577,995	6,441	.19	.70	20-1/4 — 13-3/4
1992	659,408	(64,150)[d]	(1.84)[d]	.70	23-3/4 — 14-1/4
1991	704,225	31,025	.89	.70	27 — 15-3/4
1990	716,088	40,671	1.15	.70	26-3/4 — 19

[a]Restated.
[b]Adjusted to reflect a 2-for-1 stock split in the form of a 100% distribution of Class B non-voting common stock effective April 26, 1991.
[c]Class A common stock.
[d]Includes FAS 109, resulting in additional income of $1,200,000 ($.03 per share); FAS 106, resulting in a cumulative charge of $49,800,000 ($1.43 per share); and FAS 112, resulting in a charge of $1,900,000 ($.05 per share).

Transfer Agent & Registrar: Harris Trust and Savings Bank

General Counsel:	Mary Ann Hynes	Auditors:	Deloitte & Touche LLP
Investor Relations:	Kathleen Arney	Traded (Symbol):	NASDAQ (CCHIA, CCHIB)
		Stockholders:	8,505
Human Resources:	Ralph C. Whitley	Employees:	5,299
Mgt. Info. Svcs.:	Ken McBeath	Annual Meeting:	Last Thursday in March

CDW Computer Centers, Inc.

1020 East Lake Cook Road, Buffalo Grove, Illinois 60089
Telephone: (708) 465-6000

CDW Computer Centers, Inc., is a direct marketer of more than 20,000 MS-DOS/Microsoft Windows- and Apple Macintosh-based microcomputer products at discounted prices. The company sells a broad range of microcomputer hardware and peripherals, accessories, networking products and software through in-bound telemarketing account executives who service customers that call the company's "800" telephone numbers. Incorporated in Illinois in 1984; reincorporated in Delaware in 1993; and reincorporated in Illinois in 1995.

Directors   (In addition to indicated officers)

Joseph Levy, Jr.

Frank H. Resnik

Officers   (Directors*)

*Michael P. Krasny, Chm., C.E.O., Secy. & Treas.
*Gregory C. Zeman, Pres.
Daniel F. Callen, V.P.—Fin., Cont. & Chf. Acct. Officer

Mary C. Gerlits, V.P.—Hum. Res.
*Daniel B. Kass, V.P.—Oper.
Paul A. Kozak, V.P.—Purchasing
Chuck Meister, V.P.—Sales
Harry J. Harczak, Jr., C.F.O.

Consolidated Balance Sheet   As of December 31, 1994 (000 omitted)

Assets		Liabilities & Stockholders' Equity	
Current assets	$71,403	Current liabilities	$22,186
Net property, plant & equipment	2,904	*Stockholders' equity	55,843
Other assets	3,722		
Total	$78,029	Total	$78,029

*13,800,000 shares common stock outstanding.

Consolidated Income Statement

Years Ended Dec. 31	Thousands — — — — Net Sales	Net Income[b]	Per Share[a] — — — Earnings[b]	Cash Dividends	Common Stock Price Range[a] Calendar Year
1994	$413,270	$12,113	$ .91	$ .00	34-3/4 — 13-3/8
1993[c]	270,919	11,158	.89	.00	14-1/4 — 6-3/4[d]
1992[e]	138,769	3,371	.28		
1992[f]	138,632	1,265			
1991[f]	101,465	3,709			

[a]Adjusted to reflect a 2-for-1 stock split in May 1994.
[b]Pro forma for 1993 and 1992(e).
[c]Includes a one-time tax benefit of $3,807,000 ($.30 per share).
[d]Initial public offering in May 1993.
[e]Nine months.
[f]March 31 fiscal yearend.

Transfer Agent & Registrar: American Stock Transfer & Trust Co.

General Counsel:
  Rallo & Tepper; Saitlin, Patzik, Frank & Samotny, Ltd.

Investor Relations:
  Harry J. Harczak, Jr., C.F.O.

Human Resources: Mary C. Gerlits, V.P.

Mgt. Info. Svcs.:   James Shanks
Auditors: Coopers & Lybrand L.L.P.
Traded (Symbol):   NASDAQ (CDWC)
Stockholders: 1,200
Employees: 431
Annual Meeting: In April

CELEX Group, Inc.

919 Springer Drive, Lombard, Illinois 60148-6416
Telephone: (708) 953-8440

CELEX Group, Inc., is an innovative specialty retailer and catalog company that designs, manufactures and markets proprietary products for business and personal motivation. The products the company creates for this rapidly growing market include high-quality lithographs, posters, books, cards, apparel and awards. The company sells its products through four distribution channels: Successories® direct mail catalog, Successories® retail stores, a direct sales force, and international distributors. Incorporated in Illinois in 1990.

Directors   (In addition to indicated officers)

Joseph C. LaBonte
Mervyn C. Phillips, Jr.

Sam Raich, Jr.
Michael Singletary

Officers   (Directors*)

*Mac Anderson, Chm. & C.E.O.
James M. Beltrame, Pres. & C.O.O.
*James Allison, Sr. V.P., C.F.O. & Secy.
*Michael McKee, Sr. V.P. & Creative Dir.
John Querio, Sr. V.P.

Richard Secrest, Sr. V.P.—Oper.
Neil Sexton, Sr. V.P.
*Peter Walts, Sr. V.P.
John B. Corrigan, V.P.—Fin.

Consolidated Balance Sheet   As of April 30, 1994 (000 omitted)

Assets		Liabilities & Stockholders' Equity	
Current assets	$15,129	Current liabilities	$ 4,596
Net property, plant & equipment	4,121	Long-term debt	218
Other assets	2,540	Minority interest	534
		*Stockholders' equity	16,442
Total	$21,790	Total	$21,790

*4,735,174 shares common stock outstanding.

Consolidated Income Statement

Years Ended April 30	Thousands — — — — Revenues	Net Income	Per Share[a] — — — Earnings	Cash Dividends	Common Stock Price Range[a] Calendar Year	
1994	$29,785	$2,214	$ .50	$ .00	22	— 12
1993	13,274	1,605[b]	.47[b]	.00	18	— 10-7/8
1992	5,737	102[c]	.04[c]			

[a]Adjusted to reflect a 3-for-2 stock split in March 1994.
[b]Includes a gain to reflect FAS 109, resulting in a cumulative effect of $580,000 ($.17 per share).
[c]Includes an extraordinary gain of $26,300 ($.01 per share) for the tax benefit of utilization of net operating loss carryforward.

Transfer Agent & Registrar:	Illinois Stock Transfer Co.		
General Counsel:	Keck, Mahin & Cate	Auditors:	Price Waterhouse LLP
Investor Relations:	James Allison, Sr. V.P.	Traded (Symbol):	NASDAQ (CLXG)
Human Resources:	Tracy Temple	Stockholders:	600
		Employees:	332
Mgt. Info. Svcs.:	Jim Cates	Annual Meeting:	In September

Central Steel & Wire Company

3000 West 51st Street, Chicago, Illinois 60632-2198
Telephone: (312) 471-3800

Central Steel & Wire Company is an independent metals distributor that engages in the business of warehousing and distributing processed and unprocessed ferrous and nonferrous metals in forms produced generally by rolling mills. The company's principal facility is in Chicago with other warehouses in Detroit, Cincinnati and Milwaukee. Incorporated in Illinois in 1909; reincorporated in Delaware in 1958.

Officers (Directors*)

* James R. Lowenstine, Chm., Pres. & C.E.O.
* Frank A. Troike, Exec. V.P. & Treas.
* Alfred G. Jensen, Sr. V.P.
  Michael X. Cronin, V.P. & Secy.
  Edward J. Kentra, V.P.

* John M. Tiernan, V.P.
* Richard L. Schroer, Asst. V.P.
  Richard P. Ugolini, Compt., Asst. Secy. & Asst. Treas.

Consolidated Balance Sheet As of December 31, 1994 (000 omitted)

Assets		Liabilities & Stockholders' Equity	
Current assets	$206,600	Current liabilities	$ 95,300
Net property, plant & equipment	34,900	Other liabilities	16,100
Other assets	6,700	*Stockholders' equity	136,800
Total	$248,200	Total	$248,200

*286,000 shares common stock outstanding.

Income Statement

| Years Ended Dec. 31 | Thousands — — — — | | Per Share — — — | | Common Stock |
	Net Sales	Net Income	Earnings	Cash Dividends	Price Range Calendar Year
1994	$595,000	$14,200	$49.56	$40.00	605 — 570
1993	503,200	5,600	19.58	22.00	625 — 575
1992	459,200	2,300[a]	7.98[a]	22.00	630 — 550
1991	447,400	6,300	21.85	17.00	600 — 565
1990	524,100	10,600	35.84	31.50	675 — 575

[a]Before cumulative effect of FAS 106, resulting in a charge of $8,600,000 ($29.84 per share).

Transfer Agent & Registrar:	First Chicago Trust Co. of New York		
General Counsel:	Schiff, Hardin & Waite	**Traded:**	OTC
Investor Relations:	Michael X. Cronin, V.P.	**Stockholders:**	300
Mgt. Info. Svcs.:	Richard P. Ugolini, Compt.	**Employees:**	1,400
Auditors:	KPMG Peat Marwick LLP	**Annual Meeting:**	Third Monday in April

CFI Industries, Inc.

935 West Union Avenue, Wheaton, Illinois 60187
Telephone: (708) 668-2838

CFI Industries, Inc., is a fully integrated custom thermoformer of plastic packaging for the hospital/medical, consumer products, electronics and cosmetics markets. The company designs, markets and manufactures functional and innovative packaging for its customers through its wholly owned subsidiary, Plastofilm Industries, Inc. Plastofilm produces custom thermoformed packaging, point of purchase displays, and a variety of disposable packaging products for the hospital/medical, consumer products, electronics and cosmetics industries. Most applications involve design of custom molds or dies by Plastofilm's design and engineering departments. Incorporated in Delaware in 1972.

Directors   (In addition to indicated officers)

Sheli Z. Rosenberg, Co-Chm.
C. Clifford Brake

Marshall L. Burman
Richard M. Harris

Officers   (Directors*)

*Philip C. Calian, Co-Chm. & C.E.O.
 Robert W. George, Pres. & C.O.O.
*Donald J. Liebentritt, V.P.

Susan S. Obuchowski, Secy.
Robert W. Zimmer, Treas. & Cont.

Consolidated Balance Sheet   As of June 26, 1994 (000 omitted)

Assets		Liabilities & Stockholders' Equity	
Current assets	$ 9,049	Current liabilities	$ 8,780
Net property, plant & equipment	7,509	Long-term debt	2,618
Other assets	2,656	Deferred items	762
		Other liabilities	232
		*Stockholders' equity	6,822
Total	$19,214	Total	$19,214

*1,991,418 shares common stock outstanding.

Consolidated Income Statement[a]

Years Ended Abt. June 30	Thousands — — — —		Per Share — — —		Common Stock Price Range Calendar Year
	Net Sales	Net Income	Earnings	Cash Dividends	
1994	$28,730	$ (842)	$ (.42)	$ .00	4-7/8 — 2-1/2
1993	30,164	(448)	(.22)	.00	3-1/2 — 2-1/4
1992	29,737	(1,900)	(.95)	.00	4 — 3
1991[b]	38,897	(182)	(.09)	.00	4-1/2 — 2-3/4
1990[b]	44,255	(1,525)	(.76)	.00	4-7/8 — 2-1/2

[a]Results of heavy gauge manufacturing operations are included for the fiscal year ended June 30, 1990.
[b]1991 results include the operations of Form-Fit until date of sale (April 15, 1991). Results of 1990 include a full year of Form-Fit operations.

Transfer Agent & Registrar: American Stock Transfer & Trust Co.

Investor Relations:
  Susan S. Obuchowski, Secy.

Auditors: Deloitte & Touche LLP

Traded (Symbol):   NASDAQ (CFIB)

Stockholders: 1,700

Employees: 270

Annual Meeting: In December

First Chicago Guide

Champion Parts, Inc.

2525 22nd Street, Oak Brook, Illinois 60521
Telephone: (708) 573-6600

Champion Parts, Inc., is a remanufacturer and marketer of automotive, truck, and farm replacement parts. Major products include carburetors and fuel injection parts, water pumps, clutches, starters, alternators, and constant velocity (CV) driveshaft assemblies for domestic and imported cars, trucks, farm and industrial equipment. Automotive warehouse dealers are the company's primary customers, while other customers include automotive, truck and tractor vehicle manufacturers, heavy duty fleet specialists, and retail organizations. Domestic remanufacturing operations are conducted in plants located in Hope, Arkansas; Fresno, California; Beech Creek, Pennsylvania; and Maple, Ontario, Canada. Champion Parts (Canada) Ltd. is a foreign subsidiary. Incorporated in Illinois in 1947.

Directors   (In addition to indicated officers)

Calvin A. Campbell, Jr.
John R. Gross
Raymond F. Gross

Gary S. Hopmayer
Barry L. Katz
Edward R. Kipling

Officers   (Directors*)

*Raymond G. Perelman, Chm.
*Donald G. Santucci, Pres. & C.E.O.

*Thomas W. Blashill, Exec. V.P., C.F.O., Secy. & Treas.
Roger L. Wilson, V.P.—Sales & Mktg.

Consolidated Balance Sheet   As of January 1, 1995 (000 omitted)

Assets		Liabilities & Stockholders' Equity	
Current assets	$40,723	Current liabilities	$35,104
Net property, plant & equipment	11,494	Long-term debt	1,451
Other assets	1,095	Deferred items	1,393
		*Stockholders' equity	15,364
Total	$53,312	Total	$53,312

*3,655,266 shares common stock outstanding.

Consolidated Income Statement

Years Ended Abt. Dec. 31	Thousands — — — — Net Sales	Net Income	Per Share — — — Earnings	Cash Dividends	Common Stock Price Range Calendar Year	
1994[a]	$ 95,337	$(5,839)	$(1.60)	$ .00	5	— 2-7/8
1993	100,040	1,813	.50	.00	7-1/4	— 2-7/8
1992[a]	96,743	(7,784)	(2.13)	.00	6-1/4	— 3-1/4
1991	111,741	(653)[b]	(.18)[b]	.00	5	— 2-5/8
1990	122,288	1,125	.31	.00	5-1/8	— 2-5/8

[a]Includes restructuring charges of $3,400,000 in 1994; and the reclassification of a foreign joint venture and restructuring charges of $3,223,000 in 1992.
[b]Includes nonrecurring plant consolidation and restructuring cost of $1,034,000 and extraordinary charge of $419,000, net of taxes ($.12 per share) due to early retirement of the company's subordinated debt.

Transfer Agent & Registrar: Harris Trust and Savings Bank	
General Counsel: Lord, Bissell & Brook	**Auditors:** Arthur Andersen LLP
Investor Relations: Thomas W. Blashill, Exec. V.P.	**Traded (Symbol):** NASDAQ (CREB)
	Stockholders: 830
Human Resources: Fred Pochowicz	**Employees:** 1,470
Mgt. Info. Svcs.: Frank Vanek	**Annual Meeting:** In December

The Cherry Corporation

3600 Sunset Avenue, Waukegan, Illinois 60087-3298
Telephone: (708) 662-9200

The Cherry Corporation designs, manufactures, and sells proprietary and custom electrical, electronic, and semiconductor components to original equipment manufacturers and distributors in three market segments: Automotive, Computer, and Consumer and Commercial. Products sold to these markets include switches, keyboards and related products, electronic assemblies and displays, and semiconductor devices. The company has facilities in the U.S., Germany, England, France, the Czech Republic, Australia, Japan, and Hong Kong. Some products are assembled in China, Malaysia, the Philippines, South Korea, and Mexico. The company also participates in 50 percent joint ventures in Japan and India. Wholly owned subsidiaries are Cherry Semiconductor Corporation; Cherry Mikroschalter, GmbH; Plastech, GmbH; Cherry SRO; Cherry Electrical Products Ltd.; Cherry SARL; Cherry Australia Pty., Ltd.; Cherry Systems Corporation; and Cherasia Limited. Cherry Electrical Products operates as a division of The Cherry Corporation, and the company also has a branch sales and engineering office in Japan named Cherry Automotive—Japan. The joint ventures are Hirose Cherry Precision Company Limited in Japan and TVS Cherry Private Limited in India. Incorporated in Illinois in 1953; reincorporated in Delaware in 1978.

Directors   (In addition to indicated officers)

Walter L. Cherry
Charles W. Denny
Peter A. Guglielmi

Thomas L. Martin, Jr.
Robert B. McDermott

Officers   (Directors*)

*Peter B. Cherry, Chm., Pres. & C.E.O.
*Alfred S. Budnick, V.P.
Grant T. Hollett, Jr., V.P.

Klaus D. Lauterbach, V.P.
Dan A. King, Treas., Secy. & Corp. Cont.

Consolidated Balance Sheet   As of February 28, 1995 (000 omitted)

Assets		Liabilities & Stockholders' Equity	
Current assets	$115,282	Current liabilities	$ 69,281
Net property, plant & equipment	132,055	Deferred credits and taxes	18,422
Other assets	13,856	Long-term debt	25,863
		*Stockholders' equity	147,627
Total	$261,193	Total	$261,193

*7,560,652 shares Class A common and 4,712,341 shares Class B common stock outstanding.

Consolidated Income Statement

Years Ended Abt. Feb. 28	Thousands — — — — Net Sales	Net Income	Per Share[a] — — — Earnings	Cash Dividends	Common Stock Price Range[a] Fiscal Year
1995	$339,237	$ 14,823	$ 1.36	$ .00	17-1/4 — 11-1/2
1994	275,269	11,033[b]	1.19[b]	.00	17 — 6-7/8
1993	266,231	10,257[c]	1.12[c]	.00	15-1/2 — 4-1/2
1992	228,631	4,665[d]	.51[d]	.00	4-3/4 — 2-1/2
1991	245,887	(5,718)[e]	(.63)	.03	6-1/8 — 2-1/2

[a]Class B common stock. Adjusted to reflect a 2-for-1 stock split in the form of a Class A stock dividend in July 1994.
[b]Includes a gain to reflect FAS 109, resulting in a cumulative effect of $1,542,000 ($.17 per share).
[c]Includes $2,539,000 ($.28 per share) extraordinary tax credit from utilization of operating loss carryforwards.
[d]Includes $891,000 ($.10 per share) extraordinary tax credit from utilization of operating loss carryforwards and $1,976,000 tax benefit for German repatriation of earnings.
[e]Includes $5,600,000 provision for restructuring costs.

Transfer Agent & Registrar: Harris Trust and Savings Bank

General Counsel: McDermott, Will & Emery

Investor Relations: Dan A. King, Treas.

Auditors: Arthur Andersen LLP

Traded (Symbol):   NASDAQ (CHERA; CHERB)
Stockholders: 4,000
Employees: 3,986
Annual Meeting: Third Thursday in June

Chicago Rivet & Machine Co.

901 Frontenac Road, P.O. Box 3061, Naperville, Illinois 60566
Telephone: (708) 357-8500

Chicago Rivet & Machine Co. operates within the fastener industry. Fastener operations consist of the production and sale of rivets, automatic rivet setting machines, parts and tooling, and the leasing of such machines. The product line includes semi-tubular rivets, tubular and split rivets, cold-headed parts, and brake relining machines. Facilities are located in Naperville, Illinois; Tyrone, Pennsylvania; Norwell, Massachusetts; and Albia and Jefferson, Iowa. Incorporated in Illinois in 1927.

Directors (In addition to indicated officers)

Robert K. Brown
Stephen L. Levy

John R. Madden
Walter W. Morrissey

Officers (Directors*)

*John A. Morrissey, Chm. & C.E.O.
*John C. Osterman, Pres., C.O.O. & Treas.
 Donald P. Long, V.P.—Sales

Kimberly A. Kirhofer, Secy.
Stephen D. Voss, Asst. Treas. & Cont.

Consolidated Balance Sheet As of December 31, 1994 (000 omitted)

Assets		Liabilities & Stockholders' Equity	
Current assets	$14,194	Current liabilities	$ 3,225
Net property, plant & equipment	5,671	Deferred items	996
Other assets	58	*Stockholders' equity	15,702
Total	$19,923	Total	$19,923

*586,648 shares common stock outstanding.

Consolidated Income Statement

Years Ended Dec. 31	Thousands — — — — —		Per Share — — — —		Common Stock
	Total Revenues[a]	Net Income	Earnings	Cash Dividends[b]	Price Range Calendar Year
1994	$23,013	$1,909	$3.25	$1.55	34-3/8 — 25-7/8
1993	20,390	1,403	2.39	1.30	29-1/4 — 24
1992	15,758	952	1.62	1.20	28-3/4 — 19-5/8
1991	15,272	750	1.25	1.35	24-1/4 — 18-1/2
1990	17,041	1,250	1.97	1.45	22-7/8 — 18-3/4

[a]Continuing operations.
[b]Dividends declared per share.

Transfer Agent & Registrar:	First Chicago Trust Co. of New York		
Investor Relations:	Kimberly A. Kirhofer, Secy.	Traded (Symbol):	AMEX (CVR)
Mgt. Info. Svcs.:	John C. Osterman, Pres.	Stockholders:	591
		Employees:	318
Auditors:	Price Waterhouse LLP	Annual Meeting:	In May

First Chicago Guide

CILCORP Inc.

300 Hamilton Boulevard, Suite 300, Peoria, Illinois 61602-1238
Telephone: (309) 675-8850

CILCORP Inc. is a holding company for Central Illinois Light Company (CILCO), its principal business subsidiary, which is engaged in the generation, transmission, distribution and sale of electric energy in an area of about 3,700 square miles, and the purchase, distribution, transportation and sale of natural gas in an area of approximately 4,500 square miles in central and east central Illinois. CILCO's electric service area comprises 139 communities including Peoria; the gas service area covers 129 communities including Peoria and Springfield. CILCO owns and operates two steam-electric base load generating plants and two natural gas combustion turbine-generators, which are used for peaking service. CILCO is interconnected with CIPSCO Inc., Commonwealth Edison Company, Illinois Power Company and the City of Springfield (City Water, Light and Power Department) to provide for the interchange of electric energy on an emergency and mutual-help basis. Other CILCORP subsidiaries include: CILCORP Ventures Inc., which pursues investment opportunities in new ventures and the expansion of existing ventures in energy, environmental services, biotechnology and healthcare; CILCORP Investment Management Inc., which administers the company's investment policy and manages its investment portfolio comprised primarily of leveraged leases; and Environmental Science & Engineering, Inc., which provides engineering and environmental consulting, analysis, and laboratory services to a variety of government and private customers. Incorporated in Illinois in 1985 as a holding company for CILCO, which was incorporated in Illinois in 1913.

Directors (In addition to indicated officer)

Marcus Alexis	H. Safford Peacock
John R. Brazil	Katherine E. Smith
Willard Bunn III	Richard N. Ullman
David E. Connor	Murray M. Yeomans
Homer J. Holland	

Officers (Director*)

*Robert O. Viets, Pres. & C.E.O.
John G. Sahn, V.P., Gen. Coun. & Secy.
Michael D. Austin, Treas. & Asst. Secy.

Jeffrey L. Barnett, Cont.
Robert D. Moushon, Asst. Treas.

Consolidated Balance Sheet   As of December 31, 1994 (000 omitted)

Assets		Liabilities & Stockholders' Equity	
Current assets	$ 159,239	Current liabilities	$ 138,004
Net property, plant & equipment	891,693	Long-term debt	326,695
Other assets	187,452	Deferred items	362,850
		Preferred stock of subsidiary	66,120
		*Stockholders' equity	344,715
Total	$1,238,384	Total	$1,238,384

*13,035,756 shares common stock outstanding.

Consolidated Income Statement

Years Ended Dec. 31	Thousands — — — — Operating Revenues	Net Income[a]	Per Share — — — — Earnings	Cash Dividends	Common Stock Price Range Calendar Year
1994	$605,139	$32,586	$2.50	$2.46	37-1/2 — 28-3/4
1993	584,511	33,583	2.60	2.46	43-3/4 — 35-3/4
1992	581,225	32,097	2.48	2.46	40-5/8 — 33-5/8
1991	590,165	39,656	3.14	2.46	38-1/4 — 31
1990	542,847	34,504	2.69	2.46	38-5/8 — 29-3/4

[a]Available for common stockholders.

Transfer Agents: CILCORP Inc.; Continental Stock Transfer & Trust Co. of N.Y.

Registrars: First of America Trust Co.; Continental Stock Transfer & Trust Co. of N.Y.	Auditors: Arthur Andersen LLP
	Traded (Symbol): NYSE, CSE (CER)
General Counsel: John G. Sahn, V.P.	Stockholders: 15,095
Investor Relations: Gary A. Ebeling, Dir.	Employees: 2,941
Human Resources: Thomas F. Broderick, Prin. Atty.	Annual Meeting: Fourth Tuesday in April

CIPSCO Incorporated

607 East Adams Street, Springfield, Illinois 62739
Telephone: (217) 523-3600

CIPSCO Incorporated is a holding company whose principal subsidiary is Central Illinois Public Service Company (CIPS), an electric and natural gas utility. Another subsidiary, CIPSCO Investment Company, manages non-utility investments and provides investment management services for affiliates. CIPS is engaged in the generation, transmission and distribution of electricity. The utility also distributes natural gas which it purchases from pipeline suppliers and from producers. In addition, transportation service is provided for customers that purchase gas directly from suppliers. The CIPS service area is in a 20,000-square-mile region of central and southern Illinois. Electric service is provided to about 317,000 customers in 557 communities. Power also is furnished to other utility systems, rural electric cooperative and municipal electric systems. CIPS owns and operates five interconnected electric generating stations with a combined capacity of about 2,850 megawatts. No generating facilities are under construction or planned. All generating capacity is coal fired with the exception of a small, oil-fired unit. Natural gas service is provided to about 165,500 customers in 267 communities. Maximum natural gas sendout capability is about 330-million cubic feet per day. Incorporated in Illinois in 1986.

Directors   (In addition to indicated officer)

William J. Alley	Richard A. Lumpkin
John L. Heath	Hanne M. Merriman
Robert W. Jackson	Thomas L. Shade
Gordon R. Lohman	James W. Wogsland

Officers   (Director*)

*Clifford L. Greenwalt, Pres. & C.E.O.
William A. Koertner, V.P., C.F.O. & Secy.
John C. Fiaush, Cont. & Asst. Treas.
Craig D. Nelson, Treas., Asst. Secy. & Asst. Cont.
Lowell A. Dodd, Sr. V.P.—Oper. (CIPS)

James G. Bachman, V.P.—Mktg. (CIPS)
Gilbert W. Moorman, V.P.—Power Supp. (CIPS)
William R. Morgan, V.P.—Div. Oper. (CIPS)
D.R. Patterson, V.P.—Corp. Svc. (CIPS)
William R. Voisin, V.P.—Pub. Rel. (CIPS)

Consolidated Balance Sheet   As of December 31, 1994 (000 omitted)

Assets		Liabilities & Stockholders' Equity	
Current assets	$ 200,115	Current liabilities	$ 147,364
Net property, plant & equipment	1,439,560	Long-term debt	459,619
Other assets	137,682	Deferred items	442,761
		Preferred stock of subsidiaries	80,000
		*Stockholders' equity	647,613
Total	$1,777,357	Total	$1,777,357

*34,069,542 shares common stock outstanding.

Consolidated Income Statement

Years Ended Dec. 31	Thousands — — — —		Per Share — — — —		Common Stock
	Operating Revenues	Net Income	Earnings	Dividends Declared	Price Range Calendar Year
1994	$844,615	$83,954	$2.46	$1.99	30-5/8 — 25-1/4
1993	844,760	85,498	2.51	1.95	33-5/8 — 29-1/4
1992	739,877	72,499	2.13	1.91	30-7/8 — 26
1991	722,081	72,065	2.11	1.87	28-1/8 — 21-3/8
1990	699,721	65,756	1.92	1.83	23-1/4 — 19-1/2

Transfer Agents: Illinois Stock Transfer Company; Harris Trust and Savings Bank

Registrar:
   Harris Trust and Savings Bank

General Counsel:
   Jones, Day, Reavis & Pogue

Investor Relations:
   Robert C. Porter, Asst. Secy.—CIPS

Human Resources: D.R. Patterson, V.P.—CIPS

Mgt. Info. Svcs.:   D.R. Patterson, V.P.—CIPS

Auditors: Arthur Andersen LLP

Traded (Symbol):   NYSE, CSE (CIP)

Stockholders: 40,221

Employees: 2,669

Annual Meeting: Fourth Wednesday in April

Circle Fine Art Corporation

303 East Wacker Drive, Suite 830, Chicago, Illinois 60601
Telephone: (312) 616-1300

Circle Fine Art Corporation publishes, purchases and distributes fine art and related products. The company sells fine art at retail through 25 galleries in the U.S. and Canada. Art is also sold on a wholesale basis through the company's own sales force, independent overseas distributors, and to one 50 percent-owned joint venture which operates an art gallery. Products include signed and numbered, limited-edition fine art graphics, such as original lithographs, etchings and serigraphs; and fine art multiples, three-dimensional works and "Art to Wear" jewelry in limited editions. Circle Fine Art publishes its own editions of graphics and multiples. In addition, the company owns and operates an artists' workshop in New York City; two framing facilities, one each in New York and California; and publishes fine art posters and art books to sell through its retail galleries and through its wholesale distribution system. Art-to-Wear, signed, limited edition jewelry, designed by major artists, is created in precious metals and gemstones at Circle's Jewelry Atelier in Scottsdale, Arizona. The company's retail art galleries are located in California, Colorado, Florida, Georgia, Illinois, Louisiana, Michigan, Missouri, New Jersey, New York, Nevada, Washington and Toronto, Canada. The galleries operate under a variety of names, principally Circle Gallery and Circle Gallery of Animation & Cartoon Art. Incorporated in Delaware in 1964.

Directors (In addition to indicated officers)

Jack Solomon, Jr.   John P. Sorin

Officers (Directors*)

*Joel Stone, Chm.   Joseph R. Atkin, V.P.—Fin. & C.F.O.
*Louis Yaseen, Pres. & C.E.O.   Barry S. Podgorsky, V.P. & Dir.—East Coast Oper.
*Carolyn Solomon, Exec. V.P.   Brian Bettencourt, Cont.

Consolidated Balance Sheet   As of December 31, 1994 (000 omitted) Unaudited

Assets		Liabilities & Stockholders' Equity	
Current assets	$15,931	Current liabilities	$ 8,864
Net property, plant & equipment	5,479	Long-term debt	16,937
Other assets	5,178	*Stockholders' equity	787
Total	$26,588	Total	$26,588

*9,165,870 shares common stock outstanding.

Consolidated Income Statement

Years Ended Sept. 30	Thousands — — — —		Per Share[a] — — —		Common Stock Price Range[a] Calendar Year
	Net Sales	Net Income	Earnings	Cash Dividends	
1994	$19,170	$(7,417)	$(6.58)	$ .00	1-1/2 — 3/8[b]
1993	22,820	(7,540)	(6.67)	.00	4-1/8 — 3/8[b]
1992	25,660	(6,366)	(7.29)	.00	4-1/2 — 1-1/8
1991	35,595	(3,652)	(4.42)	.00	11-5/8 — 3
1990	41,326	475	.56	.00	24-3/8 — 7-7/8

[a]Adjusted to reflect a 1-for-3 reverse stock split in November 1994.
[b]Fiscal year.

Transfer Agent & Registrar: Registrar and Transfer Company

General Counsel: Rudnick & Wolfe

Investor Relations: Joseph R. Atkin, V.P.

Human Resources: Nancy Graham

Mgt. Info. Svcs.:   Joseph R. Atkin, V.P.

Auditors:
  Altschuler, Melvoin and Glasser LLP

Traded (Symbol):   OTC Bulletin

Stockholders: 380

Employees: 237

Annual Meeting: In December

Circuit Systems, Inc.

2350 East Lunt Avenue, Elk Grove Village, Illinois 60007-5699
Telephone: (708) 439-1999

Circuit Systems, Inc., is a manufacturer of single-sided, double-sided, and multilayer printed circuit boards for the electronics industry. Its customers are primarily original equipment manufacturers of computers, telecommunication equipment, and computer peripherals. Circuit boards are used in large quantities in the electronics industry to mount and interconnect microprocessors, integrated circuits, and other electronic components. The company has a 22 percent-interest in SigmaTron International, Inc., which is engaged in electronics contract manufacturing. Incorporated in Illinois in 1967.

Directors (In addition to indicated officers)

Richard J. Augustine

Martin Henderson

Officers (Directors*)

*D.S. Patel, Chm., Pres. & C.E.O.
Roger S. McLain, V.P.—Mktg.
*Magan H. Patel, V.P. & Asst. Secy.

Vithal V. Patel, V.P.—Reg. Compliance & Assets
*Dilip S. Vyas, V.P.—Bus. Devel. & Treas.
*Thomas W. Rieck, Secy.

Consolidated Balance Sheet   As of April 30, 1994 (000 omitted)

Assets		Liabilities & Stockholders' Equity	
Current assets	$12,596	Current liabilities	$11,018
Net property, plant & equipment	17,398	Long-term obligations	5,612
Investment in affiliates	1,778	Deferred income taxes	953
Other assets	1,329	*Stockholders' equity	15,518
Total	$33,101	Total	$33,101

*5,267,973 shares common stock outstanding.

Consolidated Income Statement

Years Ended April 30	Thousands — — — — Net Sales	Net Income	Per Share — — — Earnings	Cash Dividends	Common Stock Price Range Calendar Year
1994	$60,411	$4,989	$ .95	$ .00	8-7/8 — 4-3/8
1993	51,419	3,056	.59	.00	9-1/8 — 3-3/4
1992	47,234	1,785	.35	.00	5-1/4 — 1-3/8
1991	35,586	523	.10	.00	2-7/8 — 7/8
1990	37,181	1,421	.28	.00	6-7/8 — 1-3/8

Transfer Agent & Registrar: American Stock Transfer & Trust Co.

Legal Counsel:	Rieck and Crotty, P.C.	Auditors:	Grant Thornton LLP
Investor Relations:	Elaine Douglass	Traded (Symbol):	NASDAQ (CSYI)
		Stockholders:	1,100
Human Resources:	Bill Blair	Employees:	550
Mgt. Info. Svcs.:	Kiran Patel	Annual Meeting:	Second Friday after Labor Day

First Chicago Guide

CLARCOR Inc.

2323 Sixth Street, P.O. Box 7007, Rockford, Illinois 61125
Telephone: (815) 962-8867

CLARCOR Inc. is a diversified provider of filtration and packaging products. The company is divided into two groups: Filtration Products Group supplies filtration and purification products and systems for the over-the-road trucking, construction, farm, automotive, railroad, food/beverage processing and industrial markets; and Consumer Products Group develops and manufactures custom-decorated metal- and plastic-lithographed containers, composite containers and plastic closures for the food, gift, arts & crafts, pharmaceutical and household product markets. Significant wholly owned subsidiaries include: Baldwin Filters, Inc.; J.L. Clark, Inc.; Airguard Industries, Inc.; and Clark Filter, Inc. In November 1992, the company divested the Precision Products Group. CLARCOR Inc., formerly J.L. Clark Manufacturing Co., was organized in 1904 as an Illinois corporation; reincorporated in Delaware in 1969.

Directors (In addition to indicated officer)

J. Marc Adam	Dudley J. Godfrey, Jr.
Milton R. Brown	Stanton K. Smith, Jr.
Carl J. Dargene	Richard A. Snell
Frank A. Fiorenza	Don A. Wolf

Officers (Director*)

*Lawrence E. Gloyd, Chm. & C.E.O.	William F. Knese, V.P., Cont. & Treas.
Norman E. Johnson, Pres. & C.O.O.	David J. Lindsay, V.P.—Admin.
David J. Anderson, V.P.—Int'l./Corp. Dev.	Peter F. Nangle, V.P.—Info. Svcs.
Marshall C. Arne, V.P.	Ronald A. Moreau, Grp. V.P.—Cons. Prods.
Bruce A. Klein, V.P.—Fin. & C.F.O.	Marcia S. Blaylock, Corp. Secy.

Consolidated Balance Sheet As of December 3, 1994 (000 omitted)

Assets		Liabilities & Stockholders' Equity	
Current assets	$ 98,450	Current liabilities	$ 39,461
Net property, plant & equipment	52,615	Long-term debt	17,013
Other assets	37,383	Deferred items	5,686
		Other liabilities	8,826
		*Stockholders' equity	117,462
Total	$188,448	Total	$188,448

*14,760,888 shares common stock outstanding.

Consolidated Income Statement

Years Ended Abt. Nov. 30	Thousands — — — — —		Per Share[a] — — — —		Common Stock Price Range[ab] Calendar Year
	Net Sales	Net Income	Earnings	Cash Dividends	
1994	$270,123	$21,255[c]	$1.43[c]	$ .62	22-3/8 — 15-7/8
1993	225,319	17,251	1.16	.61	21-1/8 — 16
1992	188,625	14,139[d]	.94[d]	.60	22-1/2 — 15
1991	179,538	18,475[e]	1.24[e]	.55	22-5/8 — 14
1990	170,279	19,205[e]	1.29[e]	.52	17-7/8 — 11-7/8

[a]Adjusted to reflect 3-for-2 stock splits in February 1992 and January 1990.
[b]For 1991-90, common stock was listed on NASDAQ under the symbol CLRK.
[c]Includes a gain of $630,000 ($.04 per share), which is the cumulative effect of FAS 109.
[d]Includes a charge of $2,370,000 ($.16 per share), which is the cumulative effect of FAS 106.
[e]From continuing operations.

Transfer Agent & Registrar: First Chicago Trust Co. of New York

General Counsel: Sidley & Austin

Investor Relations:
Marcia S. Blaylock, Corp. Secy.

Human Resources: David J. Lindsay, V.P.

Mgt. Info. Svcs.: Peter F. Nangle, V.P.

Auditors: Coopers & Lybrand L.L.P.

Traded (Symbol): NYSE (CLC)

Stockholders: 1,900

Employees: 2,211

Annual Meeting: In March

Classics International Entertainment, Inc.

919 North Michigan Avenue, Suite 3400, Chicago, Illinois 60611-1901
Telephone: (312) 482-9006

Classics International Entertainment, Inc., is engaged in the comic book business through retailing, publishing and merchandising. The company owns Dream Factory, Inc., and Moondog's, which are comic book retailers. Dream Factory operates a chain of 11 specialty stores selling comic books, pop culture items, graphic novels, T-shirts, collectible cards, role playing games, and related items. Moondog's operates a chain of five company-owned specialty stores, selling comic books, pop culture items, and other merchandise. The Dream Factory stores are in the process of changing their names to Moondog's. First Classics, Inc., is another wholly owned subsidiary. Incorporated in Delaware in 1992.

Director   (In addition to indicated officers)

Rocco J. Martino

Officers   (Directors*)

*Richard S. Berger, Chm. & C.E.O.
*Gary Colabuono, Pres. & C.O.O.

Lawrence Strauss, V.P.—Hum. Res.
James M. Doré, C.F.O., Treas. & Secy.

Consolidated Balance Sheet   As of December 31, 1994 (000 omitted)

Assets		Liabilities & Stockholders' Equity	
Current assets	$1,473	Current liabilities	$2,192
Net property, plant & equipment	967	Deferred income	100
Other assets	947	*Stockholders' equity	1,095
Total	$3,387	Total	$3,387

*7,369,576 shares common stock outstanding.

Consolidated Income Statement

Years Ended Dec. 31	Thousands — — — —		Per Share — — —		Common Stock Price Range[a] Calendar Year
	Net Sales	Net Income	Earnings	Cash Dividends	
1994	$5,387	$(5,139)	$ (.79)	$ .00	7-1/8 — 2-7/8
1993	4,301	(2,728)	(.58)	.00	4-1/4 — 3
1992	2,417	2,127[b]	1.69[b]		

[a]Initial public offering in October 1993.
[b]Includes an extraordinary gain of $2,799,093 ($2.22 per share).

Transfer Agent & Registrar: Continental Stock Transfer & Trust Co.

General Counsel:
    Sotiroff Abramczyk & Rauss P.C.

Investor Relations: Channel Marketing inc.

Human Resources: Lawrence Strauss, V.P.

Auditors: Feldman Radin & Co., P.C.

Traded (Symbol):   NASDAQ (CIEI)

Stockholders: 1,500

Employees: 93

Annual Meeting: In June

CNA Financial Corporation

CNA Plaza, 333 South Wabash Avenue, Chicago, Illinois 60685
Telephone: (312) 822-5000

CNA Financial Corporation is a holding company originally formed by Continental Assurance Company and Continental Casualty Company. Continental Assurance writes a complete line of individual and group life and health insurance policies. Continental Casualty and its subsidiary companies write a comprehensive line of accident, health, liability, property and surety insurance policies. Commercial business includes such lines as workers' compensation, general liability, multiple peril, professional and specialty, and reinsurance. Personal lines primarily consist of automobile and homeowners insurance. Other subsidiaries include National Fire Insurance Co. and American Casualty Company of Reading, Pennsylvania. Loews Corporation holds an 84 percent ownership position in CNA Financial Corp. In May 1995, CNA Financial completed its acquisition of Continental Corp., a New York property and casualty insurer. Incorporated in Delaware in 1967.

Directors   (In addition to indicated officers)

Edward J. Noha, Chm.
Antoinette Cook Bush
Robert P. Gwinn
Richard L. Thomas

James S. Tisch
Preston R. Tisch
Marvin Zonis

Officers   (Directors*)

*Laurence A. Tisch, C.E.O.
Peter E. Jokiel, Sr. V.P. & C.F.O.
Donald M. Lowry, Sr. V.P., Gen. Coun. &
Secy.
Patricia L. Kubera, V.P. & Cont.
Mary A. Ribikawskis, Asst. Secy.

Robert E. Wetzel, Asst. Secy.
*Dennis H. Chookaszian, Chm./C.E.O.—CNA
Insurance Cos.
*Philip L. Engel, Pres.—CNA Insurance Cos.
Carolyn L. Murphy, Sr. V.P.—CNA Insurance Cos.
Jae L. Wittlich, Sr. V.P.—CNA Insurance Cos.

Consolidated Balance Sheet   As of December 31, 1994 (000 omitted)

Assets		Liabilities & Stockholders' Equity	
Investments	$26,942,903	Insurance reserves	$28,937,695
Insurance receivables	6,921,644	Long-term debt	911,813
Property & equipment	263,276	Short-term debt	2,000
Other assets	10,192,610	Other liabilities	9,922,988
		*Stockholders' equity	4,545,937
Total	$44,320,433	Total	$44,320,433

*61,798,262 shares common stock outstanding.

Consolidated Income Statement

Years Ended Dec. 31	Thousands — — — —		Per Share — — — —		Common Stock Price Range Calendar Year
	Revenues	Net Income	Earnings	Cash Dividends	
1994	$10,999,545	$ 36,548	$ .51	$ .00	82-1/4 — 60
1993	11,010,813	267,523	4.26	.00	101 — 74-1/4
1992	10,793,442	(330,552)[a]	(5.42)[a]	.00	104-1/2 — 78-1/2
1991	11,131,353	612,512	9.80	.00	99-1/4 — 62-3/4
1990	9,944,388	366,509	5.77	.00	100 — 49-1/2

[a]Includes a gain to reflect FAS 106, FAS 109, and the discounting of certain workers' compensation and disability claim reserves, resulting in a cumulative effect of $331,892,000 ($5.37 per share).

Transfer Agent & Registrar: The First National Bank of Chicago

General Counsel:	Donald M. Lowry, Sr. V.P.	Auditors:	Deloitte & Touche LLP
Investor Relations:	Mary A. Ribikawskis	Traded (Symbol):	CSE, NYSE, PHSE, PSE (CNA)
		Stockholders:	3,326
Human Resources:	John P. McGinley, Dir.	Employees:	15,600
Mgt. Info. Svcs.:	Mary A. Ribikawskis	Annual Meeting:	First Wednesday in May

First Chicago Guide

Cobra Electronics Corporation

6500 West Cortland Street, Chicago, Illinois 60635
Telephone: (312) 889-8870

Cobra Electronics Corporation (formerly Dynascan Corporation) designs and markets consumer electronics products, including telecommunications products, CB radios, and safety/radar detection systems in the U.S. and around the world. Subsidiaries include Cobra Electronics (Hong Kong) Limited and Dynascan Europe Ltd. In October 1993, the company sold its rights to market professional recording devices under the Marantz name to a private party. Incorporated in Delaware in 1961; present name adopted in 1993.

Directors (In addition to indicated officers)

William P. Carmichael
Samuel B. Horberg

Harold D. Schwartz

Officers (Directors*)

*Carl Korn, Chm.
*Jerry Kalov, Pres. & C.E.O.

*Gerald M. Laures, V.P.—Fin. & Corp. Secy.
Stephen M. Yanklowitz, C.O.O.

Consolidated Balance Sheet As of December 31, 1994 (000 omitted)

Assets		Liabilities & Stockholders' Equity	
Current assets	$27,503	Current liabilities	$20,913
Net property, plant & equipment	6,984	*Stockholders' equity	19,429
Other assets	5,855		
Total	$40,342	Total	$40,342

*6,226,648 shares common stock outstanding.

Consolidated Income Statement

Years Ended Dec. 31	Thousands — — — — Net Sales	Net Income[a]	Per Share — — — Earnings[a]	Cash Dividends	Common Stock Price Range Calendar Year
1994	$ 82,131	$(1,515)	$ (.24)	$ .00	3-7/8 — 1-3/4
1993	98,844	(4,392)	(.70)	.00	4-3/8 — 2-1/8
1992	117,733	(9,514)[b]	(1.52)[b]	.00	6-1/4 — 3
1991	135,901	(5,656)	(.90)	.00	5-7/8 — 3-3/8
1990	168,987	(1,589)	(.26)	.00	8-1/4 — 2-3/4

[a]From continuing operations.
[b]Includes FAS 109, resulting in a charge of $835,000 ($.13 per share).

Transfer Agent & Registrar: American Stock Transfer & Trust Co.

General Counsel: Sidley & Austin

Investor Relations: Gerald M. Laures, V.P.

Human Resources: Celeste Boucher, Dir.

Mgt. Info. Svcs.: Dean Marino

Auditors: Deloitte & Touche LLP

Traded (Symbol): NASDAQ (COBR)

Stockholders: 1,400

Employees: 146

Annual Meeting: In May

Cole Taylor Financial Group, Inc.

350 East Dundee Road, Suite 300, Wheeling, Illinois 60090-3199
Telephone: (708) 459-1111

Cole Taylor Financial Group, Inc., and its subsidiaries provide financial services to individual customers and middle-market companies. Cole Taylor Financial Group is the holding company for Cole Taylor Bank, which has nine full-service banking centers, and Cole Taylor Finance Co. Cole Taylor Finance Co., through its wholly owned subsidiaries, operating as Reliance Acceptance Corp., is engaged in the acquisition of sales finance contracts primarily collateralized by used automobiles. In 1989, Cole Taylor Financial Group completed the merger of its four Cook County banks with Cole Taylor Bank, creating a commercial branch banking system. In 1992, Cole Taylor Bank/Yorktown merged with Cole Taylor Bank. The company was founded by Irwin H. Cole and Sidney J. Taylor in 1969. In May 1994, the company completed an initial public offering of 2,300,000 shares of common stock. Incorporated in Delaware in 1978.

Directors   (In addition to indicated officers)

Irwin H. Cole
Solway F. Firestone
Dean L. Griffith
Ross J. Mangano

Melvin E. Pearl
Howard B. Silverman
Sidney J. Taylor

Officers   (Directors*)

*Jeffrey W. Taylor, Chm. & C.E.O.
*Bruce W. Taylor, Pres.
 Richard M. Schwartz, Exec. V.P.
 Jean C. Schmidt, Sr. V.P. & Dir.—Hum.
   Res./Bus. Plan.

Daniel S. Bleil, V.P.
James I. Kaplan, Gen. Coun. & Corp. Secy.
*William S. Race, C.F.O.

Consolidated Balance Sheet   As of December 31, 1994 (000 omitted)

Assets		Liabilities & Stockholders' Equity	
Cash & due from banks	$ 69,715	Total deposits	$1,292,981
Federal funds sold	23,600	Short-term borrowing	238,797
Investment securities	464,419	Long-term debt	131,207
Loans, net	1,195,545	Other liabilities	19,918
Property & equipment	15,153	*Stockholders' equity	130,711
Other assets	45,182		
Total	$1,813,614	Total	$1,813,614

*14,508,353 shares common stock outstanding.

Consolidated Income Statement

Years Ended Dec. 31	Thousands — — — —		Per Share[b] — — — —		Common Stock Price Range[bc] Calendar Year
	Total Income[a]	Net Income	Earnings	Dividends	
1994	$143,771	$17,759	$1.26	$ .18	22-7/8 — 13-1/4
1993	119,534	11,233	.91	.13	
1992	114,093	8,245	.67	.13	
1991	120,415	6,462	.61	.13	
1990	128,214	2,370	.22	.13	

[a]Total interest income and non-interest income.
[b]Adjusted to reflect a 40-for-1 stock split in January 1994.
[c]Initial public offering in May 1994.

Transfer Agent & Registrar: Cole Taylor Bank

Corporate Counsel: Katten Muchin & Zavis

Investor Relations: William S. Race, C.F.O.

Human Resources: Jean C. Schmidt, Sr. V.P.

Mgt. Info. Svcs.:   Alan R. Gunnerson

Auditors: KPMG Peat Marwick LLP
Traded (Symbol):   NASDAQ (CTFG)
Stockholders: 769
Employees: 842
Annual Meeting: In May

First Chicago Guide

Comdisco, Inc.

6111 North River Road, Rosemont, Illinois 60018-5159
Telephone: (708) 698-3000

Comdisco, Inc., is a leading provider of solutions that help businesses acquire, manage, and protect their high-tech equipment. These services include equipment leasing, remarketing, and refurbishing, business continuity, consulting, strategic and financial planning, asset management software tools, data center moves, and consolidations. Comdisco has more than 100 locations around the world and serves more than 8,000 customers in North and South America, Europe, the Pacific Rim, and Australia, providing a full range of solutions for reducing technology cost and risk. Incorporated in Delaware in 1971.

Directors (In addition to indicated officers)

Edward H. Fiedler, Jr.
C. Keith Hartley
Rick Kash

Thomas H. Patrick
Basil R. Twist, Jr.

Officers (Directors*)

* John F. Slevin, Pres. & C.E.O.
* Alan J. Andreini, Exec. V.P.
* Robert A. Bardagy, Exec. V.P.—Leasing Prods.
* Nicholas K. Pontikes, Exec. V.P. & Pres.—Bus. Contin. Svcs.
* William N. Pontikes, Exec. V.P.—Oper.
* John J. Vosicky, Exec. V.P., C.F.O. & Treas.
James D. Duncan, Sr. V.P.—N. Amer. Sales
Rosemary P. Geisler, Sr. V.P.—High Tech. Trade Ctr.
Kenneth A. Halverson, Jr., Sr. V.P.—Medical Equip. Grp.
Stephen W. Hamilton, Sr. V.P.—Int'l.
* Philip A. Hewes, Sr. V.P.—Legal & Secy.
Joseph A. Kafka, Sr. V.P.
Vincent L. Ricci, Sr. V.P.
Hugh L. Roberts, Sr. V.P.—N. Amer. Sales
Roy A. Wagner, Sr. V.P.—N. Amer. Sales
Martin R. Walsh, Sr. V.P.—High Tech. Trade Ctr.
Richard B. Zane, Sr. V.P.—N. Amer. Sales

Stanley M. Abes, V.P.—COPAM
William O. Bray, V.P.—Syst. Integration
Lucie A. Buford, V.P.—Hum. Res.
Richard A. Finocchi, V.P.—Fin.
Jeremiah M. Fitzgerald, V.P.—Legal & Gen. Coun.
Vincent J. Fricas, V.P.—Disaster Recov.
Allan J. Graham, V.P.—Disaster Recov.
H. Scott Harvey, V.P.—Mktg. Admin.
Michael F. Herman, V.P.—Electronics
James J. Hyland, V.P.—Inv. Rel.
David J. Keenan, V.P. & Cont.
Mary C. Moster, V.P.—Corp. Comm.
David Nolan, V.P.—Disaster Recov.
Edward A. Pacewicz, V.P.—Fin.
Robert A. Plowman, V.P.—Private Placement
Gregory D. Sabatello, V.P.—Info. Svcs.
Russell S. West, V.P.—Leasing Prods.
W. Bradford Wheatley, V.P.—Private Placement

Consolidated Balance Sheet As of September 30, 1994 (000 omitted)

Assets		Liabilities & Stockholders' Equity	
Current assets	$ 402,000	Current liabilities	$ 677,000
Net property, plant & equipment	4,008,000	Long-term debt	2,912,000
Other assets	397,000	Deferred items	229,000
		Other liabilities	248,000
		*Stockholders' equity	741,000
Total	$4,807,000	Total	$4,807,000

*36,695,908 shares common stock outstanding.

Consolidated Income Statement

Years Ended Sept. 30	Total Revenue	Net Income	Earnings[b]	Cash Dividends	Common Stock Price Range[a] Calendar Year
	Thousands — — — —		Per Share[a] — — — —		
1994	$2,098,000	$ 44,000[c]	$ 1.16[c]	$ .35	24-1/4 — 17-3/4
1993	2,153,000	80,000[d]	1.97[d]	.29	21 — 13-1/8
1992	2,205,000	(9,000)	(.21)	.28	23-1/4 — 12-1/2
1991	2,174,000	69,000	1.69	.27	27 — 17-1/4
1990	1,920,000	95,000	2.23	.26	27-1/8 — 13-7/8

[a]Adjusted to reflect 5% stock dividend in March 1992.
[b]Based on common and common equivalent shares.
[c]Includes a one-time, aftertax charge of $42,000,000 ($1.09 per share).
[d]Includes a gain to reflect FAS 109, resulting in a cumulative effect of $20,000,000 ($.50 per share).

Transfer Agent & Registrar: Chemical Bank

Corporate Counsel: McBride, Baker & Coles

Investor Relations: James J. Hyland, V.P.

Human Resources: Lucie A. Buford, V.P.

Mgt. Info. Svcs.:   Gregory D. Sabatello, V.P.

Auditors: KPMG Peat Marwick LLP
Traded (Symbol):   NYSE, CSE (CDO)
Stockholders: 2,240
Employees: 2,000
Annual Meeting: In January

First Chicago Guide

Continental Materials Corporation

225 West Wacker Drive, Suite 1800, Chicago, Illinois 60606-1229
Telephone: (312) 541-7200

Continental Materials Corporation is a holding company that operates in two business segments: Heating and Air-Conditioning; and Construction Materials. In the Heating and Air-Conditioning segment, Williams Furnace Co. manufactures and sells heating and cooling equipment including wall furnaces, console heaters, and fan coil units. Phoenix Manufacturing, Inc., manufactures and sells evaporative air coolers. In the Construction Materials segment, Transit Mix Concrete Co. produces and distributes ready mix concrete, sand, gravel, and other building materials. Castle Concrete Company produces limestone, sand, and gravel. The sales of the Construction Materials segment are confined to the Colorado Springs area. Sales of heating and cooling equipment are nationwide. Through Continental Catalina, Inc., the company holds a 30 percent-interest in Oracle Ridge Mining Partners, a partnership which owns a copper property near Tuscon, Arizona. Through Continental Quicksilver, Inc., the company owns a 3.56 percent net-profits interest in the DeLamar Mine, a gold and silver property in southern Idaho. Incorporated in Delaware in 1954.

Directors (In addition to indicated officers)

Thomas H. Carmody
Ralph W. Gidwitz
Ronald J. Gidwitz

William G. Shoemaker
Theodore R. Tetzlaff

Officers (Directors*)

*James G. Gidwitz, Chm. & C.E.O.
*Joseph L. Gidwitz, V. Chm.
*William A. Ryan, Pres. & C.O.O.

*Joseph J. Sum, V.P. & Treas.
Mark S. Nichter, Secy. & Cont.

Consolidated Balance Sheet   As of December 31, 1994 (000 omitted)

Assets		Liabilities & Stockholders' Equity	
Current assets	$32,156	Current liabilities	$16,131
Net property, plant & equipment	13,726	Long-term debt	3,512
Other assets	2,280	Deferred items	1,730
		*Stockholders' equity	26,789
Total	$48,162	Total	$48,162

*1,140,278 shares common stock outstanding.

Consolidated Income Statement[a][b]

Years Ended Abt. Dec. 31	Thousands — — — — Net Sales	Net Income	Per Share — — — — Earnings	Cash Dividends	Common Stock Price Range Calendar Year
1994	$75,294	$ 1,385	$ 1.21	$ .00	13-7/8 — 7-7/8
1993	62,495	40[c]	.03[c]	.00	9-3/4 — 6-3/4
1992	60,982	137	.12	.00	10-1/8 — 6-1/8
1991	58,043	598	.51	.00	11-3/8 — 5-3/4
1990	55,120	(1,151)	(.98)	.00	16-7/8 — 6

[a]Imeco, Inc., was sold June 30, 1993. This operation is reported as discontinued and, therefore, net sales do not include Imeco for any year shown. Net income and earnings per share, however, include the effects of the discontinued operation.
[b]Certain prior years' amounts have been reclassified to conform with the current presentation.
[c]Includes an extraordinary charge of $1,335,000 ($1.15 per share).

Transfer Agent & Registrar: LaSalle National Trust, N.A.

Corporate Counsel:
  Wildman, Harrold, Allen & Dixon

Investor Relations: Mark S. Nichter, Secy.

Human Resources:
  Annemarie Bruckner, Office Mgr.

Mgt. Info. Svcs.:   Mark S. Nichter, Secy.

Auditors: Coopers & Lybrand L.L.P.

Traded (Symbol):   AMEX (CUO)

Stockholders: 3,400

Employees: 552

Annual Meeting: Fourth Wednesday in May

Corcom, Inc.

844 East Rockland Road, Libertyville, Illinois 60048
Telephone: (708) 680-7400

Corcom, Inc., is a supplier of radio frequency interference filters and power entry products. The company's catalog of 450 standard filter designs and 96 power entry devices offers the most complete variety of sizes, configurations, power ratings, and environmental capabilities to the commercial and industrial electronic industries. Corcom filters are sold by 35 independent distributors in the U.S. and by 36 distributors in 22 foreign countries. The catalog is available in German and Japanese, as well as English. Company subsidiaries include: Corcom S.A. de C.V.; Corcom Far East Ltd.; and Corcom GmbH. Facilities are located in Illinois, Mexico, Germany and Hong Kong. Incorporated in Illinois in 1955.

Directors (In addition to indicated officer)

George B. Berry
David B. Pivan
Herbert L. Roth

James A. Steinback
Gene F. Straube
Renato Tagiuri

Officers (Director*)

*Werner E. Neuman, Pres.
 Thomas J. Buns, V.P.—Fin. & Treas.

Walter Roth, Secy.

Consolidated Balance Sheet   As of December 31, 1994 (000 omitted)

Assets		Liabilities & Stockholders' Equity	
Current assets	$11,417	Current liabilities	$ 3,171
Net property, plant & equipment	3,399	Long-term debt	213
		*Stockholders' equity	11,432
Total	$14,816	Total	$14,816

*3,619,386 shares common stock outstanding.

Consolidated Income Statement

Years Ended Dec. 31	Thousands — — — — Net Sales	Net Income	Per Share — — — Earnings	Cash Dividends	Common Stock Price Range Calendar Year		
1994	$26,726	$ 1,243	$ .33	$ .00	5	—	1-1/2
1993	25,854	(2,047)	(.58)	.00	2-1/4	—	1
1992a	26,990	(305)	(.09)	.00	1-1/2	—	1
1991a	27,345	(1,759)	(.50)	.00	1-7/8	—	1
1990a	29,667	(2,233)	(.63)	.00	2-5/8	—	1-1/8

aNet income and earnings per share restated.

Transfer Agent & Registrar:	American Stock Transfer & Trust Co.

General Counsel:	D'Ancona & Pflaum	Traded (Symbol):	NASDAQ (CORC)
Investor Relations:	Thomas J. Buns, V.P.	Stockholders:	500
Human Resources:	Sherril W. Bishop	Employees:	588
Auditors:	Coopers & Lybrand L.L.P.	Annual Meeting:	In May

Dean Foods Company

3600 North River Road, Franklin Park, Illinois 60131-2185
Telephone: (708) 678-1680

Dean Foods Company purchases, processes and distributes dairy and specialty food products. Primarily a dairy company until the early 1960s, Dean Foods has achieved product diversification through internal development and acquisition. Its dairy products include fluid milk and related products, ice cream and frozen novelties. Specialty food products include processed vegetables, pickles, relishes, dips, puddings, sauces and powdered products. In addition to its own and acquired brand names, the company processes and distributes private-label products to supermarkets, food service outlets, various food service distributors, and other food processors. Dean Foods operates in 62 plants and 52 distribution warehouses in 21 states, Mexico and the Caribbean. Subsidiaries include: Dean Foods Vegetable Company; Dean Pickle and Specialty Products (consolidating Green Bay Foods Company, Charles F. Cates & Sons, W.B. Roddenbery Co., Inc.); Mayfield Dairy Farms; and Reiter Dairy. In June 1994, Dean Foods acquired dairy operations in New Mexico. In November 1993, Dean Foods acquired Longlife Dairy Products, a Florida processor of extended shelf life dairy products. In December 1993, Dean Foods acquired the *Birds Eye* line of frozen vegetable products, adding the company's first location in Mexico. Incorporated in Illinois in 1929; reincorporated in Delaware in 1968.

Directors (In addition to indicated officers)

Lewis M. Collens	Bert A. Getz
Paula H. Crown	John S. Llewellyn, Jr.
William D. Fischer	Andrew J. McKenna
John P. Frazee, Jr.	Alexander J. Vogl

Officers (Directors*)

*Howard M. Dean, Chm. & C.E.O.	*Thomas A. Ravencroft, Sr. V.P. & Pres.—Dairy Div.
*Thomas L. Rose, Pres. & C.O.O.	Eric A. Blanchard, V.P., Secy. & Gen. Coun.
Daniel E. Green, Grp.V.P.—Specialty Dairy Products	Gary A. Corbett, V.P.—Govt. & Dairy Industry Reg.
James R. Greisinger, Grp. V.P. & Pres.—Dean Pickle and Specialty Prod.	Gary D. Flickinger, V.P.—Prod.
	Charles D. Kinser, V.P.—Eng.
Dennis J. Purcell, Grp. V.P.	George A. Muck, V.P.—R&D
Roger A. Ragland, Grp. V.P.—Int'l. Sales	Douglas A. Parr, V.P.—Sales & Mktg., Milk & Ice Cream
Jeffrey P. Shaw, Grp. V.P. & Pres.—Dean Foods Vegetable Co.	Terrence J. Smith, V.P.—Ind. Rel.
	Dale I. Hecox, Treas.

Consolidated Balance Sheet As of May 29, 1994 (000 omitted)

Assets		Liabilities & Stockholders' Equity	
Current assets	$ 460,182	Current liabilities	$ 367,267
Net property, plant & equipment	543,211	Long-term debt	136,150
Other assets	105,761	Deferred items	80,963
		*Stockholders' equity	524,774
Total	$1,109,154	Total	$1,109,154

*39,788,613 shares common stock outstanding.

Consolidated Income Statement

Years Ended Abt. May 30	Thousands — — — —		Per Share[b] — — — —		Common Stock
	Net Sales	Net Income[a]	Earnings[a]	Cash Dividends	Price Range[b] Calendar Year
1994	$2,431,203	$71,941	$1.81	$ .64	33-1/2 — 25-1/4
1993	2,274,340	68,409	1.73	.60	32-7/8 — 23-1/8
1992	2,289,441	62,016	1.53	.56	31-1/2 — 22-3/4
1991	2,157,997	72,533	1.79	.49	33-1/2 — 24-3/4
1990	1,987,517	61,232	1.53	.44	27-1/4 — 20-1/8

[a]Includes an aftertax net gain of $1,179,000 ($.03 per share) related to changes in accounting principles in 1994 and a net charge of $9,100,000 ($.14 per share) for an unusual item in 1992.
[b]Adjusted to reflect a 3-for-2 stock split in August 1991.

Transfer Agent & Registrar: Harris Trust and Savings Bank

General Counsel:	Eric A. Blanchard, V.P.	Auditors:	Price Waterhouse LLP
Investor Relations:	Lu Ann Lilja, Dir.—Corp. Comm.	Traded (Symbol):	NYSE (DF)
		Stockholders:	8,936
Human Resources:	Gerald Berger, Dir.	Employees:	12,100
Mgt. Info. Svcs.:	John Brenner, Dir.	Annual Meeting:	In September

Deerbank Corporation

745 Deerfield Road, Deerfield, Illinois 60015
Telephone: (708) 945-2550

Deerbank Corporation is the holding company for Deerfield Federal Savings and Loan Association. The bank was incorporated in Illinois in 1927 as a mutual savings and loan association and converted to a federally chartered mutual savings and loan association in 1981. In 1987, it converted to a federally chartered stock savings and loan association. Deerfield Federal's principal sources of income are interest earned on loans and interest and dividends earned on investments. The principal expenses of the bank are interest paid on deposits, operating expenses and administrative costs. In January 1995, the company announced that it would be acquired by NBD Bancorp, Inc. Incorporated in Delaware in 1990.

Directors (In addition to indicated officers)

Edward E. Bach	John A.S. Lindemann
Forrest O. Berg	Susanne B. Roth
Phillip I. Coleman	Robert R. Rudolph

Officers (Directors*)

*Wayne V. Ecklund, Chm., Pres. & C.E.O.	Candy LoGiurato, V.P.
*David Mullins, Exec. V.P. & C.F.O.	J. Gerald Matta, V.P.
*James A. Miller, Sr. V.P.	Liomar S. Mendoza, V.P.
James Enger, V.P.	John L. Penny, V.P.
Richard Erler, V.P.	Ginger D. Tracz, V.P.
John J. Fulara, Jr., V.P.	Mark J. Babicz, Pres.—Norwood Div.
Christine Gordon, V.P.	*James M. Murphy, Pres.—Northern Div.

Consolidated Balance Sheet As of September 30, 1994 (000 omitted)

Assets		Liabilities & Stockholders' Equity	
Current assets	$748,415	Current liabilities	$665,196
Net property, plant & equipment	14,691	Other liabilities	41,067
Other assets	2,780	*Stockholders' equity	59,623
Total	$765,886	Total	$765,886

*2,582,160 shares common stock outstanding.

Consolidated Income Statement[a]

Years Ended Sept. 30	Thousands — — — —		Per Share[b] — — —		Common Stock
	Total Income	Net Income	Earnings	Cash Dividends	Price Range[b] Calendar Year
1994	$50,517	$8,504	$3.15	$ .75	38 — 28-1/2
1993	54,107	8,009	3.00	.68	37-3/4 — 23-1/8
1992	48,525	5,723	2.31	.55	23-3/4 — 15-1/4
1991	49,207	4,620	1.94	.55	15-7/8 — 8-7/8
1990	26,605	3,542	1.48	.55	12-1/8 — 9-5/8

[a]1990 financial information is for Deerfield Federal Savings and Loan Association, Deerbank Corporation's wholly owned subsidiary. Deerbank became the holding company for Deerfield Federal in February 1991.
[b]Adjusted to reflect a 2-for-1 stock split distributed to stockholders in September 1993.

Transfer Agent & Registrar: Registrar and Transfer Company

Special Counsel:
  Muldoon, Murphy & Faucette, Washington, D.C.

Investor Relations: David Mullins, Exec. V.P.

Human Resources: David Mullins, Exec. V.P.

Mgt. Info. Svcs.: David Mullins, Exec. V.P.

Auditors: Ernst & Young LLP

Traded (Symbol): NASDAQ (DEER)

Stockholders: 660

Employees: 257

Annual Meeting: In January

Deere & Company
John Deere Road, Moline, Illinois 61265-8098
Telephone: (309) 765-8000

Deere & Company and subsidiaries manufacture, distribute and finance the sale and leasing of mobile power machinery, and provide credit, insurance and health care products. The company's machine products are divided into three industry segments: agricultural equipment, industrial equipment, and lawn and grounds care equipment. Agricultural equipment includes: tractors, tillage, soil preparation, planting and harvesting equipment; and crop handling equipment. The products in the industrial equipment segment consist of: utility tractors and smaller earthmoving equipment; medium capacity construction and earthmoving equipment; and forestry machines. This segment also includes the manufacture and distribution of engines and drivetrain components for the original equipment manufacturer (OEM) market. The products in the lawn and grounds care equipment segment are manufactured and distributed for commercial and residential uses —including small tractors for lawn, garden and utility purposes; riding and walk-behind mowers; golf course equipment; utility transport vehicles; snow blowers and other outdoor power products. Company subsidiaries include: John Deere Credit Company, John Deere Finance Limited, John Deere Insurance Group, John Deere Insurance Company of Canada, and John Deere Health Care, Inc. Deere & Company operates factories in the U.S., Argentina, Canada, France, Germany, South Africa and Spain. Foreign sales branches are located in Argentina, Australia, Canada, England, France, Germany, Italy, South Africa and Spain. Incorporated in Delaware in 1958.

Directors   (In addition to indicated officers)

John R. Block	Samuel C. Johnson	William A. Schreyer
Leonard A. Hadley	Arthur L. Kelly	John R. Walter
Regina E. Herzlinger	Agustin Santamarina	Arnold R. Weber

Officers   (Directors*)

*Hans W. Becherer, Chm. & C.E.O.	Frank S. Cottrell, V.P., Gen. Coun. & Secy.
*David H. Stowe, Jr., Pres. & C.O.O.	John S. Gault, V.P.
Bernard L. Hardiek, Exec. V.P.	Dennis E. Hoffmann, V.P.
Eugene L. Schotanus, Exec. V.P.	Michael P. Orr, V.P.
Joseph W. England, Sr. V.P.	Robert W. Porter, V.P.
Michael Frank, Sr. V.P.	Mark C. Rostvold, V.P.
Ferdinand F. Korndorf, Sr. V.P.	James D. White, V.P.
John K. Lawson, Sr. V.P.	Adel A. Zakaria, V.P.
Pierre E. Leroy, Sr. V.P. & C.F.O.	John J. Jenkins, Compt.
Michael S. Plunkett, Sr. V.P.	Nathan J. Jones, Treas.

Consolidated Balance Sheet   As of October 31, 1994 (000 omitted)

Assets		Liabilities & Stockholders' Equity	
Net property, plant & equipment	$ 1,314,075	Other liabilities	$10,223,354
Other assets	11,467,140	*Stockholders' equity	2,557,861
Total	$12,781,215	Total	$12,781,215

*86,420,927 shares common stock outstanding.

Consolidated Income Statement[a]

Years Ended Oct. 31	Thousands — — — — — Equipment Revenues[b]	Net Income	Per Share — — — — Earnings	Cash Dividends	Common Stock Price Range Calendar Year
1994	$7,663,143	$ 603,563	$ 7.01	$2.00	90-7/8 — 61-1/4
1993	6,479,251	(920,860)[c]	(11.91)[c]	2.00	78-3/8 — 42-3/8
1992	5,723,446	37,426	.49	2.00	54 — 37-3/8
1991	5,847,815	(20,191)[d]	(.27)[d]	2.00	57-3/8 — 39-7/8
1990	6,778,737	411,068	5.42	1.85	78-3/8 — 37-5/8

[a]The consolidated data conforms with the requirements of FAS 94.
[b]Total revenues including finance and interest income, insurance and health care premiums, investment income and other income are $9,029,789,000 (1994); $7,753,515,000 (1993); $6,960,727,000 (1992); $7,055,208,000 (1991); and $7,875,001,000 (1990).
[c]Includes a one-time charge adopted November 1, 1992, to reflect FAS 106 and FAS 112, resulting in a cumulative effect of $1,105,300,000($14.30 per share); and restructuring costs of $80,000,000 ($1.03 per share).
[d]Includes restructuring costs of $120,000,000 ($1.58 per share).

Transfer Agent & Registrar:	Chemical Bank		
General Counsel:	Frank S. Cottrell, V.P.	Auditors:	Deloitte & Touche LLP
Investor Relations:	Marie Z. Ziegler, Dir.	Traded (Symbol):	NYSE, CSE, Frankfurt SE (DE)
Human Resources:	Michael S. Plunkett, Sr. V.P.	Stockholders:	23,380
Mgt. Info. Svcs.: Ronnie D. Sonnenburg, Dir.— Computer Systems		Employees:	34,300
		Annual Meeting:	In February

DEKALB Genetics Corporation

3100 Sycamore Road, DeKalb, Illinois 60115-9600
Telephone: (815) 758-3461

DEKALB Genetics Corporation, through its subsidiaries, engages in the development and continual improvement of important products to two segments of agriculture: seed (primarily corn, soybeans, sorghum and sunflower), and hybrid swine breeding stock. The company operates its business segments through its Seed division, and through its wholly owned subsidiaries, which include DEKALB Swine Breeders, Inc. Other subsidiaries are DEKALB Argentina, S.A., DEKALB Canada, Inc., DEKALB Europa GmbH, and DEKALB Italia, S.P.A. In April 1995, DEKALB Genetics announced that it had sold DEKALB Poultry Research, Inc. Incorporated in Delaware in 1988.

Directors (In addition to indicated officers)

Charles J. Arntzen, Ph.D.
Allan Aves
Tod R. Hamachek
Paul H. Hatfield

Douglas C. Roberts
John T. Roberts
H. Blair White

Officers (Directors*)

*Bruce P. Bickner, Chm. & C.E.O.
*Richard O. Ryan, Pres. & C.O.O.
 Richard T. Crowder, Sr. V.P.—Int'l. Seed
 Oper.
 John H. Witmer, Jr., Sr. V.P., Gen. Coun. &
 Secy.
 Gregory L. Olson, V.P.—Admin.

Thomas R. Rauman, V.P.—Fin. & C.F.O.
Janis M. Felver, Cont. & C.A.O.
David R. Wagley, Treas.
Robert W. Donaldson, Asst. Treasurer
Roy L. Poage, Pres.—DEKALB Swine Breeders,
Inc.

Consolidated Balance Sheet   As of August 31, 1994 (000 omitted)

Assets		Liabilities & Stockholders' Equity	
Current assets	$164,000	Current liabilities	$ 95,100
Net property, plant & equipment	100,600	Long-term debt	85,000
Other assets	54,400	Deferred items	17,600
		*Stockholders' equity	121,300
Total	$319,000	Total	$319,000

*786,639 shares Class A common and 4,358,186 shares Class B common stock outstanding.

Consolidated Income Statement[a]

Years Ended Aug. 31	Thousands — — — — Operating Revenues	Net Income	Per Share — — — Earnings	Cash Dividends	Common Stock Price Range[b] Calendar Year
1994	$320,000	$10,600	$2.02	$ .80	36 — 24-1/2
1993	299,300	1,700	.33	.80	34 — 22-1/2
1992	307,800	10,300	1.99	.80	34-1/2 — 23-1/2
1991	284,100	17,100	3.09	.80	43-1/4 — 26-3/4
1990	281,300	14,800	2.63	.70	44-3/4 — 27

[a]Restated to reflect an accounting change.
[b]Class B common stock only.

Transfer Agent & Registrar: American Stock Transfer & Trust Co.

General Counsel: John H. Witmer, Jr., Sr. V.P.

Investor Relations: Thomas R. Rauman, V.P.

Human Resources: Gregory L. Olson, V.P.

Mgt. Info. Svcs.:   J. Barry Markovic

Auditors: Coopers & Lybrand L.L.P.

Traded (Symbol):   NASDAQ (SEEDB)

Stockholders: 2,100

Employees: 2,131

Annual Meeting: In January

First Chicago Guide

Delphi Information Systems, Inc.

3501 Algonquin Road, Suite 500, Rolling Meadows, Illinois 60008
Telephone: (708) 506-3100

Delphi Information Systems, Inc., is a leading provider of management information and automation systems to independent property and casualty agencies and brokerages in North America. The company develops, markets, and supports computer application software systems, which enhance the efficiency and profitability of agencies, brokerages, and insurance carriers. The systems automate the areas of sales management, policy and claims administration, accounting, financial reporting, rating and electronic interface. Delphi also markets and supports computer hardware to operate its software systems. Incorporated in Delaware in 1976.

Directors   (In addition to indicated officer)

Yuval Almog	Richard R. Janssen
Larry G. Gerdes	Donald L. Lucas

Officers   (Director*)

*M. Denis Connaghan, Pres. & C.E.O.	John R. Sprieser, Sr. V.P.—Fin. & Secy.
Gustavus J. Esselen, Exec. V.P.	Michael J. Marek, Corp. Cont.

Consolidated Balance Sheet   As of March 31, 1995 (000 omitted)

Assets		Liabilities & Stockholders' Equity	
Current assets	$10,923	Current liabilities	$16,661
Net property, plant & equipment	3,630	Convertible promissory notes	1,500
Other assets	12,993	Subordinated note payable	2,750
		Other liabilities	2,082
		*Stockholders' equity	4,553
Total	$27,546	Total	$27,546

*7,979,173 shares common stock outstanding.

Consolidated Income Statement

Years Ended March 31	Thousands — — — — Revenues	Net Income	Per Share — — — Earnings	Cash Dividends	Common Stock Price Range Fiscal Year
1995	$53,040	$(1,681)	$ (.23)	$ .00	4 — 1/2
1994	53,605	(8,922)[a]	(1.34)	.00	7-1/4 — 3-1/2
1993	51,607	531	.07	.00	7-3/4 — 5-3/4
1992	44,605	(9,064)	(1.53)	.00	
1991	28,509	855	.17	.00	

[a]Includes pretax charges of $6,490,000 related to restructuring.

Transfer Agent & Registrar: Chemical Trust Co. of California

General Counsel:	Schiff, Harden & Waite	Auditors:	Arthur Andersen LLP
Investor Relations:	Sandy McQuade	Traded (Symbol):	NASDAQ (DLPH)
Human Resources:		Stockholders:	185
Meigan Putnam, V.P.—Opers.		Employees:	377
Mgt. Info. Svcs.:	Hari Srihari, V.P.—Tech.	Annual Meeting:	In August

DeSoto, Inc.

16750 South Vincennes Road, South Holland, Illinois 60473
Telephone: (708) 331-8800

DeSoto, Inc., is a marketer and contract manufacturer of detergents and household cleaning products. The company's product lines include powdered laundry detergents, liquid laundry detergents, fabric softeners, dishwashing liquids, and dishwashing powders sold to retailers, wholesalers, and direct sales companies. DeSoto participates in a diverse range of markets, including manufacturing private and control labeled products for major merchandisers and grocery chains, and contract manufacturing and packaging for brand leaders. The company maintains plants in Illinois and California. Incorporated in Delaware in 1927.

Directors (In addition to indicated officers)

Daniel T. Carroll
William P. Lyons

Paul E. Price
David M. Tobey

Officers (Directors*)

*William Spier, Chm.
*John R. Phillips, Pres. & C.E.O.
*Anders U. Schroeder, V. Chm.

N. Ron Bowen, Exec. V.P.
*Anne E. Eisele, Sr. V.P., C.F.O. & Secy.

Consolidated Balance Sheet As of December 31, 1994 (000 omitted)

Assets		Liabilities & Stockholders' Equity	
Current assets	$26,341	Current liabilities	$33,473
Net property, plant & equipment	7,968	Deferred items	16,567
Other assets	48,803	Other liabilities	11,823
		*Stockholders' equity	21,249
Total	$83,112	Total	$83,112

*4,671,707 shares common stock outstanding.

Consolidated Income Statement

Years Ended Dec. 31	Thousands — — — — Net Revenues[a]	Net Income[a]	Per Share — — — Earnings[a]	Cash Dividends[b]	Common Stock Price Range Calendar Year
1994	$ 87,182	$(1,635)	$ (.42)	$ .00	8-5/8 — 3
1993	101,175	(8,090)	(1.83)	.00	10-3/4 — 6-7/8
1992	59,799	(2,318)[c]	(.58)[c]	.00	8-1/4 — 5-3/8
1991	58,872	(402)	(.10)	.04	10-1/2 — 6
1990	74,335	4,473	1.10	.40	47-7/8 — 7-7/8

[a]From continuing operations.
[b]During the fourth quarter 1990, special dividends of $35.50 per share were declared and paid as a result of the sale of discontinued operations.
[c]Includes cumulative effect of accounting change, resulting in a charge to net earnings of $162,000 ($.04 per share).

Transfer Agent & Registrar: Harris Trust and Savings Bank

General Counsel:	Shefsky & Froelich	Traded (Symbol):	NYSE (DSO)
		Stockholders:	1,774
Investor Relations:	John R. Phillips, Pres.	Employees:	417
Auditors:	Arthur Andersen LLP	Annual Meeting:	In May

First Chicago Guide

DeVRY INC.

One Tower Lane, Oakbrook Terrace, Illinois 60181-4624
Telephone: (708) 571-7700

DeVRY INC. is a holding company which, through its wholly owned subsidiary, Keller Graduate School of Management, Inc., owns and operates the DeVRY Institutes of Technology, the Keller Graduate School of Management (KGSM), and Corporate Educational Services (CES). The DeVRY Institutes and KGSM collectively form one of the largest private degree-granting higher education systems in North America. The DeVRY Institutes were founded in 1931 and for more than 60 years have provided career-oriented technical education to high school graduates in the U.S. and Canada. KGSM, founded in 1973, employs a faculty of practicing business professionals to teach master's degree programs in business administration, project management and human resource management to working adults at multiple sites in the U.S. The DeVRY Institutes and KGSM are each accredited by the Commission on Institutions of Higher Education of the North Central Association of Colleges and Schools. The DeVRY Institutes are located on 10 campuses in the U.S. and three campuses in Canada. KGSM operates 17 campuses in Illinois, Wisconsin, Missouri, Georgia, California, and Arizona. CES offers on-site training and educational programs tailored to specific client needs. Incorporated in Delaware in 1987.

Directors (In addition to indicated officers)

David S. Brown
Sister Ann Ida Gannon
Rodney L. Goldstein

Robert E. King
Thurston E. Manning

Julie A. McGee
Hugo J. Melvoin

Officers (Directors*)

*Dennis J. Keller, Chm. & C.E.O.
*Ronald L. Taylor, Pres. & C.O.O.
David C. MacFarlane, Sr. V.P.
Norman C. Metz, Sr. V.P.
O. John Skubiak, Sr. V.P. & Dean-KGSM
Marilynn J. Cason, V.P.—Gen. Coun. & Corp. Secy.
George W. Fisher, V.P.—Oper.

Norman M. Levine, V.P.—Cont. & C.F.O.
Patrick L. Mayers, V.P.—Academic Affairs, KGSM
Robert R. Roehrich, V.P.—Academic Affairs
Kenneth Rutkowski, V.P.—Oper. Svcs. & Admin.
Vijay Shah, V.P.—Admissions
Edward J. Steffes, V.P.—Mktg.
Sharon Thomas-Parrott, V.P.—Govt. Rel.

Consolidated Balance Sheet As of June 30, 1994 (000 omitted)

Assets		Liabilities & Stockholders' Equity	
Current assets	$ 48,856	Current liabilities	$ 40,214
Net property, plant & equipment	51,857	Long-term debt	39,674
Other assets	6,085	Deferred items	222
		Other liabilities	3,710
		*Stockholders' equity	22,978
Total	$106,798	Total	$106,798

*8,303,246 shares common stock outstanding.

Consolidated Income Statement

Years Ended June 30	Thousands — — — — Net Sales	Net Income	Per Share[a] — — — Earnings	Cash Dividends	Common Stock Price Range[a] Calendar Year
1994	$211,437	$ 12,225	$ .73	$ .00	16-3/4 — 11-3/4
1993	191,915	9,431	.57	.00	14-7/8 — 9-3/4
1992	179,196	21,687[b]	1.36[b]	.00	10-7/8 — 6-5/8
1991	163,141	(3,645)	(1.50)	.00	8-1/8 — 4-3/8[c]
1990	156,736	(9,209)	(4.01)	.00	

[a]Adjusted to reflect a 2-for-1 stock split in June 1995 and a 5-for-1 stock split in May 1991.
[b]Includes a gain to reflect FAS 109, resulting in a cumulative effect of $15,798,000 ($.99 per share).
[c]Initial public offering in June 1991.

Transfer Agent & Registrar: Harris Trust and Savings Bank

General Counsel: Marilynn J. Cason, V.P.

Investor Relations: Norman M. Levine, V.P.

Human Resources: Marilynn J. Cason, V.P.

Mgt. Info. Svcs.: Richard E. Lermer

Auditors: Price Waterhouse LLP
Traded (Symbol): NASDAQ (DVRY)
Stockholders: 2,200
Employees: 1,925
Annual Meeting: In November

Discovery Zone, Inc.

205 North Michigan Avenue, Suite 3400, Chicago, Illinois 60601
Telephone: (312) 616-3800

Discovery Zone, Inc., owns and franchises indoor family entertainment and fitness facilities. Discovery Zone FunCenters, which are designed for children and which emphasize both fun and fitness, feature a distinct play zone comprised of a series of tubes, slides, ball bins, climbing mountains, air and water trampolines, obstacle courses, and other devices, all of which have been designed, tested, and constructed with a view toward safety. In September 1994, the company completed its acquisition of Leaps & Bounds, Inc. Incorporated in Delaware in 1993.

Directors   (In addition to indicated officers)

Gerald E. Seegers, V. Chm.
H. Wayne Huizenga
George D. Johnson
James R. Jorgensen

John T. McCarthy
John J. Melk
Peer Pedersen

Officers   (Directors*)

*Donald F. Flynn, Chm.
*Steven R. Berrard, C.E.O.
Donna Moore, Pres. & C.O.O.
Victor M. Casini, Sr. V.P., Secy. & Gen. Coun.
Kevin F. Flynn, Sr. V.P.—Dev.
Robert W. Flynn, Sr. V.P.—West Region
Robert D. Mitchum, Sr. V.P. & C.F.O.
James K. Dublin, V.P.—Admin.
Frank P. Erlain, V.P.—Cont.
Charles D. Gelman, V.P.—Mktg.

Fredric A. Goers, V.P.—Construction Design.
Robert E. Henry, V.P.—Western Zone
Steven J. Horowitz, V.P.—East Region
Katherine A. Hurtman, V.P.—Mktg.
Michael S. Mattes, V.P.—Planning
G. William McClintock, V.P.—Franchise Rel.
Thomas R. Raterman, V.P.—Treas. & Int'l. Dev.
Brian J. Robertson, V.P.—Info. Syst.
Frank C. Schroeder, V.P.—Foreign Dev.
Thomas J. Sulik, V.P.—Eastern Zone

Consolidated Balance Sheet   As of December 31, 1994 (000 omitted)

Assets		Liabilities & Stockholders' Equity	
Current assets	$ 43,102	Current liabilities	$ 72,454
Net property, plant & equipment	303,687	Long-term debt	18,192
Other assets	130,597	Deferred items	11,707
		Other liabilities	136,070
		*Stockholders' equity	238,963
Total	$477,386	Total	$477,386

*48,718,057 shares common stock outstanding.

Consolidated Income Statement[a]

Years Ended Dec. 31	Thousands — — — — Total Revenue	Net Income	Per Share[b] — — — Earnings	Cash Dividends	Common Stock Price Range[b] Calendar Year
1994	$180,573	$(24,897)[c]	$ (.53)[c]	$ .00	24-1/4 — 11-3/8
1993	61,585	3,306	.08	.00	34-1/4 — 16-1/8[d]
1992	19,593	(4,969)	(.14)		
1991	10,236	(809)	(.02)		
1990	5,721	(343)	(.01)		

[a]Restated to reflect pooling of interests.
[b]Adjusted to reflect a 2-for-1 stock split in September 1993.
[c]Includes a charge to reflect accounting change for preopening costs, resulting in a cumulative effect of $5,773,000 ($.12 per share).
[d]Initial public offering in June 1993.

Transfer Agent & Registrar: Harris Trust and Savings Bank

General Counsel:	Bell, Boyd & Lloyd	Auditors:	Arthur Andersen LLP
Investor Relations:	Robert D. Mitchum, Sr. V.P.	Traded (Symbol):	NASDAQ (ZONE)
		Stockholders:	950
Human Resources:	James K. Dublin, V.P.	Employees:	14,500
Mgt. Info. Svcs.:	Brian J. Robertson, V.P.	Annual Meeting:	In May

R.R. Donnelley & Sons Company

77 West Wacker Drive, Chicago, Illinois 60601-1696
Telephone: (312) 326-8000

R.R. Donnelley & Sons Company is a major participant in the information industry, providing a broad range of services in print and digital media. The company is one of the largest suppliers of commercial and print and print-related services in the U.S. It is a major supplier in the United Kingdom and also provides services in Latin America, other locations in Europe, and in Asia. Services provided to customers include presswork and binding, including on-demand customized publications; conventional and digital pre-press operations, including desktop publishing and filmless color imaging necessary to create a printed image; software replication, translation and localization; list rental, list enhancement, database management and mail production services (provided primarily through Metromail); design and related creative services (provided through Mobium); electronic communication networks for simultaneous worldwide product releases; digital services to publishers; and other services. The company provides these services to more than 5,000 customers. Incorporated in Delaware in 1956.

Directors (In addition to indicated officers)

Martha Layne Collins	M. Bernard Puckett	Bide L. Thomas
Charles C. Haffner III	John M. Richman	H. Blair White
Thomas S. Johnson	William D. Sanders	Stephen M. Wolf
Richard M. Morrow	Jerre L. Stead	

Officers (Directors*)

*John R. Walter, Chm. & C.E.O.
*James R. Donnelley, V. Chm.
Rory J. Cowan, Exec. V.P. & Pres.—Info. Resources
W. Ed Tyler, Exec. V.P. & Pres.—Networked Svcs.
Jonathan P. Ward, Exec. V.P. & Pres.—Commerc. Print
Steven J. Baumgartner, Sr. V.P.— Hum. Res., Comm. & Strat. Plan.
Ronald G. Eidell, Sr. V.P.—Treas.
Thomas J. Quarles, Sr. V.P. & Gen. Coun.
James G. Turner, Sr. V.P.—Tech. & Info. Svcs.
Jane L. Altobelli, V.P.—Hum. Res.

Steve Bono, V.P.—Comm.
Monica M. Fohrman, V.P.—Law & Asst. Gen. Coun.
Glenn T. Kelly, V.P.—Strat. Plan.
Ruby C. Kerr, V.P.—Credit
Robert E. Logan, V.P.—Corp. Dev.
Peter F. Murphy, V.P. & Cont.
Deborah M. Regan, V.P. & Secy.
Jack L. Simmons, V.P.—Taxes
Michael B. Allen, Pres.—Retail Svcs.
Ronald E. Daly, Pres.—Telecomm.
Barton L. Faber, Pres.—Info. Svcs.
Rhonda Kochlefl, Pres.—Bus. Svcs.
Fuad Lahham, Pres.—Donnelley Europe

Edward E. Lane, Pres.—Spec. Publ. Svcs.
Terence M. Leahy, Pres.—Global Software Svcs.
Rhonda S. MacQueen, Pres.—Fin. Svcs.
Robert S. Mathews, Pres.—Catalog Svcs.
Grant McGuire, Pres.—Book Publ. Svcs.
James D. McQuaid, Chm./C.E.O.— Metromail Corp.
Robert S. Pyzdrowski, Pres.—Cons. Mag. Svcs.
Terry A. Tevis, Pres.—Sterling Grp.
Ronald J. Weir, Pres.—Mfg. Support

Consolidated Balance Sheet As of December 31, 1994 (000 omitted)

Assets		Liabilities & Stockholders' Equity	
Current assets	$1,353,330	Current liabilities	$ 801,850
Net property, plant & equipment	1,856,760	Long-term debt	1,212,332
Other assets	1,242,053	Deferred items	286,904
		Other liabilities	172,688
		*Stockholders' equity	1,978,369
Total	$4,452,143	Total	$4,452,143

*153,085,318 shares common stock outstanding.

Consolidated Income Statement

Years Ended Dec. 31	Thousands — — — — Net Sales	Net Income	Per Share[a] — — — — Earnings	Cash Dividends	Common Stock Price Range[a] Calendar Year
1994	$4,888,786	$268,603	$1.75	$ .60	32-1/2 — 26-7/8
1993	4,387,761	109,420[b]	.71[b]	.54	32-3/4 — 26-1/8
1992	4,193,072	234,659	1.51	.51	33-3/4 — 23-3/4
1991	3,914,828	204,919	1.32	.50	25-5/8 — 19-1/2
1990	3,497,943	225,846	1.45	.48	26-3/8 — 17-1/8

[a]Adjusted to reflect a 2-for-1 stock split in September 1992.
[b]Includes a charge to reflect FAS 106 and FAS 109, resulting in a cumulative effect of $69,500,000 ($.45 per share); a restructuring charge of $60,800,000 ($.39 per share); and a deferred income tax charge of $6,200,000 ($.04 per share) related to the federal income tax rate increase.

Transfer Agent & Registrar: First Chicago Trust Co. of New York

General Counsel:	Thomas J. Quarles, Sr. V.P.	**Auditors:**	Arthur Andersen LLP
Investor Relations:	Ronald G. Eidell, Sr. V.P.	**Traded (Symbol):**	CSE, NYSE, PSE (DNY)
		Stockholders:	11,000
Human Resources:	Steven J. Baumgartner, Sr. V.P.	**Employees:**	39,000
Mgt. Info. Svcs.:	James G. Turner, Sr. V.P.	**Annual Meeting:**	In March

First Chicago Guide

Duff & Phelps Corporation

55 East Monroe Street, Suite 3600, Chicago, Illinois 60603
Telephone: (312) 263-2610

Duff & Phelps Corporation provides financial advisory services to institutional investors, corporations, and individuals through two operating subsidiaries: Duff & Phelps Investment Management Co. and Duff & Phelps Capital Markets Co. The company's original business, which dates back to 1932, was to provide clients with investment research on public utility companies. The investment management and capital markets businesses grew out of its investment research activity. Investment Management is now Duff & Phelps Corporation's primary business. Capital Markets, formed in response to clients' requests for special advisory projects, provides a broad range of merger and acquisition, valuation, and other investment banking services. In October 1994, the company spun off its Duff & Phelps Credit Rating Co. subsidiary to its stockholders; and in November, Duff & Phelps Corp. formed a new unit, Duff & Phelps Securities Co. In June 1995, Duff & Phelps Corporation announced a plan of merger with a subsidiary of Phoenix Home Life Mutual Insurance Co. Incorporated in Delaware in 1988.

Directors   (In addition to indicated officers)

Glen D. Churchill
Bradford M. Freeman

Donna F. Tuttle
David A. Williams

Officers   (Directors*)

*Francis E. Jeffries, Chm. & C.E.O.
*Calvin J. Pedersen, Pres. & C.O.O.
*Chester A. Gougis, Exec. V.P.

*Wayne C. Stevens, Exec. V.P.
Lorrie P. Zogg, Secy., Treas. & C.F.O.

Consolidated Balance Sheet   As of December 31, 1994 (000 omitted)

Assets		Liabilities & Stockholders' Equity	
Current assets	$ 16,547	Current liabilities	$ 8,058
Net property, plant & equipment	5,362	Long-term debt	35,500
Other assets	99,191	Other liabilities	2,083
		*Stockholders' equity	75,459
Total	$121,100	Total	$121,100

*16,985,000 shares common stock outstanding.

Consolidated Income Statement

Years Ended Dec. 31	Thousands — — — —		Per Share[a] — — —		Common Stock Price Range[a] Calendar Year
	Revenues	Net Income	Earnings	Cash Dividends	
1994	$65,893	$ 21,634	$ 1.24	$ .16	22 — 7-7/8
1993	81,167	23,139	1.30	.16	22-7/8 — 15-1/8
1992	67,075	11,548[b]	.66[b]	.00	15-3/8 — 12
1991	52,900	6,916	.55		
1990	38,600	(655)	(.05)		

[a]Adjusted to reflect a 3-for-2 stock split in March 1993 and a 2.7-for-1 stock split in the form of a stock dividend paid in January 1992. Initial public offering in March 1992.
[b]Includes a loss of $5,932,000 ($.34 per share) on early extinguishment of debt.

Transfer Agent & Registrar:	Harris Trust and Savings Bank		
General Counsel:	Lord, Bissell & Brook	Auditors:	Arthur Andersen LLP
Investor Relations:	Lorrie P. Zogg, Secy.	Traded (Symbol):	NYSE (DUF)
		Stockholders:	3,000
Human Resources:	Cynthia Tupik	Employees:	290
Mgt. Info. Svcs.:	Steve Mannina, V.P.	Annual Meeting:	In May

First Chicago Guide

Duff & Phelps Credit Rating Co.

55 East Monroe Street, 35th Floor, Chicago, Illinois 60603
Telephone: (312) 368-3100

Duff & Phelps Credit Rating Co. is an internationally recognized credit rating agency, issuing credit ratings on bonds, debentures, preferred stocks, commercial paper, certificates of deposit, and other fixed income securities, as well as structured financings and insurance company claims-paying ability. The credit rating business was established in 1980 and currently has offices in Chicago, New York, and London, and joint ventures in Mexico, Chile, Argentina, Columbia, Peru, and a designated rating agency in Japan. In October 1994, Duff & Phelps Corporation spun off Duff & Phelps Credit Rating Co. to its shareholders. Incorporated in Illinois in 1987.

Directors   (In addition to indicated officers)

Jonathan Ingham   William H. Sherer
Milton L. Meigs

Officers   (Directors*)

*Paul J. McCarthy, Jr., Pres., C.E.O. & C.F.O.   *Philip T. Maffei, Exec. V.P. & C.O.O.
Daniel J. Donoghue, Exec. V.P.   Peter J. Stahl, Exec. V.P.—Mktg.
Ernest T. Elsner, Exec. V.P.   Marie C. Becker, V.P., Cont. & Secy.

Consolidated Balance Sheet   As of December 31, 1994 (000 omitted)

Assets		Liabilities & Stockholders' Equity	
Current assets	$ 9,465	Current liabilities	$ 9,140
Net property, plant & equipment	3,302	Long-term debt	10,000
Other assets	28,207	Other liabilities	1,004
		*Stockholders' equity	20,830
Total	$40,974	Total	$40,974

*5,650,068 shares common stock outstanding.

Consolidated Income Statement

Years Ended Dec. 31	Thousands — — — —		Per Share — — — —		Common Stock Price Range[a] Calendar Year
	Revenues	Net Income	Earnings	Cash Dividends	
1994	$40,409	$6,466	$1.12	$ .03	12-1/2 — 7-7/8
1993	32,635	6,497[b]	1.10		
1992	24,697	3,400[b]	.59		
1991	18,300				
1990	11,600				

[a]Duff & Phelps Corporation spun off Duff & Phelps Credit Rating Co. in October 1994.
[b]Unaudited pro forma.

Transfer Agent & Registrar:	Harris Trust and Savings Bank			
General Counsel:	Lord, Bissell & Brook	Auditors:	Arthur Andersen LLP
Investor Relations:	Marie C. Becker, V.P.	Traded (Symbol):	NYSE (DCR)
		Stockholders:	300
Human Resources:	Marie C. Becker, V.P.	Employees:	200
Mgt. Info. Svcs.:	Mark R. Stefanic, V.P.	Annual Meeting:	In May

First Chicago Guide   79

Duplex Products Inc.

1947 Bethany Road, Sycamore, Illinois 60178
Telephone: (815) 895-2101

Duplex Products Inc. is a leading provider of business information products and technologies. The company provides custom and stock business forms and labels, electronic printing and mailing services, forms management programs, forms automation solutions, and process analysis. Products and services are provided through the company's sales force, manufacturing facilities, and business service centers throughout the U.S. and Puerto Rico. Duplex was founded in 1947 and originally incorporated in Illinois; reincorporated in Delaware in 1958.

Directors (In addition to indicated officer)

John A. Bacon, Jr.
Michael J. Birck
John C. Colman

David J. Eskra
W. Robert Reum

Officers (Director*)

*Andrew A. Campbell, Pres.
Marc A. Loomer, V.P.—Oper.
Nicholas A. Martellotto, V.P.—Research & Tech.

Rose R. Principe, V.P.—Mktg.
Laurence J. Quinn, V.P.—Sales
Michael E. Wilson, V.P.—Info. Svcs.

Consolidated Balance Sheet   As of October 29, 1994 (000 omitted)

Assets		Liabilities & Stockholders' Equity	
Current assets	$105,156	Current liabilities	$ 33,642
Net property, plant & equipment	37,000	Long-term debt	5,928
Other assets	4,052	Deferred items	6,599
		*Stockholders' equity	100,039
Total	$146,208	Total	$146,208

*7,551,000 shares common stock outstanding.

Consolidated Income Statement

Years Ended Abt. Oct. 31	Thousands — — — — —		Per Share — — —		Common Stock Price Range Calendar Year
	Net Sales	Net Income	Earnings	Cash Dividends	
1994	$265,791	$(16,127)[a]	$(2.12)[a]	$ .00	11-3/4 — 8
1993	258,867	2,454[b]	.32[b]	.00	11-7/8 — 9-1/2
1992	270,093	(563)[c]	(.07)	.48	13-3/4 — 9-1/4
1991	285,271	4,269[d]	.55	.69	15-1/2 — 10
1990	297,647	9,516	1.23	.75	20-7/8 — 9-5/8

[a]Includes a charge to reflect an accounting change, resulting in a cumulative effect of $7,084,000 ($.93 per share).
[b]Includes a gain to reflect FAS 109, resulting in a cumulative effect of $1,000,000 ($.13 per share).
[c]A provision of $7,000,000 was made to cover the cost associated with closing two manufacturing plants and the scaling back of other operations.
[d]A provision of $2,000,000 was made to cover the cost associated with closing a plant in Florida and consolidation in distribution operations.

Transfer Agent & Registrar:	Harris Trust and Savings Bank		
General Counsel:	Hinshaw & Culbertson	Traded (Symbol):	AMEX (DPX)
Investor Relations:	Beverly A. Bangs, Dir.	Stockholders:	1,297
Mgt. Info. Svcs.:	Michael E. Wilson, V.P.	Employees:	1,852
Auditors:	Grant Thornton LLP	Annual Meeting:	In March

First Chicago Guide

Dyna Group International, Inc.

1801 West 16th Street, Broadview, Illinois 60153
Telephone: (708) 450-9200

Dyna Group International, Inc., through its Great American Products, Inc., subsidiary, is engaged in the business of manufacturing consumer products for sale to the retail giftware market and the corporate premium and incentive market. Great American produces and sells cast products and pewter enhanced glassware. Incorporated in Nevada in 1986.

Officers (Directors*)

*Roger R. Tuttle, Chm./C.E.O. & Pres.—Great Amer. Prods.
*William M. Sandstrom, Treas. & Cont.

*Jeffrey L. Smith, Secy.
Kevin P. McCue, Asst. Secy.

Consolidated Balance Sheet As of December 31, 1994 (000 omitted)

Assets		Liabilities & Stockholders' Equity	
Current assets	$4,784	Current liabilities	$2,516
Net property, plant & equipment	1,060	Long-term debt	835
Other assets	196	*Stockholders' equity	2,689
Total	$6,040	Total	$6,040

*7,495,647 shares common stock outstanding.

Consolidated Income Statement[a]

Years Ended Dec. 31	Thousands — — — — Net Sales	Net Income	Per Share — — — — Earnings	Cash Dividends	Common Stock Price Range Calendar Year
1994	$10,025	$ 564	$ .08	$ .00	1-3/8 — 3/4
1993	10,703	359	.05	.00	1-1/2 — 3/4
1992	8,615	261	.04	.00	1-3/8 — 1/2
1991	5,161	(7)	.00	.00	2-1/4 — 3/8
1990	3,973	(131)	(.02)	.00	2-7/8 — 1-3/8

[a]Restated to reflect continuing operations only.

Transfer Agent & Registrar: Pacific Stock Transfer

Securities Counsel:
Siegan Barbakoff Gomberg & Kane, Ltd.

Investor Relations:
Kevin P. McCue, Asst. Secy.

Human Resources:
Kevin P. McCue, Asst. Secy.

Auditors: Arthur Andersen LLP

Traded (Symbol): NASDAQ (DGIX)

Stockholders: 425

Employees: 223

Annual Meeting: In July

Eagle Finance Corp.

1509 North Milwaukee Avenue, Libertyville, Illinois 60048-1380
Telephone: (708) 680-4555

Eagle Finance Corp. is a specialized financial services company engaged primarily in acquiring and servicing automobile retail installment sale contracts for purchases of late model used automobiles (cars and light trucks) by "non-prime" consumers, who typically have limited access to traditional credit sources. The company also makes direct consumer loans and finance leases, purchases other retail installment sale contracts, and offers, as agent, insurance and other products related to consumer finance transactions. In July 1994, the company completed an initial public offering of 1,380,000 shares of common stock. Incorporated in Delaware in 1961.

Directors   (In addition to indicated officers)

Robert H. Arnold
Edward J. Noha

Walter J. O'Brien
Anne Hamblin Schiave

Officers   (Directors*)

*Charles F. Wonderlic, Chm. & C.E.O.
*Ronald B. Clonts, Pres.
*Richard E. Wonderlic, Exec. V.P.

Robert J. Braasch, Sr. V.P., C.F.O. & Treas.
W. Timothy Parker, Sr. V.P.—Mktg.

Consolidated Balance Sheet   As of December 31, 1994 (000 omitted)

Assets		Liabilities & Stockholders' Equity	
Finance receivables, net, after	$68,944	Senior debt	$51,236
discount & allow.		Subordinated debt	1,293
Other assets	2,301	Other liabilities	3,507
		*Stockholders' equity	15,209
Total	$71,245	Total	$71,245

*4,180,000 shares common stock outstanding.

Consolidated Income Statement

Years Ended Dec. 31	Thousands — — — — Total Income	Net Income	Per Share[a] — — — — Earnings[c]	Cash Dividends	Common Stock Price Range[ab] Calendar Year
1994	$13,711	$3,951	$ .93	$ .00	16-3/4 — 9
1993	6,168	1,686	.37		
1992	5,757	1,070	.23		
1991	5,394	613	.13		
1990	6,780	543	.12		

[a]Adjusted to reflect an 11,666.667-for-1 stock split in April 1994.
[b]Initial public offering in July 1994.
[c]Pro forma.

Transfer Agent & Registrar:	Harris Trust and Savings Bank	
General Counsel:	Auditors:	KPMG Pear Marwick LLP
Barack, Ferrazzano, Kirschbaum & Perlman	Traded (Symbol):	NASDAQ (EFCW)
Investor Relations: Robert J. Braasch, Sr. V.P.	Stockholders:	1,100
Human Resources: Charles F. Wonderlic, Jr., V.P.	Employees:	184
Mgt. Info. Svcs.: Thomas Shouf	Annual Meeting:	In May

Eagle Food Centers, Inc.

Route 67 and Knoxville Road, Milan, Illinois 61264
Telephone: (309) 787-7730

Eagle Food Centers, Inc., operates a regional supermarket chain with 102 stores under the trade names "Eagle Food Centers" and "Eagle Country Markets." The stores operate in the Quad Cities area of Illinois and Iowa, northern Illinois, central Illinois, eastern Illinois, eastern Iowa, and the Chicago/Fox Valley and northwestern Indiana areas. Eagle supermarkets offer a full line of groceries, meats, fresh produce, dairy products, delicatessen and bakery products, health and beauty aids, and other general merchandise, as well as video rental and floral service. Subsidiaries include Milan Distributing Co., Eagle Country Markets, Inc., and Eagle Pharmacy Co. Incorporated in Delaware in 1987.

Directors (In addition to indicated officers)

Peter B. Foreman
Steven M. Friedman
Michael J. Knilans

Pasquale V. Petitti
William J. Snyder

Officers (Directors*)

*Martin J. Rabinowitz, Chm.
*Robert J. Kelly, Pres. & C.E.O.

*Herbert T. Dotterer, Sr. V.P.—Fin., C.F.O. & Secy.
Kenneth L. Martin, Sr. V.P.—Oper.

Consolidated Balance Sheet As of January 28, 1995 (000 omitted)

Assets		Liabilities & Stockholders' Equity	
Current assets	$114,185	Current liabilities	$113,385
Net property, plant & equipment	167,749	Long-term debt	118,216
Other assets	29,550	Deferred items	10,316
		Other liabilities	27,083
		*Stockholders' equity	42,484
Total	$311,484	Total	$311,484

*11,051,994 shares common stock outstanding.

Consolidated Income Statement

Years Ended Abt. Feb. 2	Thousands — — — — Net Sales	Net Income	Per Share — — — — Earnings	Cash Dividends	Common Stock Price Range Fiscal Year
1995	$1,015,063	$(18,874)	$(1.71)	$ .00	8-1/2 — 1-1/8
1994	1,062,348	(10,132)[a]	(.91)	.00	8-1/4 — 5
1993	1,081,538	8,222[b]	.74[b]	.00	8-3/4 — 6
1992	1,112,203	9,227	.82	.00	11 — 5-3/4
1991	1,124,930	(1,860)[c]	(.16)[c]	.00	16-1/4 — 4-1/2

[a]Includes a pretax store-closing charge of $17,000,000 and an extraordinary charge (aftertax) of $4,000,000 for the early retirement of debt.
[b]Includes a non-recurring charge of $744,000 ($.06 per share) related to the solicitation of the holders of the 13-1/2% subordinated notes to waive a restrictive covenant to allow the company to repurchase up to $20,000,000 of its common stock.
[c]Includes a one-time charge of $11,800,000 ($1.03 per share) for store closings and asset re-evaluations.

Transfer Agent & Registrar: First Chicago Trust Co. of New York

General Counsel:
Davis,Hockenberg,Wine,Brown,Koehn & Shors,P.C.

Investor Relations: Herbert T. Dotterer, Sr. V.P.

Human Resources: Randy P. Smith, V.P.

Mgt. Info. Svcs.:
Lawrence J. Fernstrom, V.P.

Auditors: Deloitte & Touche LLP

Traded (Symbol): NASDAQ (EGLE)

Stockholders: 1,800

Employees: 7,880

Annual Meeting: In June

Elco Industries, Inc.

1111 Samuelson Road, P.O. Box 7009, Rockford, Illinois 61125-7009
Telephone: (815) 397-5151

Elco Industries, Inc., is a North American-based manufacturing and distribution company comprised of two groups with distinct markets. The Elco Industrial Products Group manufactures and supplies automotive and commercial original equipment manufacturers with parts, components and assemblies made of metal and plastic. The Elco Home and Construction Products Group supplies the consumer/do-it-yourself and commercial construction markets with fasteners and related products. Subsidiaries are Elco Consumer Products Corp., Thermoplastics, Inc., and Anchor Wire Corp. of Tennessee. Incorporated in Delaware in 1969.

Directors   (In addition to indicated officer)

Robert L. Berner, Jr.
Milton R. Brown
Carl J. Dargene
G. Robert Evans

Wayne P. Lockwood
James L. Packard
David D. Peterson
James H. Rilott

Officers   (Director*)

*John C. Lutz, Pres. & C.E.O.
 August F. DeLuca, V.P.—Fin. & C.F.O.
 Derek M. Hasse, V.P.—Admin.
 Kenneth L. Heal, Secy., Treas. & Corp. Cont.

Robert H. Rothkopf, Grp. Pres.—Indust. Prods.
James R. Stenberg, Grp. Pres.—Home & Const. Prods.

Consolidated Balance Sheet   As of June 30, 1994 (000 omitted)

Assets		Liabilities & Stockholders' Equity	
Current assets	$ 64,814	Current liabilities	$ 31,434
Net property, plant & equipment	69,317	Long-term obligations	41,860
Other assets	17,333	Deferred items	13,204
		*Stockholders' equity	64,966
Total	$151,464	Total	$151,464

*4,884,554 shares common stock outstanding.

Consolidated Income Statement

Years Ended June 30	Thousands — — — — — Net Sales	Net Income	Per Share — — — — Earnings	Cash Dividends	Common Stock Price Range Calendar Year
1994	$225,901	$ 8,229	$ 1.65	$ .52	21-1/4 — 15-1/2
1993	199,179	4,869	.98	.52	20-3/4 — 10
1992	189,337	(2,525)a	(.52)a	.52	15-3/4 — 9-1/2
1991	156,391	195	.04	.52	13 — 7-1/2
1990	150,706	4,819	1.01	.52	14-3/4 — 9-1/4

aIncludes FAS 106, resulting in a cumulative effect of $1,355,000 ($.28 per share).

Transfer Agent & Registrar:	Harris Trust and Savings Bank		
General Counsel:	Baker & McKenzie	Traded (Symbol):	NASDAQ (ELCN)
Investor Relations:	August F. DeLuca, V.P.	Stockholders:	785
Human Resources:	Derek M. Hasse, V.P.	Employees:	1,971
Auditors:	Coopers & Lybrand L.L.P.	Annual Meeting:	In October

ELEK-TEK, Inc.

7350 North Linder Avenue, Skokie, Illinois 60077-3217
Telephone: (708) 677-7660

ELEK-TEK, Inc., is a full-line, regional marketer of microcomputer products (including hardware, software, related accessories and supplies). Since its origin in the Chicago area in 1979, ELEK-TEK has steadily expanded its base of operations. Its multi-channel distribution system comprises seven retail superstores (four in the Chicago metropolitan area and one each in Indianapolis, Kansas City and Denver); a national catalog operation; and direct sales divisions in all locations, including Louisville, Kentucky, geared to corporate, educational, and government buyers. ELEK-TEK carries all major brands, including IBM, Apple, COMPAQ, Hewlett-Packard, Lotus, Microsoft, and Novell. Incorporated in Illinois in 1979; reincorporated in Delaware in 1993.

Directors   (In addition to indicated officer)

Dennis G. Flanagan
Susan J. Kaiser
Harvey Kinzelberg

Alvin Richer
Louis E. Rosen

Officers   (Director*)

*Cameron B. Estes, Jr., Pres. & C.E.O.
 Steven M. Goodman, V.P.—Mdse. & Secy.

John M. Lader, V.P. & C.F.O.
Rory Zaks, V.P.—Human Res.

Consolidated Balance Sheet   As of December 31, 1994 (000 omitted)

Assets		Liabilities & Stockholders' Equity	
Current assets	$76,602	Current liabilities	$41,347
Net property, plant & equipment	16,268	Long-term debt	25,000
Other assets	174	Other liabilities	4,571
		*Stockholders' equity	22,126
Total	$93,044	Total	$93,044

*6,300,000 shares common stock outstanding.

Consolidated Income Statement

Years Ended Dec. 31	Thousands — — — — Net Sales	Net Income	Per Share[a] — — — Earnings	Cash Dividends	Common Stock Price Range[ab] Calendar Year
1994	$305,602	$3,461	$ .55	$ .00	19 — 7
1993	222,194	4,451[c]	.78[c]	.00	17-3/4 — 9-1/4
1992	176,824	2,721[c]	.51[c]		
1991	148,687	1,745			
1990	138,378	2,683			

[a]Adjusted to reflect a 48-for-1 stock split in June 1993.
[b]Initial public offering in August 1993.
[c]Pro forma.

Transfer Agent & Registrar: LaSalle National Trust, N.A.

General Counsel:	Lord, Bissell & Brook	Auditors:	Coopers & Lybrand L.L.P.
Investor Relations:	John M. Lader, V.P.	Traded (Symbol):	NASDAQ (ELEK)
Human Resources:	Rory Zaks, V.P.	Stockholders:	2,200
		Employees:	882
Mgt. Info. Svcs.:	John M. Lader, V.P.	Annual Meeting:	In June

First Chicago Guide

Envirodyne Industries, Inc.

701 Harger Road, Suite 190, Oak Brook, Illinois 60521
Telephone: (708) 571-8800

Envirodyne Industries, Inc., through Viskase Corporation, is a producer of cellulosic casings used in preparing and packaging processed meat products and is a major producer of specialty films for packaging and preserving poultry, fresh meat products, and processed meats and cheeses. Viskase Corporation is also a leading domestic and international manufacturer of plasticized polyvinyl chloride films. The company, through Clear Shield National, Inc., and Sandusky Plastics, Inc., produces thermo-formed and injection molded plastic containers and disposable plastic cutlery, drinking straws, custom dining kits, and related products. Incorporated in Delaware in 1970.

Directors   (In addition to indicated officers)

Robert N. Dangremond
Avram A. Glazer
Malcolm I. Glazer

Michael E. Heisley
Gregory R. Page
Mark D. Senkpiel

Officers   (Directors*)

*Donald P. Kelly, Chm., Pres. & C.E.O.
 J.S. Corcoran, Exec. V.P. & C.F.O.
*F. Edward Gustafson, Exec. V.P. & C.O.O.

Gordon S. Donovan, V.P. & Treas.
Stephen M. Schuster, V.P., Gen. Coun. & Secy.

Consolidated Balance Sheet   As of December 29, 1994 (000 omitted)

Assets		Liabilities & Stockholders' Equity	
Current assets	$224,106	Current liabilities	$132,379
Net property, plant & equipment	470,338	Long-term debt	489,358
Other assets	202,192	Deferred income taxes	83,333
		Other liabilities	56,217
		*Stockholders' equity	135,349
Total	$896,636	Total	$896,636

*13,515,000 shares common stock outstanding.

Consolidated Income Statement

Years Ended Abt. Dec. 31	Thousands — — — — Net Sales	Net Income	Per Share — — — Earnings	Cash Dividends	Common Stock Price Range Calendar Year
1994[a]	$599,029	$(3,612)	$ (.27)	$ .00	10-7/8 — 3-3/8
1993[a]	587,385	85,589[b]			
1992	575,705	(36,996)			
1991	543,969	(31,755)			
1990	544,138	(15,174)			

[a]Due to the implementation of the plan of reorganization and fresh start reporting, financial statements for the new restructured company (effective December 31, 1993) are not comparable to those of prior years.
[b]Includes an extraordinary gain of $183,784,000 from the implementation of the plan of reorganization.

Transfer Agent & Registrar:	Shawmut Bank Connecticut, N.A.			
General Counsel:	Stephen M. Schuster, V.P.	Traded (Symbol):	NASDAQ (EDYN)	
		Stockholders:	126	
Investor Relations:	J.S. Corcoran, Exec. V.P.	Employees:	4,900	
Auditors:	Coopers & Lybrand L.L.P.	Annual Meeting:	In May	

First Chicago Guide

Enviropur Waste Refining and Technology, Inc.

150 South Wacker Drive, Suite 675, Chicago, Illinois 60606
Telephone: (312) 251-7000

Enviropur Waste Refining and Technology, Inc. (formerly Moreco Energy, Inc.), is a re-refiner of petroleum waste products, with manufacturing, refining, and marketing capabilities. Enviropur differs from most major oil companies in that previously used lubricating oil serves as the base for a significant portion of the company's finished products. Enviropur also processes waste glycol and oily waste water streams and sells finished glycol-based products. In March 1994, Enviropur completed the acquisition of Petroleum Recycling Corporation (PRC) and its PRC Patterson subsidiary, based in Long Beach, California. Incorporated in Illinois in 1952 as Motor Oils Refining Company; present name adopted in 1992.

Directors (In addition to indicated officers)

Bryan G. Colbert
John E. McConnaughy, Jr.

Morgan F. Murphy, Jr.

Officers (Directors*)

*Robert J. Wessels, Chm. & C.E.O.
*Richard D. McAuley, Sr. V.P.—Dir. of Mktg.
Robert J. Babbitt, V.P.—Compliance
John L. Charlton, V.P.—Sales

Phillip Goodman, V.P.—West Coast Oper.
Francis J. Lappin, V.P.—Oper.
*Stuart N. Rubin, C.F.O.

Consolidated Balance Sheet   As of September 30, 1994 (000 omitted)

Assets		Liabilities & Stockholders' Equity	
Current assets	$ 5,446	Current liabilities	$11,560
Net property, plant & equipment	23,152	Long-term debt	9,085
Other assets	6,565	Other liabilities	5,982
		* Stockholders' equity	8,536
Total	$35,163	Total	$35,163

*11,729,317 shares common stock outstanding.

Consolidated Income Statement

Years Ended Sept. 30	Thousands — — — — Net Sales	Net Income	Per Share — — — Earnings	Cash Dividends	Common Stock Price Range[a] Calendar Year
1994	$17,294	$(7,895)[b]	$ (.73)	$ .00	3-5/8 — 3/4
1993	8,584	(1,577)	(.18)	.00	3-5/8 — 2
1992[c]	7,056	(5,290)	(.74)		

[a]Trading commenced October 14, 1993, on NASDAQ.
[b]Includes extraordinary charges in excess of $5,000,000 due to reimbursable charges.
[c]Nine months.

Transfer Agent & Registrar: OTR Security Transfer Inc.

General Counsel: Coffield Ungaretti & Harris

Investor Relations: Kathleen K. McDaniel

Human Resources: Erin Judd

Mgt. Info. Svcs.:   Wade Dauner

Auditors: BDO Seidman

Traded (Symbol):   NASDAQ (EPUR)

Stockholders: 2,000

Employees: 388

Annual Meeting: In April

First Chicago Guide

ERO, Inc.

585 Slawin Court, Mount Prospect, Illinois 60056-2183
Telephone: (708) 803-9200

ERO, Inc., is a leading marketer of children's leisure products. ERO's product lines include: slumber products, including indoor sleeping bags, playtents, and children's furniture; back-to-school products, including back packs, school bags, and stationery products; water sports products, including personal flotation devices, and swim and pool products; children's room decor; and sport bags and coolers. ERO's products are sold to all major mass retailers, sporting goods stores, and toy retailers. Subsidiaries are ERO Industries, Inc.; Impact, Inc.; Priss Prints, Inc.; ERO Canada, Inc.; and ERO Marketing, Inc. Incorporated in Delaware in 1988.

Directors   (In addition to indicated officers)

William T. Alldredge
Robert J. Lipsig
Elliot W. Maluth

Arthur S. Nicholas
Bruce V. Rauner

Officers   (Directors*)

*D. Richard Ryan, Jr., Chm., Pres. & C.E.O.
*Thomas M. Gasner, Exec. V.P.—Oper.

Ted J. Lueken, Sr. V.P.—Fin. & C.F.O.

Consolidated Balance Sheet   As of December 31, 1994 (000 omitted)

Assets		Liabilities & Stockholders' Equity	
Current assets	$33,910	Current liabilities	$16,920
Net property, plant & equipment	4,769	Long-term debt	11,875
Other assets	18,113	*Stockholders' equity	27,997
Total	$56,792	Total	$56,792

*10,331,300 shares common stock outstanding.

Consolidated Income Statement

Years Ended Dec. 31	Thousands — — — — Net Sales	Net Income[c]	Per Share[a] — — — — Earnings[c]	Cash Dividends	Common Stock Price Range[ab] Calendar Year
1994	$126,734	$6,459	$ .61	$ .00	10-1/4 — 6-1/4
1993	95,459	2,185	.21	.00	14-1/4 — 5-3/4
1992	101,777	4,952[d]	.50[de]	.00	18-1/4 — 7
1991	87,535	4,985	.65[e]	.00	
1990	72,118	799	.10[e]	.00	

[a]Adjusted to reflect a 10-for-1 stock split on February 27, 1992.
[b]Initial public offering in April 1992.
[c]From continuing operations, as reported.
[d]Before extraordinary expense for the early extinguishment of debt, which resulted in a charge of $1,558,000 ($.16 per share), and FAS 109, which resulted in a charge of $1,911,000 ($.19 per share).
[e]Before revaluation of warrant to purchase common stock per share of $.13, $2.30, and $.08 for 1992-90, respectively.

Transfer Agent & Registrar: The First National Bank of Chicago

General Counsel:	Kirkland & Ellis	Auditors:	Price Waterhouse LLP
Investor Relations:	Ted J. Lueken, Sr. V.P.	Traded (Symbol):	NASDAQ (EROI)
		Stockholders:	4,500
Human Resources:	Mary Ann Phelan, Dir.	Employees:	499
Mgt. Info. Svcs.:	Kathy Leable, V.P.	Annual Meeting:	In April

First Chicago Guide

Evans, Inc.

36 South State Street, Chicago, Illinois 60603
Telephone: (312) 855-2000

Evans, Inc., is a retailer of quality fur apparel in the U.S. The company also wholesales fur apparel to retailers, distributes furs through various catalogs, provides certain related fur services, and in the Chicago area only, retails women's ready-to-wear apparel in 11 stores. The company has 16 stores in the metropolitan areas of Chicago, Washington, D.C., Austin, and Dallas, and operates leased departments in more than 54 locations of five major department stores throughout the U.S. Evans operates fur departments in Marshall Field and Co., Filene's Basement, Lazarus, Strawbridge & Clothier, Dayton's, Hudson's, Rich's, and others. Some of the fur apparel offered is specially made according to designs and specifications furnished to manufacturers. In October 1994, the company acquired Gilson Inc. Incorporated in Delaware in 1963.

Directors (In addition to indicated officers)

Dennis S. Bookshester   Ernest R. Wish
Harold Sussman

Officers (Directors*)

*David B. Meltzer, Chm.   Samuel B. Garber, V.P., Secy. & Gen. Coun.
*Patrick J. Regan, Pres. & C.E.O.   William E. Koziel, V.P. & Cont.
*Robert K. Meltzer, Exec. V.P.—Gen. Mdse.   John Sarama, V.P.—Oper.
  Mgr.

Consolidated Balance Sheet As of February 26, 1995 (000 omitted)

Assets		Liabilities & Stockholders' Equity	
Current assets	$35,152	Current liabilities	$17,603
Net property, plant & equipment	10,604	Long-term debt	9,653
Other assets	3,060	Other liabilities	16
		*Stockholders' equity	21,544
Total	$48,816	Total	$48,816

*4,918,301 shares common stock outstanding.

Consolidated Income Statement

Years Ended Abt. Feb. 28	Thousands — — — —		Per Share — — —		Common Stock
	Total Revenues	Net Income	Earnings	Cash Dividends	Price Range Calendar Year
1995	$ 86,817	$(12,064)	$(2.45)		
1994	96,785	1,960[a]	.39[a]	.00	3-7/8 — 1-3/4
1993	107,072	1,620	.33	.00	4-1/2 — 2-5/8
1992	100,296	(2,551)	(.52)	.00	3-1/4 — 1
1991	117,340	(5,037)	(1.02)	.00	2-3/4 — 7/8

[a]Includes a gain to reflect FAS 109, resulting in a cumulative effect of $1,500,000 ($.30 per share).

Transfer Agent & Registrar: Harris Trust and Savings Bank

General Counsel:	Samuel B. Garber, V.P.	**Traded (Symbol):**	NASDAQ (EVAN)
Investor Relations:	Patrick J. Regan	**Stockholders:**	780
Human Resources:	Samuel B. Garber, V.P.	**Employees:**	800
Auditors:	Coopers & Lybrand L.L.P.	**Annual Meeting:**	In July

Falcon Building Products, Inc.

Two North Riverside Plaza, Suite 1100, Chicago, Illinois 60606
Telephone: (312) 906-9700

Falcon Building Products, Inc., an indirect wholly owned subsidiary of Eagle Industries, Inc., is a domestic manufacturer and distributor of products for the residential and commercial construction, and home improvement markets. The company traces its origins to businesses that have been selling products for the residential and commercial construction markets since the early 1900s. Falcon Building Products is a leading supplier of air distribution products and the leading manufacturer of residential and light commercial grilles, registers, and diffusers for the heating, ventilating, and air-conditioning market. The company also produces ceramic china bathroom fixtures, and consumer and commercial air compressors primarily for the home improvement market. Subsidiaries include DeVilbiss Air Power Company, Mansfield Plumbing Products, Inc., and Hart & Cooley, Inc. In November 1994, the company completed an initial public offering of 6,000,000 shares of Class A common stock. Incorporated in Delaware in 1994.

Directors   (In addition to indicated officers)

Rod F. Dammeyer
Bradbury Dyer III
F. Warren Hellman
Philip C. Kantz

John M. Pasquesi
Sheli Z. Rosenberg
B. Joseph White

Officers   (Directors*)

*Samuel Zell, Chm.
*William K. Hall, Pres. & C.E.O.
 Gus J. Athas, Sr. V.P., Gen. Coun. & Secy.
*C. Clifford Brake, Sr. V.P.—Oper.
*Sam A. Cottone, Sr. V.P.—Fin. & Treas.

Daniel G. Ellis, V.P.—Fin.
William E. Allen, Pres.—DeVilbiss Air Power Co.
Paul G. Fischer, Pres.—Mansfield Plumbing
 Prods., Inc.
Lawrence B. Lee, Pres.—Hart & Cooley, Inc.

Consolidated Balance Sheet   As of December 31, 1994 (000 omitted)

Assets		Liabilities & Stockholders' Equity	
Current assets	$ 60,587	Current liabilities	$ 87,785
Net property, plant & equipment	80,563	Long-term debt	103,785
Other assets	46,311	Other liabilities	20,445
		*Stockholders' equity	(24,554)
Total	$187,461	Total	$187,461

*6,070,500 shares Class A common and 14,000,000 shares Class B common stock outstanding.

Consolidated Income Statement

Years Ended Dec. 31	Thousands — — — —		Per Share — — —		Common Stock Price Range[a] Calendar Year
	Net Sales	Net Income	Earnings	Cash Dividends	
1994[b]	$440,657	$26,025	$1.30	$ .00	12-1/8 — 10
1993[b]	372,324	16,600[c]	.83[c]		
1992	345,210	18,685			
1991	281,205	10,613			

[a]Initial public offering in November 1994.
[b]Pro forma.
[c]Includes a charge to reflect FAS 109 and FAS 112, resulting in a cumulative effect of $3,607,000 ($.18 per share).

Transfer Agent & Registrar: The Bank of New York

General Counsel: Mayer, Brown & Platt

Investor Relations: Kirk E. Brewer, Sr. V.P.

Auditors: Arthur Andersen LLP

Traded (Symbol):   NYSE (FB)
Stockholders: 198
Employees: 3,400
Annual Meeting: In May

First Chicago Guide

Fansteel Inc.

Number One Tantalum Place, North Chicago, Illinois 60064-3388
Telephone: (708) 689-4900

Fansteel Inc. is a specialty metals manufacturer of fabricated precision metal products for use in the aircraft/aerospace, weapon systems, metalworking, energy and automotive industries. Its principal products include tungsten carbide cutting tools; coal mining tools and accessories; toolholding devices; wear parts; fabricated aircraft parts; space vehicles and missile components; titanium, nickel base and high alloy steel forgings; sand mold aluminum and magnesium castings; and special wire forms and investment castings. The company classifies its products into two business segments: Industrial Tools and Metal Fabrications. Sales of the company's products are made through a direct sales organization and through distributors, representatives and agents. In the Industrial Tools business segment, distributors and agents account for the majority of sales. Incorporated in Delaware in 1917.

Directors (In addition to indicated officer)

Betty B. Evans
Edward P. Evans
Robert S. Evans
Thomas M. Evans

Thomas M. Evans, Jr.
Jack S. Petrik
Charles J. Queenan, Jr.

Officers (Director*)

*William D. Jarosz, Pres., C.E.O. & C.O.O.
R. Michael McEntee, V.P. & C.F.O.

Michael J. Mocniak, V.P., Gen. Coun. & Secy.

Consolidated Balance Sheet As of December 31, 1994 (000 omitted)

Assets		Liabilities & Stockholders' Equity	
Current assets	$38,482	Current liabilities	$17,382
Net property, plant & equipment	9,364	Other liabilities	5,327
Net assets of discontinued operations	523	*Stockholders' equity	50,172
Other assets	24,512		
Total	$72,881	Total	$72,881

*8,598,858 shares common stock outstanding.

Consolidated Income Statement

Years Ended Dec. 31	Thousands — — — — Net Sales	Net Income	Per Share — — — — Earnings	Cash Dividends	Common Stock Price Range Calendar Year
1994	$ 89,287	$ 3,609	$ .42	$ .40	8 — 6-1/8
1993	89,387	906[a]	.11[a]	.40	8-7/8 — 6-3/4
1992	127,145	5,232	.61	.50	9-3/8 — 6-3/8
1991	134,943	(13,356)[a]	(1.55)[a]	.50	13 — 4-7/8
1990	168,808	6,882	.80	.75	13-1/2 — 7-1/4

[a]Results include a net loss from previously discontinued operations of $1,676,000 ($.19 per share) in 1993 and $4,118,000 ($.48 per share) in 1991.

Transfer Agent & Registrar: Mellon Bank N.A.

General Counsel: Michael J. Mocniak, V.P.

Investor Relations: Michael J. Mocniak, V.P.

Human Resources: Michael J. Mocniak, V.P.

Mgt. Info. Svcs.: Daniel K. Garrity

Auditors: Ernst & Young LLP

Traded (Symbol): CSE, NYSE (FNL)

Stockholders: 1,055

Employees: 867

Annual Meeting: In April

Federal Signal Corporation

1415 West 22nd Street, Oak Brook, Illinois 60521-9945
Telephone: (708) 954-2000

Federal Signal Corporation manufactures and supplies products through its four groups: Safety Products (formerly Signal), Sign, Tool and Vehicle. The Safety Products Group manufactures a variety of visual and audible warning and signaling devices, safety containment products for handling and storing hazardous materials, and parking, revenue and access control systems. The Sign Group designs, engineers, manufactures and installs illuminated and non-illuminated advertising sign displays. The Tool Group manufactures a variety of die components for metal stamping, precision cutting and deep grooving tools. The company's Vehicle Group manufactures custom designed fire trucks, rescue vehicles and self-propelled street sweeping, vacuum loader, and catch basin cleaning vehicles. Major subsidiaries of Federal Signal include: Dayton Progress Corporation; Elgin Sweeper Company; Emergency One, Inc.; Federal APD, Inc.; Ravo International; Superior Emergency Vehicles, Ltd.; Guzzler Manufacturing, Inc.; and Manchester Tool Company. Federal Signal has 60 plants and offices throughout North America. In addition, the company has several plants and offices located throughout Europe and the Far East. In June 1994, the company acquired Vactor Manufacturing, Inc., an Illinois-based manufacturer of municipal combination catch basin/sewer cleaning vacuum trucks. In May 1994, the company acquired Justrite Manufacturing Company, an Illinois-based manufacturer of safety containment products for handling and storing hazardous materials. Incorporated in Illinois in 1901; reincorporated in Delaware in 1969.

Directors (In addition to indicated officer)

J. Patrick Lannan, Jr.
James A. Lovell, Jr.

Thomas N. McGowen, Jr.
Walter R. Peirson

Richard R. Thomas

Officers (Director*)

*Joseph J. Ross, Chm., Pres. & C.E.O.
John A. DeLeonardis, V.P.—Taxes
Henry L. Dykema, V.P. & C.F.O.
Robert W. Racic, V.P. & Treas.

Richard L. Ritz, V.P. & Cont.
Kim A. Wehrenberg, V.P., Gen. Coun. & Secy.
Mary Ellen Penicook, Asst. Secy. & Corp. Atty.

Consolidated Balance Sheet As of December 31, 1994 (000 omitted)

Assets		Liabilities & Stockholders' Equity	
Current assets (Mfg.)	$196,296	Current liabilities (Mfg.)	$142,378
Net property, plant & equipment (Mfg.)	72,838	Long-term debt (Mfg.)	34,878
		Deferred taxes (Mfg.)	13,778
Other assets (Mfg.)	125,278	Short-term borrowings (Fin. Svcs.)	110,252
Lease financing receivables (Fin. Svcs.)	127,188	*Stockholders' equity	220,314
Total	$521,600	Total	$521,600

*45,372,000 shares common stock outstanding.

Consolidated Income Statement

Years Ended Dec. 31	Thousands — — — —		Per Share[a] — — — —		Common Stock Price Range[a] Calendar Year
	Sales	Net Income[b]	Earnings[b]	Cash Dividends	
1994	$677,228	$46,770	$1.02	$ .42	21-3/8 — 16-7/8
1993	565,163	39,780	.86	.36	21 — 15-3/4
1992	518,223	34,460	.75	.31	17-5/8 — 12-3/8
1991	466,939	31,046	.67	.27	15-1/4 — 9-1/4
1990	439,426	28,088	.61	.22	10-3/4 — 6-1/4

[a]Adjusted to reflect a 4-for-3 stock split distributed in March 1994 and 3-for-2 stock splits distributed in April 1992, March 1991 and March 1990.
[b]From continuing operations.

Transfer Agent & Registrar: Harris Trust and Savings Bank

General Counsel: Kim A. Wehrenberg, V.P.

Investor Relations: Henry L. Dykema, V.P.

Human Resources: Paul Wittig, Dir.

Mgt. Info. Svcs.: Henry L. Dykema, V.P.

Auditors: Ernst & Young LLP
Traded (Symbol): NYSE (FSS)
Stockholders: 10,000
Employees: 5,243
Annual Meeting: In April

First Chicago Guide

Fidelity Bancorp, Inc.

5455 West Belmont Avenue, Chicago, Illinois 60641
Telephone: (312) 736-4414

Fidelity Bancorp, Inc., is the holding company for Fidelity Federal Savings Bank, its only subsidiary. Fidelity Federal is a federally chartered savings bank, the deposits of which are insured by the Federal Deposit Insurance Corporation, up to applicable limits. Originally organized in 1906, the bank conducts its business through its main office and four full-service branch offices. In December 1993, Fidelity Bancorp completed an initial public offering of 3,782,350 shares of common stock. Incorporated in Delaware in 1993.

Directors   (In addition to indicated officers)

Paul Bielat
Myron H. Dudek
Patrick J. Flynn

Raymond J. Horvat
Bonnie Stolarczyk

Officers   (Directors*)

*Raymond S. Stolarczyk, Chm. & C.E.O.
*Thomas E. Bentel, Pres. & C.O.O.

*Grant M. Berntson, Sr. V.P. & Secy.
 James R. Kinney, Sr. V.P. & C.F.O.

Consolidated Balance Sheet   As of September 30, 1994 (000 omitted)

Assets		Liabilities & Stockholders' Equity	
Loans receivable	$216,657	Deposits	$238,062
Premises & equipment	2,384	Other liabilities	46,543
Other assets	119,041	*Stockholders' equity	53,477
Total	$338,082	Total	$338,082

*3,593,233 shares common stock outstanding.

Consolidated Income Statement

Years Ended Sept. 30	Thousands — — — — Total Income	Net Income	Per Share — — — Earnings	Cash Dividends	Common Stock Price Range[a] Fiscal Year	
1994	$22,284	$2,680	$ .71[b]	$ .00	13	— 10-1/4
1993	23,683	3,616				
1992	25,088	2,754				
1991	24,004	1,262				
1990	23,723	1,669				

[a]Initial public offering in December 1993.
[b]Pro forma.

Transfer Agent & Registrar: Harris Trust and Savings Bank

General Counsel:
 Muldoon, Murphy & Faucette

Investor Relations: Judi Leaf

Human Resources: Lindalee Hansen

Auditors: KPMG Peat Marwick LLP

Traded (Symbol): NASDAQ (FBCI)

Stockholders: 758

Employees: 103

Annual Meeting: In January

Financial Security Corp.

1209 North Milwaukee Avenue, Chicago, Illinois 60622
Telephone: (312) 227-7020

Financial Security Corp. is a savings and loan holding company formed at the direction of Security Federal Savings and Loan Association of Chicago to acquire all of the capital stock that the Association issued upon its conversion from the mutual to stock form of ownership. Established in 1907, Security Federal is a community-oriented thrift institution offering traditional deposit accounts and mortgage loan products. In November 1994, Financial Security opened its first branch office at 5697 Touhy Avenue in Niles, Illinois. The Association is a member of the Federal Home Loan Bank System, and its deposits are insured to the maximum allowable amount by the Federal Deposit Insurance Corporation. Incorporated in Delaware in 1991.

Directors (In addition to indicated officers)

I. Paul Brna
Robert Genetski

Julia Machalek
Ladimir C. Zidek

Officers (Directors*)

*Ivan F. Kovac, Chm.
*Daniel K. Augustine, Pres. & C.E.O.
Patrick J. Hunt, V.P.—Oper.
William C. Preissner, V.P. & C.F.O.
Edward L. Sylvestrak, V.P.—Corp. Coun.

Daniel R. Yamtich, V.P.—Lending
Philip Foltmer, Auditor
Bruce J. Michalski, Cont.
*Frank M. Swiderski, C.F.O., Treas. & Secy.

Consolidated Balance Sheet   As of December 31, 1994 (000 omitted)

Assets		Liabilities & Stockholders' Equity	
Current assets	$259,334	Current liabilities	$197,454
Net property, plant & equipment	3,407	Long-term debt	31,517
Other assets	9,621	Other liabilities	4,701
		*Stockholders' equity	38,690
Total	$272,362	Total	$272,362

*1,566,378 shares common stock outstanding.

Consolidated Income Statement[a]

Years Ended Dec. 31	Thousands — — — — Total Income	Net Income	Per Share — — — Earnings	Cash Dividends	Common Stock Price Range Calendar Year
1994	$19,884	$ 1,907	$1.17	$ .00	20-1/2— 14-1/2
1993	20,376	3,915	2.28	.00	15-1/4— 11-3/4
1992	21,141	1,675	N/M		13-1/4— 12-3/4[b]
1991	20,867	(557)			
1990	20,929	1,881			

[a]Includes the holding company since December 29, 1992. Data for prior years are for Security Federal Savings and Loan Association of Chicago, a wholly owned subsidiary of Financial Security Corp.
[b]Initial public offering in December 1992.

Transfer Agent & Registrar:	Harris Trust and Savings Bank

General Counsel:
  Muldoon, Murphy & Faucette,
  Washington, D.C.

Investor Relations: William C. Preissner, V.P.

Human Resources: Virginia Bresser

Mgt. Info. Svcs.:   Bruce J. Michalski, Cont.

Auditors: KPMG Peat Marwick LLP

Traded (Symbol):   NASDAQ (FNSC)

Stockholders: 450

Employees: 62

Annual Meeting: In April

First Alert, Inc.

780 McClure Road, Aurora, Illinois 60504-2495
Telephone: (708) 851-7330

First Alert, Inc., through its subsidiaries, is a manufacturer and marketer of a broad range of residential safety products, anchored by its leadership position in the U.S. residential smoke and carbon monoxide detector market through retail distribution channels. Additional products include fire extinguishers, rechargeable flashlights and lanterns, electronic and electromechanical timers, night lights and passive infrared motion sensors. All of the company's manufacturing occurs in its two facilities in Juarez, Mexico, except fire extinguisher manufacturing which occurs in the company's Aurora, Illinois, facility. In March 1994, the company completed an initial public offering of 8,280,000 shares of common stock. Incorporated in Delaware in 1992.

Directors (In addition to indicated officers)

Anthony J. DiNovi
David V. Harkins

Scott A. Schoen

Officers (Directors*)

*Malcolm Candlish, Chm. & C.E.O.
 James S. Amtmann, Pres. & C.O.O.
*Gary L. Lederer, Sr. V.P. & C.F.O.
 William K. Brouse, V.P.—Sales

Thomas A. Gionta, V.P.—Eng.
Fred W. Higgenbottom, V.P.—Oper.
Richard F. Timmons, V.P.—Mktg.

Consolidated Balance Sheet   As of December 31, 1994 (000 omitted)

Assets		Liabilities & Stockholders' Equity	
Current assets	$109,935	Current liabilities	$ 57,418
Net property, plant & equipment	31,066	Long-term debt	15,700
Other assets	31,304	Deferred items	3,672
		Other liabilities	102
		*Stockholders' equity	95,413
Total	$172,305	Total	$172,305

*24,025,616 shares common stock outstanding.

Consolidated Income Statement

Years Ended Dec. 31	Thousands — — — — Net Sales	Net Income	Per Share[a] — — — Earnings	Cash Dividends	Common Stock Price Range[ab] Calendar Year
1994	$248,404	$17,625	$ .78	$ .00	22-1/2 — 8-3/4
1993	157,625	5,042	.25		
1992	131,061	1,237	.08		
1991[c]	123,706	7,277			
1990[c]	107,697	2,708			

[a]Adjusted to reflect a 2-for-1 stock split in October 1994 and a 3.1-for-1 stock split in March 1994.
[b]Initial public offering in March 1994.
[c]Predecessor company.

Transfer Agent & Registrar: The First National Bank of Boston

General Counsel:
  Hutchins, Wheeler & Dittmar

Investor Relations: Michael Rohl, Corp. Cont.

Human Resources: Lisa Reynolds, Mgr.

Mgt. Info. Svcs.:   Dale Berman, Dir.

Auditors: Price Waterhouse LLP
Traded (Symbol):   NASDAQ (ALRT)
Stockholders: 100
Employees: 2,040
Annual Meeting: In May

First Bankers Trustshares, Inc.

1201 Broadway, P.O. Box 3566, Quincy, Illinois 62305-3566
Telephone: (217) 228-8000

First Bankers Trustshares, Inc., is the holding company for First Bankers Trust Company, N.A. The bank provides comprehensive financial products and services to retail, institutional, and corporate customers in the tri-state area of west central Illinois, northeast Missouri and southeast Iowa. As a community-oriented financial institution, First Bankers Trust Company, which traces its beginnings to 1946, operates three banking facilities located in Quincy, Illinois, and one facility in Mendon, Illinois, in northern Adams County. Incorporated in Delaware in 1988.

Directors   (In addition to indicated officers)

David E. Connor, Chm.
William D. Daniels

Donald E. Mitchell
Dennis R. Williams

Officers   (Directors*)

*Donald K. Gnuse, Pres. & C.E.O.
*George H. Pfister, V.P.

*Steven E. Siebers, Secy. & Treas.
Joe J. Leenerts, Asst. Secy.

Consolidated Balance Sheet   As of December 31, 1994 (000 omitted)

Assets		Liabilities & Stockholders' Equity	
Cash & due from banks	$ 6,947	Total deposits	$125,873
Investment securities	55,890	Long-term debt	5,780
Net loans	89,463	Funds & securities under	16,918
Other assets	6,104	agreement to repurchase	
		Other liabilities	1,399
		*Stockholders' equity	8,434
Total	$158,404	Total	$158,404

*316,722 shares common stock outstanding.

Consolidated Income Statement

Years Ended Dec. 31	Thousands — — — —		Per Share — — —		Common Stock Price Range Calendar Year
	Net Sales	Net Income	Earnings	Cash Dividends	
1994	$11,198	$1,010	$2.68	$ .42	25 — 20-1/2
1993	10,744	1,153	3.14	.20	20-1/2 — 11
1992	11,772	886	2.29	.00	14 — 12
1991	13,080	596	1.34	.00	14 — 12
1990	13,121	371	.53	.00	13 — 11

Transfer Agent & Registrar:	First Bankers Trust Company		
General Counsel:	Hinshaw & Culbertson	Traded (Symbol):	OTC
Investor Relations:	Joe J. Leenerts	Stockholders:	212
Human Resources:	Joe J. Leenerts	Employees:	73
Auditors:	McGladrey & Pullen, LLP	Annual Meeting:	Second Tuesday in May

First Chicago Guide

First Busey Corporation

P.O. Box 123, 102 East Main Street, Urbana, Illinois 61801
Telephone: (217) 384-4556

First Busey Corporation is a multi-bank holding company that owns two community bank subsidiaries, a trust company subsidiary, and a securities broker-dealer subsidiary. Through its subsidiaries, the company engages in retail, commercial and correspondent banking, and provides trust and investment services. Banks include Busey Bank and Busey Bank of McLean County. Non-banking subsidiaries are First Busey Trust & Investment Co., which is a full-service investment company, offering professional financial planning, and First Busey Securities, Inc., which is a full-service brokerage firm. Incorporated in Delaware in 1978; reincorporated in Nevada in 1993.

Directors (In addition to indicated officer)

Joseph M. Ambrose
Thomas O. Dawson
Martin A. Klingel
E. Phillips Knox

John W. Pollard, M.D.
Edwin A. Scharlau II
Arthur R. Wyatt

Officers (Director*)

*Douglas C. Mills, Chm., Pres. & C.E.O.
 Barbara J. Kuhl, Exec. V.P., Corp. Secy. & Treas.

Robert E. Beskow, V.P.—Acct. & Auditing
Scott L. Hendrie, V.P. & Cont.

Consolidated Balance Sheet   As of December 31, 1994 (000 omitted)

Assets		Liabilities & Stockholders' Equity	
Current assets	$687,667	Current liabilities	$661,254
Net property, plant & equipment	21,924	Long-term debt	5,000
Other assets	18,868	Other liabilities	3,189
		*Stockholders' equity	59,016
Total	$728,459	Total	$728,459

*3,801,401 Class A shares and 750,000 Class B shares common stock outstanding.

Consolidated Income Statement

| Years Ended Dec. 31 | Thousands — — — — | | Per Share[a] — — — | | Common Stock |
	Total Income	Net Income	Earnings	Cash Dividends[b]	Price Range[ab] Calendar Year
1994	$55,132	$8,238	$1.78	$ .80	25-1/4 — 21-1/2
1993	54,527	7,364	1.60	.80	22 — 16-3/8
1992	54,376	5,938	1.43	.69	16-3/8 — 15
1991	55,495	5,215	1.27	.67	15-5/8 — 11-1/2
1990	54,530	4,680	1.11	.67	16 — 13-5/8

[a]Adjusted to reflect a 3-for-2 stock split in May 1993.
[b]Class A common stock.

Transfer Agent & Registrar: First Busey Corporation

General Counsel:	Chapman & Cutler	Traded (Symbol):	OTC (FBSYA)
Investor Relations:	Barbara J. Kuhl, Exec. V.P.	Stockholders:	867
		Employees:	366
Auditors:	McGladrey & Pullen, LLP	Annual Meeting:	In April

First Chicago Corporation

One First National Plaza, Chicago, Illinois 60670
Telephone: (312) 732-4000

First Chicago Corporation (the Corporation) is a multi-bank holding company. The principal asset of the Corporation is the capital stock of The First National Bank of Chicago. The Corporation also owns all the outstanding capital stock of American National Corporation (ANC) and FCC National Bank. ANC is the holding company for American National Bank and Trust Company of Chicago. FCC National Bank is a Delaware-based bank primarily engaged in the issuance of VISA and MasterCard credit cards. In addition to these banking organizations, the Corporation, directly or indirectly, owns the stock of various nonbank companies engaged in businesses related to banking and finance, including venture capital, leasing, and investment management subsidiaries. Incorporated in Delaware in 1969. On July 12, 1995, First Chicago Corporation announced that it had signed a definitive agreement providing for a merger of equals with NBD Bancorp, Inc.

Directors (In addition to indicated officers)

John H. Bryan	Earl L. Neal
Dean L. Buntrock	James J. O'Connor
James S. Crown	Jerry K. Pearlman
Donald V. Fites	Jack F. Reichert
Donald P. Jacobs	Patrick G. Ryan
Andrew J. McKenna	Adele Simmons
Richard M. Morrow	Roger W. Stone

Officers (Directors*)

* Richard L. Thomas, Chm., Pres. & C.E.O.	Thomas H. Hodges, Exec. V.P.
* David J. Vitale, V. Chm.	Donald R. Hollis, Exec. V.P.
Marvin James Alef, Jr., Exec. V.P.	William G. Jurgensen, Exec. V.P.
John W. Ballantine, Exec. V.P.	Scott P. Marks, Jr., Exec. V.P.
Sherman I. Goldberg, Exec. V.P., Gen. Coun. & Secy.	Robert A. Rosholt, Exec. V.P. & C.F.O.

Consolidated Balance Sheet   As of December 31, 1994 (000 omitted)

Assets		Liabilities & Stockholders' Equity	
Cash & due from banks	$ 12,331,000	Deposits	$31,666,000
Securities	7,559,000	Funds borrowed	20,691,000
Other short-term investments	13,302,000	Long-term debt	2,271,000
Net loans & lease financing	25,224,000	Other liabilities	6,739,000
Properties & equipment	665,000	* Stockholders' equity	4,533,000
Other assets	6,819,000		
Total	$65,900,000	Total	$65,900,000

*89,859,798 shares common stock outstanding.

Consolidated Income Statement

Years Ended Dec. 31	Thousands — — — Operating Income	Net Income	Per Share— — — Earnings	Cash Dividends	Common Stock Price Range Calendar Year
1994	$5,094,600	$689,700	$7.04	$1.80	55 - 1/2 — 41 - 1/8
1993	4,826,500	804,500	8.78	1.20	50 - 5/8 — 35 - 1/2
1992	4,357,800	93,500 [a]	.64 [a]	1.40	37 - 3/4 — 22 - 7/8
1991	4,829,800	116,300	1.15	2.00	28 - 3/4 — 15 - 5/8
1990	5,693,300	249,300	3.35	1.95	38 - 1/4 — 13 - 1/8

[a]Includes the cumulative effect of accounting changes, resulting in a gain to net earnings of $208,000,000 ($2.72 per share).

Transfer Agent & Registrar: First Chicago Trust Co. of New York

General Counsel:
Sherman I. Goldberg, Exec. V.P.

Investor Relations: Susan L. Temple, V.P.

Human Resources:
Marvin James Alef, Jr., Exec. V.P.

Auditors: Arthur Andersen LLP

Traded (Symbol):
NYSE, CSE, PSE, London (FNB)

Stockholders: 14,773

Employees: 17,630

Annual Meeting: In April

First Evergreen Corporation

3101 West 95th Street, Evergreen Park, Illinois 60642
Telephone: (708) 422-6700

First Evergreen Corporation is the holding company for First National Bank of Evergreen Park. The bank offers full-service banking, including transaction services, investment services, trust services, and depository and transfer services. The bank also offers IRA and Keogh accounts and assists customers wishing to purchase or sell corporate stocks and bonds, municipal bonds, or U.S. Treasury bills, notes, and bonds. Incorporated in 1978.

Directors (In addition to indicated officers)

Alfred E. Bleeker
Jerome J. Cismoski

Martin F. Ozinga

Officers (Directors*)

*Kenneth J. Ozinga, Chm. & Pres.
 Robert C. Wall, V.P.

*Stephen M. Hallenbeck, Treas. & Secy.

Consolidated Statement of Condition   As of December 31, 1994 (000 omitted)

Assets		Liabilities & Stockholders' Equity	
Current assets	$ 221,777	Current liabilities	$ 403,163
Net property, plant & equipment	28,462	Other liabilities	1,311,408
Other assets	1,621,796	*Stockholders' equity	157,464
Total	$1,872,035	Total	$1,872,035

*404,584 shares common stock outstanding.

Consolidated Income Statement

Years Ended Dec. 31	Thousands — — — — Operating Income	Net Income	Per Share — — — Earnings	Cash Dividends	Common Stock Price Range Calendar Year
1994	$121,539	$20,415	$50.29	$13.00	391-1/2 — 344-3/4
1993	126,706	21,970	53.77	9.00	357-3/4 — 309-1/4
1992	126,484	18,959	45.95	8.00	315-1/4 — 269-5/8
1991	115,498	16,814	40.39	7.00	277 — 236-3/4
1990	108,108	13,995	33.39	6.00	243-3/4 — 201-3/4

Transfer Agent & Registrar: First Evergreen Corporation

General Counsel:
  Barry N. Voorn—FNB of Ever. Pk.

Investor Relations: Kenneth J. Ozinga, Chm.

Human Resources:
  John A. Camphouse, V.P.-FNB of Ever. Pk.

Mgt. Info. Svcs.:
  Barbara L. Heidegger, Sr. V.P.-FNB of Ever. Pk.

Auditors: Arthur Andersen LLP

Traded: OTC (When-issued basis)

Stockholders: 498

Employees: 3

Annual Meeting: In April

First Financial Bancorp, Inc.

121 East Locust Street, Belvidere, Illinois 61008
Telephone: (815) 544-3167

First Financial Bancorp, Inc., is the holding company of First Federal Savings Bank of Belvidere. First Federal is a federally chartered savings institution engaged primarily in the business of originating one- to four-family residential mortgage loans in its primary market area. As a community-oriented savings bank, it offers traditional deposit and loan products through its two full-service offices in Belvidere and its loan origination office in Rockford. The bank has a wholly owned subsidiary, First Financial Services of Belvidere Illinois, Inc., which offers annuities and insurance products on an agency basis at the bank's full-service locations. Incorporated in Delaware in 1993.

Directors (In addition to indicated officers)

Jack R. Manley
Morton I. Silver

Richard E. Winkelman

Officers (Directors*)

*Steven C. Derr, Pres. & C.E.O.
Thomas R. Montgomery, V.P.

*Larry A. Hall, Secy.

Consolidated Balance Sheet   As of December 31, 1994 (000 omitted)

Assets		Liabilities & Stockholders' Equity	
Cash & cash equivalents	$ 1,899	Deposits	$59,797
Investment securities	10,474	Short-term borrowings	3,000
Loans receivable	45,390	Advance payment by borrow-	262
Mortgage-backed securities	10,696	ers for taxes & insur.	
Other assets	2,706	Other liabilities	456
		*Stockholders' equity	7,650
Total	$71,165	Total	$71,165

*485,974 shares common stock outstanding.

Consolidated Income Statement

Years Ended Dec. 31	Thousands ———— Total Income	Net Income	Per Share ——— Earnings	Cash Dividends	Common Stock Price Range Calendar Year
1994	$5,079	$572	$1.23	$ .00	13-1/2 — 9-1/4
1993	5,513	496		.00	10 — 8[a]
1992	6,222	740			
1991	6,896	545			
1990	7,154	633			

[a]Initial public offering in October 1993.

Transfer Agent & Registrar: Registrar and Transfer Company

General Counsel:
  Strom Sewell Larson & Popp

Investor Relations: Steven C. Derr

Auditors:
  Lindgren Callihan Van Osdol & Co., Ltd.

Traded (Symbol): NASDAQ (FFBI)

Stockholders: 210

Employees: 38

Annual Meeting: In April

First Merchants Acceptance Corporation

570 Lake Cook Road, Suite 126, Deerfield, Illinois 60015
Telephone: (708) 948-9300

First Merchants Acceptance Corporation is a specialty consumer finance company engaged in financing the purchase of used automobiles through the acquisition of dealer-originated retail installment contracts. Such contracts are entered into by automobile dealers with borrowers who do not have access to credit from traditional lending sources. The company currently operates 32 regional dealer service centers in 21 states. In September 1994, the company completed an initial public offering of 1,640,000 shares of common stock. Incorporated in Delaware in 1991.

Directors (In addition to indicated officer)

Thomas A. Hiatt
William N. Plamondon
Marcy H. Shockey

Richard J. Uhl
Solomon A. Weisgal
Stowe W. Wyant

Officers (Director*)

*Mitchell C. Kahn, Pres. & C.E.O.
Thomas R. Ehmann, V.P.—Fin. & Asst. Secy.
Brian W. Hausmann, V.P.—Oper.
Allen D. Rice, V.P.—Sales & Mktg.

Paul Van Eyl, V.P.—Corp. Planning
Charles L. Lanzrath, Cont.
Christopher R. Manning, Secy.

Consolidated Balance Sheet   As of May 31, 1994 (000 omitted)

Assets		Liabilities & Stockholders' Equity	
Finance receivables, net	$53,474	Total liabilities	$45,575
Net property, plant & equipment	652	Common stock warrants	1,511
Other assets	1,325	*Stockholders' equity	8,365
Total	$55,451	Total	$55,451

*2,309,594 shares common and 161,758 shares non-voting common stock outstanding, after September 1994 stock split.

Consolidated Income Statement

Years Ended May 31	Thousands — — — — Total Revenues	Net Income	Per Share[a] — — — — Earnings	Cash Dividends	Common Stock Price Range[ab] Fiscal Year
1994[c]	$10,048	$ 2,276	$ .53	$ .00	16-1/2 — 9
1993	3,609	697	.30		
1992[d]	579	(335)	(.19)		

[a]Adjusted to reflect a 23.184-for-1 stock split in September 1994.
[b]Initial public offering in September 1994.
[c]Pro forma.
[d]First year of operations.

Transfer Agent & Registrar: Harris Trust and Savings Bank	
General Counsel: Burke, Warren & MacKay, P.C.	Traded (Symbol): NASDAQ (FMAC)
	Stockholders: 1,100
Investor Relations: Thomas R. Ehmann, V.P.	Employees: 175
Auditors: Deloitte & Touche LLP	Annual Meeting: In October

First Chicago Guide   101

First Midwest Bancorp, Inc.

300 Park Boulevard, Suite 405, Itasca, Illinois 60143-2636
Telephone: (708) 875-7450

First Midwest Bancorp, Inc., is headquartered in the Chicago suburb of Itasca and is a leading Illinois publicly traded bank holding company. First Midwest is engaged in the business of commercial banking, investment management, trust, mortgage, and related services through one bank and four other affiliates. The commercial bank operates 43 offices in northern Illinois with approximately 80 percent of bank assets being situated in Metro Chicago. The four nonbank affiliates operate in the same markets served by the bank. Company affiliates are: First Midwest Bank, N.A., First Midwest Insurance Company, First Midwest Trust Company, First Midwest Asset Management Company, and First Midwest Mortgage Company. In May 1995, First Midwest Bancorp merged its four commercial banks — First Midwest Bank/Illinois, N.A., First Midwest Bank, N.A., First Midwest Bank/Danville, N.A., and First Midwest Bank/Western Illinois, N.A. — into one entity, First Midwest Bank, N.A. Incorporated in Delaware in 1982.

Directors (In addition to indicated officers)

Bruce S. Chelberg
O. Ralph Edwards
Joseph W. England
Thomas M. Garvin
Alan M. Hallene

Sister Norma Janssen
Robert E. Joyce
Frank J. Turk, Sr.
J. Stephen Vanderwoude

Officers (Directors*)

* C.D. Oberwortmann, Chm.
* Robert P. O'Meara, Pres. & C.E.O.
* Andrew B. Barber, V. Chm.
* John M. O'Meara, Exec. V.P. & C.O.O.

Donald J. Swistowicz, Sr. V.P.—Corp. Admin. & C.F.O.
Alan R. Milasius, Corp. Secy.

Consolidated Statement of Condition   As of December 31, 1994 (000 omitted)

Assets		Liabilities & Stockholders' Equity	
Cash & cash equivalents	$ 107,180	Total deposits	$1,994,408
Federal funds sold & short-term investments	15,694	Short-term borrowings	665,500
		Other liabilities	29,078
Investment securities	168,644	*Stockholders' equity	186,115
Securities available for sale	696,384		
Net loans	1,761,117		
Net property, plant & equipment	40,329		
Other assets	85,753		
Total	$2,875,101	Total	$2,875,101

*12,197,480 shares common stock outstanding.

Consolidated Income Statement

Years Ended Dec. 31	Thousands — — — — Total Oper. Income[a]	Net Income	Per Share — — — Earnings	Cash Dividends	Common Stock Price Range Calendar Year
1994	$215,645	$20,368[b]	$1.67[b]	$ .68	28-3/4 — 22
1993	197,862	20,784	1.68	.60	28-1/4 — 19-1/4
1992[c]	199,671	17,908	1.43	.52	20-1/4 — 14-1/4
1991[c]	229,418	17,807	1.42	.52	20 — 13
1990[c]	224,373	22,604	1.80	.52	23 — 11-3/4

[a]Restated to reflect FAS 91.
[b]Includes an aftertax restructuring charge of $2,379,000 ($.20 per share).
[c]Certain reclassifications have been made to the consolidated financial statements to conform to the 1994 presentation.

Transfer Agent & Registrar: American Stock Transfer & Trust Co.

General Counsel: Hinshaw & Culbertson

Investor Relations:
   James M. Roolf, Corp. Comm. Dir.

Human Resources: Phillip E. Glotfelty

Mgt. Info. Svcs.:   Kent S. Belasco

Auditors: KPMG Peat Marwick LLP

Traded (Symbol):   NASDAQ (FMBI)

Stockholders: 2,693

Employees: 1,269

Annual Meeting: In April

First Chicago Guide

First National Bancorp, Inc.

78 North Chicago Street, Joliet, Illinois 60431
Telephone: (815) 726-4371

First National Bancorp, Inc., is a multi-bank holding company providing financial and other banking services to customers located primarily in suburban Will, Grundy and Kendall Counties, Illinois. First National Bancorp originated with the merger of First National Bank of Joliet in 1986. Expansion has continued to occur through the acquisition in 1989 of Southwestern Suburban Bank, Bolingbrook, and the Bank of Lockport in 1990. The subsidiary banks make loans to both individuals and commercial entities. In October 1994, First National Bancorp acquired Plano Bancshares, Inc., the parent of Community Bank of Plano. Incorporated in Illinois in 1986.

Directors (In addition to indicated officers)

Sheldon C. Bell
George H. Buck
Watson A. Healy
Paul A. Lambrecht
Harvey J. Lewis

Walter F. Nolan
Charles R. Peyla
Louis R. Peyla
Howard E. Reeves

Officers (Directors*)

*Kevin T. Reardon, Chm. & C.E.O.

*Albert G. D'Ottavio, Pres., C.O.O., Treas. & Secy.

Consolidated Balance Sheet As of December 31, 1994 (000 omitted)

Assets		Liabilities & Stockholders' Equity	
Cash & due from banks	$ 42,832	Total deposits	$556,162
Interest-bearing deposits in other fin. insts.	4,198	Short-term borrowings	59,614
		Long-term debt	8,326
Investments in debt securities	189,874	Accrued interest & other liabilities	6,883
Loans, net	418,918		
Premises and equipment	14,660	*Stockholders' equity	61,657
Other assets	22,160		
Total	$692,642	Total	$692,642

*1,215,902 shares common stock outstanding.

Consolidated Income Statement

Years Ended Dec. 31	Thousands — — — —		Per Share[a] — — — —		Common Stock Price Range[a] Calendar Year
	Total Income	Net Income	Earnings	Cash Dividends	
1994	$45,908	$7,507	$6.17	$2.68	64 — 57
1993	43,637	7,366	6.06	2.50	57-1/8 — 51-3/8
1992	45,232	6,826	5.61	2.50	51-3/8 — 46-3/8
1991	47,311	5,805	4.77	1.91	52-1/8 — 44-1/4
1990	40,234	5,307	5.01	2.09	52-1/8 — 45

[a]Adjusted to reflect a 7-for-5 stock split in 1994 and a 20% stock dividend in 1991.

Transfer Agent & Registrar: First National Bancorp, Inc.

General Counsel:
  Herschbach, Tracy, Johnson, Bertani & Wilson

Investor Relations: Albert G. D'Ottavio, Pres.

Human Resources: Betty J. McTee

Mgt. Info. Svcs.: Jack A. Podlesny

Auditors: McGladrey & Pullen, LLP
Traded (Symbol): OTC
Stockholders: 1,674
Employees: 357
Annual Meeting: In March

First Chicago Guide

First Oak Brook Bancshares, Inc.

1400 Sixteenth Street, Oak Brook, Illinois 60521
Telephone: (708) 571-1050

First Oak Brook Bancshares, Inc., is a bank holding company formed under the Bank Holding Company Act of 1956, as amended. The company owns all of the outstanding capital stock of Oak Brook Bank, an Illinois state-chartered bank. The bank has seven locations in Du Page County and two in Cook County. The business of First Oak Brook Bancshares consists primarily of the ownership, supervision and control of its subsidiary. The company provides its subsidiary with advice, counsel and specialized services in various fields of financial, legal, and banking policy and operations. First Oak Brook Bancshares also engages in negotiations designed to lead to the acquisition of other banks and closely related businesses. Oak Brook Bank is engaged in the general retail and commercial banking business. The services offered include demand, savings, time deposits, corporate cash management services, commercial lending products such as commercial loans, mortgages and letters of credit, and personal lending products such as residential mortgages, home equity lines, and Gold and Silver MasterCard. In addition, private banking products and services are offered, including discount brokerage, mutual funds and precious metal sales. Oak Brook Bank has a full-service trust and land trust department. In August 1994, 1st Oak Brook Bank merged with Oak Brook Bank. Incorporated in Delaware in 1983.

Directors (In addition to indicated officers)

Miriam Lutwak Fitzgerald, M.D.
Geoffrey R. Stone

Alton M. Withers

Officers (Directors*)

*Eugene P. Heytow, Chm. & C.E.O.
*Frank M. Paris, V. Chm.
*Richard M. Rieser, Jr., Pres.
Rosemarie Burget, V.P., C.F.O. & Treas.
Mary C. Campbell, V.P. & Chf. Hum. Res.
Officer

George C. Clam, V.P. & Chf. Banking Officer
William E. Navolio, V.P., Gen. Coun. & Secy.
Dennis E. O'Hara, V.P.—Mktg.
Susanne Griffith, Auditor
Joseph Garro, Assoc. Gen. Coun.
Lola Donofrio, Asst. Treas.

Consolidated Balance Sheet As of December 31, 1994 (000 omitted)

Assets		Liabilities & Stockholders' Equity	
Current assets	$606,066	Current liabilities	$582,200
Net property, plant & equipment	18,989	Long-term debt	6,000
Other assets	9,650	Other liabilities	3,596
		*Stockholders' equity	42,909
Total	$634,705	Total	$634,705

*1,526,876 shares common and 1,835,666 shares Class A common stock outstanding.

Consolidated Income Statement

Years Ended Dec. 31	Thousands — — — —		Per Share[ab] — — —		Common Stock
	Total Income	Net Income	Earnings	Cash Dividends	Price Range[ab] Calendar Year
1994	$45,305	$6,194	$1.81	$ .28	20-1/2 — 14-1/2
1993	42,001	5,533	1.62	.24	15-1/2 — 10-1/8
1992	39,733	4,313	1.27	.22	11-3/4 — 8-5/8
1991	39,948	3,425	1.01	.21	10-1/2 — 5-1/8
1990	38,889	3,474	1.03	.21	8-5/8 — 5-1/8

[a]Class A common stock; common stock dividends for the years 1994-1990 were $.22, $.19, $.18, $.17, and $.17 per share, respectively.
[b]Adjusted for 50% stock dividends distributed in September 1994 and November 1992, and the 25% stock dividend distributed in December 1993.

Transfer Agent & Registrar: Oak Brook Bank

General Counsel: William E. Navolio, V.P.

Investor Relations: Rosemarie Burget, V.P.

Human Resources: Mary C. Campbell, V.P.

Mgt. Info. Svcs.: Dennis J. Reidy

Auditors: Ernst & Young LLP

Traded (Symbol): NASDAQ (FOBBA, Class A)

Stockholders: 437

Employees: 278

Annual Meeting: In May

Firstbank of Illinois Co.

205 South Fifth Street, Springfield, Illinois 62701
Telephone: (217) 753-7543

Firstbank of Illinois Co. is a multi-bank holding company for eight subsidiary banks. They include: Central Bank (Fairview Heights); City Bank of Bloomington-Normal (Bloomington); Colonial Bank (Des Peres, Missouri); Elliott State Bank (Jacksonville); Farmers & Merchants Bank of Carlinville (Carlinville); The First National Bank of Springfield (Springfield); First Trust and Savings Bank of Taylorville (Taylorville); and United Illinois Bank of Southern Illinois (Benton). During 1994, Firstbank completed the acquisitions of FFG Investments Inc. (formerly known as Rowe, Henry & Deal, Inc.), a registered securities broker/dealer, in March; and Colonial Bancshares, Inc., and its wholly owned subsidiary, Colonial Bank, in April. It also established FFG Trust, Inc., in July 1994, to enhance and expand trust and farm management services companywide through the reorganization and consolidation of those services. The majority of business is commercial and retail banking, trust and investment management, business lending, agriculture credit, and management services. Incorporated in Delaware in 1974.

Directors (In addition to indicated officers)

Leo J. Dondanville, Jr.
William T. Grant, Jr.
Robert W. Jackson
William R. Schnirring

Robert L. Sweney
E. Jack Thornburg
P. Richard Ware
Richard E. Zemenick

Officers (Directors*)

*Mark H. Ferguson, Chm., Pres. & C.E.O.
*William B. Hopper, V. Chm.
Larry A. Burton, Exec. V.P.—Fin. Svcs.
Sandra L. Stolte, Exec. V.P.
David W. Waggoner, Exec. V.P.
Chris R. Zettek, Exec. V.P., C.F.O. & Treas.
Duane L. Gerlach, Sr. V.P. & C.L.O.

Jeffrey B. Coultas, V.P.—Affiliate Bank Serv.
Daniel R. Davis, V.P. & Cont.
Jack Griggs, V.P.—Mktg.
William V. Peterman, V.P. & Corp. Aud.
Steven Schweizer, V.P. & Opers. Center Mgr.
John R. Smith, V.P. & Chf. Invest. Officer

Consolidated Balance Sheet As of December 31, 1994 (000 omitted)

Assets		Liabilities & Stockholders' Equity	
Current assets	$ 599,378	Current liabilities	$ 480,473
Net property, plant & equipment	41,784	Long-term debt	3,463
Other assets	1,111,899	Other liabilities	1,110,641
		*Stockholders' equity	158,484
Total	$1,753,061	Total	$1,753,061

*6,552,908 shares common stock outstanding.

Consolidated Income Statement[a]

Years Ended Dec. 31	Thousands — — — — — Total Revenue	Net Income	Per Share[b] — — — — Earnings	Cash Dividends	Common Stock Price Range[b] Calendar Year
1994	$120,029	$23,454	$2.37	$ .80	25-7/8 — 22-5/8
1993	126,144	20,643	2.20	.72	26-1/8 — 23-3/8
1992	139,713	17,067	1.83	.64	25-3/8 — 18-1/2
1991	141,319	14,726	1.63	.59	20 — 11-1/2
1990	125,098	12,409	1.41	.53	13-5/8 — 10-3/8

[a]Restated for First Highland Corp. acquisition and accounted as a pooling-of-interests.
[b]Adjusted to reflect a 3-for-2 stock split in the form of a stock dividend in March 1995.

Transfer Agent & Registrar: Firstbank of Illinois Co.

General Counsel:
  Brown, Hay & Stephens—Springfield, Illinois
Investor Relations: Chris R. Zettek, Exec. V.P.
Human Resources: Diane Schwab, Coordinator
Auditors: KPMG Peat Marwick LLP

Traded (Symbol): NASDAQ (FBIC)
Stockholders: 2,135
Employees: 840
Annual Meeting: In May

First Chicago Guide

The Florsheim Shoe Company

130 South Canal Street, Chicago, Illinois 60606-3999
Telephone: (312) 559-2500

The Florsheim Shoe Company designs, manufactures, and sources a diverse and extensive range of products in the middle- to upper-price range of the men's quality footwear market. Florsheim markets its products to more than 6,000 department and specialty store locations worldwide and through 355 company-owned specialty stores and outlet stores. In November 1994, INTERCO INCORPORATED spun off Florsheim in a distribution to stockholders. Incorporated in Delaware in 1987.

Directors (In addition to indicated officer)

Richard B. Loynd, Chm.
Michael S. Gross
John J. Hannan

Joshua J. Harris
John H. Kissick
John Madden

Officers (Director*)

*Ronald J. Mueller, Pres. & C.E.O.
Steve L. Bick, V.P.
Harry S. Bock, V.P.
George M. Chrislu, V.P.
Thomas W. Joseph, V.P.
Bruce Polcek, V.P.

Roy J. Sauer, V.P.
Larry J. Svoboda, V.P., C.F.O. & Secy.
James J. Tunney, V.P.
Gregory J. Van Gasse, V.P.
Henry W. Wachholz, V.P.

Consolidated Balance Sheet As of December 31, 1994 (000 omitted)

Assets		Liabilities & Stockholders' Equity	
Current assets	$168,942	Current liabilities	$ 27,642
Net property, plant & equipment	21,687	Long-term debt	105,533
Other assets	24,641	Deferred items	20,785
		Other liabilities	1,162
		*Stockholders' equity	60,148
Total	$215,270	Total	$215,270

*8,346,051 shares common stock outstanding.

Consolidated Income Statement

Years Ended Abt. Dec. 31	Thousands — — — —		Per Share — — —		Common Stock Price Range[a] Calendar Year
	Net Sales	Net Income	Earnings	Cash Dividends	
1994[b]	$302,001	$1,573	$ .19	$ .00	9-1/4 — 5-5/8
1993[b]	299,625	7,221	.87		
1992[c]	311,888				

[a]INTERCO INCORPORATED spun off The Florsheim Shoe Company to stockholders in November 1994.
[b]Pro forma.
[c]Due to fresh start reporting, net income figure is not meaningful.

Transfer Agent & Registrar:	KeyCorp Shareholder Services, Inc.		
Investor Relations:	Larry J. Svoboda, V.P.	Stockholders:	2,200
Auditors:	KPMG Peat Marwick LLP	Employees:	3,248
Traded (Symbol):	NASDAQ (FLSC)	Annual Meeting:	In May

FluoroScan Imaging Systems, Inc.

650-B Anthony Trail, Northbrook, Illinois 60062
Telephone: (708) 564-5400

FluoroScan Imaging Systems, Inc., manufactures and distributes the FluoroScan® Imaging System, a low intensity, real-time X-ray imaging device which provides high resolution images at radiation levels and at a cost well below those of conventional X-ray and fluoroscopic equipment. The FluoroScan technology, which the company licenses on an exclusive basis in the U.S. from the United States of America, as represented by the National Aeronautics and Space Administration, is based on a micro-channel plate image intensifier commonly known as a "night vision" intensifier. In July 1994, the company completed an initial public offering of 1,000,000 units, which consist of common stock and redeemable common stock warrants. Incorporated in Delaware in 1984.

Directors (In addition to indicated officers)

Larry Bier
Bruce W. Johnson

Theodore Sall, Ph.D.

Officers (Directors*)

*Larry S. Grossman, Chm., C.E.O. & Secy.
*Arlen L. Issette, Pres. & Treas.

George T. Knackstedt, V.P.—Mfg. & Eng.
Bernard M. Klos, C.F.O.

Consolidated Balance Sheet   As of December 31, 1994 (000 omitted)

Assets		Liabilities & Stockholders' Equity	
Current assets	$7,081	Current liabilities	$ 802
Net property, plant & equipment	478	*Stockholders' equity	7,371
Other assets	614		
Total	$8,173	Total	$8,173

*3,346,039 shares common stock outstanding.

Consolidated Income Statement

Years Ended Dec. 31	Thousands — — — —		Per Share[a] — — — —		Common Stock Price Range[ab] Calendar Year
	Net Sales	Net Income	Earnings	Cash Dividends	
1994	$9,171	$1,773	$ .57	$ .00	8-3/8 — 5-5/8
1993	6,928	1,458	.52		
1992	5,983	418	.15		

[a]Adjusted to reflect a 1,344-for-1 stock split in April 1994.
[b]Initial public offering in July 1994.

Transfer Agent & Registrar: American Stock Transfer & Trust Co.

General Counsel: Katten Muchin & Zavis

Investor Relations: Bernard M. Klos, C.F.O.

Auditors: BDO Seidman

Traded (Symbol): NASDAQ (FLRO)
Stockholders: 1,000
Employees: 24
Annual Meeting: In June

FMC Corporation

200 East Randolph Drive, Chicago, Illinois 60601
Telephone: (312) 861-6000

FMC Corporation participates on a worldwide basis in five broad markets: Industrial Chemicals, Performance Chemicals, Precious Metals, Defense Systems, and Machinery and Equipment. Chemical products include industrial and agricultural chemicals and food additives. Precious metals produces primarily gold and silver. The machinery manufactured includes equipment for defense, energy and transportation, as well as food and agricultural machinery. FMC, through its subsidiaries, operates 97 manufacturing facilities and mines in 21 countries, and two research facilities. In January 1994, the company and Harsco Corp. completed the formation of a joint venture, United Defense L.P., which combines their defense operations. Incorporated in Delaware in 1928.

Directors (In addition to indicated officers)

William W. Boeschenstein
B.A. Bridgewater, Jr.
Patricia A. Buffler, Ph.D.
Albert J. Costello
Paul L. Davies, Jr.
Jean A. Francois-Poncet

Robert H. Malott
Edward C. Meyer
William F. Reilly
James R. Thompson
Clayton K. Yeutter

Officers (Directors*)

*Robert N. Burt, Chm. & C.E.O.
*Larry D. Brady, Pres.
William F. Beck, Exec. V.P.
Michael J. Callahan, Exec. V.P. & C.F.O.
William J. Kirby, Sr. V.P.—Admin.
Alfredo Bernad, V.P. & Pres.—FMC Europe
Charles H. Cannon, Jr., V.P. & Gen. Mgr.—Food Mach.
Robert J. Fields, V.P.
Cheryl A. Francis, V.P. & Treas.
W. Reginald Hall, V.P. & Gen. Mgr.—Specialty Chem.
Robert I. Harries, V.P. & Gen. Mgr.—Chem. Prod.
Patrick J. Head, V.P. & Gen. Coun.

Lawrence P. Holleran, V.P.
William R. Jenkins, V.P.—Comm.
James A. McClung, V.P.—Exec. Mktg.
Michael W. Murray, V.P.—Hum. Res.
Joseph H. Netherland, V.P. & Gen. Mgr.—Energy & Trans. Equip.
Thomas W. Rabaut, V.P. & Pres./C.E.O.—United Defense, L.P.
Harold S. Russell, V.P.—Gov't. Aff.
William H. Schumann, V.P. & Gen. Mgr.—Ag. Chem.
Peter E. Weber, V.P.—Latin Amer./Middle East/Africa
William J. Wheeler, V.P.—Asia Pacific
Scott H. Williamson, V.P.—Corp. Dev.
Robert L. Day, Secy. & Asst. Gen. Coun.

Consolidated Balance Sheet As of December 31, 1994 (000 omitted)

Assets		Liabilities & Stockholders' Equity	
Current assets	$1,376,300	Current liabilities	$1,268,900
Net property, plant & equipment	1,537,400	Long-term debt	901,200
Other assets	437,800	Other liabilities	764,900
		*Stockholders' equity	416,500
Total	$3,351,500	Total	$3,351,500

*36,515,304 shares common stock outstanding.

Consolidated Income Statement

Years Ended Dec. 31	Thousands — — — — Total Revenue	Net Income[a]	Per Share — — — Earnings[a]	Cash Dividends	Common Stock Price Range Calendar Year	
1994	$4,051,300	$ 173,400	$ 4.66	$ .00	65	— 45-1/2
1993	3,788,953	36,284	.98	.00	53	— 41-1/2
1992	4,003,459	(75,746)	(2.06)	.00	53	— 42-5/8
1991	3,923,529	163,877	4.52	.00	51-5/8 — 29-1/2	
1990	3,742,993	155,288	4.30	.00	38-3/4 — 25-3/8	

[a]Reflects extraordinary items, net of taxes, of $4,683,000 ($.13 per share) in 1993; extraordinary items, net of taxes, of $11,417,000 ($.31 per share) and FAS 106, net of taxes, of $183,730,000 ($4.99 per share) and provision for discontinued operations, net of taxes, of $73,200,000 ($1.99 per share) in 1992; and extraordinary items, net of taxes, of $9,206,000 ($.25 per share) in 1991.

Transfer Agent & Registrar:	Harris Trust and Savings Bank		
General Counsel:	Patrick J. Head, V.P.	Traded (Symbol):	CSE, NYSE, PSE (FMC)
Investor Relations:	Elisabeth D. Azzarello, Dir.	Stockholders:	12,438
Human Resources:	Michael W. Murray, V.P.	Employees:	21,344
Auditors:	KPMG Peat Marwick LLP	Annual Meeting:	In April

Fort Dearborn Income Securities, Inc.

209 S. LaSalle St., Eleventh Floor, Chicago, Illinois 60604-1295
Telephone: (312) 346-0676

Fort Dearborn Income Securities, Inc., is a diversified, closed-end investment management company, advised by Brinson Partners, Inc. Fort Dearborn invests principally in investment grade, long-term, fixed-income debt securities. The primary objective of the company is to provide shareholders with a stable stream of current income consistent with external interest rate conditions and provide a total return over time that is above what they could receive by investing individually in the investment grade and long-term maturity sectors of the bond market. Incorporated in Delaware in 1972; reincorporated in Illinois in 1991.

Directors

Richard M. Burridge, Chm.
Walter E. Auch
C. Roderick O'Neil

Frank K. Reilly
Edward M. Roob

Officers

Gary P. Brinson, Pres.
Dennis L. Hesse, V.P. & Portfolio Mgr.
Michael J. Jacobs, Secy. & Treas.

Joseph A. Anderson, Asst. Secy. & Asst. Treas.
Gregory P. Smith, Asst. Portfolio Mgr.

Consolidated Balance Sheet   As of September 30, 1994 (000 omitted)

Assets		Liabilities & Stockholders' Equity	
Portfolio of investments	$131,048	Current liabilities	$ 223
Other assets	2,613	*Stockholders' equity	133,438
Total	$133,661	Total	$133,661

*8,872,365 shares common stock outstanding.

Consolidated Income Statement

Years Ended Sept. 30	Thousands — — — — Net Income	Per Share — — — — Net Income	Cash Dividends	Common Stock Price Range Calendar Year
1994	$9,840	$1.15	$1.12	16-1/8 — 12-5/8
1993	8,684	1.22	1.24	18-1/4 — 15-1/4
1992	8,736	1.24	1.24	17　 — 15-1/4
1991	8,910	1.28	1.33	16-5/8 — 14-1/2
1990	9,249	1.34	1.36	15-1/4 — 13-1/4

Transfer Agent & Registrar:	First Chicago Trust Co. of New York		
General Counsel:	Winston & Strawn	Traded (Symbol):	NYSE, CSE (FTD)
Investor Relations:	Michael J. Jacobs, Secy.	Stockholders:	13,238
Auditors:	KPMG Peat Marwick LLP	Annual Meeting:	In December

Ben Franklin Retail Stores, Inc.

500 East North Avenue, Carol Stream, Illinois 60188-2168
Telephone: (708) 462-6100

Ben Franklin Retail Stores, Inc., franchises retail variety and crafts stores under the names Ben Franklin®
and Ben Franklin Crafts®, and sells variety and crafts merchandise to its franchisees and independent
selected retail outlets on a wholesale basis. As of December 31, 1994, there were 575 franchisee-owned
variety stores and 309 franchisee-owned crafts stores located in 47 states. The company also owns and
operates 28 Ben Franklin Crafts "superstores." Variety stores sell a broad mix of merchandise, including
apparel, housewares, hardware, paper products, health and beauty aids, toys, sporting goods,
stationery, party supplies, and greeting cards. The company is a 67 percent-owned subsidiary of
Foxmeyer Health Corporation. Incorporated in Delaware in 1985.

Directors (In addition to indicated officers)

Harvey A. Fain
Sheldon W. Fantle

Alfred H. Kingon
William A. Lemer

Officers (Directors*)

* Abbey J. Butler, Co-Chm.
* Melvyn J. Estrin, Co-Chm.
* John B. Menzer, Pres. & C.O.O.
David A. Brainard, Sr. V.P. & C.F.O.
Robert A. Kendig, Sr. V.P.—Mdse. & Adv.
Richard T. Krubeck, Sr. V.P., Gen. Coun. &
  Secy.
Richard Siska, Sr. V.P.—Sales
Edward D. Walker, Sr. V.P.—Franchise Bus.
  Svcs.

Phyllis A. Dinaro, V.P.—Fin. Planning
Kenneth L. Fisher, V.P.—Distr. & Transp.
David Larson, V.P.—N. Central Reg.
Thomas Peterson, V.P.—Eastern Reg.
C. Wayne Pyrant, V.P.—Franchise Sales
Scott B. Sayers, V.P.—MIS
Donald V. Streu, V.P.—Mdse.
Kent L. Wise, V.P.—Western Reg.

Consolidated Balance Sheet As of March 31, 1995 (000 omitted)

Assets		Liabilities & Stockholders' Equity	
Current assets	$154,286	Current liabilities	$ 88,656
Net property, plant & equipment	40,979	Long-term debt	60,990
Deferred tax asset	8,778	Long-term insurance claim	1,717
Other assets	15,430	reserves	
		Other liabilities	8,724
		*Stockholders' equity	59,386
Total	$219,473	Total	$219,473

*5,504,250 shares common stock outstanding.

Consolidated Income Statement

Years Ended March 31	Thousands — — — — Net Sales	Net Income	Per Share[a] — — — — Earnings	Cash Dividends	Common Stock Price Range[ab] Calendar Year
1995	$354,788	$ 1,558	$ .28		
1994	337,933	5,717[c]	1.02[c]	.00	6-1/4 — 3-1/2
1993	346,174	3,139[d]	.56[d]	.00	8-3/4 — 4-1/2
1992	340,643	(6,910)[e]	(1.26)[e]	.00	8-3/8 — 3-5/8
1991	339,269	1,901	.35[f]		

[a]Adjusted to reflect a 5,500-for-1 stock split in the form of a dividend in November 1991.
[b]Initial public offering in April 1992.
[c]Includes FAS 109, resulting in a credit to net earnings of $8,042,000 ($1.44 per share).
[d]Includes an extraordinary gain of $1,035,000 ($.18 per share).
[e]Includes FAS 106, resulting in a charge to net earnings of $9,664,000 ($1.76 per share); and an extraordinary gain
  of $1,006,000 ($.18 per share).
[f]Pro forma.

Transfer Agent & Registrar:	LaSalle National Trust, N.A.
General Counsel:	Richard T. Krubeck, Sr. V.P.
Investor Relations:	David A. Brainard, Sr. V.P.
Mgt. Info. Svcs.:	Scott B. Sayers, V.P.
Auditors:	Deloitte & Touche LLP

Traded (Symbol): NASDAQ (BFRS)
Stockholders: 535
Employees: 1,600
Annual Meeting: In August

Fruit of the Loom, Inc.

5000 Sears Tower, 233 South Wacker Drive, Chicago, Illinois 60606
Telephone: (312) 876-1724

Fruit of the Loom, Inc., is a vertically integrated international basic apparel company, emphasizing branded products for consumers ranging from infants to senior citizens. It is the largest domestic producer of underwear and of activewear for the imprinted market, selling products principally under the FRUIT OF THE LOOM®, BVD®, SCREEN STARS®, BEST℠, MUNSINGWEAR®, WILSON®, BOTANY 500® and JOHN HENRY® brand names. The company also manufactures and markets sports licensed apparel bearing the names, tradenames, and logos of the National Football League, the National Basketball Association, Major League Baseball, the National Hockey League, professional sports teams, and most major colleges and universities, as well as the likenesses of certain popular professional athletes under the PRO PLAYER®, SALEM®, SALEM SPORTSWEAR®, and OFFICIAL FAN® brands. Fruit of the Loom designs, manufactures, arranges for the manufacture of, and markets women's and men's jeanswear and jeans-related sportswear under the GITANO® name. Major subsidiaries are Union Underwear Company, Inc., and NWI Land Management Inc. Incorporated in Delaware in 1985.

Directors (In addition to indicated officers)

Omar Z. Al Askari
Dennis S. Bookshester
Lee W. Jennings

Henry A. Johnson
A. Lorne Weil
Sir Brian G. Wolfson

Officers (Directors*)

*William Farley, Chm. & C.E.O.
*Richard C. Lappin, V. Chm.
*John B. Holland, Pres. & C.O.O.
Richard M. Cion, Sr. Exec. V.P.—Corp. Dev.
Larry K. Switzer, Exec. V.P. & C.F.O.

Michael F. Bogacki, V.P. & Cont.
Burgess D. Ridge, V.P.—Admin.
Earl C. Shanks, V.P.—Treas.
Mark A. Steinkraus, V.P.—Inv. Rel.

Consolidated Balance Sheet   As of December 31, 1994 (000 omitted)

Assets		Liabilities & Stockholders' Equity	
Current assets	$1,076,600	Current liabilities	$ 331,800
Net property, plant & equipment	1,058,200	Long-term debt	1,440,200
Other assets	1,028,700	Deferred taxes	43,400
		Other liabilities	222,300
		*Stockholders' equity	1,125,800
Total	$3,163,500	Total	$3,163,500

*69,160,349 shares Class A and 6,690,976 shares Class B common stock outstanding.

Consolidated Income Statement

Years Ended Dec. 31	Thousands — — — — Net Sales	Net Income[a]	Per Share — — — Earnings[a]	Cash Dividends	Common Stock Price Range[b] Calendar Year	
1994	$2,297,800	$ 60,300[c]	$ .79[c]	$ .00	33	— 23
1993	1,884,400	212,800[d]	2.80[d]	.00	49-1/4	— 22-7/8
1992	1,855,100	188,500	2.48	.00	49-5/8	— 26-5/8
1991	1,628,100	111,000[e]	1.60[e]	.00	28	— 7-5/8
1990	1,426,800	77,100[f]	1.25[f]	.00	15-1/4	— 6-1/8

[a]From continuing operations before extraordinary items and cumulative effect of change in accounting principles.
[b]Class A common stock.
[c]Includes pretax charges of approximately $40,000,000 to write down inventories to net realizable value and a pretax charge of $18,000,000 related to the writeoff of Artex intangibles.
[d]Includes a pretax gain of $67,300,000 ($.55 per share) from the company's investment in Acme Boot Co., Inc.
[e]Includes a court-ordered refund of federal income taxes of $10,500,000 plus interest of $49,400,000 ($.57 per share), a pretax charge of $10,200,000 ($.12 per share), and a pretax charge of $39,200,000 ($.45 per share) to write down the company's investment in Acme Boot to its then market value.
[f]Includes a pretax charge of $16,300,000 ($.17 per share) for certain obligations related to former subsidiaries.

Transfer Agent & Registrar:	Chemical Bank		
Investor Relations:	Mark A. Steinkraus, V.P.	Traded (Symbol):	NYSE (FTL)
		Stockholders:	2,593
Human Resources:	Burgess D. Ridge, V.P.	Employees:	37,400
Auditors:	Ernst & Young LLP	Annual Meeting:	In May

Arthur J. Gallagher & Co.

The Gallagher Centre, Two Pierce Place, Itasca, Illinois 60143-3141
Telephone: (708) 773-3800

Arthur J. Gallagher & Co. and its subsidiaries are engaged in providing insurance brokerage, risk management, and related services to clients in the U.S. and abroad. The company's principal activity is the negotiation and placement of insurance for its clients. The company places insurance for and services commercial, industrial, institutional, governmental, religious and personal accounts. Arthur J. Gallagher also specializes in furnishing risk management services. Risk management involves assisting clients in analyzing risks and in determining whether proper protection is best obtained through the purchase of insurance or through retention of all or a portion of those risks and the adoption of corporate risk management policies and cost-effective loss control and prevention programs. Risk management services also include claims management, loss control consulting, and property appraisals. Gallagher Bassett Services, Inc., the company's principal subsidiary, is a provider of risk management services dedicated to serving the needs of corporations and institutions worldwide. Services include claims management, risk management consulting, information management, property appraisals, and other specialized services. Other major subsidiaries and divisions include: The Brokerage Services Division; Gallagher Benefit Services; Gallagher Bassett Benefit Administrators; Gallagher Bassett International Ltd.; Arthur J. Gallagher International, Inc.; Arthur J. Gallagher (UK) Limited; Arthur J. Gallagher & Co. (Bermuda) Limited; International Special Risk Services, Inc.; and Corporate Information Services. Arthur J. Gallagher operates through a network of approximately 140 offices located throughout the U.S. and five abroad. Founded in 1927; reincorporated in Delaware in 1972.

Directors (In addition to indicated officers)

T. Kimball Brooker
Jack M. Greenberg

Philip A. Marineau
James R. Wimmer

Officers (Directors*)

*Robert E. Gallagher, Chm.
*J. Patrick Gallagher, Jr., Pres. & C.E.O.
*John P. Gallagher, V. Chm.
 Bill G. Jensen, Sr. V.P.
*Walter F. McClure, Sr. V.P.
 Bette J. Brinkerhoff, V.P.
*John G. Campbell, V.P.
*Michael J. Cloherty, V.P.—Fin.
 Peter J. Durkalski, V.P.
 James W. Durkin, Jr., V.P.
 Nicholas M. Elsberg, V.P.
 Joseph W. Fahey, V.P.
 Frank M. Heffernan, Jr., V.P.

Clark W. Johnson, V.P.
Jack H. Lazzaro, V.P.
David R. Long, V.P.
David E. McGurn, Jr., V.P.
Richard J. McKenna, V.P.
George A. McWeeney, V.P.
Richard R. Rothman, V.P.
John D. Stancik, V.P.
Gary M. Van der Voort, V.P.
Warren G. Van der Voort, Jr., V.P.
Carl E. Fasig, Secy.
David B. Hoch, Cont.
Mark P. Strauch, Treas.
Christine D. Greb, Asst. Secy.

Consolidated Balance Sheet   As of December 31, 1994 (000 omitted)

Assets		Liabilities & Stockholders' Equity	
Current assets	$351,072	Current liabilities	$341,726
Net property, plant & equipment	20,012	Long-term debt	3,390
Marketable securities	37,836	Deferred items and other	9,263
Leveraged leases & other assets	34,294	liabilities	
Intangible assets--net	7,896	*Stockholders' equity	96,731
Total	$451,110	Total	$451,110

*14,784,000 shares common stock outstanding.

Consolidated Income Statement[a]

Years Ended Dec. 31	Thousands — — — —		Per Share — — — —		Common Stock Price Range Calendar Year
	Revenues	Net Income	Earnings	Cash Dividends	
1994	$356,377	$34,540	$2.17	$ .88	36-3/8 — 28-1/8
1993	329,263	29,446	1.79	.72	37-3/8 — 25-1/2
1992	299,685	23,923	1.50	.64	29-1/4 — 21
1991	273,806	19,516	1.20	.64	28-3/8 — 19
1990	262,086	21,584	1.33	.60	25 — 19-3/4

[a]The financial information for all periods prior to 1994 has been restated for significant acquisitions accounted for using the pooling-of-interests method.

Transfer Agent & Registrar:	Harris Trust and Savings Bank		
Outside Counsel:	Lord, Bissell & Brook	Traded (Symbol):	NYSE (AJG)
Investor Relations:	Michael J. Cloherty, V.P.—Fin.	Stockholders:	600
Mgt. Info. Svcs.:	Nicholas M. Elsberg, V.P.	Employees:	3,308
Auditors:	Ernst & Young LLP	Annual Meeting:	In May

First Chicago Guide

GATX Corporation

500 West Monroe Street, Chicago, Illinois 60661-3676
Telephone: (312) 621-6200

GATX Corporation is a holding company whose subsidiaries engage in the leasing and management of railroad tank cars and specialized freight cars; provide equipment and capital asset financing and related services; own and operate tank storage terminals, pipelines and related facilities; engage in Great Lakes shipping; and provide distribution and logistics support services, warehousing facilities, and related real estate services. Major subsidiaries include: General American Transportation Corporation, a tank car and specialized railcar lessor; GATX Terminals Corporation, an independent bulk liquid storage and pipeline company; GATX Financial Services, Inc., which, through its principal subsidiary, GATX Capital Corp., is one of the larger non-bank related financial service companies; American Steamship Company, which competes with other Great Lakes commercial fleets and with all steel companies which operate captive fleets; and GATX Logistics, Inc., which is one of the largest full-service third-party providers in North America of warehousing, distribution, and logistics support services. Incorporated in New York in 1916.

Directors (In addition to indicated officers)

Franklin A. Cole
James W. Cozad
James M. Denny
William C. Foote
Deborah M. Fretz

Richard A. Giesen
Miles L. Marsh
Charles Marshall
Michael E. Murphy

Officers (Directors*)

* James J. Glasser, Chm. & C.E.O.
* Ronald H. Zech, Pres. & C.O.O.
  David B. Anderson, V.P.—Corp. Dev., Gen. Coun. & Secy.

William L. Chambers, V.P.—Hum. Res.
David M. Edwards, V.P.—Fin. & C.F.O.
E. Paul Dunn, Jr., Treas.
Ralph L. O'Hara, Cont.

Consolidated Balance Sheet   As of December 31, 1994 (000 omitted)

Assets		Liabilities & Stockholders' Equity	
Current assets	$ 176,300	Current liabilities	$ 587,300
Net property, plant & equipment	2,192,300	Long-term debt	1,805,100
Other assets	1,282,100	Deferred items	595,900
		*Stockholders' equity	662,400
Total	$3,650,700	Total	$3,650,700

*19,894,636 shares common stock outstanding.

Consolidated Income Statement

Years Ended Dec. 31	Thousands — — — —		Per Share[a] — — —		Common Stock Price Range[a] Calendar Year
	Gross Income	Net Income	Earnings	Cash Dividends	
1994	$1,155,000	$ 91,500	$ 3.88	$1.50	44-5/8 — 38-1/4
1993	1,086,900	72,700	2.99	1.40	42-1/4 — 31-3/8
1992	1,019,100	(16,500)[b]	(1.53)[b]	1.30	33-3/4 — 24-1/4
1991	989,100	82,700	3.56	1.20	40-1/4 — 21-1/2
1990	870,400	82,900	3.61	1.10	35-3/4 — 17-5/8

[a]Adjusted to reflect a 2-for-1 stock split in May 1990.
[b]Includes a charge to reflect FAS 106 and FAS 109, resulting in a cumulative effect of $45,800,000 ($2.35 per share).

Transfer Agent & Registrar: Chemical Bank

General Counsel: David B. Anderson, V.P.

Investor Relations:
  George S. Lowman, Dir.—Commun.

Human Resources: William L. Chambers, V.P.

Mgt. Info. Svcs.:   Robert A. Kane, Dir.

Auditors: Ernst & Young LLP

Traded (Symbol):   NYSE, CSE, London SE (GMT)

Stockholders: 3,503

Employees: 5,800

Annual Meeting: In April

Gaylord Container Corporation

500 Lake Cook Road, Suite 400, Deerfield, Illinois 60015-4921
Telephone: (708) 405-5500

Gaylord Container Corporation manufactures and markets corrugated containers, corrugated sheets, containerboard, unbleached kraft paper, multiwall bags, and grocery bags and sacks. Facilities include three containerboard and paper mills, 14 corrugated container plants, three sheetfeeder plants, two multiwall bag facilities, two grocery bag and sack plants, one preprint linerboad plant, and marketing operations throughout the U.S. Gaylord serves more than 3,000 local and national account customers in the industrial, agricultural, commercial and consumer markets. The company's three paper mills use both virgin and recycled fiber to produce linerboard and unbleached kraft paper in a wide variety of grades and weights. Gaylord's corrugated container plants manufacture corrugated shipping containers, and such specialty products as label-laminated and precision die-cut boxes, point-of-purchase and display containers, solid fiber products, and bulk boxes. Gaylord's multiwall bag plants service the agricultural, food, pet supply, pet food, and plastics industries. Incorporated in Delaware in 1986.

Directors (In addition to indicated officer)

Frank E. Babb	David B. Hawkins	Richard S. Levitt
Norman H. Brown, Jr.	John Hawkinson	Ralph L. MacDonald, Jr.
Harve A. Ferrill	Warren J. Hayford	Thomas H. Stoner
John E. Goodenow		

Officers (Director*)

*Marvin A. Pomerantz, Chm. & C.E.O.
Dale E. Stahl, Pres. & C.O.O.
Daniel P. Casey, Exec.V.P., C.F.O. & Treas.
Lawrence G. Rogna, Sr. V.P.
Kathryn J. Chieger, V.P.—Corp. Aff.
Donald C. Devine, V.P.—Bag Oper.
Ray C. Dillon, V.P.—Mill Oper.

R. Bruce Grimm, V.P.—Primary Prods. Sales & Mktg.
Michael J. Keough, V.P.—Container Oper.
Robert E. Kramer, V.P.
E. Larry Mizell, V.P.—Bogalusa Mill
Jeffrey B. Park, V.P.—Cont.
David F. Tanaka, V.P., Gen. Coun. & Secy.

Consolidated Balance Sheet As of September 30, 1994 (000 omitted)

Assets		Liabilities & Stockholders' Equity	
Current assets	$206,700	Current liabilities	$135,100
Net property, plant & equipment	592,900	Long-term debt	696,800
Other assets	43,500	Deferred taxes	4,300
		Other liabilities	30,700
		*Stockholders' equity	(23,800)
Total	$843,100	Total	$843,100

*48,427,881 shares Class A common and 5,266,273 shares Class B common stock outstanding.

Consolidated Income Statement

Years Ended Abt. Sept. 30	Thousands — — — — Net Sales	Net Income[a]	Per Share — — — Earnings[a]	Cash Dividends	Common Stock Price Range[b] Calendar Year
1994	$784,400	$(84,000)	$(1.57)	$ .00	9-3/4 — 4-3/8
1993	733,500	130,200	2.61	.00	4-3/4 — 1-7/8
1992	722,800	(132,500)	(8.54)	.00	4-7/8 — 1-7/8
1991[c]	723,800	(180,300)	(11.68)	.00	5-7/8 — 2-3/8
1990	718,300	(23,200)	(1.47)	.00	9-1/4 — 2-1/2

[a]1993 includes an extraordinary gain of $201,500,000 ($4.04 per share) on the retirement of subordinated debt in connection with the financial restructuring; 1991 includes a charge of $101,200,000 ($6.56 per share) for an asset writedown.
[b]Class A common stock.
[c]The company consolidated the results of Gaylord Bag Partnership. In fiscal 1990, the company used the equity method of accounting for its investment in Gaylord Bag Partnership.

Transfer Agent & Registrar:	Harris Trust and Savings Bank		
General Counsel:	Kirkland & Ellis	Auditors:	Deloitte & Touche LLP
Investor Relations:	Kathryn J. Chieger, V.P.	Traded (Symbol):	AMEX (GCR)
		Stockholders:	598
Human Resources:	Lawrence G. Rogna, Sr. V.P.	Employees:	4,100
Mgt. Info. Svcs.:	Jim Adams, Dir.	Annual Meeting:	In February

General Binding Corporation

One GBC Plaza, Northbrook, Illinois 60062-4195
Telephone: (708) 272-3700

General Binding Corporation (GBC) designs, manufactures, and distributes a broad line of business machines and related supplies. Products manufactured include binding and laminating machines, paper shredders, and photo identification systems. GBC also manufactures consumable supply items, including plastic bindings; customized binders; laminating films; standard and specialty metal looseleaf elements; and plastic sheeting for covers and binders. GBC products are marketed under the GBC, Shredmaster, U.S. RingBinder, Bates, Sickinger, and VeloBind names. International operations are located in Australia, Austria, Belgium, Canada, France, Germany, India, Italy, Japan, Mexico, the Netherlands, New Zealand, Spain, Switzerland, and the United Kingdom. Subsidiaries include U.S. RingBinder Corp. In 1994, GBC acquired the Sickinger Company of Auburn Hills, Michigan. Incorporated in Delaware in 1947.

Directors (In addition to indicated officers)

Harry J. Bruce
James M. Denny
Theodore Dimitriou
Thomas V. Kalebic

Arthur C. Nielsen, Jr.
Warren R. Rothwell
Robert J. Stucker

Officers (Directors*)

*William N. Lane III, Chm.
*Govi C. Reddy, Pres. & C.E.O.
*Rudolph Grua, V. Chm.
Steven R. Baumhardt, Sr. V.P.—Int'l.
Walter M. Hebb, Sr. V.P.—Mktg. & Prod. Dev.
Elliott L. Smith, Sr. V.P.—N. Amer. Opers.
Eugene J. Angel, V.P. & Pres.—U.S.
  RingBinder Corp.

Govind K. Arora, V.P.—Mfg.
Thomas F. Gueth, V.P.—R&D
William P. Heffernan, V.P.—Bus. Tech.
Joseph J. LaPorte, V.P.—Corp. Rel.
John G. Lindroth, V.P.—Sales
Edward J. McNulty, V.P. & C.F.O.
Steven Rubin, V.P., Secy. & Gen. Coun.
Charles K. Shattuck, V.P.—Off. Prod.

Consolidated Balance Sheet As of December 31, 1994 (000 omitted)

Assets		Liabilities & Stockholders' Equity	
Current assets	$171,154	Current liabilities	$ 84,604
Net property, plant & equipment	65,530	Long-term debt	42,020
Other assets	47,594	Deferred income taxes	7,225
		Other liabilities	9,340
		*Stockholders' equity	141,089
Total	$284,278	Total	$284,278

*13,349,512 shares common and 2,398,275 shares Class B common stock outstanding.

Consolidated Income Statement

Years Ended Dec. 31	Thousands — — — —		Per Share — — — —		Common Stock
	Net Sales	Net Income[a]	Earnings[a]	Cash Dividends	Price Range Calendar Year
1994	$420,449	$15,703	$1.00	$ .41	22 — 14-3/8
1993	376,138	14,994	.95	.40	19-1/4 — 11-1/2
1992	368,643	16,380	1.04	.37	21-1/2 — 14-1/2
1991	311,199	12,599	.80	.33	20-1/2 — 10-3/4
1990	303,670	13,655	.86	.29	28-1/4 — 13

[a]From continuing operations.

Transfer Agent & Registrar: Harris Trust and Savings Bank

Corporate Counsel: Steven Rubin, V.P.

Investor Relations: Joseph J. LaPorte, V.P.

Human Resources: Joseph J. LaPorte, V.P.

Mgt. Info. Svcs.: Willaim P. Heffernan, V.P.

Auditors: Arthur Andersen LLP

Traded (Symbol): NASDAQ (GBND)

Stockholders: 828

Employees: 3,226

Annual Meeting: In May

General Employment Enterprises, Inc.

Oakbrook Terrace Tower, One Tower Lane, Suite 2100, Oakbrook Terrace, Illinois 60181-4600
Telephone: (708) 954-0400

General Employment Enterprises, Inc., provides contract temporary staffing and permanent placement services for business and industry. Essentially, the company finds people for jobs and jobs for people. Its 24 offices are located in major metropolitan and suburban business centers in 12 states. The company's wholly owned subsidiary, Triad Personnel Services, Inc., is principally engaged in the business of providing clients with data processing and technical employees for contract temporary assignments. The company markets its permanent placement services under the trade styles General Employment, Business Management Personnel, Craig Agency, and Omni One. Permanent job placements range from entry-level trainee to senior-level management positions, with the primary focus on the placement of computer, engineering, technical, and accounting personnel. Incorporated in Illinois in 1962.

Directors (In addition to indicated officers)

Sheldon Brottman
Leonard Chavin
Delain G. Danehey

Walter T. Kerwin, Jr.
Howard S. Wilcox

Officers (Directors*)

*Herbert F. Imhoff, Chm. & Pres.
*Herbert F. Imhoff, Jr., Exec V.P. & Gen. Coun.
Nancy C. Frohnmaier, V.P. & Corp. Secy.

Kent M. Yauch, Treas. & Cont.
John J. Derby, Sr. V.P.—Triad Personnel Services, Inc.

Consolidated Balance Sheet As of September 30, 1994 (000 omitted)

Assets		Liabilities & Stockholders' Equity	
Current assets	$3,561	Current liabilities	$2,343
Net property & equipment	347	Long-term obligations	550
Other assets	138	*Stockholders' equity	1,153
Total	$4,046	Total	$4,046

*1,829,823 shares common stock outstanding.

Consolidated Income Statement

Years Ended Sept. 30	Thousands — — — — Net Revenues	Net Income	Per Share[a] — — — Earnings	Cash Dividends	Common Stock Price Range[a] Calendar Year
1994	$14,212	$ 663	$ .34	$ .00	11-5/8 — 1-7/8
1993	10,865	61	.03	.00	2-7/8 — 1-5/8
1992	10,209	(605)	(.33)	.00	3-7/8 — 1
1991	13,005	(1,492)	(.82)	.00	3-3/8 — 1-1/4
1990	17,831	(11)	(.01)	.00	3-7/8 — 1-7/8

[a]Adjusted for a 15% stock dividend paid in November 1994.

Transfer Agent & Registrar: Continental Stock Transfer & Trust Co.

General Counsel:
 Herbert F. Imhoff, Jr., Exec. V.P.

Investor Relations: Nancy C. Frohnmaier, V.P.

Human Resources: S.L. Hubacek

Auditors: Ernst & Young LLP

Traded (Symbol): AMEX (JOB)

Stockholders: 1,170

Employees: 300

Annual Meeting: In February

General Instrument Corporation

181 West Madison Street, Chicago, Illinois 60602
Telephone: (312) 541-5000

General Instrument Corporation (GI) is a world leader in developing technology, systems, and product solutions for the interactive delivery of video, voice, and data. As a leader in digital television, GI is adapting and integrating its technology to deliver new and advanced services. GI offers complete digital compression and transmission systems — from the equipment that encodes and transmits the signal up to the satellite, to the intelligent set-top terminal in the consumer's home and everything in between. GI's analog and digital technologies are in use worldwide, making enriched forms of information and entertainment available to customers around the globe. In addition, GI's Power Semiconductor Division is a world-class provider of rectifiers and transient voltage suppressors. Incorporated in Delaware in 1990.

Directors (In addition to indicated officers)

John S. Brown
Lynn Forester
Nicholas C. Forstmann
Theodore J. Forstmann
Steven B. Klinsky

Morton H. Meyerson
J. Tracy O'Rourke
Felix G. Rohatyn
Paul G. Stern
Robert S. Strauss

Officers (Directors*)

*Daniel F. Akerson, Chm. & C.E.O.
*Richard S. Friedland, Pres. & C.O.O.
Paul J. Berzenski, V.P. & Cont.
Edward D. Breen, V.P.
Charles T. Dickson, V.P. & C.F.O.
Thomas A. Dumit, V.P., Gen. Coun. & Secy.
Ronald A. Ostertag, V.P. & Pres.—Power
  Semiconductor Div.

Laurence L. Osterwise, V.P. & Pres.—GI
  Communications Div.
Richard C. Smith, V.P.—Taxes & Treas.
*Frank M. Drendel, Pres./C.E.O.—CommScope,
  Inc.

Consolidated Balance Sheet As of December 31, 1994 (000 omitted)

Assets		Liabilities & Stockholders' Equity	
Current assets	$ 641,764	Current liabilities	$ 428,474
Net property, plant & equipment	343,868	Long-term debt	794,694
Other assets	1,123,319	Deferred items	21,990
		*Stockholders' equity	863,793
Total	$2,108,951	Total	$2,108,951

*122,220,089 shares common stock outstanding.

Consolidated Income Statement

Years Ended Dec. 31	Thousands — — — —		Per Share[a] — — — —		Common Stock Price Range[a] Calendar Year
	Net Sales	Net Income	Earnings	Cash Dividends	
1994	$2,036,323	$ 246,535	$ 2.00	$ .00	34-5/8 — 21-1/4
1993	1,392,522	90,583	.74	.00	30-1/8 — 11-5/8
1992	1,074,695	(52,993)[b]	(.54)[b]	.00	13 — 5-3/4[c]
1991[d]	928,826	(110,657)	(1.52)		

[a]Adjusted to reflect a 2-for-1 stock split in August 1994.
[b]Includes an extraordinary charge of $11,598,000 ($.12 per share).
[c]Initial public offering in June 1992.
[d]Unaudited pro forma for the 12 months ending December 31.

Transfer Agent & Registrar: Chemical Bank

Outside Counsel:
  Fried, Frank, Harris, Shriver & Jacobson

Investor Relations: Charles T. Dickson, V.P.

Auditors: Deloitte & Touche LLP

Traded (Symbol): NYSE (GIC)
Stockholders: 551
Employees: 12,300
Annual Meeting: In April

The Goodheart-Willcox Company, Inc.

123 West Taft Drive, South Holland, Illinois 60473-2089
Telephone: (708) 333-7200

The Goodheart-Willcox Company, Inc., publishes textbooks and workbooks for junior and senior high schools, vocational, technical and private trade schools, colleges and universities. Its books are also used for apprentice training, adult education, home study and do-it-yourselfers. The current catalogs list approximately 366 texts, workbooks, computer software supplements, and instructor's guides published by the company. The publishing activities of the company encompass the search for and development of authors in the preparation of their product, editing manuscripts, designing textbooks, and arranging for art work and illustrations, typesetting the manuscript, contracting for printing and binding, and marketing its textbooks. The company's subsidiary is G/W Investment Company, Inc. Incorporated in Delaware in 1972.

Directors (In addition to indicated officers)

Walter C. Brown, Ed.D
Robert C. DeBolt
Wilma Pitts Griffin, Ph.D.

Clois E. Kicklighter, Ed.D
Loraine J. Mix

Officers (Directors*)

*George A. Fischer, Chm.
*John F. Flanagan, Pres. & C.E.O.

Donald A. Massucci, V.P.—Admin. & Treas.
Dick G. Snyder, V.P.—Sales & Secy.

Consolidated Balance Sheet   As of April 30, 1994 (000 omitted)

Assets		Liabilities & Stockholders' Equity	
Current assets	$ 9,142	Current liabilities	$ 1,638
Property and equipment	702	Deferred income taxes	105
Other assets	1,292	Other liabilities	2,696
		*Stockholders' equity	6,697
Total	$11,136	Total	$11,136

*747,900 shares common stock outstanding.

Consolidated Income Statement

Years Ended April 30	Thousands — — — — Net Sales	Net Income[a]	Per Share — — — Earnings	Cash Dividends	Common Stock Price Range Fiscal Year
1994	$12,641	$1,357	$1.81	$ .70	20 — 16
1993	11,873	1,220	1.63	.60	26 — 18
1992	11,081	940	1.25	.60	25 — 18
1991	11,661	1,001	1.31	.60	27 — 25
1990	8,871	214	.28	.60	27-3/4 — 27

[a]1990 restated.

Transfer Agent & Registrar: The First National Bank of Chicago

General Counsel:
  Hedberg, Tobin, Flaherty & Whalen

Investor Relations: John F. Flanagan, Pres.

Human Resources: John F. Flanagan, Pres.

Mgt. Info. Svcs.:   Donald A. Massucci, V.P.

Auditors: Grant Thornton LLP
Traded (Symbol):   NASDAQ (GWOX)
Stockholders: 150
Employees: 50
Annual Meeting: In July

First Chicago Guide

W.W. Grainger, Inc.

5500 West Howard Street, Skokie, Illinois 60077-2699
Telephone: (708) 982-9000

W.W. Grainger, Inc., is a leading nationwide distributor of maintenance, repair, and operating supplies and related information to commercial, industrial, contractor, and institutional customers. The company's core branch-based business, Grainger, distributes air compressors, air-conditioning and refrigeration equipment and components, air tools and paint spraying equipment. Other products include: blowers, computer supplies, electric motors, fans, gas engine driven power plants, gearmotors, heating equipment and controls. Additional products are: hydraulic equipment, janitorial supplies, lighting fixtures and components, liquid pumps, material handling and storage equipment, motor controls, office equipment, outdoor equipment, plant and office maintenance equipment. An important selling tool, the General Catalog, lists more than 61,000 items. Grainger also is an important resource for both product and procurement process information. The company operates regional distribution centers in the Chicago area; Kansas City, Missouri; and Greenville County, South Carolina; zone distribution centers in Ontario, California; Atlanta, Georgia; Arlington, Texas; and Cranbury, New Jersey; and a network of 338 branches in all 50 states and Puerto Rico. The company's other businesses include Lab Safety Supply, a leader in business-to-business direct marketing of safety products, and Parts Company of America, a distributor of repair and replacement parts. Incorporated in Illinois in 1928.

Directors (In addition to indicated officers)

George R. Baker
Robert E. Elberson
Wilbur H. Gantz

John W. McCarter, Jr.
James D. Slavik

Harold B. Smith
Fred L. Turner

Officers (Directors*)

*David W. Grainger, Chm.
*Richard L. Keyser, Pres. & C.E.O.
*Jere D. Fluno, V. Chm.
James M. Baisley, Sr. V.P., Gen. Coun. & Secy.
Donald E. Bielinski, Sr. V.P.—Mktg. & Sales
John W. Slayton, Jr., Sr. V.P.—Prod. Mgt.
Edward C. Bender, V.P.
Barbara M. Chilson, V.P. & Pres.—Parts Co. of Amer.
Wesley M. Clark, V.P.—Field Opers. & Qual.
Timothy M. Ferrarell, V.P.—Prod. Line Dev.
Robert J. Gariano, Grp. V.P.
Raymond R. Greabe, V.P.—Personnel
Richard H. Hantke, V.P.—Distr. Oper.

Michael R. Kight, V.P. & Gen. Mgr.—Integr. Supply
Fred E. Loepp, V.P.—Prod. Line Dev.
P. Ogden Loux, V.P.—Fin.
Max C. Mielecki, V.P. — Mkt. Comm.
Micheal G. Murray, V.P.—Adm. Svcs.
Neal Ormond III, V.P.—Hum. Res.
Robert D. Pappano, V.P.—Fin. Rept./Inv. Rel.
Richard D. Quast, V.P.—Real Estate
John J. Rozwat, V.P. & Gen. Mgr.—Dir. Sales
James T. Ryan, V.P.—Info. Svcs.
John A. Schweig, V.P. & Gen. Mgr.—Dir. Mktg.
Peggy H. Stitch, V.P. & Pres.—Lab Safety Supply, Inc.
Paul J. Wallace, V.P.—Fin. Svcs.
Douglas E. Witt, V.P.—Nat. Accts.

Consolidated Balance Sheet As of December 31, 1994 (000 omitted)

Assets		Liabilities & Stockholders' Equity	
Current assets	$ 963,646	Current liabilities	$ 459,051
Net property, plant & equipment	469,142	Long-term debt	1,023
Other assets	101,963	Deferred items	15,177
		Other liabilities	26,695
		*Stockholders' equity	1,032,805
Total	$1,534,751	Total	$1,534,751

*50,749,681 shares common stock outctanding.

Consolidated Income Statement

Years Ended Dec. 31	Thousands — — — —		Per Share[a] — — — —		Common Stock Price Range[a] Calendar Year
	Net Sales	Net Income	Earnings	Cash Dividends	
1994	$3,023,076	$127,874[b]	$2.50[b]	$ .78	69-1/8 — 51-1/2
1993	2,628,398	148,447[c]	2.86[c]	.70	66-3/4 — 51-5/8
1992	2,364,421	137,242	2.58	.65	61 — 39
1991	2,077,235	127,737	2.37	.61	55-1/2 — 30-1/4
1990	1,935,209	126,775	2.31	.57	39-1/4 — 27-1/4

[a]Adjusted to reflect a 2-for-1 stock split effective in May 1991.
[b]Includes restructuring charges of $49,779,000 ($.97 per share).
[c]Includes a charge to reflect FAS 106, FAS 109 and FAS 112, resulting in a cumulative effect of $820,000 ($.02 per share).

Transfer Agent & Registrar: The First National Bank of Boston

Corporate Counsel: Lord, Bissell & Brook

Investor Relations: Robert D. Pappano, V.P.

Human Resources: Neal Ormond III, V.P.

Mgt. Info. Svcs.: James T. Ryan, V.P.

Auditors: Grant Thornton LLP
Traded (Symbol): NYSE, CSE (GWW)
Stockholders: 2,200
Employees: 11,343
Annual Meeting: Last Wednesday in April

Great American Management and Investment, Inc.

Two North Riverside Plaza, Chicago, Illinois 60606
Telephone: (312) 648-5656

Great American Management and Investment, Inc., is a diversified holding company. Major subsidiaries include: Eagle Industries, Inc., a diversified holding company with businesses producing capital goods and other products serving industrial, commercial, and consumer markets; Falcon Building Products, Inc.; and The Vigoro Corporation (formerly KAC Holdings, Inc.), 30 percent-owned, a holding company for three agricultural chemical and fertilizer companies. Great American also has investments in real estate; mortgage loans; real estate syndications; and a manufacturer of mobile homes. Incorporated in Delaware in 1979.

Directors   (In addition to indicated officers)

Mitchell R. Cohen
Bradbury Dyer III
David A. Gardner
William K. Hall

F. Philip Handy
John M. Pasquesi
Sheli Z. Rosenberg
Joseph P. Sullivan

Officers   (Directors*)

*Samuel Zell, Chm.
*Rod F. Dammeyer, Pres. & C.E.O.
Gus J. Athas, Sr. V.P. & Gen. Coun.

Sam A. Cottone, Sr. V.P. & C.F.O.
Susan S. Obuchowski, Secy.

Consolidated Balance Sheet   As of December 31, 1994 (000 omitted)

Assets		Liabilities & Stockholders' Equity	
Current assets	$ 285,700	Current liabilities	$ 194,300
Net property, plant & equipment	185,100	Long-term debt	378,000
Other assets	564,200	Other liabilities	213,600
		*Stockholders' equity	249,100
Total	$1,035,000	Total	$1,035,000

*11,178,586 shares common stock outstanding.

Consolidated Income Statement[a]

Years Ended Dec. 31	Thousands — — — —		Per Share — — — —		Common Stock Price Range Calendar Year
	Net Sales & Revenues	Net Income[b]	Earnings[b]	Cash Dividends	
1994	$1,010,300	$ 49,000[c]	$ 4.38[c]	$ .00	34-1/4 — 29
1993	881,200	(100,200)[d]	(9.03)[d]	.00	33-1/2 — 25-1/2
1993[e]	385,700	(79,700)	(7.18)	.00	
1992[f]	813,500	29,600	2.67	.00	30-1/2 — 23-1/8
1991[f]	743,300	37,700	3.40	.84	32 — 25

[a]Restated to give retroactive effect to businesses accounted for as discontinued operations.
[b]Available to common stockholders.
[c]Includes a loss of $24,000,000 ($2.14 per share) from discontinued operations and a loss of $16,300,000 ($1.45 per share) from early retirement of debt.
[d]Includes a loss of $87,300,000 ($7.87 per share) from discontinued operations, a loss of $14,200,000 ($1.28 per share) from early retirement of debt, and a gain of $5,100,000 ($.46 per share) to reflect adoption of FAS 109.
[e]Five months ended December 31.
[f]July 31 yearend.

Transfer Agent & Registrar: Chemical Trust Co. of California

General Counsel: Gus J. Athas, Sr. V.P.

Investor Relations:
  Susan S. Obuchowski, Secy.

Auditors: Arthur Andersen LLP

Traded (Symbol):   NASDAQ (GAMI)

Stockholders: 900

Employees: 7,000

Annual Meeting: In June

First Chicago Guide

Growth Environmental, Inc.

2211 South York Road, Suite 115, Oak Brook, Illinois 60521
Telephone: (708) 990-2751

Growth Environmental, Inc., provides consulting, engineering, remediation, and analytical laboratory services to assist its clients in complying with environmental laws and regulations, such as those concerning leaking underground storage tanks. The company's environmental services range from the initial assessment and evaluation of sites for contamination by hazardous substances through the design and implementation of remediation systems to control, treat or remove contamination. Incorporated in Illinois in 1984 as Nutri-Cheese Co.; present name adopted in 1991.

Director   (In addition to indicated officers)

Leo C. Culligan

Officers   (Directors*)

*Mervyn C. Phillips, Jr., Chm.
*Alvin K. Eaton, Pres. & C.E.O.
*Gary P. Adams, V.P.
Michael N. Marsh, V.P.
Timothy E. Meyer, V.P., C.F.O. & Treas.

Darryl L. Peake, V.P. & Gen. Coun.
*David B. Schuurman, V.P.
*Joseph J. Lickteig, Secy.
David W. Stasiewicz, Cont.

Consolidated Balance Sheet   As of December 31, 1994 (000 omitted)

Assets		Liabilities & Stockholders' Equity	
Current assets	$15,068	Current liabilities	$ 9,695
Net property, plant & equipment	4,780	Long-term debt	6,717
Other assets	7,480	Other liabilities	31
		*Stockholders' equity	10,885
Total	$27,328	Total	$27,328

*5,187,835 shares common stock outstanding.

Consolidated Income Statement

Years Ended Dec. 31	Thousands — — — —		Per Share[a] — — — —		Common Stock Price Range[ab] Calendar Year
	Revenues	Net Income[c]	Earnings	Cash Dividends	
1994	$19,920	$ 349	$ .07	$ .00	4-5/8 — 3
1993[d]	7,942	448	.16	.00	3-5/8 — 1
1992[d]	2,213	(595)	(.45)	.00	4 — 1
1991[d]	432	351	.33		

[a]Adjusted to reflect a 1-for-2 reverse stock split in July 1993.
[b]Trading commenced on NASDAQ, November 10, 1993, the date of the stock offering.
[c]Attributable to common shares.
[d]Restated.

Transfer Agent & Registrar: Illinois Stock Transfer Co.

General Counsel:	Darryl L. Peake, V.P.	Auditors:	Deloitte & Touche LLP
Investor Relations:	Darryl L. Peake, V.P.	Traded (Symbol):	NASDAQ (GCER)
Human Resources:	Darryl L. Peake, V.P.	Stockholders:	1,585
		Employees:	275
Mgt. Info. Svcs.:	Timothy E. Meyer, V.P.	Annual Meeting:	In June

HA-LO Industries, Inc.

5980 Touhy Avenue, Niles, Illinois 60714
Telephone: (708) 647-2300

HA-LO Industries, Inc., is a distributor in the specialty and premium advertising products industry. The company's revenue base largely comprises Fortune 500 companies, professional sports teams, and other organizations with high name recognition. Specialty and premium advertising products are generally articles of merchandise imprinted or otherwise customized with an advertiser's name, logo or message, and used by the advertiser for marketing, sales incentives and awards, and development of goodwill for a targeted audience. Because such products are designed to be useful to the recipient, messages imprinted on these products enjoy repeated exposure. Examples of these products include jackets, hats, T-shirts, calendars, pens, coffee mugs and key chains, as well as more upscale items such as crystalware and desk accessories. The company functions as a single source to meet its customers' needs for specialty and premium advertising products. HA-LO utilizes its in-house art and production departments to assist its customers in creating innovative specialty and premium programs. Incorporated in Illinois in 1986.

Directors   (In addition to indicated officers)

Thomas Herskovits
Jordan R. Katz
Marshall J. Katz

Dominic M. Mangone
Neil A. Ramo
Marc S. Simon

Officers   (Directors*)

* Lou Weisbach, Chm., Pres. & C.E.O.
* David C. Robbins, Exec. V.P.

Barbara G. Berman, V.P.
* Richard A. Magid, V.P.—Fin., Treas. & C.F.O.

Consolidated Balance Sheet   As of December 31, 1994 (000 omitted)

Assets		Liabilities & Stockholders' Equity	
Current assets	$27,205	Current liabilities	$13,542
Net property, plant & equipment	1,886	Long-term debt	11,960
Other assets	7,038	Deferred items	1,739
		*Stockholders' equity	8,888
Total	$36,129	Total	$36,129

*4,369,402 shares common stock outstanding.

Consolidated Income Statement

Years Ended Dec. 31	Thousands — — — — Net Sales	Net Income[b]	Per Share[a] — — — — Earnings[b]	Cash Dividends	Common Stock Price Range[a] Calendar Year
1994	$68,603	$ 1,288	$ .30	$ .00	7-3/4 — 5
1993	35,717	224	.05	.00	7 — 3-5/8
1992	23,505	467	.16	.72	7-1/2 — 5-1/2
1991	22,423	839	.30	.00	
1990	17,468	(66)	(.02)	.00	

[a]Adjusted to reflect the 2,776.428-for-1 stock split effective September 1, 1992.
[b]Pro forma 1992-90. HA-LO elected to be treated as an S corporation for federal income tax purposes through the IPO completed November 4, 1992. Accordingly, the company was not subject to federal income taxes for such periods. Pro forma net income includes a provision for federal and state taxes at an effective rate of 38%.

Transfer Agent & Registrar:	Harris Trust and Savings Bank		
General Counsel:	Neal Gerber & Eisenberg	Traded (Symbol):	NASDAQ (HALO)
Investor Relations:	Richard A. Magid, V.P.	Stockholders:	680
Human Resources:	Sabina Filipovic	Employees:	202
Auditors:	Arthur Andersen LLP	Annual Meeting:	In June

Hartmarx Corporation

101 North Wacker Drive, Chicago, Illinois 60606-7389
Telephone: (312) 372-6300

Hartmarx Corporation is the holding company for Hart Schaffner & Marx and other subsidiaries, manufacturing and marketing quality clothing, including men's suits, sportcoats, slacks, men's and women's sportswear, including golfwear, and women's career apparel. In addition to Hart Schaffner & Marx, men's apparel is sold under the following labels: Hickey-Freeman, Graham & Gunn, Karl Lagerfeld, Pierre Cardin, Society Brand, Tommy Hilfiger, Austin Reed, Henry Grethel, Jack Nicklaus, Bobby Jones, Gieves & Hawkes, Perry Ellis, Daniel Hechter, Nicklaus, Fumagalli's, Nino Cerruti, KM by Krizia, Confezioni Riserva, Racquet Club, Allyn St. George, Sansabelt, Kuppenheimer, John Alexander, and J.G. Hook. Women's apparel is sold under the following labels: Barrie Pace, Austin Reed, Suburbans, Nicklaus for women, and Bobby Jones for women. Hartmarx subsidiaries operate 22 apparel manufacturing and distribution facilities in 11 states. Kuppenheimer is a manufacturer of popular-priced men's tailored clothing and operates approximately 92 retail stores. The company's Trans-Apparel Group subsidiary (formerly Jaymar-Ruby) also operates nine Sansabelt shops. In May 1995, Hartmarx agreed to sell its Kuppenheimer subsidiary. Incorporated in Delaware in 1983.

Directors   (In addition to indicated officers)

A. Robert Abboud	Donald P. Jacobs	Talat M. Othman
Letitia Baldrige	Miles L. Marsh	Stuart L. Scott
Jeffrey A. Cole	Charles Marshall	Sam F. Segnar
Raymond F. Farley	Charles K. Olson	

Officers   (Directors*)

*Elbert O. Hand, Chm. & C.E.O.
*Homi B. Patel, Pres. & C.O.O.
Mary D. Allen, Exec. V.P., Gen. Coun. & Secy.
Wallace L. Rueckel, Exec. V.P. & C.F.O.
Glenn R. Morgan, Sr. V.P.—Fin./Admin. & Chf. Acct. Off.

Frank A. Brenner, V.P.—Mkt. Services
James E. Condon, V.P.—Long-Term Plan. & Inv. Rel.
Linda J. Valentine, V.P.—Compensation & Benefits
Steven R. Davison, Treas.
Andrew A. Zahr, Cont.

Consolidated Balance Sheet   As of November 30, 1994 (000 omitted)

Assets		Liabilities & Stockholders' Equity	
Current assets	$312,437	Current liabilities	$ 96,748
Net property, plant & equipment	51,543	Long-term debt	167,085
Other assets	28,220	*Stockholders' equity	128,367
Total	$392,200	Total	$392,200

*32,477,800 shares common stock outstanding.

Consolidated Income Statement

Years Ended Nov. 30	Thousands — — — — Net Sales	Net Income[a]	Per Share — — — Earnings[a]	Cash Dividends	Common Stock Price Range Calendar Year
1994	$ 717,706	$ 16,148	$ .50	$ .00	7-3/8 — 5
1993	731,980	6,220	.20	.00	8-1/4 — 5-1/8
1992	1,053,949	(220,245)	(8.59)	.00	8-5/8 — 3
1991	1,215,310	(38,365)	(1.74)	.60	13-1/4 — 6-7/8
1990	1,295,840	(61,545)	(3.11)	.90	19-7/8 — 5-1/2

[a]1994 includes an extraordinary charge, net of tax benefit, of $3,862,000 ($.12 per share); 1992 includes an aftertax restructuring charge of $190,800,000 ($7.44 per share); 1991 includes an aftertax retail consolidation charge of $8,900,000 ($.40 per share); and 1990 includes an aftertax restructuring charge of $51,000,000 ($2.59 per share).

Transfer Agent & Registrar:	The First National Bank of Chicago; First Chicago Trust Co. of New York		
General Counsel:	Mary D. Allen, Exec. V.P.	Traded (Symbol):	CSE, NYSE (HMX)
Investor Relations:	James E. Condon, V.P.	Stockholders:	6,900
Human Resources:	Linda J. Valentine, V.P.	Employees:	11,000
Auditors:	Price Waterhouse LLP	Annual Meeting:	In April

HealthCare COMPARE Corp.

3200 Highland Avenue, Downers Grove, Illinois 60515-1223
Telephone: (708) 241-7900

HealthCare COMPARE Corp. is an independent provider of health care utilization review and cost management services. These services control a client's health care costs by reducing unnecessary hospital admissions and lengths of stay — and by monitoring the medical necessity and appropriateness of other health care services. AFFORDABLE Health Care Concepts, a wholly owned subsidiary, negotiates medical provider prices in order to develop and maintain preferred provider networks for the exclusive use of its clients. In addition, AFFORDABLE collects and analyzes health care cost data. The company's current clients include corporate employers, group health insurance carriers, third party administrators, government employee groups, unions and trusts, HMO's, and worker's compensation carriers. Incorporated in Delaware in 1982.

Directors (In addition to indicated officers)

Robert J. Becker, M.D.
Michael J. Boskin, Ph.D.
Robert S. Colman

J. Patrick Foley
Burton W. Kanter
David E. Simon

Officers (Directors*)

*Thomas J. Pritzker, Chm.
*James C. Smith, Pres. & C.E.O.
*Daniel S. Brunner, Exec. V.P.—Gov't. Aff.
 Mary Anne Carpenter, Exec. V.P.—Clinical
 Opers. & Claims Admin.

Patrick G. Dills, Exec. V.P.—Managed Care Sales
*Ronald H. Galowich, Exec. V.P., Secy. & Gen.
 Coun.
Edward L. Wristen, Exec. V.P.—Risk Prods.
Joseph E. Whitters, V.P.—Fin. & C.F.O.

Consolidated Balance Sheet   As of December 31, 1994 (000 omitted)

Assets		Liabilities & Stockholders' Equity	
Current assets	$163,070	Current liabilities	$ 15,452
Net property, plant & equipment	45,300	*Stockholders' equity	199,557
Other assets	6,639		
Total	$215,009	Total	$215,009

*34,201,826 shares common stock outstanding.

Consolidated Income Statement[a]

Years Ended Dec. 31	Thousands — — — —		Per Share[b] — — — —		Common Stock Price Range[b] Calendar Year
	Revenues	Net Income	Earnings	Cash Dividends	
1994	$186,606	$50,669	$1.45	$ .00	34-3/8 — 15-1/2
1993	157,650	38,471	1.08	.00	31-7/8 — 10-1/2
1992	133,501	18,116	.51	.00	43-1/4 — 25
1991	101,345	17,867	.51	.00	40-1/2 — 7-1/2
1990	62,795	8,568	.26	.00	9-3/8 — 2-5/8

[a]A wholly owned subsidiary of the company merged with Occupational-Urgent Care Health Systems, Inc. in February 1992. The transaction was accounted for as a pooling of interests. Therefore, financial statements have been restated to include the accounts of OUCH. In connection with the merger, the company recorded in 1992 a one-time charge of $16,000,000 for costs and expenses incurred by the company and OUCH. As a result of this charge, the company's net income in 1992 was reduced by $11,500,000 ($.33 per share).
[b]Adjusted to reflect 2-for-1 stock splits in June 1991 and December 1990.

Transfer Agent & Registrar:	LaSalle National Bank		
Corporate Counsel:	Neal Gerber & Eisenberg	Auditors:	Deloitte & Touche LLP
Investor Relations:	Joseph E. Whitters, V.P.	Traded (Symbol):	NASDAQ (HCCC)
		Stockholders:	15,000
Human Resources:	Nancy Zambon, Dir.	Employees:	1,500
Mgt. Info. Svcs.:	Ron Boeving, V.P.	Annual Meeting:	In May

Heartland Partners, L.P.

547 West Jackson Boulevard, Suite 1510, Chicago, Illinois 60661
Telephone: (312) 294-0440

Heartland Partners, L.P., engages in the ownership, development, leasing, and sale of real estate properties. Heartland was organized by Chicago Milwaukee Corporation, an open-end, management investment company. Milwaukee Land Company is the general partner of Heartland. Incorporated as a Delaware limited partnership in 1988.

Directors/Milwaukee Land Company[a]

Robert S. Davis
Jack Nash

Ezra K. Zilkha

[a]Milwaukee Land Company is the general partner of Heartland Partners, L.P.

Officers/CMC Heartland Partners[b]

Clarence G. Frame, Chm.
Edwin Jacobson, Pres. & C.E.O.
Lawrence S. Adelson, V.P.—Gen. Coun.
Richard Brandstatter, V.P.—Cont.

Wayne J. Delfino, V.P.—Dev.
Leon F. Fiorentino, V.P.—Fin., Secy. & Treas.
James G. Righeimer, V.P.—Sales & Prop. Mgt.
David L. Kozisek, Asst. Treas.

[b]CMC Heartland Partners is an operating general partnership owned 99.99% by Heartland and .01% by Milwaukee Land Company, which is the general partner of Heartland.

Consolidated Balance Sheet   As of December 31, 1994 (000 omitted)

Assets		Liabilities & Partners' Capital	
Cash & cash equivalents	$ 8,691	Accounts payable	$ 1,031
Net property, plant & equipment	20,552	Accrued liabilities	1,324
Other assets	1,000	Allowance for claims & liabilities	1,895
		Other liabilities	680
		*Partners' capital	25,313
Total	$30,243	Total	$30,243

*2,142,438 Class A limited partner units outstanding.

Consolidated Income Statement

Years Ended Dec. 31	Thousands — — — — Net Revenues	Net Income	Per Share — — — Earnings	Cash Dividends	Common Stock Price Range Calendar Year
1994[a]	$3,498	$(2,608)	$(1.20)	$ .00	14-5/8 — 10-1/2
1993	7,304	(38)	(.02)	.00	14-5/8 — 7-3/4
1992	6,377	(572)	(.26)	.00	11 — 7-1/4
1991	5,841	(769)	(.35)	.00	11 — 6-5/8
1990[b]	3,878	686	.32	.00	14-7/8 — 6-1/4[c]

[a]Includes a loss of $462,000 on the sale of a plant.
[b]For the period June 28, 1990, to December 31, 1990.
[c]Spinoff of Heartland Partners, L.P., into independent publicly held limited partnership completed June 20, 1990. Unit price range is for the period June 20, 1990, to December 31, 1990.

Transfer Agent & Registrar: Norwest Bank Minnesota, N.A.

Investor Relations: Leon F. Fiorentino, V.P.

Human Resources: Diane Barango

Auditors: Ernst & Young LLP

Traded (Symbol):   AMEX (HTL)
Stockholders: 741
Employees: 25
Annual Meeting: As set by General Partner

Helene Curtis Industries, Inc.

325 North Wells Street, Chicago, Illinois 60610-4713
Telephone: (312) 661-0222

Helene Curtis Industries, Inc., is the holding company for Helene Curtis, Inc., and has two strategic business units: Helene Curtis North America and Helene Curtis International. Helene Curtis North America manufactures and sells Helene Curtis consumer and professional salon products throughout the United States, Canada, and Mexico. Brand name consumer products — such as Suave, Finesse, Salon Selectives, Vibrance, and Degree — are sold through supermarkets, drug stores, and mass merchandisers. Professional brands — such as Quantum permanent wave products — are sold for beauty salon use and for retail to salon clients. Helene Curtis International sells Helene Curtis consumer and professional products in more than 100 countries, including subsidiary operations in Australia, Japan, New Zealand, Scandinavia, the United Kingdom, and Italy. Incorporated in Delaware in 1984.

Directors (In addition to indicated officers)

Marshall L. Burman
Frank W. Considine

Abbie J. Smith, Ph.D.
John C. Stetson

Officers (Directors*)

*Gerald S. Gidwitz, Chm.
*Ronald J. Gidwitz, Pres. & C.E.O.
*Joseph L. Gidwitz, V. Chm.
*Michael Goldman, Exec. V.P. & C.O.O.
*Gilbert P. Smith, Exec. V.P.
*Charles G. Cooper, Sr. V.P.
Colin J. Morgan, Sr. V.P.
Robert K. Niles, Sr. V.P.
Eugene Zeffren, Sr. V.P.

Thomas J. Gildea, V.P. & Chf. Info. Off.
Lawrence A. Gyenes, V.P. & C.F.O.
Robert G. Kelly, V.P.
V. James Marino, V.P.
Mary J. Oyer, V.P. & Cont.
Jack D. Pogue, V.P.
Robert Sack, V.P.
Roy A. Wentz, V.P., Secy. & Gen. Coun.
Arthur A. Schneider, Treas.

Consolidated Balance Sheet   As of February 28, 1995 (000 omitted)

Assets		Liabilities & Stockholders' Equity	
Current assets	$406,167	Current liabilities	$253,582
Net property, plant & equipment	215,336	Long-term debt	137,248
Other assets	25,329	Deferred income taxes	11,686
		Other liabilities	23,898
		*Stockholders' equity	220,418
Total	$646,832	Total	$646,832

*6,809,621 shares common and 3,060,529 shares Class B common stock outstanding.

Consolidated Income Statement[a]

Years Ended Abt. Feb. 28	Thousands — — — — Net Sales	Net Income	Per Share — — — Earnings	Cash Dividends[b]	Common Stock Price Range Fiscal Year
1995	$1,265,600	$19,169	$2.02	$ .24	36-3/8 — 22-3/4
1994	1,187,081	12,942[c]	1.37[c]	.24	43-3/4 — 24-7/8
1993	1,167,819	22,109	2.33	.24	47-3/8 — 30-1/4
1992	1,019,911	19,236	2.04	.20	43-3/4 — 26-1/2
1991	867,708	6,502	.70	.20	28-3/8 — 20

[a]From continuing operations.
[b]Excludes Class B common stock.
[c]Includes a charge to reflect FAS 106, resulting in a cumulative effect of $1,351,000 ($.14 per share).

Transfer Agent & Registrar: Harris Trust and Savings Bank

General Counsel:	Roy A. Wentz, V.P.	Auditors:	Coopers & Lybrand L.L.P.
Investor Relations:	Mary J. Oyer, V.P. & Cont.	Traded (Symbol):	NYSE (HC)
		Stockholders:	1,516
Human Resources:	Robert K. Niles, Sr. V.P.	Employees:	3,400
Mgt. Info. Svcs.:	Thomas J. Gildea, V.P.	Annual Meeting:	In June

First Chicago Guide

Heritage Financial Services, Inc.

17500 South Oak Park Avenue, Tinley Park, Illinois 60477
Telephone: (708) 532-8000

Heritage Financial Services, Inc., is a bank holding company for Heritage Bank, Blue Island, which has 13 banking locations in the southwestern suburbs of Chicago; and Heritage Trust Company, Tinley Park. As a commercial banking institution, Heritage Bank serves a number of diverse light manufacturing and service businesses as well as provides a broad range of banking services to retail customers. Heritage Financial Services has centralized a number of functions to provide a comprehensive system of support services for all of its locations. Reincorporated in Illinois in 1984 as the successor to County Bankshares, Inc.

Directors (In addition to indicated officers)

John J. Gallagher
Lael W. Mathis
Jack Payan
Arthur E. Sieloff

John L. Sterling
Chester Stranczek
Arthur G. Tichenor
Dominick J. Velo

Officers (Directors*)

*Richard T. Wojcik, Chm. & C.E.O.
*Frederick J. Sampias, Pres.

*Ronald P. Groebe, Sr. Exec. V.P. & Secy.
Paul A. Eckroth, Exec. V.P. & Treas.

Consolidated Balance Sheet As of December 31, 1994 (000 omitted)

Assets		Liabilities & Stockholders' Equity	
Net loans	$516,095	Total deposits	$823,590
Cash & due from banks	36,870	Securities sold	33,018
Federal funds sold & interest-bearing deposits	49,286	Notes payable	6,500
		Other liabilities	6,631
Securities, held-to-maturity	236,810	*Stockholders' equity	83,111
Securities, available-for-sale	71,478		
Net property, plant & equipment	17,079		
Other assets	25,232		
Total	$952,850	Total	$952,850

*7,915,972 shares common stock outstanding.

Consolidated Income Statement

Years Ended Dec. 31	Thousands — — — —		Per Share[a] — — — —		Common Stock
	Total Income	Net Income	Earnings	Cash Dividends	Price Range[a] Calendar Year
1994	$66,645	$12,417	$1.50	$ .36	19-3/4 — 15-3/4
1993	61,360	11,025	1.34	.32	17-1/2 — 12-3/4
1992	60,697	9,618	1.18	.30	14 — 10-1/4
1991	60,686	7,754	.96	.28	11-3/4 — 6-3/4
1990	61,063	6,197	.76	.25	10-3/4 — 5-3/4

[a]Adjusted to reflect a 2-for-1 stock split in April 1992.

Transfer Agent & Registrar: Harris Trust and Savings Bank

Corporate Counsel: Albert A. Stroka

Investor Relations:
Paul A. Eckroth, Exec. V.P. & Treas.

Human Resources: Karen Myers, Dir.

Mgt. Info. Svcs.: Linda Duggan, Dir.

Auditors: Arthur Andersen LLP

Traded (Symbol): NASDAQ (HERS)

Stockholders: 825

Employees: 485

Annual Meeting: In April

Hinsdale Financial Corporation

One Grant Square, Hinsdale, Illinois 60521
Telephone: (708) 323-1776

Hinsdale Financial Corporation is a holding company for Hinsdale Federal Bank for Savings. The bank is a federal savings bank chartered under the authority of the Office of Thrift Supervision. Originally organized in 1934, the bank is a community-oriented financial institution that conducts its business through 10 retail banking offices located in DuPage County and western Cook County, Illinois. The bank is principally engaged in the business of attracting retail deposits from the general public and investing those funds in mortgage loans and mortgage-backed securities, secured primarily by one- to four-family residential real estate, consumer loans, and investment securities. Hinsdale Financial Corporation was recently organized by the bank for the purpose of acquiring all of the capital stock of the bank issued in the conversion to a federally chartered stock savings bank from a federally chartered mutual savings bank. In April 1995, Hinsdale Financial entered into a letter of intent to purchase Preferred Mortgage Associates, LTD., a mortgage brokerage company. Incorporated in Delaware in 1992.

Directors   (In addition to indicated officer)

William R. Rybak, Chm.
Thomas R. Anderson
Howard R. Jones

Russell F. Stephens, Jr.
Donald E. Sveen

Officers   (Director*)

*Kenne P. Bristol, Pres. & C.E.O.
 Richard A. Hojnicki, Exec. V.P. & C.F.O.

Andrew W. Malawy, Exec. V.P. & Secy.

Consolidated Balance Sheet   As of September 30, 1994 (000 omitted)

Assets		Liabilities & Stockholders' Equity	
Cash & cash equivalents	$ 20,385	Deposits	$419,436
Investment securities	22,734	Borrowings	166,920
Mortgage-backed securities	30,701	Deferred taxes	2,704
Loans, net	544,284	Other liabilities	7,513
Other assets	25,185	*Stockholders' equity	46,716
Total	$643,289	Total	$643,289

*2,118,543 shares common stock outstanding.

Consolidated Income Statement[a]

Years Ended Sept. 30	Thousands — — — — — Total Income	Net Income	Per Share — — — — Earnings	Cash Dividends	Common Stock Price Range Calendar Year
1994	$42,110	$ 4,716	$2.11	$ .00	25-3/4— 19-3/4
1993	39,820	4,598	2.06	.00	23-1/2— 15-1/2
1992	45,051	(1,946)[bc]	.43[d]	.00	17-1/4— 11-1/4[e]
1991	58,755	(21,464)[f]			
1990	61,613	(785)			

[a]1991-90 financial information is for Hinsdale Federal Bank for Savings, a wholly owned subsidiary of Hinsdale Financial Corporation.
[b]Includes a gain to reflect FAS 109, resulting in a cumulative effect of $2,102,000.
[c]The remaining carrying value of goodwill was charged to expense.
[d]Based upon net income from July 7 through September 30, 1992.
[e]Initial public offering in July 1992.
[f]The bank recorded a writedown of goodwill of approximately $27,600,000 due to the recent enactment of FIRREA and changing economic conditions in the thrift industry.

Transfer Agent & Registrar: Harris Trust and Savings Bank

Corporate Counsel:
  Gomberg, Sharfman, Gold and Ostler, P.C.

Investor Relations:
  Richard A. Hojnicki, Exec. V.P.

Human Resources: Margaret Perfetto

Mgt. Info. Svcs.:
  Richard A. Hojnicki, Exec. V.P.

Auditors: KPMG Peat Marwick LLP

Traded (Symbol):   NASDAQ (HNFC)

Stockholders: 485

Employees: 257

Annual Meeting: In February

HomeCorp, Inc.

1107 East State Street, P.O. Box 4779, Rockford, Illinois 61110-4779
Telephone: (815) 987-2200

HomeCorp, Inc., is the holding company for HomeBanc, a federal savings bank, one of northern Illinois' oldest financial institutions. HomeCorp was formed in 1989 as part of the conversion from mutual to stock ownership of HomeBanc. The bank operates 10 full-service offices in northern Illinois, including six in Rockford and two each in Freeport and Dixon. HomeBanc serves its customers with a wide range of contemporary retail banking products. Mortgage and consumer installment lending are emphasized, as well as financing and investment services for small business. Stock, bond and annuity sales are promoted through a relationship with INVEST Financial Corporation. Incorporated in Delaware in 1989.

Directors (In addition to indicated officers)

Karl H. Erickson, Chm.
Marvin E. Johnson, V. Chm.
Robert C. Hauser
Adam A. Jahns

Larry U. Larson
Richard W. Malmgren
David R. Rydell

Officers (Directors*)

*C. Steven Sjogren, Pres. & C.E.O.
*John R. Perkins, Exec. V.P. & C.F.O.

*Wesley E. Lindberg, Secy.
Dirk J. Meminger, Treas. & Chf. Acct. Officer

Consolidated Balance Sheet As of December 31, 1994 (000 omitted)

Assets		Liabilities & Stockholders' Equity	
Total cash & cash equivalents	$ 17,983	Deposits	$307,605
Investment securities	14,837	Other liabilities	3,778
Securities held for sale	7,022	*Stockholders' equity	19,029
Mortgage-backed securities	28,431		
Loans receivable, net	244,860		
Other assets	17,279		
Total	$330,412	Total	$330,412

*1,121,971 shares common stock outstanding.

Consolidated Income Statement

Years Ended Dec. 31	Thousands — — — — Net Sales	Net Income	Per Share[a] — — — Earnings	Cash Dividends	Common Stock Price Range[ab] Calendar Year
1994	$23,601	$(3,712)[c]	$(3.21)[c]	$ .00	18-1/2 — 9-3/4
1993	24,406	1,606[d]	1.39[d]	.00	15-1/2 — 10-3/8
1992	28,330	1,641	1.43	.00	10-1/2 — 5-3/8
1991	33,515	2,099	1.87	.00	11 — 8-1/2
1990	37,521	3,823	5.19		

[a]Adjusted to reflect a 3-for-2 stock split in March 1993.
[b]Initial public offering in June 1990.
[c]Includes a charge to reflect FAS 72, resulting in a cumulative effect of $4,340,424 ($3.75 per share).
[d]Includes a gain to reflect FAS 109, resulting in a cumulative effect of $440,000 ($.38 per share).

Transfer Agent & Registrar: Firstar Trust Co.

General Counsel:
  Reno, Zahm, Folgate, Lindberg & Powell

Investor Relations: C. Steven Sjogren, Pres.

Human Resources: Kathy Bergstrom

Mgt. Info. Svcs.: Marsha Abramson

Auditors: Ernst & Young LLP

Traded (Symbol): NASDAQ (HMCI)

Stockholders: 1,350

Employees: 185

Annual Meeting: In April

Household International, Inc.

2700 Sanders Road, Prospect Heights, Illinois 60070
Telephone: (708) 564-5000

Household International, Inc., is a major provider of consumer finance and banking services, and consumer insurance and investment products. Major subsidiaries include Household Finance Corporation, Household Bank, f.s.b., Household Credit Services, Alexander Hamilton Life Insurance Co. of America, and Household Retail Services. Incorporated in Delaware in 1925; reincorporated in Delaware in 1981.

Directors   (In addition to indicated officers)

Robert J. Darnall
Gary G. Dillon
John A. Edwardson
Mary Johnston Evans
Cyrus F. Freidheim, Jr.
Louis E. Levy

George A. Lorch
John D. Nichols
James B. Pitblado
S. Jay Stewart
Louis W. Sullivan, M.D.
Raymond C. Tower

Officers   (Directors*)

*Donald C. Clark, Chm.
*William F. Aldinger, Pres. & C.E.O.
Lawrence N. Bangs, Grp. Exec.—UK, Life Insur.
Robert F. Elliott, Grp. Exec.—HFC
Glen O. Fick, Grp. Exec.—Commercial
Joseph W. Saunders, Grp. Exec.—Credit Cards
David A. Schoenholz, Sr. V.P. & C.F.O.
Charles A. Albright, V.P.—Credit Cycle Mgt.
Edgar D. Ancona, V.P.—Treas.

David B. Barany, V.P.—Chf. Info. Off.
Michael A. DeLuca, V.P.—Taxes
H. Kirk Henry, V.P.—Gov't. Rel.
Colin P. Kelly, V.P.—Hum. Res.
Theresa F. Kendziorski, V.P.—Analysis & Projects
Richard J. Kolb, V.P.—Cont.
Michael H. Morgan, V.P.—Corp. Comm.
Randall L. Raup, V.P.—Strategy & Dev.
Kenneth H. Robin, V.P.—Gen. Coun.
Gregory L. Snyder, V.P.—Internal Audit
John W. Blenke, Asst. Gen. Coun. & Secy.

Consolidated Balance Sheet   As of December 31, 1994 (000 omitted)

Assets		Liabilities & Stockholders' Equity	
Receivables	$30,324,000	Current liabilities	$19,526,900
Net property, plant & equipment	512,000	Long-term debt	10,274,100
Other assets	3,502,400	Other liabilities	2,014,400
		*Stockholders' equity	2,523,000
Total	$34,338,400	Total	$34,338,400

*96,602,598 shares common stock outstanding.

Consolidated Income Statement

Years Ended Dec. 31	Thousands — — — — Net Revenues	Net Income	Per Share[b] — — — Earnings[a]	Cash Dividends	Common Stock Price Range[b] Calendar Year
1994	$3,360,600	$367,600	$3.50	$1.23	39-3/4 — 28-1/2
1993	3,305,000	298,700	2.85	1.18	40-3/8 — 26-7/8
1992	2,760,400	190,900	1.93	1.15	30-1/4 — 20-3/4
1991	2,707,000	149,800	1.55	1.12	31-1/2 — 13-3/4
1990	2,293,800	235,300	2.88	1.09	26-5/8 — 9-3/4

[a]Fully diluted earnings per share. Fully diluted earnings per share from continuing operations for 1994-90 were $3.50, $2.85, $1.93, $1.55, and $2.88, respectively.
[b]Adjusted to reflect a 2-for-1 stock split in the form of a 100% stock dividend in October 1993.

Transfer Agent & Registrar: Harris Trust and Savings Bank

General Counsel:	Kenneth H. Robin, V.P.	Auditors:	Arthur Andersen LLP
Investor Relations:	Michael H. Morgan, V.P.	Traded (Symbol):	NYSE, CSE, PHSE, BSE, PSE (HI)
		Stockholders:	14,379
Human Resources:	Colin P. Kelly, V.P.	Employees:	15,119
Mgt. Info. Svcs.:	David B. Barany, V.P.	Annual Meeting:	Second Wednesday in May

IDEX Corporation

630 Dundee Road, Northbrook, Illinois 60065-3001
Telephone: (708) 498-7070

IDEX Corporation, through its subsidiaries, designs, manufactures, and markets a broad range of fluid handling and industrial products, including industrial pumps; fire-fighting pumps and rescue tools; lubrication systems; tooling and machinery; stainless steel banding and clamping devices; sign-mounting systems; and energy absorption devices. Subsidiaries are organized into two segments: Fluid Handling and Industrial Products. The Fluid Handling Group consists of Corken, a producer of vane pumps, compressors, and valves for the LP gas industry; Hale, a manufacturer of truck-mounted and portable fire pumps and products which form the Hurst Jaws of Life® rescue systems; Lubriquip, a producer of automatic lubrication systems for use in machinery, compressors, and vehicles; Micropump, a manufacturer of small, precision-engineered, magnetically driven pumps used in industrial, medical, and electronic applications; Pulsafeeder, a manufacturer of specialty pumps, controls, and systems for the process industries; Viking Pump, a producer of positive displacement rotary interval gear pumps sold to process industries; and Warren Rupp, a manufacturer of air-operated double diaphragm pumps used in industrial applications. The Industrial Products Group consists of Band-It, a worldwide producer of stainless steel bands, buckles, and preformed clamps and related installation tools for industrial, automotive, energy, and maintenance applications; Signfix, a U.K.-based manufacturer of sign-mounting devices and related equipment; Strippit, a manufacturer of tooling and computer-controlled turret punching machinery sold to the precision metal fabrication industry; and Vibratech, a producer of mechanical energy absorption devices for use in transportation equipment and machinery. Incorporated in Delaware in 1987.

Directors (In addition to indicated officer)

Richard E. Heath	Clifton S. Robbins
Henry R. Kravis	George R. Roberts
William H. Luers	Neil A. Springer
Paul E. Raether	Michael T. Tokarz

Officers (Director*)

*Donald N. Boyce, Chm., Pres. & C.E.O.	Mark W. Baker, V.P.—Grp. Exec.
Frank J. Hansen, Sr. V.P.—Oper. & C.O.O.	Jerry N. Derck, V.P.—Hum. Res.
Wayne P. Sayatovic, Sr. V.P.—Fin., C.F.O. & Secy.	Wade H. Roberts, Jr., V.P.—Grp. Exec.

Consolidated Balance Sheet As of December 31, 1994 (000 omitted)

Assets		Liabilities & Stockholders' Equity	
Current assets	$151,357	Current liabilities	$ 69,350
Net property, plant & equipment	66,241	Long-term debt	168,166
Other assets	153,498	Other liabilities	17,275
		*Stockholders' equity	116,305
Total	$371,096	Total	$371,096

*19,078,671 shares common stock outstanding. Includes a $96,500,000 charge to net worth to write off excess of purchase price of businesses comprising IDEX over the carrying value of assets at the time IDEX was formed in 1988.

Consolidated Income Statement

Years Ended Dec. 31	Thousands — — — — Net Sales	Net Income[a]	Per Share[b] — — — Earnings[a]	Cash Dividends	Common Stock Price Range[b] Calendar Year
1994	$399,502	$33,610	$1.72	$ .00	29-1/4 — 22-5/8
1993	308,638	25,326	1.31	.00	24 — 14-5/8
1992	277,129	20,146	1.06	.00	15-7/8 — 11-1/8
1991	228,181	15,917	.94	.00	13-3/8 — 6-3/8
1990	228,397	15,703	.97	.00	11-5/8 — 6-7/8

[a]Before extraordinary items.
[b]Adjusted to reflect a 3-for-2 stock split in January 1995.

Transfer Agent & Registrar:	Harris Trust and Savings Bank		
Investor Relations:	Wayne P. Sayatovic, Sr. V.P.—Fin.	Traded (Symbol):	NYSE (IEX)
Human Resources:	Jerry N. Derck, V.P.	Stockholders:	1,388
		Employees:	3,000
Auditors:	Deloitte & Touche LLP	Annual Meeting:	In April

Illinois Central Corporation

455 North Cityfront Plaza Drive, Chicago, Illinois 60611-5504
Telephone: (312) 755-7500

Illinois Central Corporation, through its wholly owned subsidiary, Illinois Central Railroad Company, operates about 2,700 route miles in six states, including a major north-south line from Chicago to New Orleans, primarily carrying chemicals, coal and paper north, with coal, grain and milled grain products moving south along its lines. Incorporated in Delaware in 1989; present name adopted in 1989.

Directors (In addition to indicated officer)

Gilbert H. Lamphere, Chm.
Thomas A. Barron
George D. Gould
William B. Johnson
Alexander P. Lynch

Samuel F. Pryor IV
F. Jay Taylor
John V. Tunney
Alan H. Washkowitz

Officers (Director*)

*E. Hunter Harrison, Pres. & C.E.O.
John D. McPherson, Sr. V.P.—Oper.
Gerald F. Mohan, Sr. V.P.—Mktg.
James M. Harrell, V.P.—Hum. Res.
David C. Kelly, V.P.—Maint.

Ronald A. Lane, V.P., Gen. Coun. & Secy.
Dale W. Phillips, V.P. & C.F.O.
Donald H. Shelton, V.P.—Mktg. & Sales
John V. Mulvaney, Cont.

Consolidated Balance Sheet   As of December 31, 1994 (000 omitted)

Assets		Liabilities & Stockholders' Equity	
Current assets	$ 108,000	Current liabilities	$ 173,400
Net property, plant & equipment	1,171,300	Long-term debt	328,600
Other assets	29,400	Deferred taxes	218,200
		Other liabilities	134,400
		*Stockholders' equity	454,100
Total	$1,308,700	Total	$1,308,700

*42,609,591 shares common stock outstanding.

Consolidated Income Statement

Years Ended Dec. 31	Thousands — — — — Net Revenues	Net Income	Per Share[a] — — — Earnings	Cash Dividends	Common Stock Price Range[a] Calendar Year
1994	$593,900	$113,900	$2.67	$ .84	38-5/8 — 28-5/8
1993	564,700	91,700[b]	2.14[b]	.64	36 — 23-5/8
1992	547,400	72,500[c]	1.70[c]	.35	25-5/8 — 16-1/2
1991	549,700	65,400	1.64	.00	23-3/8 — 7-3/8
1990	544,200	46,200	1.31	.00	11-3/8 — 5-5/8[d]

[a]Adjusted for 3-for-2 stock split in February 1992.
[b]Before extraordinary charge of $23,400,000 ($.55 per share) and the cumulative effect of FAS 106 and FAS 112.
[c]Before FAS 109, which resulted in a cumulative effect of $23,400,000 ($.55 per share).
[d]Commenced trading on NASDAQ August 21, 1990, and on NYSE April 3, 1991.

Transfer Agent & Registar: The First National Bank of Boston

General Counsel: Ronald A. Lane, V.P.

Investor Relations: Ann G. Thoma

Human Resources: James M. Harrell, V.P.

Mgt. Info. Svcs.:   Dale W. Phillips, V.P.

Auditors: Arthur Andersen LLP
Traded (Symbol):   NYSE (IC)
Stockholders: 15,000
Employees: 3,000
Annual Meeting: In April

Illinois Tool Works Inc.

3600 West Lake Avenue, Glenview, Illinois 60025-5811
Telephone: (708) 724-7500

Illinois Tool Works Inc. manufactures and markets a variety of highly engineered products and systems that provide specific, problem-solving solutions to a diverse customer base worldwide. The company's products include Engineered Components — plastic and metal components, small assemblies, metal fasteners, adhesives, and welding equipment; and Industrial Systems and Consumables — systems and related consumables for packaging, finishing, quality assurance, tools, and specialty applications. Illinois Tool Works has small flexible units operating in more than 33 countries. In April 1990, the company acquired substantially all of the net assets of The DeVilbiss Industrial/Commercial businesses of Eagle Industries, Inc. The DeVilbiss businesses manufacture and sell products and engineered systems used for product finishing and coating applications, including conventional air spray equipment, powder coating devices, and robotic finishing systems. Ransburg, a major subsidiary, is primarily a manufacturer and distributor of electrostatic finishing systems for liquid and powder coatings. In February 1993, the company agreed to acquire Appleton, Wisconsin-based Miller Group Ltd., a maker of arc-welding equipment. Incorporated in Delaware in 1961.

Directors (In addition to indicated officers)

Julius W. Becton, Jr.	Richard M. Jones	Phillip B. Rooney
Silas S. Cathcart	George D. Kennedy	Harold B. Smith
Susan Crown	Richard H. Leet	Ormand J. Wade
H. Richard Crowther	Robert C. McCormack	Calvin A.H. Waller

Officers (Directors*)

*John D. Nichols, Chm. & C.E.O.
*W. James Farrell, Pres.
Russell M. Flaum, Exec. V.P.—Signode
  Packaging Systems
Robert H. Jenkins, Exec. V.P.—Const. Prod.
  & Eng. Polymers, Miller
Frank S. Ptak, Exec. V.P.—Auto. & Spec.
  Components
F. Ronald Seager, Exec. V.P.—Cons. Pack.
  Prod. & Syst.

Michael W. Gregg, Sr. V.P. & Cont., Acct.
Stewart S. Hudnut, Sr. V.P., Gen. Coun. & Secy.
John Karpan, Sr. V.P.—Hum. Res.
Thomas W. Buckman, V.P.—Patents & Tech.
Jon Kinney, V.P. & Cont., Oper.
Robert V. McGrath, V.P.—Tax
Michael J. Robinson, V.P. & Treas.
Donald L. Van Erden, V.P.—Res. & Adv. Devel.

Consolidated Balance Sheet   As of December 31, 1994 (000 omitted)

Assets		Liabilities & Stockholders' Equity	
Current assets	$1,262,933	Current liabilities	$ 628,433
Net property, plant & equipment	641,235	Long-term debt	272,987
Other assets	676,330	Deferred items	69,516
		Other liabilities	68,041
		*Stockholders' equity	1,541,521
Total	$2,580,498	Total	$2,580,498

*113,957,932 shares common stock outstanding.

Consolidated Income Statement

Years Ended Dec. 31	Thousands — — — —		Per Share[b] — — — —		Common Stock
	Operating Revenues	Net Income[a]	Earnings	Cash Dividends	Price Range[b] Calendar Year
1994	$3,461,315	$277,783	$2.45	$ .54	45-1/2 — 36-3/4
1993	3,159,181	206,570	1.83	.49	40-1/2 — 32-1/2
1992	2,811,645	192,080	1.72	.45	34-3/8 — 28-1/2
1991	2,639,650	180,559	1.62	.40	34-5/8 — 22-3/4
1990	2,544,153	182,383	1.68	.33	28-5/8 — 19-5/8

[a]Based on weighted average shares outstanding.
[b]Adjusted to reflect a 2-for-1 stock split in June 1993.

Transfer Agent & Registrar:	Harris Trust and Savings Bank		
General Counsel:	Stewart S. Hudnut, Sr. V.P.	Traded (Symbol):	CSE, NYSE (ITW)
Investor Relations:	Linda Williams, Dir.	Stockholders:	3,700
Human Resources:	John Karpan, Sr. V.P.	Employees:	19,500
Auditors:	Arthur Andersen LLP	Annual Meeting:	In May

Illinova Corporation

500 South 27th Street, Decatur, Illinois 62525-1805
Telephone: (217) 424-6600

Illinova Corporation (formerly Illinois Power Company) is a public utility holding company, which through its subsidiaries, is engaged principally in the generation, transmission, distribution, and the sale of electric energy, and the distribution, transportation, and sale of natural gas in parts of northern, central, and southern Illinois. Illinois Power Company (IP), a wholly owned subsidiary, serves Belleville, Bloomington, Champaign, Danville, Decatur, East St. Louis, Galesburg, Granite City, Normal and Urbana. The company's territory spans about 15,000 square miles, and it serves more than one-half million people. Illinois Power operates five major electric generating stations and one nuclear generating station. It also owns eight gas storage fields, predominantly in southern Illinois. Illinova Generating Company (formerly IP Group, Inc.), another wholly owned subsidiary, is a developer of and investor in independent power projects worldwide. In February 1994, shareholders approved the formation of Illinova Corporation. Incorporated in Illinois in 1994.

Directors (In addition to indicated officers)

Richard R. Berry
Donald E. Lasater
Donald S. Perkins
Robert M. Powers
Walter D. Scott

Ronald L. Thompson
Walter M. Vannoy
Marilou M. von Ferstel
John D. Zeglis
Vernon K. Zimmerman

Officers (Directors*)

*Larry D. Haab, Chm., Pres. & C.E.O.
Larry F. Altenbaumer, C.F.O., Treas. & Cont.
Leah Manning Stetzner, Gen. Coun. & Corp.
  Secy.
*Charles W. Wells, Exec. V.P.—Illinois Power
Larry S. Brodsky, Sr. V.P.—Illinois Power

Paul L. Lang, Sr. V.P.—Illinois Power
Wilfred Connell, V.P.—Illinois Power
John G. Cook, V.P.—Illinois Power
Larry L. Idleman, V.P.—Illinois Power
Alec G. Dreyer, Treas. & Cont.—Illinois Power

Consolidated Balance Sheet   As of December 31, 1994 (000 omitted)

Assets		Liabilities & Stockholders' Equity	
Current assets	$ 439,400	Current liabilities	$ 530,400
Net property, plant & equipment	4,644,200	Long-term debt	1,946,100
Other assets	493,100	Deferred items	1,292,300
		Other liabilities	357,700
		*Stockholders' equity	1,450,200
Total	$5,576,700	Total	$5,576,700

*75,643,937 shares common stock outstanding.

Consolidated Income Statement

Years Ended Dec. 31	Thousands — — — — Operating Revs.[a]	Net Income[b]	Per Share — — — Earnings	Cash Dividends	Common Stock Price Range Calendar Year
1994	$1,589,500	$ 158,200	$ 2.09	$ .80	22-5/8 — 18-1/8
1993	1,581,200	(81,900)	(1.08)	.80	25-7/8 — 20-1/8
1992	1,479,500	93,200	1.23	.80	25-1/8 — 19-1/4
1991	1,474,905	109,244	1.04	.20	24-1/8 — 15-3/8
1990	1,469,480	(78,484)	(1.53)	.00	19-3/8 — 12-3/4

[a]Operating revenues and purchased power expenses for the prior periods have been adjusted to show the reclassification of electric interchange revenues to operating revenues to conform with the 1991 presentation. In prior periods, interchange revenues were recorded as a credit to power purchased.
[b]Applicable to common stock.

Transfer Agent & Registrar: Illinois Power Company

General Counsel: Leah Manning Stetzner

Investor Relations: Russell J. Naylor, Dir.

Human Resources:
  Larry S. Brodsky, Sr. V.P.—Illinois Power

Mgt. Info. Svcs.:
  Larry S. Brodsky, Sr. V.P.—Illinois Power

Auditors: Price Waterhouse LLP
Traded (Symbol):   CSE, NYSE (ILN)
Stockholders: 51,000
Employees: 4,350
Annual Meeting: Second Wednesday in April

IMC Global Inc.

2100 Sanders Road, Northbrook, Illinois 60062-6139
Telephone: (708) 272-9200

IMC Global Inc. (formerly IMC Fertilizer Group, Inc.) is one of the world's leading producers of soil nutrients for agriculture. It mines and processes potash in the U.S. and Canada; and is a joint-venture partner in IMC-Agrico Company, the nation's largest producer, marketer and distributor of phosphate soil nutrients. The company also produces sulphur, oil and natural gas through other joint-venture operations. IMC Global also manufactures retail crop nutrient products at four large granulation plants, which it markets under the Rainbow name in the southeastern U.S., principally through unaffiliated farm centers and local dealers. The company maintains a large distribution and warehouse system which utilizes a unit train arrangement, leased railcars, trucks, barges and ships to transport its crop nutrient products. The company's North America customers include wholesale and retail crop nutrient producers and regional agricultural cooperatives. Internationally, IMC Global's products are sold through one Canadian and three U.S. export associations, mainly to Japan, India, the People's Republic of China, Pakistan, Turkey, Brazil and several European countries. The company's major subsidiaries are IMC Global Operations Inc. and International Minerals and Chemical Corporation (Canada) Global Limited. Incorporated in Delaware in 1987; present name adopted in 1994.

Directors (In addition to indicated officers)

Raymond F. Bentele
Frank W. Considine
James M. Davidson
Richard A. Lenon

David B. Mathis
Thomas H. Roberts, Jr.
Billie B. Turner

Officers (Directors*)

*Wendell F. Bueche, Chm. & C.E.O.
*James D. Speir, Pres. & C.O.O.
Robert C. Brauneker, Exec. V.P. & C.F.O.
Robert Felsenthal, Sr. V.P.—Bus. Dev.
C. Steven Hoffman, Sr. V.P.

Allen C. Miller, Sr. V.P.—Human Resources
Marschall I. Smith, Sr. V.P., Secy. & Gen. Coun.
Peter Hong, V.P. & Treas.
Don R. McCombs, V.P.—Env., Health & Safety
Louis Spillone, Jr., Dir. of Taxes & Secy.

Consolidated Balance Sheet   As of June 30, 1994 (000 omitted)

Assets		Liabilities & Stockholders' Equity	
Current assets	$ 534,000	Current liabilities	$ 209,400
Net property, plant & equipment	1,927,400	Long-term debt	688,100
Other assets	316,900	Deferred income taxes	372,600
		Other liabilities	275,100
		Minority interest	578,100
		*Stockholders' equity	655,000
Total	$2,778,300	Total	$2,778,300

*29,462,606 shares common stock outstanding.

Consolidated Income Statement

Years Ended June 30	Thousands — — — — — Net Sales	Net Income	Per Share — — — Earnings	Cash Dividends	Common Stock Price Range Calendar Year
1994	$1,441,500	$(28,800)[a]	$(1.14)[a]	$ .00	49-1/4 — 30-3/4
1993	897,100	(167,100)[b]	(7.57)[b]	.81	47-1/4 — 24-3/8
1992	1,058,500	(74,600)[c]	(3.38)[c]	1.08	68 — 37-1/4
1991	1,131,200	95,800	3.85	1.08	60 — 33
1990	1,105,700	82,600	3.13	1.08	38-5/8 — 30-3/8

[a]Includes a one-time charge of $25,200,000 ($1.00 per share) related to the early extinguishment of debt.
[b]Includes a one-time charge of $47,100,000 ($2.13 per share) for the cumulative effect on prior years of FAS 106 as of July 1, 1992.
[c]Includes a one-time charge of $165,500,000 ($7.50 per share) for the cumulative effect on prior years of FAS 109 as of July 1, 1991.

Transfer Agent & Registrar: American Stock Transfer & Trust Co.

General Counsel:	Marschall I. Smith, Sr. V.P.	Auditors:	Ernst & Young LLP
Investor Relations:	Peter Hong, V.P.	Traded (Symbol):	NYSE, CSE (IGL)
		Stockholders:	280
Human Resources:	Allen C. Miller, Sr. V.P.	Employees:	6,700
Mgt. Info. Svcs.:	Alan C. Paveza, V.P.	Annual Meeting:	In October

Information Resources, Inc.

150 North Clinton Street, Chicago, Illinois 60661-1416
Telephone: (312) 726-1221

Information Resources, Inc., provides a variety of information and software services. In the information sector, the company offers computerized proprietary databases, analytical models, and software products to assist consumer packaged goods companies in testing, monitoring, evaluating and executing their sales and marketing plans. The company's software products, with applications for executive information systems, planning, marketing, sales, finance and operations, are licensed across a wide variety of industries and governmental agencies. The company's services are marketed in 26 countries around the world. Incorporated in Delaware in 1982.

Directors   (In addition to indicated officers)

Thomas W. Wilson, Jr., Chm.
Edwin E. Epstein
John D.C. Little, Ph.D.
Leonard M. Lodish, Ph.D.

Edward E. Lucente
Edith W. Martin, Ph.D.
George G. Montgomery, Jr.
Glen L. Urban, Ph.D.

Officers   (Directors*)

*James G. Andress, Pres., Co-C.E.O. &
   C.O.O.
*Gian M. Fulgoni, Co-C.E.O.
*Gerald J. Eskin, Ph.D., V. Chm.
   Edward S. Berger, Secy. & Gen. Coun.
   Gary M. Hill, C.F.O.

George R. Garrick, Pres.—IRI N. Amer. Grp.
Randall S. Smith, Pres.—Int'l. Info. Svcs. Grp.
*Jeffrey P. Stamen, Pres.—IRI Software Grp.
Kenneth J. Giacomino, Div. Exec. V.P. & Corp.
   Cont.

Consolidated Balance Sheet   As of December 31, 1994 (000 omitted)

Assets		Liabilities & Stockholders' Equity	
Current assets	$143,189	Current liabilities	$ 73,615
Net property, plant & equipment	60,293	Long-term debt	31,452
Other assets	151,072	Deferred items	16,122
		Other liabilities	6,164
		*Stockholders' equity	227,201
Total	$354,554	Total	$354,554

*26,493,277 shares common stock outstanding.

Consolidated Income Statement[a]

Years Ended Dec. 31	Thousands — — — — Revenues[b]	Net Income	Per Share — — — Earnings	Cash Dividends	Common Stock Price Range Calendar Year
1994	$376,570	$(15,515)[c]	$ (.60)[c]	$ .00	39-1/4 — 11-1/4
1993	334,544	24,079[d]	.89[d]	.00	44 — 27
1992	276,362	19,247	.78	.00	35-3/4 — 18-1/2
1991	222,689	15,386	.66	.00	29 — 9-1/2
1990	179,789	4,299[e]	.22[e]	.00	16-1/2 — 8-1/8

[a]Restated to reflect the Towne-Oller acquisition.
[b]From continuing operations.
[c]Includes a charge to reflect a change in accounting method to recognize revenue, resulting in a cumulative effect of $6,594,000 ($.26 per share).
[d]Includes a gain to reflect FAS 109, resulting in a cumulative effect of $1,864,000 ($.07 per share).
[e]Restated to reflect Statement of Position No. 91-1 Software Revenue Recognition, resulting in a cumulative effect of $1,369,000 ($.07 per share).

Transfer Agent & Registrar: Harris Trust and Savings Bank

General Counsel:	Freeborn & Peters	Traded (Symbol):	NASDAQ (IRIC)
Investor Relations:	Edward S. Berger, Secy.	Stockholders:	644
Human Resources:	Julie Chandler, V.P.	Employees:	6,360
Auditors:	Grant Thornton LLP	Annual Meeting:	In May

Inland Steel Industries, Inc.

30 West Monroe Street, Chicago, Illinois 60603
Telephone: (312) 346-0300

Inland Steel Industries, Inc., is a materials management, logistics, and technical services company that provides value-added steel products and materials-related services to manufacturers in the automotive, appliance, furniture, equipment, electric motor, and a wide variety of other industries. The company is best known as a steel manufacturer and as the nation's largest operator of material service centers. The company has three primary business units. Inland Steel Company, an integrated steel producer in the U.S., mines iron ore, makes iron, and produces carbon and high-strength, low-allow steels. Its sole steelmaking facility is the 1,900-acre Indiana Harbor Works at East Chicago, Indiana, with an annual raw steelmaking capacity of six-million tons. Inland Materials Distribution Group, Inc., is the nation's largest metal distributor, with 54 centers that process and distribute carbon, stainless and alloy steels, aluminum, nickel, brass, copper, and industrial plastics to 60,000 customers. Inland International, Inc., is the company's international marketing, trading, and distribution arm. Based in Chicago, Inland International was formed in January 1994. Inland Steel Industries, Inc., also is involved in several joint ventures through its business units. Incorporated in Delaware in 1986.

Directors (In addition to indicated officers)

A. Robert Abboud	Donald S. Perkins
James W. Cozad	Joshua I. Smith
James A. Henderson	Nancy H. Teeters
Robert B. McKersie	Arnold R. Weber

Officers (Directors*)

*Robert J. Darnall, Chm., Pres. & C.E.O.	H. William Howard, V.P.—Info. Tech.
*Maurice S. Nelson, Jr., Exec. V.P.	Vicki L. Avril, Treas.
Earl L. Mason, Sr. V.P. & C.F.O.	James M. Hemphill, Cont.
Neil S. Novich, Sr. V.P.	George A. Ranney, Jr., Interim Gen. Coun.
Judd R. Cool, V.P.—Hum. Res.	

Consolidated Balance Sheet As of December 31, 1994 (000 omitted)

Assets		Liabilities & Stockholders' Equity	
Current assets	$1,081,500	Current liabilities	$ 564,800
Net property, plant & equipment	1,610,300	Long-term debt	705,900
Other assets	661,600	Deferred items	1,316,500
		Other liabilities	34,100
		Temporary equity	222,900
		*Stockholders' equity	509,200
Total	$3,353,400	Total	$3,353,400

*44,550,228 shares common stock outstanding.

Consolidated Income Statement

Years Ended Dec. 31	Thousands — — — — Net Sales	Net Income[a]	Per Share — — — — Earnings[a]	Cash Dividends	Common Stock Price Range Calendar Year	
1994	$4,497,000	$ 107,400	$ 1.81	$ .00	42	— 29-3/8
1993	3,888,200	(37,600)[b]	(1.96)[b]	.00	35	— 20
1992	3,494,300	(815,600)[c]	(25.82)[c]	.00	27	— 16-1/4
1991	3,404,500	(275,100)	(9.88)	.15	26-1/8	— 17-3/8
1990	3,870,400	(20,600)	(1.41)	1.40	36-3/8	— 20-7/8

[a]Includes special charges of $165,100,000 aftertax in 1991 ($5.33 per share).
[b]Includes facility shutdown provision of $14,700,000 aftertax ($.41 per share).
[c]Includes a charge to reflect FAS 106, resulting in a cumulative aftertax effect of $656,200,000 ($19.99 per share).

Transfer Agent & Registrar:	Harris Trust and Savings Bank		
Corporate Counsel:	Mayer, Brown & Platt	Auditors:	Price Waterhouse LLP
Investor Relations:	M. Robert Weidner III, Dir.	Traded (Symbol):	NYSE, CSE (IAD)
		Stockholders:	16,000
Human Resources:	Judd R. Cool, V.P.	Employees:	15,479
Mgt. Info. Svcs.:	H. William Howard, V.P.	Annual Meeting:	In May

Intercargo Corporation

1450 East American Lane, 20th Floor, Schaumburg, Illinois 60173-6090
Telephone: (708) 517-2510

Intercargo Corporation is a holding company that serves as a management and administrative organization for its insurance company subsidiaries, which mainly provide specialized insurance coverages for companies involved in international trade. The primary coverages underwritten by the subsidiaries are surety bonds, marine insurance, errors and omissions insurance, and other property and casualty coverages. Intercargo's market consists primarily of importers and exporters, custom brokers and freight forwarders (service firms engaged in the movement of international cargo for their clients), and other global traders. Intercargo serves customers in all major trading centers across the U.S. and has established a presence in Canada and the United Kingdom. The company's subsidiaries are Intercargo Insurance Company, Kingsway Financial Services, Inc., International Advisory Services, Inc. (IAS), Interocean Company, Ltd., TRM Insurance Services, Inc., and Oceanic Insurance and Surety Company (wholly owned by Intercargo Insurance Co.). Incorporated in Delaware in 1985.

Directors (In addition to indicated officer)

Kenneth A. Bodenstein
Arthur J. Fritz, Jr.
Albert J. Gallegos

Arthur L. Litman
John H. Robinson
Robert B. Sanborn

Officers (Director*)

*James R. Zuhlke, Chm., Pres. & C.E.O.
Brian D. Freund, V.P.

Lawrence P. Goecking, C.F.O., Treas. & Secy.
Robert S. Kielbas, Dir.—Int'l. Bus. Dev.

Consolidated Balance Sheet As of December 31, 1994 (000 omitted)

Assets		Liabilities & Stockholders' Equity	
Cash & cash equivalents	$ 19,011	Losses & loss adj. expense	$ 38,836
Investments	60,778	Unearned premiums	31,586
Premiums receivable	21,887	Notes payable	8,636
Equipment	2,496	Other liabilities	9,444
Other assets	24,251	*Stockholders' equity	39,921
Total	$128,423	Total	$128,423

*7,640,981 shares common stock outstanding.

Consolidated Income Statement

Years Ended Dec. 31	Thousands — — — — Total Revenues	Net Income	Per Share — — — Earnings[a]	Cash Dividends	Common Stock Price Range Calendar Year
1994	$80,885	$4,981	$ .65	$ .18	12-1/4 — 7-1/4
1993	50,712	2,138	.30	.17	14-1/2 — 10
1992	46,376	4,379	.68	.08	17 — 10
1991	45,071	4,015	.73	.00	15-3/4 — 4-1/4
1990	24,844	2,397	.46	.00	5-7/8 — 4-5/8

[a]From continuing operations.

Transfer Agent & Registrar: Harris Trust and Savings Bank

Investor Relations:
Lawrence P. Goecking, C.F.O.

Human Resources: Sheila H. Lake, Dir.

Mgt. Info. Svcs.: Phillip Bernard

Auditors: KPMG Peat Marwick LLP

Traded (Symbol): NASDAQ (ICAR)

Stockholders: 2,163

Employees: 287

Annual Meeting: Third Friday in May

First Chicago Guide

The Interlake Corporation

550 Warrenville Road, Lisle, Illinois 60532-4387

Telephone: (708) 852-8800

The Interlake Corporation is a diversified multinational company that operates in two business segments. The Engineered Materials segment includes Special Materials (ferrous metal powder used to manufacture precision parts) and Aerospace Components (manufactures precision jet engine components and repairs jet engine fan blades). The Handling/Packaging Systems segment includes automated systems, hardware, and supplies used to convey, store, retrieve, sort and package. Interlake's sales offices, warehouses and manufacturing plants are located in the U.S., Australia, Belgium, Canada, England and Germany. Major subsidiaries include: Chem-tronics, Inc.; Dexion (Australia) Pty. Ltd.; Dexion Group plc; Hoeganaes Corporation; Interlake Material Handling; and Interlake Packaging Corp. Incorporated in New York in 1905; reincorporated in Delaware in 1986.

Directors (In addition to indicated officer)

John A. Canning, Jr.
James C. Cotting
John E. Jones
Frederick C. Langenberg

Quentin C. McKenna
William G. Mitchell
Erwin E. Schulze

Officers (Director*)

*W. Robert Reum, Chm., Pres. & C.E.O.
Craig A. Grant, V.P.—Hum. Res.
Stephen Gregory, V.P.—Fin., Treas. & C.F.O.

Stephen R. Smith, V.P., Gen. Coun. & Secy.
John P. Miller, Cont.

Consolidated Balance Sheet   As of December 25, 1994 (000 omitted)

Assets		Liabilities & Stockholders' Equity	
Current assets	$248,990	Current liabilities	$ 181,371
Net property, plant & equipment	145,734	Long-term debt	417,898
Other assets	50,229	Deferred tax liabilities	6,038
		Other liabilities	96,926
		Preferred stock	39,155
		*Stockholders' equity	(296,435)
Total	$444,953	Total	$ 444,953

*22,026,695 shares common stock outstanding.

Consolidated Income Statement[a]

Years Ended Abt. Dec. 31	Thousands — — — — —		Per Share — — —		Common Stock Price Range Calendar Year
	Net Sales	Net Income	Earnings	Cash Dividends	
1994	$752,592	$(40,751)[b]	$(1.85)[b]	$ .00	3-7/8 — 1-1/2
1993	681,330	(25,962)[c]	(1.18)[c]	.00	4-3/4 — 2-1/2
1992	708,199	(27,698)[d]	(1.67)[d]	.00	9-3/8 — 3-1/4
1991	714,742	(13,744)[e]	(1.31)[e]	.00	6-1/8 — 2-3/4
1990	786,279	(12,843)[f]	(1.22)[f]	.00	14-3/8 — 3-1/8

[a]From continuing operations.
[b]Includes goodwill writedown of $34,174,000.
[c]Includes a restructuring charge of $5,611,000 and a non-operating charge of $4,750,000 for environmental matters.
[d]Includes an extraordinary loss on early extinguishment of debt of $7,567,000 ($.46 per share) and the cumulative loss effect of FAS 106 and FAS 109 of $6,141,000 ($.37 per share).
[e]Includes a special non-operating charge of $6,000,000 for environmental matters and $3,344,000 of unusual items of expense.
[f]Excludes loss from discontinued operations of $8,908,000 ($.85 per share) and includes $13,482,000 of unusual expense items.

Transfer Agent & Registrar: First Chicago Trust Co. of New York

General Counsel:
  Jones, Day, Reavis & Pogue

Investor Relations: Stephen R. Smith, V.P.

Human Resources: Craig A. Grant, V.P.

Mgt. Info. Svcs.:   Bruce E. Steimle, Dir.

Auditors: Price Waterhouse LLP

Traded (Symbol):   NYSE, CSE (IK)

Stockholders: 7,432

Employees: 4,536

Annual Meeting: In April

International Jensen Incorporated

25 Tri-State International Office Center, Suite 400, Lincolnshire, Illinois 60069

Telephone: (708) 317-3700

International Jensen Incorporated designs, manufactures, and markets quality loudspeakers and loudspeaker components for the domestic and international automotive original equipment manufacturer market, automotive aftermarket, and home audio market. The company also designs and markets related audio electronics products. Its products are sold under the brand names *Advent, Jensen, Phase Linear, AR, NHT, Day Sequerra, MAGNAT,* and *MAC AUDIO.* The company's customers include major automobile manufacturers, retail chains as well as specialty audio retailers. Incorporated in Delaware in 1986.

Directors (In addition to indicated officer)

David G. Chandler
Donald W. Jenkins

Robert H. Jenkins
Norman H. McMillan

Officers (Director*)

*Robert G. Shaw, Chm., Pres. & C.E.O.
Donald J. Cowie, Grp. V.P.—OEM
David M. Marinello, Sr. V.P.—Branded
Prods., Mktg. & Sales

James Braun, V.P.—Mktg. & Sales
Willie L. Carter, V.P.—Quality
Marc T. Tanenberg, V.P.—Fin. & C.F.O.

Consolidated Balance Sheet   As of February 28, 1995 (000 omitted)

Assets		Liabilities & Stockholders' Equity	
Current assets	$112,590	Current liabilities	$ 63,914
Net property, plant & equipment	18,564	Total debt	15,881
Other assets	11,394	[a]Other liabilities	8,509
		*Stockholders' equity	54,244
Total	$142,548	Total	$142,548

[a]Includes $5,982,000 excess of fair value of acquired net assets over cost, net.
*5,703,755 shares common stock outstanding.

Consolidated Income Statement

Years Ended Abt. Feb. 28	Thousands — — — — Net Sales	Net Income	Per Share[a] — — — Earnings	Cash Dividends	Common Stock Price Range[ab] Fiscal Year
1995	$252,772	$6,942	$1.21	$ .00	10-1/4 — 6-1/2
1994	220,601	3,167[c]	.55	.00	10 — 6
1993	188,318	5,385	.93	.00	15-3/4 — 7-3/4
1992	153,346	6,530[d]	1.59	.00	16 — 7-3/4
1991	138,763	4,774	1.17		

[a]Adjusted to reflect a 4.25-for-1 stock split in December 1991.
[b]Initial public offering in February 1992.
[c]Includes $3,595,000 of income for cumulative effect of FAS 109.
[d]Includes a pretax charge of $1,120,000 from sale of investment in joint venture.

Transfer Agent & Registrar: Harris Trust and Savings Bank

General Counsel:
  Vedder, Price, Kaufman & Kammholz

Investor Relations: Marc T. Tanenberg, V.P.

Human Resources: Larry P. Bentley, V.P.

Auditors: Coopers & Lybrand L.L.P.

Traded (Symbol):   NASDAQ (IJIN)

Stockholders: 1,800

Employees: 1,725

Annual Meeting: In June

Itel Corporation

Two North Riverside Plaza, Suite 1900, Chicago, Illinois 60606
Telephone: (312) 902-1515

Itel Corporation, through its ownership of Anixter and a 30 percent interest in ANTEC Corporation, supplies wiring systems for data, voice and energy, and supplies and develops products employing broadband and fiber networks for video, voice and data applications. Anixter, with a global network of 160 locations, is a $1.7 billion value-added provider of integrated communications systems and services. ANTEC is an international technology integration company that specializes in the design, engineering, manufacturing, and distribution of products for fiber and coaxial broadband networks. Incorporated in Delaware in 1967.

Directors   (In addition to indicated officers)

James Blyth	John R. Petty
Bernard F. Brennan	Sheli Z. Rosenberg
F. Philip Handy	Stuart Sloan
Melvyn N. Klein	Thomas C. Theobald

Officers   (Directors*)

*Samuel Zell, Chm.	Philip F. Meno, V.P.—Taxes
*Rod F. Dammeyer, Pres. & C.E.O.	John M. Egan, Pres./C.E.O.—ANTEC
Kirk E. Brewer, Sr. V.P.—Corp. & Inv. Rel.	J. George Miller, Pres./C.E.O.—Anixter
James E. Knox, Sr. V.P., Gen. Coun. & Secy.	Eben Moulton, Pres./C.E.O.—Signal Cap. Mer. Bank

Consolidated Balance Sheet   As of December 31, 1994 (000 omitted)

Assets		Liabilities & Stockholders' Equity	
Current assets	$ 620,800	Current liabilities	$ 266,500
Net property, plant & equipment	33,400	Long-term debt	280,500
Other assets	456,700	Deferred items	600
		Other liabilities	11,200
		Minority interests	8,200
		*Stockholders' equity	543,900
Total	$1,110,900	Total	$1,110,900

*29,400,000 shares common stock outstanding.

Consolidated Income Statement[a][b]

Years Ended Dec. 31	Thousands — — — — Net Sales	Net Income	Per Share — — — Earnings	Cash Dividends	Common Stock Price Range Calendar Year
1994	$1,732,600	$ 246,900	$ 7.71	$ .00	36- 1/4 — 22- 3/4
1993	1,756,200	(1,200)	(.14)	.00	33- 5/8 — 20- 1/4
1992	1,464,600	(104,300)	(3.79)	.00	24- 3/8 — 16
1991	1,591,100	(55,700)	(1.79)	.00	20- 1/4 — 9- 3/4
1990	1,617,400	128,700	2.60	.00	24 — 7- 5/8

[a]Restated to reflect FAS 109.
[b]Consolidated results in 1993 included ANTEC, while 1994 consolidated results present ANTEC as an equity investment. Itel reduced its interest in ANTEC to 30 percent of ANTEC's outstanding shares in 1994.

Transfer Agent & Registrar:	Chemical Trust Company of California		
General Counsel:	James E. Knox, Sr. V.P.	Traded (Symbol):	NYSE (ITL)
Investor Relations:	Kirk E. Brewer, Sr. V.P.	Stockholders:	6,005
		Employees:	5,300
Auditors:	Ernst & Young LLP	Annual Meeting:	In May

JG Industries, Inc.

1615 West Chicago Avenue, Chicago, Illinois 60622
Telephone: (312) 421-5300

JG Industries, Inc., is a Chicago-based retailing concern that operates, through its various subsidiaries, 14 Goldblatt's department stores with 13 locations in the Chicago area and one in Indiana; and 13 Huffman Koos furniture stores in New Jersey and New York. Goldblatt's stores offer a broad range of fashion-wearing apparel for the entire family. The department stores also sell hard-line merchandise, including toys, sporting goods, cosmetics, luggage, housewares, textiles, and domestics. Jupiter Industries, Inc., owns about 55 percent of the outstanding shares of common stock. Sussex Group, Ltd., conducts the retail furniture operations. Incorporated in Illinois in 1928.

Directors   (In addition to indicated officers)

Peter C.B. Bynoe
Sheldon C. Collen
Max Dressler

Charles H. Jamison
Michael Kurzman
Wallace W. Schroeder

Officers   (Directors*)

*William Hellman, Chm. & C.E.O.
*Edward W. Ross, V. Chm.
 Clarence Farrar, Pres. & C.O.O.
*Lionel H. Goldblatt, V.P.

William M. Guzik, V.P., C.F.O. & Secy.
*Philip Rootberg, V.P.
 Evelyn P. Egan, Treas. & Asst. Secy.

Consolidated Balance Sheet   As of January 28, 1995 (000 omitted)

Assets		Liabilities & Stockholders' Equity	
Current assets	$56,215	Current liabilities	$35,871
Net property, plant & equipment	16,349	Long-term debt, less current portion	11,269
Other assets	3,443	Minority interest	17,268
		Redeemable preferred stock	3,183
		*Stockholders' equity	8,416
Total	$76,007	Total	$76,007

*7,054,873 shares common stock outstanding.

Consolidated Income Statement

Years Ended Abt. Jan. 31	Thousands — — — —		Per Share — — —		Common Stock Price Range Calendar Year
	Net Sales	Net Income[a]	Earnings[a]	Cash Dividends	
1995	$196,195	$ 487	$ .04		
1994	176,273	(1,346)	(.23)	.00	2-1/4 — 1
1993	168,939	691	(.08)	.00	3-1/2 — 1-1/8
1992	153,589	136	(.21)	.00	1-7/8 — 1/2
1991	137,768	(446)	(.29)	.00	2-3/8 — 5/8

[a]From continuing operations.

Transfer Agent & Registrar: The First National Bank of Chicago

Investor Relations: Evelyn P. Egan, Treas.

Human Resources: Darlene Wisneski, V.P.

Auditors: Coopers & Lybrand L.L.P.

Traded (Symbol):   NASDAQ, CSE (JGIN)
Stockholders: 2,592
Employees: 1,597
Annual Meeting: In June

Johnstown America Industries, Inc.

980 North Michigan Avenue, Suite 1000, Chicago, Illinois 60611
Telephone: (312) 280-8844

Johnstown America Industries, Inc., through its wholly owned subsidiary, Johnstown America Corporation, is a leading manufacturer of a variety of railroad freight cars that are used principally for hauling coal, intermodal containers (which are used on trucks and ships as well as on freight cars), highway trailers, and agricultural and mining products. Johnstown America is the leading manufacturer of coal gondola cars and a leading manufacturer of intermodal cars, two of the fastest growing segments of the freight car market. The company also completely rebuilds cars and sells car kits to railroads and car repair shops for assembly. Other subsidiaries are Freight Car Services Inc. and JAIX Leasing Company. In January 1995, the company acquired Bostrom Seating, Inc., a manufacturer of air suspension and static seats for the Class 8 heavy truck market. In June 1995, the company agreed to acquire Truck Components Inc. Incorporated in Delaware in 1991.

Directors (In addition to indicated officers)

Anthony J. Garcia
Camillo Santomero

R. Philip Silver
Francis A. Stroble

Officers (Directors*)

*Thomas M. Begel, Chm., Pres. & C.E.O.
*Andrew M. Weller, Exec. V.P., C.F.O. & Secy.
 Gary Ouderkirk, Pres.—Bostrom Seating, Inc.

Thomas Uhlig, Pres.—Johnstown America Corp.
Edward J. Whalen, Pres.—JAIX Leasing Co./Freight Car Svcs. Inc.

Consolidated Balance Sheet As of December 31, 1994 (000 omitted)

Assets		Liabilities & Stockholders' Equity	
Current assets	$ 82,208	Current liabilities	$ 58,241
Net property, plant & equipment	33,453	Long-term liabilities	7,600
Other assets	27,693	Other liabilities	14,279
		*Stockholders' equity	63,234
Total	$143,354	Total	$143,354

*9,722,862 shares common stock outstanding.

Consolidated Income Statement

Years Ended Dec. 31	Thousands — — — — Net Sales	Net Income	Per Share[a] — — — Earnings	Cash Dividends	Common Stock Price Range[ab] Calendar Year
1994	$468,525	$ 5,697	$ .58	$ .00	30-1/4 — 10-1/2
1993	329,122	2,463[c]	.30[c]	.00	26-1/4 — 14
1992	204,500	(731)	(.13)		
1991[d]	48,548	778	.12		

[a]Adjusted to reflect a 2-for-5 reverse stock split in July 1993.
[b]Initial public offering in July 1993.
[c]Includes an extraordinary charge of $2,918,000 ($.36 per share) from the repayment of debt.
[d]From October 28, 1991, when Johnstown America Corporation acquired substantially all of the assets of the Freight Car Division of Bethlehem Steel Corporation.

Transfer Agent & Registrar: Mellon Securities Trust Co.

General Counsel:
 Skadden, Arps, Slate, Meagher & Flom
Investor Relations:
 Andrew M. Weller, Exec. V.P.
Auditors: Arthur Andersen LLP

Traded (Symbol): NASDAQ (JAII)
Stockholders: 100
Employees: 1,700
Annual Meeting: In May

Joslyn Corporation

30 South Wacker Drive, Chicago, Illinois 60606
Telephone: (312) 454-2900

Joslyn Corporation and its subsidiaries are suppliers of diversified products and services to the electric utility, industrial controls, telecommunications, defense and aerospace markets. The company manufactures antenna lightning arresters and electromagnetic pulse protection devices for the aerospace and defense industries. Joslyn manufactures communication transient voltage suppression devices, and manufactures and supplies electrical hardware, apparatus, protective equipment and services used in the construction and maintenance of transmission and distribution facilities to electrical power and telephone companies. Joslyn's subsidiaries are Joslyn Canada, Inc.; Joslyn Hi-Voltage Corporation; Joslyn Manufacturing Co.; Joslyn Power Products Corporation; Joslyn Clark Controls, Inc.; ADK Pressure Equipment Corporation; Joslyn Jennings Corporation; Joslyn Research and Development Corporation; Joslyn Foreign Sales Corporation; Joslyn Electronic Systems Corporation; and The Sunbank Family of Companies, Inc. Facilities are located in California, Illinois, Ohio, South Carolina, Texas and Canada. Incorporated in Illinois in 1902.

Directors (In addition to indicated officer)

William E. Bendix, Chm.
John H. Deininger
Richard C. Osborne

James M. Reed
Lawrence A. Reed

Officers (Director*)

*Lawrence G. Wolski, Acting C.E.O.
George W. Diehl, V.P.
Daniel Dumont, V.P.

Wayne M. Koprowski, V.P., Gen. Coun. & Secy.
Steven L. Thunander, V.P.
Raymond G. Bjorseth, Cont.

Consolidated Balance Sheet As of December 31, 1994 (000 omitted)

Assets		Liabilities & Stockholders' Equity	
Current assets	$119,625	Current liabilities	$ 43,666
Net property, plant & equipment	37,955	Other liabilities	53,212
Other assets	19,924	*Stockholders' equity	80,626
Total	$177,504	Total	$177,504

*7,154,000 shares common stock outstanding.

Consolidated Income Statement

Years Ended Dec. 31	Thousands — — — — Net Sales	Net Income	Per Share[a] — — — Earnings	Cash Dividends	Common Stock Price Range[a] Calendar Year
1994	$216,177	$(11,180)[b]	$(1.57)	$1.20	32 — 22-3/4
1993	217,707	14,870	2.10	1.16	28-1/2 — 23-1/4
1992	217,889	14,308	2.03	1.13	27-3/4 — 20-1/8
1991	203,736	6,937[c]	.98[c]	1.07	21-5/8 — 13-5/8
1990	197,006	(10,990)[d]	(1.55)[d]	1.07	19-1/2 — 12-5/8

[a]Adjusted to reflect a 3-for-2 stock split in December 1992.
[b]Includes charges of $35,000,000 and $6,200,000.
[c]Includes a charge to reflect FAS 106, resulting in a cumulative effect of $10,963,000 ($.89 per share).
[d]Includes non-recurring charges of $21,500,000 after taxes ($4.56 per share), primarily for the writedown of goodwill.

Transfer Agent & Registrar: The First National Bank of Chicago

General Counsel:	Wayne M. Koprowski, V.P.	Auditors:	Arthur Andersen LLP
Investor Relations:	William J. Rotenberry, Dir.	Traded (Symbol):	NASDAQ (JOSL)
		Stockholders:	3,075
Human Resources:	Lewis M. Jacobson	Employees:	1,975
Mgt. Info. Svcs.:	Rachel A. Murdock	Annual Meeting:	In April

Juno Lighting, Inc.

2001 South Mt. Prospect Road, P.O. Box 5065, Des Plaines, Illinois 60017-5065

Telephone: (708) 827-9880

Juno Lighting, Inc., manufactures and markets a full line of recessed and track lighting fixtures for use in new construction and remodeling of commercial, institutional and residential buildings. The company produces more than 300 styles of fixtures and related equipment of both contemporary and traditional design with a variety of finishes. Principal products use incandescent light sources (filament lamps as distinguished from fluorescent tubes). Examples of new product introductions in 1994 include: a line of energy conserving Compact Fluorescent trac fixtures; two new design-patented series of halogen trac fixtures marketed under the names Delta 200 and Flyback; and additional trac and recessed products incorporating White Baffles. More than 94 percent of the company's sales are to electrical distributors and wholesale lighting outlets in the U.S. Warehouse facilities are located in the metropolitan areas of Atlanta, Dallas, Indianapolis, Los Angeles, Philadelphia and Toronto. Subsidiaries include Juno Lighting, Ltd.; and Indy Lighting, Inc., Indianapolis, a manufacturer of commercial lighting products for department and chain stores. Incorporated in Illinois in 1976; reincorporated in Delaware in 1983.

Directors (In addition to indicated officers)

George M. Ball   Allan Coleman

Officers (Directors*)

*Robert S. Fremont, Chm. & C.E.O.
*Ronel W. Giedt, Pres. & C.O.O.
George J. Bilek, V.P.—Fin. & Treas.
Glenn R. Bordfeld, V.P.—Sales

Charles F. Huber, V.P.—Corp. Dev.
*Thomas W. Tomsovic, V.P.—Oper.
*Julius Lewis, Secy.

Consolidated Balance Sheet As of November 30, 1994 (000 omitted)

Assets		Liabilities & Stockholders' Equity	
Current assets	$100,005	Current liabilities	$ 10,554
Net property, plant & equipment	31,195	Long-term debt	6,404
Other assets	14,556	Deferred items	2,050
		*Stockholders' equity	126,748
Total	$145,756	Total	$145,756

*18,457,112 shares common stock outstanding.

Consolidated Income Statement

Years Ended Nov. 30	Thousands — — — — Net Sales	Net Income	Per Share[a] — — — Earnings	Cash Dividends	Common Stock Price Range[a] Calendar Year	
1994	$126,777	$22,907	$1.23	$ .26	21	— 16-1/4
1993	109,098	18,213	.98	.22	21	— 15-1/2
1992	96,633	15,321	.83	.17	18-1/4	— 10
1991	79,538	12,773	.69	.14	12-1/8	— 8-1/4
1990	85,474	13,353	.73	.12	11-5/8	— 6

[a]Adjusted to reflect a 2-for-1 stock split in April 1992 in the form of a 100% stock dividend.

Transfer Agent & Registrar: First Chicago Trust Co. of New York

General Counsel:
  Sonnenschein Nath & Rosenthal

Investor Relations: George J. Bilek, V.P.

Human Resources: George J. Bilek, V.P.

Mgt. Info. Svcs.: Thomas W. Tomsovic, V.P.

Auditors: Price Waterhouse LLP
Traded (Symbol): NASDAQ (JUNO)
Stockholders: 349
Employees: 915
Annual Meeting: In April

Kemper Corporation

One Kemper Drive, Long Grove, Illinois 60049-0001
Telephone: (708) 320-4700

Kemper Corporation is a financial services holding company focused on its core asset management, life insurance, and securities brokerage businesses. The asset management business primarily consists of the mutual fund products and investment advisory services provided by Kemper Financial Services, Inc., and its subsidiaries. Assets under management totaled about $63 billion at December 31, 1994. The life insurance business is produced by Federal Kemper Life Assurance Company, which sells mortality-based and interest-sensitive life insurance and annuities through independent general agents, brokerage general agents, and other organizations such as savings institutions, securities brokerage firms, and property-casualty insurance agents; and Kemper Investors Life Insurance Company, which provides a variety of fixed and variable annuities as well as interest-sensitive and variable life products. The two life subsidiaries had over $97 billion of insurance in-force and invested assets of more than $7 billion at December 31, 1994. The securities brokerage business, represented by Kemper Securities, Inc., is primarily retail oriented, with a measure of diversification in investment banking, municipal finance and institutional sales. Nationwide, KSI had 155 offices and more than 1,300 registered representatives at December 31, 1994. Kemper Corporation also has a real estate segment, which owns equity interests in mainly commercial real estate properties and projects. In April 1995, Kemper announced that the Kemper Securities, Inc., employee stock ownership plan would purchase 55 percent of the brokerage unit while 44 percent would be spun off to Kemper Corp. stockholders; and that Kemper Corp. would be acquired by an investor group led by Zurich Insurance Group. Incorporated in Delaware in 1967.

Directors   (In addition to indicated officers)

John T. Chain, Jr.	George D. Kennedy
J. Reed Coleman	Richard D. Nordman
Raymond F. Farley	Kenneth A. Randall
Peter B. Hamilton	Daniel R. Toll

Officers   (Directors*)

*David B. Mathis, Chm. & C.E.O.	Kathleen A. Gallichio, Sr. V.P., Gen. Coun. & Corp. Secy.
*Stephen B. Timbers, Pres. & C.O.O.	Arthur J. McGivern, Sr. V.P. & Corp. Coun.
James R. Boris, Exec. V.P.—Sales & Distr.	John E. Neal, Sr. V.P.—Asset Mgt.
*John H. Fitzpatrick, Exec. V.P. & C.F.O.	Joseph R. Sitar, Sr. V.P. & Chf. Acct. Off.
John B. Scott, Exec. V.P.—Life & Annuities	Frederick L. Stephens, Sr. V.P.—Real Est.
Alan J. Baltz, Sr. V.P.—Adm.	John W. Burns III, Treas.
Stanley R. Fallis, Sr. V.P.—Planning	Thomas B. Sabol, Gen. Auditor

Consolidated Balance Sheet   As of December 31, 1994 (000 omitted)

Assets		Liabilities & Stockholders' Equity	
Investments	$ 7,390,261	Life policy benefits	$ 7,871,160
Accounts receivable	1,363,073	Long-term debt	358,891
Deferred insurance acquis. costs	696,804	Convert. debent. of subsid.	33,113
Deferred invest. prod. sales costs	166,397	Liabilities of separate accounts	1,871,777
Assets of separated accounts	1,871,777	Other liabilities	1,761,669
Other assets	1,665,655	*Stockholders' equity	1,257,357
Total	$13,153,967	Total	$13,153,967

*34,417,484 shares common stock outstanding.

Consolidated Income Statement

Years Ended Dec. 31	Thousands — — — —		Per Share — — —		Common Stock
	Total Revenue[a]	Net Income[ab]	Earnings[ab]	Cash Dividends	Price Range Calendar Year
1994	$1,601,821	$ 85,713	$ 1.80	$ .92	64-5/8 — 35-3/8
1993	1,549,174	(101,284)	(2.80)	.92	43 — 26-1/8
1992	1,503,724	(214,675)	(4.39)	.92	46-1/8 — 20-3/4
1991	1,815,843	76,063	1.58	.92	41 — 19-3/4
1990	1,829,263	(69,858)	(1.44)	.92	51 — 17-1/8

[a]Continuing operations, including accounting changes.
[b]Includes realized investment results.

Transfer Agent & Registrar: Harris Trust and Savings Bank

General Counsel:	Kathleen A. Gallichio, Sr. V.P.	Auditors:	KPMG Peat Marwick LLP
Investor Relations:	John A. Effrein, Dir.	Traded (Symbol):	NYSE (KEM)
		Stockholders:	12,200
Human Resources:	Sharon R. Quay, V.P.	Employees:	6,059
Mgt. Info. Svcs.:	Ira Nathanson, Sr. V.P.	Annual Meeting:	In May

Landauer, Inc.

2 Science Road, Glenwood, Illinois 60425-1586
Telephone: (708) 755-7000

Landauer, Inc., engages in the detection of personal exposure to occupational and environmental hazards in the workplace and at home. The company specializes in providing complete radiation dosimetry programs, which include the manufacture of various types of personal radiation exposure detection monitors, the distribution and collection of the monitors to and from clients, and the analysis and reporting of exposure findings. Services are used by hospitals, universities, national laboratories, nuclear power plants, medical and dental offices, and other industries in which radiation poses a potential threat to employees. Landauer also offers assessment of the concentration of radon gas in homes and other buildings through its long-term alpha-track radon gas detectors. The company also operates a 50 percent-owned subsidiary in Japan, Nagase-Landauer, Ltd., which is involved in radiation monitoring in that country. Landauer branch offices are located in New Jersey, California, Texas and the United Kingdom. Incorporated in Delaware in 1987.

Directors (In addition to indicated officers)

Gary D. Eppen, Ph.D.
Richard H. Leet
Paul B. Rosenberg

Herbert Roth, Jr.
C. Vincent Vappi
Michael D. Winfield

Officers (Directors*)

*Marvin G. Schorr, Chm.
*Thomas M. Fulton, Pres. & C.E.O.
Brent A. Latta, V.P.—Mktg.
James M. O'Connell, V.P., C.F.O., Treas. & Secy.

R. Craig Yoder, V.P.—Oper.
Larry A. Barden, Gen. Coun.
Lester A. Core, Asst. Secy.

Consolidated Balance Sheet   As of September 30, 1994 (000 omitted)

Assets		Liabilities & Stockholders' Equity	
Current assets	$14,108	Current liabilities	$13,109
Net property, plant & equipment	7,079	*Stockholders' equity	22,531
Other assets	14,453		
Total	$35,640	Total	$35,640

*8,477,285 shares common stock outstanding.

Consolidated Income Statement

Years Ended Sept. 30	Thousands — — — — Net Revenue	Net Income	Per Share[a] — — — — Earnings	Cash Dividends	Common Stock Price Range[a] Calendar Year
1994	$31,653	$8,903	$1.05	$ .88	17 — 13-1/8
1993	29,406	8,023	.95	.80	17-1/4 — 14-5/8
1992	27,823	7,882	.93	1.15	21-3/8 — 14-1/2
1991	26,932	7,440	.88	.50	17-7/8 — 14-1/8
1990	24,736	6,509	.77	.80	15-1/8 — 10-3/4

[a]Adjusted to reflect a 2-for-1 stock split effective January 17, 1992.

Transfer Agent & Registrar: The Bank of Boston, Boston, Massachusetts

Corporate Counsel: Sidley & Austin

Investor Relations: James M. O'Connell, V.P.

Human Resources: James M. O'Connell, V.P.

Mgt. Info. Svcs.:   Emil A. Plecko

Auditors: Arthur Andersen LLP

Traded (Symbol): AMEX, CSE (LDR)

Stockholders: 600

Employees: 260

Annual Meeting: In February

Lawson Products, Inc.

1666 East Touhy Avenue, Des Plaines, Illinois 60018
Telephone: (708) 827-9666

Lawson Products, Inc., is an international distributor of approximately 28,000 expendable maintenance, repair and replacement fasteners, parts, chemical specialties, welding rod and supplies, hydraulic and other flexible hose fittings, electrical and shop supplies. These products are used for the repair and maintenance of capital equipment of all types in the industrial, heavy duty equipment, in-plant, buildings and grounds maintenance, and transportation fields. Sales are made to a wide variety of industrial, mining, institutional, governmental, agricultural, automotive, and apartment building maintenance customers through approximately 1,600 agents in the U.S., Puerto Rico, Canada, Mexico, and England. Distribution centers are located in Georgia, Illinois, Nevada, New Jersey, Texas, Canada and England. Specialized subsidiaries include Cronatron Welding Systems, Inc., and Drummond American Corporation. Incorporated in Illinois in 1952; reincorporated in Delaware in 1982.

Directors   (In addition to indicated officers)

James T. Brophy
Louis L. Carrol
Ronald B. Port, M.D.

Robert G. Rettig
Thomas W. Smith

Officers   (Directors*)

*Bernard Kalish, Chm. & C.E.O.
*Sidney L. Port, Chm. of the Exec. Comm.
*Peter G. Smith, Pres. & C.O.O.
 Hugh L. Allen, Exec. V.P.—Sales & Mktg.
 Jeffrey B. Belford, Exec. V.P.—Oper.
 Leslie R. White, Sr. V.P.—Corp. Admin. Syst.
 Walter L. Anderson, V.P.—Eng.
 George H. Buckingham, V.P.—East. Field
 Sales
 James N. Buckingham, V.P.—Mexico & Latin
 Amer. Dev.

Roger F. Cannon, V.P.—Cent. Field Sales
John M. Del Sasso, V.P.—Dist.
Henry Kvintus, V.P.—Hum. Res.
Joseph L. Pawlick, V.P. & Cont.
James L. Schmidt, V.P.—Credit Admin.
Donald A. Schneider, V.P.—Int'l. Dev.
*Jerome Shaffer, V.P. & Treas.
James J. Smith, V.P.—Personnel
Robert J. Spedale, V.P.—Purch. & Prod. Dev.
Robert J. Washlow, Secy.

Consolidated Balance Sheet   As of December 31, 1994 (000 omitted)

Assets		Liabilities & Stockholders' Equity	
Current assets	$ 92,249	Current liabilities	$ 19,815
Net property, plant & equipment	35,858	Other liabilities	17,085
Other assets	40,023	*Stockholders' equity	131,230
Total	$168,130	Total	$168,130

*12,603,814 shares common stock outstanding.

Consolidated Income Statement

Years Ended Dec. 31	Thousands — — — — Net Sales	Net Income	Per Share — — — Earnings	Cash Dividends	Common Stock Price Range Calendar Year
1994	$213,097	$20,524	$1.55	$ .48	31 — 21-3/4
1993	195,735	18,117	1.34	.44	30-3/4 — 23-1/4
1992	186,709	15,343	1.13	.40	31-1/4 — 22
1991	181,729	16,647	1.23	.40	35-1/4 — 22-1/2
1990	185,571	22,571	1.67	.37	30-1/2 — 22-3/4

Transfer Agent & Registrar: The First National Bank of Chicago

General Counsel:
 McDermott, Will & Emery; Vedder, Price, Kaufman & Kammholz

Investor Relations: Bernard Kalish, Chm.

Human Resources: Henry Kvintus, V.P.

Auditors: Ernst & Young LLP
Traded (Symbol):   NASDAQ (LAWS)
Stockholders: 1,375
Employees: 750
Annual Meeting: In May

Lawter International, Inc.

990 Skokie Boulevard, Northbrook, Illinois 60062
Telephone: (708) 498-4700

Lawter International, Inc., manufactures and markets specialty chemicals. Products include: printing ink vehicles and components, which enable printing inks to carry color onto a variety of printing surfaces; synthetic and hydrocarbon resins for the production of printing inks, varnishes and other coatings, adhesives, rubber compounds and plastics; thermographic compounds used in the production of embossed lettering; and fluorescent pigments and coatings used in the production of paint, printing ink, paper coatings, plastic products and rubber compounds. Lawter also manufactures thermographic and rota-matic machines. The company's domestic plants are located in Alabama, California, Illinois, New Jersey, Tennessee and Wisconsin. Plants outside the U.S. are located in Belgium, Canada, Denmark, England, Germany, Ireland, Italy, the People's Republic of China, Spain, and Singapore. Incorporated in Delaware in 1958 to succeed a company established in 1940.

Directors (In addition to indicated officers)

William P. Clark
Arthur A. Hartman

Leonard P. Judy
Fred G. Steingraber

Officers (Directors*)

*Daniel J. Terra, Chm. & C.E.O.
*Richard D. Nordman, Pres. & C.O.O.
Richard A. Hacker, V.P.
Ludwig P. Horn, V.P.
John P. Jilek, V.P.

Hermann Mueller, V.P.
John O'Mahoney, V.P.—Eur. Oper.
William S. Russell, V.P., Treas. & Secy.
Victoria J. Patrick, Asst. Secy.

Consolidated Balance Sheet   As of December 31, 1994 (000 omitted)

Assets		Liabilities & Stockholders' Equity	
Current assets	$150,129	Current liabilities	$ 64,528
Net property, plant & equipment	52,465	Long-term obligations	4,152
Other assets	29,233	Deferred items	35,354
		*Stockholders' equity	127,793
Total	$231,827	Total	$231,827

*44,923,729 shares common stock outstanding.

Consolidated Income Statement

Years Ended Dec. 31	Thousands — — — — Net Sales	Net Income	Per Share[a] — — — Earnings	Cash Dividends	Common Stock Price Range[a] Calendar Year
1994	$191,056	$29,405	$ .66	$ .40	13-3/4 — 10-3/4
1993	172,249	5,027[b]	.11[b]	.40	15-1/2 — 12-1/8
1992	167,568	27,015	.62	.40	14-7/8 — 11-7/8
1991	152,893	26,470	.61	.35	13-3/4 — 7-7/8
1990	150,005	23,420	.54	.29	8-1/2 — 6-1/2

[a]Adjusted to reflect 4-for-3 stock splits in November 1991 and 1990.
[b]Includes adjustments of $21,600,000 ($.48 per share) for taxes on foreign earnings; $6,400,000 ($.14 per share) for other charges; and a credit of $4,025,000 ($.09 per share) for FAS 109.

Transfer Agent & Registrar:	Harris Trust and Savings Bank		
General Counsel:	Bell, Boyd & Lloyd	Traded (Symbol):	NYSE (LAW)
Investor Relations:	William S. Russell, V.P.	Stockholders:	3,400
Human Resources:	Sue Vollmer	Employees:	577
Auditors:	Arthur Andersen LLP	Annual Meeting:	In April

Liberty Bancorp, Inc.

5700 North Lincoln Avenue, Chicago, Illinois 60659
Telephone: (312) 334-1200

Liberty Bancorp, Inc., is the savings and loan holding company for Liberty Federal Savings Bank. Liberty Federal, which was established in 1887, is a member of the Federal Home Loan Bank System, and its deposit accounts are insured to the maximum allowable amount by the Federal Deposit Insurance Corporation. The savings bank is a community-oriented institution offering traditional deposit and mortgage loan products. It operates three offices, one in northwestern Chicago, one in Morton Grove, and one in Glenview, Illinois, and its deposit-gathering area is concentrated in the neighborhoods surrounding its offices. Incorporated in Delaware in 1991.

Directors (In addition to indicated officers)

Whit G. Hughes
H. Verne Loeppert
David D. Mill, D.D.S.

William C. O'Donnell
Vernon B. Thomas, Jr.

Officers (Directors*)

*Edward J. Burns, Chm.
*Fredric G. Novy, Pres. & C.E.O.
 Joseph W. Stachnik, V.P., C.F.O., Treas. &
 Asst. Secy.

Cynthia M. Mallo, Secy.

Consolidated Balance Sheet As of December 31, 1994 (000 omitted)

Assets		Liabilities & Stockholders' Equity	
Cash & due from banks	$ 6,798	Deposits	$453,084
Other current assets	10,301	Borrowed funds	62,000
Loans receivable, net	502,359	Advance payments by borrowers for taxes & insur.	4,512
Net property, plant & equipment	3,141		
Investment securities	21,061	Accrued expenses & other liabilities	6,006
Mortgage-backed securities	37,494		
Other assets	14,290	*Stockholders' equity	69,842
Total	$595,444	Total	$595,444

*2,872,716 shares common stock outstanding.

Consolidated Income Statement

Years Ended Dec. 31	Thousands — — — —		Per Share — — —		Common Stock
	Total Income	Net Income	Earnings	Cash Dividends	Price Range Calendar Year
1994	$38,016	$5,182	$1.65	$2.10	32　— 20-3/4
1993	39,949	6,897	2.17	.45	26-3/4— 18
1992	41,631	6,843[a]	2.06[a]	.00	18-3/4— 12-3/4
1991[b]	41,085	3,494			13-1/2— 12-1/4[c]
1990	39,812	2,976			

[a]Includes a gain to reflect FAS 106 and FAS 109, resulting in a cumulative effect of $481,000 ($.14 per share).
[b]Earnings per share not meaningful as the stock conversion was not completed until December 23, 1991.
[c]Initial public offering in December 1991. Financial information for 1990 is for Liberty Federal Savings Bank.

Transfer Agent & Registrar: Harris Trust and Savings Bank

General Counsel:
 Muldoon, Murphy & Faucette

Investor Relations:
 James K. Mair, Mgr.—Shareholder Services

Human Resources: Susan Schliep

Mgt. Info. Svcs.: Joseph W. Stachnik, V.P.

Auditors: KPMG Peat Marwick LLP

Traded (Symbol): NASDAQ (LBCI)

Stockholders: 750

Employees: 150

Annual Meeting: In April

Lindberg Corporation

6133 North River Road, Suite 700, Rosemont, Illinois 60018
Telephone: (708) 823-2021

Lindberg Corporation provides heat treating services and produces a variety of metal parts. The company serves many industries, including the automotive, truck, construction equipment, consumer durables, defense and aerospace, and tool and die industries. Commercial heat treating services are provided from 17 plants offering a variety of thermal processes. These include hardening and tempering; carburizing; nitriding; selective hardening; solution treating and aging; stress relieving; normalizing; and other specialty or proprietary processes. Technical and Management services are also provided to customers with in-house heat treating facilities. Aluminum and zinc die castings and assemblies are produced at Impact Industries and Arrow-Acme. Harris Metals provides precision aluminum castings. The Allow Wire Belt division manufactures conveyor belting products used in food processing industries. Incorporated in Illinois in 1924; reincorporated in Delaware in 1976.

Directors (In addition to indicated officers)

Raymond F. Decker
John W. Puth

J. Thomas Schanck

Officers (Directors*)

*George H. Bodeen, Chm.
*Leo G. Thompson, Pres. & C.E.O.
 Gary E. Miller, Sr. V.P.
 Michael W. Nelson, Sr. V.P.
 Stephen S. Penley, Sr. V.P. & C.F.O.
 Terrence D. Brown, V.P.

Geoffrey S. Calhoun, V.P.
Roger J. Fabian, V.P.
Paul J. McCarren, V.P.
Jerome R. Sullivan, V.P. & Mgr.—Hum. Res.
Brian J. McInerney, Asst. Treas.

Consolidated Balance Sheet As of December 31, 1994 (000 omitted)

Assets		Liabilities & Stockholders' Equity	
Current assets	$25,887	Current liabilities	$17,279
Net property, plant & equipment	38,858	Long-term debt	16,700
Other assets	5,777	Deferred items	6,491
		Other liabilities	5,383
		*Stockholders' equity	24,669
Total	$70,522	Total	$70,522

*4,717,016 shares common stock outstanding.

Consolidated Income Statement

Years Ended Dec. 31	Thousands — — — —		Per Share — — —		Common Stock Price Range Calendar Year
	Revenues	Net Income	Earnings	Cash Dividends	
1994	$99,858	$ 4,374	$ .92	$ .21	8-3/4 — 4-1/8
1993[a]	69,619	(1,318)	(.28)	.20	5-3/4 — 3-1/2
1992	71,039	942	.20	.24	5-1/2 — 3
1991	73,819	127	.03	.28	7-3/4 — 3-3/4
1990	76,141	3,205	.68	.28	6-1/4 — 4-1/2

[a]Includes a charge of $8,261,000 ($5,122,000 aftertax) for the restructuring of the company's heat treat operations and a $1,500,000 ($.32 per share) gain for an accounting change. Excluding those items, net earnings for 1993 were $2,304,473 ($.49 per share).

Transfer Agent & Registrar:	Harris Trust and Savings Bank			
General Counsel:	Bell, Boyd & Lloyd	Traded (Symbol):	NASDAQ (LIND)	
Investor Relations:	Stephen S. Penley, Sr. V.P.	Stockholders:	1,300	
Human Resources:	Jerome R. Sullivan, V.P.	Employees:	1,168	
Auditors:	Arthur Andersen LLP	Annual Meeting:	In April	

Littelfuse, Inc.

800 East Northwest Highway, Des Plaines, Illinois 60016
Telephone: (708) 824-1188

Littelfuse, Inc., is a leading world designer, manufacturer, and marketer of fuses and other circuit protection devices for use in the electronic, automotive, and general industrial markets. The company manufactures its products on fully integrated manufacturing and assembly equipment, much of which is designed and built by its own engineers. Littelfuse conducts a majority of its own fabrication and maintains product quality through a rigorous quality assurance program. In addition to its Des Plaines world headquarters, the company has research and manufacturing facilities in England, Switzerland, China, and Mexico, as well as in Centralia, Arcola and Watseka, Illinois. It also has sales, engineering, and distribution facilities in the Netherlands, Singapore, England, and Illinois. Littelfuse, Inc., is the successor to the business and assets of a corporation bearing the same name, which was originally formed in 1927 and subsequently acquired by Tracor, Inc., in 1968. Incorporated in Delaware in 1991.

Directors (In addition to indicated officer)

Anthony Grillo
Bruce A. Karsh

John E. Major
John J. Nevin

Officers (Director*)

*Howard B. Witt, Chm., Pres. & C.E.O.
Kenneth R. Audino, V.P.—Quality Assurance
  & Reliability
William S. Barron, V.P.—Sales & Mktg.
James F. Brace, V.P., Treas. & C.F.O.

David J. Krueger, V.P.—Eng.
Scott M. Nease, V.P. & Corp. Cont.
Lloyd J. Turner, V.P.—Oper.
Mary S. Muchoney, Secy.

Consolidated Balance Sheet   As of December 31, 1994 (000 omitted)

Assets		Liabilities & Stockholders' Equity	
Current assets	$ 58,791	Current liabilities	$ 38,068
Net property, plant & equipment	57,087	Long-term debt	60,344
Other assets	83,450	Deferred items	5,217
		*Stockholders' equity	95,699
Total	$199,328	Total	$199,328

*10,086,000 shares common stock outstanding.

Consolidated Income Statement[a]

Years Ended Abt. Dec. 31	Thousands — — — — Net Sales	Net Income	Per Share — — — Earnings	Cash Dividends	Common Stock Price Range Calendar Year
1994	$194,454	$ 15,227	$1.25	$ .00	31 — 20
1993	160,712	9,987	.83	.00	27-1/2 — 17
1992	149,832	654	.06	.00	19-1/4 — 7[b]
1991	136,388	158,372			
1990	133,894	(119,482)			

[a]1991-90 financial data for predecessor operations.
[b]Began trading on NASDAQ in September 1992.

Transfer Agent & Registrar: LaSalle National Trust, N.A.

General Counsel: Chapman & Cutler

Investor Relations: Art Skwerski, Dir.

Human Resources: Jon B. Anderson, Dir.

Mgt. Info. Svcs.:   Lisa Finch, Dir.

Auditors: Ernst & Young LLP
Traded (Symbol):   NASDAQ (LFUS)
Stockholders: 1,750
Employees: 2,270
Annual Meeting: In May

The Lori Corporation

500 Central Avenue, Northfield, Illinois 60093-8902
Telephone: (708) 441-7300

The Lori Corporation operates in the jewelry industry through two wholly owned subsidiaries: Rosecraft, Inc., and Lawrence Jewelry Corporation. Rosecraft is a creator, designer, importer and distributor of popular-priced fashion costume jewelry and related accessories for children. It offers more than 1,700 styles of earrings, necklaces, bracelets, hair and other fashion accessories. Lawrence is engaged in the distribution and sale of a full line of popular-priced fashion costume jewelry and fashion accessories to mass merchandise retailers, department stores, and specialty stores throughout the U.S. The Lori Corporation is 64 percent-owned by ARTRA GROUP, Inc. Lori's largest customer is Target stores. Incorporated in Delaware in 1969.

Directors (In addition to indicated officers)

Peter R. Harvey

Alexander Verde

Officers (Directors*)

*John Harvey, Chm.
*Austin A. Iodice, V. Chm., Pres. & C.E.O.
James D. Doering, V.P. & C.F.O.

Lawrence D. Levin, Cont.
Edwin G. Rymek, Secy.

Consolidated Balance Sheet   As of December 31, 1994 (000 omitted)

Assets		Liabilities & Stockholders' Equity	
Current assets	$ 4,512	Current liabilities	$ 5,358
Net property, plant & equipment	444	Other liabilities	8,068
Other assets	13,748	*Stockholders' equity	5,278
Total	$18,704	Total	$18,704

*3,165,019 shares common stock outstanding.

Consolidated Income Statement

| Years Ended Dec. 31 | Thousands — — — — | | Per Share — — — — | | Common Stock |
	Net Sales	Net Income	Earnings	Cash Dividends	Price Range Calendar Year
1994[a]	$ 34,431	$(9,537)	$(2.99)	$ .00	8-1/8 — 1-7/8
1993[b]	46,054	20,385	5.58	.00	8-1/2 — 3/4
1992[c]	75,484	(34,619)	(10.99)	.00	3-1/4 — 5/8
1991	106,834	(7,099)	(2.25)	.00	5 — 1-3/4
1990	114,604	1,686	.54	.00	5-5/8 — 1-1/4

[a]Includes an extraordinary credit of $8,965,000 ($2.81 per share) and a $10,800,000 writeoff of goodwill.
[b]Includes an extraordinary credit of $22,057,000 ($6.03 per share) from net discharge of indebtedness as a result of New Dimensions Accessories, Ltd, subsidiary emerging from Chapter 11 bankruptcy protection (May 3, 1993); and a charge of $767,000 related to reorganization.
[c]Includes non-recurring charges of $18,150,000.

Transfer Agent & Registrar: Mellon Securities Transfer Services

General Counsel:
Kwiatt, Silverman & Ruben Ltd.

Investor Relations:
Robert S. Gruber—(212) 628-2554

Human Resources: John P. Conroy

Auditors: Coopers & Lybrand L.L.P.

Traded (Symbol):   AMEX (LRC)

Stockholders: 5,600

Employees: 600

Annual Meeting: As set by Directors

M~Wave, Inc.

216 Evergreen Street, Bensenville, Illinois 60106
Telephone: (708) 860-9542

M~Wave, Inc., through its wholly owned subsidiary, Poly Circuits, Inc., manufactures microwave frequency components (MFC) and high frequency circuit boards (HFCB) on Teflon-based laminates (TBL). The company's MFC and HFCB are used in wireless communication systems and other devices and equipment operating in the microwave frequency spectrum of 800 Mhz and above, such as cellular telephone, direct broadcast satellite television, global positioning satellite systems, personal communication networks, and military smart weapons and antenna systems. Another subsidiary is PC Dynamics Corp. Incorporated in Delaware in 1992.

Directors (In addition to indicated officer)

Timothy A. Dugan
Irwin Katz
Lavern D. Kramer

Eric C. Larson
Daniel M. Morris

Officers (Director*)

*Joseph A. Turek, Chm., Pres. & C.E.O.

Paul H. Schmitt, Secy. & Treas.

Consolidated Balance Sheet As of December 31, 1994 (000 omitted)

Assets		Liabilities & Stockholders' Equity	
Current assets	$15,317	Current liabilities	$ 4,271
Net property, plant & equipment	6,456	Long-term debt	424
Other assets	1,485	Deferred items	920
		*Stockholders' equity	17,643
Total	$23,258	Total	$23,258

*3,005,750 shares common stock outstanding.

Consolidated Income Statement[a]

Years Ended Dec. 31	Thousands — — — — — Net Sales	Net Income	Per Share[b] — — — — Earnings	Cash Dividends	Common Stock Price Range[b] Calendar Year
1994	$28,009	$3,746[c]	$1.25	$ .00	17-3/4 — 9-3/4
1993	19,606	3,534	1.20	.00	27 — 3-3/4
1992	10,658	1,050	.40	.00	7-3/4 — 2-1/4
1991	14,418	3,012	1.51	.00	
1990	6,802	399	.20	.00	

[a]Initial public offering in April 1992.
[b]Adjusted to give effect to the 100-for-1 share exchange with the former stockholders of Poly Circuits, Inc., in January 1992.
[c]Includes a $425,000 non-recurring gain.

Transfer Agent & Registrar: Harris Trust and Savings Bank

General Counsel:
  Sonnenschein Nath & Rosenthal

Investor Relations: Paul H. Schmitt, Secy.

Human Resources: Diane DuVall, Mgr.

Mgt. Info. Svcs.: Paul H. Schmitt, Secy.

Auditors: Deloitte & Touche LLP

Traded (Symbol): NASDAQ (MWAV)

Stockholders: 2,200

Employees: 200

Annual Meeting: In June

First Chicago Guide

MAF Bancorp, Inc.

55th Street and Holmes Avenue, Clarendon Hills, Illinois 60514-1596
Telephone: (708) 325-7300

MAF Bancorp, Inc., is a registered savings and loan holding company and is engaged in the savings and loan business through its wholly owned subsidiary, Mid America Federal Savings Bank. The bank is a community-oriented financial institution offering various financial services to its customers through 13 retail banking offices. The bank's market area is generally defined as the western suburbs of Chicago, including DuPage County. It is principally engaged in the business of attracting deposits from the general public and using such deposits, along with other borrowings, to make loans secured by real estate, primarily single-family residential and, to a lesser extent, various types of consumer loans. Through its wholly owned subsidiaries, MAF Developments, Inc., and Mid America Development Services, Inc., the holding company and the bank are engaged in real estate development activities. Additionally, the bank operates an insurance agency, Mid America Insurance Agency, Inc., which provides general insurance service. As a federally chartered savings bank, the bank's deposits are insured up to the applicable limits by the Federal Deposit Insurance Corporation. Incorporated in Delaware in 1989.

Directors (In addition to indicated officers)

Robert J. Bowles, M.D.	Terry Ekl	Richard A. Kallal
Nicholas J. DiLorenzo, Sr.	Joe F. Hanauer	F. William Trescott

Officers (Directors*)

*Allen H. Koranda, Chm. & C.E.O.	Gerard J. Buccino, First V.P. & Cont.
*Kenneth Koranda, Pres.	Michael J. Janssen, First V.P.
Jerry A. Weberling, Exec. V.P. & C.F.O.	David W. Kohlsaat, First V.P.
Tom Miers, Sr. V.P.	Carolyn Pihera, V.P. & Corp. Secy.
Kenneth B. Rusdal, Sr. V.P.	Alan Schatz, V.P.
*Lois B. Vasto, Sr. V.P.	William Haider, Pres.—MAF and Mid America
Sharon Wheeler, Sr. V.P.	Developments

Consolidated Balance Sheet As of June 30, 1994 (000 omitted)

Assets		Liabilities & Stockholders' Equity	
Cash & due from banks	$ 28,635	Total deposits	$1,292,531
Interest-bearing deposits	29,922	Other liabilities	198,653
Federal funds sold	17,450	*Stockholders' equity	95,150
Investment securities	97,260		
Mortgage-backed securities	347,902		
Loans receivable/net	1,010,992		
Net property & equipment	20,416		
Other assets	33,757		
Total	$1,586,334	Total	$1,586,334

*5,158,739 shares common stock outstanding.

Consolidated Income Statement

Years Ended June 30	Thousands — — — — Total Income	Net Income	Per Share[a] — — — — Earnings	Cash Dividends	Common Stock Price Range[a] Fiscal Year
1994	$123,426	$13,450	$2.44	$ .00	24-1/2 — 17-5/8
1993	127,167	13,946	2.50	.00	19-5/8 — 9-1/8
1992	138,391	9,796	1.83	.00	9-7/8 — 4-1/2
1991	143,707	4,978	.94	.00	6-1/8 — 3
1990	156,388	4,968	.96	.00	6-1/8 — 4-3/8[b]

[a]Adjusted to reflect a 3-for-2 stock split in August 1993.
[b]Initial public offering in January 1990.

Transfer Agent & Registrar: Harris Trust and Savings Bank

General Counsel:	Muldoon, Murphy & Faucette	Auditors:	KPMG Peat Marwick LLP
Investor Relations:	Michael J. Janssen, First V.P.	Traded (Symbol):	NASDAQ (MAFB)
		Stockholders:	3,500
Human Resources:	David W. Kohlsaat, First V.P.	Employees:	493
Mgt. Info. Svcs.:	Kenneth B. Rusdal, Sr. V.P.	Annual Meeting:	In October

Magna Group, Inc.

One Magna Place, 1401 South Brentwood Boulevard, St. Louis, MO
63144-1401
Telephone: (314) 963-2500

Magna Group, Inc., is a retail banking franchise with 103 community banking locations and is a multi-bank holding company serving the greater St. Louis area and southern and central Illinois. More than 70 offices are located in the metropolitan St. Louis area. Magna focuses on community banking, serving customers and small to mid-sized businesses in its markets. Through its subsidiaries, the company engages in retail, commercial and correspondent banking, and provides trust services and investment services. Subsidiaries include Magna Bank of Illinois, Magna Bank of Missouri, Magna Trust Company, MGI Group, Inc., and InBank Group, Inc. Incorporated in Delaware in 1974.

Directors (In addition to indicated officer)

James A. Auffenberg, Jr.	Wendell J. Kelley
William E. Cribbin	S. Lee Kling
Wayne T. Ewing	Ralph F. Korte
Donald P. Gallop	Robert E. McGlynn
C.E. Heiligenstein	Frank R. Trulaske III
Carl G. Hogan, Sr.	George T. Wilkins, Jr., M.D.
Franklin A. Jacobs	

Officers (Director*)

*G. Thomas Andes, Chm. & C.E.O.
David L. Bramlet, Exec. V.P.—Branch
  Network
Linda K. Fabel, Exec. V.P.—Retail Banking
David D. Harris, Exec. V.P.—Credit Admin.

Gary D. Hemmer, Exec. V.P.—Admin.
James D. Jolley, Exec. V.P.—Invest.
Luckett G. Maynard, Exec. V.P. & C.F.O.
Robert M. Olson, Jr., Exec. V.P.—Opers. & Tech.

Consolidated Balance Sheet As of December 31, 1994 (000 omitted)

Assets		Liabilities & Stockholders' Equity	
Cash & due from banks	$ 264,434	Total deposits	$3,672,755
Federal funds sold	17,496	Short-term borrowings	436,515
Investment securities	1,217,174	Long-term borrowings	104,453
Net loans	2,920,205	Other liabilities	53,467
Premises & equipment	72,986	*Stockholders' equity	371,312
Other assets	146,207		
Total	$4,638,502	Total	$4,638,502

*27,512,462 shares common stock outstanding.

Consolidated Income Statement

Years Ended Dec. 31	Thousands — — — — Total Income	Net Income	Per Share[a] — — — Earnings[b]	Cash Dividends[c]	Common Stock Price Range[a] Calendar Year
1994	$337,064	$45,030	$1.69	$ .76	21-1/2 — 16-3/4
1993	290,128	37,487	1.50	.72	20-1/4 — 15-3/4
1992	312,496	30,192	1.38	.68	17-3/8 — 10-5/8
1991	219,650	3,838	.28	.68	13-1/2 — 8-1/2
1990	236,510	18,116	1.31	.65	16-1/2 — 8-1/2

[a]Adjusted to reflect mergers and 5% stock dividends, including one in January 1991.
[b]Fully diluted.
[c]Dividends declared.

Transfer Agent & Registrar:	Magna Trust Company		
General Counsel:	Thompson & Mitchell	Auditors:	Ernst & Young LLP
Investor Relations:	Gary D. Hemmer, Exec. V.P.	Traded (Symbol):	NASDAQ (MAGI)
Human Resources:	Leslie Mehrtens, Sr. V.P.	Stockholders:	8,912
Mgt. Info. Svcs.: Robert M. Olson, Jr., Exec. V.P.		Employees:	2,379
		Annual Meeting:	In May

Horace Mann Educators Corporation

1 Horace Mann Plaza, Springfield, Illinois 62715-0001
Telephone: (217) 789-2500

Horace Mann Educators Corporation is an insurance holding company, which through its subsidiaries, markets and underwrites personal lines of property/casualty and life insurance, and retirement annuities to individuals in all states except Hawaii, New York and New Jersey. The company also underwrites and markets a limited line of group life and health insurance products. Horace Mann markets its products primarily to educators and other employees of public schools and their families. The company sells and services its products through its own sales force. Subsidiaries are Horace Mann Insurance Company, Teachers Insurance Company, Allegiance Insurance Company, and Horace Mann Life Insurance Company. Incorporated in Delaware in 1968.

Directors (In addition to indicated officers)

Edward Gibbons
Todd Goodwin
Stafford R. Grady
Leonard I. Green

Donald G. Heth
Ralph S. Saul
Charles M. Williams

Officers (Directors*)

*John T. Gurash, Chm.
*Paul J. Kardos, Pres. & C.E.O.
Richard W. Stilwell, Sr. Exec. V.P.
Larry K. Becker, Exec. V.P. & C.F.O.
Clark W. McKee, Exec. V.P.
Edward L. Najim, Exec. V.P.
Walter E. Stooksbury, Exec. V.P.
Paul C. Tarr III, Exec. V.P.—Info. Svcs.

A. Thomas Arisman, Sr. V.P.
H. Albert Inkel, Sr. V.P.
George J. Zock, Sr. V.P. & Treas.
Ann M. Caparros, V.P., Gen. Coun. & Corp. Secy.
Valerie A. Chrisman, V.P.—Hum. Res.
Charles M. de St. Germain, Jr., V.P.
Roger W. Fisher, V.P. & Cont.
Frank L. Purcell, V.P.

Consolidated Balance Sheet   As of December 31, 1994 (000 omitted)

Assets		Liabilities & Stockholders' Equity	
Total investments	$2,533,441	Total policy liabilities & accruals	$2,217,440
Other assets	752,092	Long-term debt	100,000
		Other liabilities	555,553
		Warrants, subject to redemption	577
		*Stockholders' equity	411,963
Total	$3,285,533	Total	$3,285,533

*28,958,229 shares common stock outstanding.

Consolidated Income Statement

Years Ended Dec. 31	Thousands — — — —		Per Share[b] — — — —		Common Stock
	Total Revenues[a]	Net Income	Earnings	Cash Dividends	Price Range[bc] Calendar Year
1994	$711,916	$ 62,855	$ 2.17[d]	$ .29	28-3/4 — 19-1/8
1993	707,581	77,233	2.67	.24	32-1/2 — 22-1/4
1992	704,221	58,160	2.01[d]	.20	29 — 18-3/8
1991	657,229	(16,964)	(1.07)[d]	.00	22-1/4 — 17-3/8
1990	628,578	2,077	.15	.00	

[a]The company has reclassified certain information in the prior periods to conform with the 1994 presentation.
[b]Adjusted to reflect a 6.36-for-1 stock split in November 1991.
[c]Initial public offering in November 1991.
[d]Includes an extraordinary charge to earnings of $.06 per share in 1994, $.47 per share in 1992, and $2.64 per share in 1991, due to debt retirement.

Transfer Agent & Registrar: American Stock Transfer & Trust Co.

General Counsel: Ann M. Caparros, V.P.

Investor Relations: George J. Zock, Sr. V.P.

Human Resources: Valerie A. Chrisman, V.P.

Mgt. Info. Svcs.:   Paul C. Tarr III, Exec. V.P.

Auditors: KPMG Peat Marwick LLP

Traded (Symbol):   NYSE (HMN)

Stockholders: 2,500

Employees: 2,501

Annual Meeting: As set by Directors

Market Facts, Inc.

3040 West Salt Creek Lane, Arlington Heights, Illinois 60005
Telephone: (708) 590-7000

Market Facts, Inc., gathers and analyzes information to help private companies and other organizations make better decisions. This objective is accomplished through consumer and industrial surveys or other forms of marketing research. Most of Market Facts' revenues derive from sales of custom marketing research services to major consumer goods manufacturers. However, company clients also include medium- and smaller-sized marketers of products and services, as well as public agencies, trade associations and other institutions. Market Facts has established a wide array of data collection facilities and information processing systems, and is one of the largest companies of its kind in the world. Offices are located in Illinois, California, Massachusetts, Virginia, and Ohio. Major subsidiaries include: Market Facts—New York, Inc., and Market Facts of Canada, Ltd. Incorporated in Illinois in 1946; reincorporated in Delaware in 1966.

Directors (In addition to indicated officers)

William W. Boyd
Karen E. Predow-James

Wesley S. Walton, Secy.
Jack R. Wentworth

Officers (Directors*)

*Verne B. Churchill, Chm. & C.E.O.
*Thomas H. Payne, Pres. & C.O.O.
*Glenn W. Schmidt, Exec. V.P.
*Sanford M. Schwartz, Exec. V.P. &
    Pres.—Market Facts—New York, Inc.
Ronald P. Duda, Sr. V.P.
Michael H. Freehill, Sr. V.P.
Janith P. Fuller, Sr. V.P.
*Lawrence W. Labash, Sr. V.P.
Peter J. LaSalle, Sr. V.P.

Lawrence R. Levin, Sr. V.P.
Gregory J. McMahon, Sr. V.P.
Donald J. Morrison, Sr. V.P.
*Timothy Q. Rounds, Sr. V.P.
William E. Seymour III, Sr. V.P.
Stephen J. Weber, Sr. V.P.
Timothy J. Sullivan, V.P. & Treas.
*John C. Robertson, Pres.—Market Facts of
    Canada, Ltd.

Consolidated Balance Sheet   As of December 31, 1994 (000 omitted)

Assets		Liabilities & Stockholders' Equity	
Current assets	$14,037	Current liabilities	$10,413
Net property, plant & equipment	16,863	Long-term liabilities	10,532
Other assets	782	Deferred items	39
		Other liabilities	952
		*Stockholders' equity	9,746
Total	$31,682	Total	$31,682

*1,788,839 shares common stock outstanding.

Consolidated Income Statement[a]

Years Ended Dec. 31	Thousands — — — —		Per Share — — — —		Common Stock Price Range Calendar Year	
	Revenues	Net Income	Earnings	Cash Dividends		
1994	$55,483	$ 1,434	$ .76	$ .29	11	—6-1/2
1993	45,609	1,074	.61	.22	7-1/4	—3-3/4
1992	40,718	(437)	(.26)	.20	7	—3-1/2
1991	39,681	797	.47	.29	6-1/4	—3-3/4
1990	38,997	1,085	.62	.32	8	—5-3/4

[a]Restated for 1991-90 to conform with latest year's presentation.

Transfer Agent & Registrar: First Chicago Trust Co. of New York

General Counsel: Keck, Mahin & Cate

Investor Relations:
  Glenn W. Schmidt, Exec. V.P.

Human Resources:
  Charise D. Davis-Moubel, V.P.

Mgt. Info. Svcs.:   Peter J. LaSalle, Sr. V.P.

Auditors: KPMG Peat Marwick LLP

Traded (Symbol):   NASDAQ (MFAC)

Stockholders: 930

Employees: 1,100

Annual Meeting: In April

Material Sciences Corporation

2300 East Pratt Boulevard, Elk Grove Village, Illinois 60007-5995
Telephone: (708) 439-8270

Material Sciences Corporation is a diversified coated-materials company with operations in laminates, coil coating, structural composites, metallizing, coating, and electrogalvanizing. Coated and electro-plated sheet-metal coils, structural composites, and laminate materials are used by other manufacturers in motor vehicles, industrial and commercial building products, appliances, office equipment, furniture, lighting fixtures, containers, and a wide range of other products. Metallized materials are used in the manufacture of energy-control films, high-efficiency reflectors, and electronic displays, as well as in food packaging and data storage applications. Subsidiaries include Pre Finish Metals Incorporated and Deposition Technologies, Inc. Incorporated in Delaware in 1983.

Directors (In addition to indicated officer)

Jerome B. Cohen
Roxanne J. Decyk
Eugene W. Emmerich

E.F. Heizer, Jr.
J. Frank Leach
Irwin P. Pochter

Officers (Director*)

*G. Robert Evans, Chm. & C.E.O.
Gerald G. Nadig, Pres. & C.O.O.
Frank D. Graziano, Sr. V.P.—Tech.
Anton F. Vitzthum, Sr. V.P.—Mfg.
William H. Vrba, Sr. V.P., C.F.O. & Secy.
Paul G. Guttman, V.P.—Int'l.

Frank J. Lazowski, Jr., V.P.—Human Res.
Robert J. Mataya, V.P.—Bus. Plan. & Dev.
Gene F. Nutoni, V.P.—Eng.
James J. Waclawik, V.P. & Cont.
David B. Baker, Asst. Treas.
John J. Glazier, Jr., Asst. Cont.

Consolidated Balance Sheet   As of February 28, 1995 (000 omitted)

Assets		Liabilities & Stockholders' Equity	
Current assets	$ 61,799	Current liabilities	$ 39,093
Net property, plant & equipment	92,913	Long-term liabilities	27,860
Other assets	17,645	*Stockholders' equity	105,404
Total	$172,357	Total	$172,357

*15,150,426 shares common stock outstanding.

Consolidated Income Statement

Years Ended Abt. Feb. 28	Thousands — — — —		Per Share[a] — — —		Common Stock Price Range[a] Fiscal Year
	Net Sales	Net Income	Earnings	Cash Dividends	
1995	$227,658	$16,740	$1.10	$ .00	17-3/4 — 13-3/4
1994	187,701	11,802	.78	.00	17-5/8 — 10-5/8
1993	156,230	7,617[b]	.56[b]	.00	12 — 7-7/8
1992	142,599	7,141	.63	.00	10-3/8 — 4-7/8
1991	139,459	4,688[c]	.42	.00	7-5/8 — 4-1/8

[a]Adjusted to reflect 3-for-2 stock splits paid in June 1994 and April 1992.
[b]Includes FAS 106 and 109, resulting in a cumulative charge to net earnings of $1,283,000 ($.11 per share).
[c]Includes pretax charge of $2,000,000 related to restructuring.

Transfer Agent & Registrar:	Mellon Securities Transfer Services		
General Counsel:	Kirkland & Ellis	Traded (Symbol):	NYSE (MSC)
Investor Relations:	Robert J. Mataya, V.P.	Stockholders:	1,110
Human Resources:	Frank J. Lazowski, Jr., V.P.	Employees:	925
Auditors:	Arthur Andersen LLP	Annual Meeting:	In June

McDonald's Corporation

McDonald's Plaza, Oak Brook, Illinois 60521
Telephone: (708) 575-3000

McDonald's Corporation is a leading foodservice organization. The company, restaurant managers, franchisees, and joint-venture partners operate more than 15,000 McDonald's restaurants in 79 countries, each offering a limited menu of high-quality food. McDonald's has pioneered food quality specifications, equipment technology, marketing and training programs, and operational and supply systems that are considered the standards of the industry throughout the world. Approximately 70 percent of McDonald's restaurants are locally owned and operated by independent entrepreneurs who provide capital and management skills. There are more than 5,460 restaurants outside of the United States, through wholly owned subsidiaries, joint-venture, and franchise arrangements. In order to fix occupancy costs, about 60 percent of McDonald's restaurants are owned, and the remainder are generally leased under various long-term lease arrangements. Reincorporated in Delaware in 1965 to continue a business established in 1955.

Directors (In addition to indicated officers)

Hall Adams, Jr.
Gordon C. Gray
Donald R. Keough
Donald G. Lubin

Andrew J. McKenna
Terry Savage
Ballard F. Smith

Roger W. Stone
Robert N. Thurston
B. Blair Vedder, Jr.

Officers (Directors*)

*Fred L. Turner, Sr. Chm.
*Michael R. Quinlan, Chm. & C.E.O.
*James R. Cantalupo, Pres. & C.E.O.—Int'l.
*Edward H. Rensi, Pres. & C.E.O.—U.S.A.
*Jack M. Greenberg, V. Chm. & C.F.O.
*Paul D. Schrage, Sr. Exec. V.P. & Chf. Mktg. Off.
Thomas S. Dentice, Exec. V.P.
Patrick J. Flynn, Exec. V.P.
Thomas W. Glasgow, Jr., Exec. V.P. & C.O.O.
James A. Skinner, Exec. V.P.—Int'l.
O. Thomas Albrecht, Sr. V.P. & Chf. Purch. Off.
Thomas B. Allin, Sr. V.P.—U.S. Zone Mgr.
*Robert M. Beavers, Jr., Sr. V.P.
John S. Charlesworth, Sr. V.P.—U.S. Zone Mgr.
Winston B. Christiansen, Sr. V.P.
Burton D. Cohen, Sr. V.P.
Michael L. Conley, Sr. V.P. & Cont.
Carl F. Dill, Jr., Sr. V.P.

Robert J. Doran, Sr. V.P.—U.S. Zone Mgr.
Henry Gonzalez, Sr. V.P.
David B. Green, Sr. V.P.
Robbin L. Hedges, Sr. V.P.—Int'l. Rel. Ptnr., Eur.
William Hockett, Sr. V.P.
Noel Kaplan, Sr. V.P.—Int'l. Rel. Ptnr., Asia/Pacific
Debra A. Koenig, Sr. V.P.—U.S. Zone Mgr.
Raymond C. Mines, Jr., Sr. V.P.—U.S. Zone Mgr.
Paul S. Preston, Sr. V.P.—Int'l. Rel. Ptnr., Eur.
Lynal A. Root, Sr. V.P. & Chm.—Purch. Div.
W. Robert Sanders, Sr. V.P.—U.S. Zone Mgr.
Richard G. Starmann, Sr. V.P.
Stanley R. Stein, Sr. V.P.
Delbert H. Wilson, Jr., Sr. V.P.—U.S. Zone Mgr.
S. Bruce Wunner, Sr. V.P.—Int'l. Rel. Ptnr., Latin Amer.
Shelby Yastrow, Sr. V.P., Gen. Coun. & Secy.
Peter D. Ritchie, Chm.—Australia, Int'l. Rel. Ptnr., Pacif.

Consolidated Balance Sheet   As of December 31, 1994 (000 omitted)

Assets		Liabilities & Stockholders' Equity	
Current assets	$ 740,700	Current liabilities	$ 2,451,300
Net property and equipment	11,328,400	Long-term debt	3,358,200
Intangible assets	483,100	Deferred items	840,800
Other assets	1,039,700	Other liabilities	56,200
		*Stockholders' equity	6,885,400
Total	$13,591,900	Total	$13,591,900

*693,700,000 shares common stock outstanding.

Consolidated Income Statement

| Years Ended Dec. 31 | Thousands — — — — | | Per Share[a] — — — | | Common Stock |
	Total Revenues	Net Income	Earnings	Cash Dividends[b]	Price Range[a] Calendar Year
1994	$8,321,800	$1,224,400	$1.68	$ .23	31-3/8 — 25-5/8
1993	7,408,100	1,082,500	1.45	.21	29-5/8 — 22-3/4
1992	7,133,300	958,600	1.30	.20	25-1/4 — 19-1/4
1991	6,695,000	859,600	1.17	.18	19-7/8 — 13-1/8
1990	6,640,000	802,000	1.10	.17	19-1/4 — 12-1/2

[a]Adjusted to reflect a 2-for-1 stock split in June 1994.
[b]Cash dividends declared.

Transfer Agent & Registrar: First Chicago Trust Co. of New York

Corporate Counsel: Sonnenschein Nath & Rosenthal

Investor Relations: Sharon L. Vuinovich, V.P.

Human Resources: Stanley R. Stein, Sr. V.P.

Mgt. Info. Svcs.:   Carl F. Dill, Jr., Sr. V.P.

Auditors: Ernst & Young LLP

Traded (Symbol):
  CSE,NYSE,Par.,Mun.,Frank.,Tky.,Swtz. (3) (MCD)

Stockholders: 529,000

Employees: 183,000

Annual Meeting: In May

McWhorter Technologies, Inc.

400 East Cottage Place, Carpentersville, Illinois 60110
Telephone: (708) 428-2657

McWhorter Technologies, Inc., is a leading manufacturer of resins used in the paint and coatings industry in the U.S., and is a manufacturer of resins used in the reinforced fiberglass plastics industry. These resins are a primary component of paint and coatings used in a variety of protective and decorative applications. Resins used for reinforced fiberglass plastics are a primary component for a variety of fiberglass products. In February 1994, McWhorter Technologies acquired the Resin Products Division of Cargill, Incorporated. In April 1994, The Valspar Corporation spun off McWhorter Technologies, its former wholly owned subsidiary. Incorporated in Delaware in 1994.

Directors (In addition to indicated officers)

Michelle L. Collins
Edward Giles
D. George Harris

John G. Johnson, Jr.
Heinn F. Tomfohrde III
Nathan L. Zutty

Officers (Directors*)

*John R. Stevenson, Pres. & C.E.O.
*Jeffrey M. Nodland, Exec. V.P. & C.O.O.
Patrick T. Heffernan, Sr. V.P.—Coatings
Resins

Kevin W. Brolsma, V.P.—Oper.
Douglas B. Rahrig, V.P.—Tech.

Consolidated Balance Sheet   As of October 31, 1994 (000 omitted)

Assets		Liabilities & Stockholders' Equity	
Current assets	$ 67,131	Current liabilities	$ 40,211
Net property, plant & equipment	69,464	Long-term debt	30,087
Other assets	1,968	Deferred items	3,389
		Other liabilities	2,749
		*Stockholders' equity	62,127
Total	$138,563	Total	$138,563

*10,864,899 shares common stock outstanding.

Consolidated Income Statement[a]

Years Ended Abt. Oct. 31	Thousands — — — — Net Sales	Net Income	Per Share — — — Earnings	Cash Dividends	Common Stock Price Range Calendar Year
1994[b]	$281,340	$10,010[c]	$ .92[c]	$ .00	19-1/4 — 13-1/4
1993[b]	272,432	10,125	.93		
1992	103,545	4,748			
1991	106,161	3,904			
1990	107,776	5,519			

[a]McWhorter Technologies, Inc, was spun off by The Valspar Corporation on April 29, 1994.
[b]Pro forma combined, McWhorter Technologies, Inc., and the Resin Products Division of Cargill, Incorporated.
[c]Includes an aftertax charge of $1,497,000 ($.14 per share) for the writedown of the Los Angeles resin facility.

Transfer Agent & Registrar: Wachovia Bank of North Carolina, N.A.

General Counsel: Bell, Boyd & Lloyd

Investor Relations: Sue Riley

Auditors: Ernst & Young LLP

Traded (Symbol):   NYSE (MWT)
Stockholders: 1,800
Employees: 550
Annual Meeting: In February

First Chicago Guide

Medicus Systems Corporation

One Rotary Center, Suite 400, Evanston, Illinois 60201-4802
Telephone: (708) 570-7500

Medicus Systems Corporation provides software products, contract management, systems integration, and related services to help its customers effectively manage the care of the patient and improve the health status of the populations that they serve. Medicus Systems offers three main product lines: patient focused systems; clinical data systems; and decision support systems. It also supports its clients with related contract management services. In February 1995, the company announced that it would spin off MCM Managed Care, Inc., its managed care business. Incorporated in Delaware in 1984.

Directors   (In addition to indicated officers)

Jon E.M. Jacoby
Risa Lavizzo-Mourey, M.D.

Walter J. McNerney
Gail L. Warden

Officers   (Directors*)

*Richard C. Jelinek, Ph.D., Chm. & C.E.O.
James Alland, Exec. V.P. & C.O.O.
Susan P. Dowell, Exec. V.P. & C.O.O.
Frank A. Pierce, Sr. V.P.
Donald W. Simborg, M.D., Sr. V.P.
Robert C. Steffel, Sr. V.P.
William D. Carswell, V.P.
Gerald Hansberger, V.P. & C.F.O.

Sandra K. Lichty, Ph.D., V.P.
Michael N. Minear, V.P.
Timothy K. Rutledge, V.P.
Bradley G. Scherzer, V.P.
Victor W. Sterne, V.P.
Arlene J. Verona, V.P.
*William G. Brown, Secy.

Consolidated Balance Sheet   As of May 31, 1994 (000 omitted)

Assets		Liabilities & Stockholders' Equity	
Current assets	$30,724	Current liabilities	$ 7,520
Net property, plant & equipment	1,638	Deferred items	696
Other assets	2,745	*Stockholders' equity	26,891
Total	$35,107	Total	$35,107

*6,382,307 shares common stock outstanding.

Consolidated Income Statement

Years Ended May 31	Thousands — — — — Total Revenues	Net Income	Per Share[a] — — — Earnings[b]	Cash Dividends	Common Stock Price Range[a] Calendar Year	
1994	$34,485	$3,848	$ .61	$ .00	22	— 10
1993	24,459	2,656	.49	.00	19	— 8-1/4
1992	22,370	2,431	.45	.00	15-3/4	— 8-1/4
1991	17,342	1,628	.35	.00	14-3/4	— 8-3/4[c]
1990	12,770	610	.11			

[a]Adjusted to reflect a 2.2-for-1 stock split effected in June 1991.
[b]After payment to controlling stockholder of dividend on preferred shares, which were redeemed on August 1, 1990.
[c]Initial public offering in August 1991.

Transfer Agent & Registrar:	Harris Trust and Savings Bank		
General Counsel:	Bell, Boyd & Lloyd	Traded (Symbol):	NASDAQ (MECS)
Investor Relations:	Ted Bucknam	Stockholders:	2,100
Human Resources:	Mary Stewart	Employees:	285
Auditors:	Price Waterhouse LLP	Annual Meeting:	In October

Merchants Bancorp, Inc.

34 South Broadway Avenue, Aurora, Illinois 60507
Telephone: (708) 896-9000

Merchants Bancorp, Inc., is the holding company for The Merchants National Bank in Aurora, Illinois. Merchants National Bank conducts a full-service community banking and trust business. Along with three locations and its main office in Aurora, the bank has an additional location in Oswego, Illinois. In April 1995, Merchants Bancorp signed a letter of intent to acquire Valley Banc Services Corp. of St. Charles, Illinois. Incorporated in Delaware in 1981.

Directors (In addition to indicated officer)

C. Tell Coffey
James R. Flynn
William C. Glenn
James D. Pearson

Frank A. Sarnecki
John J. Swalec
Norman L. Titiner
William S. Wake

Officers (Director*)

*Calvin R. Myers, Chm., Pres. & C.E.O.
 J. Douglas Cheatham, V.P. & C.F.O.

Frank K. Voris, V.P.
Dana K. Hopp, Treas. & Secy.

Consolidated Balance Sheet   As of December 31, 1994 (000 omitted)

Assets		Liabilities & Stockholders' Equity	
Cash & due from banks	$ 28,922	Deposits	$413,741
Total securities	166,831	Federal funds purchased	33,299
Net loans	280,433	Notes payable	3,000
Net property, plant & equipment	9,337	Other liabilities	2,793
Loans held for sale	2,033	*Stockholders' equity	43,456
Other assets	8,733		
Total	$496,289	Total	$496,289

*2,567,282 shares common stock outstanding.

Consolidated Income Statement

Years Ended Dec. 31	Thousands — — — — Total Income	Net Income	Per Share[a] — — — — Earnings	Cash Dividends	Common Stock Price Range[abc] Calendar Year	
1994	$39,797	$5,459	$2.13	$ .37	27	— 21
1993	36,152	4,734[d]	2.25[d]	.34	22-1/2	— 15
1992	34,117	4,050	2.03	.28	15	— 11-3/8
1991	33,284	2,574	1.29	.24	12	— 6-3/8
1990	31,550	1,681	.84	.23		

[a]Adjusted to reflect a 3-for-1 stock split in April 1993.
[b]Initial public offering in October 1993.
[c]The company's common stock previously did not trade on any national or regional exchange, but certain brokerage firms did make a market in the common stock.
[d]Includes a gain to reflect FAS 109, resulting in a cumulative effect of $300,000 ($.14 per share).

Transfer Agent & Registrar: Harris Trust and Savings Bank

General Counsel:
  Barack, Ferrazzano, Kirschbaum & Perlman

Investor Relations: J. Douglas Cheatham, V.P.

Human Resources: Susan M. Anderson, V.P.

Auditors: Crowe, Chizek & Co.

Traded (Symbol):   NASDAQ (MBIA)

Stockholders: 791

Employees: 265

Annual Meeting: In April

First Chicago Guide 163

Mercury Finance Company

40 Skokie Boulevard, Suite 200, Northbrook, Illinois 60062
Telephone: (708) 564-3720

Mercury Finance Company specializes in financing the sale of previously owned automobiles for new and used car dealers. The company also makes direct cash loans and sells credit insurance to its customers. Mercury operates 247 branch offices in 25 states. In April 1993, the company completed the acquisition of Louisiana-based Gulfco Investment Inc., a consumer finance company. Incorporated in Delaware in 1988.

Directors   (In addition to indicated officers)

Dennis H. Chookaszian
William C. Croft
Clifford R. Johnson
Andrew McNally IV

Bruce I. McPhee
Fred G. Steingraber
Philip J. Wicklander

Officers   (Directors*)

*Daniel J. Terra, Chm.
*John N. Brincat, Pres. & C.E.O.
 James A. Doyle, Sr. V.P., Cont. & Secy.
 Richard P. Bosson, V.P.—Oper.
 Jeffrey R. Brincat, V.P.—Adm.
 John N. Brincat, Jr., V.P.—Oper.

Michael H. Caul, V.P.—Oper.
Steven G. Gould, V.P.—Oper.
John J. Pratt, V.P.—Oper.
Edward G. Stautzenbach, V.P.—Marketing
Sheila M. Tilson, Asst. V.P. & Asst. Secy.

Consolidated Balance Sheet   As of December 31, 1994 (000 omitted)

Assets		Liabilities & Stockholders' Equity	
Finance receivables, net	$ 950,902	Short-term debt	$ 449,945
Net property, plant & equipment	3,492	Long-term debt	300,875
Other assets	82,009	Income taxes payable	4,668
		Other liabilities	53,401
		*Stockholders' equity	227,514
Total	$1,036,403	Total	$1,036,403

*116,079,703 shares common stock outstanding.

Consolidated Income Statement

Years Ended Dec. 31	Thousands — — — — Interest Income	Net Income	Per Share[a] — — — Earnings	Cash Dividends	Common Stock Price Range[a] Calendar Year
1994	$211,565	$86,545	$ .74	$ .29	19-1/8 — 11-1/8
1993	165,054	64,927	.56	.20	20-3/8 — 11-1/4
1992	121,531	45,723	.39	.14	12-5/8 — 7-3/4
1991	99,199	32,816	.29	.09	9-1/2 — 2-3/4
1990	81,053	23,211	.21	.07	3-7/8 — 2-1/4

[a]Adjusted to reflect a 4-for-3 stock split in June 1993, a 2-for-1 stock split in May 1992, and 4-for-3 stock splits in December 1991, April 1991, and September 1990.

Transfer Agent & Registrar: Harris Trust Company of New York

Investor Relations: James A. Doyle, Sr. V.P.

Human Resources: Robert Lutgen

Auditors: KPMG Peat Marwick LLP

Traded (Symbol):   NYSE, CSE (MFN)

Stockholders: 12,000

Employees: 1,500

Annual Meeting: In April

Methode Electronics, Inc.

7444 West Wilson Avenue, Chicago, Illinois 60656-4549
Telephone: (708) 867-9600

Methode Electronics, Inc., and its wholly owned subsidiaries are engaged principally in the development and manufacture of component devices that connect, convey, and control electrical energy, pulse and signal. Production is centered around space-saving circuitry under the general headings of controls, connectors, power distribution systems, fiber optic components, printed circuits, and cables. These products are basic components used in the production of electrical and electronic apparatus, instruments and systems. Principal customers include equipment manufacturers in the computer, automotive, communication, industrial, military, and aerospace industries. Methode serves the component needs of more than 2,000 different businesses in North America and overseas. The company has 18 manufacturing and two testing facilities. Subsidiaries include: Graphic Research, Inc.; Technical Components, Inc.; Methode of California; Methode Electronics Far East P.T.E. Ltd.; Methode Electronics Europe Ltd.; Intertrace Technology; Methode Development Co.; Methode Mikon Ltd.; Methode New England Co. Inc.; and Methode Electronics Ireland Ltd. Incorporated in Illinois in 1946; reincorporated in Delaware in 1966.

Directors (In addition to indicated officers)

William C. Croft
Raymond J. Roberts

George C. Wright

Officers (Directors*)

*William J. McGinley, Chm.
*William T. Jensen, Pres.
*Michael G. Andre, Sr. Exec. V.P.
*Kevin J. Hayes, V.P. & Treas.

*Robert C. Keck, Secy.
James W. Ashley, Asst. Secy.
*James W. McGinley, Pres.—ElectroOptics Grp.

Consolidated Balance Sheet   As of October 31, 1994 (000 omitted) Unaudited

Assets		Liabilities & Stockholders' Equity	
Current assets	$104,461	Current liabilities	$ 37,560
Net property, plant & equipment	53,013	Deferred items	6,166
Other assets	14,994	Other liabilities	8,695
		*Stockholders' equity	120,047
Total	$172,468	Total	$172,468

*21,957,362 shares Class A common and 1,268,766 shares Class B common stock outstanding.

Consolidated Income Statement

Years Ended Apr. 30	Thousands — — — — — Net Sales	Net Income	Per Share[a] — — — Earnings	Cash Dividends[c]	Common Stock Price Range[ab] Fiscal Year
1994	$213,298	$20,976	$ .91	$ .05	17-1/4 — 10-1/2
1993	172,038	14,748[d]	.65[d]	.04	13-3/4 — 5-7/8
1992	148,085	9,529[d]	.43[d]	.04	10-3/4 — 4-7/8
1991	143,717	7,941	.36	.04	6-1/4 — 2-7/8
1990	126,426	5,096	.23	.04	4-1/2 — 2-1/2

[a]Adjusted to reflect 100% stock dividend paid January 15, 1993, in Class A stock for each share of Class A and Class B outstanding.
[b]Class A common stock.
[c]Represents dividends paid on Class A common stock. Dividends for Class B common stock were $.04 for 1994, 1993, and $.03 for every other fiscal year. (The cash dividend on the Class A and Class B common stock was increased to $.12 and $.10 per share, respectively, for fiscal 1995.)
[d]From continuing operations.

Transfer Agent & Registrar:	Mellon Financial Services		
General Counsel:	Keck, Mahin & Cate	Auditors:	Ernst & Young LLP
Investor Relations:	Kevin J. Hayes, V.P.	Traded (Symbol):	NASDAQ (METH)
		Stockholders:	1,820
Human Resources:	Robert Kuehnau	Employees:	2,500
Mgt. Info. Svcs.:	Ronald Duffy	Annual Meeting:	In September

MFRI, Inc.

7720 Lehigh Avenue, Niles, Illinois 60714-3491
Telephone: (708) 966-1000

MFRI, Inc. (formerly Midwesco Filter Resources, Inc.), is engaged in the manufacture and sale of filter bags for use in industrial air pollution control systems known as "baghouses," and also engineers, designs, and manufactures specialty piping systems, and leak detection and location systems. MFRI is the successor corporation to Midwesco Filter Resources, Inc. On January 28, 1994, MFRI acquired the Perma-Pipe business from Midwesco, Inc., for cash and common stock. Pursuant to the merger, each share of common stock of Midwesco Filter was exchanged for one share of common stock of MFRI. Midwesco Filter, now a wholly owned subsidiary of MFRI, manufactures and sells a wide variety of filter bags for baghouse air pollution control and particulate collection systems. Baghouses are used in a wide variety of industries in the U.S. and abroad to limit particulate emissions, primarily to comply with environmental regulations The company manufactures bags in standard industry sizes, shapes, and fabrics, and to custom specifications, maintaining manufacturing standards for more than 8,000 styles of filter bags. Midwesco Filter manufactures substantially all the seamless tube filter bags sold in the U.S. Perma-Pipe's piping system products include secondary containment piping systems for transporting hazardous fluids and petroleum products; and insulated and jacketed district heating and cooling piping systems for efficient energy distribution to multiple locations from central energy plants. Perma-Pipe's leak detection and location systems are sold as part of an increasing number of its piping system products, and on a stand-alone basis, to monitor areas where fluid intrusion may contaminate the environment, endanger personal safety, cause a fire hazard, or damage equipment or property. Incorporated in Delaware in 1993.

Directors   (In addition to indicated officers)

Arnold F. Brookstone	Eugene Miller
Bradley E. Mautner	Stephen B. Schwartz

Officers   (Directors*)

*David Unger, Chm., Pres. & C.E.O.	Joseph P. Findley, V.P.
*Henry M. Mautner, V. Chm.	J. Tyler Headley, V.P.
Michael D. Bennett, V.P., Secy. & Treas.	Robert Maffei, V.P.
*Fati A. Elgendy, V.P.	*Gene K. Ogilvie, V.P.
Bill Ervin, V.P.	Herbert J. Sturm, V.P.

Consolidated Balance Sheet   As of January 31, 1995 (000 omitted)

Assets		Liabilities & Stockholders' Equity	
Current assets	$33,587	Current liabilities	$16,297
Net property, plant & equipment	8,098	Long-term debt	6,902
Other assets	6,232	Deferred items	778
		*Stockholders' equity	23,940
Total	$47,917	Total	$47,917

*4,289,000 shares common stock outstanding.

Consolidated Income Statement

Years Ended Abt. Jan. 31	Thousands — — — — Net Sales	Net Income	Per Share — — — Earnings	Cash Dividends	Common Stock Price Range Calendar Year
1995	$75,495	$1,203	$ .27		
1994[a]	62,390	2,569	.60	.00	9-1/4 — 4-3/4
1993[a]	51,490	1,132	.26	.00	8-3/4 — 6-3/8
1992	21,659	695	.25	.00	8-1/4 — 4-3/4
1991	22,740	1,337	.48	.00	8-1/2 — 3-5/8

[a]Pro forma results as if the acquisition of Perma-Pipe had taken place at the beginning of fiscal 1993.

Transfer Agent & Registrar: Harris Trust and Savings Bank

Legal Counsel:	Rudnick & Wolfe	Auditors:	Deloitte & Touche LLP
Investor Relations:	Michael D. Bennett, V.P.	Traded (Symbol):	NASDAQ (MFRI)
		Stockholders:	1,200
Human Resources:	Michael D. Bennett, V.P.	Employees:	483
Mgt. Info. Svcs.:	Steve Harbaugh	Annual Meeting:	In June

The Middleby Corporation

1400 Toastmaster Drive, Elgin, Illinois 60120
Telephone: (708) 741-3300

The Middleby Corporation is engaged in the manufacture and sale of commercial foodservice equipment. It designs, develops, manufactures, and markets a broad line of equipment used for the preparation, cooking, and refrigeration of food in commercial and institutional kitchens and restaurants, along with a line of refrigerated display coolers used primarily by soft drink bottlers in supermarkets and other retail outlets, in the U.S. and internationally. Founded in 1888 as The Middleby Marshall Oven Company, the company's principal business units today include: Middleby Marshall, which produces automated conveyor cooking systems and processing equipment; Toastmaster, which produces cooking and warming equipment for commercial use; Southbend, which specializes in heavy-duty cooking and steam equipment; and Victory, which produces refrigeration systems. Incorporated in Delaware in 1985.

Directors (In addition to indicated officers)

Newell Garfield, Jr.
A. Don Lummus
John R. Miller III

Philip G. Putnam
Sabin C. Streeter

Officers (Directors*)

*William F. Whitman, Jr., Chm.
*David P. Riley, Pres. & C.E.O.

John J. Hastings, Exec. V.P., C.F.O., Secy. & Treas.

Consolidated Balance Sheet As of December 31, 1994 (000 omitted)

Assets		Liabilities & Stockholders' Equity	
Current assets	$41,241	Current liabilities	$24,153
Net property, plant & equipment	23,260	Long-term debt	42,650
Other assets	12,121	Other liabilities	1,782
		*Stockholders' equity	8,037
Total	$76,622	Total	$76,622

*8,341,000 shares common stock outstanding.

Consolidated Income Statement

Years Ended Abt. Dec. 31	Thousands — — — — Net Sales[a]	Net Income	Per Share — — — — Earnings	Cash Dividends	Common Stock Price Range Calendar Year
1994	$129,967	$ 3,050	$ .36	$ .00	4-7/8 — 2-5/8
1993	119,355	3,432[b]	.41[b]	.00	4-1/8 — 1-3/4
1992	109,219	(1,894)	(.23)	.00	3-3/8 — 1-1/8
1991	102,518	(7,510)	(.90)	.02	2-5/8 — 3/4
1990	113,016	(978)	(.12)	.08	6-3/8 — 1

[a]Certain amounts in the prior year's financial data have been reclassified to be consistent with the fiscal 1994 presentation.
[b]Includes unusual income item of $7,716,000 ($.92 per share) related to settlement of legal dispute.

Transfer Agent & Registrar: Continental Stock Transfer & Trust Co.

General Counsel: D'Ancona & Pflaum

Auditors: Arthur Andersen LLP

Investor Relations:
  John J. Hastings, Exec. V.P.

Traded (Symbol): AMEX (MBY)

Human Resources:
  John J. Hastings, Exec. V.P.

Stockholders: 2,000

Mgt. Info. Svcs.:
  John J. Hastings, Exec. V.P.

Employees: 994

Annual Meeting: In May

Minuteman International, Inc.

111 South Rohlwing, Addison, Illinois 60101
Telephone: (708) 627-6900

Minuteman International, Inc. (formerly Hako Minuteman, Inc.), manufactures and distributes commercial and industrial vacuums, floor, carpet and lawn care equipment, and chemical cleaning and coating products. The company's products include vacuums, floor maintenance machines, carpet maintenance machines, sweepers and automatic scrubbers, chemical cleaning and coating products, and complementary accessories. The company's products are distributed throughout the U.S. and Canada by more than 550 independent distributors and also are sold in many foreign markets. The company's products generally are not sold to consumers for home use. Subsidiaries include: Minuteman Canada Inc., Multi-Clean and Parker Sweeper Divisions of Minuteman International, Inc., and Minuteman International Foreign Sales Corp. Incorporated in Illinois in 1951.

Directors   (In addition to indicated officer)

Frederick W. Hohage
Tyll Necker

Frank R. Reynolds, Jr.
James C. Schrader, Jr.

Officers   (Director*)

*Jerome E. Rau, Pres. & C.E.O.
Gary E. Palmer, V.P.—Eng.
Gregory J. Rau, V.P.—Sales

Thomas J. Nolan, C.F.O., Secy. & Treas.
Michael Gravelle, Pres.—Minuteman Canada Inc.

Consolidated Balance Sheet   As of December 31, 1994 (000 omitted)

Assets		Liabilities & Stockholders' Equity	
Current assets	$20,392	Current liabilities	$ 3,185
Net property, plant & equipment	7,421	Deferred taxes	183
Other assets	254	*Stockholders' equity	24,699
Total	$28,067	Total	$28,067

*3,568,385 shares common stock outstanding.

Consolidated Income Statement

Years Ended Dec. 31	Thousands — — — — Net Sales	Net Income	Per Share — — — Earnings	Cash Dividends	Common Stock Price Range Calendar Year
1994	$41,518	$3,203	$ .90	$ .34	13 — 9-1/2
1993	38,237	2,349	.66	.28	11-1/2 — 6-1/4
1992	32,659	1,611	.45	.28	10 — 5-1/2
1991	30,238	2,503	.70	.23	9-1/4 — 5
1990	29,238	2,108	.58	.20	10-3/4 — 4-5/8

Transfer Agent & Registrar: Mellon Securities

General Counsel: Frank R. Reynolds, Jr.

Investor Relations: Thomas J. Nolan, C.F.O.

Human Resources: Thomas J. Nolan, C.F.O.

Mgt. Info. Svcs.:   Thomas J. Nolan, C.F.O.

Auditors: Ernst & Young LLP

Traded (Symbol):   NASDAQ (MMAN)

Stockholders: 1,100

Employees: 221

Annual Meeting: In April

First Chicago Guide

MMI Companies, Inc.

540 Lake Cook Road, Deerfield, Illinois 60015-5290
Telephone: (708) 940-7550

MMI Companies, Inc., is an international healthcare risk management company providing liability insurance, clinical risk management services, managed care, and strategic planning consultation to healthcare organizations, physicians, and allied healthcare professionals nationwide. Through its subsidiaries, the company offers products and services that enable its clients to manage insurance, clinical, and business risks associated with providing healthcare. In May 1995, MMI acquired all of the outstanding capital stock of Health Provider Insurance Company. Incorporated in Delaware in 1983.

Directors (In addition to indicated officer)

Richard R. Barr
James A. Block, M.D.
George B. Caldwell
F. Laird Facey, M.D.
Ronald J. French, M.D.
William M. Kelley
Timothy R. McCormick

Gerald L. McManis
Scott S. Parker
Edward C. Peddie
Anthony J. Perry
Joseph D. Sargent
Marshall Whisnant

Officers (Director*)

*B. Frederick Becker, Chm. & C.E.O.
Paul M. Orzech, Exec. V.P. & C.F.O.
John E. Groskopf, Sr. V.P. & Pres.—MMI
  Agency, Inc.
Anna Marie Hajek, Sr. V.P. & Pres.—MMI
  Risk Mgt. Resources, Inc.
William E. Lape, Sr. V.P. & Pres.—ACLIC
Wayne A. Sinclair, Sr. V.P., Gen. Coun. &
  Secy.

William R. Spence, Sr. V.P. & Pres.—ACIC
James E. DeWald, V.P. & Actuary
Merrilee Hepler, V.P.—Hum. Res.
Joseph R. Herman, V.P. & Cont.
Barbara R. Herrington, V.P.—Claims
Michael S. LaSala, V.P.
Richard A. Linden, V.P.—Info. Syst.
Scott T. Veech, V.P.—Fin.
Peter C. Gunder, Treas.

Consolidated Balance Sheet As of December 31, 1994 (000 omitted)

Assets		Liabilities & Stockholders' Equity	
Investments	$497,679	Policy liabilities	$502,173
Other assets	196,125	Other liabilities	68,572
		*Stockholders' equity	123,059
Total	$693,804	Total	$693,804

*8,677,000 shares common stock outstanding.

Consolidated Income Statement

Years Ended Dec. 31	Thousands — — — — Total Revenues	Net Income	Per Share[a] — — — Earnings	Cash Dividends	Common Stock Price Range[a] Calendar Year
1994	$177,205	$15,051	$1.73	$ .16	15-7/8 — 12-1/8
1993	154,864	14,181	1.90	.12	16-3/8 — 13-1/8
1992	142,074	5,078[b]	.77[b]	.11	
1991	144,895	11,107	1.62	.09	
1990	129,892	10,950	1.32	.07	

[a]Adjusted to reflect a 1.375-for-1 stock split in March 1993. Initial public offering in June 1993.
[b]Includes a gain to reflect FAS 109, resulting in a cumulative effect of $5,419,000 ($.82 per share).

Transfer Agent & Registrar: Mellon Securities Trust Co.

General Counsel: Wayne A. Sinclair, Sr. V.P.

Investor Relations: Paul M. Orzech, Exec. V.P.

Human Resources: Merrilee Hepler, V.P.

Mgt. Info. Svcs.: Richard A. Linden, V.P.

Auditors: Ernst & Young LLP

Traded (Symbol): NYSE (MMI)

Stockholders: 335

Employees: 400

Annual Meeting: In April

First Chicago Guide

Molex Incorporated

2222 Wellington Court, Lisle, Illinois 60532-1682
Telephone: (708) 969-4550

Molex Incorporated is a worldwide designer, manufacturer, marketer, and distributor for the high technology electronics industry. Molex supplies connectors, conductor cable, terminals, interconnection systems (including fiberoptic), associated application equipment, and switches to manufacturers of business machines, telecommunications equipment, video tape recorders, computers and computer peripheral equipment, home entertainment products, medical electronics, testing apparatus, home appliances, premise wiring systems, and automobiles. Molex's 30,000 products are sold through direct sales offices and representatives in 20 countries. Manufacturing facilities include over 40 plants on six continents. The domestic operations are divided into six profit-centers: DataComm Products Division; Commercial Products Division; Ulti-Mate, Inc.; Mod-Tap W Corp.; Molex Fiber Optic Interconnect Technologies, Inc.; and Molex-ETC Inc. Incorporated in Delaware in 1972 as the successor to an Illinois corporation of the same name formed in 1957.

Directors   (In addition to indicated officers)

Robert H. Hayes
Edgar D. Jannotta
Fred L. Krehbiel
Donald G. Lubin

Masahisa Naitoh
Lewis E. Platt
Robert J. Potter

Officers   (Directors*)

*Frederick A. Krehbiel, Chm. & C.E.O.
*John H. Krehbiel, Jr., Pres.
 Werner W. Fichtner, V.P.
 James E. Fleischhacker, V.P.
 J. Joseph King, V.P.—Int'l. Oper.
 John C. Psaltis, V.P., Treas. & C.F.O.

Kathi M. Regas, V.P.
Ronald L. Schubel, V.P.
Martin P. Slark, V.P.
Goro Tokuyama, V.P.
Raymond C. Wieser, V.P.
Louis A. Hecht, Corp. Secy. & Gen. Coun.

Consolidated Balance Sheet   As of June 30, 1994 (000 omitted)

Assets		Liabilities & Stockholders' Equity	
Current assets	$ 586,612	Current liabilities	$ 205,394
Net property, plant & equipment	440,995	Long-term debt	7,350
Other assets	110,910	Deferred items	14,612
		Other liabilities	29,547
		*Stockholders' equity	881,614
Total	$1,138,517	Total	$1,138,517

*31,871,000 shares common, 31,633,000 shares Class A common, and 94,255 shares Class B common stock outstanding.

Consolidated Income Statement

Years Ended June 30	Thousands — — — — Net Revenue	Net Income	Per Share[a] — — — Earnings	Cash Dividends	Common Stock Price Range[a] Calendar Year
1994	$964,108	$94,852	$1.20	$ .03	36 — 24-1/4
1993	859,283	71,055	.90	.02	30-5/8 — 20-5/8
1992	776,192	67,464	.86	.02	25-1/4 — 18-7/8
1991	707,950	64,631	.83	.02	23-1/4 — 14-1/8
1990	594,372	62,087	.79	.02	16-1/2 — 10-5/8

[a]Adjusted to reflect 5-for-4 stock splits in November 1994 and 1992, and a 2-for-1 stock split in June 1990.

Transfer Agent & Registrar: Harris Trust and Savings Bank

General Counsel: Louis A. Hecht, Secy.

Investor Relations: G. Neil Lefort

Human Resources:
  Kathi Regas, V.P. (U.S.), Malou Roth (Int'l.)

Mgt. Info. Svcs.:   Richard R. Haugen

Auditors: Deloitte & Touche LLP

Traded (Symbol):
  NASDAQ, London SE (MOLX, Common stock; MOLXA, Class A)

Stockholders: 5,550

Employees: 8,167

Annual Meeting: In October

Morton International, Inc.

100 North Riverside Plaza, Chicago, Illinois 60606-1596
Telephone: (312) 807-2000

Morton International, Inc., operates three commercial businesses consisting of specialty chemicals, salt, and automotive inflatable restraint systems. The specialty chemicals segment manufactures high technology chemical products for a wide variety of customer applications. The salt segment produces and sells salt principally in the U.S. and Canada, under the MORTON and WINDSOR trademarks, respectively, for human and animal consumption, water conditioning, highway ice melting, and for industrial and chemical uses. The inflatable restraint systems segment designs, develops, manufactures, and sells gas generators ("inflators") and modules for use in automotive airbag passive restraint systems. Incorporated in Indiana in 1989.

Directors   (In addition to indicated officer)

Ralph M. Barford	Richard L. Keyser	Charles A. Sanders, M.D.
William T. Creson	Frank W. Luerssen	George A. Schaefer
Dennis C. Fill	Edward J. Mooney, Jr.	Roger W. Stone

Officers   (Director*)

*S. Jay Stewart, Chm. & C.E.O.
William E. Johnston, Jr., Exec. V.P.—Adm.
Walter W. Becky II, Grp. V.P.—Salt
Daniel D. Feinberg, Grp. V.P.—Electronic Mat.
James J. Fuerholzer, Grp. V.P.—Spec. Chem. Prod.
Stephen A. Gerow, Grp. V.P.—Coatings
Fred J. Musone, Grp. V.P.—Auto. Safety Prod.
Thomas S. Russell, Grp. V.P.—Adhesives & Spec. Polymers

Albert E. Greene, V.P.—Health, Safety & Envir.
Nancy A. Hobor, V.P.—Comm. & Inv. Rel.
Christopher K. Julsrud, V.P.—Hum. Res.
Donald L. Kidd, V.P.—Mgt. Info. & Svcs.
Lewis N. Liszt, V.P.—Mgt. Svcs.
Thomas F. McDevitt, V.P.—Fin. & C.F.O.
P. Michael Phelps, V.P. & Corp. Secy.
James R. Stanley, V.P.—Legal Affs. & Gen. Coun.
Bruce G. Wolfe, Treas.
Lisa F. Zumbach, Cont.

Consolidated Balance Sheet   As of June 30, 1994 (000 omitted)

Assets		Liabilities & Stockholders' Equity	
Current assets	$ 996,400	Current liabilities	$ 557,200
Net property, plant & equipment	1,004,900	Long-term debt	198,600
Other assets	461,300	Deferred items	55,100
		Other liabilities	252,100
		*Stockholders' equity	1,399,600
Total	$2,462,600	Total	$2,462,600

*49,196,174 shares common stock outstanding.

Consolidated Income Statement

Years Ended June 30	Thousands — — — — Net Sales	Net Income	Per Share[a] — — — Earnings	Cash Dividends	Common Stock Price Range[a] Calendar Year
1994	$2,849,600	$226,500	$1.51[b]	$ .37	37-1/4 — 25-3/4
1993	2,309,800	32,500[b]	.22[b]	.32	33-1/2 — 19-1/4
1992	2,043,900	144,500	.98	.32	21-5/8 — 16-7/8
1991	1,905,900	138,300	.95	.31	19-1/2 — 12-7/8
1990	1,638,700	134,800[c]	.93[c]	.29	15-7/8 — 11-1/8

[a]Adjusted to reflect a 3-for-1 stock split in August 1994.
[b]Includes a charge to reflect FAS 106 and FAS 112, resulting in a cumulative effect of $94,400,000 ($.64 per share).
[c]Includes gain of $13,100,000 ($.09 per share) on sale of 40% interest in foreign affiliate and unusual charges of $7,300,000 ($.05 per share) for additional anticipated costs related primarily to previously divested operations.

Transfer Agent & Registrar: First Chicago Trust Co. of New York

General Counsel:	James R. Stanley, V.P.	Auditors:	Ernst & Young LLP
Investor Relations:	Nancy A. Hobor, V.P.	Traded (Symbol):	NYSE, CSE (MII)
Human Resources:	Christopher K. Julsrud, V.P.	Stockholders:	8,860
		Employees:	13,100
Mgt. Info. Svcs.:	Donald L. Kidd, V.P.	Annual Meeting:	In October

Motorola, Inc.

1303 East Algonquin Road, Schaumburg, Illinois 60196-1065
Telephone: (708) 576-5000

Motorola, Inc., is a leading provider of electronic equipment, systems, components, and services produced for both U.S. and international markets. The Land Mobile Products Sector is a principal supplier of mobile and portable FM two-way radio and radio data communications systems. The Messaging, Information and Media Sector designs, manufactures and distributes products for paging and radio data systems worldwide. Products include modems, multiplexers and integrated network management systems. The Semiconductor Products Sector manufactures discrete semiconductors and integrated circuits, including microprocessors, memories, logic, analog and application specific ICs. The General Systems Sector manufactures cellular mobile and portable telephones, cellular systems, microcomputer boards, and multi-function computer systems. The Government and Space Technology Group produces diversified military and space electronics equipment, including communications equipment, and strategic and tactical electronic systems. The Automotive, Energy and Controls Group manufactures electronic engine controls, sensors, and power conversion equipment as well as electronic components such as batteries, crystals and ceramics. Incorporated in Illinois in 1928; reincorporated in Delaware in 1973.

Directors (In addition to indicated officers)

William J. Weisz, Chm.	Donald R. Jones	John E. Pepper, Jr.
David R. Clare	Judy C. Lewent	Samuel C. Scott III
H. Laurance Fuller	Walter E. Massey	Gardiner L. Tucker
John T. Hickey	John F. Mitchell	B. Kenneth West
Anne P. Jones	Thomas J. Murrin	John A. White

Officers (Directors*)

*Robert W. Galvin, Chm. of Exec. Comm.
*Gary L. Tooker, V. Chm. & C.E.O.
*Christopher B. Galvin, Pres. & C.O.O.
Keith J. Bane, Exec. V.P. & Chf. Corp. Staff Officer
Arnold S. Brenner, Exec. V.P. & Gen. Mgr.—Japan Group
James Donnelly, Exec. V.P. & Hum. Res. Dir.
Thomas D. George, Exec. V.P. & Pres./Gen. Mgr.—Semicond. Prod.
Merle L. Gilmore, Exec. V.P. & Pres./Gen. Mgr.—Land Mobile Prod.
Robert L. Growney, Exec. V.P. & Pres./Gen. Mgr.-Mess., Info. & Media

Carl F. Koenemann, Exec. V.P. & C.F.O.
James A. Norling, Exec. V.P. & Pres.—Europe, Middle E. & Africa
Edward F. Staiano, Exec. V.P. & Pres./Gen. Mgr.—Gen. Syst.
Frederick T. Tucker, Exec. V.P. & Gen. Mgr.—Auto., Energy & Control
David G. Wolfe, Exec. V.P. & Gen. Mgr.—Govt. & Space
Richard W. Younts, Exec. V.P. & Dir.—Int'l.
William V. Braun, Sr. V.P. & Dir.—R&D
Garth L. Milne, Sr. V.P. & Treas.
Richard H. Weise, Sr. V.P., Gen. Coun. & Secy.

Consolidated Balance Sheet   As of December 31, 1994 (000 omitted)

Assets		Liabilities & Stockholders' Equity	
Current assets	$ 8,925,000	Current liabilities	$ 5,917,000
Net property, plant & equipment	7,073,000	Long-term debt	1,127,000
Other assets	1,538,000	Deferred income taxes	509,000
		Other liabilities	887,000
		*Stockholders' equity	9,096,000
Total	$17,536,000	Total	$17,536,000

*588,000,000 shares common stock outstanding.

Consolidated Income Statement

Years Ended Dec. 31	Thousands — — — — Sales[a]	Net Income	Per Share[d] — — — — Earnings[b]	Cash Dividends[c]	Common Stock Price Range[d] Calendar Year
1994	$22,245,000	$1,560,000	$2.65	$ .31	61-1/8 — 42-1/8
1993	16,963,000	1,022,000	1.78	.22	53-3/4 — 24-3/8
1992	13,303,000	576,000[e]	1.05[e]	.20	26-5/8 — 16-1/8
1991	11,341,000	454,000	.84	.19	17-1/2 — 11-5/8
1990	10,885,000	499,000	.93	.19	22-1/8 — 12-3/8

[a]Includes FAS 94, consolidation of majority-owned subsidiaries.
[b]Fully diluted.
[c]Cash dividends declared.
[d]Adjusted to reflect 2-for-1 stock splits declared in February 1994 and November 1992.
[e]Before a charge to reflect FAS 106, which resulted in a cumulative effect of $123,000,000 ($.22 per share).

Transfer Agent & Registrar: Harris Trust and Savings Bank

General Counsel: Richard H. Weise, Sr. V.P.

Investor Relations: Edward Gams, V.P.

Human Resources: James Donnelly, Exec. V.P.

Mgt. Info. Svcs.: John Major, Sr. V.P.

Auditors: KPMG Peat Marwick LLP

Traded (Symbol): CSE, NYSE, London, Tokyo (MOT)

Stockholders: 40,000

Employees: 132,000

Annual Meeting: In May

The L.E. Myers Co. Group

2550 West Golf Road, Suite 200, Rolling Meadows, Illinois 60008-4007
Telephone: (708) 290-1891

The L.E. Myers Co. Group is a holding company whose principal asset consists of all of the outstanding shares of capital stock of The L.E. Myers Co. The company is also the owner of all of the issued and outstanding stock of Hawkeye Construction, Inc. The L.E. Myers Co. Group's principal business is the construction of transmission lines, distribution systems, and substations for electric utilities. In addition to new construction, the maintenance and upgrading of existing facilities constitute an important part of the company's construction work. The L.E. Myers Co. Group has installed electrical systems in commercial, industrial and institutional facilities, electrical transportation systems, and power generating stations. The company also installs and maintains municipal street lighting and traffic control systems. The company generally serves the electric utility industry as a prime construction contractor. Designs and specifications for a project are usually prepared by the utilities or their agents. Contracts generally require the company to supply the management, labor, equipment, and tools necessary to construct the project. Construction materials are generally supplied by the utilities. Incorporated in Delaware in 1982.

Directors (In addition to indicated officer)

William G. Brown
Allen E. Bulley, Jr.

John M. Harlan
Bide L. Thomas

Officers (Director*)

*Charles M. Brennan III, Chm. & C.E.O.
William S. Skibitsky, Pres. & C.O.O.
Byron D. Nelson, Sr. V.P., Secy. & Gen. Coun.

Elliott C. Robbins, Sr. V.P., Treas. & C.F.O.
Betty R. Johnson, Cont.

Consolidated Balance Sheet As of December 31, 1994 (000 omitted)

Assets		Liabilities & Stockholders' Equity	
Current assets	$22,364	Current liabilities	$13,769
Net property, plant & equipment	14,652	Long-term debt	318
Other assets	2,628	Deferred items	1,675
		Other liabilities	260
		*Stockholders' equity	23,622
Total	$39,644	Total	$39,644

*2,379,156 shares common stock outstanding.

Consolidated Income Statement[a]

Years Ended Dec. 31	Thousands — — — — Contract Revenues[b]	Net Income[b]	Per Share — — — Earnings[b]	Cash Dividends	Common Stock Price Range Calendar Year
1994	$ 86,842	$2,329	$ .93	$ .22	13-5/8 — 9-3/4
1993	108,515	1,633	.65	.21	17-7/8 — 8-1/2
1992	110,251	3,584	1.37	.19	25-3/8 — 15-1/4
1991[c]	96,097	3,045	1.18	.16	17-5/8 — 12-1/2
1990	65,846	2,201	.86	.13	21 — 6-5/8

[a]Includes FAS 109, resulting in a charge to net income of $867,000 ($.33 per share) in 1992, $1,302,000 ($.50 per share) in 1991, and $1,250,000 ($.49 per share) in 1990.
[b]Adjusted to reflect continuing operations only.
[c]Includes Hawkeye Construction, Inc., since May 31, 1991, effective date of acquisition.

Transfer Agent & Registrar: Harris Trust and Savings Bank

General Counsel: Byron D. Nelson, Sr. V.P.

Investor Relations:
  Charles M. Brennan III, Chm.

Human Resources: Becky Matthews

Mgt. Info. Svcs.: Richard Beemster

Auditors: Deloitte & Touche LLP

Traded (Symbol): NYSE (MYR)

Stockholders: 1,297

Employees: 1,120

Annual Meeting: In May

N.S. Bancorp, Inc.

2300 North Western Avenue, Chicago, Illinois 60647-3195
Telephone: (312) 489-2300

N.S. Bancorp, Inc., is the savings bank holding company for Northwestern Savings Bank (formerly Northwestern Savings and Loan Association), a thrift with six locations in Chicago, Berwyn, and Norridge, Illinois. The principal business of Northwestern Savings consists of attracting deposits from the general public and investing those deposits, together with funds generated from operations and borrowings, into one- to four-family mortgage loans. Incorporated in Delaware in 1990.

Directors (In addition to indicated officers)

Ramona Castillo
Robert E. Chamberlain
Stanley C. Wielgos

Chester J. Zaleski
Edward J. Zych

Officers (Directors*)

*Henry R. Smogolski, Chm., Pres. & C.E.O.
*Andrew J. Zych, Exec. V.P.
Stephen G. Skiba, Sr. V.P., C.F.O. & Treas.

Gary M. Smogolski, Sr. V.P.—Hum. Res. & Secy.
Trent N. Fotopoulos, Asst. Secy.

Consolidated Balance Sheet   As of December 31, 1994 (000 omitted)

Assets		Liabilities & Stockholders' Equity	
Loans receivable, net	$ 826,812	Deposits	$ 839,876
Mortgage-backed securities	252,009	Borrowed funds	190,522
Marketable equity sec.	14,242	Other liabilities	7,953
Investment securities	96,912	*Stockholders' equity	215,660
Real estate	39,953		
Other assets	24,083		
Total	$1,254,011	Total	$1,254,011

*6,199,140 shares common stock outstanding.

Consolidated Income Statement

| Years Ended Dec. 31 | Thousands — — — — | | Per Share — — — | | Common Stock |
	Operating Income	Net Income	Earnings	Cash Dividends	Price Range Calendar Year
1994	$ 78,262	$14,048	$1.87	$ .32	33 — 25-3/8
1993	96,984	28,039	3.31	.32	34-7/8 — 26-1/4
1992	122,200	32,780	3.61	.32	31-1/2 — 18
1991	128,741	24,048[a]	2.46	.32	19-1/4 — 7-7/8
1990	130,699	12,626[a]			8-3/8 — 7-7/8[b]

[a]Restated for FAS 109.
[b]Initial public offering in December 1990.

Transfer Agent & Registrar: Harris Trust and Savings Bank

General Counsel:
  Stone, Pogrund, Korey & Spagat

Investor Relations: Stephen G. Skiba, Sr. V.P.

Human Resources: Gary M. Smogolski, Sr. V.P.

Mgt. Info. Svcs:
  Marie L. Phillips, Asst. V.P.—Data Syst.

Auditors: Ernst & Young LLP

Traded (Symbol): NASDAQ (NSBI)

Stockholders: 468

Employees: 312

Annual Meeting: In April

Nalco Chemical Company

One Nalco Center, Naperville, Illinois 60563-1198
Telephone: (708) 305-1000

Nalco Chemical Company manufactures and sells highly specialized chemicals and technology used in water treatment, pollution control, energy conservation, oil production and refining, steelmaking, papermaking, mining, automotive, food and beverage, and other industries. Nalco markets programs to improve operating efficiencies and minimize energy consumption and pollution in industrial water and process systems. Outside the U.S., Nalco products and services are marketed in nearly 130 countries through a network of 67 subsidiaries and three affiliated companies. Incorporated in Delaware in 1928.

Directors (In addition to indicated officer)

Jose Luis Ballesteros
Harold G. Bernthal
Harry Corless
Howard M. Dean
John P. Frazee, Jr.

Arthur L. Kelly
Frederick A. Krehbiel
William A. Pogue
John J. Shea

Officers (Director*)

*Edward J. Mooney, Jr., Chm., Pres. & C.E.O.
Milford B. Harp, Exec. V.P.—Oper.
W. Steven Weeber, Exec. V.P.—Oper. Staff
Peter Dabringhausen, Grp. V.P. &
  Pres.—Process. Chem. Div.
Stephen D. Newlin, Grp. V.P. & Pres.
  —Europe Division

J. David Tinsley, Grp. V.P. & Pres.—Water &
  Waste Treat. Div.
Ronald J. Allain, Sr. V.P.—R&D
David R. Bertran, Sr. V.P.—Mfg. & Logistics
James F. Lambe, Sr. V.P.—Hum. Res.
William E. Buchholz, V.P.—C.F.O.
William E. Parry, V.P.—Gen. Coun.

Consolidated Balance Sheet As of December 31, 1994 (000 omitted)

Assets		Liabilities & Stockholders' Equity	
Current assets	$ 362,100	Current liabilities	$ 274,300
Net property, plant & equipment	523,900	Long-term debt	245,300
Other assets	396,200	Deferred items	56,800
		Accrued postretirement benefits	95,200
		Other liabilities	66,400
		*Stockholders' equity	544,200
Total	$1,282,200	Total	$1,282,200

*67,900,145 shares common stock outstanding.

Consolidated Income Statement

Years Ended Dec. 31	Thousands — — — —		Per Share[a] — — —		Common Stock
	Net Sales	Net Income	Earnings	Cash Dividends	Price Range[a] Calendar Year
1994	$1,345,600	$ 97,100	$1.25	$ .95	37-7/8 — 29-3/4
1993	1,389,400	85,600[b]	1.07[b]	.89	37-7/8 — 30-1/4
1992	1,374,529	144,989	1.90	.84	40-7/8 — 30-3/8
1991	1,237,291	137,791	1.82	.83	42-1/4 — 26-1/8
1990	1,068,067	131,077	1.71	.76	30-5/8 — 22

[a]Adjusted to reflect a 2-for-1 stock split in May 1991.
[b]Includes a charge to reflect FAS 106, resulting in a cumulative effect of $56,500,000 ($.81 per share); and an extraordinary loss from retirement of debt, net of taxes, of $10,600,000 ($.15 per share).

Transfer Agent & Registrar:	First Chicago Trust Co. of New York		
Corporate Counsel:	Mayer, Brown & Platt	Traded (Symbol):	CSE, NYSE (NLC)
Investor Relations:	William E. Buchholz, V.P.	Stockholders:	6,005
Human Resources:	James F. Lambe, Sr. V.P.	Employees:	5,601
Auditors:	Price Waterhouse LLP	Annual Meeting:	In April

Navistar International Corporation

455 North Cityfront Plaza Drive, Chicago, Illinois 60611
Telephone: (312) 836-2000

Navistar International Corporation is a holding company whose principal operating subsidiary, Navistar International Transportation Corp., manufactures and markets medium and heavy diesel trucks, school bus chassis, mid-range diesel engines, and replacement parts in North America, and also distributes them in selected export markets. Its products are sold worldwide through 951 independent dealers and distribution outlets. Navistar International's brand of trucks include: diesel powered truck/tractors used for local and long distance hauling of freight; cab and chassis units used for medium hauling and for hauling heavy loads over rugged terrain and highways; and chassis units for school buses. Navistar International also provides wholesale and retail financing, product leasing, and casualty insurance coverage services through wholly owned finance subsidiaries. Other major subsidiaries include Navistar Financial Corporation and Navistar International Corporation Canada. Incorporated in Delaware in 1965.

Directors (In addition to indicated officers)

James C. Cotting, Chm.
Jack R. Anderson
William F. Andrews
Wallace W. Booth
Andrew F. Brimmer
Bill Casstevens
Richard F. Celeste

John D. Correnti
William C. Craig
Jerry E. Dempsey
Mary Garst
Charles Haggerty
Arthur G. Hansen

Officers (Directors*)

*John R. Horne, Pres. & C.E.O.
*Robert C. Lannert, Exec. V.P. & C.F.O.
Robert A. Boardman, Sr. V.P. & Gen. Coun.

Thomas M. Hough, V.P. & Treas.
Robert I. Morrison, V.P. & Cont.
Steven K. Covey, Secy.

Consolidated Balance Sheet As of October 31, 1994 (000 omitted)

Assets		Liabilities & Stockholders' Equity	
Cash & cash equivalents	$ 557,000	Long-term debt	$ 696,000
Property and equipment, net	578,000	Other liabilities	3,543,000
Other assets	3,921,000	*Stockholders' equity	817,000
Total	$5,056,000	Total	$5,056,000

*49,319,200 shares common and 25,034,861 shares Class B common stock outstanding.

Consolidated Income Statement

Years Ended Oct. 31	Thousands — — — — Sales & Revenues	Net Income	Per Share[a] — — — — Earnings	Cash Dividends	Common Stock Price Range[a] Calendar Year
1994	$5,337,000	$ 82,000	$ .72	$ .00	26-5/8 — 12-1/4
1993	4,721,000	(501,000)[b]	(15.19)[b]	.00	33-3/4 — 19-1/4
1992	3,897,000	(212,000)[c]	(9.55)[c]	.00	40 — 17-1/2
1991	3,496,000	(165,000)	(7.71)	.00	42-1/2 — 21-1/4
1990	3,903,000	(11,000)	(1.56)	.00	46-1/4 — 20

[a]Adjusted to reflect a 1-for-10 reverse stock split in August 1993.
[b]Includes a charge of $513,000,000 for the issuance of Class B common stock to a retiree supplemental trust in settlement of a reduction in retiree health and life insurance benefits, and a charge to reflect FAS 106 and FAS 109, resulting in a cumulative effect of $228,000,000 ($6.56 per share).
[c]Includes a $65,000,000 ($2.58 per share) charge to discontinued operations for the settlement of two Wisconsin Steel lawsuits brought by the Pension Benefit Guaranty Corporation.

Transfer Agent: Harris Trust and Savings Bank

Registrar:
The First National Bank of Chicago

General Counsel:
Robert A. Boardman, Sr. V.P.

Investor Relations: Thomas M. Hough, V.P.

Human Resources:
John M. Sheahin, Sr. V.P.—Employee Rel. & Adm.

Auditors: Deloitte & Touche LLP

Traded (Symbol): NYSE, CSE, PSE (NAV)

Stockholders: 70,394

Employees: 14,910

Annual Meeting: In March

First Chicago Guide

Newell Co.

Newell Center, 29 East Stephenson Street, Freeport, Illinois 61032
Telephone: (815) 235-4171

Newell Co. is a manufacturer and marketer of staple, volume consumer and industrial products for the volume purchaser. Newell's multi-product offering includes: Mirro and WearEver cookware and bakeware, Amerock cabinet hardware, Anchor Hocking glassware and plasticware, EZ Paintr paint applicators, Newell window furnishings, Dorfile shelving systems, Bulldog home hardware, and BernzOmatic torches. These consumer products are sold to national and regional discount, variety, department and hardware stores, home improvement centers, supermarket chains, mail order houses, paint stores, independent distributors, catalog showrooms, and military post exchanges. Newell also sells industrial products to large institutional purchasers. Newell companies include: Amerock, Amerock Window Hardware, Anchor Hocking Glass, Anchor Hocking Industrial, Anchor Hocking Plastics, Plastics Inc., Stuart Hall Co., BernzOmatic, Bulldog, Dorfile, Sanford Corp., Levolor Corp., EZ Paintr, Mirro, Goody Products, Inc., Intercraft Company, Newell International, Newell Venture Group, and Newell Window Furnishings. In November 1994, Newell acquired Corning's European divisions, now called Newell Europe. Newell acquired Faber-Castell Corp. in October 1994. In 1993, the company acquired Goody Products, Inc., Jareen Co., Lee-Rowan Co., and PI Industries. Incorporated in Delaware in 1903.

Directors   (In addition to indicated officers)

Alton F. Doody
Gary H. Driggs
Robert L. Katz
John J. McDonough

Elizabeth C. Millett
Allan P. Newell
Henry B. Pearsall

Officers   (Directors*)

*Daniel C. Ferguson, Chm.
*William P. Sovey, V. Chm. & C.E.O.
*Thomas A. Ferguson, Jr., Pres. & C.O.O.
 Richard C. Dell, Grp. Pres.
 William J. Denton, Grp. Pres.
 James E. Gillies, Sr. V.P.—Canadian Mktg. Dev.
 Donald L. Krause, Sr. V.P.—Cont.
 Byron H. Stebbins, Sr. V.P.—Mktg. Devel.
 William T. Alldredge, V.P.—Fin.
 Thomas F. Bradley, V.P. & Grp. Cont.

Clarence R. Davenport, V.P.—Treas., Chf. Info. Off. & Asst. Corp. Secy.
William K. Doppstadt, V.P.—Person. Rel.
Brett E. Gries, V.P.—Acct. & Tax
Peter J. Martin, V.P. & Grp. Cont.
Dale L. Matschullat, V.P. & Gen. Coun.
John G. Miles, V.P.—Corp. Retail Svcs.
Richard H. Wolff, Corp. Secy. & Assoc. Gen. Coun.
Shirley K. Martin, Asst. Corp. Secy.

Consolidated Balance Sheet   As of December 31, 1994 (000 omitted)

Assets		Liabilities & Stockholders' Equity	
Current assets	$ 917,671	Current liabilities	$ 784,024
Net property, plant & equipment	454,597	Long-term debt	408,986
Other assets	1,116,008	Deferred items	17,243
		Other liabilities	152,697
		*Stockholders' equity	1,125,326
Total	$2,488,276	Total	$2,488,276

*157,843,590 shares common stock outstanding.

Consolidated Income Statement

Years Ended Dec. 31	Thousands — — — — Net Sales	Net Income	Per Share[a] — — — Earnings	Cash Dividends	Common Stock Price Range[a] Calendar Year
1994	$2,074,934	$195,575	$1.24	$ .68	23 - 7/8 — 19
1993	1,645,036	165,334	1.05	.30	21 - 1/2 — 15 - 3/8
1992	1,451,656	119,137[b]	.77[b]	.30	26 - 1/2 — 16 - 1/2
1991[c]	1,258,958	135,637	.89	.27	22 - 7/8 — 11 - 5/8
1990[c]	1,204,442	125,502	.84	.22	17 - 1/8 — 9 - 1/4

[a]Adjusted to reflect a 2-for-1 stock split in September 1994.
[b]Includes FAS 106, resulting in a cumulative charge of $44,134,000 ($.29 per share).
[c]Restated to include the merger with Sanford Corporation, which has been accounted for as a pooling-of-interests.

Transfer Agent & Registrar: First Chicago Trust Co. of New York

General Counsel: Dale L. Matschullat, V.P.

Investor Relations: Ross Porter, Dir.

Human Resources: James Peters

Mgt. Info. Svcs.:   Clarence R. Davenport, V.P.

Auditors: Arthur Andersen LLP
Traded (Symbol):   NYSE, CSE (NWL)
Stockholders: 10,290
Employees: 21,000
Annual Meeting: In May

NICOR Inc.

1844 Ferry Road, P.O. Box 3014, Naperville, Illinois 60566-7014
Telephone: (708) 305-9500

NICOR Inc. is a holding company whose principal subsidiary is Northern Illinois Gas, a gas distribution company. NICOR's non-utility business is engaged in containerized shipping. Northern Illinois Gas delivers natural gas to more than 1.8 million customers and provides transportation service, gas storage, and gas supply backup to approximately 18,000 commercial and industrial customers who purchase their own natural gas supplies. Tropical Shipping transports containerized freight between the Port of Palm Beach, Florida, and 22 ports in the Caribbean, Central America and Mexico. Tropical Shipping has leading market shares in many of the ports it serves. Incorporated in Illinois in 1976.

Directors (In addition to indicated officers)

Robert M. Beavers, Jr.
John H. Birdsall III
W.H. Clark
John E. Jones
Dennis J. Keller

Charles S. Locke
Sidney R. Petersen
Daniel R. Toll
Patricia A. Wier

Officers (Directors*)[a]

*Richard G. Cline, Chm.
*Thomas L. Fisher, Pres. & C.E.O.
 David L. Cyranoski, Sr. V.P., Secy. & Cont.
 Thomas A. Nardi, Sr. V.P.—Nonutility Opers.
   & Bus. Dev.

John C. Flowers, V.P.—Hum. Res.
Edwin M. Werneke, V.P.—Supply Ventures
Donald W. Lohrentz, Treas.

[a]Fisher will become Chairman in December 1995, when Cline retires.

Consolidated Balance Sheet As of December 31, 1994 (000 omitted)

Assets		Liabilities & Stockholders' Equity	
Current assets	$ 418,000	Current liabilities	$ 600,400
Net property, plant & equipment	1,717,000	Long-term debt	458,900
Other assets	74,900	Deferred items	312,700
		Other liabilities	145,100
		*Stockholders' equity	692,800
Total	$2,209,900	Total	$2,209,900

*51,540,327 shares common stock outstanding.

Consolidated Income Statement

Years Ended Dec. 31	Thousands — — — — Operating Revenues[a]	Net Income	Per Share[b] — — — — Earnings	Cash Dividends[c]	Common Stock Price Range[b] Calendar Year
1994	$1,609,400	$109,500	$2.07	$1.26	29-1/4 — 21-7/8
1993	1,673,900	111,700	2.01	1.22	31-5/8 — 24-1/8
1992	1,546,500	108,300	1.91	1.18	25-3/4 — 19
1991	1,457,100	108,600	1.85	1.12	23-3/4 — 19-1/2
1990	1,471,700	113,500	1.93	1.06	23-1/2 — 17-3/8

[a]Restated to reflect the sale of oil and gas operations.
[b]Adjusted to reflect the 2-for-1 stock split in April 1993.
[c]Cash dividends declared.

Transfer Agent & Registrar: Harris Trust and Savings Bank

General Counsel: Mayer, Brown & Platt

Investor Relations: Randall S. Horn, Dir.

Human Resources: John C. Flowers, V.P.

Mgt. Info. Svcs.: Kathleen L. Halloran, V.P.

Auditors: Arthur Andersen LLP
Traded (Symbol): CSE, NYSE (GAS)
Stockholders: 43,800
Employees: 3,400
Annual Meeting: In May

NIPSCO Industries, Inc.

5265 Hohman Avenue, Hammond, Indiana 46320-1775
Telephone: (219) 853-5200

NIPSCO Industries, Inc. (Industries), serves as the holding company for a number of subsidiaries, including three public utility operating companies: Northern Indiana Public Service Company, Kokomo Gas and Fuel Company, and Northern Indiana Fuel and Light Company, Inc. Northern Indiana supplies natural gas and electric energy to the public, operating in 30 counties in northern Indiana, serving an area of about 12,000 square miles with a population of approximately 2.1 million. Kokomo Gas supplies natural gas to the public, operating in Kokomo and the surrounding six-county area with a population of approximately 100,000. Northern Indiana Fuel and Light Co. supplies natural gas, operating in five counties in northeast Indiana with a population of approximately 66,700. Industries' major non-utility subsidiaries include NIPSCO Development Company, Inc., which makes various investments, including real estate, and is a 95 percent shareholder in Elm Energy and Recycling (UK) Ltd., the owner and operator of a tire-fueled electric generating plant in Wolverhampton, England, which commenced operations in late 1993; NIPSCO Energy Services, Inc., which coordinates the energy-related diversification ventures of Industries and has four wholly owned subsidiaries; and NIPSCO Capital Markets, Inc., which handles financing for ventures of Industries other than those for Northern Indiana Public Service Co. Incorporated in Indiana in 1987.

Directors (In addition to indicated officer)

Steven C. Beering
Arthur J. Decio
Ernestine M. Raclin
Denis E. Ribordy

Ian M. Rolland
Edmund A. Schroer
John W. Thompson
Robert J. Welsh, Jr.

Officers (Director*)

*Gary L. Neale, Chm., Pres. & C.E.O.
Stephen P. Adik, Exec. V.P., C.F.O. & Treas.
Patrick J. Mulchay, Exec. V.P. &
C.O.O.—Electric
Jeffrey W. Yundt, Exec. V.P. & C.O.O.—Gas
William R. Elliott, V.P.—Subsidiary Opers.,
Electric

Owen C. Johnson, Jr., V.P.—Hum. Res.
David A. Kelly, V.P.—Real Estate & Taxes
Nina M. Rausch, Secy.
Jerry M. Springer, Cont. & Asst. Secy.
Dennis E. Senchak, Asst. Treas.

Consolidated Balance Sheet   As of December 31, 1994 (000 omitted)

Assets		Liabilities & Stockholders' Equity	
Current assets	$ 327,945	Current liabilities	$ 640,988
Net property, plant & equipment	3,230,957	Long-term debt	1,180,338
Other assets	385,641	Deferred items	743,505
		Other liabilities	271,864
		*Stockholders' equity	1,107,848
Total	$3,944,543	Total	$3,944,543

*63,905,389 shares common stock outstanding.

Consolidated Income Statement

Years Ended Dec. 31	Thousands — — — — Operating Revenues	Net Income[a]	Per Share — — — Earnings	Cash Dividends	Common Stock Price Range Calendar Year
1994	$1,676,401	$160,924	$2.48	$1.44	33 — 26-1/8
1993	1,677,872	153,077	2.31	1.32	34-7/8 — 26-1/8
1992	1,582,356	133,585	2.00	1.24	26-5/8 — 22-1/2
1991	1,535,161	130,325	1.94	1.16	27 — 18-1/2
1990	1,520,995	125,088	1.81	1.04	19-1/4 — 15-3/4

[a]Adjusted to reflect income after dividend requirements on preferred and preference stocks.

Transfer Agent & Registrar: Harris Trust and Savings Bank

General Counsel: Schiff, Hardin & Waite

Investor Relations: Dennis E. Senchak, Asst. Treas.

Human Resources: Owen C. Johnson, Jr., V.P.

Mgt. Info. Svcs.:   Wayne L. Hall, Dir.—N. Indiana

Auditors: Arthur Andersen LLP
Traded (Symbol):   CSE, NYSE, PSE (NI)
Stockholders: 39,172
Employees: 4,441
Annual Meeting: In April

North Bancshares, Inc.

100 West North Avenue, Chicago, Illinois 60610-1399
Telephone: (312) 664-4320

North Bancshares, Inc., is the holding company recently organized for North Federal Savings Bank, a federally chartered stock savings bank. The bank primarily serves the Old Town, Lincoln Park, Gold Coast, and Lake View areas of Chicago. Originally organized in 1886, the bank converted to a federal mutual savings bank in 1986. It changed to a stock savings bank in connection with its initial public offering in 1993. The bank attracts retail deposits from the general public and invests those funds primarily in first mortgages on owner-occupied and non-owner occupied, one- to four-family residences and mortgage-backed and investment securities. Incorporated in Delaware in 1993.

Directors (In addition to indicated officers)

James L. Ferstel
Elmer L. Hass
Michael J. Perri

Paul E. Rose
Robert H. Rusher

Officers (Directors*)

*Mary Ann Hass, Chm. & C.E.O.
*Joseph A. Graber, Pres. & C.O.O.

Victor E. Caputo, Exec. V.P. & Secy.
Martin W. Trofimuk, V.P. & Treas.

Consolidated Balance Sheet   As of December 31, 1994 (000 omitted)

Assets		Liabilities & Stockholders' Equity	
Total cash & cash equivalents	$ 6,385	Deposits	$ 70,178
Investments	35,984	Other liabilities	15,179
Loans receivable	45,288	*Stockholders' equity	21,602
Mortgage-backed securities	17,015		
Premises & equipment	804		
Other assets	1,483		
Total	$106,959	Total	$106,959

*1,360,626 shares common stock outstanding.

Consolidated Income Statement

Years Ended Dec. 31	Thousands — — — — Total Income	Net Income	Per Share — — — — Earnings	Cash Dividends	Common Stock Price Range[a] Calendar Year	
1994	$6,060	$ 45	$ .03	$ .25	14	— 11
1993	6,691	622			13	— 10-1/2[b]
1992	7,559	988[c]				
1991	7,898	600				
1990	7,818	415				

[a]Initial public offering in December 1993.
[b]Common stock began trading December 21, 1993, on NASDAQ.
[c]Includes a charge to reflect FAS 109, resulting in a cumulative effect of $96,000.

Transfer Agent & Registrar: Harris Trust and Savings Bank

General Counsel:
  Silver, Freedman & Taff, L.L.P.

Investor Relations: Joseph A. Graber, Pres.

Human Resources: Joseph A. Graber, Pres.

Mgt. Info. Svcs.:   Joseph A. Graber, Pres.

Auditors: KPMG Peat Marwick LLP

Traded (Symbol):   NASDAQ (NBSI)

Stockholders: 900

Employees: 35

Annual Meeting: In April

Northern States Financial Corporation

1601 North Lewis Avenue, Waukegan, Illinois 60085
Telephone: (708) 244-6000

Northern States Financial Corporation is a holding company for Bank of Waukegan and First Federal Bank, fsb. The principal business of the company consists of attracting deposits from the general public, making commercial loans, loans secured by residential and commercial real estate, making consumer loans, and operating a trust business. Bank of Waukegan is an Illinois-chartered bank with two banking offices located in Waukegan and one located in Antioch, Illinois. First Federal Bank primarily offers traditional deposit services and mortgage loans. Incorporated in Delaware in 1984.

Directors (In addition to indicated officers)

Jack H. Blumberg
Frank Furlan
Harry S. Gaples
Laurence A. Guthrie
James A. Hollensteiner

Frank Ryskiewicz
Sol Siegel
Henry G. Tewes
Arthur J. Wagner

Officers (Directors*)

*Fred Abdula, Chm. & C.E.O.
Howard A. Jaffe, Exec. V.P. & C.F.O.
*Kenneth W. Balza, V.P. & Treas.

Joseph F. Tomasello, V.P.
*Helen Rumsa, Secy.

Consolidated Balance Sheet As of December 31, 1994 (000 omitted)

Assets		Liabilities & Stockholders' Equity	
Cash & due from banks	$ 25,952	Deposits	$329,363
Investments	154,841	Other borrowings	30,654
Loans, net	212,823	Other liabilities	5,918
Other assets	18,019	*Stockholders' equity	45,700
Total	$411,635	Total	$411,635

*886,131 shares common stock outstanding.

Consolidated Income Statement[ab]

Years Ended Dec. 31	Thousands — — — — Total Income	Net Income	Per Share[c] — — — Earnings	Cash Dividends[d]	Common Stock Price Range[c] Calendar Year
1994	$30,139	$4,475	$5.05	$1.45	67-1/2 — 55
1993	30,376	4,434	5.01	1.30	55 — 42
1992	33,029	4,170	4.71	1.15	47 — 38
1991	36,150	3,675	4.16	1.00	42-1/2 — 38
1990	37,410	3,863	4.37	.92	42-1/2 — 37[e]

[a]The company acquired First Federal Bank on July 1, 1991, in a transaction accounted for as a pooling-of-interests. Accordingly, the consolidated results of operations include First Federal Bank for each of the years ended December 31, 1991, and 1990.
[b]The company changed its fiscal yearend to December 31 from September 30 effective for the fiscal year ended December 31, 1991. All information presented has been restated as if the change in the fiscal year occurred December 31, 1990.
[c]Adjusted to reflect a 5-for-1 stock split in June 1991.
[d]Cash dividends declared.
[e]The company began trading on NASDAQ Market System on July 2, 1991. Prior to the offering, there was no established public trading market for the common stock.

Transfer Agent & Registrar:	Firstar Trust Co.		
General Counsel:	Chapman & Cutler	Auditors:	Crowe, Chizek & Co.
Investor Relations:	Howard A. Jaffe, Exec. V.P.	Traded (Symbol):	NASDAQ (NSFC)
Human Resources:	Kerry J. Biegay, V.P.	Stockholders:	625
		Employees:	154
Mgt. Info. Svcs.:	Howard A. Jaffe, Exec. V.P.	Annual Meeting:	In April

Northern Trust Corporation

50 South LaSalle Street, Chicago, Illinois 60675
Telephone: (312) 630-6000

Northern Trust Corporation is a multi-bank holding company with subsidiaries in Illinois, Arizona, California, New York, Florida, Georgia, and Texas. Its principal subsidiary, The Northern Trust Company, was established in 1889. Northern Trust Corporation also is the parent company of: Northern Trust Bank of Arizona N.A.; Northern Trust Bank/O'Hare N.A.; Northern Trust Bank/Lake Forest N.A.; Northern Trust Bank/DuPage; Northern Trust Bank of Florida N.A., Miami, Florida; Northern Trust Bank of California N.A.; Northern Trust Bank of Texas N.A.; The Northern Trust Company of New York; Northern Securities Services, Canada, Ltd.; Northern Futures Corporation; Northern Trust Securities, Inc.; Hazlehurst & Associates, Inc.; Berry, Hartell, Evers & Osborne, Inc.; and Northern Trust Services, Inc. The Northern Trust Company offers a full range of banking, trust, savings, international, and bond services to individuals and corporations. All Illinois, Florida, Arizona, California, and Texas affiliate banks are full-service commercial banks. Northern Trust Securities, Inc., is a securities distribution unit for individual investors, correspondent banks, and corporations. Incorporated in Delaware in 1971.

Directors (In addition to indicated officers)

W.H. Clark	Robert D. Krebs
Dolores E. Cross	Frederick A. Krehbiel
Robert S. Hamada	William G. Mitchell
Robert A. Helman	Harold B. Smith
Arthur L. Kelly	William D. Smithburg
Ardis Krainik	Bide L. Thomas

Officers (Directors*)[a]

*David W. Fox, Chm.	Sheila A. Penrose, Exec. V.P.
*William A. Osborn, Pres. & C.E.O.	Peter L. Rossiter, Exec. V.P., Gen. Coun. & Secy.
*Barry G. Hastings, V. Chm. & C.O.O.	William S. Trukenbrod, Exec. V.P.
Perry R. Pero, Sr. Exec. V.P. & C.F.O.	David L. Eddy, Sr. V.P. & Treas.
J. David Brock, Exec. V.P.	William H. Miller, Sr. V.P.
John V.N. McClure, Exec. V.P.	Daniel S. O'Keefe, Sr. V.P. & Gen. Auditor
James J. Mitchell, Exec. V.P.	Harry W. Short, Sr. V.P. & Cont.

[a]Fox will retire on October 3, 1995, at which time Osborn will add the title of Chairman, and Hastings will become President and C.O.O.

Statement of Condition   As of December 31, 1994 (000 omitted)

Assets		Liabilities & Stockholders' Equity	
Cash & due from banks	$ 1,192,500	Deposits	$11,734,400
Securities	5,053,100	Funds borrowed	4,146,300
Other short-term investments	2,651,200	Senior medium-term notes	547,000
Net loans & lease financing	8,445,800	Notes payable	244,800
Properties & equipment	274,700	Other liabilities	608,400
Other assets	944,300	*Stockholders' equity	1,280,700
Total	$18,561,600	Total	$18,561,600

*54,089,259 shares common stock outstanding.

Consolidated Income Statement

Years Ended Dec. 31	Thousands — — — — Operating Income	Net Income	Per Share[a] — — — Earnings	Cash Dividends	Common Stock Price Range[a] Calendar Year
1994	$1,478,500	$174,900	$3.17	$ .92	43-1/4 — 32-1/4
1993	1,258,800	161,600	2.96	.77	50-1/2 — 37
1992	1,231,300	142,700	2.64	.66	43-1/8 — 32-5/8
1991	1,260,200	121,400	2.29	.58	34-5/8 — 18
1990	1,322,900	109,200	2.06	.52	22-1/2 — 13

[a]Adjusted to reflect a 3-for-2 stock split in December 1992 and a 2-for-1 stock split in April 1990.

Transfer Agent & Registrar: Harris Trust and Savings Bank

General Counsel:	Peter L. Rossiter, Exec. V.P.	Auditors:	Arthur Andersen LLP
Investor Relations:	Laurie K. McMahon, V.P.	Traded (Symbol):	NASDAQ (NTRS)
		Stockholders:	2,962
Human Resources:	William N. Setterstrom, Sr. V.P.	Employees:	6,608
Mgt. Info. Svcs.:	John P. Archer, Sr. V.P.	Annual Meeting:	Third Tuesday in April

Northwestern Steel and Wire Company

121 Wallace Street, Sterling, Illinois 61081-3558
Telephone: (815) 625-2500

Northwestern Steel and Wire Company is a major mini-mill producer of structural steel, rod, and fabricated wire products. The company's structural steel products include wide flange beams, light structural shapes, and merchant bars, which are sold nationwide for use in the construction and manufacturing industries. The company's rod and wire products include nails, concrete reinforcing mesh, residential and agricultural fencing, and a wide range of other wire products. Incorporated in Illinois in 1879.

Directors   (In addition to indicated officer)

William F. Andrews
Warner C. Frazier
Darius W. Gaskins, Jr.
James A. Kohlberg

Christopher Lacovara
Albert G. Pastino
George W. Peck IV
Richard F. Williams

Officers   (Director*)

*Robert N. Gurnitz, Chm., Pres. & C.E.O.
Edward G. Maris, Sr. V.P., C.F.O., Secy. & Treas.
William H. Hillpot, V.P.—Purch. & Bus. Dev.

John C. Meyer, V.P.—Hum. Res.
Richard D. Way, Sr. V.P.—Oper., Sterling
Kenneth J. Burnett, V.P.—Oper., Houston
David C. Oberbillig, V.P.—Sales, Wire Prods. Div.

Consolidated Balance Sheet   As of July 31, 1994 (000 omitted)

Assets		Liabilities & Stockholders' Equity	
Current assets	$168,999	Current liabilities	$ 90,082
Net property, plant & equipment	217,178	Long-term debt	166,942
Other assets	7,999	Deferred items	86,648
		*Stockholders' equity	50,504
Total	$394,176	Total	$394,176

*24,715,022 shares common stock outstanding.

Consolidated Income Statement

Years Ended July 31	Thousands — — — — Net Sales	Net Income	Per Share — — — Earnings	Cash Dividends	Common Stock Price Range Calendar Year
1994	$603,609	$ 10,010	$ .40	$ .00	13-1/8 — 5-1/2
1993	539,210	(47,695)[a]	(2.62)[a]	.00	10-1/2 — 7-5/8[b]
1992	470,049	(22,372)	(1.72)		
1991	477,429	(19,751)	(1.53)		
1990	464,365	10,316	.80		

[a]Includes an extraordinary loss related to early retirement of debt and a charge to reflect FAS 106, resulting in a cumulative effect of $46,173,000 ($2.54 per share).
[b]Initial public offering in June 1993.

Transfer Agent & Registrar: Fleet National Bank
General Counsel: Kirkland & Ellis
Investor Relations: Edward G. Maris, Sr. V.P.
Human Resources: John C. Meyer, V.P.
Mgt. Info. Svcs.:   Larry See

Auditors: Coopers & Lybrand L.L.P.
Traded (Symbol):   NASDAQ (NWSW)
Stockholders: 1,387
Employees: 2,500
Annual Meeting: In January

First Chicago Guide

The John Nuveen Company

333 West Wacker Drive, Chicago, Illinois 60606
Telephone: (312) 917-7700

The John Nuveen Company, through its wholly owned subsidiaries — John Nuveen & Co. Incorporated, Nuveen Advisory Corp., and Nuveen Institutional Advisory Corp. — is a specialist in the municipal securities business. Founded in 1898 as an underwriter of municipal bonds, the company specializes in the sponsorship, marketing, and management of tax-free investment products for individual investors and in municipal finance. Nuveen began to develop and market Tax-Free Investment Products in 1961 with the introduction of its first tax-free unit investment trust. Currently, the company sponsors more than 100 Tax-Free Investment Products, including UITs, short-term money market funds, long-term mutual funds, and closed-end funds that issue common stock that is traded on stock exchanges in the U.S., and in some cases also issue preferred stock. The John Nuveen Company is 76 percent-owned by St. Paul Cos. Incorporated in Delaware in 1992 as a successor to the business formed in 1898 by John Nuveen.

Directors (In addition to indicated officers)

Willard L. Boyd
Andrew I. Douglass
W. John Driscoll

Duane R. Kullberg
Douglas W. Leatherdale
Patrick A. Thiele

Officers (Directors*)

*Richard J. Franke, Chm. & C.E.O.
*Donald E. Sveen, Pres. & C.O.O.
John Amboian, Exec. V.P. & C.F.O.
*Anthony T. Dean, Exec. V.P.
*Timothy R. Schwertfeger, Exec. V.P.
William Adams IV, V.P.

Robert B. Kuppenheimer, V.P.
O. Walter Renfftlen, V.P. & Cont.
H. William Stabenow, V.P. & Treas.
James J. Wesolowski, V.P., Secy. & Gen. Coun.
Paul C. Williams, V.P.

Consolidated Balance Sheet   As of December 31, 1994 (000 omitted)

Assets		Liabilities & Stockholders' Equity	
Current assets	$318,305	Current liabilities	$ 38,465
Net property, plant & equipment	17,615	Deferred items	19,303
Other assets	12,927	Other liabilities	5,147
		*Stockholders' equity	285,932
Total	$348,847	Total	$348,847

*37,222,727 shares common stock outstanding.

Consolidated Income Statement

Years Ended Dec. 31	Thousands Total Revenues	Net Income	Per Share Earnings	Cash Dividends	Common Stock Price Range[a] Calendar Year
1994	$220,303	$58,211	$1.52	$ .64	27-1/8 — 19-1/8
1993	245,732	70,444	1.76	.56	41-5/8 — 23-7/8
1992	221,212	59,440[b]	1.58[b]	.24	30-3/8 — 15-1/8
1991	180,238	47,886			
1990	131,474	30,527			

[a]Initial public offering in May 1992.
[b]Includes two one-time accounting changes.

Transfer Agent & Registrar: The Bank of New York

General Counsel:	Sidley & Austin	Auditors:	KPMG Peat Marwick LLP
Investor Relations:	Jeffrey Kratz	Traded (Symbol):	NYSE (JNC)
		Stockholders:	9,600
Human Resources:	Michael G. Gaffney	Employees:	558
Mgt. Info. Svcs.:	Stuart Rogers	Annual Meeting:	In May

First Chicago Guide

Oil•Dri Corporation of America

410 North Michigan Avenue, Suite 400, Chicago, Illinois 60611
Telephone: (312) 321-1515

Oil•Dri Corporation of America is a leading developer, manufacturer, and marketer of sorbent products for consumer, industrial, environmental, agricultural, and specialty markets. Consumer products include Cat's Pride® and Lasting Pride™ brand cat litters as well as premium private label products. These products are marketed by food brokers to the grocery products industry and by inside sales to major mass merchandisers. Floor absorbents under the trademark Oil-Dri® are sold to factories, automotive service establishments, and industrial distributors. Environmental clean-up materials include Oil-Dri Lite™ sorbents. These non-clay products are light weight, very absorbent, and offer recycling and incineration options to end users. The Agrisorbents™ Product Group markets Agsorb® carriers for crop protection chemicals, Pel-Unite® and ConditionAde™ feed binders, and other agriculturally related products. The Pure-Flo Products Group provides sorbent technologies under the brand names Pure-Flo® and Ultra-Clear® for the bleaching, filtration, and clarifying of all processed oils and oleo chemicals. Oil•Dri also manufactures Fresh Step® and Control® for The Clorox Company. Corporate headquarters are located in Chicago; research & development is in Vernon Hills; and domestic mining and processing facilities are located in Georgia, Mississippi, and Oregon. Foreign offices and facilities are located in Canada, the United Kingdom, and Switzerland. Incorporated in Delaware in 1969 as successor to a company founded in 1941.

Directors (In addition to indicated officers)

J. Steven Cole	Paul J. Miller
Robert D. Jaffee	Haydn H. Murray
Edgar D. Jannotta	Allan H. Selig

Officers (Directors*)

*Richard M. Jaffee, Chm. & C.E.O.	James T. Davis, V.P.—Mfg.
*Joseph C. Miller, V. Chm.	*Norman B. Gershon, V.P.—Int'l.
*Daniel S. Jaffee, Pres. & C.O.O.	William F. Moll, Ph.D., V.P.—R&D
Herbert V. Pomerantz, Sr. V.P.—R&D,	Richard Pietrowski, Treas.
Agrisorbents, Pure-Flo Prods. Grps.	Albert L. Swerdlik, Secy.
Richard V. Hardin, Grp. V.P.—Tech.	*Bruce H. Sone, V.P.—Consumer Prod. Div.

Consolidated Balance Sheet As of July 31, 1994 (000 omitted)

Assets		Liabilities & Stockholders' Equity	
Current assets	$ 44,362	Current liabilities	$ 15,601
Net property, plant & equipment	60,243	Long-term debt	23,606
Other assets	7,662	*Stockholders' equity	73,060
Total	$112,267	Total	$112,267

*4,818,927 shares common and 2,132,895 shares Class B common stock outstanding.

Consolidated Income Statement

Years Ended July 31	Thousands — — — — Net Sales	Net Income[a]	Per Share[b] — — — — Earnings[a]	Cash Dividends	Common Stock Price Range[b] Calendar Year
1994	$139,809	$9,852	$1.41	$ .28	23-3/8 — 17-1/8
1993	134,760	9,420	1.34	.25	25 — 18-1/2
1992	118,750	7,100	1.01	.24	22-1/2 — 15
1991	102,283	7,079	1.00	.21	24 — 15-7/8
1990	94,192	6,787[c]	.96[c]	.20	23-3/4 — 15-3/4

[a]Restated to reflect FAS 109.
[b]Adjusted for a 5-for-4 stock split in March 1990 in the form of a stock dividend.
[c]Includes a one-time benefit related to a tax accounting change of $160,000 (.02 per share).

Transfer Agent & Registrar: Harris Trust and Savings Bank

Legal Counsel: Sonnenschein Nath & Rosenthal		Auditors:	Blackman Kallick Bartelstein
		Traded (Symbol):	NYSE (ODC)
Investor Relations:	Kelly McGrail, Mgr.	Stockholders:	1,346
Human Resources:	Karen Jaffee-Cofsky	Employees:	650
Mgt. Info. Svcs.:	Daniel S. Jaffee, Pres.	Annual Meeting:	In December

First Chicago Guide   185

Old Republic International Corporation

307 North Michigan Avenue, Chicago, Illinois 60601-5382
Telephone: (312) 346-8100

Old Republic International Corporation is an insurance holding company whose principal subsidiaries underwrite and market specialty insurance lines in the property, liability, title, mortgage guaranty, life and disability insurance fields. Old Republic has a leadership position in workers' compensation insurance by virtue of the company's 40 years of experience and service to the coal and other industries. Since 1978 the company has been engaged in the title insurance business, following the acquisition of Minnesota Title Financial Corporation and its subsidiaries. In early 1980, the company entered the mortgage guaranty insurance business through its acquisition of Republic Mortgage Insurance Company. In early 1985, the company expanded its property and liability insurance with the acquisition of Bitco Corporation and its insurance subsidiaries. Principal insurance subsidiaries include: Old Republic Insurance Company, Old Republic Life Insurance Company, Bituminous Casualty Corporation, Great West Casualty Company, Old Republic National Title Insurance Company, Old Republic General Title Insurance Corporation, Republic Mortgage Insurance Company, and International Business and Mercantile REassurance Co. Incorporated in Delaware in 1969.

Directors   (In addition to indicated officers)

John C. Collopy
Jimmy A. Dew
Kurt W. Kreyling
Peter Lardner
Wilbur S. Legg

John W. Popp
Arnold L. Steiner
William R. Stover
David Sursa
William G. White, Jr.

Officers   (Directors*)

*A.C. Zucaro, Chm., Pres. & C.E.O.
 Paul D. Adams, Sr. V.P., C.F.O. & Treas.
*Anthony F. Colao, Sr. V.P.

 Spencer LeRoy III, Sr. V.P., Gen. Coun. & Secy.
 William F. Schumann, Sr. V.P.
*William A. Simpson, Sr. V.P.

Consolidated Balance Sheet   As of December 31, 1994 (000 omitted)

Assets		Liabilities and Stockholders' Equity	
Cash & invested assets	$3,906,400	Policy liabilities	$ 669,600
Reinsurance reserves recoverable	1,526,200	Benefit & claim reserves	3,514,700
Other assets	830,300	Debt & debt equivalents	314,700
		Sundry liabilities	359,200
		Preferred stock	75,400
		*Stockholders' equity	1,329,300
Total	$6,262,900	Total	$6,262,900

*51,536,412 shares common stock outstanding.

Consolidated Income Statement

Years Ended Dec. 31	Thousands — — — — Total Revenue	Net Income	Per Share[a] — — — — Earnings	Cash Dividends	Common Stock Price Range[a] Calendar Year
1994	$1,679,000	$151,000	$2.55	$ .47	24-3/8 — 18-7/8
1993	1,736,300	175,100[b]	2.98[b]	.43	27-3/8 — 21-5/8
1992	1,617,000	174,700	3.09	.39	26-1/2 — 17-1/2
1991	1,374,500	131,000	2.48	.37	17-3/4 — 10-1/8
1990	1,242,700	104,600	2.02	.34	12-1/4 — 8-5/8

[a]Adjusted for the 2-for-1 stock split in March 1992.
[b]Includes a gain to reflect FAS 106 and FAS 109, resulting in a cumulative effect of $8,600,000 ($.15 per share).

Transfer Agent & Registrar:	First Chicago Trust Co. of New York		
General Counsel:	Spencer LeRoy III, Sr. V.P.	Traded (Symbol):	NYSE (ORI)
Investor Relations:	A.C. Zucaro, Pres.	Stockholders:	3,799
Human Resources:	Charles Strizak, Dir.	Employees:	5,400
Auditors:	Coopers & Lybrand L.L.P.	Annual Meeting:	In May

First Chicago Guide

OPTION CARE, Inc.

100 Corporate North, Suite 212, Bannockburn, Illinois 60015
Telephone: (708) 615-1690

OPTION CARE, Inc., is a franchisor of businesses which provide home infusion therapy and related services. As of December 31, 1994, 199 OPTION CARE offices were operating in exclusive territories in 40 states. Existing offices include 183 offices owned and operated by franchise owners and 16 offices controlled and operated by the company. OPTION CARE'S home infusion therapy business involves the in-home or other non-hospital administration of nutrients, antibiotics, and other medications to patients parenterally or through inhalation or enteral feedings, as well as the provision of equipment, supplies, and nursing care incidental to such services. Subsidiaries are Option Care Capital Services, Inc.; Option Care Enterprises, Inc.; Cordesys Healthcare Management, Inc.; Women's Health of Option Care, Inc.; and Option Care, Inc. (California). Incorporated in Delaware in 1991.

Directors   (In addition to indicated officer)

James G. Andress
Jerome F. Sheldon

Roger W. Stone

Officers   (Director*)

*John N. Kapoor, Ph.D., Chm., Pres. & C.E.O.
Erick "Rick" Hanson, Sr. V.P.
Cathy Bellehumeur, V.P.—Gen. Coun. & Secy.
J. Jeffrey Fox, V.P. & C.F.O.

Michael T. Prime, V.P.—Oper. Support & Dev., West
Daniel F. Skalecki, V.P.—Procurement
Catherine Young, V.P.—Managed Care

Consolidated Balance Sheet   As of December 31, 1994 (000 omitted)

Assets		Liabilities & Stockholders' Equity	
Current assets	$23,270	Current liabilities	$ 7,258
Net property, plant & equipment	3,285	Long-term debt	9,517
Other assets	31,888	Deferred items	991
		Other liabilities	667
		*Stockholders' equity	40,010
Total	$58,443	Total	$58,443

*9,935,835 shares common stock outstanding.

Consolidated Income Statement

Years Ended Dec. 31	Thousands — — — — Total Revenues	Net Income	Per Share[a] — — — — Earnings	Cash Dividends	Common Stock Price Range[a] Calendar Year
1994	$59,395	$(1,958)[b]	$ (.20)	$ .00	4-1/4 — 1-7/8
1993	50,221	145[c]	.01	.00	12-1/4 — 3-1/4
1992	41,496	3,488	.36	.00	12 — 6-1/4[d]
1991	23,462	(3,032)[c]	(.39)	.00	
1990	15,859	625	.08	.04	

[a]Adjusted to reflect a 10-for-1 exchange of the stock of the company for shares of stock of OPTION CARE, Inc., a California corporation, which occurred on September 3, 1991; and a 6-for-5 stock split effected in the form of a stock dividend on February 13, 1992.
[b]Includes $6,560,000 charge for asset writeoffs and other unusual expenses.
[c]The company recorded charges of $4,250,000 and $6,633,000 for restructuring expenses in 1993 and 1991, respectively.
[d]Initial public offering in April 1992.

Transfer Agent & Registrar: U.S. Stock Transfer Corp.

General Counsel: Cathy Bellehumeur, V.P.

Investor Relations: J. Jeffrey Fox, V.P.

Auditors: KPMG Peat Marwick LLP

Traded (Symbol):   NASDAQ (OPTN)
Stockholders: 321
Employees: 280
Annual Meeting: In May

Outboard Marine Corporation

100 Sea-Horse Drive, Waukegan, Illinois 60085-2195
Telephone: (708) 689-6200

Outboard Marine Corporation (OMC) designs, manufactures, and distributes a broad range of boats, marine engines and accessories, and provides related services throughout the world. Its major products fall into three areas: marine power products, boat-building (comprised of the fishing boat group, recreational boat group and aluminum boat group), and marine services. Principal marine products include Evinrude® and Johnson® outboard motors. OMC sells 18 brands of boats ranging from 10 to 42 feet, including Chris-Craft®, Four Winns®, Stratos®, Lowe®, Sea Nymph® and Sunbird®; others are Seaswirl®, Javelin®, Suncruiser®, Ryds® and Hydra-Sports®. In the marine services area, the company distributes various marine parts and accessories under the OMC SysteMatched® brand through its dealer network. All of OMC's products are sold in the U.S. and Canada, and most of its principal products are sold throughout the world. Major subsidiaries include Outboard Marine Corp. of Canada, Ltd., OMC Europe, Outboard Marine Asia, Outboard Marine Australia, Outboard Marine Belgium, OMC Aluminum Boat Group, OMC Fishing Group, and OMC Recreational Boat Group. In July 1993, the company, AB Volvo Penta, and Volvo Penta North America, Inc., formed a joint venture company that produces gasoline stern drive and gasoline inboard marine power systems. Incorporated in Delaware in 1936.

Directors (In addition to indicated officer)

Frank Borman
William C. France
Urban T. Kuechle
Richard T. Lindgren

J. Willard Marriott, Jr.
Richard J. Stegemeier
Charles D. Strang
Richard F. Teerlink

Officers (Director*)

*Harry W. Bowman, Chm., Pres. & C.E.O.
D. Jeffrey Baddeley, V.P. & Gen. Coun.
L. Earl Bentz, V.P. & Pres.—Fishing Boat Grp.
William J. Ek, V.P. & Pres.—Alum. Boat Grp.
John D. Flaig, V.P.—Eng.
Ronald J. Jensen, V.P. & Pres.—Int'l. Group
James R. Maurice, V.P. & Cont.

Richard H. Medland, V.P.—Hum. Res.
Howard Malovany, Secy. & Sr. Coun.
Christopher R. Sachs, Treas.
R. Warren Comstock, Asst. Secy.
Robert J. Moerchen, Asst. Treas.
David R. Lumley, V.P.—Sales & Mktg., Mar. Power Prods. Grp.

Consolidated Balance Sheet As of September 30, 1994 (000 omitted)

Assets		Liabilities & Stockholders' Equity	
Current assets	$429,800	Current liabilities	$233,600
Net property, plant & equipment	217,100	Long-term debt	178,200
Other assets	170,200	Deferred items	102,300
		Other liabilities	94,000
		*Stockholders' equity	209,000
Total	$817,100	Total	$817,100

*20,000,000 shares common stock outstanding.

Consolidated Income Statement

Years Ended Sept. 30	Thousands — — — — Net Sales	Net Income	Per Share — — — Earnings	Cash Dividends	Common Stock Price Range Calendar Year
1994	$1,078,400	$ 48,500	$ 2.42	$ .40	25-7/8 — 17-3/8
1993	1,034,600	(282,500)[a]	(14.42)[a]	.40	25-1/4 — 15-1/4
1992	1,064,600	1,900	.10	.40	26-5/8 — 15-1/8
1991	983,600	(84,300)	(4.34)	.50	19-3/8 — 11-1/2
1990	1,145,600	(75,500)	(3.89)	.80	28-1/4 — 9

[a]Includes restructuring charges and FAS 106 and FAS 109, resulting in a cumulative effect of $117,500,000 ($6.00 per share).

Transfer Agent & Registrar: First Chicago Trust Co. of New York

General Counsel:	D. Jeffrey Baddeley, V.P.	Auditors:	Arthur Andersen LLP
Investor Relations:	Stanley R. Main, Dir.	Traded (Symbol):	NYSE, BSE, CSE, PHSE, PSE (OM)
		Stockholders:	4,519
Human Resources:	Richard H. Medland, V.P.	Employees:	8,472
Mgt. Info. Svcs.:	Harry Adams, Dir.	Annual Meeting:	Third Thursday in January

First Chicago Guide

Ozite Corporation

1755 Butterfield Road, Libertyville, Illinois 60048
Telephone: (708) 362-8210

Ozite Corporation conducts its business in two industry segments: plastics processing and non-woven textile products. Its subsidiary, Plastics Specialties and Technologies, Inc., has three operating divisions: Colorite Plastics Company, which manufactures proprietary specialty polyvinyl chloride compounds, including nontoxic medical grade and vinyl garden hose; Action Technology, which produces extruded plastic tubing, tubing, diaphragm, static seals, rubber and thermoplastic gaskets; and Ozite Manufacturing Company, which confines its fabric manufacturing to non-woven textile products for the automotive aftermarket, music, wall covering, marine, and secondary markets. In July 1994, Ozite entered into an agreement and plan of merger with Pure Tech International, Inc. Incorporated in Texas in 1967; reincorporated in Delaware in 1990.

Directors (In addition to indicated officers)

Murray Fox
Yitz Grossman

John Harvey
Peter R. Harvey

Officers (Directors*)

*Fred W. Broling, Chm. & C.E.O.
Terence K. Brennan, Pres. & C.O.O.
Craig H. Boss, V.P.—Admin. & Secy.

*David Katz, V.P.
Melvin R. Miller, Cont.
Michael Nafish, Asst. Secy.

Consolidated Balance Sheet As of July 31, 1994 (000 omitted)

Assets		Liabilities & Stockholders' Equity	
Current assets	$ 68,010	Current liabilities	$ 58,277
Net property, plant & equipment	41,418	Long-term debt	126,739
Other assets	51,122	Deferred items	745
		Other liabilities	914
		*Stockholders' equity	(26,125)
Total	$160,550	Total	$160,550

*5,378,416 shares common stock outstanding.

Consolidated Income Statement[a]

Years Ended July 31	Thousands — — — — — Net Sales	Net Income	Per Share — — — — Earnings	Cash Dividends	Common Stock Price Range Fiscal Year	
1994	$203,575	$ 867[b]	$ (.62)[b]	$ .00	1-1/8 —	1/2
1993	179,880	(6,161)	(1.93)	.00	1-1/2 —	5/8
1992	175,669	(1,780)	(1.09)	.00	1-3/4 —	3/8
1991	166,454	(4,690)	(1.59)	.00	1-1/2 —	1/4
1990	158,848	(2,762)	.54	.00	4	— 1-1/4[c]

[a]The merger between Ozite and Sage Group, Inc, in 1990 has been accounted for at historical cost in a manner similar to the pooling-of-interests method. 1990 was restated to reflect the combined financial positions.
[b]Includes an extraordinary loss of $3,061,000 ($.57 per share), and a gain of $916,000 ($.17 per share) to reflect FAS 109.
[c]Calendar year.

Transfer Agent & Registrar: Mellon Securities Transfer Services

General Counsel:
  Kwiatt, Silverman & Ruben Ltd.

Investor Relations: Terence K. Brennan, Pres.

Human Resources: Craig H. Boss, V.P.

Mgt. Info. Svcs.:   Melvin R. Miller, Cont.

Auditors: Deloitte & Touche LLP
Traded: OTC
Stockholders: 1,300
Employees: 1,420
Annual Meeting: In December

PC Quote, Inc.

300 South Wacker Drive, Suite 300, Chicago, Illinois 60606-6688
Telephone: (312) 913-2800

PC Quote, Inc., is a software developer and vendor of last-sale and bid/ask information for the Consolidated Tape Associations, the Option Price Reporting Authority, the National Association of Security Dealers, and all major U.S. commodity exchanges. The company subscribes to the high-speed vendor lines provided by each of the above authorities and maintains a real-time database which provides last-sale, bid/ask, theoretical values to various application programs developed by the company and available to customers. Its principal product and service is PC QUOTE. The principal users of the company's products and services are professional investors, such as securities brokers, dealers or traders, and portfolio managers. PC Quote maintains sales offices in Chicago, New York, Los Angeles and San Diego. Incorporated in Illinois in 1980; reincorporated in Delaware in 1987.

Directors (In addition to indicated officer)

Phillip W. Arneson
James M. Casty

Karl R. Orellana

Officers (Director*)

*Louis J. Morgan, Chm. & Treas.
Richard F. Chappetto, V.P.—Fin.
Michael J. Kreutzjans, V.P.—Sys. Dev.

Jerry M. Traver, V.P.—Sales
Darlene E. Czaja, Corp. Secy.

Consolidated Balance Sheet As of December 31, 1994 (000 omitted)

Assets		Liabilities & Stockholders' Equity	
Current assets	$2,541	Current liabilities	$3,188
Net property, plant & equipment	3,840	Capital lease obligations	714
Other assets	2,691	Other liabilities	339
		*Stockholders' equity	4,831
Total	$9,072	Total	$9,072

*6,969,174 shares common stock outstanding.

Consolidated Income Statement

Years Ended Dec. 31	Thousands — — — —		Per Share — — —		Common Stock Price Range Calendar Year
	Operating Revenues	Net Income	Earnings	Cash Dividends	
1994	$12,904	$ 305	$ .04	$ .00	3-1/8 — 1
1993	12,206	185	.03	.00	3-3/4 — 3/4
1992	10,951	118	.02	.00	1-3/4 — 5/8
1991	10,169	(524)	(.08)	.00	1-1/8 — 5/8
1990	9,963	(1,429)	(.21)	.00	2-3/8 — 3/4

Transfer Agent & Registrar: American Securities Transfer, Inc.

General Counsel:
Wildman, Harrold, Allen & Dixon

Investor Relations:
Darlene E. Czaja, Corp. Secy.

Human Resources:
Darlene E. Czaja, Corp. Secy.

Mgt. Info. Svcs.: Michael J. Kreutzjans, V.P.
Auditors: Coopers & Lybrand L.L.P.
Traded (Symbol): AMEX (PQT)
Stockholders: 402
Employees: 76
Annual Meeting: In June

Peoples Energy Corporation

130 East Randolph Drive, Chicago, Illinois 60601-6207
Telephone: (312) 240-4000

Peoples Energy Corporation (Peoples) is solely a holding company with its principal business centered in the retail distribution of natural gas. Peoples is the parent of: The Peoples Gas Light and Coke Company and North Shore Gas Company. Both public utility subsidiaries are engaged primarily in the purchase, production, storage, distribution, sale, and transportation of natural gas. Peoples Gas also owns and operates a synthetic natural gas plant near Joliet, Illinois, and an underground gas storage reservoir and a liquefied natural gas plant at Manlove Field near Champaign, Illinois. Peoples Gas serves nearly 842,000 residential, commercial, and industrial retail sales and transportation customers within the City of Chicago. North Shore Gas, headquartered in Waukegan, Illinois, serves more than 129,000 residential, commercial, and industrial retail sales and transportation customers within its 275 square-mile service area in northeastern Illinois. Peoples District Energy Corporation, a wholly owned subsidiary of Peoples formed in May 1992, is a 50 percent participant in a partnership that provides heating and cooling services to the McCormick Place Exposition and Convention Center in Chicago. The services are supplied from a central plant, a concept known as district energy. Neither the partnership nor Peoples District Energy Corp. is regulated as a public utility. Two other wholly owned subsidiaries of Peoples are: Peoples Energy Services Corporation, a seller and distributor of carbon monoxide detectors; and Peoples NGV Corp., a participant in a partnership to develop on-site fueling services for natural gas-powered fleet vehicles. Neither the partnership nor Peoples NGV Corp. is regulated as a public utility. Incorporated in Illinois in 1967.

Directors (In addition to indicated officers)

Pastora San Juan Cafferty	William G. Mitchell
Franklin A. Cole	Earl L. Neal
Frederick C. Langenberg	Richard P. Toft
Homer J. Livingston, Jr.	Arthur R. Velasquez

Officers (Directors*)

*Richard E. Terry, Chm. & C.E.O.	James Hinchliff, Sr. V.P. & Gen. Coun.
*J. Bruce Hasch, Pres. & C.O.O.	Kenneth S. Balaskovits, V.P., C.F.O. & Cont.
*Michael S. Reeves, Exec. V.P.	Emmet P. Cassidy, Secy. & Treas.

Consolidated Balance Sheet As of September 30, 1994 (000 omitted)

Assets		Liabilities & Stockholders' Equity	
Current assets	$ 397,185	Current liabilities	$ 267,966
Net property, plant & equipment	1,341,932	Long-term debt	626,075
Other assets	70,169	Deferred credits & reserves	273,867
		*Stockholders' equity	641,378
Total	$1,809,286	Total	$1,809,286

*34,868,069 shares common stock outstanding.

Consolidated Income Statement

Years Ended Sept. 30	Thousands ———— Operating Revenues	Net Income	Per Share ———— Earnings	Cash Dividends[a]	Common Stock Price Range Calendar Year
1994	$1,279,488	$74,399	$2.13	$1.80	32-1/8 — 23-3/8
1993	1,258,941	73,375	2.11	1.78	35 — 27-1/2
1992	1,096,752	70,384	2.06	1.75	31-5/8 — 24-3/8
1991	1,103,703	66,975	2.05	1.71	28-1/4 — 21-3/4
1990	1,165,168	67,516	2.07	1.65	26-1/2 — 20

[a]Declared.

Transfer Agent & Registrar: Harris Trust and Savings Bank

General Counsel: James Hinchliff, Sr. V.P.

Investor Relations: Emmet P. Cassidy, Secy.

Human Resources: John C. Ibach, V.P.

Mgt. Info. Svcs.: Frank H. Blackmore, V.P.

Auditors: Arthur Andersen LLP

Traded (Symbol): NYSE, CSE, PSE (PGL)

Stockholders: 29,222

Employees: 3,278

Annual Meeting: Fourth Friday in February

Pinnacle Banc Group, Inc.

2215 York Road, Suite 208, Oak Brook, Illinois 60521
Telephone: (708) 574-3550

Pinnacle Banc Group, Inc., is a multi-bank holding company registered under the Bank Holding Company Act of 1956, as amended, and is engaged in the business of banking through the ownership of subsidiary banks. Subsidiaries are Pinnacle Bank and Pinnacle Bank of the Quad-Cities, each organized as state banking corporations; and Batavia Savings Bank, F.S.B., a federally chartered savings bank. Pinnacle Banc Group is a legal entity separate and distinct from its subsidiary banks. The major source of the corporation's revenues is dividends from its subsidiary banks. Each of the subsidiary banks is a full-service bank encompassing most of the usual functions of commercial and savings banking including commercial, consumer, and real estate lending; installment credit lending; collections; safe deposit operations; and other services tailored for individual customer needs. The banks also offer a full range of deposit services, which include demand, savings and time deposits. Pinnacle Bank and Pinnacle Bank of the Quad-Cities also provide trust services to their clients. Lending activities of the subsidiary banks include term loans, lines and letters of credit, revolving credits, participations, indirect automobile financing, personal loans, student loans, and residential and commercial mortgages. Incorporated in Illinois in 1979.

Directors   (In addition to indicated officers)

William J. Finn, Jr.
Samuel M. Gilman
Albert Giusfredi
James L. Greene
Donald G. King

James A. Maddock
James J. McDonough
William C. Nickels
James R. Phillip, Jr.

Officers   (Directors*)

*John J. Gleason, Sr., Chm. & C.E.O.
*John J. Gleason, Jr., V. Chm.
*Mark P. Burns, Pres.
 William P. Gleason, Exec. V.P. & Treas.

*Kenneth C. Whitener, Jr., Exec. V.P. & Chf.
  Investment Off.
*Richard W. Burke, Secy.

Consolidated Balance Sheet   As of December 31, 1994 (000 omitted)

Assets		Liabilities & Stockholders' Equity	
Current assets	$ 20,265	Total deposits	$599,879
Interest bearing deposits	2,815	Short-term borrowings	4,800
Securities	386,500	Long-term debt	5,400
Net loans	244,176	Other liabilities	5,977
Net property, plant & equipment	9,714	*Stockholders' equity	68,836
Other assets	21,422		
Total	$684,892	Total	$684,892

*4,406,046 shares common stock outstanding.

Consolidated Income Statement

Years Ended Dec. 31	Thousands — — — — Total Income	Net Income	Per Share[a] — — — Earnings	Cash Dividends	Common Stock Price Range[a] Calendar Year
1994	$38,537	$ 2,255	$ .51	$1.08	36-1/2 — 26-1/2
1993	55,136	12,993[b]	2.87[b]	.96	36-3/4 — 30
1992	58,418	12,914	2.82	.88	31 — 18
1991	54,037	10,538	2.25	.80	24-1/2 — 18
1990	50,032	10,676	2.19	.69	22-1/8 — 16-1/4

[a]Adjusted to reflect a 4-for-3 stock split in February 1991 and a 5-for-4 stock split in January 1990.
[b]Includes a gain to reflect FAS 109, resulting in a cumulative effect of $1,700,000 ($.37 per share).

Transfer Agent & Registrar:	Harris Trust and Savings Bank		
General Counsel:	Burke, Warren & MacKay, P.C.	Auditors:	Arthur Andersen LLP
Investor Relations:	John J. Gleason, Jr., V. Chm.	Traded (Symbol):	NASDAQ (PINN)
		Stockholders:	340
Human Resources:	Denise Medema, Dir.	Employees:	277
Mgt. Info. Svcs.:	David F. Spiewak, Dir.	Annual Meeting:	In April

Pioneer Financial Services, Inc.

1750 East Golf Road, Schaumburg, Illinois 60173
Telephone: (708) 995-0400

Pioneer Financial Services, Inc., through its subsidiaries, provides health and life insurance underwriting, marketing, and managed healthcare services throughout the nation. The company's largest operating subsidiary is Pioneer Life Insurance Company of Illinois, a successor to a company organized in 1926. Other primary subsidiaries include National Group Life Insurance Company, Health and Life Insurance Company of America, Manhattan National Life Insurance Company, National Health Services, Inc., Design Benefit Plans, Continental Life & Accident Co., Connecticut National Life Insurance Co., Association Management Corporation, Network Air Medical Systems, and United Group Holdings of Delaware, Inc. Incorporated in Delaware in 1982.

Directors (In addition to indicated officers)

R. Richard Bastian III
Michael A. Cavataio
Richard R. Haldeman
Carl A. Hulbert

Michael K. Keefe
Karl-Heinz Klaeser
Robert F. Nauert

Officers (Directors*)

*Peter W. Nauert, Chm. & C.E.O.
*Thomas J. Brophy, Pres.—Health
*Charles R. Scheper, Pres.—Life
 Ernest T. Giambra, Jr., Exec. V.P.
 Anthony J. Pino, Exec. V.P.
*William B. Van Vleet, Exec. V.P. & Gen. Coun.
 Philip J. Fiskow, Sr. V.P. & C.I.O.
 Mark S. Fischer, V.P.—Corp. Planning

Rodman Nichols, V.P.
David H. Popplewell, V.P.
Val Rajic, V.P. & Secy.
Lee H. Resnick, V.P. & Chf. Actuary
David I. Vickers, V.P., Treas. & C.F.O.
Nancy L. Zalud, V.P.—Corp. Comm.
Traci J. Schmerse, Asst. Secy.

Consolidated Balance Sheet   As of December 31, 1994 (000 omitted)

Assets		Liabilities & Stockholders' Equity	
Cash & receivables	$ 28,714	Policy liabilities	$ 868,608
Investments	723,837	General liabilities	59,655
Deferred policy acquis. costs	225,618	Convertible subord. debentures	57,427
Net property, plant & equipment	20,314	Preferred stock	21,682
Other assets	77,217	*Stockholders' equity	68,328
Total	$1,075,700	Total	$1,075,700

*5,917,757 shares common stock outstanding.

Consolidated Income Statement

Years Ended Dec. 31	Thousands — — — — Total Income[a]	Net Income	Per Share — — — Earnings	Cash Dividends	Common Stock Price Range Calendar Year
1994	$774,155	$ 17,149	$ 2.36	$ .15	14-3/4 — 8-3/4
1993	699,128	12,145	1.51	.00	14 — 4-3/4
1992	655,973	(16,959)	(2.85)	.00	9-1/8 — 4
1991	708,738	8,872	1.02	.00	11 — 4-5/8
1990	611,017	(9,346)	(1.72)	.00	26 — 5-3/8

[a]Certain amounts in the 1992 and 1993 financial statements have been reclassified to conform to the 1994 presentation.

Transfer Agent & Registrar: First Chicago Trust Co. of New York

General Counsel:
  McDermott, Will & Emery

Investor Relations: Nancy L. Zalud, V.P.

Human Resources: Peter J. Gulatto

Mgt. Info. Svcs.:
  Thomas J. Brophy, Pres.—Health

Auditors: Ernst & Young LLP
Traded (Symbol): CSE, NYSE (PFS)
Stockholders: 550
Employees: 1,900
Annual Meeting: In May

Pioneer Railcorp

1318 South Johanson Road, Peoria, Illinois 61607
Telephone: (309) 697-1400

Pioneer Railcorp is a short-line railroad holding company operating in one business segment, railroad transportation. The company's rail system provides shipping links for customers along its routes, and interchanges with six major railroads and three smaller railroads. Pioneer's rail system is devoted to carrying freight. Wholly owned subsidiaries include: Pioneer Railroad Equipment Co., Ltd., which leases equipment to the company's subsidiary railroads, and also purchases and sells equipment to and from unrelated parties; and Pioneer Railroad Services, Inc., which provides accounting, management, and agency services to the company's subsidiary railroads, and also sells computer technical services and equipment to unrelated parties. Incorporated in Iowa in 1986.

Director   (In addition to indicated officers)

John S. Fulton

Officers   (Directors*)

*Guy L. Brenkman, Chm., Pres. & C.E.O.
*J. Michael Carr, C.F.O. & Asst. Treas.

*Orvel L. Cox, Secy.
*John P. Wolk, Treas.

Consolidated Balance Sheet   As of December 31, 1994 (000 omitted)

Assets		Liabilities & Stockholders' Equity	
Current assets	$ 1,464	Current liabilities	$ 2,320
Net property, plant & equipment	10,228	Long-term debt	6,470
Other assets	604	Deferred taxes	491
		*Stockholders' equity	3,015
Total	$12,296	Total	$12,296

*2,098,042 shares common stock outstanding.

Consolidated Income Statement

Years Ended Dec. 31	Thousands — — — — Operating Revenue	Net Income	Per Share[a] — — — — Earnings	Cash Dividends	Common Stock Price Range[a] Calendar Year
1994	$6,367	$ 516	$ .10	$ .00	3-1/8 — 1-3/8
1993	4,947	244[b]	.04[b]	.00	2-1/8 — 1
1992	3,200	180	.04	.00	
1991	1,150	130	.04	.00	
1990	512	(33)	(.01)	.00	

[a]Adjusted to reflect a 2-for-1 stock split in July 1995. No established trading market before July 28, 1993.
[b]Includes a charge to reflect FAS 109, resulting in a cumulative effect of $155,000 ($.04 per share).

Transfer Agent & Registrar:	Pioneer Railcorp		
General Counsel:	Daniel A. LaKemper	Traded (Symbol):	CSE (PRR)
Investor Relations:	Kevin L. Williams	Stockholders:	1,994
		Employees:	63
Auditors:	McGladrey & Pullen, LLP	Annual Meeting:	In June

Pittway Corporation

200 South Wacker Drive, Suite 700, Chicago, Illinois 60606-5802
Telephone: (312) 831-1070

Pittway Corporation and its subsidiaries manufacture professional fire and burglar alarm equipment and systems, and other security products; publish technical journals and directories; produce trade shows and conferences; and operate mail marketing services. Pittway and its subsidiaries also develop real estate and participate in joint ventures with Metco Properties in real estate development. The company's security products divisions operate plants in Northford, Connecticut; St. Charles, Illinois; Syosset, New York; Milan and Trieste, Italy; Brighton, England, and Juarez, Mexico. Publishing divisions are headquartered in Cleveland, with a division in New York City. Real estate operations are located in Wesley Chapel, Florida, and Chicago, Illinois. Major subsidiaries and divisions include: Ademco Security Group, Ademco Distribution, Inc., Pittway Systems Technology Group, Pittway Real Estate, and Penton Publishing, Inc. Incorporated in Delaware in 1925.

Directors (In addition to indicated officers)

Eugene L. Barnett
E. David Coolidge III
Anthony Downs

William W. Harris
Jerome Kahn, Jr.

Officers (Directors*)

*Neison Harris, Chm.
*Irving B. Harris, Chm. Exec. Comm.
*King Harris, Pres. & C.E.O.
*Sidney Barrows, V. Chm.
*Leo A. Guthart, V. Chm.
*Fred J. Conforti, V.P.

Sal F. Marino, V.P.
Daniel J. Ramella, V.P.
Edward J. Schwartz, V.P.
Paul R. Gauvreau, Fin. V.P., Treas. & Asst. Secy.
Nicholas J. Caccamo, Cont. & Secy.

Consolidated Balance Sheet   As of December 31, 1994 (000 omitted)

Assets		Liabilities & Stockholders' Equity	
Current assets	$336,904	Current liabilities	$169,849
Net property, plant & equipment	89,773	Long-term debt	5,088
Investments	79,013	Deferred liabilities	60,220
Other assets	57,597	*Stockholders' equity	328,130
Total	$563,287	Total	$563,287

*2,626,024 shares common and 11,314,700 shares Class A common stock outstanding.

Consolidated Income Statement

| Years Ended Dec. 31 | Thousands — — — — | | Per Share — — — | | Common Stock |
	Net Sales[a]	Net Income[a]	Earnings[a]	Cash Dividends[bc]	Price Range[bc] Calendar Year
1994	$778,026	$33,060[d]	$2.37[d]	$ .50	40-5/8 — 31-3/8
1993	650,105	21,240	1.52	.55	39-1/8 — 17-7/8
1992	568,301	12,460	.90	1.10	34-3/4 — 25-5/8
1991	516,343	4,371	.32	1.10	30-1/4 — 15-1/2
1990	505,243	10,596	.77	.90	40-3/4 — 16-1/4

[a]From continuing operations.
[b]Class A common stock.
[c]Common stock price range in 1994 was 40-3/4 — 31-1/2. Dividends paid per share of common stock were $.40 in 1994.
[d]Excludes a gain of $11,800,000 ($.85 per share) on sale of investment.

Transfer Agent & Registrar:	Chemical Bank		
General Counsel:	Kirkland & Ellis	Traded (Symbol):	AMEX (PRY, Common; PRYA, Class A)
Investor Relations:	Edward J. Schwartz, V.P.	Stockholders:	1,800
		Employees:	5,400
Auditors:	Price Waterhouse LLP	Annual Meeting:	In May

PLATINUM technology, inc.

1815 S. Meyers Road, Oakbrook Terrace, Illinois 60181
Telephone: (708) 620-5000

PLATINUM technology, inc., provides software solutions for managing the open enterprise environment. By leveraging its expertise in relational technology, PLATINUM offers open enterprise systems management products and integrated solutions that help information services organizations manage the prevailing complex, multi-platform, multi-operating system, multi-vendor computing environment. PLATINUM's products and services increase the efficiency of individual computing systems and databases as well as the interoperability of these systems and databases in distributed environments. PLATINUM has sales offices across the U.S., in Canada, and in Japan, with wholly owned subsidiaries in 11 countries and international affiliates in 33 countries. Incorporated in Delaware in 1987.

Directors   (In addition to indicated officers)

Casey G. Cowell
James E. Cowie

Steven D. Devick
Gian M. Fulgoni

Officers   (Directors*)

*Andrew J. Filipowski, Chm., Pres. & C.E.O.
*Michael P. Cullinane, Exec. V.P., C.F.O.,
  Secy. & Treas.

*Paul L. Humenansky, Exec. V.P.—C.O.O.
Thomas A. Slowey, Exec. V.P.—Sales
Paul A. Tatro, Exec. V.P.—Int'l. Opers.

Consolidated Balance Sheet   As of December 31, 1994 (000 omitted)

Assets		Liabilities & Stockholders' Equity	
Current assets	$123,509	Current liabilities	$ 45,402
Property, plant & equipment	11,542	Acquisition-related payments	8,450
Other assets	55,274	Deferred items	5,302
		*Stockholders' equity	131,171
Total	$190,325	Total	$190,325

*24,158,000 shares common stock outstanding.

Consolidated Income Statement[a]

Years Ended Dec. 31	Thousands — — — —		Per Share[b] — — — —		Common Stock Price Range[b] Calendar Year
	Revenues	Net Income[c]	Earnings[c]	Cash Dividends	
1994	$95,749	$(3,200)	$ (.16)	$ .00	23-3/4 — 10
1993	62,165	3,002	.14	.00	25 — 7-1/4
1992	49,040	9,343	.43	.00	25-1/4 — 11-1/4
1991	27,889	4,521	.22	.00	23-1/2 — 9[d]
1990	14,462	2,458	.15	.00	

[a]1991-90 restated to reflect adoption of the new method of accounting for first year maintenance revenue.
[b]Adjusted to reflect a 2-for-1 stock split in September 1991 and a 1-for-5 reverse stock split in March 1991.
[c]Results in 1994 and 1993 include charges for acquired in-process technology of $19,125,000 ($.94 per share) and $7,632,000 ($.39 per share), respectively.
[d]Initial public offering in April 1991.

Transfer Agent & Registrar: Harris Trust and Savings Bank	
General Counsel: Katten Muchin & Zavis	**Auditors:** KPMG Peat Marwick LLP
Investor Relations: Michael P. Cullinane, Exec. V.P.	**Traded (Symbol):** NASDAQ (PLAT)
Human Resources: Michael P. Cullinane, Exec. V.P.	**Stockholders:** 175
Mgt. Info. Svcs.: Paul L. Humenansky, Exec. V.P.	**Employees:** 894
	Annual Meeting: In May

Playboy Enterprises, Inc.

680 North Lake Shore Drive, Chicago, Illinois 60611
Telephone: (312) 751-8000

Playboy Enterprises, Inc., is an international publishing and entertainment company that publishes *Playboy* magazine and related media, including newsstand specials and calendars; operates a direct marketing business, including the *Playboy*, *Collectors' Choice Music* and *Critics' Choice Video* catalogs; creates and distributes programming for Playboy's domestic pay television network, worldwide home video, and international television; and markets Playboy trademarks on apparel, accessories, and products for consumers around the world. Foreign editions of *Playboy* magazine are published in the following countries: Argentina, Australia, Brazil, Czech Republic, Germany, Greece, Italy, Japan, Mexico, the Netherlands, Poland, South Africa, and Spain. The company's publishing interests include a 20 percent stake in the *duPont Registry*, a monthly guide to classical and luxury automobiles. Major subsidiaries of the company include: Lifestyle Brands, Ltd.; Playboy Preferred, Inc.; Playboy Models, Inc.; Playboy Products and Services International, B.V.; Playboy Entertainment Group, Inc.; Alta Loma Productions, Inc.; Critics' Choice Video, Inc.; Special Editions, Ltd.; Lake Shore Press, Inc.; Impulse Productions, Inc.; Playboy Clubs International, Inc.; After Dark Video, Inc.; Playboy Records, Inc.; and Playboy Shows, Inc. Incorporated in Illinois in 1953, the company was merged into a wholly owned Delaware subsidiary in 1964; present name adopted in 1971.

Directors (In addition to indicated officers)

Dennis S. Bookshester
Robert Kamerschen

John R. Purcell
Sol Rosenthal

Officers (Directors*)

*Christie Hefner, Chm. & C.E.O.
Hugh M. Hefner, Chm. Emer. & Ed.-in-Chf.
David I. Chemerow, Exec. V.P.—Fin./Oper. & C.F.O.
Anthony J. Lynn, Exec. V.P. & Pres.—Ent. Grp.
*Richard S. Rosenzweig, Exec. V.P.
Howard Shapiro, Exec. V.P.—Law/Admin. & Gen. Coun.
Robert B. Beleson, Sr. V.P. & Chf. Mktg. Off.

Rebecca S. Maskey, Sr. V.P.—Fin. & Treas.
Denise Bindelglass, V.P.—Hum. Res.
Martha O. Lindeman, V.P.—Corp. Comm. & Investor Rel.
Cindy Rakowitz, V.P.—Public Rel.
John A. Ullrick, V.P.—MIS
Irma Villarreal, Sr. Corp. Coun. & Secy.
Robert D. Campbell, Asst. Treas.
Michael Dannhauser, Asst. Corp. Cont.

Consolidated Balance Sheet As of June 30, 1994 (000 omitted)

Assets		Liabilities & Stockholders' Equity	
Current assets	$ 87,668	Current liabilities	$ 76,762
Net property & equipment	15,654	Long-term debt	1,020
Other assets	28,599	Other liabilities	7,828
		*Stockholders' equity	46,311
Total	$131,921	Total	$131,921

*4,709,454 shares Class A common and 15,254,889 shares Class B common stock outstanding.

Consolidated Income Statement

Years Ended June 30	Thousands — — — — — Net Revenues[a]	Net Income[bc]	Per Share — — — — Earnings[bc]	Cash Dividends	Common Stock Price Range[d] Calendar Year	
1994	$218,987	$(9,484)	$ (.48)	$ .00	11	— 6
1993	214,875	365	.02	.00	11	— 6-5/8
1992	193,749	3,510	.19	.00	9-1/2	— 5-7/8
1991	174,042	4,510	.24	.00	8-1/2	— 3-7/8
1990	167,697	6,228	.33	.00	7-5/8	— 3-1/8

[a]From continuing operations.
[b]Includes restructuring expenses, unusual items, nonrecurring expenses, and a gain to reflect FAS 109, which resulted in a cumulative gain of $2,887,000 ($.14 per share) in 1994.
[c]Includes a loss from discontinued operations of $120,000 ($.01 per share) in 1991; and extraordinary credits of $1,688,000 ($.09 per share) in 1992; $2,219,000 ($.12 per share) in 1991; and $2,632,000 ($.14 per share) in 1990.
[d]Class A common stock.

Transfer Agent & Registrar: Harris Trust and Savings Bank

General Counsel: Howard Shapiro, Exec. V.P.

Investor Relations: Martha O. Lindeman, V.P.

Human Resources: Denise Bindelglass, V.P.

Mgt. Info. Svcs.: John A. Ullrick, V.P.

Auditors: Coopers & Lybrand L.L.P.

Traded (Symbol):
NYSE, PSE (PLA A, Class A; PLA, Class B)

Stockholders: 8,633 Class A; 8,982 Class B

Employees: 578

Annual Meeting: In November

First Chicago Guide   197

PORTEC, Inc.

One Hundred Field Drive, Suite 120, Lake Forest, Illinois 60045-2597
Telephone: (708) 735-2800

PORTEC, Inc., is a diversified manufacturer and marketer of engineered products for the construction equipment, materials handling, and railroad industries. The Construction Equipment segment manufactures and markets the Kolberg and Pioneer product lines. These product lines include machinery and systems used in the construction, mining, and road-building industries. The Innovator product line consists of grinders and screens for the processing of green yard waste, waste wood, and demolition debris. The Materials Handling segment, consisting of the Flomaster Division, Pathfinder Division, and Count Recycling Systems Division, manufactures and markets materials handling equipment, such as electronic wire guidance lift-truck controls and systems, specialty conveyor products, and conveyor systems for solid waste recycling. The Railroad segment manufactures and markets a variety of railroad products. The Railway Maintenance Products Division manufactures and markets a variety of track components, including rail joints, rail anchors and lubricators, and jacking systems for railroad car repair facilities. The Shipping Systems Division is a major supplier of railroad load securement systems and devices for shipping containers, building products, automobiles, military vehicles, farm implements, and heavy construction equipment. Portec, Ltd., the company's Canadian subsidiary, engineers and markets a broad range of railway track products in Canada. Portec (U.K.) Ltd., the company's British subsidiary, manufactures and markets railway track products and materials handling equipment. Incorporated in Delaware in 1928.

Directors (In addition to indicated officers)

J. Grant Beadle	Arthur McSorley, Jr.
Frederick J. Mancheski	Robert D. Musgjerd
John F. McKeon	L.L. White, Jr.

Officers (Directors*)

*Albert Fried, Jr., Chm.	John S. Cooper, Sr. V.P. & Grp. Mgr.—Railway
*Michael T. Yonker, Pres. & C.E.O.	Nancy A. Kindl, V.P., C.F.O., Treas. & Secy.

Consolidated Balance Sheet As of December 31, 1994 (000 omitted)

Assets		Liabilities & Stockholders' Equity	
Current assets	$35,561	Current liabilities	$22,764
Net property, plant & equipment	13,372	Long-term debt	7,623
Other assets	8,589	Deferred items	2,176
		*Stockholders' equity	24,959
Total	$57,522	Total	$57,522

*4,283,260 shares common stock outstanding.

Consolidated Income Statement

Years Ended Dec. 31	Thousands — — — —		Per Share[a] — — —		Common Stock Price Range Calendar Year
	Net Sales	Net Income	Earnings	Cash Dividends	
1994	$96,474	$6,825	$1.49	$ .00	16-7/8 — 10-1/4
1993	76,324	4,696	1.05	.00	15-1/8 — 6-5/8
1992	68,638	5,513	1.37	.00	7-5/8 — 3-5/8
1991	65,027	807	.20	.00	4-5/8 — 2-5/8
1990	80,551	3,481	.89	.00	5-5/8 — 2-1/4

[a]Adjusted to reflect 10% stock dividends paid in December 1994, 1993 and 1992.

Transfer Agent & Registrar:	Harris Trust and Savings Bank		
General Counsel:	Schiff, Hardin & Waite	Traded (Symbol):	NYSE, CSE (POR)
Investor Relations:	Nancy A. Kindl, V.P.	Stockholders:	1,335
Human Resources: Patricia A. Riccio, Employee Benefits Mgr.		Employees:	779
Auditors:	Price Waterhouse LLP	Annual Meeting:	In April

Premark International, Inc.

1717 Deerfield Road, Deerfield, Illinois 60015-3900
Telephone: (708) 405-6000

Premark International, Inc., comprises three business segments: Tupperware; Food Equipment Group; and Consumer and Decorative Products Group. Tupperware, headquartered in Orlando, Florida, is a leading world manufacturer and marketer of premium quality plastic products for preparing, serving and storing food. It also markets children's products, including educational toys. The Food Equipment Group, headquartered in Troy, Ohio, manufactures, sells and services commercial products worldwide for food preparation, cooking, weighing, wrapping, baking, refrigeration and warewashing. The Consumer and Decorative Products Group consists of Ralph Wilson Plastics Co., headquartered in Temple, Texas, one of the largest manufacturers of decorative laminates in the U.S.; Hartco, a maker of prefinished hardwood flooring products; Florida Tile, a leading U.S. ceramic tile manufacturer; The West Bend Company, headquartered in West Bend, Wisconsin, a manufacturer of small electric kitchen appliances and direct-to-the-home stainless steel cookware; and Precor, a maker of aerobic physical fitness equipment. Incorporated in Delaware in 1986.

Directors (In addition to indicated officers)

William O. Bourke	Joseph E. Luecke	David R. Parker
Ruth M. Davis, Ph.D.	Bob Marbut	Robert M. Price
Lloyd C. Elam, M.D.	John B. McKinnon	Janice D. Stoney
Clifford J. Grum		

Officers (Directors*)

*Warren L. Batts, Chm. & C.E.O.
*James M. Ringler, Pres. & C.O.O.
*E.V. (Rick) Goings, Exec. V.P. & Pres.—Tupperware
James C. Coleman, Sr. V.P.—Hum. Res.
John M. Costigan, Sr. V.P., Gen. Coun. & Secy.
Lawrence B. Skatoff, Sr. V.P. & C.F.O.
Joseph W. Deering, Grp. V.P. & Pres.—Food Eq.
Thomas W. Kieckhafer, Corp. V.P. & Pres.—West Bend

L. John Fletcher, V.P. & Asst. Gen. Coun.
Isabelle C. Goossen, V.P.—Planning
Robert W. Hoaglund, V.P.—Control & Info. Syst.
Wendy R. Katz, V.P.—Internal Audit
William R. Reeb, V.P. & Pres.—R. Wilson Plastics
Lisa K. Richardson, V.P.—Treas.
James E. Rose, Jr., V.P.—Taxes & Govt. Aff.

Consolidated Balance Sheet As of December 31, 1994 (000 omitted)

Assets		Liabilities & Stockholders' Equity	
Current assets	$1,274,100	Current liabilities	$ 920,600
Net property, plant & equipment	711,800	Long-term debt	122,300
Other assets	372,000	Deferred items	9,900
		Other liabilities	332,800
		*Stockholders' equity	972,300
Total	$2,357,900	Total	$2,357,900

*3,898,493 shares common stock outstanding.

Consolidated Income Statement

Years Ended Abt. Dec. 31	Thousands — — — —		Per Share[b] — — — —		Common Stock
	Net Sales[a]	Net Income	Earnings	Dividends Declared	Price Range[b] Calendar Year
1994	$3,394,559	$ 225,500	$ 3.39	$ .74	48 — 33-5/8
1993	3,043,190	172,500	2.57	.55	41-7/8 — 19-1/8
1992	2,939,777	(79,300)[c]	(1.20)	.48	25-5/8 — 14-7/8
1991	2,842,790	102,300	1.62	.42	20-3/8 — 8-1/8
1990	2,721,400	52,000[d]	.82	.42	15-1/2 — 6-3/8

[a]1994-91 restated to reflect new Tupperware sales reporting.
[b]Adjusted to reflect a 2-for-1 stock split in June 1994.
[c]Includes pretax charges of $136,700,000 ($111,400,000 aftertax) primarily for restructuring the Tupperware U.S. business; includes a $140,000,000 charge ($98,900,000 aftertax) for adoption of FAS 106; and includes a $15,000,000 credit for adoption of FAS 109.
[d]Includes pretax charges of $25,300,000 for manufacturing streamlining and organizational changes, and $11,900,000 for settlement of lawsuits.

Transfer Agent & Registrar:	Chemical Bank		
General Counsel:	John M. Costigan, Sr. V.P.	Auditors:	Price Waterhouse LLP
Investor Relations:	Christine J. Hanneman, Dir.	Traded (Symbol):	NYSE, PSE, London SE (PMI)
Human Resources:	James C. Coleman, Sr. V.P.	Stockholders:	25,300
Mgt. Info. Svcs.:		Employees:	24,000
Robert W. Hoaglund, V.P.—Control/Info. Syst.		Annual Meeting:	In May

First Chicago Guide

Premier Financial Services, Inc.

27 West Main Street, Suite 101, Freeport, Illinois 61032
Telephone: (815) 233-3671

Premier Financial Services, Inc., is a registered bank holding company whose operations consist primarily of financial activities common to the commercial banking industry, including trust and investment services, electronic banking and insurance. The primary function of the company is to coordinate the banking policies and operations of its subsidiaries. The company's banking subsidiaries include First Bank North, First Bank South, First National Bank of Northbrook, and First Security Bank of Cary Grove, which are chartered as commercial banks. All banks serve as general sales offices providing a full array of financial services and products to individuals, businesses, local governmental units, and institutional customers throughout northwestern Illinois. Other subsidiaries include: Premier Trust Services, Inc., Premier Operating Systems, Inc., and Premier Insurance Services, Inc. Incorporated in Delaware in 1976.

Directors (In addition to indicated officers)

Donald E. Bitz
R. Gerald Fox
Charles M. Luecke

Edward G. Maris
H. Barry Musgrove
Joseph C. Piland

Officers (Directors*)

*Richard L. Geach, Pres. & C.E.O.

*David L. Murray, Exec. V.P. & C.F.O.

Consolidated Balance Sheet   As of December 31, 1994 (000 omitted)

Assets		Liabilities & Stockholders' Equity	
Cash & cash equivalents	$ 45,870	Deposits	$523,693
Investment securities	248,478	Short-term borrowings	26,185
Net loans	280,768	Other liabilities	18,150
Bank premises & equipment	14,255	*Stockholders' equity	52,476
Other assets	31,133		
Total	$620,504	Total	$620,504

*6,504,876 shares common stock outstanding.

Consolidated Income Statement

Years Ended Dec. 31	Thousands Total Income	Net Income	Per Share[a] Earnings	Cash Dividends	Common Stock Price Range[a] Calendar Year
1994	$43,213	$5,710	$ .68	$ .18	8-1/4 — 5-7/8
1993	36,435	4,011	.55	.16	7-7/8 — 6-1/8
1992	33,128	4,352	.74	.15	8-3/8 — 4-3/8
1991	34,550	3,618	.64	.11	4-7/8 — 2-3/4
1990	35,333	2,882	.49	.08	4-1/4 — 2-5/8

[a]Adjusted to reflect a 200% stock dividend declared in May 1994, a 10% stock dividend declared in 1992, and 5% stock dividends declared in 1991 and 1990.

Transfer Agent & Registrar:	First Bank North		
General Counsel:	Schiff, Hardin & Waite	Auditors:	KPMG Peat Marwick LLP
Investor Relations:	David L. Murray, Exec. V.P.	Traded (Symbol):	NASDAQ (PREM)
		Stockholders:	658
Human Resources:	Jack Croffoot	Employees:	280
Mgt. Info. Svcs.:	Katie Vasi	Annual Meeting:	In April

Prime Capital Corporation

10275 West Higgins Road, Suite 200, Rosemont, Illinois 60018
Telephone: (708) 294-6000

Prime Capital Corporation is a publicly held provider of merchant banking and financial services. Prime has provided a variety of services since its inception in 1977, including: equipment leasing and rentals, financial consulting, private placement of long-term debt, tax-exempt financing, off-balance sheet real estate financing, joint ventures, project development, diagnostic imaging center development, and healthcare equipment remarketing. Prime has regional offices throughout the U.S. Incorporated in 1977; reincorporated in Delaware in 1986.

Directors   (In addition to indicated officer)

Lee W. Jennings
Marvin T. Keeling

William D. Smithburg
Robert R. Youngquist, D.D.S.

Officers   (Director*)

*James A. Friedman, Chm., Pres. & C.E.O.
Charles G. Schultz, Exec. V.P.

David L. Daum, Sr. V.P.

Consolidated Balance Sheet   As of December 31, 1994 (000 omitted)

Assets		Liabilities & Stockholders' Equity	
Cash & cash equivalents	$ 1,945	Notes payable to banks	$ 7,889
Receivables	2,235	Accounts payable for equipment	11,920
Net invest. in direct fin. leases	16,847	Accrued expenses & other liabilities	1,996
Other assets	5,914	Deposits & advances	513
		*Stockholders' equity	4,623
Total	$26,941	Total	$26,941

*4,374,365 shares common stock outstanding.

Consolidated Income Statement

Years Ended Dec. 31	Thousands — — — — Revenues	Net Income	Per Share — — — Earnings	Cash Dividends	Common Stock Price Range Calendar Year
1994	$ 4,678	$(1,998)	$ (.47)	$ .00	1-1/2 — 3/4
1993	7,559	2,008	.47	.00	1-1/2 — 1/2
1992	10,695	1,808	.42	.00	1-1/2 — 1/2
1991	23,480	258	.06	.00	1/4 — 1/8
1990	32,589	(2,739)	(.64)	.00	3/4 — 1/8

Transfer Agent & Registrar: Lake Forest Bank & Trust

General Counsel:
  Bischoff, Maurides & Swabowski, Ltd.

Investor Relations: Teri A. Folisi

Human Resources: Teri A. Folisi

Auditors: KPMG Peat Marwick LLP

Traded (Symbol):   OTC Bulletin Board (PMCP)

Stockholders: 560

Employees: 44

Annual Meeting: In August

First Chicago Guide

Princeton National Bancorp, Inc.

606 South Main Street, Princeton, Illinois 61356-2080
Telephone: (815) 875-4444

Princeton National Bancorp, Inc., a bank holding company, is a commercial banking and trust institution in north central Illinois (Bureau, LaSalle, DeKalb, Marshall, Grundy, and Kendall counties). PNB conducts a full-service community banking and trust business through its subsidiary, Citizens First National Bank. Incorporated in Delaware in 1981.

Directors   (In addition to indicated officers)

Thomas R. Lasier, Chm.
Don S. Browning
John Ernat
Donald E. Grubb

Harold C. Hutchinson, Jr.
Thomas M. Longman
Ervin I. Pietsch
Stephen W. Samet

Officers   (Directors*)

*D.E. Van Ordstrand, Pres. & C.E.O.
*Tony J. Sorcic, Exec. V.P.
 Lou Ann Birkey, Secy.

Todd D. Fanning, Cont.
Dennis B. Guthrie, Treas.
Patricia L. Boesch, Auditor

Consolidated Balance Sheet   As of December 31, 1994 (000 omitted)

Assets		Liabilities & Stockholders' Equity	
Cash & due from banks	$ 16,346	Total deposits	$352,987
Federal funds sold	5,400	Short-term borrowings	5,622
Interest-bearing time deposits in	200	Long-term borrowings	5,300
other banks		Other liabilities	1,986
Investment securities	154,957	*Stockholders' equity	34,636
Net loans	204,179		
Premises & equipment	9,280		
Other assets	10,169		
Total	$400,531	Total	$400,531

*2,710,643 shares common stock outstanding.

Consolidated Income Statement

Years Ended Dec. 31	Thousands — — — — Total Income	Net Income	Per Share[a] — — — Earnings	Cash Dividends[b]	Common Stock Price Range[a] Calendar Year	
1994	$28,902	$3,758	$1.39	$ .33	16	— 12-3/4
1993	25,136	3,750	1.38	.32	17	— 11
1992	25,180	3,240	1.32	.30	11-5/8 —	9-7/8
1991	23,848	2,735	1.35	.27	10-3/8 —	8-3/8
1990	24,218	2,719	1.30	.27	10	— 8-7/8

[a]Adjusted to reflect a 3-for-2 stock split paid in December 1994 and common stock dividends paid in December 1991.
[b]Cash dividends declared.

Transfer Agent & Registrar: Princeton National Bancorp, Inc.

General Counsel: Schiff, Hardin & Waite

Investor Relations: Lou Ann Birkey, Secy.

Human Resources: Betty Walters

Mgt. Info. Svcs.:   D.E. Van Ordstrand, Pres.

Auditors: KPMG Peat Marwick LLP
Traded (Symbol):   NASDAQ (PNBC)
Stockholders: 591
Employees: 188
Annual Meeting: In April

The Quaker Oats Company

321 North Clark Street, Chicago, Illinois 60610-4714
Telephone: (312) 222-7111

The Quaker Oats Company is an international marketer of consumer grocery products. The Grocery Products Group includes Quaker Oats, Aunt Jemima products, Quaker 100% Natural Cereal, Cap'n Crunch cereals, and Quaker Life and Quaker Toasted Oatmeal cereals. Other products are Quaker Chewy Granola Bars, Quaker Rice Cakes, Celeste frozen pizza, Gatorade thirst quencher, Snapple iced teas and fruit juice drinks, Van Camp's pork and beans, and Rice-A-Roni and Noodle Roni. Major subsidiaries are The Gatorade Company, Continental Coffee Products Co., Golden Grain Co., Stokely-Van Camp, Inc., Quaker Oats Limited, UK, Quaker-Chiari & Forti S.p.A., Italy, and The Quaker Oats Company of Canada Limited. In March 1995, the company sold its U.S. and Canadian pet foods business and in April 1995 sold its European pet foods business. In December 1994, Quaker Oats acquired New York-based Snapple Beverage Co., a maker of ready-to-drink iced teas and fruit juice drinks. Incorporated in New Jersey in 1901.

Directors (In addition to indicated officers)

Frank C. Carlucci	Judy C. Lewent	Gertrude G. Michelson
Silas S. Cathcart	Vernon R. Loucks, Jr.	Walter J. Salmon
Kenneth I. Chenault	Thomas C. MacAvoy	William L. Weiss

Officers (Directors*)

*William D. Smithburg, Chm. & C.E.O.
*Philip A. Marineau, Pres. & C.O.O.
Barbara R. Allen, Exec. V.P.—Int'l. Food Prods.
James F. Doyle, Exec. V.P.—Worldwide Beverages
Douglas W. Mills, Exec. V.P.—U.S./Can. Quaker Foods Prods.
Walter G. VanBenthuysen, Exec. V.P.—Worldwide Quaker Food Serv.
*Luther C. McKinney, Sr. V.P.—Law & Corp. Aff.
Douglas J. Ralston, Sr. V.P.—Human Res.
Robert S. Thomason, Sr. V.P.—Fin. & C.F.O.
John A. Boynton, V.P. & Chf. Cust. Officer

John H. Calhoun, V.P.—Int'l. Law
Penelope C. Cate, V.P.—Govt. Rel.
Janet K. Cooper, V.P. & Treas.
Margaret M. Eichman, V.P.—Investor Rel.
Thomas L. Gettings, V.P. & Corp. Cont.
R. Thomas Howell, Jr., V.P., Gen. Corp. Coun. & Secy.
John G. Jartz, V.P.—Bus. Dev.
Mart C. Matthews, V.P. & Assoc. Gen. Corp. Coun.
Kenneth W. Murray, V.P.—Internal Auditing
W. Stephen Perry, V.P.—Corp. Tax
Arthur R. Skantz, V.P.—Corp. Growth
Russell A. Young, V.P.—Supply Chain

Consolidated Balance Sheet As of June 30, 1994 (000 omitted)

Assets		Liabilities & Stockholders' Equity	
Current assets	$1,253,600	Current liabilities	$1,259,100
Net property, plant & equipment	1,214,200	Long-term debt	759,500
Other assets	575,500	Deferred taxes	82,200
		Other liabilities	481,400
		*Stockholders' equity	461,100
Total	$3,043,300	Total	$3,043,300

*66,804,296 shares common stock outstanding.

Consolidated Income Statement

Years Ended June 30	Thousands — — — — Net Sales[a]	Net Income	Per Share[c] — — — Earnings	Cash Dividends[b]	Common Stock Price Range[c] Calendar Year
1994	$5,955,000	$231,500[d]	$1.68[d]	$1.06	42-1/2 — 29-3/4
1993	5,730,600	171,300[e]	1.17[e]	.96	38-1/2 — 30-1/4
1992	5,576,400	247,600	1.63	.86	37-1/8 — 25-1/8
1991	5,491,200	205,800	1.33	.78	37-7/8 — 23-7/8
1990	5,030,600	169,000	1.07	.70	29-3/4 — 20-7/8

[a]Adjusted to exclude Fisher-Price, which is accounted for as a discontinued operation in 1991 and 1990.
[b]Cash dividends declared.
[c]Adjusted to reflect a 2-for-1 stock split in November 1994.
[d]Includes restructuring charges and gains on divestitures, which together net to a pretax charge of $108,600,000 ($.48 per share).
[e]Includes a charge to reflect FAS 106 and FAS 109, resulting in a cumulative effect of $115,500,000 ($.79 per share); and restructuring charges and gains on divestitures, which together net to a pretax charge of $20,500,000 ($.09 per share).

Transfer Agent & Registrar: Harris Trust and Savings Bank

General Counsel:	R. Thomas Howell, Jr., V.P.	Traded (Symbol):	NYSE, CSE, PSE, London, Amsterdam (OAT)
Investor Relations:	Margaret M. Eichman, V.P.		
Human Resources:	Douglas J. Ralston, Sr. V.P.	Stockholders:	28,197
Mgt. Info. Svcs.:	James E. LeGere, V.P.	Employees:	20,000
Auditors:	Arthur Andersen LLP	Annual Meeting:	In November

Quixote Corporation

One East Wacker Drive, Chicago, Illinois 60601
Telephone: (312) 467-6755

Quixote Corporation, through its wholly owned subsidiaries, engages primarily in three lines of business. Energy Absorption Systems, Inc., develops, manufactures, and markets energy-absorbing highway crash cushions for the protection of motorists. Legal Technologies, Inc., is a leading designer and supplier of advanced technologies and services for the legal, judicial, and court reporting markets through its subsidiaries, Stenograph Corporation, Discovery Products, Inc., Integrated Information Services, Inc., and Litigation Sciences, Inc. Disc Manufacturing, Inc., manufactures compact discs, CD-ROMs, and CD-i discs. Facilities are located in Chicago and Mt. Prospect, Illinois; Culver City, Rocklin and Anaheim, California; Pell City and Huntsville, Alabama; and South Bend and Carmel, Indiana. Incorporated in Delaware in 1969.

Directors (In addition to indicated officers)

William G. Fowler
Lawrence C. McQuade

David S. Ruder
Robert D. van Roijen, Jr.

Officers (Directors*)

*Philip E. Rollhaus, Jr., Chm., Pres. & C.E.O.
*James H. DeVries, Exec. V.P. & Secy.
Myron R. Shain, Exec. V.P.—Fin. & Treas.

Daniel P. Gorey, V.P. & Cont.
Joan R. Riley, Asst. Gen. Coun. & Asst. Secy.

Consolidated Balance Sheet   As of June 30, 1994 (000 omitted)

Assets		Liabilities & Stockholders' Equity	
Current assets	$ 52,325	Current liabilities	$ 26,552
Net property, plant & equipment	60,946	Long-term debt	38,975
Other assets	9,518	Deferred items	3,193
		*Stockholders' equity	54,069
Total	$122,789	Total	$122,789

*7,792,555 shares common stock outstanding.

Consolidated Income Statement[a]

Years Ended June 30	Thousands — — — — —		Per Share — — —		Common Stock Price Range Calendar Year
	Net Sales[b]	Net Income[b]	Earnings[b]	Cash Dividends	
1994	$176,938	$11,644	$1.44	$ .21	22-3/4 — 10-3/4
1993	145,111	9,441	1.20	.20	18 — 11-3/4
1992	129,433	8,280	1.07	.00	15-3/4 — 9-1/2
1991	111,811	1,915	.26	.00	13-1/4 — 3-3/8
1990	65,775	5,039	.68	.00	6-1/2 — 4-1/8

[a]Reflects Source Scientific Systems, Inc. (1991-90), as a discontinued operation.
[b]From continuing operations.

Transfer Agent & Registrar:	Bank of Boston			
Outside Counsel:	McBride Baker & Coles	Traded (Symbol):	NASDAQ (QUIX)
Investor Relations:	Joan R. Riley, Dir.	Stockholders:	2,124
Human Resources:	Dorothy French	Employees:	1,586
Auditors:	Coopers & Lybrand L.L.P.	Annual Meeting:	In November

Richardson Electronics, Ltd.

40W267 Keslinger Road, P.O. Box 393, LaFox, Illinois 60147-0393
Telephone: (708) 208-2200

Richardson Electronics, Ltd., is an international distributor and manufacturer of electron tubes and power semiconductors used primarily to control electrical power or as display devices in a variety of industrial, communication, and scientific applications. In addition, the company distributes a variety of closed circuit television equipment. Richardson distributes more than 100,000 products including small power tubes, traveling wave tubes, klystrons, thyratrons, rectifiers, RF power transistors, ignitrons, planar triodes, magnetrons, and cathode ray tubes. Richardson sells electron tubes primarily to the replacement market. Sales offices include ones in California, Georgia, Illinois, Massachusetts, New York, and Texas; and in the following foreign countries: Brazil, Canada, France, Germany, Italy, Japan, Mexico, Singapore, Spain, the Netherlands (European headquarters), Taiwan, and the United Kingdom. Major subsidiaries include: Richardson International and Richardson Electronics (Europe) Ltd. Richardson has a manufacturing facility located in LaFox, Illinois. Incorporated in Illinois in 1947; reincorporated in Delaware in 1986.

Directors (In addition to indicated officers)

Arnold R. Allen	Scott Hodes, Asst. Secy.
Jacques Bouyer	Harold L. Purkey
Kenneth J. Douglas	Samuel Rubinovitz

Officers (Directors*)

*Edward J. Richardson, Chm., Pres. & C.E.O.	*William J. Garry, V.P.—Fin. & C.F.O.
Flint Cooper, Exec. V.P.—Security Systems	David Gilden, V.P.—Latin Amer Sales
*Dennis R. Gandy, Exec. V.P. & Asst. Secy.	Joseph C. Grill, V.P.—Hum. Res.
Ad Ketelaars, Exec. V.P. & Man. Dir.—Euro. Oper.	Kathleen M. McNally, V.P.—Mktg. Oper.
*Joel Levine, Sr. V.P.—Solid State Components	Bart F. Petrini, V.P.—Electron Device Grp.
William G. Seils, Sr. V.P., Corp. Secy. & Gen. Coun.	*Robert L. Prince, V.P.—Sales
Charles J. Acurio, V.P.—Display Prods.	Kevin F. Reilly, V.P.—Info. Sys.

Consolidated Balance Sheet As of May 31, 1994 (000 omitted)

Assets		Liabilities & Stockholders' Equity	
Current assets	$136,967	Current liabilities	$ 40,473
Net property, plant & equipment	16,932	Long-term debt	86,421
Investments	17,836	*Stockholders' equity	52,573
Other assets	7,732		
Total	$179,467	Total	$179,467

*8,055,877 shares common and 3,247,296 shares Class B common stock outstanding.

Consolidated Income Statement

Years Ended May 31	Thousands — — — — Net Sales	Net Income	Per Share — — — Earnings	Cash Dividends	Common Stock Price Range Calendar Year	
1994[a]	$172,094	$(19,809)	$(1.75)	$ .16	9	— 3-3/4
1993	159,215	2,802	.25	.16	10-1/2 — 5-1/2	
1992	158,789	1,707	.15	.16	10-1/4 — 6-3/4	
1991[bc]	161,146	(13,923)	(1.25)	.16	9-1/2 — 5-1/4	
1990[d]	160,101	1,012	.09	.16	11	— 5-1/4

[a]The company established a $26,500,000 provision, which included $21,400,000 for the estimated costs of a plan to dispose of its manufacturing operations in Brive, France, and $5,100,000 for incremental costs related to the phasedown of its LaFox, Illinois, manufacturing facility.
[b]The company repurchased $7,265,000 at face value of its 7-1/4% Convertible Debentures, resulting in an extraordinary gain of $2,290,000 ($.21 per share).
[c]The company established a $20,000,000 provision for the estimated costs of the settlement of the Department of Justice investigation and the phasedown of domestic manufacturing operations.
[d]Includes $8,000,000 in pretax charges for manufacturing, restructuring, and disposal of inventory at reduced values.

Transfer Agent & Registrar: Harris Trust and Savings Bank

General Counsel:	William G. Seils, Sr. V.P.	Auditors:	Ernst & Young LLP
Investor Relations:	William J. Garry, V.P.—Fin.	Traded (Symbol):	NASDAQ (RELL)
		Stockholders:	785
Human Resources:	Joseph C. Grill, V.P.	Employees:	654
Mgt. Info. Svcs.:	Kevin F. Reilly, V.P.	Annual Meeting:	In October

River Forest Bancorp, Inc.

Lincoln National Bank Building, 3959 North Lincoln Avenue, Chicago, Illinois 60613

Telephone: (312) 549-7100

River Forest Bancorp, Inc., is a multi-bank holding company in the business of providing financial services, primarily through its banking subsidiaries, to customers in the Chicago metropolitan area. Bank subsidiaries include: River Forest Bank, Lincoln National Bank, Commercial National Bank, First State Bank of Calumet City, Madison Bank N.A., First National Bank of Wheeling, Aetna Bank, and Belmont National Bank. The company's subsidiary banks offer general banking services such as checking accounts, savings and time deposit accounts; commercial, mortgage, home equity, student and personal loans; safe deposit boxes; and a variety of additional services. River Forest, Commercial and Aetna provide trust services. Lincoln serves more than 400 state-licensed check-cashing facilities in the Chicago area. Incorporated in Minnesota in 1958.

Directors (In addition to indicated officers)

Karl H. Horn
Michael Levitt
Rodney D. Lubeznik

Michael Tang
William H. Wendt III

Officers (Directors*)

*Joseph C. Glickman, Chm.
*Robert J. Glickman, Pres. & C.E.O.
David H. Johnson III, Exec. V.P.
Leona A. Gleason, Sr. V.P.
Terence W. Keenan, Sr. V.P.
Jay B. Kaun, V.P. & Chf. Acct. Off.

Barbara J. Kessner, V.P.—Hum. Res.
James Kolovos, V.P.—Taxes
Alan J. Lorr, V.P., Secy., Treas. & Cont.
James E. Murnane, V.P.
Timothy H. Taylor, V.P.—Invest.

Consolidated Balance Sheet   As of December 31, 1994 (000 omitted)

Assets		Liabilities & Stockholders' Equity	
Cash & due from banks	$ 109,880	Total deposits	$1,698,498
Federal funds sold	96,785	Short term borrowings	10,165
Securities	499,364	Other liabilities	22,191
Net loans, net of allowance	1,080,352	Minority interest	1,742
Net property, plant & equipment	27,268	*Stockholders' equity	156,859
Other assets	75,806		
Total	$1,889,455	Total	$1,889,455

*7,621,171 shares common stock outstanding.

Consolidated Income Statement

Years Ended Dec. 31	Thousands — — — —		Per Share — — — —		Common Stock Price Range Calendar Year
	Total Income[a]	Net Income	Earnings	Cash Dividends	
1994	$127,776	$24,016	$3.14	$ .58	38-1/2 — 32-3/4
1993	113,864	25,322	3.32	.53	45-3/4 — 35-1/2
1992	120,110	23,278	3.05	.45	42 — 32-1/4
1991	115,736	19,536	2.57	.31	35-1/4 — 22-3/4
1990	127,529	18,187	2.40	.24	32-1/2 — 18-3/4

[a]Certain prior-year amounts have been reclassified to conform with the 1993 presentation.

Transfer Agent & Registrar:	Mellon Securities Transfer Services		
Investor Relations:	Alan J. Lorr, V.P.	**Traded (Symbol):**	NASDAQ (RFBC)
		Stockholders:	570
Human Resources:	Barbara J. Kessner, V.P.	**Employees:**	581
Auditors:	KPMG Peat Marwick LLP	**Annual Meeting:**	In May

RLI Corp.

9025 North Lindbergh Drive, Peoria, Illinois 61615-1499
Telephone: (309) 692-1000

RLI Corp. is a holding company which, through nine operating entities, underwrites specialty property and casualty insurance. The principal specialty insurance coverages currently written by the company are: commercial property, personal and commercial umbrella, and directors' and officers' liability. In addition, the company provides various products and services to the ophthalmic industry, including Rx lab spectacles and frames, extended service programs, computerized office automation software, and the manufacture and distribution of contact lenses. It also provides licensing services for agents and brokers, and writes miscellaneous surety bonds. Major subsidiaries include: RLI Insurance Company, Mt. Hawley Insurance Company, and RLI Ophthalmic Group Inc. Incorporated in Delaware in 1984 as the successor to an Illinois corporation incorporated in 1965; reincorporated in Illinois in 1993.

Directors (In addition to indicated officer)

Bernard J. Daenzer, J.D.
Richard J. Haayen
William R. Keane
Gerald I. Lenrow

John S. McGuinness, Ph.D.
Edwin S. Overman, Ph.D.
Edward F. Sutkowski
Robert O. Viets

Officers (Director*)

*Gerald D. Stephens, Pres. & C.E.O.
Joseph E. Dondanville, V.P. & C.F.O.
Mary Beth Nebel, V.P. & Gen. Coun.
Kim J. Hensey, Corp. Secy.
Timothy J. Krueger, Treas.
Michael W. Dalton, Pres. (RLI Ophthalmic Grp. Inc.)
Jonathan E. Michael, Pres. & C.O.O. (RLI Ins. Grp.)

Gregory J. Tiemeier, Sr. V.P.—Branch Oper. (RLI Ins. Grp.)
Gary P. Bonham, V.P.—Claims (RLI Ins. Grp.)
Roger M. Buss, V.P.—Mgmt. Info. Svcs. (RLI Ins. Grp.)
Michael E. Quine, V.P.—Admin. (RLI Ins. Grp.)

Consolidated Balance Sheet As of December 31, 1994 (000 omitted)

Assets		Liabilities & Stockholders' Equity	
Cash and investments	$425,067	Unearned premiums	$119,818
Ceded unearned premiums	40,978	Unpaid losses & settlement exp.	394,966
Reins. balances recov. on unpaid losses/sett. exp.	199,737	Reinsurance balances payable	39,860
Net property, plant & equipment	14,906	Long-term debt	52,255
Other assets	71,613	Other liabilities	15,805
		*Stockholders' equity	129,597
Total	$752,301	Total	$752,301

*6,028,892 shares common stock outstanding.

Consolidated Income Statement

Years Ended Dec. 31	Thousands — — — —		Per Share — — —		Common Stock Price Range Calendar Year
	Revenues	Net Income	Earnings	Cash Dividends	
1994	$171,902	$(5,001)[a]	$ (.84)[a]	$ .58	27-3/4 — 19-7/8
1993	155,125	15,797[b]	2.71[b]	.54	28-5/8 — 24-1/8
1992	129,757	16,207	2.83	.50	25-3/4 — 16
1991	102,343	16,800	2.97	.46	16-3/8 — 11-3/8
1990	92,958	14,267	2.52	.42	14-7/8 — 8-3/8

[a]Losses incurred as a result of the Northridge, California, earthquake on January 17, 1994, reduced net income and earnings per share by $25,000,000 ($4.19 per share).
[b]Includes a gain to reflect FAS 109, resulting in a cumulative effect of $1,665,000 ($.29 per share).

Transfer Agent & Registrar: Norwest Bank Minnesota, N.A.

Outside Counsel:	Sutkowski & Washkuhn Ltd.	Auditors:	KPMG Peat Marwick LLP
Investor Relations:	Timothy J. Krueger, Treas.	Traded (Symbol):	NYSE (RLI)
		Stockholders:	745
Human Resources:	Michael E. Quine, V.P.	Employees:	515
Mgt. Info. Svcs.:	Roger M. Buss, V.P.	Annual Meeting:	In May

Rodman & Renshaw Capital Group, Inc.

233 South Wacker Drive, Suite 4500, Chicago, Illinois 60606
Telephone: (312) 977-7800

Rodman & Renshaw Capital Group, Inc., is a holding company which, through its principal subsidiary, Rodman & Renshaw, Inc., engages in securities brokerage and trading, domestic and international commodities and financial futures, underwriting of municipal and corporate securities, private placement of securities, and the sale of interests in real estate limited partnerships. Through its other subsidiaries, the company also provides investment advisory and other financial services, acts as a general and limited partner of real estate limited partnerships, and sells insurance products. Those subsidiaries include Rodman Advisory Services, River West Development, and Rodman & Renshaw Futures Management, Inc. In December 1993, Abaco Casa de Bolsa, S.A. de C.V., Abaco Grupo Financiero acquired a majority of the company. Incorporated in Delaware in 1980.

Directors   (In addition to indicated officers)

Jorge Lankenau Rocha, Chm.
Alexander C. Anderson
Jorge Antonio Garcia Garza
Eduardo Camarena Legaspi
Federico Richardson Lemas

Thomas E. Meade
Richard Pigott
David S. Ruder
Joseph P. Shanahan

Officers   (Directors*)

*Charles W. Daggs III, Pres. & C.E.O.
*Paul C. Blackman, Exec. V.P.
 John T. Hague, Exec. V.P. & C.F.O.
*Francis L. Kirby, Exec. V.P.
*Keith F. Pinsoneault, Exec. V.P. & C.O.O.
*David H. Shulman, Exec. V.P.

James D. Van De Graaff, Exec. V.P., Gen. Coun.
 & Secy.
*Peter Boneparth, Managing Dir.—Investment
 Banking
 Edwin J. McGuinn, Jr., Managing Dir.—Equities

Consolidated Balance Sheet   As of December 31, 1994 (000 omitted)

Assets		Liabilities & Stockholders' Equity	
Current assets	$442,970	Current liabilities	$424,032
Net property, plant & equipment	2,298	Long-term debt	3,874
Other assets	9,063	*Stockholders' equity	26,425
Total	$454,331	Total	$454,331

*4,576,837 shares common stock outstanding.

Consolidated Income Statement

Years Ended Abt. June 30	Thousands — — — — Revenues	Net Income	Per Share — — — Earnings	Cash Dividends	Common Stock Price Range Calendar Year
1994[a]	$32,194	$(4,164)	$ (.91)	$ .00	7-7/8 — 3-5/8
1994	77,317	(16,501)	(3.69)	.00	
1993	87,309	256	.06	.00	9-3/4 — 5
1992	84,378	1,989	.46	.00	5-3/4 — 4
1991	76,590	(1,595)	(.37)	.00	5-1/2 — 3-1/4
1990	71,882	1,752	.42	.00	7-3/8 — 3-1/2

[a]The company's fiscal year has been changed to December 31. Financial results are from June 25 through December 31, 1994.

Transfer Agent & Registrar: Continental Stock Transfer & Trust Co.

General Counsel:
 James D. Van De Graaff, Exec. V.P.

Investor Relations: Eileen Kelly; Linda Sauer

Human Resources: Charles Henry, V.P.

Mgt. Info. Svcs.:   Scott Denewellis, V.P.

Auditors: Coopers & Lybrand L.L.P.
Traded (Symbol):   CSE, NYSE (RR)
Stockholders: 232
Employees: 494
Annual Meeting: In June

Rymer Foods Inc.

4600 South Packers Avenue, Suite 400, Chicago, Illinois 60609
Telephone: (312) 927-7777

Rymer Foods Inc. is engaged in the production of frozen, pre-seasoned, portion-controlled entrees for restaurants, foodservice and retail customers. Subsidiaries include: Rymer International Seafood Inc. and Rymer Meat Inc. Rymer International Seafood is primarily a seafood importer and distributor, serving major foodservice distributors, restaurant chains, processors and retail customers. Rymer Meat is a further processor of beef into ready-to-cook, portion-controlled seasoned steaks and other beef products. All operating companies engage in the development and production of proprietary "signature" recipes for chain restaurant customers. The company also offers its customers services such as menu planning, new product development, and other marketing services, such as training. These programs, products and services are custom-designed for each chain restaurant. Rymer has plants in Illinois, Florida and Arkansas. Incorporated in Delaware in 1969.

Directors   (In addition to indicated officers)

Samuel I. Bailin
David E. Jackson
Anders J. Maxwell

Barry Rymer
Hannah H. Strasser

Officers   (Directors*)

*John L. Patten, Chm. & C.E.O.
*Jeffrey Rymer, Pres. & C.O.O.
 Edward M. Hebert, Sr. V.P.—Fin. & Treas.

Ludwig A. Streck, Sr. V.P. & C.F.O.
Barbara A. McNicholas, Secy.

Consolidated Balance Sheet   As of October 29, 1994 (000 omitted)

Assets		Liabilities & Stockholders' Equity	
Current assets	$32,014	Current liabilities	$16,034
Net property, plant & equipment	1,969	Long-term debt	18,843
Other assets	24,509	Deferred items	810
		Other liabilities	341
		*Stockholders' equity	22,464
Total	$58,492	Total	$58,492

*10,741,451 shares common stock outstanding.

Consolidated Income Statement

Years Ended Abt. Oct. 31	Thousands — — — — Net Sales[a]	Net Income	Per Share — — — Earnings	Cash Dividends	Common Stock Price Range Calendar Year
1994	$162,256	$ 6,478[b]	$ .61	$ .00	4-1/2 — 1-5/8
1993	147,850	(11,441)[c]	(1.68)[c]	.00	3-3/8 — 7/8
1992	159,427	(9,423)	(3.80)	.00	4-7/8 — 1
1991	152,509	(4,376)	(2.09)	.00	9-1/8 — 4
1990	147,293	(1,649)	(1.16)	.00	11-7/8 — 3-3/4

[a]Restated to reclassify the results of Rymer Chicken Inc. as a discontinued operation.
[b]Includes gain on dispositions (primarily Rymer Chicken) of $4,474,000.
[c]Includes an extraordinary gain from restructuring of subordinated debentures of $11,388,000 ($1.67 per share); a restructuring charge of $2,020,000; and restructuring expense resulting from goodwill writedown of $20,828,000.

Transfer Agent & Registrar: Mellon Securities Transfer Services

General Counsel:
  Berlack, Israels & Liberman

Investor Relations: Ludwig A. Streck, Sr. V.P.

Human Resources:
  Joan Kielbasa, Mgr.—Rymer Meat Inc.

Mgt. Info. Svcs.:
  Paul Dowd, Mgr.—Rymer Meat Inc.

Auditors: Coopers & Lybrand L.L.P.

Traded (Symbol):   NYSE (RYR)

Stockholders: 791

Employees: 408

Annual Meeting: In March

Safety-Kleen Corp.

1000 North Randall Road, Elgin, Illinois 60123-7857
Telephone: (708) 697-8460

Safety-Kleen Corp. is a business-to-business marketing and service company focusing on the environmental needs of business through recycling and reuse of fluid waste. It is a leading provider of services to generators of spent solvents and other hazardous and non-hazardous liquid wastes and by-products, the world's largest provider of parts cleaner services, and one of the world's largest collectors and re-refiners of used oil. The services offered are broadly grouped into the following categories: Small Quantity Generator Resource Recovery Services, Envirosystems, and Oil Recovery Services. The company's primary focus is on servicing small quantity hazardous waste generators who are typically in businesses such as auto and auto body repair, fleet operations, dry cleaning, manufacturing, and a variety of other activities. The original and largest Safety-Kleen service is the parts cleaner service, which provides equipment and solvents to customers and collects spent solvent, considered to be a hazardous waste, for recycling and reuse. At yearend 1994, the company and its subsidiaries had 179 branch service centers in North America and 57 additional branch service centers located across seven western European countries. Major subsidiaries include Safety-Kleen Canada Inc., Safety-Kleen Parts Washer Service LTD., and Safety-Kleen Envirosystem Co. of Puerto Rico. Incorporated in Wisconsin in 1963.

Directors (In addition to indicated officers)

Richard T. Farmer
Russell A. Gwillim
Edgar D. Jannotta
Karl G. Otzen

Paul D. Schrage
Marcia E. Williams
W. Gordon Wood

Officers (Directors*)

*Donald W. Brinckman, Chm.
*John G. Johnson, Jr., Pres. & C.E.O.
 Hyman K. Bielsky, Sr. V.P.—Gen. Coun.
 Roy D. Bullinger, Sr. V.P.—Bus. Mgmt. & Mktg.
 Robert J. Burian, Sr. V.P.—Hum. Res.
 Michael H. Carney, Sr. V.P.—Mktg. Svcs. & Cust. Care
 Joseph Chalhoub, Sr. V.P.—Proc., Eng. & Oil Rec.
 David A. Dattilo, Sr. V.P.—Sales & Svcs.

Scott E. Fore, Sr. V.P.—Envir., Health & Safety
F. Henry Habicht II, Sr. V.P.—Strat./Env. Plan.
William P. Kasko, Sr. V.P.—Oper. & Info.
Robert W. Willmschen, Jr., Sr. V.P.—Fin. & Secy.
Glenn R. Casbourne, V.P.—Eng.
Clark J. Rose, V.P.—Tech. Svcs.
Laurence M. Rudnick, Treas.
C. James Schulz, Cont.

Consolidated Balance Sheet As of December 31, 1994 (000 omitted)

Assets		Liabilities & Stockholders' Equity	
Current assets	$ 191,394	Current liabilities	$ 166,305
Net property, plant & equipment	634,647	Long-term debt	284,125
Other assets	189,945	Deferred items	69,545
		Other liabilities	99,675
		*Stockholders' equity	396,336
Total	$1,015,986	Total	$1,015,986

*57,754,963 shares common stock outstanding.

Consolidated Income Statement

Years Ended Abt. Dec. 31	Thousands — — — — Revenues	Net Income	Per Share[a] — — — — Earnings	Cash Dividends	Common Stock Price Range[a] Calendar Year
1994	$791,267	$ 50,094	$ .87	$ .36	18-1/2 — 12-3/4
1993	795,508	(101,346)[b]	(1.76)[b]	.36	24-3/4 — 13-1/8
1992	794,542	45,637[c]	.79[c]	.34	32-1/4 — 22-5/8
1991	695,001	51,551	.90	.32	37-7/8 — 22
1990	588,987	55,198	1.05	.27	29-5/8 — 18-3/8

[a]Adjusted to reflect a 3-for-2 stock split in March 1991.
[b]Includes restructuring and special charges of $136,000,000 ($2.36 per share), net of tax benefits.
[c]Includes FAS 106 and FAS 109, resulting in an increase to net earnings of $300,000 ($.01 per share).

Transfer Agent & Registrar:	First Chicago Trust Co. of New York		
General Counsel:	Hyman K. Bielsky, Sr. V.P.	Auditors:	Arthur Andersen LLP
Investor Relations:	Marian Miller, Fin. Rel.	Traded (Symbol):	NYSE (SK)
		Stockholders:	7,258
Human Resources:	Robert J. Burian, Sr. V.P.	Employees:	6,600
Mgt. Info. Svcs.:	William P. Kasko, Sr. V.P.	Annual Meeting:	In May

First Chicago Guide

St. Paul Bancorp, Inc.

6700 West North Avenue, Chicago, Illinois 60635
Telephone: (312) 622-5000

St. Paul Bancorp, Inc., is the holding company for St. Paul Federal Bank For Savings, which is primarily engaged in attracting checking, savings, and certificates of deposit accounts from the general public and investing those funds in a variety of mortgage and consumer loan products, and high quality investment securities. Fifty-two branch offices are located in the Chicago metropolitan area. In addition, St. Paul offers its customers a variety of allied financial services through subsidiaries of the bank and holding company. St. Paul Financial Development Corp. purchases and develops real estate. St. Paul Service, Inc., provides a wide range of insurance services. Investment Network, Inc., a discount brokerage firm, offers execution and clearance services for stocks, bonds, and mutual funds. Annuity Network, Inc., is engaged in sales of insurance annuity products. Incorporated in Delaware in 1987.

Directors (In addition to indicated officers)

William A. Anderson
John W. Croghan
Alan J. Fredian
Kenneth J. James

Jean C. Murray, O.P.
Michael R. Notaro
John J. Viera
James B. Wood

Officers (Directors*)

*Joseph C. Scully, Chm. & C.E.O.
*Patrick J. Agnew, Pres. & C.O.O.
James R. Lutsch, Sr. V.P.—Info. Svcs.
Robert N. Parke, Sr. V.P.—Fin. & C.F.O.
Robert N. Pfeiffer, Sr. V.P.—Hum. Res.

Thomas J. Rinella, Sr. V.P.—Community Lend.
Donald G. Ross, Sr. V.P.—Retail Banking
John J. Schukay, Sr. V.P.—Cust. Oper.
Clifford M. Sladnick, Sr. V.P., Gen. Coun. & Secy.

Consolidated Balance Sheet   As of December 31, 1994 (000 omitted)

Assets		Liabilities & Stockholders' Equity	
Cash & cash equivalents	$ 159,948	Deposit accounts	$3,232,903
Investments	99,643	FHLB advances	336,959
Mortgage-backed securities	1,126,617	Other borrowed funds	155,968
Loans receivable (net of reserves)	2,568,381	Deposits for payment of taxes & insurance	21,842
Net property, plant & equipment	44,112	Other liabilities	32,468
FHLB stock	29,847	*Stockholders' equity	351,397
Other assets	102,989		
Total	$4,131,537	Total	$4,131,537

*18,781,480 shares common stock outstanding.

Consolidated Income Statement[a]

Years Ended Dec. 31	Thousands — — — —		Per Share[b] — — — —		Common Stock Price Range[b] Calendar Year
	Total Income	Net Income	Earnings	Cash Dividends	
1994	$283,033	$34,512	$1.70	$ .30	24-1/8 — 16-1/4
1993[c]	289,443	41,387	2.03	.27	20-5/8 — 13-1/4
1992	307,035	37,685	2.00	.27	15-3/4 — 8-5/8
1991	343,938	27,192	1.48	.27	10-7/8 — 4-3/4
1990	338,558	8,400	.46	.27	12-1/8 — 3-3/4

[a]Restated for 1990 to reflect FAS 109.
[b]Adjusted to reflect a 3-for-2 stock split in January 1994.
[c]Includes the operations of Elm Financial Services as of the acquisition date, February 23, 1993.

Transfer Agent & Registrar: The First National Bank of Boston

General Counsel: Clifford M. Sladnick, Sr. V.P.

Investor Relations:
  Maryellen T. Thielen, Asst. V.P.

Human Resources: Robert N. Pfeiffer, Sr. V.P.

Mgt. Info. Svcs.:   James R. Lutsch, Sr. V.P.

Auditors: Ernst & Young LLP

Traded (Symbol):   NASDAQ (SPBC)

Stockholders: 7,510

Employees: 1,103

Annual Meeting: In May

Salton/Maxim Housewares, Inc.

550 Business Center Drive, The Kensington Center, Mount Prospect, Illinois 60056
Telephone: (708) 803-4600

Salton/Maxim Housewares, Inc., designs and markets a broad range of small kitchen appliances, and personal and beauty care appliances under the brand names of Salton®, Maxim®, and Salton Creations™. The kitchen appliances currently marketed by the company include espresso-cappuccino makers, coffee makers, sandwich makers, toasters, bread makers, Hotray® warming trays, juice extractors, ice cream and yogurt makers, and a wide variety of other food preparation appliances. The company's personal and beauty care appliances include hair dryers, Wet Tunes® shower radios, curling irons and brushes, make-up mirrors, massagers, manicure systems, and facial salons. The company contracts for the manufacture of most of its products with independent manufacturers located overseas, primarily in the Far East and Europe. The company also manufactures and assembles certain appliances in its plant located in Newark, New Jersey. Incorporated in Delaware in 1991.

Directors (In addition to indicated officers)

Bert Doornmalen
Thomas E. Galuhn

James C. Tyree

Officers (Directors*)

*David C. Sabin, Chm. & Secy.
*Leonhard Dreimann, Pres. & C.E.O.

William B. Rue, V.P., C.F.O. & Treas.

Consolidated Balance Sheet   As of July 2, 1994 (000 omitted)

Assets		Liabilities & Stockholders' Equity	
Current assets	$32,816	Current liabilities	$23,525
Net property, plant & equipment	2,736	Long-term debt	4,374
Other assets	3,083	*Stockholders' equity	10,736
Total	$38,635	Total	$38,635

*5,100,000 shares common stock outstanding.

Consolidated Income Statement

Years Ended Abt. June 30	Thousands — — — — Net Sales	Net Income	Per Share[a] — — — Earnings	Cash Dividends	Common Stock Price Range[a] Calendar Year
1994	$48,807	$(2,944)	$ (.58)	$ .00	3-1/2 — 1-1/4
1993	50,661	(3,151)	(.64)	.00	3-5/8 — 3/4
1992	48,699	(4,867)	(1.18)	.00	6-3/4 — 2
1991[b]	52,677	1,095	.56	.00	12-3/4 — 4[c]
1990	24,786	(1,443)	(.76)		

[a]Adjusted to reflect an approximately 3.16-for-1 stock split in August 1991.
[b]Includes extraordinary item of $425,000, an income tax benefit from operating loss carryforwards.
[c]Initial public offering in October 1991.

Transfer Agent & Registrar: LaSalle National Trust, N.A.

General Counsel:		Auditors:	Deloitte & Touche LLP
Sonnenschein Nath & Rosenthal		Traded (Symbol):	NASDAQ (SALT)
Investor Relations:	David C. Sabin, Chm.	Stockholders:	1,000
Human Resources:	William B. Rue, V.P.	Employees:	70
Mgt. Info. Svcs.:	William B. Rue, V.P.	Annual Meeting:	In December

John B. Sanfilippo & Son, Inc.

2299 Busse Road, Elk Grove Village, Illinois 60007-6057
Telephone: (708) 593-2300

John B. Sanfilippo & Son, Inc., is a processor, packager, marketer, and distributor of shelled and inshell nuts, which are sold under a variety of private labels and under the company's Evon's™ brand name. The company also markets and distributes, and in most cases, manufactures or processes a diverse product line of food and snack items including peanut butter, candy and confections, natural snacks and trail mixes, corn snacks and sesame sticks. The company sells its products to more than 6,000 retailers, wholesalers, and industrial, government and food service customers. Incorporated in Delaware in 1979 as the successor by merger to an Illinois corporation that was incorporated in 1959.

Directors (In addition to indicated officers)

John W.A. Buyers

William D. Fischer

Officers (Directors*)

*Jasper B. Sanfilippo, Chm., Pres. & C.E.O.
*Matthias A. Valentine, Sr. Exec. V.P., Treas. & Secy.
*Larry D. Ray, Exec. V.P.—Sales & Mktg.

Gary P. Jensen, V.P.—Fin. & C.F.O.
William R. Pokrajac, Cont.
Michael J. Valentine, Asst. Secy.

Consolidated Balance Sheet As of December 31, 1994 (000 omitted)

Assets		Liabilities & Stockholders' Equity	
Current assets	$115,236	Current liabilities	$ 78,818
Net property, plant & equipment	72,358	Long-term debt	52,804
Other assets	12,120	*Stockholders' equity	68,092
Total	$199,714	Total	$199,714

*3,687,426 shares Class A common and 5,392,150 shares common stock outstanding.

Consolidated Income Statement

Years Ended Dec. 31	Thousands — — — — Net Sales	Net Income	Per Share[a] — — — — Earnings	Cash Dividends	Common Stock Price Range[a] Calendar Year
1994	$208,970	$ 49	$ .00	$ .00	15-1/2 — 4-1/2
1993	202,583	6,123	.74	.05	18 — 13-1/4
1992	191,373	6,431	.95	.05	20-3/4 — 12-1/8
1991	161,095	8,208	.83	.00	13-3/4 — 11-1/2[b]
1990	151,990	3,713	.48		

[a]Adjusted to reflect a 407.61-for-1 split of outstanding common and Class A common stock.
[b]Initial public offering in December 1991.

Transfer Agent & Registrar: American Stock Transfer & Trust Co.

General Counsel:
  Katz, Karacic & Helmin; Jenner & Block

Investor Relations: Gary P. Jensen, V.P.

Human Resources: David Meyers

Mgt. Info. Svcs.: Jim Valentine

Auditors: Price Waterhouse LLP

Traded (Symbol): NASDAQ (JBSS)

Stockholders: 2,000

Employees: 1,100

Annual Meeting: In May

Santa Fe Pacific Corporation

Two Century Centre, 1700 East Golf Road, Schaumburg, Illinois
60173-5860
Telephone: (708) 995-6000

Santa Fe Pacific Corporation (SFP) is a holding company which owns subsidiaries engaged in two segments of business: Rail, consisting principally of The Atchison, Topeka and Santa Fe Railway Company, a major Class I railroad operating in 12 midwestern, western, and southwestern states; and Pipeline, reflecting SFP's interest in a refined petroleum products pipeline system operating in six western and southwestern states. Santa Fe Railway, an indirect wholly owned subsidiary of SFP, Santa Fe Pacific Pipeline Partners, L.P., the general partner of which is an indirect wholly owned subsidiary of SFP, and SFP Pipeline Holdings, Inc., an indirect wholly owned subsidiary of SFP, all are public companies subject to the filing requirements of the Securities Exchange Act of 1934, as amended. In February 1995, the company's shareholders approved a merger with Burlington Northern Inc., following regulatory approval. Incorporated in Delaware in 1983.

Directors   (In addition to indicated officer)

Joseph F. Alibrandi	Michael A. Morphy	Jean Head Sisco
John J. Burns, Jr.	Roy S. Roberts	Edward F. Swift
George Deukmejian	John S. Runnells II	Robert H. West
Bill M. Lindig		

Officers   (Director*)

*Robert D. Krebs, Chm., Pres. & C.E.O.
Russ Hagberg, Sr. V.P. & Chf. of Staff
Steven F. Marlier, Sr. V.P. & Chf. Mktg. Off.
Donald G. McInnes, Sr. V.P. & C.O.O.
Denis E. Springer, Sr. V.P. & C.F.O.
Thomas N. Hund, V.P. & Cont.
Jeffrey R. Moreland, V.P.—Law & Gen. Coun.

Patrick J. Ottensmeyer, V.P.—Fin.
Daniel J. Westerbeck, V.P. & Tax Coun.
Catherine Westphal, V.P.—Corp. Comm.
Linda J. Hurt, Treas.
Marsha K. Morgan, Secy.
Irvin Toole, Jr., Chm., Pres. & C.E.O.—S.F. Pacific
Pipelines, Inc.

Consolidated Balance Sheet   As of December 31, 1994 (000 omitted)

Assets		Liabilities & Stockholders' Equity	
Current assets	$ 493,700	Current liabilities	$ 928,400
Net property, plant & equipment	4,741,300	Long-term debt	1,067,400
Other assets	337,900	Deferred items	1,191,900
		Other liabilities	1,128,300
		*Stockholders' equity	1,256,900
Total	$5,572,900	Total	$5,572,900

*188,300,000 shares common stock outstanding.

Consolidated Income Statement

Years Ended Dec. 31	Thousands — — — —		Per Share — — —		Common Stock Price Range Calendar Year
	Revenuesª	Net Incomeᵇ	Earningsᵇ	Cash Dividendsᶜ	
1994	$2,680,900	$ 181,380	$ .95	$ .10	26-1/4 — 12
1993	2,409,200	114,507	.61	.10	22-1/2 — 12-3/4
1992	2,251,700	96,448	.52	.10	14-1/8 — 10-5/8
1991	2,153,500	96,400	.54	.10	14 — 5-1/8
1990	2,111,600	(57,677)	(.35)	.10	23-1/8 — 6

ª1993-90 have been reclassified to reflect SFP Corp.'s former gold subsidiary as a discontinued operation as a result of the distribution to shareholders on September 30, 1994.
ᵇ1994 excludes aftertax effect of the gain on sale of an investment, favorable outcome of litigation, changes in postretirement medical benefits eligibility requirements, and merger related costs. 1993 excludes aftertax effect of gain on sale of California lines, arbitration and litigation settlements, Pipelines special charges and retroactive impact of federal income tax rate increase. 1992 excludes gain on sale of California lines, aftertax effect of Rail and Pipelines special charges, cumulative effect of a change in accounting, and extraordinary charge for early retirement of debt. 1990 excludes litigation and property tax settlements.
ᶜ1994 excludes the distribution of SFP's former gold subsidiary in September 1994. 1990 excludes the distribution of SFP's former energy and real estate subsidiaries in December 1990.

Transfer Agent & Registrar:	First Chicago Trust Co. of New York		
General Counsel:	Jeffrey R. Moreland, V.P.—Law	Auditors:	Price Waterhouse LLP
		Traded (Symbol):	NYSE, CSE, PSE (SFX)
Investor Relations:	Marsha K. Morgan, Secy.	Stockholders:	70,000
Human Resources:	Dennis J. Cech, Asst. V.P.	Employees:	15,000
Mgt. Info. Svcs.:	William R. Smith	Annual Meeting:	In April

Sara Lee Corporation

Three First National Plaza, Chicago, Illinois 60602-4260
Telephone: (312) 726-2600

Sara Lee Corporation is a global manufacturer and marketer of packaged food and consumer products. The company markets its brand name products in more than 120 countries around the world. Sara Lee is organized into two business segments: Sara Lee Packaged Foods manufactures and markets frozen baked goods, fresh and processed meats, nuts, snacks, coffee, tea and other beverages; and Sara Lee Packaged Consumer Products manufactures and markets hosiery, intimate apparel, knitwear, and other consumer products, along with a variety of household and personal products sold through retail outlets or directly to consumers. Incorporated in Maryland in 1939.

Directors (In addition to indicated officers)

Paul A. Allaire	Allen F. Jacobson	Arvi Hillar Parbo
Frans H.J.J. Andriessen	Vernon E. Jordan, Jr.	Rozanne L. Ridgway
Duane L. Burnham	James L. Ketelsen	Richard L. Thomas
Charles W. Coker	Joan D. Manley	Hans B. van Liemt
Willie D. Davis	Newton N. Minow	

Officers (Directors*)

*John H. Bryan, Chm. & C.E.O.	Frank L. Meysman, Sr. V.P.	Floyd G. Hoffman, V.P. & Dep. Gen.
*Michael E. Murphy, V. Chm. & C.A.O.	Lucien Nessim, Sr. V.P.	Coun.
*Donald J. Franceschini, Exec. V.P.	Judith A. Sprieser, Sr. V.P. & C.F.O.	Ronald D. Hubble, V.P.—Internal
*C. Steven McMillan, Exec. V.P.	Jacques A.N. van Dijk, Sr. V.P.	Audit
George W. Bryan, Sr. V.P.	John F. Ward, Sr. V.P.	E.L. (Lee) Kramer, V.P.
Lew Frankfort, Sr. V.P.	Kirk Beaudin, V.P.	Donald L. Meier, V.P.—Taxes
Gary C. Grom, Sr. V.P.—Hum. Res.	Janet E. Bergman, V.P.—Inv. Rel. &	Richard Oberdorf, V.P.
Joseph E. Heid, Sr. V.P.	Corp. Aff.	John A. Piazza, V.P.
Janet Langford Kelly, Sr. V.P., Gen.	James R. Carlson, V.P.	Steven P. Stanbrook, V.P.
Coun. & Secy.	Lee A. Chaden, V.P.	Wayne R. Szypulski, V.P.—Cont.
Jan H. Konings, Sr. V.P.	Charles W. Chambers, V.P.	N. Robert Utecht, V.P.
Paul J. Lustig, Sr. V.P.	Maureen M. Culhane, V.P.—Fin. &	Douglas C. Volz, V.P.—Employee
Mark J. McCarville, Sr. V.P.—Corp.	Treas.	Relations
Devel.	William A. Geoppinger, V.P.	Elynor A. Williams, V.P.—Public
	Simon C. Hemus, V.P.	Responsibility

Consolidated Balance Sheet As of July 2, 1994 (000 omitted)

Assets		Liabilities & Stockholders' Equity	
Current assets	$ 4,469,000	Current liabilities	$ 4,919,000
Net property, plant & equipment	2,900,000	Long-term debt	1,496,000
Other assets	4,296,000	Deferred income taxes	290,000
		Other liabilities	1,303,000
		Redeemable preferred stock	331,000
		*Stockholders' equity	3,326,000
Total	$11,665,000	Total	$11,665,000

*480,765,240 shares common stock outstanding.

Consolidated Income Statement

Years Ended Abt. June 30	Thousands — — — — Net Sales	Net Income	Per Share[a] — — — Earnings	Cash Dividends	Common Stock Price Range[a] Calendar Year
1994	$15,536,000	$199,000[b]	$ .37[b]	$ .63	26 — 19-3/8
1993	14,580,000	704,000	1.40	.56	31-1/8 — 21
1992	13,243,000	761,000	1.54[c]	.61[d]	32-1/2 — 23-3/8
1991	12,381,000	535,000	1.08	.46	29-1/8 — 14-7/8
1990	11,606,000	470,000	.96	.41	16-7/8 — 12-1/8

[a]Adjusted to reflect a 2-for-1 stock split in October 1992.
[b]Includes a restructuring expense and a charge to reflect FAS 109, resulting in a cumulative effect of $530,000,000 ($1.10 per share).
[c]Includes unusual items resulting in a net gain of $.30 per share.
[d]Includes a $.12 per share special dividend.

Transfer Agent: Sara Lee Corporation	
Registrar: The First National Bank of Chicago	Traded (Symbol): NYSE,CSE,PSE,London,Amsterdam, Paris Bourse, Swtz. (3) (SLE)
General Counsel: Janet Langford Kelly, Sr. V.P.	
Investor Relations: Janet E. Bergman, V.P.	Stockholders: 96,470
Human Resources: Gary C. Grom, Sr. V.P.	Employees: 145,900
Auditors: Arthur Andersen LLP	Annual Meeting: In October

First Chicago Guide

Schawk, Inc.

1695 River Road, Des Plaines, Illinois 60018-3013
Telephone: (708) 827-9494

Schawk, Inc., has two operating divisions, the Graphics Group and the Plastics Group. The Graphics Group is a leader in the U.S. prepress industry, primarily serving consumer products businesses. The group offers a complete line of prepress services and products for the production of consumer product packaging and related marketing and advertising materials. The Plastics Group manufactures injection molded plastic filtration, custom specialty plastic, and thermoformed products. In December 1994, the corporation previously known as Schawk, Inc., and certain affiliated corporations were merged with and into the company's predecessor, Filtertek, Inc. Upon consummation of the merger, Filtertek changed its name to Schawk, Inc. Incorporated in Illinois in 1965; reincorporated in Delaware in 1972.

Directors   (In addition to indicated officers)

Judith W. McCue
John T. McEnroe

Robert F. Meinken
Hollis W. Rademacher

Officers   (Directors*)

*Clarence W. Schawk, Chm.
*David A. Schawk, Pres. & C.E.O.
*A. Alex Sarkisian, Exec. V.P., Secy. &
  Pres.—Graphics Grp.
*Marie Meisenbach Graul, Treas., C.F.O. &
  Public Info. Officer

*Ronald J. Kay, Pres.—Plastics Grp., N. Amer.
  Oper.
*Larry Larkin, Exec. V.P.—Plastics Grp.

Consolidated Balance Sheet   As of December 31, 1994 (000 omitted)

Assets		Liabilities & Stockholders' Equity	
Current assets	$ 56,736	Current liabilities	$ 31,482
Net property, plant & equipment	81,450	Long-term debt	75,059
Other assets	55,240	Deferred taxes	3,370
		Other liabilities	7,240
		*Stockholders' equity	76,275
Total	$193,426	Total	$193,426

*19,388,852 shares common stock outstanding.

Consolidated Income Statement

Years Ended Dec. 31	Thousands — — — —		Per Share — — — —		Common Stock Price Range Calendar Year
	Net Sales	Net Income	Earnings	Cash Dividends	
1994[a]	$186,145	$12,585	$ .64		13-3/8 — 8-1/4[b]
1993[a]	169,038	9,907	.49		
1992	110,999	12,466			

[a]Unaudited pro forma to account for merger between Schawk, Inc., and Filtertek, Inc., on December 30, 1994.
[b]Stock price for Filtertek, Inc.

Transfer Agent & Registrar: First Chicago Trust Co. of New York

General Counsel: Vedder, Price, Kaufman & Kammholz		Auditors:	Ernst & Young LLP
		Traded (Symbol):	NYSE (SGK)
Investor Relations:	Anita L. Fletcher	Stockholders:	2,400
Human Resources:	Robert Drew	Employees:	1,902
Mgt. Info. Svcs.:	William Shay	Annual Meeting:	In May

First Chicago Guide

Scotsman Industries, Inc.

775 Corporate Woods Parkway, Vernon Hills, Illinois 60061-3112
Telephone: (708) 215-4500

Scotsman Industries, Inc., is a worldwide supplier of refrigeration products and technologies to the foodservice, hospitality, beverage, and health care industries. Products include ice machines, refrigerators, freezers, food preparation workstations, and drink dispensing equipment, and are sold internationally under the brand names "Scotsman," "Crystal Tips," "Booth," "Tecnomac," "Simag," "Rapid Freeze," "Delfield," "Whitlenge," and "Icematic." The company manufactures its products through six operations: Scotsman; Booth/Crystal Tips; Frimont; The Delfield Company; Whitlenge Drink Equipment Limited; and Castel MAC. Incorporated in Delaware in 1989.

Directors (In addition to indicated officer)

Donald C. Clark	George D. Kennedy
Timothy C. Collins	James J. O'Connor
Frank W. Considine	Robert G. Rettig
Matthew O. Diggs, Jr.	

Officers (Director*)

*Richard C. Osborne, Chm., Pres. & C.E.O.
Emanuele Lanzani, Exec. V.P. & Man. Dir.—Frimont & Castel MAC
Michael de St. Paer, V.P. & Man. Dir.—Whitlenge Drink Equip. Ltd.
Richard M. Holden, V.P.—Human Res.
Donald D. Holmes, V.P.—Fin. & Secy.

Christopher D. Hughes, V.P. & Pres.— Booth/Crystal Tips
Kevin E. McCrone, V.P. & Pres.—The Delfield Co.
Randall C. Rossi, V.P. & Pres.—Scotsman Ice Systems
Paolo Faenza, Gen. Mgr.—Castel MAC
Gerardo Palmieri, Dir.—Sales & Mktg., Frimont

Consolidated Balance Sheet As of January 1, 1995 (000 omitted)

Assets		Liabilities & Stockholders' Equity	
Current assets	$116,382	Current liabilities	$ 61,817
Net property, plant & equipment	40,657	Long-term debt	84,900
Other assets	87,752	Other liabilities	11,611
		*Stockholders' equity	86,463
Total	$244,791	Total	$244,791

*8,267,938 shares common stock outstanding.

Consolidated Income Statement

Years Ended Abt. Dec. 31	Thousands — — — —		Per Share — — — —		Common Stock Price Range Calendar Year
	Net Sales	Net Income	Earnings	Cash Dividends	
1994[a]	$266,632	$ 12,785	$ 1.49	$ .10	18-1/4 — 13
1993	163,952	7,411	1.06	.10	14-1/2 — 9-1/8
1992	168,674	6,392	.90	.10	10-5/8 — 7-1/8
1991	164,126	(1,674)	(.24)	.10	9-5/8 — 6
1990	179,857	7,412	1.05	.10	10-1/2 — 4-5/8

[a]Includes the results of Delfield and Whitlenge subsequent to their acquisitions on April 29, 1994.

Transfer Agent & Registrar:	Harris Trust and Savings Bank		
General Counsel:	Schiff, Hardin & Waite	Traded (Symbol):	NYSE (SCT)
Investor Relations:	Donald D. Holmes, V.P.	Stockholders:	5,400
Human Resources:	Richard M. Holden, V.P.	Employees:	2,200
Auditors:	Arthur Andersen LLP	Annual Meeting:	In May

Sears, Roebuck and Co.

Sears Tower, Chicago, Illinois 60684
Telephone: (312) 875-2500

Sears, Roebuck and Co. consists of domestic merchandising, which sells goods and services in the U.S.; credit, which initiates and maintains customer credit accounts; and international, which conducts retail and credit operations in Canada and Mexico. In June 1995, the company spun off The Allstate Corporation and planned to divest Homart to focus on its core retail operations. In 1993, Sears completed the initial fundamental repositioning of the company that included Dean Witter, Discover and Co.'s sale of 20 percent of its stock to the public and a distribution of the Dean Witter stock held by Sears to Sears common shareholders; the offer by Allstate of up to 20 percent of its stock to the public; and the sale of the Coldwell Banker Residential Services businesses. Incorporated in New York in 1906.

Directors (In addition to indicated officers)

Hall Adams, Jr.
Warren L. Batts
James W. Cozad
William E. LaMothe
Michael A. Miles

Sybil C. Mobley
Nancy C. Reynolds
Clarence B. Rogers, Jr.
Donald H. Rumsfeld
Dorothy A. Terrell

Officers (Directors*)[a]

*Edward A. Brennan, Chm., Pres. & C.E.O.
*Arthur C. Martinez, Chm./C.E.O.—Merchandise Grp.
James M. Denny, V. Chm. & Acting C.F.O.

David Shute, Sr. V.P., Corp. Gen. Coun. & Secy.
James A. Blanda, V.P.—Cont.
Gerald E. Buldak, V.P.—Public Aff.
Alice M. Peterson, V.P. & Treas.

[a]Brennan will retire and Martinez will become Chairman and C.E.O. after the completion of The Allstate Corporation spinoff.

Consolidated Balance Sheet · As of December 31, 1994 (000 omitted)

Assets		Liabilities & Stockholders' Equity	
Investments	$46,942,000	Long-term debt	$10,854,000
Receivables	21,969,000	Insurance reserves	40,136,000
Other assets	22,985,000	Short-term borrowings	6,190,000
		[a]Other liabilities	23,915,000
		*Stockholders' equity	10,801,000
Total	$91,896,000	Total	$91,896,000

[a]Includes minority interest.
*351,740,000 shares common stock outstanding.

Consolidated Income Statement

Years Ended Dec. 31	Thousands — — — —		Per Share — — — —		Common Stock Price Range Calendar Year
	Revenues[a]	Net Income	Earnings	Cash Dividends	
1994	$54,559,000	$ 1,454,000[b]	$ 3.66[b]	$1.60	55-1/8 — 42-1/8
1993	51,486,000	2,374,400[c]	6.13[c]	1.60	60-1/8 — 39-7/8
1992	53,110,000	(3,932,300)[d]	(10.72)[d]	2.00	48 — 37
1991	51,592,000	1,278,900	3.71	2.00	43-1/2 — 24-3/8
1990	50,889,000	902,200	2.63	2.00	41-7/8 — 22

[a]Restated to reflect Homart Development Co., Dean Witter, Discover & Co., and the Coldwell Banker Residential Services businesses as discontinued operations.
[b]Includes an extraordinary gain related to early extinguishment of debt of $195,000,000 ($.50 per share).
[c]Includes an extraordinary loss related to early extinguishment of debt of $210,800,000 ($.55 per share).
[d]Includes a charge to reflect FAS 106 and FAS 112, resulting in a cumulative effect of $1,873,400,000 ($5.07 per share).

Transfer Agent & Registrar: First Chicago Trust Co. of New York

General Counsel: David Shute, Sr. V.P.

Investor Relations: Harry E. Wren, Dir./Asst. Treas.

Auditors: Deloitte & Touche LLP

Traded (Symbol):
NYSE,CSE,PSE,London,Amsterdam,Paris,Frankf., Geneva, Tokyo, Swiss (S)

Stockholders: 262,605

Employees: 361,000

Annual Meeting: In May

First Chicago Guide

Selfix, Inc.

4501 West 47th Street, Chicago, Illinois 60632
Telephone: (312) 890-1010

Selfix, Inc., designs, manufactures and markets a broad range of consumer home products, including more than 300 houseware products and a line of plastic exterior shutters. The company markets its products in four categories: home bathwares, home helpers, home organization products, and home improvement products. Selfix's houseware products are designed to satisfy everyday household storage and organizational needs, and its shutters are designed for easy assembly from standard components into custom lengths. Houseware products are sold in the U.S. and other countries, principally to mass merchandisers, drug and hardware store chains, variety outlets and supermarkets. Shutters are sold primarily in the eastern U.S. and Canada through building product distributors. Subsidiaries are Shutters, Inc., Selfix of Canada, Ltd., Selfix (Housewares) Ltd., Selfix (H.K.) Ltd., and Selfix International Ltd. (V.I.). Incorporated in Illinois in 1962; reincorporated in Delaware in 1987.

Directors (In addition to indicated officer)

Charles Campbell
William P. Mahoney

Jeffrey C. Rubenstein
Daniel Shure

Officers (Director*)

*James R. Tennant, Chm. & C.E.O.
William Englehart, Sr. V.P.—Sales
Edgar L. Freer, Sr. V.P. & Man. Dir.—Int'l.

Ted Lucore, Sr. V.P.—Oper.
James Winslow, Sr. V.P., Secy. & C.F.O.
Raymond E. Anderson, V.P.—Sales

Consolidated Balance Sheet As of December 31, 1994 (000 omitted)

Assets		Liabilities & Stockholders' Equity	
Current assets	$18,742	Current liabilities	$ 7,717
Net property, plant & equipment	10,466	Long-term debt	9,421
Other assets	1,553	*Stockholders' equity	13,623
Total	$30,761	Total	$30,761

*3,603,637 shares common stock outstanding.

Consolidated Income Statement

Years Ended Abt. Dec. 31	Thousands — — — — Net Sales	Net Income	Per Share — — — Earnings	Cash Dividends	Common Stock Price Range Calendar Year
1994[a]	$40,985	$(6,003)	$(1.70)	$ .00	9-1/4 — 4
1993	39,711	1,515	.43	.00	7-1/2 — 2-3/4
1992	35,209	(781)	(.23)	.00	7 — 2-7/8
1991	37,013	574	.17	.00	7 — 3-1/4
1990[b]	20,764	(165)	(.05)	.00	9 — 3-1/4

[a]Includes restructuring charges of $1,701,000.
[b]Seven months ended December 31, 1990.

Transfer Agent & Registrar: Mellon Financial Services

General Counsel:
  Much Shelist Freed Denenberg Ament
  & Eiger, P.C.

Investor Relations: James Winslow, Sr. V.P.

Human Resources: Robert Anderson

Mgt. Info. Svcs.: Ross Gosnell

Auditors: Grant Thornton LLP

Traded (Symbol): NASDAQ (SLFX)

Stockholders: 600

Employees: 394

Annual Meeting: In June

First Chicago Guide

ServiceMaster Limited Partnership

One ServiceMaster Way, Downers Grove, Illinois 60515-9969
Telephone: (708) 271-1300

ServiceMaster Limited Partnership is a portfolio of quality service companies with two major operating units, ServiceMaster Consumer Services and ServiceMaster Management Services, and other developing segments, ServiceMaster Diversified Health Services and International and New Business Development. ServiceMaster Consumer Services includes five market leading companies — ServiceMaster Residential and Commercial Services; Terminix; TruGreen-ChemLawn; Merry Maids; and American Home Shield — which operate through the ServiceMaster Quality Services Network of more than 5,700 company-owned and franchised businesses. ServiceMaster Management Services is a leading company serving 2,300 health care, education, and industrial and commercial facilities with management of plant operations and maintenance, housekeeping, clinical equipment maintenance, food service, laundry, grounds and energy. ServiceMaster Diversified Health Services provides a broad range of services to home care, subacute and long-term care markets, serving 133 health care facilities. ServiceMaster Limited Partnership serves more than five-million customers in the U.S. and in 28 foreign countries. Incorporated in Delaware in 1986.

Directors (In addition to indicated officers)

Henry O. Boswell
Brian Griffiths
Sidney E. Harris
Herbert P. Hess

Gunther H. Knoedler
James D. McLennan
Vincent C. Nelson
Kay A. Orr

Phillip B. Rooney
Burton E. Sorensen
David K. Wessner

Officers (Directors*)

*C. William Pollard, Chm.
*Carlos H. Cantu, Pres. & C.E.O.
*Charles W. Stair, V. Chm.
Ernest J. Mrozek, Sr. V.P., Treas. & C.F.O.
Vernon T. Squires, Sr. V.P. & Gen. Coun.
Susan D. Krause, V.P., Secy. & Legal Coun.
Deborah A. O'Connor, V.P. & Cont.
Eric R. Zarnikow, V.P. & Treas.

William C. Dowdy, Pres.—Healthcare Mgt. Svcs.
Robert D. Erickson, Pres./C.O.O.—Int'l. & New Bus.
Robert F. Keith, Pres./C.O.O.—Consumer Svcs.
Jerry D. Mooney, Pres./C.E.O.—Divers. Health Svcs.
Brian D. Oxley, Pres./C.O.O.—Mgmt. Svcs.
Dallen W. Peterson, Chm.—Merry Maids

Consolidated Balance Sheet   As of December 31, 1994 (000 omitted)

Assets		Liabilities & Stockholders' Equity	
Current assets	$ 331,045	Current liabilities	$ 304,395
Net property, plant & equipment	128,448	Long-term debt	386,511
Other assets	771,346	Other liabilities	232,667
		*Stockholders' equity	307,266
Total	$1,230,839	Total	$1,230,839

*76,022,000 shares common stock outstanding.

Consolidated Income Statement

Years Ended Dec. 31	Thousands — — — — Operating Revenues	Net Income	Per Share[a] — — — Earnings	Cash Dividends	Common Stock Price Range[a] Calendar Year
1994	$2,985,207	$139,883	$1.81	$ .92	28-3/8 — 21-1/2
1993	2,758,859	145,947	1.90	.89	31 — 17-5/8
1992	2,488,854	122,065	1.61	.87	19-7/8 — 14-5/8
1991	2,109,941	85,982	1.19	.85	17-3/8 — 9-3/4
1990	1,825,750	83,053	1.17	.82	10-5/8 — 8-3/4

[a]Adjusted to reflect 3-for-2 stock splits in June 1993 and January 1992.

Transfer Agent: Harris Trust and Savings Bank
General Counsel: Vernon T. Squires, Sr. V.P.
Investor Relations: Bruce T. Duncan, V.P.
Human Resources: William W. Hargreaves, V.P.
Mgt. Info. Svcs.: Douglas E. Nies, V.P.

Auditors: Arthur Andersen LLP
Traded (Symbol): NYSE (SVM)
Stockholders: 65,000
Employees: 34,000
Annual Meeting: In May

Shelby Williams Industries, Inc.

1348 Merchandise Mart, Chicago, Illinois 60654
Telephone: (312) 527-3593

Shelby Williams designs, manufactures, and distributes products for the contract furniture market. The company has a significant position in the hospitality and foodservice markets through its "Shelby Williams" seating line and "King Arthur" line of function room furniture and "Sterno" Accessories. The company provides contemporary upholstered seating products under the names "Preview" and "Madison." It serves the health care, university, office furniture, and other institutional markets through its "Thonet" division with health care and dormitory furniture, including chairs and tables, and ergonomically designed office seating products, desks and credenzas. The company also distributes vinyl wall coverings for residential, hotel and office use under the name "Sellers & Josephson," and markets other textile products to the architectural and design community through "SW Textiles." The company distributes floor coverings and other textile products, as well as Shelby Williams products, in Hawaii and the entire Pacific Basin, through "PHF." Incorporated in Delaware in 1976.

Directors   (In addition to indicated officers)

Robert L. Haag
William B. Kaplan

Herbert L. Roth
Trisha Wilson

Officers   (Directors*)

*Manfred Steinfeld, Chm.
*Paul N. Steinfeld, V. Chm. & C.E.O.
*Robert P. Coulter, Pres. & C.O.O.
 Peter W. Barile, Exec. V.P.
 Dennis E. Gurley, Sr. V.P.—Mfg.

Sam Ferrell, V.P.—Fin., Treas. & C.F.O.
James R. Goldner, V.P.—Subs. Oper.
William Lau, V.P.—Int'l. Oper.
Michael E. Moore, V.P.—Sales
Walter Roth, Secy.

Consolidated Balance Sheet   As of December 31, 1994 (000 omitted)

Assets		Liabilities & Stockholders' Equity	
Current assets	$57,079	Current liabilities	$28,987
Net property, plant & equipment	29,874	Long-term debt	8,895
Other assets	1,567	Deferred items	1,980
		*Stockholders' equity	48,658
Total	$88,520	Total	$88,520

*8,999,000 shares common stock outstanding.

Consolidated Income Statement

Years Ended Dec. 31	Thousands — — — — Net Sales	Net Income	Per Share — — — — Earnings	Cash Dividends	Common Stock Price Range Calendar Year
1994	$159,072	$ 365[a]	$ .04[a]	$ .28	14-3/8 — 7-1/2
1993	153,527	4,150	.46	.28	14-7/8 — 10-1/8
1992	140,262	3,594	.39	.24	11 — 6-3/8
1991	139,703	(3,143)[b]	(.34)[b]	.24	8-3/4 — 5-7/8
1990	163,915	3,448	.38	.24	11-1/8 — 5-1/4

[a]Reflects restructuring charge of $3,850,000 ($.43 per share).
[b]Reflects restructuring charge of $5,325,000 ($.58 per share).

Transfer Agent & Registrar: Wachovia Bank of North Carolina, N.A.

General Counsel:	D'Ancona & Pflaum	Auditors:	Ernst & Young LLP
Investor Relations:	Robert P. Coulter, Pres.	Traded (Symbol):	NYSE (SY)
		Stockholders:	3,000
Human Resources:	Robert P. Coulter, Pres.	Employees:	1,728
Mgt. Info. Svcs.:	Sam Ferrell, V.P.	Annual Meeting:	In May

First Chicago Guide

SigmaTron International, Inc.

2201 Landmeier Road, Elk Grove Village, Illinois 60007
Telephone: (708) 956-8000

SigmaTron International, Inc., is an independent contract manufacturer of electronic components, printed circuit board assemblies, and turnkey (completely assembled) electronic products. Included among the wide range of services that the company offers its customers are manual and automatic assembly and testing of customer products; material sourcing, procurement and control; design, manufacturing and test engineering support; warehousing and shipment services; and assistance in obtaining product approvals from governmental and other regulatory bodies. The company provides these services through an international network of facilities located in North America and the Far East. In February 1994, the company completed an initial public offering of 1,100,000 shares of common stock. Incorporated in Delaware in 1993.

Directors   (In addition to indicated officer)

Franklin D. Sove, Chm.
John P. Chen
William C. Mitchell
D.S. Patel

Thomas W. Rieck
Steven A. Rothstein
Dilip S. Vyas

Officers   (Director*)

*Gary R. Fairhead, Pres. & C.E.O.
Linda K. Blake, V.P.—Fin., C.F.O., Treas. & Secy.
Gregory A. Fairhead, V.P., Asst. Secy. & Gen. Mgr.—Mexico Oper.

John P. Sheehan, V.P.—Dir. of Mat. & Asst. Secy.
Nunzio A. Truppa, V.P.—Dom. Oper.

Consolidated Balance Sheet   As of April 30, 1994 (000 omitted)

Assets		Liabilities & Stockholders' Equity	
Current assets	$13,850	Current liabilities	$ 5,101
Net property, plant & equipment	3,485	Long-term debt	3,807
Other assets	502	Deferred items	418
		*Stockholders' Equity	8,511
Total	$17,837	Total	$17,837

*2,737,500 shares common stock outstanding.

Consolidated Income Statement[a]

Years Ended April 30	Thousands — — — — Net Sales	Net Income	Per Share — — — Earnings	Cash Dividends	Common Stock Price Range[b] Calendar Year
1994	$36,690	$ 1,862[c]	$ .59[d]	$ .00	9-1/2 — 6
1993	29,764	1,383			
1992	22,123	288			
1991	20,558	(373)			

[a]In February 1991, SigmaTron, Inc., the predecessor, was restructured as a partnership. SigmaTron International, Inc., is the successor to all of the assets and liabilities of SigmaTron L.P., through a reorganization.
[b]Initial public offering in February 1994.
[c]Includes a charge to reflect FAS 109, resulting in a cumulative effect of $527,000.
[d]Unaudited pro forma.

Transfer Agent & Registrar:	American Stock Transfer & Trust Co.		
General Counsel:	D'Ancona & Pflaum	Traded (Symbol):	NASDAQ (SGMA)
		Stockholders:	76
Investor Relations:	Linda K. Blake, V.P.	Employees:	1,000
Auditors:	Ernst & Young LLP	Annual Meeting:	In September

Southwest Bancshares, Inc.

4062 Southwest Highway, Hometown, Illinois 60456-1134
Telephone: (708) 636-2700

Southwest Bancshares, Inc., is the holding company for Southwest Federal Savings and Loan Association of Chicago, which has operated for 111 years and was originally organized in 1883, and Southwest Bancshares Development Corporation. Southwest Federal is a community-oriented, federally insured savings institution, focused on developing long-term deposit relationships with customers and providing residential lending, primarily in southwest Chicago and neighboring suburbs. It serves its customers from five offices, the last of which was opened during 1993. It maintains one office in the Chicago Lawn community of Chicago, two offices in Oak Lawn, one in Hometown and one in Cicero. Incorporated in Delaware in 1992.

Directors (In addition to indicated officers)

James W. Gee, Sr.
Joseph A. Herbert
Robert E. Lawler, D.D.S.

Frank J. Muriello
Albert Rodrigues

Officers (Directors*)

*Lawrence M. Cox, Chm.
*Richard E. Webber, Pres. & C.E.O.
 Robert J. Eckert, V.P.
 Michael J. Gembara, V.P.

Ronald D. Phares, V.P.
Mary A. McNally, Secy.
Robert C. Olson, Compt.
Noralee Goossens, Asst. Secy.

Consolidated Balance Sheet As of December 31, 1994 (000 omitted)

Assets		Liabilities & Stockholders' Equity	
Total cash & cash equivalents	$ 6,831	Deposits	$235,679
Loans receivable	238,103	Borrowed funds	60,375
Mortgage-backed securities, net	32,626	Other liabilities	5,937
Other investments	58,228	*Stockholders' equity	48,409
Other assets	14,612		
Total	$350,400	Total	$350,400

*2,300,719 shares common stock outstanding.

Consolidated Income Statement[a]

Years Ended Dec. 31	Thousands — — — — Total Income	Net Income	Per Share — — — Earnings	Cash Dividends	Common Stock Price Range Calendar Year
1994	$26,125	$6,067	$2.41	$ .25	25 — 19
1993	25,948	6,402	2.39	1.20[b]	22-1/4 — 15-1/4
1992	26,369	5,348	1.89[c]	.00	17-1/4 — 11-1/2[d]
1991	26,382	3,004			
1990	26,427	2,793			

[a]1991-90 financial information is for Southwest Federal Savings and Loan Association, a wholly owned subsidiary of Southwest Bancshares, Inc.
[b]Special dividend.
[c]Pro forma.
[d]Initial public offering in June 1992.

Transfer Agent & Registrar: Harris Trust and Savings Bank

General Counsel:
  Muldoon, Murphy & Faucette

Investor Relations: Ronald D. Phares, V.P.

Human Resources: Robert J. Eckert, V.P.

Mgt. Info. Svcs.: Michael J. Gembara, V.P.

Auditors:
  Cobitz, VandenBerg and Fennessy

Traded (Symbol): NASDAQ (SWBI)
Stockholders: 422
Employees: 101
Annual Meeting: In April

First Chicago Guide

Spiegel, Inc.
3500 Lacey Road, Downers Grove, Illinois 60515-5432
Telephone: (708) 986-8800

Spiegel, Inc., markets wearing apparel, household furnishings, and other general merchandise through catalogs distributed to more than 30-million households throughout the U.S. The company features upscale American designer and brand-name merchandise such as Liz Claiborne, Ralph Lauren, Calvin Klein and Laura Ashley. Spiegel's merchandise is marketed under its own tradenames and trademarks, and under tradenames licensed from others. The company purchases all of its merchandise on the open market from about 7,000 suppliers, selling both domestically produced and imported merchandise. Customers may order merchandise either by calling a toll-free number or mailing an order form located inside the catalog. Telephone orders constitute approximately 93 percent of the total number of the company's orders. Eddie Bauer, a specialty retailer, sells men's and women's casual sportswear, gifts, and outdoor equipment through catalogs and 353 retail stores. Spiegel Holdings, Inc., holds 99.7 percent of the company's Class B voting common stock. Spiegel and its predecessors date back to 1865, and since 1905, Spiegel has operated as a catalog merchandiser. Incorporated in Delaware in 1965.

Directors (In addition to indicated officers)

Michael Otto, Chm.
Thomas Bohlmann
Michael E. Crusemann
Hans-Christoph Fischer
Hans-Jorg Hammer

Horst R. Hansen
Karl-August Hopmann
Peter Muller
Peer Witten

Officers (Directors*)

*John J. Shea, V. Chm., Pres. & C.E.O.
*David C. Moon, Exec. V.P.—Mdse.
*Kenneth A. Bochenski, Sr. V.P.—Oper. & Info. Svcs.
*Harold S. Dahlstrand, Sr. V.P.—Hum. Res.
James J. Broderick, V.P.—Mdse.
Robert E. Conradi, V.P.—Mdse.

Davia L. Kimmey, V.P.—Advert.
Stanley D. Leibowitz, V.P.—Corp. Plan.
Alois J. Lohn, V.P.—Mfg.
Michael R. Moran, V.P., Secy. & Gen. Coun.
James W. Sievers, V.P.—Fin. & C.F.O.
Karl A. Steigerwald, V.P.—Mktg.
John R. Steele, Treas.

Consolidated Balance Sheet As of December 31, 1994 (000 omitted)

Assets		Liabilities & Stockholders' Equity	
Current assets	$1,908,402	Current liabilities	$ 628,346
Net property & equipment	335,103	Long-term debt	1,300,364
Other assets	316,782	Deferred items	52,360
		*Stockholders' equity	579,217
Total	$2,560,287	Total	$2,560,287

*15,065,244 shares Class A non-voting common and 93,141,654 shares Class B voting common stock outstanding.

Consolidated Income Statement

Years Ended Dec. 31	Thousands — — — — Net Sales	Net Income	Per Share[a] — — — — Earnings	Cash Dividends	Common Stock Price Range[ab] Calendar Year
1994	$3,015,985	$25,100	$ .23	$ .20	26-3/4 — 8-3/4
1993	2,596,147	48,705	.47	.20	23-3/8 — 7-3/4
1992	2,218,732	43,224[c]	.42[c]	.18	9 — 5
1991	1,976,308	16,921	.16	.18	10-1/2 — 5-3/8
1990	1,993,428	61,522	.59	.18	13-1/2 — 4-7/8

[a]Adjusted to reflect a 2-for-1 stock split in October 1993.
[b]Class A non-voting common stock only.
[c]Includes a gain to reflect FAS 109, resulting in a cumulative effect of $4,101,000 ($.04 per share).

Transfer Agent & Registrar:	Harris Trust and Savings Bank		
Outside Counsel:	Rooks, Pitts and Poust	Auditors:	KPMG Peat Marwick LLP
Investor Relations:	Deborah L. Koopman, Dir.	Traded (Symbol):	NASDAQ (SPGLA)
Human Resources:	Harold S. Dahlstrand, Sr. V.P.	Stockholders:	11,000
Mgt. Info. Svcs.:	Kenneth A. Bochenski, Sr. V.P.	Employees:	15,000

Sportmart, Inc.

1400 South Wolf Road, Suite 200, Wheeling, Illinois 60090
Telephone: (708) 520-0100

Sportmart, Inc., is a leading sporting goods superstore retailer in the Chicago metropolitan and southern California markets. The company operates 17 superstores in the Chicago metropolitan area, 14 marts in the Los Angeles metropolitan area, 10 marts in the San Francisco area, two marts in the San Diego area, four marts in the Minneapolis metropolitan area, three marts in Seattle, three in Portland, two in Columbus, Ohio, and three in Toronto, Ontario, Canada. The company pioneered the sporting goods superstore concept in 1971. Incorporated in Illinois in 1971; reincorporated in Delaware in 1992.

Directors (In addition to indicated officers)

Charles G. Cooper
Jerome S. Gore

Stuart C. Nathan

Officers (Directors*)

*Larry J. Hochberg, Chm. & C.E.O.
*Sanford Cantor, V. Chm. & Secy.
*Andrew S. Hochberg, Pres.
*John A. Lowenstein, Exec. V.P.—Opers.
Thomas T. Hendrickson, Sr. V.P. & C.F.O.
James D. Peters, Sr. V.P.—Mdse.
Jim Conroy, V.P.—Construction
Joseph A. DeFalco, V.P.—Hum. Res.

Gregory Fix, V.P.—Legal
Michelle K. Garvey, V.P.—MIS
Lawrence R. Job, V.P.—Advertising
Mitchell P. Kahn, V.P.—Real Est./Construction
Jeffrey Matekaitis, V.P.—Mart Planning
Dena McKinley, V.P.—Mdse. Planning &
  Allocation
Stephen Reed, V.P.—Western Reg.

Consolidated Balance Sheet   As of January 29, 1995 (000 omitted)

Assets		Liabilities & Stockholders' Equity	
Current assets	$173,018	Current liabilities	$ 84,240
Net property, plant & equipment	52,509	Long-term debt	25,600
Other assets	1,285	Capitalized lease obligations	5,514
		Deferred items	802
		Other liabilities	3,609
		*Stockholders' equity	107,047
Total	$226,812	Total	$226,812

*10,911,000 shares common stock outstanding.

Consolidated Income Statement

Years Ended Abt. Jan. 31	Thousands — — — — Net Sales	Net Income[b]	Per Share[a] — — — — Earnings[b]	Cash Dividends	Common Stock Price Range[a] Calendar Year
1995	$424,189	$8,935	$ .82		
1994	338,427	7,879	.77	.00	16-1/2 — 9-5/8
1993[c]	250,529	5,362	.60	.00	17-3/4 — 7-1/4
1992[c]	216,043	5,385	.63	.00	19-1/4 — 14-1/4[d]
1991	187,195	2,984			

[a]Adjusted to reflect a 54.4-for-1 stock split in September 1992.
[b]Pro forma. Prior to the offering, the company was an S corporation and not subject to federal (and some state) corporate income taxes. 1993-1991 are adjusted to reflect a pro forma tax provision as if the company were subject to corporate income taxes for such periods.
[c]Restated.
[d]Initial public offering in October 1992.

Transfer Agent & Registrar: LaSalle National Bank

General Counsel: Katten Muchin & Zavis

Investor Relations:
  Thomas T. Hendrickson, Sr. V.P.

Human Resources: Joseph A. DeFalco, V.P.

Mgt. Info. Svcs.:   Michelle K. Garvey, V.P.

Auditors: Coopers & Lybrand L.L.P.

Traded (Symbol):   NASDAQ (SPMT)

Stockholders: 202

Employees: 3,804

Annual Meeting: In June

SPS Transaction Services, Inc.

2500 Lake Cook Road, Riverwoods, Illinois 60015
Telephone: (708) 405-0200

SPS Transaction Services, Inc., is a leader in the rapidly growing transaction processing industry and is one of the largest third-party providers in its two primary businesses, the electronic processing of point-of-sale transactions (predominantly credit card transactions) and the development, implementation, and administration of private label credit card programs. The company develops and provides technology-based systems, including proprietary software, for the cost effective and efficient processing of information generated by a broad range of business transactions. The company operates its business through two wholly owned subsidiaries, SPS Payment Systems, Inc., and Hurley State Bank. SPS Transaction Services, Inc., is a 74 percent-owned subsidiary of Novus Credit Services, Inc., which is a wholly owned subsidiary of Dean Witter, Discover and Co. Incorporated in Delaware in 1991.

Directors   (In addition to indicated officers)

Thomas R. Butler	Mitchell M. Merin
Thomas J. Campbell	Charles F. Moran
Frank T. Cary	Dennie M. Welsh

Officers   (Directors*)

*Philip J. Purcell, Chm.	Robert J. Ferkenhoff, V.P. & Chf. Info. Off.
*Robert L. Wieseneck, Pres. & C.E.O.	Thomas M. Goldstein, V.P.—Fin.
Robert W. Archer, Sr. V.P.—Sales	Larry H. Myatt, V.P.—Mktg. & Prod. Dev.
Richard F. Atkinson, Sr. V.P.—Oper.	Mary Ann Warniment, V.P.—Electronic Info. Svcs.
Russell J. Bonaguidi, V.P. & Cont.	Christine A. Edwards, Secy. & Gen. Coun.
Thomas W. Clarke, V.P.—Network Svcs. Oper.	Birendra Kumar, Treas.
David D. Field, V.P.—Customer Relations	*Thomas C. Schneider, C.F.O.

Consolidated Balance Sheet   As of December 31, 1994 (000 omitted)

Assets		Liabilities & Stockholders' Equity	
Current assets	$706,252	Current liabilities	$591,860
Net property, plant & equipment	12,703	Other liabilities	20,929
Other assets	49,538	*Stockholders' equity	155,704
Total	$768,493	Total	$768,493

*27,062,000 shares common stock outstanding.

Consolidated Income Statement

Years Ended Dec. 31	Thousands — — — — Operating Revenues	Net Income	Per Share[a] — — — Earnings	Cash Dividends	Common Stock Price Range[ab] Calendar Year
1994	$245,802	$37,735	$1.40	$ .00	32-3/8 — 24
1993	205,494	30,648	1.14	.00	35-5/8 — 18-1/8
1992	165,630	19,663	.76	.00	23-1/8 — 8-1/8
1991	128,446	8,608			
1990	94,440	5,821			

[a]Adjusted to reflect a 2-for-1 stock split in November 1994.
[b]Initial public offering in February 1992.

Transfer Agent & Registrar: First Chicago Trust Co. of New York

General Counsel:	Kirkland & Ellis	Auditors:	Deloitte & Touche LLP
Investor Relations:	Larry H. Myatt, V.P.	Traded (Symbol):	NYSE (PAY)
		Stockholders:	3,984
Human Resources:	Larry H. Myatt, V.P.	Employees:	3,480
Mgt. Info. Svcs.:	Robert J. Ferkenhoff, V.P.	Annual Meeting:	In April

SPSS Inc.

444 North Michigan Avenue, Chicago, Illinois 60611-3962
Telephone: (312) 329-2400

SPSS Inc. develops, markets, and supports an integrated line of statistical software products that enable users to effectively bring marketplace and enterprise data to bear on decision-making. The primary users of the company's software are managers and data analysts involved in marketing, quality improvement, scientific research, education, and data reporting in both the public and private sectors. Incorporated in Illinois in 1975; reincorporated in Delaware in 1993.

Directors (In addition to indicated officers)

Guy de Chazal
Bernard Goldstein

Fredric Harman
Merritt Lutz

Officers (Directors*)

*Norman H. Nie, Chm.
*Jack Noonan, Pres. & C.E.O.
 Edward Hamburg, Ph.D., Sr. V.P.—Corp.
 Oper., C.F.O. & Secy.
 Louise Rehling, Sr. V.P.—Prod. Dev.

Mark V. Battaglia, V.P.—Corp. Mktg.
Ian S. Durrell, V.P.—Int'l.
Susan Phelan, V.P.—Domestic Sales & Svcs.

Consolidated Balance Sheet   As of December 31, 1994 (000 omitted)

Assets		Liabilities & Stockholders' Equity	
Current assets	$15,074	Current liabilities	$24,744
Net property, plant & equipment	3,878	Deferred items	2,191
Other assets	12,478	Other liabilities	550
		*Stockholders' equity	3,945
Total	$31,430	Total	$31,430

*6,210,105 shares common stock outstanding.

Consolidated Income Statement[a]

Years Ended Dec. 31	Thousands — — — — Net Revenues	Net Income	Per Share[b] — — — Earnings	Cash Dividends	Common Stock Price Range[b] Calendar Year
1994[c]	$51,757	$ 3,560	$ .55	$ .00	14-1/4 — 8-3/8
1993	42,724	3,209	.67	.00	10-1/8 — 7[d]
1992	37,863	(3,493)[e]	(.91)		
1991	34,592	(1,687)	(.44)		
1990	33,791	(2,683)			

[a]Restated to reflect FAS 109.
[b]Adjusted to reflect a 1-for-3 reverse stock split in August 1993.
[c]Includes $1,928,000 in one-time charges related to the acquisition of SYSTAT, Inc., in September 1994.
[d]Initial public offering in August 1993.
[e]Includes a pretax charge of $3,024,000 related to writeoff of software.

Transfer Agent & Registrar:	Harris Trust and Savings Bank		
General Counsel:	Ross & Hardies	Auditors:	KPMG Peat Marwick LLP
Investor Relations:	Mark V. Battaglia, V.P.	Traded (Symbol):	NASDAQ (SPSS)
		Stockholders:	110
Human Resources:	Theresa Dear	Employees:	414
Mgt. Info. Svcs.:	Rick Goddard	Annual Meeting:	In June

First Chicago Guide

Standard Financial, Inc.

4192 South Archer Avenue, Chicago, Illinois 60632-1890
Telephone: (312) 847-1140

Standard Financial, Inc., is the holding company for Standard Federal Bank for savings. The bank is a community-oriented thrift institution offering a variety of retail financial services to meet the needs of the communities it serves. Its deposit-gathering and lending markets are primarily concentrated in the communities surrounding its full-service offices, located in the southwestern and western parts of the city of Chicago and neighboring suburbs in Cook and DuPage counties, Illinois. In July 1994, the company completed an offering of 18,630,000 shares of common stock in connection with the bank converting to a federal stock savings bank from a federal mutual savings bank. Incorporated in Delaware in 1994.

Directors   (In addition to indicated officers)

Stasys J. Baras
John A. Brdecka
Sharon Reese Dalenberg
Simon P. Gary

Fred V. Gwyer, M.D.
Tomas A. Kisielius, M.D.
George W. Lane
Chester K. McMillen

Officers   (Directors*)

*David H. Mackiewich, Chm., Pres. & C.E.O.
 Thomas C. Halm, Sr. V.P.
 Kurtis D. Mackiewich, Sr. V.P.
*Thomas M. Ryan, Sr. V.P. & C.F.O.

Ruta M. Juska Staniulis, Sr. V.P.
Leonard A. Metheny, V.P. & Secy.
Randall R. Schwartz, V.P. & Gen. Coun.

Consolidated Balance Sheet   As of December 31, 1994 (000 omitted)

Assets		Liabilities & Stockholders' Equity	
Cash & cash equivalents	$ 76,097	Total deposits	$1,392,558
Investment securities	253,604	Advances from FHLB	50,000
Mortgage-backed certificates	759,860	Advance payments by borrowers	6,199
Loans receivable	593,047	for taxes & insur.	
FHLB stock	11,932	Other liabilities	13,947
Property & equipment	28,647	*Stockholders' equity	276,659
Other assets	16,176		
Total	$1,739,363	Total	$1,739,363

*18,630,000 shares common stock outstanding.

Consolidated Income Statement[a]

Years Ended Dec. 31	Thousands — — — — Total Income	Net Income	Per Share — — — Earnings	Cash Dividends	Common Stock Price Range[b] Calendar Year
1994	$104,682	$11,055	$ .37	$ .00	11-3/4 — 9
1993	97,189	3,868			
1992	114,820	10,007			
1991	130,411	8,004			
1990	125,858	6,099			

[a]1993-90 financial information is for Standard Federal Bank for savings.
[b]Initial public offering in July 1994.

Transfer Agent & Registrar: Harris Trust and Savings Bank

General Counsel:	Randall R. Schwartz, V.P.	Auditors:	Ernst & Young LLP
Investor Relations:	Thomas M. Ryan, Sr. V.P.	Traded (Symbol):	NASDAQ (STND)
		Stockholders:	5,317
Human Resources:	Patricia Barrera	Employees:	575
Mgt. Info. Svcs.:	Mark Collins, V.P.	Annual Meeting:	In April

First Chicago Guide

Stepan Company

Edens Expressway and Winnetka Road, Northfield, Illinois 60093
Telephone: (708) 446-7500

Stepan Company is a major manufacturer of basic and intermediate chemicals used in a broad range of industries. Stepan produces surfactants, which are the key ingredient in consumer and industrial cleaning compounds. Manufacturers of detergents, shampoos, lotions, toothpaste, and cosmetics depend on surfactants to achieve the foaming and cleaning qualities required of their products. Stepan also produces germicidal quaternary compounds. Stepan produces other specialty products which are often custom-made to meet individual needs. These include emulsifiers which facilitate spreading of insecticides and herbicides, and lubricant and cutting-oil ingredients. The company also is a principal supplier of phthalic anhydride, a commodity chemical intermediate which is used in polyester resins, alkyd resins, and plasticizers. Polyurethane polyols and foam systems sold by the company are used in the expanding thermal insulation market primarily by the construction and refrigeration industries. Stepan utilizes a North and South American and European network of modern production facilities. Incorporated in Illinois in 1940; reincorporated in Delaware in 1959.

Directors (In addition to indicated officers)

Robert D. Cadieux
Thomas F. Grojean

Robert G. Potter
Paul H. Stepan

Officers (Directors*)

*F. Quinn Stepan, Chm., Pres. & C.E.O.
*James A. Hartlage, Ph.D., Sr. V.P.—Tech. & Oper.
Jeffrey W. Bartlett, V.P., Gen. Coun. & Corp. Secy.
Charles W. Given, V.P. & Gen. Mgr.—Surfactants

Walter J. Klein, V.P.—Fin.
M. Mirghanbari, V.P.—Mfg. & Eng.
Charles P. Riley, Jr., V.P.—Admin. & Reg. Aff.
Ronald L. Siemon, V.P. & Gen. Mgr.—Polymers
Earl H. Wagener, Ph.D., V.P.—R&D

Consolidated Balance Sheet   As of December 31, 1994 (000 omitted)

Assets		Liabilities & Stockholders' Equity	
Current assets	$129,371	Current liabilities	$ 80,456
Net property, plant & equipment	183,657	Long-term debt	89,795
Other assets	11,920	Deferred items	43,395
		*Stockholders' equity	111,302
Total	$324,948	Total	$324,948

*9,944,264 shares common stock outstanding.

Consolidated Income Statement

Years Ended Dec. 31	Thousands — — — — Net Sales	Net Income	Per Share[a] — — — Earnings	Cash Dividends	Common Stock Price Range[a] Calendar Year
1994	$443,948	$13,845	$1.29	$ .43	17-3/4 — 12-3/8
1993	438,825	10,776	.98	.41	18-7/8 — 12-5/8
1992	435,764	15,829[b]	1.46[b]	.37	22-7/8 — 13-1/8
1991	414,069	12,547	1.15	.33	14-7/8 — 10-5/8
1990	389,612	14,491	1.32	.29	13-5/8 — 8-3/8

[a]Adjusted to reflect a 2-for-1 stock split in December 1994.
[b]Includes a gain to reflect FAS 109 and the accounting change related to investment tax credits, resulting in a cumulative effect of $5,406,000 ($.51 per share).

Transfer Agent & Registrar:	Harris Trust and Savings Bank		
General Counsel:	Mayer, Brown & Platt	Traded (Symbol):	AMEX, CSE (SCL)
Investor Relations:	Walter J. Klein, V.P.	Stockholders:	1,792
Human Resources:	Craig O. Gardiner, Dir.	Employees:	1,265
Auditors:	Arthur Andersen LLP	Annual Meeting:	In May

Stimsonite Corporation

7542 Natchez Avenue, Niles, Illinois 60714
Telephone: (708) 647-7717

Stimsonite Corporation is a manufacturer and marketer of reflective highway safety products. The company makes a range of high performance products which are designed to offer enhanced visual guidance to vehicle operators in a variety of driving conditions. These products include: highway delineation products, such as raised reflective pavement markers, construction work zone markers, and roadside and other delineators; highway signing materials, such as high performance reflective sheeting used in the construction of highway signs and Protected Legend pre-printed sign faces; and precision embossed film, which is used in internally illuminated airport runway signs, reflective truck markings, and a variety of other products that require optical grade film. Incorporated in Delaware in 1990.

Directors (In addition to indicated officers)

Edward K. Crawford
Lawrence S. Eagleburger
Donald H. Haider

Edward T. Harvey, Jr.
Anthony R. Ignaczak
Richard J.M. Poulson

Officers (Directors*)

*Terrence D. Daniels, Chm.
*Jay R. Taylor, Pres. & C.E.O.
Robert E. Claude, Exec. V.P.
Michael A. Cherwin, V.P.—Hum. Res.
Richard J. Cisek, V.P.—Int'l. Opers.

Clifford S. Deremo, V.P.—Sales & Mktg.
Charles L. Hulsey, V.P.—Oper.
Robert M. Pricone, V.P.—Eng.
Thomas C. Ratchford, V.P.—Fin., C.F.O., Treas. & Secy.

Consolidated Balance Sheet As of December 31, 1994 (000 omitted)

Assets		Liabilities & Stockholders' Equity	
Current assets	$22,653	Current liabilities	$10,814
Net property, plant & equipment	8,125	Long-term debt	15,523
Other assets	20,158	Other liabilities	631
		*Stockholders' equity	23,968
Total	$50,936	Total	$50,936

*8,903,900 shares common stock outstanding.

Consolidated Income Statement

Years Ended Dec. 31	Thousands — — — — Net Sales	Net Income	Per Share[a] — — — Earnings	Cash Dividends	Common Stock Price Range[a] Calendar Year
1994	$55,941	$ 6,136[b]	$ .68[b]	$ .00	14-1/4 — 9-1/2
1993	45,929	(1,286)[c]	(.17)[c]	.00	11 — 9
1992	39,658	2,110[d]	.28[d]		
1991	28,844	(3,595)	(.48)		
1990[ef]	26,470	(2,897)	(.38)		

[a]Adjusted to reflect a 35-for-1 stock split in December 1993. Initial public offering in December 1993.
[b]Includes an extraordinary charge of $104,000 ($.01 per share).
[c]Includes an extraordinary charge of $3,829,000 ($.50 per share).
[d]Includes a charge of $630,000 ($.08 per share) for an accounting change.
[e]Includes seven months of predecessor operations, $14,529,000 of net sales, and a net loss of $84,000.
[f]Predecessor company. Prior to August 1990, Stimsonite was a division of Amerace Corp.

Transfer Agent & Registrar: LaSalle National Trust, N.A.

General Counsel:		Auditors:	Coopers & Lybrand L.L.P.
Jones, Day, Reavis & Pogue		Traded (Symbol):	NASDAQ (STIM)
Investor Relations:	Thomas C. Ratchford, V.P.	Stockholders:	500
Human Resources:	Michael A. Cherwin, V.P.	Employees:	265
Mgt. Info. Svcs.:	Thomas C. Ratchford, V.P.	Annual Meeting:	In May

Stone Container Corporation

150 North Michigan Avenue, Chicago, Illinois 60601-7568
Telephone: (312) 346-6600

Stone Container Corporation is a vertically integrated producer and seller of commodity paper and packaging products. Products include: kraft linerboard, corrugating medium, kraft paper, newsprint, groundwood paper, market pulp, corrugated containers, folding cartons, paper bags, sacks, flexible packaging, and wood products. Subsidiaries include: Stone-Consolidated Corporation, Stone Container (Canada), Europa Carton AG (Germany), Bridgewater Paper Co. (U.K.), Seminole Kraft Corp., Stone Container International Corp., Stone Savannah River Pulp & Paper Corp., and Stone Forest Industries, Inc. The company, including its subsidiaries and affiliates, maintains manufacturing facilities throughout North America and Europe, and in Australia. Incorporated in Illinois in 1945 to continue a business established in 1926; reincorporated in Delaware in 1987.

Directors (In addition to indicated officers)

Richard A. Giesen
James J. Glasser
Jack M. Greenberg
George D. Kennedy
Howard C. Miller, Jr.
John D. Nichols

Jerry K. Pearlman
Richard J. Raskin
Alan Stone
Avery J. Stone
James H. Stone

Officers (Directors*)

*Roger W. Stone, Chm., Pres. & C.E.O.
Arnold F. Brookstone, Exec. V.P., C.F.O. & C.P.O.
Morty Rosenkranz, Exec. V.P.
John D. Bence, Sr. V.P.—Euro. Pack. Oper.
Thomas W. Cadden, Sr. V.P. & Gen. Mgr.—Ind. & Retail Pkg. Div.
Thomas P. Cutilletta, Sr. V.P. & Corp. Cont.
Gerald M. Freeman, Sr. V.P. & Gen. Mgr.—Forest Prod. Div.

James B. Heider, Sr. V.P. & Gen. Mgr.—Containerbd., Paper & Pulp
*Ira N. Stone, Sr. V.P.—Corp. Mktg., Comm. & Pub. Aff.
Gordon L. Jones, V.P. & Gen. Mgr.—Market Pulp & Export Sales
William J. Klaisle, V.P.—Corp. Dev.
Leslie T. Lederer, V.P., Secy. & Counsel
Michael B. Wheeler, V.P., Treas. & Asst. Secy.
Matthew S. Kaplan, Sr. V.P.—Corrug. Container Div.

Consolidated Balance Sheet As of December 31, 1994 (000 omitted)

Assets		Liabilities & Stockholders' Equity	
Current assets	$1,816,900	Current liabilities	$1,031,500
Net property, plant & equipment	3,359,000	Long-term debt	4,431,900
Other assets	1,829,000	Deferred items	381,400
		Other liabilities	512,000
		*Stockholders' equity	648,100
Total	$7,004,900	Total	$7,004,900

*90,400,000 shares common stock outstanding.

Consolidated Income Statement

Years Ended Dec. 31	Thousands — — — —		Per Share[a] — — —		Common Stock
	Net Sales	Net Income	Earnings[b]	Cash Dividends	Price Range[a] Calendar Year
1994	$5,748,700	$(204,600)	$(2.46)	$ .00	21-1/8 — 9-5/8
1993	5,059,600	(358,700)	(5.15)	.00	19-1/2 — 6-3/8
1992	5,520,700	(269,400)[c]	(3.89)[c]	.35	32 — 12-1/2
1991	5,384,300	(49,100)	(.78)	.71	25-1/2 — 8-7/8
1990	5,755,900	95,400	1.56	.71	25-1/4 — 8-1/8

[a]Adjusted to reflect a 2% stock dividend in September 1992.
[b]Fully diluted.
[c]Restated to reflect adoption of FAS 109 retroactive to January 1, 1992.

Transfer Agent & Registrar: The First National Bank of Chicago

General Counsel:	Leslie T. Lederer, V.P.	Auditors:	Price Waterhouse LLP
Investor Relations:	Arnold F. Brookstone, Exec. V.P.	Traded (Symbol):	NYSE (STO)
		Stockholders:	6,900
Human Resources:	Gayle M. Sparapani, Staff. V.P.	Employees:	29,100
Mgt. Info. Svcs.:	Joseph P. Thompson, Staff. V.P.	Annual Meeting:	Second Tuesday in May

SuburbFed Financial Corp.

3301 West Vollmer Road, Flossmoor, Illinois 60422-2093
Telephone: (708) 333-2200

SuburbFed Financial Corp. is the holding company for Suburban Federal Savings, A Federal Savings Bank. Suburban Federal's offices are located throughout the southern, southwestern, and western Chicago metropolitan area and in Dyer, Indiana. Its deposits are insured up to applicable limits by the Federal Deposit Insurance Corporation. The savings bank is principally engaged in the business of attracting deposits from the general public and using such deposits to originate residential mortgage and, to a lesser extent, consumer, construction or development, non-residential real estate, and multi-family loans. Suburban Federal also invests in mortgage-backed and investment securities and makes deposits in other financial institutions. Incorporated in Delaware in 1991.

Directors (In addition to indicated officers)

Robert L. Harris
Bruce E. Huey
Raymond J. Kalinsky
Wilbur L. Morrison

William E. Ricketts, M.D.
August R. Rump
Alan Wischhover
Robert E. Zell

Officers (Directors*)

*Vernon P. Vollbrecht, Chm.
*Daniel P. Ryan, V. Chm., Pres. & C.E.O.
Byron G. Thoren, Exec. V.P. & C.O.O.
Peter A. Ruhl, Sr. V.P.—Lending & Savings

Steven E. Stock, Sr. V.P., C.F.O. & Treas.
Lester J. Wolf, Sr. V.P.—Hum. Res. & Mktg.
Lisa F. Morris, Asst. V.P.
Lynn M. Nevills, Corp. Secy.

Consolidated Balance Sheet As of December 31, 1994 (000 omitted)

Assets		Liabilities & Stockholders' Equity	
Total cash & cash equivalents	$ 9,448	Deposits	$256,669
Loans receivable, net	105,630	Total borrowings	39,623
Mortgage-backed securities	188,313	Other liabilities	4,083
Investment securities	11,778	*Stockholders' equity	22,882
Other assets	8,088		
Total	$323,257	Total	$323,257

*901,235 shares common stock outstanding.

Consolidated Income Statement

Years Ended Dec. 31	Thousands — — — — Total Income	Net Income	Per Share — — — Earnings	Cash Dividends	Common Stock Price Range Calendar Year
1994	$22,064	$1,939	$2.07	$ .44	25-3/4 — 19-1/2
1993	20,913	2,291	2.47	.39	23 — 16-1/2
1992	22,218	1,707	1.89	.18	17-1/4 — 10[a]
1991	20,011	354	N/A		
1990	17,899	384	N/A		

[a]Initial public offering in February 1992. Financial data for 1991-90 are for Suburban Federal Savings, A Federal Savings Bank.

Transfer Agent & Registrar: American Stock Transfer & Trust Co.

General Counsel:
  Silver, Freedman & Taff, L.L.P.

Investor Relations: Lisa F. Morris, Asst. V.P.

Human Resources: Lester J. Wolf, Sr. V.P.

Mgt. Info. Svcs.:   Ronald H. LeClaire, V.P.

Auditors:
  Cobitz, VandenBerg & Fennessy

Traded (Symbol):   NASDAQ (SFSB)
Stockholders: 579
Employees: 175
Annual Meeting: In April

Sundance Homes, Inc.

1375 East Woodfield Road, Suite 600, Schaumburg, Illinois 60173
Telephone: (708) 255-5555

Sundance Homes, Inc., is a builder of affordably priced, single-family homes in the Chicago metropolitan area. The company currently offers diverse product lines of single-family homes within each project, with a variety of front elevations and architectural designs that complement each other and create a sense of community within the project. Incorporated in Illinois in 1981.

Directors   (In addition to indicated officers)

Dennis S. Bookshester
Charles Engles

Gerald Ginsburg

Officers   (Directors*)

*Maurice Sanderman, Chm., Pres. & C.E.O.
*Daniel J. O'Brien, Sr. V.P. & C.F.O.
Vincent Deligio, V.P.—Construction
Robert Hinz, V.P. & Cont.
Caren Holland, V.P.—Contracts
Kalman Rowen, V.P.—Land Acquis.

*Michael Schall, V.P.—Mktg. & Sales
Thomas Small, V.P.—Land Dev.
Linda Spinelli, V.P.—Purch.
Arthur Titus, V.P.—C.O.O.
David Apter, Corp. Secy.

Consolidated Balance Sheet   As of December 31, 1994 (000 omitted)

Assets		Liabilities & Stockholders' Equity	
Cash & equivalents	$ 5,096	Current liabilities	$66,489
Real estate inventories	86,721	Minority interest	1,049
Prepaid expenses & other assets	881	*Stockholders' equity	31,369
Net property, plant & equipment	2,688		
Other assets	3,521		
Total	$98,907	Total	$98,907

*7,805,000 shares common stock outstanding.

Consolidated Income Statement

Years Ended Dec. 31	Thousands — — — — Residential Sales	Net Income[c]	Per Share[a] — — — Earnings[c]	Cash Dividends	Common Stock Price Range[ab] Calendar Year
1994	$118,659	$1,930	$ .25	$ .00	12-3/4 — 1-7/8
1993	77,764	4,709	.76	.00	14-1/2 — 8
1992	86,208	5,010	1.00		
1991	29,444	24			
1990	42,960	565			

[a]Adjusted to reflect a 4,700-for-1 stock split in July 1993.
[b]Initial public offering in July 1993.
[c]Unaudited pro forma, 1993-90, based on historical net income, as adjusted to reflect a provision for income taxes, as if the company had been a C corporation since inception.

Transfer Agent & Registrar: LaSalle National Trust, N.A.

General Counsel:	Katten Muchin & Zavis	Traded (Symbol):	NASDAQ (SUNH)
Investor Relations:	Daniel J. O'Brien, Sr. V.P.	Stockholders:	650
Human Resources:	Karen Chamberlain	Employees:	140
Auditors:	Price Waterhouse LLP	Annual Meeting:	In May

First Chicago Guide

Sundstrand Corporation

4949 Harrison Avenue, P.O. Box 7003, Rockford, Illinois 61125-7003
Telephone: (815) 226-6000

Sundstrand Corporation designs, manufactures, and sells a variety of proprietary, technology-based components and systems requiring significant research, development engineering, and processing expertise. The company is divided into two segments: aerospace and industrial. Systems and components for aerospace applications include: electrical power generating systems; constant speed drives; variable speed constant frequency systems; high power semiconductors; engine fuel and lubricating systems; actuation systems; pneumatic systems; and turbopower systems. Products in the industrial segment include: hydrostatic transmissions; hydromechanical transmissions and hydraulic equipment for agricultural, construction, and material-handling equipment; a comprehensive line of gear drives and flexible couplings; high-speed pumps, blowers, and compressors; and rotary screw air and gas compressors. Major subsidiaries include: Falk Corp.; Sullair Corp; and Milton Roy Company. Incorporated in Illinois in 1910; reincorporated in Delaware in 1966.

Directors (In addition to indicated officers)

J.P. Bolduc
Gerald Grinstein
Charles Marshall
Klaus H. Murmann

Donald E. Nordlund
Thomas G. Pownall
John A. Puelicher
Ward Smith

Officers (Directors*)

*Don R. O'Hare, Chm. & C.E.O.
Paul Donovan, Exec. V.P. & C.F.O.
*Robert J. Smuland, Exec. V.P. &
  C.O.O.—Aerospace
Patrick L. Thomas, Exec. V.P. &
  C.O.O.—Industrial

*Berger G. Wallin, Exec. V.P.—Spec. Projects
DeWayne J. Fellows, V.P. & Cont.
James F. Ricketts, V.P. & Treas.
Richard M. Schilling, V.P., Gen. Coun. & Secy.

Consolidated Balance Sheet   As of December 31, 1994 (000 omitted)

Assets		Liabilities & Stockholders' Equity	
Current assets	$ 735,200	Current liabilities	$ 431,900
Net property, plant & equipment	459,100	Long-term debt	235,700
Other assets	392,600	Accrued postretire. benefits other than pensions	356,800
		Other liabilities	68,700
		*Stockholders' equity	493,800
Total	$1,586,900	Total	$1,586,900

*31,635,971 shares common stock outstanding.

Consolidated Income Statement

Years Ended Dec. 31	Thousands — — — — Net Sales	Net Income	Per Share[a] — — — Earnings	Cash Dividends	Common Stock Price Range[a] Calendar Year	
1994[b]	$1,372,700	$ 95,600	$ 2.92	$1.20	52	— 41
1993[c]	1,383,100	140,700	3.97	1.20	44-3/4	— 35
1992[de]	1,479,100	(121,700)	(3.37)	1.18	47-1/4	— 31-1/8
1991[d]	1,453,900	108,800	3.02	1.10	37	— 23-3/8
1990[d]	1,380,900	114,300	3.11	1.10	40	— 21-3/4

[a]Adjusted to reflect a 2-for-1 stock split in June 1990.
[b]Includes a reduction of depreciation expense related to a change in depreciable lives of $5,500,000 after taxes ($.17 per share).
[c]Includes a gain of $55,700,000 after taxes ($1.57 per share) on the sale of the Data Control business.
[d]Restated to reflect the Data Control business, sold in 1993, as a discontinued operation.
[e]Includes charges of $24,200,000 after tax ($.67 per share) for restructuring of and reduction in employment in the aerospace segment; and charges of $217,500,000 after tax ($6.03 per share) for adoption of FAS 106.

Transfer Agent & Registrar:	Harris Trust and Savings Bank		
General Counsel:	Richard M. Schilling, V.P.	Traded (Symbol):	CSE, NYSE, PSE (SNS)
Investor Relations:	Craig Watson, Dir.	Stockholders:	4,000
Human Resources:	Paul Donovan, Exec. V.P.	Employees:	9,200
Auditors:	Ernst & Young LLP	Annual Meeting:	In April

System Software Associates, Inc.

500 West Madison Street, 32nd Floor, Chicago, Illinois 60661
Telephone: (312) 641-2900

System Software Associates, Inc. (SSA), provides open client/server business-process integration across all operations, including R&D, finance, manufacturing, facilities management, sales and distribution. SSA markets four product lines that run on the IBM AS/400, Unix-based IBM RS/6000, and Hewlett-Packard HP 9000 business systems: BPCS/AS (Business Planning and Control System/Advanced Solution), which includes more than 50 applications for world-class operational processes, such as JIT (just-in-time), TQM (total quality management) and electronic commerce; EDI/SET (Electronic Data Interchange/Software Enabling Technology), which allows businesses to communicate electronically with trading partners through wide-area networks following international and industry-specific EDI standards; Main/Tracker, which automates the planning and control of all equipment and facilities maintenance, safety inspections, and warranty tracking; and AS/SET, which is open CASE (computer-aided systems engineering) technology that simplifies and speeds application development and allows clients to build mission-critical client/server applications. More than 5,000 professionals globally provide support for clients. With offices and business affiliates in 67 countries, SSA provides companies with global coordination. With more than 150 affiliates, country operations provide a full array of services in all major markets, including Brazil, Mexico, Argentina, Italy, France, Spain, Germany, the Netherlands, the United Kingdom, Australia, Singapore, Japan, and China. SSA products are translated into 20 languages. Incorporated in Illinois in 1981; reincorporated in Delaware in 1985.

Directors   (In addition to indicated officers)

Warren J. Hayford
John W. Puth

William N. Weaver, Jr.

Officers   (Directors*)

*Roger E. Covey, Chm. & C.E.O.
*Larry J. Ford, V. Chm.
 Terence H. Osborne, Pres. & C.O.O.
 James Franch, V.P.—Tech.

Terry E. Notari, V.P.—N. Amer.
Joseph J. Skadra, V.P. & C.F.O.
Adam Bartkowski, Area V.P.—Prods.
Martin Taylor-Smith, Area V.P.—Client Services

Consolidated Balance Sheet   As of October 31, 1994 (000 omitted)

Assets		Liabilities & Stockholders' Equity	
Current assets	$237,700	Current liabilities	$145,000
Net property, plant & equipment	27,600	Deferred revenue	30,300
Other assets	67,900	Deferred income taxes	8,600
		Other long-term obligations	32,700
		Other liabilities	1,900
		*Stockholders' equity	114,700
Total	$333,200	Total	$333,200

*26,994,000 shares common stock outstanding.

Consolidated Income Statement

Years Ended Oct. 31	Thousands — — — — Total Revenues	Net Income	Per Share[a] — — — — Earnings	Cash Dividends	Common Stock Price Range[a] Calendar Year
1994	$334,400	$15,400	$ .57	$ .12	18 — 10-5/8
1993	263,400	23,400	.86	.12	25-1/2 — 10
1992	228,800	26,600	.99	.12	25-3/8 — 11-7/8
1991[b]	146,000	15,400	.58	.11	16-1/2 — 5-1/2
1990	108,500	8,800	.33	.00	12-3/4 — 5-5/8

[a]Adjusted to reflect 3-for-2 stock splits in December 1992, December 1991, and January 1990.
[b]Financial information for fiscal 1991 and prior was restated to reflect the adoption of Statement of Position 91-1.

Transfer Agent & Registrar: The First National Bank of Chicago

General Counsel: Kirk Isaacson

Investor Relations: Joseph J. Skadra, V.P.

Human Resources: Rick Steel, Dir.

Mgt. Info. Svcs.:   John Norenberg

Auditors: Price Waterhouse LLP
Traded (Symbol):   NASDAQ (SSAX)
Stockholders: 560
Employees: 1,800
Annual Meeting: In March

Technology Solutions Company

205 North Michigan Avenue, Suite 1500, Chicago, Illinois 60601
Telephone: (312) 819-2250

Technology Solutions Company (TSC) provides business benefits to corporations through the application of computer technology. TSC offers a comprehensive package of the services and resources necessary to design, develop, and implement major computer systems. TSC addresses the entire spectrum of systems development, including feasibility studies, business case justification, project management, logical and physical systems design, hardware and software selection, programming, application and foundation software development, implementation change management and training, and benefits realization. TSC focuses exclusively on systems consulting and implementation, offering a comprehensive package of services and resources relating thereto and emphasizing active project involvement of its senior project managers. TSC currently has more than 250 systems professionals serving six practice areas: Financial Services, Products-East, Products-Central, Call Center, Managed Health Care, and Applications and Training. TSC's services are provided primarily to large corporate clients that require effectively integrated information systems to better operate their businesses. In addition to its Chicago office, the company maintains offices in the New York, Los Angeles, Dallas, and Atlanta metropolitan areas. Incorporated in Delaware in 1988.

Directors (In addition to indicated officer)

Jeffrey T. Chambers
Michael J. Murray

Stephen B. Oresman
John R. Purcell

Officers (Director*)

*William H. Waltrip, Chm.
John T. Kohler, Pres., C.E.O. & C.O.O.
James S. Carluccio, Exec. V.P.
Kelly D. Conway, Sr. V.P.
Jack N. Hayden, Sr. V.P.

Robert J. Hoyt, Sr. V.P.
Emmett H. Zahn, Sr. V.P.
Diann Bilderback, V.P.—Mktg. & Comm.
Martin "Tork" Johnson, V.P. & C.F.O.
Paul R. Peterson, V.P., Gen. Coun. & Secy.

Consolidated Balance Sheet As of May 31, 1994 (000 omitted)

Assets		Liabilities & Stockholders' Equity	
Current assets	$41,838	Current liabilities	$15,240
Net property, plant & equipment	2,687	*Stockholders' equity	54,100
Other assets	24,815		
Total	$69,340	Total	$69,340

*9,751,929 shares common stock outstanding.

Consolidated Income Statement

Years Ended May 31	Thousands — — — — Total Revenues	Net Income	Per Share[a] — — — Earnings	Cash Dividends	Common Stock Price Range[a] Calendar Year
1994	$53,157	$ 35	$ .00	$ .00	9-1/4 — 4-3/4
1993	62,475	5,706	.46	.00	15 — 7
1992	70,987	12,059	1.01	.00	30-3/4 — 6-3/4
1991	52,439	8,469	.81	.00	25-3/4 — 15[b]
1990	43,869	3,238	.31		

[a]Adjusted to reflect a 125-for-1 stock split in June 1991.
[b]Initial public offering in September 1991.

Transfer Agent & Registrar: Mellon Securities Transfer Services

General Counsel:	Sidley & Austin	Auditors:	Price Waterhouse LLP
Investor Relations:	Martin "Tork" Johnson, V.P.	Traded (Symbol):	NASDAQ (TSCC)
		Stockholders:	160
Human Resources:	Jackie Hilt	Employees:	274
Mgt. Info. Svcs.:	Dave Glogowski	Annual Meeting:	In September

Telephone and Data Systems, Inc.

30 North LaSalle Street, Suite 4000, Chicago, Illinois 60602-2507
Telephone: (312) 630-1900

Telephone and Data Systems, Inc. (TDS), is a diversified telecommunications company. As of December 31, 1994, TDS Telecommunications Corporation, a subsidiary, operated 96 telephone companies serving 392,500 access lines in 29 states. These states comprise three TDS operating regions: Northeast, Southeast, and Central. United States Cellular Corp., a subsidiary that owns or has the rights to acquire cellular interests representing about 25.2-million population equivalents, had its initial public offering in May 1988. American Paging, Inc., a paging subsidiary, which operates 17 customer operations centers and serves 652,800 units, had its initial public offering in February 1994. Other subsidiaries include: TDS Computing Services, Inc., a systems development, data processing, and education services company; Suttle Press, Inc., a custom printing company; Integrated Communications Services, Inc.; and American Portable Telecommunications Inc., a personal communications company. In 1994, the company announced the following telephone acquisitions: Arvig Telephone Co., Bridge Water Telephone Co., and McDaniel Telephone Co. Incorporated in Iowa in 1968.

Directors (In addition to indicated officers)

James Barr III
Donald R. Brown
Walter C.D. Carlson
Robert J. Collins

Lester O. Johnson
Donald C. Nebergall
Herbert S. Wander

Officers (Directors*)

*LeRoy T. Carlson, Chm.
*LeRoy T. Carlson, Jr., Pres. & C.E.O.
*Murray L. Swanson, Exec. V.P.—Fin. & C.F.O.
Michael K. Chesney, V.P.—Corp. Dev.
George L. Dienes, V.P.—Corp. Dev.
C. Theodore Herbert, V.P.—Hum. Res.
*Rudolph E. Hornacek, V.P.—Eng.
Ronald D. Webster, V.P. & Treas.

Byron A. Wertz, V.P.—Corp. Dev.
Gregory J. Wilkinson, V.P. & Cont.
Michael G. Hron, Secy.
William S. DeCarlo, Asst. Secy.
Ross J. McVey, Asst. Cont. & Dir.—Tax
Karen M. Stewart, Asst. Cont.—External Rept.
James W. Twesme, Asst. Treas.
Joyce M. Zeasman, Asst. Cont.—Corp. Reengineering

Consolidated Balance Sheet   As of December 31, 1994 (000 omitted)

Assets		Liabilities & Stockholders' Equity	
Current assets	$ 185,918	Current liabilities	$ 346,184
Net property, plant & equipment	2,153,575	Long-term debt	536,509
Other assets	450,634	Deferred credits	119,076
		Preferred stock & minority interests	315,320
		*Common stockholders' equity	1,473,038
Total	$2,790,127	Total	$2,790,127

*47,937,570 shares common and 6,886,684 shares Series A common stock outstanding.

Consolidated Income Statement

Years Ended Dec. 31	Thousands — — — — Operating Revenues[a]	Net Income	Per Share — — — — Earnings	Cash Dividends	Common Stock Price Range Calendar Year
1994	$730,810	$60,544[b]	$1.07[b]	$ .36	51-1/2 — 35-1/2
1993	557,795	33,896	.67	.34	57 — 33-1/4
1992	432,740	38,520[b]	.91[b]	.32	41-1/4 — 30-1/8
1991	340,160	21,113[b]	.59[b]	.30	40-3/8 — 28-1/2
1990	286,743	27,208	.86	.28	48 — 21-3/4

[a]Prior years have been restated to conform with the 1994 presentation.
[b]Before extraordinary charge of $769,000 ($.02 per share) in 1992; and charges of $723,000 ($.01 per share) in 1994 to reflect the cumulative effect of FAS 112; of $6,866,000 ($.17 per share) in 1992 to reflect FAS 106; and of $5,035,000 ($.15 per share) in 1991 to reflect an accounting change.

Transfer Agent:	Harris Trust and Savings Bank		
General Counsel:	Sidley & Austin	Traded (Symbol):	AMEX (TDS)
Investor Relations:	Julie Matthews, Coord.	Stockholders:	4,266
Human Resources:	C. Theodore Herbert, V.P.	Employees:	5,322
Auditors:	Arthur Andersen LLP	Annual Meeting:	In May

First Chicago Guide

Tellabs, Inc.

4951 Indiana Avenue, Lisle, Illinois 60532-1698
Telephone: (708) 969-8800

Tellabs, Inc., designs, manufactures, markets, and services voice and data transport and network access systems used in public and private communication networks worldwide. Customers include public telephone companies, long-distance carriers, government agencies, business end-users, alternate service providers, cellular and other wire service providers, cable operators, and original equipment manufacturers. The company has 30 locations in the U.S., Canada, Great Britain, Hong Kong, Belgium, Ireland, Finland, Korea, Mexico, New Zealand, Australia, and the U.S. Virgin Islands. Major subsidiaries include: Tellabs Operations, Inc., Telecommunications Laboratories, Inc., Tellabs International, Inc., Martis Oy, and Tellabs Mexico, Inc. Incorporated in Delaware in 1992.

Directors (In addition to indicated officers)

John D. Foulkes, Ph.D.
Frederick A. Krehbiel
Robert P. Reuss

William F. Souders
Thomas H. Thompson

Officers (Directors*)

*Michael J. Birck, Pres. & C.E.O
*Peter A. Guglielmi, Exec.
 V.P.,C.F.O.,Secy.,Treas. & Pres.—T. Int'l.
*Brian J. Jackman, Exec. V.P. &
 Pres.—Tellabs Oper.
Charles C. Cooney, V.P.—Sales & Service
Carol C. Gavin, V.P. & Gen. Coun.
Jon C. Grimes, V.P. & Gen. Mgr.—Network
 Access Systems Div.

James Peter Johnson, V.P.—Fin. & Treas.
John C. Kohler, V.P.—Manuf.
James L. Melsa, Ph.D., V.P.—Strategic Qual. &
 Proc. Mgt.
Harvey R. Scull, V.P.—Advanced Tech.
Richard T. Taylor, V.P.—Digital Syst.
Jeffrey J. Wake, V.P.—Int'l.
Nicholas J. Williams, V.P.—Int'l.

Consolidated Balance Sheet As of December 30, 1994 (000 omitted)

Assets		Liabilities & Stockholders' Equity	
Current assets	$220,556	Current liabilities	$ 82,239
Net property, plant & equipment	97,631	Long-term debt	2,850
Other assets	71,880	Deferred income taxes	1,772
		Other liabilities	10,416
		*Stockholders' equity	292,790
Total	$390,067	Total	$390,067

*43,644,346 shares common stock outstanding.

Consolidated Income Statement

Years Ended Abt. Dec. 31	Thousands — — — — Net Sales	Net Income	Per Share[a] — — — Earnings	Cash Dividends	Common Stock Price Range[a] Calendar Year
1994	$494,153	$72,389	$ .80	$ .00	28 — 10-7/8
1993	320,463	31,967	.36	.00	13-5/8 — 3-1/8
1992	258,560	16,854	.20	.00	4-3/8 — 2-5/8
1991	212,751	6,631	.08	.00	3-5/8 — 2-1/8
1990	211,046	8,102	.11	.00	2-5/8 — 1-3/8

[a]Adjusted to reflect 2-for-1 stock splits in the form of 100% stock dividends in May 1995 and May 1994, and a 3-for-2 stock split in the form of a 50% stock dividend effective in November 1993.

Transfer Agent & Registrar: Harris Trust and Savings Bank

Outside Counsel:
 Vedder, Price, Kaufman & Kammholz
Investor Relations: Carol C. Gavin, V.P.
Mgt. Info. Svcs.: James Peter Johnson, V.P.
Auditors: Grant Thornton LLP

Traded (Symbol): NASDAQ (TLAB)
Stockholders: 1,832
Employees: 2,585
Annual Meeting: In April

Teltrend Inc.

620 Stetson Avenue, St. Charles, Illinois 60174
Telephone: (708) 377-1700

Teltrend Inc. designs, manufactures, and markets a broad range of transmission products, such as channel units, repeaters, and termination units, used by telephone companies to provide voice and data services over the telephone network. Substantially all of the company's products are sold directly to the Regional Bell Operating Companies and their local affiliates for use with copper wireline in the local telephone subscriber loop. In June 1995, the company completed an initial public offering of 3,250,000 shares of common stock. Incorporated in Delaware in 1987.

Directors (In addition to indicated officers)

Carl M. Mueller, Chm.

Frank T. Cary

Officers (Directors*)

*Howard L. Kirby, Jr., Pres. & C.E.O.
Donald G. Bozeman, V.P.—Mktg.
Michael S. Grzeskowiak, V.P.—Opers.
Douglas P. Hoffmeyer, V.P.—Fin., Secy. & Treas.
Gilbert H. Hosie, V.P.—Sales

Laurence L. Sheets, V.P.—Eng.
*Henry F. Skelsey, V.P., Asst. Secy. & Asst. Treas.
Norman C. Guenther, Asst. V.P.—Quality
Theodor A. Maxeiner, Cont, Asst. Secy. & Asst. Treas.

Consolidated Balance Sheet[a]   As of January 28, 1995 (000 omitted)

Assets		Liabilities & Stockholders' Equity	
Current assets	$15,914	Current liabilities	$10,040
Net property, plant & equipment	3,252	Long-term debt	3,057
Other assets	222	*Stockholders' equity	6,291
Total	$19,388	Total	$19,388

[a]Unaudited pro forma.
*5,431,542 shares common and 125,074 shares Class A common stock outstanding.

Consolidated Income Statement

Years Ended Abt. July 31	Thousands — — — — Net Sales	Net Income	Per Share — — — Earnings	Cash Dividends	Common Stock Price Range[a] Calendar Year
1994[b]	$49,454	$ 3,580	$ .64		
1993	39,365	(3,307)			
1992	28,994	(54,945)			
1991	35,120	(5,160)			
1990	43,735	(4,741)			

[a]Initial public offering in June 1995.
[b]Unaudited pro forma.

Transfer Agent & Registrar: LaSalle National Trust, N.A.

General Counsel:	Jenner & Block	Auditors:	Ernst & Young LLP
Investor Relations:	Douglas P. Hoffmeyer, V.P.	Traded (Symbol):	NASDAQ (TLTN)
Human Resources:	Lucy Golding	Stockholders:	N/A
		Employees:	293
Mgt. Info. Svcs.:	Cindy Feldman	Annual Meeting:	As set by Directors

Telular Corporation

920 Deerfield Parkway, Buffalo Grove, Illinois 60089
Telephone: (708) 465-4500

Telular Corporation is a leader in the fixed wireless telecommunications equipment industry. The company designs, develops, manufactures, and markets products based on its proprietary interface technology, which provides the capability to bridge wireless telecommunications customer premises equipment and wireless communications networks, whether cellular, ESMR, PCS or satellite-based. Subsidiaries are Telular International, Inc., and Adcor-Telular Security Products, Inc. The company was formerly known as The Telular Group L.P., a limited partnership established in May 1992. On May 13, 1993, Telular Corporation entered into various agreements whereby all of the outstanding partnership interests in The Telular Group L.P. were exchanged for shares of common stock. In January 1994, Telular Corporation completed an initial public offering of 4,000,000 shares of common stock. Incorporated in Delaware in 1993.

Directors (In addition to indicated officers)

Joel J. Bellows
John A. Blanchard III
Robert B. Blow
Larry J. Ford

Brian R. Groh
Rick Hanning
David P. Mixer
William E. Spencer

Officers (Directors*)

*William L. DeNicolo, Chm.
*Richard T. Gerstner, Pres. & C.E.O.
Rodney J. Puleo, Sr. V.P.
Michael J. Quinlan, Sr. V.P.—Mktg. & Sales
Daniel O. Wagster, Sr. V.P. & C.F.O.
John R. Wilkins, Jr., Sr. V.P.—Mfg. & Dev.

Stephen P. Wolfe, Sr. V.P.
George Claudio, Jr., V.P.—Tech.
Loretta Elliott, V.P.—Corp. Strategy
Patrick L. Murtha, V.P.—Dev.
Timothy L. Walsh, Treas. & Compt.

Consolidated Balance Sheet   As of September 30, 1994 (000 omitted)

Assets		Liabilities & Stockholders' Equity	
Current assets	$50,995	Current liabilities	$ 4,924
Net property, plant & equipment	3,984	*Stockholders' equity	56,318
Other assets	6,263		
Total	$61,242	Total	$61,242

*23,167,104 shares common stock outstanding.

Consolidated Income Statement

Years Ended Sept. 30	Thousands — — — — — Net Sales	Net Income	Per Share[a] — — — — Earnings	Cash Dividends	Common Stock Price Range[ab] Calendar Year
1994	$17,734	$(27,933)	$(1.25)[c]	$ .00	24-1/2 — 6
1993[d]	6,575	(3,708)	(.18)[c]		
1992[e]	3,032	(1,552)			

[a]Adjusted to reflect a 14-for-1 stock split in January 1994.
[b]Initial public offering in January 1994.
[c]Pro forma.
[d]Nine months ending September 30. Includes results of The Telular Group L.P. for the period from January 1 to May 13, 1993, and thereafter the results of the company, which has selected a fiscal yearend of September 30.
[e]Unaudited pro forma data give effect to the formation of The Telular Group L.P. and the combination of the operations of the limited partnership with the predecessor as if the limited partnership had been formed on January 1, 1992.

Transfer Agent & Registrar: Harris Trust and Savings Bank

General Counsel:	Bellows & Bellows	Auditors:	Ernst & Young LLP
Investor Relations:	Steve McConnell, Mgr.	Traded (Symbol):	NASDAQ (WRLS)
		Stockholders:	4,600
Human Resources:	Sheryl Eskenazi, Dir.	Employees:	250
Mgt. Info. Svcs.:	Timothy Andeen, Dir.	Annual Meeting:	In January

Titan Wheel International, Inc.

2701 Spruce Street, Quincy, Illinois 62301
Telephone: (217) 228-6011

Titan Wheel International, Inc., is a leading manufacturer of steel wheels and rims for off-highway vehicles used in the agriculture, construction, military, and grounds care markets, and complete wheel and tire assemblies for the recreation and mining markets. Additionally, with the August 1994 acquisition of Titan Tire Corporation (formerly Pirelli-Armstrong Tire Corp.'s Des Moines, Iowa, plant), Titan has become a leading manufacturer of tires for the agriculture market. Other recent acquisitions for the company include the Titan Wheel—Specialty Wheel Division, a specialty wheel manufacturing facility in Greenwood, South Carolina; Nieman's Ltd., a distribution facility; Lemmerz UK Limited (renamed Steel Wheels, Ltd.), an off-road and specialty wheel manufacturing facility in Kidderminster, England; and the SIRMAC group of companies of Italy (including SIRMAC, SIRIA and AGM), a major European earthmoving/construction wheels, specialty truck wheels, and gear manufacturer. Additional subsidiaries of Titan Wheel include Automation International Inc. of Danville, Illinois; Automotive Wheels Inc. of Brea, California; Dico Inc. of Des Moines, Iowa; Dico Tire of Clinton, Tennessee; Dico Inc. of Slinger, Wisconsin; Nieman's Ltd. of Ventura, Iowa; TD Wheel Company of Saltville, Virginia; Titan Wheel of Walcott, Iowa; Titan Wheel of Merseyside, England; Tractech of Warren, Michigan; and Tractech Ltd. of Sligo, Ireland. The company also operates seven other distribution facilities throughout the U.S. Incorporated in Illinois in 1983.

Directors   (In addition to indicated officer)

Erwin H. Billig
Edward J. Campbell
Richard M. Cashin, Jr.

Albert J. Febbo
Anthony L. Soave

Officers   (Director*)

*Maurice M. Taylor, Jr., Pres. & C.E.O.
 Kent W. Hackamack, Treas.

Cheri T. Holley, Secy.
Michael R. Samide, C.O.O.

Consolidated Balance Sheet   As of December 31, 1994 (000 omitted)

Assets		Liabilities & Stockholders' Equity	
Current assets	$192,358	Current liabilities	$ 72,396
Net property, plant & equipment	143,323	Long-term debt	178,341
Other assets	64,779	Deferred income taxes	10,778
		Other liabilities	31,209
		*Stockholders' equity	107,736
Total	$400,460	Total	$400,460

*7,233,464 shares common stock outstanding.

Consolidated Income Statement

Years Ended Dec. 31	Thousands — — — — Net Sales	Net Income	Per Share[a] — — — Earnings	Cash Dividends	Common Stock Price Range[a] Calendar Year
1994	$407,000	$ 18,480	$ 1.71	$ .04	20-1/2 — 14-1/2
1993	150,441	6,361	.69	.02	17-3/8 — 10
1992	113,170	4,072[b]	.31[b]		
1991	100,054	(3,616)	(.28)		
1990	103,854	4,189	.33		

[a]Adjusted to reflect a 3-for-2 stock split in March 1995 and an 858-for-1 stock split in March 1993. Initial public offering in May 1993.
[b]Net income before an extraordinary charge of $258,000 ($.03 per share) and for FAS 109, resulting in a charge of $275,000 ($.04 per share).

Transfer Agent & Registrar: Harris Trust and Savings Bank

General Counsel:
  Schmiedeskamp, Robertson, Neu & Mitchell

Investor Relations: Jennifer Ryan Swartz

Human Resources: Henry Washington

Auditors: Price Waterhouse LLP

Traded (Symbol):   NYSE (TWI)

Stockholders: 750

Employees: 5,000

Annual Meeting: In May

TNT Freightways Corporation

9700 Higgins Road, Suite 570, Rosemont, Illinois 60018
Telephone: (708) 696-0200

TNT Freightways Corporation operates a group of regional less-than-truckload (LTL) general commodities motor carriers — or carriers that fill their trucks with partial loads from multiple customers. The company's regional trucking subsidiaries focus on overnight and second-day delivery and provide service throughout the United States and Puerto Rico, and to certain points in Canada. The company also operates logistics subsidiaries which provide complete solutions to customers' logistics and distribution requirements. The company's largest subsidiary is TNT Holland Motor Express, Inc., which operates throughout the central and southeastern United States. The company's other trucklines include TNT Red Star Express Inc. in the Northeast, TNT Bestway Transportation Inc. in the Southwest, TNT Dugan, Inc., in the Plains and southeastern states, TNT Reddaway Truck Line, Inc., on the West coast, and TNT United Truck Lines, Inc., in the Northwest. Incorporated in Delaware in 1991.

Directors   (In addition to indicated officer)

Morley Koffman, Chm.
Robert V. Delaney
Robert P. Neuschel

John W. Puth
Neil A. Springer
William N. Weaver

Officers   (Director*)

*John Campbell Carruth, Pres. & C.E.O.
Peter D. Boulais, Sr. V.P.

Christopher L. Ellis, Sr. V.P.—Fin. & C.F.O.

Consolidated Balance Sheet   As of December 31, 1994 (000 omitted)

Assets		Liabilities & Stockholders' Equity	
Current assets	$144,615	Current liabilities	$118,447
Net property, plant & equipment	272,264	Long-term debt	105,667
Other assets	84,123	Deferred income taxes	33,059
		Other liabilities	35,735
		*Stockholders' equity	208,094
Total	$501,002	Total	$501,002

*21,923,149 shares common stock outstanding.

Consolidated Income Statement

Years Ended Abt. Dec. 31	Thousands — — — — — Operating Revenue	Net Income	Per Share[a] — — — Earnings	Cash Dividends	Common Stock Price Range[a] Calendar Year
1994	$1,016,464	$32,065	$1.45[b]	$ .37	29-3/4 — 19-1/4
1993	898,920	27,348	1.20	.37	27-1/2 — 12
1992	774,678	21,092[c]	.79[c]	.28	14-3/8 — 9-3/8[d]
1991	649,775	14,872	.59		
1990	577,526	15,709	.63		

[a]Adjusted to reflect a 3-for-2 stock split in September 1993.
[b]After extraordinary charge of $.06 per share.
[c]Before cumulative effect of FAS 109.
[d]Initial public offering in February 1992.

Transfer Agent & Registrar:	Harris Trust and Savings Bank			
General Counsel:	Sachnoff & Weaver, Ltd.	Traded (Symbol):	NASDAQ (TNTF)	
Investor Relations:	Kenneth F. Ball, Dir.	Stockholders:	6,800	
Mgt. Info. Svcs.:	Tim Harvie, V.P.	Employees:	12,000	
Auditors:	KPMG Peat Marwick LLP	Annual Meeting:	In April	

TODAY'S BANCORP, INC.

P.O. Box 30, 50 West Douglas Street, 12th Floor, Freeport, Illinois 61032
Telephone: (815) 235-8459

TODAY'S BANCORP, INC. (formerly Northwest Illinois Bancorp, Inc.), is a bank holding company engaged in the business of commercial banking. Its two bank subsidiaries, TODAY'S BANK-EAST and TODAY'S BANK-WEST, operate in northwestern Illinois. Through these affiliates, the company offers commercial and consumer financial services to all aspects of the community: business, agriculture, industry, families and individuals. Services include various types of deposit accounts, lending, and trust and investment management. In 1994, the company purchased Tri-State Bank and Trust in East Dubuque, Illinois. Incorporated in Delaware in 1977; present name adopted in 1995.

Directors (In addition to indicated officers)

Allen E. Fehr
Thomas A. Ferguson, Jr.
Frank E. Furst
Craig D. Hartman
Edward D. Higgins

J. Michael Hillard
Raymond E. Johnson
James C. Skyrms
Ruth Mercedes Smith

Officers (Directors*)

*Dan Heine, Pres. & C.E.O.
*R. William Owen, Exec. V.P. & C.F.O.
Ellison W. Powell, Sr. V.P.
Douglas J. Groebner, V.P.
Ray A. Johnson, V.P. & Corp. Cont.
Daniel M. Lashinski, V.P., Secy. & Treas.
Cynthia L. Lower, V.P.—Hum. Res.

Ellen K. Poppen, V.P. & Corp. Auditor
Cindy S. Werkheiser, Asst. V.P.
Jeffrey L. Brotherson, Asst. Corp. Cont.
Rob S. Barron, Tech. Officer
Susan J. Leverton, Tech. Officer
Peggy A. Wohlford, Admin. Credit Officer
Karen S. Woker, Deposit Opers. Officer

Consolidated Balance Sheet As of December 31, 1994 (000 omitted)

Assets		Liabilities & Stockholders' Equity	
Current assets	$ 26,714	Total deposits	$417,747
Net loans	327,638	Other liabilities	30,787
Net property, plant & equipment	12,637	*Stockholders' equity	40,832
Time deposits and investment securities	108,786		
Other assets	13,591		
Total	$489,366	Total	$489,366

*2,705,257 shares common stock outstanding.

Consolidated Income Statement

Years Ended Dec. 31	Thousands — — — —		Per Share[a] — — —		Common Stock Price Range[a] Calendar Year
	Total Income	Net Income	Earnings	Cash Dividends	
1994	$35,502	$3,679	$1.37	$ .50	20 — 16
1993	34,125	4,351	1.65	.44	18-1/4 — 14-5/8
1992	32,542	3,662	1.39	.39	15-7/8 — 9-7/8
1991	33,855	3,373	1.29	.37	11-5/8 — 8-5/8
1990	34,404	3,184	1.22	.33	10-1/2 — 7-7/8

[a]Adjusted to reflect a 3-for-2 stock split in the form of a stock dividend in February 1993.

Transfer Agent & Registrar: Chemical Mellon Shareholder Services

General Counsel: Hinshaw & Culbertson

Investor Relations: R. William Owen, Exec. V.P.

Human Resources: Cynthia L. Lower, V.P.

Mgt. Info. Svcs.: R. William Owen, Exec. V.P.

Auditors: KPMG Peat Marwick LLP

Traded (Symbol): NASDAQ (TDAY)

Stockholders: 850

Employees: 250

Annual Meeting: In April

Tootsie Roll Industries, Inc.

7401 South Cicero Avenue, Chicago, Illinois 60629
Telephone: (312) 838-3400

Tootsie Roll Industries, Inc., has been engaged in the manufacture and sale of candy since 1896. The company's products are primarily sold under the familiar brand names Tootsie Roll, Tootsie Roll Pops, Child's Play, Charms Blow Pop, Blue Razz, Cella's, Mason Dots, Mason Crows, Junior Mints, Charleston Chew, Sugar Daddy, and Sugar Babies. Tootsie Roll customers include wholesale distributors of candy and groceries, variety and drug store chains, discount houses, cooperative grocery associations, vending machine operators, and fundraising religious and charitable organizations. Tootsie Roll owns subsidiaries in Mexico and Canada and five plants, located in Chicago; New York; Covington, Tennessee; Cambridge, Massachusetts; and Mexico City. Major subsidiaries include: Charms Company; Cambridge Brands, Inc.; TRI Sales Co; Henry Eisen Advertising Agency, Inc.; Tootsie Roll of Canada, Ltd.; Cella's Confections, Inc.; World Trade and Marketing, Ltd.; Tri-Mass. Inc.; and Tutsi S.A. de C.V. Incorporated in Virginia in 1919.

Directors (In addition to indicated officers)

Lana Jane Lewis-Brent

Charles W. Seibert

Officers (Directors*)

*Melvin J. Gordon, Chm. & C.E.O.
*Ellen R. Gordon, Pres. & C.O.O.
Thomas E. Corr, V.P.—Mktg. & Sales
G. Howard Ember, V.P.—Fin. & Asst. Secy.
James M. Hunt, V.P.—Phys. Distrib.

John W. Newlin, Jr., V.P.—Mfg.
Barry P. Bowen, Treas.
Daniel P. Drechney, Cont.
*William Touretz, Secy.

Consolidated Balance Sheet   As of December 31, 1994 (000 omitted)

Assets		Liabilities & Stockholders' Equity	
Current assets	$118,887	Current liabilities	$ 26,261
Net property, plant & equipment	85,648	Deferred items	7,716
Other assets	105,548	Industrial dev. bonds & notes payable	27,500
		Other liabilities	8,145
		*Stockholders' equity	240,461
Total	$310,083	Total	$310,083

*7,306,000 shares common and 3,542,000 shares Class B common stock outstanding.

Consolidated Income Statement

Years Ended Dec. 31	Thousands — — — —		Per Share[ab] — — — —		Common Stock
	Net Sales	Net Income	Earnings	Cash Dividends	Price Range[ab] Calendar Year
1994	$296,932	$37,931	$1.75	$ .21	38-1/4 — 27-1/8
1993	259,593	35,442	1.64	.18	41-5/8 — 32-1/2
1992	245,424	32,032	1.48	.14	40-1/2 — 29
1991	207,875	25,495[c]	1.18[c]	.12	36-1/8 — 18
1990	194,299	22,556	1.04	.10	24-1/8 — 15-5/8

[a]Adjusted for a 2-for-1 stock split in June 1995 and for stock dividends.
[b]In addition, a 3% stock dividend has been distributed each year in April.
[c]Includes a charge to reflect FAS 106 and FAS 109, resulting in a cumulative effect of $1,038,000 ($.05 per share).

Transfer Agent & Registrar: Chemical Bank
General Counsel:
  Becker Ross Stone DeStefano & Klein—N.Y.
Investor Relations: G. Howard Ember, V.P.
Auditors: Price Waterhouse LLP

Traded (Symbol): NYSE (TR)
Stockholders: 9,500
Employees: 1,700
Annual Meeting: In May

First Chicago Guide

Trans Leasing International, Inc.

3000 Dundee Road, Northbrook, Illinois 60062
Telephone: (708) 272-1000

Trans Leasing International, Inc., specializes in leasing medical and general office equipment to physicians and other health care and business professionals. A large portion of the equipment leased by the company is technologically advanced. The company markets its leasing services through salespeople representing the various equipment suppliers with which the company does business and through its own sales force. Trans Leasing has developed and is marketing an exclusive credit card called LeaseCard (a registered servicemark of the company), which it provides to qualified applicants for use in leasing equipment from the company. Trans Leasing Insurance Services Inc., a subsidiary of the company which sells property, casualty, and credit-life insurance to its lessees, was formed in 1982. The company maintains a separate subsidiary, Nuvotron, Inc., to handle the sale of used equipment which is returned to the company by lessees who elect not to exercise the purchase option at the end of the lease. Nuvotron, which was formed in 1991, also sells or disposes of repossessed equipment. The company formed TLI Auto Leasing Group, Inc., in fiscal 1991 to handle leasing services in the automobile market. Other subsidiaries are Trans Leasing Finance Corp., TL Lease Funding Corp. II, TL Lease Funding Corp. III, and TL Lease Funding Corp. IV. Incorporated in Illinois in 1972; reincorporated in Delaware in 1983.

Directors (In addition to indicated officer)

Clifford V. Brokaw III
Larry S. Grossman
Michael J. Heyman

Mark C. Matthews
John W. Stodder

Officers (Director*)

*Richard Grossman, Chm., Pres. & C.E.O.
Brian F. Cascarano, V.P.—Sales & Mktg.
Joseph Rabito, V.P.—Oper.

Norman Smagley, V.P.—Fin. & C.F.O.
Terry Frey, Secy.

Consolidated Balance Sheet   As of June 30, 1994 (000 omitted)

Assets		Liabilities & Stockholders' Equity	
Current assets	$187,401	Current liabilities	$ 5,288
Net property, plant & equipment	2,019	Long-term debt	161,841
Other assets	4,315	Deferred taxes	1,827
		*Stockholders' equity	24,779
Total	$193,735	Total	$193,735

*4,371,900 shares common stock outstanding.

Consolidated Income Statement

Years Ended June 30	Thousands — — — — Total Revenues	Net Income	Per Share — — — Earnings	Cash Dividends	Common Stock Price Range Fiscal Year
1994	$27,088	$ 441[a]	$ .10[a]	$ .00	6 — 3-1/8
1993	24,622	2,034	.52	.00	6-3/8 — 3-3/4
1992[b]	20,966	1,877	.64	.00	6-1/4 — 2-1/8
1991	18,482	1,159	.39	.00	3-5/8 — 2-1/4
1990	16,640	1,252	.43	.00	3-1/8 — 2

[a]Includes a charge to reflect FAS 109, resulting in a cumulative effect of $155,000 ($.03 per share).
[b]Certain reclassifications have been made to prior years to conform with the presentation in 1992.

Transfer Agent & Registrar: Harris Trust and Savings Bank

Corporate Counsel:	Kirkland & Ellis	Auditors:	Deloitte & Touche LLP
Investor Relations:	Norman Smagley, V.P.	Traded (Symbol):	NASDAQ (TLII)
Human Resources:	Norman Smagley, V.P.	Stockholders:	1,500
Mgt. Info. Svcs.:		Employees:	118
Martin G. Lewandowski, Dir.		Annual Meeting:	In November

First Chicago Guide

Tribune Company

435 North Michigan Avenue, Chicago, Illinois 60611-4001
Telephone: (312) 222-9100

Tribune Company is a leading information and entertainment company. It publishes six daily newspapers, operates eight television and six radio stations, produces and syndicates information and programming, publishes books and information in print and digital formats, and has an ownership interest in one of Canada's largest newsprint manufacturers. Tribune Company has business units in 13 major markets. Its leading businesses include the Chicago Tribune, The Orlando Sentinel, the Fort Lauderdale-based Sun-Sentinel, WGN-TV and WGN Radio in Chicago, WPIX-TV in New York, KTLA-TV in Los Angeles, WPHL-TV in Philadelphia, WLVI-TV in Boston, Tribune Media Services, and the Chicago Cubs. Recent acquisitions include Compton's, known for its CD-ROM encyclopedia and other interactive multimedia titles; Contemporary Books, a leading nonfiction publisher known for its adult and continuing education materials; and The Wright Group, a publisher of supplementary education materials for grades K-6. Incorporated in Illinois in 1861; reincorporated as a holding company in Delaware in 1968.

Directors   (In addition to indicated officers)

Stanton R. Cook	Andrew J. McKenna	James J. O'Connor
Diego E. Hernandez	Kristie M. Miller	Donald H. Rumsfeld
Robert E. La Blanc	Newton N. Minow	Arnold R. Weber
Nancy Hicks Maynard		

Officers   (Directors*)[a]

* Charles T. Brumback, Chm.
* John W. Madigan, Pres. & C.E.O.
* James C. Dowdle, Exec. V.P.—Media Opers.
  Donald C. Grenesko, Sr. V.P. & C.F.O.
  David D. Hiller, Sr. V.P.—Dev.
  John S. Kazik, Sr. V.P.—Info. Syst.
  John T. Sloan, Sr. V.P.—Admin.
  James E. Cushing, Jr., V.P. & Gen. Coun.
  Stanley J. Gradowski, Jr., V.P. & Secy.

David J. Granat, V.P. & Treas.
Joseph A. Hays, V.P.
M. Catherine Jaros, V.P.—Mktg.
R. Mark Mallory, V.P. & Cont.
Ruthellyn Musil, V.P.—Corp. Rel.
William B. Nelson, V.P.—Fin. Oper.
Andrew J. Oleszczuk, V.P.—Dev.
Shaun M. Sheehan, V.P.—Wash.

[a]Brumback will retire as Chairman on December 31, 1995.

Consolidated Balance Sheet   As of December 25, 1994 (000 omitted)

Assets		Liabilities & Stockholders' Equity	
Current assets	$ 543,544	Current liabilities	$ 529,686
Net property, plant & equipment	641,031	Long-term debt	411,200
Investment in & advances to QUNO	265,818	Deferred taxes	149,521
Other assets	1,335,432	Other liabilities	362,438
		* Stockholders' equity	1,332,980
Total	$2,785,825	Total	$2,785,825

*66,701,442 shares common stock outstanding.

Consolidated Income Statement

Years Ended Abt. Dec. 31	Thousands — — — — Operating Revenues[a]	Net Income	Per Share — — — Earnings	Cash Div. (Common)	Common Stock Price Range Calendar Year
1994	$2,154,917	$ 242,047	$ 3.32	$1.04	64-1/2 — 48-7/8
1993	1,947,525	188,606	2.56	.96	61-1/4 — 47-5/8
1992	2,099,705	119,825[b]	1.56[b]	.96	50-3/4 — 38-3/4
1991	2,039,173	141,981	1.94	.96	48-3/8 — 33-1/8
1990	2,358,950	(63,533)[c]	(1.22)[c]	.96	48-1/4 — 31-1/4

[a]From continuing operations.
[b]Includes FAS 106, FAS 109 and FAS 112, resulting in a cumulative charge of $16,800,000 ($.26 per share).
[c]Includes charges of $255,000,000 ($3.86 per share) for disposition of New York Daily News.

Transfer Agent & Registrar:	First Chicago Trust Co. of New York		
Outside Counsel:	Sidley & Austin	Auditors:	Price Waterhouse LLP
		Traded (Symbol):	CSE, NYSE, PSE (TRB)
Investor Relations:	Ruthellyn Musil, V.P.	Stockholders:	4,500
Human Resources:	John T. Sloan, Sr. V.P.	Employees:	10,500
Mgt. Info. Svcs.:	John S. Kazik, Sr. V.P.	Annual Meeting:	In May

First Chicago Guide

TRO Learning, Inc.

Woodfield Corporate Center, 150 North Martingale Road, Suite 700,
Schaumburg, Illinois 60173
Telephone: (708) 517-5100

TRO Learning, Inc., is a leading developer and marketer of microcomputer-based, interactive, self-paced instructional and educational systems used in a wide variety of applications. The company's products provide flexible, effective, cost-efficient education and training alternatives to traditional classroom instruction. TRO Learning offers a comprehensive selection of educational courseware designed for use by adults and young adults (ages 13 and older) and aviation training courseware developed for use by commercial airline pilots, ground crew, and cabin personnel. The company's education products are marketed as integrated learning systems under the PLATO® trademark to middle and secondary schools, community colleges, the military, job training programs, correctional institutions, and other government-funded programs, as well as to private industry for use in basic skills training and enhancement. Aviation training systems are marketed to airlines worldwide under the TRO label. The company was organized in 1989 to acquire certain assets and properties of Control Data Corporation's computer-based education, training and testing business. Its operating subsidiaries are The Roach Organization Inc., TRO Learning (Canada), Inc., and TRO Learning (U.K.) Limited. Incorporated in Delaware in 1989 as EduCorp; present name adopted in 1992.

Directors (In addition to indicated officer)

Jack R. Borsting, Ph.D.
Tony J. Christianson
John L. Krakauer

Maj. Gen. Vernon B. Lewis, Jr.
John Patience

Officers (Director*)

*William R. Roach, Chm., Pres. & C.E.O.
Sharon Fierro, Sr. V.P., C.F.O., Treas. & Secy.
G. Thomas Ahern, V.P.—U.S. Sales, PLATO Educ.
Jerry L. Duewel, V.P.—Curr. Dev.
Wellesley R. Foshay, Ph.D., V.P.—Qual. Assur. and Standards

Michael A. Hill, V.P.—PLATO Ed. Sales & Mktg.
David H. LePage, V.P.—Syst. Dev. & Client Supp. and Operations
Mary Jo Murphy, V.P.—Corp. Cont. & Chf. Acct. Off.
John Murray, V.P.—Aviation Sales & Opers.
Tim J. Walsh, V.P.—PLATO Asia/Pacific Sales

Consolidated Balance Sheet   As of October 31, 1994 (000 omitted)

Assets		Liabilities & Stockholders' Equity	
Current assets	$15,814	Current liabilities	$ 9,026
Net property, plant & equipment	1,436	Deferred revenue	371
Other assets	9,681	Other liabilities	1,593
		*Stockholders' equity	15,941
Total	$26,931	Total	$26,931

*6,073,097 shares common stock outstanding.

Consolidated Income Statement

Years Ended Oct. 31	Thousands — — — —		Por Share[a] — — — —		Common Stock Price Range[a] Calendar Year
	Total Revenues	Net Income	Earnings	Cash Dividends	
1994	$28,365	$ 3,361[b]	$ .53[b]	$ .00	10-1/2 — 3-3/4
1993[c]	26,533	4,577[d]	.76[d]	.00	17-3/4 — 5-3/4
1992[c]	22,864	3,858[d]	.86[d]	.00	14-1/4 — 10[e]
1991	19,050	(3,992)			
1990	15,998	(12,041)			

[a]Adjusted to reflect a 3.6-for-1 stock split in the form of a stock dividend of 3.6 shares for every share of common stock outstanding on November 6, 1992.
[b]Includes a gain to reflect FAS 109, resulting in a cumulative effect on $5,500,000 ($.87 per share).
[c]Pro forma.
[d]Includes extraordinary gains of $1,530,000 ($.25 per share) in 1993 and $1,380,000 ($.31 per share) in 1992, tax benefits resulting from utilization of loss carryforwards.
[e]Initial public offering in December 1992.

Transfer Agent & Registrar: Harris Trust and Savings Bank

General Counsel: Sidley & Austin

Investor Relations: Sharon Fierro, Sr. V.P.

Human Resources: Patricia Hawver, Dir.

Mgt. Info. Svcs.: Sharon Fierro, Sr. V.P.

Auditors: Coopers & Lybrand L.L.P.

Traded (Symbol): NASDAQ (TUTR)

Stockholders: 1,600

Employees: 267

Annual Meeting: In March

Truck Components Inc.

302 Peoples Avenue, Rockford, Illinois 61104-7092
Telephone: (815) 964-3301

Truck Components Inc. is a leading North American supplier of wheel-end components (such as brake drums, disc wheel hubs, spoke wheels and rotors) for the heavy duty truck market. The company designs, manufactures, and markets wheel-end components and gray and ductile iron castings for the trucking, trailer, and automotive industries. Wholly owned subsidiaries of the company are Gunite Corporation, Brillion Iron Works, Inc., and Fabco Automotive Corporation. In August 1994, the company completed an initial public offering of 3,844,500 shares of common stock. In June 1995, Truck Components announced that it would be acquired by Johnstown America Industries Inc. Incorporated in Delaware in 1987.

Directors (In addition to indicated officer)

John K. Castle
John J. Connolly, Ed.D.
Joel D. Goldhar

Kevin A. Melich
Erick A. Reickert

Officers (Director*)

*Thomas W. Cook, Pres. & C.E.O.

Stephen E.K. Graham, V.P.—Fin., C.F.O. & Secy.

Consolidated Balance Sheet As of December 31, 1994 (000 omitted)

Assets		Liabilities & Stockholders' Equity	
Current assets	$ 75,249	Current liabilities	$ 50,249
Net property, plant & equipment	81,620	Long-term debt	86,532
Other assets	110,438	Deferred income taxes	39,696
		Other liabilities	29,125
		*Stockholders' equity	61,705
Total	$267,307	Total	$267,307

*10,494,500 shares common stock outstanding.

Consolidated Income Statement

Years Ended Dec. 31	Thousands — — — — Net Sales	Net Income	Per Share[a] — — — Earnings	Cash Dividends	Common Stock Price Range[ab] Calendar Year	
1994[cd]	$312,800	$ 16,163	$ 1.54	$ .00	13	— 9-1/4
1993[ce]	265,609	(5,008)	(.50)			
1992	220,136	6,687				
1991	179,732	(2,494)				
1990	207,430	(207)				

[a]Adjusted to reflect a 4.7-for-1 stock split in August 1994.
[b]Initial public offering in August 1994.
[c]Unaudited pro forma.
[d]Before extraordinary item.
[e]Includes a charge to reflect FAS 106, resulting in a cumulative effect of $2,549,000 ($.26 per share).

Transfer Agent & Registrar: Harris Trust and Savings Bank	
General Counsel: Skadden, Arps, Slate, Meagher & Flom	**Auditors:** Ernst & Young LLP
Investor Relations: Stephen E.K. Graham, V.P.	**Traded (Symbol):** NASDAQ (TRCK)
Human Resources: Steven Smith, Gunite; Richard Menozz, Brillion; Mark Niemela, Fabco	**Stockholders:** 100
Mgt. Info. Svcs.: John Aldrich, Gunite; Dennis Graven, Brillion; Louis Keane, Fabco	**Employees:** 2,000
	Annual Meeting: In May

True North Communications Inc.

101 East Erie Street, Chicago, Illinois 60611-2897
Telephone: (312) 751-7000

True North Communications Inc. (formerly Foote, Cone & Belding Communications, Inc.) is a global marketing communications company that offers advertising, direct marketing, sales promotion, and other specialized marketing services. It has 190 offices located in 57 countries, including such regions as Canada, Europe, Latin America, Asia, the Pacific, and the U.S. True North's clients represent many industries, primarily consumer goods and services. The company offers its clients yellow pages advertising through Wahlstrom & Company; direct marketing through FCB Direct; health care/pharmaceutical advertising through FCB Healthcare; sales promotion through IMPACT; and Hispanic advertising through Siboney. Incorporated in Delaware in 1942; present name adopted in 1994.

Directors (In addition to indicated officers)

Richard S. Braddock
Laurel Cutler
Newton N. Minow

William A. Schreyer
Louis E. Scott
Stephen T. Vehslage

Officers (Directors*)

*Bruce Mason, Chm. & C.E.O.
*Craig R. Wiggins, V. Chm.
*Terry M. Ashwill, Exec. V.P. & C.F.O.
*Gregory W. Blaine, Exec. V.P. & Dir.—Global Oper. Syst.
Mary A. Carragher, V.P.—Gen. Coun.
Owen J. Dougherty, V.P.—Corp. Comm.

Dale F. Perona, V.P., Treas. & Secy.
John J. Rezich, V.P.—Cont.
Susan J. Schroeder, V.P.—Corp. Comm.
*Maurice Lévy, Chm.—Group Publicis S.A.
*J. Brendan Ryan, Pres. & C.E.O.—FCB/Leber Katz Ptnrs.
*John B. Balousek, Pres. & C.O.O.—FCB

Consolidated Balance Sheet As of December 31, 1994 (000 omitted)

Assets		Liabilities & Stockholders' Equity	
Current assets	$382,728	Current liabilities	$399,537
Net property, plant & equipment	45,660	Long-term debt	5,496
Other assets	245,356	Deferred items	60,954
		*Stockholders' equity	207,757
Total	$673,744	Total	$673,744

*22,842,000 shares common stock outstanding.

Consolidated Income Statement

Years Ended Dec. 31	Thousands — — — —		Per Share[a] — — —		Common Stock Price Range[a] Calendar Year	
	Revenues	Net Income	Earnings	Cash Dividends		
1994	$403,690	$ 30,277	$ 1.34	$ .60	24	— 19-7/8
1993	372,666	25,714	1.15	.60	24	— 14-3/4
1992	353,340	21,728[b]	1.00[b]	.60	15-3/4	— 11-7/8
1991	341,987	(19,148)[c]	(.91)[c]	.60	13-3/4	— 9-3/8
1990	338,138	21,624	1.05	.60	15	— 9-1/4

[a]Adjusted to reflect a 2-for-1 stock split in the form of a 100% stock dividend in February 1995.
[b]Includes a gain to reflect FAS 109, resulting in a cumulative effect of $3,681,577 ($.17 per share).
[c]Reflects unusual loss of $35,981,000 ($1.70 per share), primarily due to restructuring.

Transfer Agent & Registrar: First Chicago Trust Co. of New York

General Counsel:	Mary A. Carragher, V.P.	Auditors:	Arthur Andersen LLP
Investor Relations:	Owen J. Dougherty, V.P.	Traded (Symbol):	NYSE (TNO)
Human Resources:	Paul Sollitto, V.P.	Stockholders:	6,800
		Employees:	3,929
Mgt. Info. Svcs.:	Michael Johnson	Annual Meeting:	In May

First Chicago Guide

U.S. Can Corporation

900 Commerce Drive, Suite 302, Oak Brook, Illinois 60521
Telephone: (708) 571-2500

U.S. Can Corporation is a producer of steel containers for personal care, household, automotive, paint, and industrial products manufactured in the United States. The company conducts its principal business operations in the general packaging (non-food and non-beverage) segment of the metal container industry. The company produces aerosol, round and oblong, and specialty containers, which are sold to many well-known companies. The Sherwin-Williams Company is the company's largest customer. Personal care and household products represent the primary end-use of the company's containers. U.S. Can's 28 plants are located in 11 states, strategically positioned near principal customers and suppliers. The company was formed in 1983 by an investor group led by William J. Smith, the company's chairman and chief executive officer, to acquire the container division of Sherwin-Williams. Incorporated in Delaware in 1983.

Directors (In addition to indicated officer)

Calvin W. Aurand, Jr.
Benjamin F. Bailar
Eugene B. Connolly
Carl Ferenbach

Ricardo Poma
Francisco A. Soler
Michael J. Zimmerman

Officers (Director*)

*William J. Smith, Chm., Pres. & C.E.O.
Frank J. Galvin, Exec. V.P.—Oper.
Timothy W. Stonich, Exec. V.P.—Fin. & C.F.O.
Peter J. Andres, V.P. & Treas.
Anthony F. Bonadonna, V.P.—Hum. Res.
Charles E. Foster, V.P. & Grp. Exec.—Custom & Spec. Prods.
Richard J. Krueger, V.P.—MIS
Paul J. Mangiafico, V.P.—Mfg., Paint/Gen. Line
John R. McGowan, V.P. & Cont.
Lawrence T. Messina, V.P.—Western & Machine Ctr. Oper.

Gene A. Papes, V.P.—Sales & Mktg., Aerosol Containers
Raymond J. Parker, V.P.—Tech. & Facilities
David C. Schuermann, V.P. & Grp. Exec.—Paint/Gen. Line
William J. Smith, Jr., V.P.—Elgin & Midwest Opers.
Jack J. Tunnell, V.P.—Southern & East. Oper.
David J. West, V.P.—Sales & Mktg., Custom/Spec. Prods.
Thomas J. Yurco, V.P.—Mat. Mgt. & Logistics

Consolidated Balance Sheet As of December 31, 1994 (000 omitted)

Assets		Liabilities & Stockholders' Equity	
Current assets	$134,279	Current liabilities	$ 95,475
Net property, plant & equipment	210,048	Long-term debt	186,209
Other assets	56,397	Other long-term liabilities	44,130
		*Stockholders' equity	74,910
Total	$400,724	Total	$400,724

*12,472,748 shares Class A common stock outstanding.

Consolidated Income Statement

Years Ended Dec. 31	Thousands — — — — Net Sales	Net Income[a]	Per Share — — — Earnings	Cash Dividends	Common Stock Price Range[b] Calendar Year
1994	$563,153	$ 18,570	$ 1.73	$ .00	19-1/2 — 15
1993	455,127	7,522	.79	.00	17-1/8 — 11-1/4
1992	396,604	(12,115)[c]	(2.98)[c]		
1991	351,178	(10,036)	(.59)		
1990	323,191	(8,416)	(2.03)		

[a]Includes extraordinary losses of $3,402,000, $5,244,000 and $1,441,000 (net of income taxes) in 1993, 1991 and 1990, respectively, in each case, in connection with early extinguishment of debt.
[b]Initial public offering in March 1993.
[c]Includes FAS 106, resulting in a net noncash charge, net of income taxes, of $12,537,000 ($2.83 per share).

Transfer Agent & Registrar: Harris Trust and Savings Bank

General Counsel:	Ross & Hardies	Auditors:	Arthur Andersen LLP
Investor Relations:	Timothy W. Stonich, Exec. V.P.	Traded (Symbol):	NYSE (USC)
		Stockholders:	2,300
Human Resources:	Anthony F. Bonadonna, V.P.	Employees:	3,400
Mgt. Info. Svcs.:	Richard J. Krueger, V.P.	Annual Meeting:	In April

First Chicago Guide

U.S. Robotics Corporation

8100 North McCormick Boulevard, Skokie, Illinois 60076-2999
Telephone: (708) 982-5010

U.S. Robotics Corporation (formerly U.S. Robotics, Inc.) designs, manufactures, markets, and supports high performance data communications products and systems targeted to business, professional, and personal users worldwide. The company currently sells a broad product line of dial-up modems, local area network access products, and wide area network hubs. The company's high speed modems are designed using digital signal processor-based proprietary architectures, which enable the company to deliver high performance products. U.S. Robotics addresses the home office, portable, organizational desktop, and data center market sectors, and sells its products under four different brands: Sportster modems; Courier modems; Shared Access LAN access products; and Total Control wide area network hubs. The company's two-tiered distribution channel includes about 90 national, regional, and international distributors, which in turn sell to more than 7,000 resellers. Subsidiaries are U.S. Robotics Access Corp., Megahertz Holding Corporation, U.S. Robotics Ltd., PNB s.a., and U.S. Robotics S.A. In February 1995, shareholders approved the merger of Megahertz Holding Corporation, a producer of credit card-size modems for portable computers, with and into the company; and the formation of a new holding company, U.S. Robotics Corporation. Incorporated in Delaware in 1994.

Directors (In addition to indicated officers)

James E. Cowie
Gian M. Fulgoni

Peter I. Mason
Paul G. Yovovich

Officers (Directors*)

*Casey G. Cowell, Chm., Pres. & C.E.O.
*John McCartney, Exec. V.P.—Int'l. Oper.
*Jonathan N. Zakin, Exec. V.P.—Bus. Dev. & Corp. Strategy
Ross W. Manire, Sr. V.P. & Gen. Mgr.—Corp. Syst.
Gary R. Boss, V.P.—Mfg.
G. Christopher Coffin, V.P.—Strategic Plan.
Cheryl E. Mayberry, V.P.—Corp. Sales & Mktg.
Mark O. Remissong, V.P.—Fin. & C.F.O.

Elizabeth S. Ryan, V.P.—Hum. Res.
Michael S. Seedman, V.P. & Gen. Mgr.—Personal Comm.
Semir D. Sirazi, V.P.—R&D
George A. Vinyard, V.P., Gen. Coun. & Secy.
Dale M. Walsh, V.P.—Adv. Dev.
C. David Hall, Treas.
Martha S. Hauber, Cont.

Consolidated Balance Sheet[a] As of October 2, 1994 (000 omitted)

Assets		Liabilities & Stockholders' Equity	
Current assets	$245,214	Current liabilities	$ 56,291
Net property, plant & equipment	56,027	Long-term debt	69,464
Other assets	22,036	Deferred items	1,805
		*Stockholders' equity	195,717
Total	$323,277	Total	$323,277

[a]Pro forma combined financial information for U.S. Robotics Corporation and Megahertz Holding Corporation.
*11,824,807 shares common stock outstanding.

Consolidated Income Statement[a]

Years Ended Abt. Sept. 30	Thousands — — — —		Per Share[b] — — — —		Common Stock Price Range[b] Calendar Year
	Net Sales	Net Income	Earnings	Cash Dividends	
1994	$499,075	$36,121	$1.89	$ .00	46 — 24
1993	242,652	24,119	1.42	.00	35-1/4 — 17
1992	129,678	11,859	.78	.00	24-1/4 — 13-3/8
1991	89,030	7,459	.54	.00	16-3/4 — 12-1/4[c]
1990	64,736	5,504	.37		

[a]Pro forma combined financial information for U.S. Robotics Corporation and Megahertz Holding Corporation.
[b]Adjusted to reflect a 6-for-1 stock split in August 1991.
[c]Initial public offering in October 1991.

Transfer Agent & Registrar: Harris Trust and Savings Bank

General Counsel:	George A. Vinyard, V.P.	Auditors:	Grant Thornton LLP
Investor Relations:	Susan Lloyd	Traded (Symbol):	NASDAQ (USRX)
		Stockholders:	5,000
Human Resources:	Elizabeth S. Ryan, V.P.	Employees:	1,976
Mgt. Info. Svcs.:	James Harris	Annual Meeting:	In March

UAL Corporation

P.O. Box 66919, Chicago, Illinois 60666
Telephone: (708) 952-4000

UAL Corporation is a holding company whose principal subsidiary is United Air Lines, Inc., a major commercial air transportation company. United has been engaged in the air transportation of persons, property, and mail since 1934, and certain of its predecessors began operations as early as 1926. In 1994, United served 152 airports worldwide. During 1994, United flew a total of 108-billion revenue passenger miles and carried an average of 203,400 passengers a day, averaging 2,000 scheduled departures daily. United provides service to its domestic markets principally through a system of hub airports at major cities. Each hub provides United flights to a network of spoke destinations as well as flights to other United hubs. Currently, United flies from four domestic hubs — Chicago O'Hare International, Denver International, San Francisco International, and Dulles International near Washington, D.C. — and is the principal carrier at each of these hubs. United also has a Pacific hub operation at Tokyo Narita Airport, and an Atlantic hub operation at London Heathrow Airport. United has developed a route system covering North America, Asia, the South Pacific, Europe, and Latin America. In October 1994, United launched a new service named Shuttle by United. In July 1994, shareholders approved a recapitalization plan through which employee stock ownership plans acquired a 55 percent majority ownership of the company. Incorporated in Delaware in 1968.

Directors (In addition to indicated officers)

Duane D. Fitzgerald	Harlow B. Osteboe	Joseph V. Vittoria
Richard D. McCormick	John F. Peterpaul	Paul A. Volcker
John F. McGillicuddy	Paul E. Tierney, Jr.	
James J. O'Connor	John K. Van de Kamp	

Officers (Directors*)

*Gerald M. Greenwald, Chm. & C.E.O.
*John A. Edwardson, Pres. & C.O.O.
Joseph R. O'Gorman, Jr., Exec. V.P.

Stuart I. Oran, Exec. V.P.—Corp. Affairs & Gen. Coun.
Douglas A. Hacker, Sr. V.P.—Fin.
Francesca M. Maher, V.P.—Law & Corp. Secy.

Consolidated Balance Sheet   As of December 31, 1994 (000 omitted)

Assets		Liabilities & Stockholders' Equity	
Current assets	$ 3,192,000	Current liabilities	$ 4,906,000
Net property, plant & equipment	6,723,000	Long-term debt & capital leases	3,617,000
Other assets	1,849,000	Other liabilities	3,557,000
		*Stockholders' equity	(316,000)
Total	$11,764,000	Total	$11,764,000

*12,439,106 shares common stock outstanding.

Consolidated Income Statement

Years Ended Dec. 31	Thousands — — — — — Operating Revenues	Net Income	Per Share — — — — Earnings	Cash Dividends	Common Stock Price Range Calendar Year
1994	$13,950,000	$ 51,000[a]	$ (.61)[a]	$ .00	105— 83-1/8[b]
1993	13,325,000	(50,000)[c]	(3.40)[c]	.00	
1992	11,853,000	(956,800)[d]	(39.75)[d]	.00	
1991	10,706,000	(331,939)	(14.31)	.00	
1990	10,296,000	94,465	4.33	.00	

[a]Includes a charge to reflect FAS 112, resulting in a cumulative effect of $26,000,000 ($1.37 per share).
[b]Stock price range for the period from the date of the recapitalization through yearend. Comparisons of 1994 amounts to prior periods are not meaningful due to changes in the number of shares outstanding as a result of the recapitalization.
[c]Includes an extraordinary loss of $19,000,000 ($.76 per share) on early extinguishment of debt.
[d]Includes a charge to reflect FAS 106 and FAS 109, resulting in a cumulative effect of $539,600,000 ($22.41 per share).

Transfer Agent & Registrar:	First Chicago Trust Co. of New York		
General Counsel:	Stuart I. Oran, Exec. V.P.	Traded (Symbol):	CSE, NYSE, PSE (UAL)
Investor Relations:	Lynn Hughitt, Staff. Exec.	Stockholders:	18,000
Human Resources:	Paul G. George	Employees:	78,000
Auditors:	Arthur Andersen LLP	Annual Meeting:	In April

First Chicago Guide

Unicom Corporation

One First National Plaza, 10 S. Dearborn St., P.O. Box A-3005, Chicago, Illinois 60690-3005

Telephone: (312) 394-7399

Unicom Corporation (formerly Commonwealth Edison Company) is principally engaged in the production, purchase, transmission, distribution, and sale of electricity to a diverse base of residential, commercial, and industrial customers. The company's electric service territory has an area of about 11,540 square miles and an estimated population of eight million. It includes the City of Chicago, an area of about 225 square miles with an estimated population of three million, from which the company derived approximately one-third of its electric operating revenues in 1994. Unicom has more than 3,317,000 electric customers. In May 1994, shareholders approved the formation of Unicom Corporation, a holding company, and Commonwealth Edison Company became a wholly owned subsidiary. Other wholly owned subsidiaries are: Unicom Enterprises Inc., which is the parent company of Unicom Thermal Technologies Inc. Commonwealth Edison incorporated in Illinois in 1913; Holding company incorporated in Illinois in 1994.

Directors (In addition to indicated officers)

Jean Allard	Donald P. Jacobs	Edward A. Mason
James W. Compton	Edgar D. Jannotta	Frank A. Olson
Sue L. Gin	George E. Johnson	

Officers (Directors*)

*James J. O'Connor, Chm. & C.E.O.
*Samuel K. Skinner, Pres.
Thomas J. Maiman, Sr. V.P.
Robert J. Manning, Sr. V.P.
Donald A. Petkus, Sr. V.P.
Cordell Reed, Sr. V.P.
Michael J. Wallace, Sr. V.P.
John C. Bukovski, V.P. & C.F.O.
Louis O. DelGeorge, V.P.
Harlan M. Dellsy, V.P.—Strategic Plan.
William H. Downey, V.P.

William H. Dunbar, Jr., V.P.
J. Stanley Graves, V.P.
Emerson W. Lacey, V.P.
Paul D. McCoy, V.P.
Robert A. Paul, V.P.
J. Stephen Perry, V.P.
James A. Small, V.P.
Pamela B. Strobel, V.P. & Gen. Coun.
Roger F. Kovack, Compt.
Dennis F. O'Brien, Treas.
David A. Scholz, Secy.

Consolidated Balance Sheet As of December 31, 1994 (000 omitted)

Assets		Liabilities & Stockholders' Equity	
Current assets	$ 1,401,852	Current liabilities	$ 1,541,377
Net utility, plant & equipment	17,323,333	Long-term debt	7,453,206
Other assets	4,396,303	Deferred items	7,878,468
		Other liabilities	800,310
		*Stockholders' equity	5,448,127
Total	$23,121,488	Total	$23,121,488

*214,340,067 shares common stock outstanding.

Consolidated Income Statement

Years Ended Dec. 31	Thousands — — — — Elec. Oper. Revs.[a]	Net Income[b]	Per Share — — — — Earnings[b]	Cash Dividends[bc]	Common Stock Price Range Calendar Year
1994	$6,277,521	$354,934	$1.66	$1.60	28-3/4 — 20-5/8
1993	5,260,440	46,388[d]	.22[de]	1.60	31-5/8 — 22-7/8
1992	6,026,321	443,442	2.08	2.30	40-1/8 — 21-3/4
1991	6,275,533	16,599	.08	3.00	42-5/8 — 33-5/8
1990	5,310,819	45,796	.22	3.00	37-7/8 — 27-1/4

[a]1990 electric operating revenues have been increased to reflect the reclassification of interchange sales which were previously recorded net with purchased power under electric operating expenses.
[b]Available for common stock.
[c]Cash dividends declared.
[d]Includes a gain to reflect FAS 109, resulting in a cumulative effect of $9,738,000 ($.05 per share).
[e]Net writedown of $1.61 per share occurred during the year 1993.

Transfer Agent & Registrar: First Chicago Trust Co. of New York

General Counsel:	Pamela B. Strobel, V.P.	Auditors:	Arthur Andersen LLP
Investor Relations:	Kathryn Houtsma, Dir.	Traded (Symbol):	CSE, NYSE, PSE (UCM)
		Stockholders:	182,000
Human Resources:	J. Stanley Graves, V.P.	Employees:	18,460
Mgt. Info. Svcs.:	Robert J. Manning, Sr. V.P.	Annual Meeting:	In May

UNIMED Pharmaceuticals, Inc.

2150 East Lake Cook Road, Buffalo Grove, Illinois 60089-1862
Telephone: (708) 541-2525

UNIMED Pharmaceuticals, Inc., and its consolidated subsidiaries develop, manufacture, and distribute proprietary pharmaceutical products in niche medical markets. The company is a successor to another company incorporated in 1948. Over its history, UNIMED Pharmaceuticals has developed pharmaceuticals for a number of therapeutic categories. The most significant pharmaceuticals developed by the company are Serc®, for recurrent vertigo associated with Meniere's disease; and Marinol®, for use as an appetite stimulant in AIDS patients and antiemetic in cancer patients. Incorporated in Delaware in 1981.

Directors (In addition to indicated officers)

Fred Holubow
Robert D. Hunter

James J. Lempenau
Roland Weiser

Officers (Directors*)

* John N. Kapoor, Ph.D., Chm.
* Stephen M. Simes, Pres. & C.E.O.
  David E. Riggs, Sr. V.P.—Fin./Admin. & C.F.O.

Robert E. Dudley, Ph.D., V.P.—Clinical & Regulatory Affairs
Phillip B. Donenberg, Asst. Treas.

Consolidated Balance Sheet As of December 31, 1994 (000 omitted)

Assets		Liabilities & Stockholders' Equity	
Current assets	$10,533	Current liabilities	$ 2,334
Net property, plant & equipment	1,098	*Stockholders' equity	9,471
Other assets	174		
Total	$11,805	Total	$11,805

*6,127,161 shares common stock outstanding.

Consolidated Income Statement

Years Ended Dec. 31	Thousands — — — — Net Sales	Net Income	Per Share — — — — Earnings	Cash Dividends	Common Stock Price Range Calendar Year
1994	$7,992	$ 41	$ .01	$ .00	5-1/4 — 2
1993	7,203	(852)	(.14)	.00	11-3/4 — 3-3/4
1992[a]	3,697	(4,210)[b]	(.79)	.00	11-3/4 — 6-1/2
1991[a]	2,440	(517)	(.13)	.00	9-1/4 — 1-1/8
1990[a]	1,856	(1,601)	(.50)	.00	

[a]September 30 fiscal yearend.
[b]Includes a pretax charge of $2,519,000 related to restructuring.

Transfer Agent & Registrar:	Harris Trust and Savings Bank		
General Counsel:	Katherine A. Letourneau	Auditors:	Coopers & Lybrand L.L.P.
Securities Counsel:	Schwartz & Freeman	Traded (Symbol):	NASDAQ (UMED)
Investor Relations:	David E. Riggs, Sr. V.P.	Stockholders:	1,239
Human Resources:	David E. Riggs, Sr. V.P.	Employees:	20
Mgt. Info. Svcs.:	David E. Riggs, Sr. V.P.	Annual Meeting:	In April

United States Cellular Corporation

8410 West Bryn Mawr Avenue, Suite 700, Chicago, Illinois 60631-3486
Telephone: (312) 399-8900

United States Cellular Corporation owns, operates and invests in cellular telephone systems in metropolitan and rural areas in the U.S. Through subsidiaries and joint ventures, the company has interests or the right to acquire interests in systems in 207 metropolitan and rural areas in 36 states, including 69 metropolitan systems and 138 rural systems in operation as of December 1994. Of these systems, the company owned a majority interest in 130 operational cellular systems as of December 1994. In addition, the company has the right to acquire a majority interest in two additional metropolitan systems and eight additional rural systems. United States Cellular coordinates sales and marketing efforts through market clusters, which will offer improved operational efficiency and customer service. Telephone and Data Systems, Inc., owns 81 percent of the outstanding common stock of the company. Incorporated in Delaware in 1983.

Directors (In addition to indicated officers)

LeRoy T. Carlson
Walter C.D. Carlson
Paul-Henri Denuit

Allan Z. Loren
Murray L. Swanson

Officers (Directors*)

*Leroy T. Carlson, Jr., Chm.
*H. Donald Nelson, Pres. & C.E.O.
Douglas S. Arnold, V.P.—Hum. Res.
Richard W. Goehring, V.P.—Eng.
Kari L. Jordan, V.P.—Opers., National Region
Joyce V. Gab Kneeland, V.P.—Opers.,
    Central Region

Kenneth R. Meyers, V.P.—Fin. & C.F.O.
Michael A. Mutz, V.P.—Opers., Eastern Region
David P. Rivoira, V.P.—Cust. Serv.
Edward W. Towers, V.P.—Mkt. & Bus. Dev.
James D. West, V.P.—Info. Services
Stephen P. Fitzell, Secy.
Phillip A. Lorenzini, Cont.

Consolidated Balance Sheet As of December 31, 1994 (000 omitted)

Assets		Liabilities & Stockholders' Equity	
Current assets	$ 64,560	Current liabilities	$ 98,373
Net property, plant & equipment	368,181	Long-term debt	290,645
Other assets	1,102,046	Deferred items	8,653
		Minority interest	33,552
		*Stockholders' equity	1,103,564
Total	$1,534,787	Total	$1,534,787

*45,504,028 shares common and 33,005,877 shares Series A common stock outstanding.

Consolidated Income Statement

Years Ended Dec. 31	Thousands — — — —		Per Share — — — —		Common Stock Price Range Calendar Year
	Total Revenues[a]	Net Income	Earnings	Cash Dividends	
1994	$332,404	$ 16,393	$ .21	$ .00	35-1/4 — 22-3/8
1993	214,310	(25,441)	(.45)	.00	39-1/4 — 20-3/4
1992	139,929	6,194	.11	.00	24-1/4 — 17-1/2
1991	84,956	(34,642)[b]	(.89)[b]	.00	24-5/8 — 14-7/8
1990	54,621	(14,723)	(.51)	.00	33-5/8 — 12-3/4

[a]1993-90 amounts restated.
[b]Includes cumulative effect of change in accounting principle of $10,269,000 ($.26 per share).

Transfer Agent & Registrar: Harris Trust and Savings Bank

General Counsel:	Sidley & Austin	Auditors:	Arthur Andersen LLP
Investor Relations:	Kenneth R. Meyers, V.P.	Traded (Symbol):	AMEX (USM)
		Stockholders:	463
Human Resources:	Douglas S. Arnold, V.P.	Employees:	2,250
Mgt. Info. Svcs.:	James D. West, V.P.	Annual Meeting:	In May

First Chicago Guide

United Stationers Inc.

2200 East Golf Road, Des Plaines, Illinois 60016-1267
Telephone: (708) 699-5000

United Stationers Inc. is a wholesale distributor of business products. Its offerings of more than 25,000 items are available only to resellers; the company does not sell directly to end users. Through its sophisticated computer-based physical distribution network, the company provides 14,000 resellers with products from 500 manufacturers within 24 hours. An extensive truck fleet extends the reach of 39 regional distribution centers and 28 local distribution points. Products include office supplies, office furniture, janitorial and sanitation products, information systems supplies, microcomputers, peripherals, and retail specialty products. Comprehensive computer capabilities integrate forecasting, buying, inventory control, order entry, shipping, and invoicing. The company further supports its dealers through a variety of pricing, inventory control, catalog, and promotional program services. The company's major subsidiary is United Stationers Supply Co. In March 1995, United Stationers merged with Associated Holdings Inc., with United Stationers being the surviving entity. Incorporated in Delaware in 1981.

Directors   (In addition to indicated officer)

James Callier, Jr.
Daniel Good
Fred Hegi, Jr.
Jeffrey K. Hewson

James Johnson
Gary Miller
Joel D. Spungin

Officers   (Director*)

*Thomas W. Sturgess, Chm., Pres. & C.E.O.
Michael Rowsey, Exec. V.P.
Steven R. Schwarz, Exec. V.P.
Robert H. Cornell, V.P—Hum. Res.

Ted S. Rzeszuto, V.P. & Cont.
Ergin Uskup, V.P.—MIS & Chf. Info. Officer
Daniel H. Bushnell, C.F.O.
James A. Pribel, Treas.

Consolidated Balance Sheet   As of March 31, 1995 (000 omitted)

Assets		Liabilities & Stockholders' Equity	
Current assets	$643,887	Current liabilities	$303,261
Net property, plant & equipment	222,330	Long-term debt	560,120
Goodwill, net	71,628	Deferred items	31,469
Other assets	38,104	Redeemable preferred stock	23,761
		Redeemable warrants	11,879
		*Stockholders' equity	45,459
Total	$975,949	Total	$975,949

*6,028,392 shares common stock outstanding.

Consolidated Income Statement

Years Ended Abt. Aug. 31	Thousands — — — — Net Sales	Net Income	Per Share — — — Earnings	Cash Dividends	Common Stock Price Range Calendar Year
1994	$1,473,024	$15,749	$ .85	$ .40	15-3/4 — 8-7/8
1993	1,470,115	21,360	1.15	.40	20 — 12-3/4
1992	1,094,275	11,364ᵃ	.71	.40	17-1/8 — 8-3/4
1991	951,109	9,910	.64	.40	12 — 8-1/8
1990	993,178	12,838	.83	.40	16-1/4 — 7-3/4

ªIncludes a $5,900,000 pretax restructuring charge.

Transfer Agent & Registrar: The First National Bank of Boston

General Counsel: Otis H. Halleen

Investor Relations: Kathleen S. Dvorak, Dir.

Human Resources: Robert H. Cornell, V.P.

Mgt. Info. Svcs.:   Ergin Uskup, V.P.

Auditors: Ernst & Young LLP

Traded (Symbol):   NASDAQ (USTR)

Stockholders: 1,393

Employees: 5,000

Annual Meeting: As set by Directors

Unitrin, Inc.

One East Wacker Drive, Chicago, Illinois 60601
Telephone: (312) 661-4600

Unitrin, Inc., is a financial services company with subsidiaries engaged in three business areas: Life and Health Insurance, Property and Casualty Insurance, and Consumer Finance. Unitrin's leading life insurance product is a traditional life insurance policy sold to individuals. Traditional life insurance products offered by Unitrin include both permanent and term insurance. The company also offers individual and group health and hospitalization insurance. The Property and Casualty Insurance segment provides personal and commercial insurance consisting of automobile, homeowners, fire, casualty, workers' compensation, and related lines. Unitrin is engaged in the consumer finance business through its subsidiary, Fireside Thrift Co., which is organized under California law as an industrial loan company. Fireside's principal business is automobile financing, primarily of used automobiles, through the purchase of conditional sales contracts from automobile dealers, and direct loans. Other Unitrin subsidiaries are: United Insurance Company of America (life and health insurance); Trinity Universal Insurance Company (property and casualty insurance); Union National Fire Insurance Company; and other direct and indirect subsidiaries. Incorporated in Delaware in 1990.

Directors   (In addition to indicated officers)

James E. Annable
Reuben L. Hedlund
George A. Roberts

Fayez S. Sarofim
Henry E. Singleton

Officers   (Directors*)

*Jerrold V. Jerome, Chm.
*Richard C. Vie, Pres. & C.E.O.
 David F. Bengston, V.P.

James W. Burkett, V.P.
Eric J. Draut, Treas. & Cont.
Thomas H. Maloney, Secy.

Consolidated Balance Sheet   As of December 31, 1994 (000 omitted)

Assets		Liabilities & Stockholders' Equity	
Investments	$3,321,100	Insurance reserves	$1,828,300
Receivables	646,800	Investment cert. & passbook	437,600
Other assets	601,900	accounts	
		Other liabilities	538,800
		*Stockholders' equity	1,765,100
Total	$4,569,800	Total	$4,569,800

*47,052,820 shares common stock outstanding.

Consolidated Income Statement

Years Ended Dec. 31	Thousands — — — — Total Revenues	Net Income	Per Share — — — Earnings	Cash Dividends	Common Stock Price Range Calendar Year
1994	$1,365,500	$148,400	$2.96	$1.50	51-1/2 — 38-1/2
1993	1,363,200	95,000	1.83	1.30	46-3/4 — 39
1992	1,362,600	123,400[a]	2.38[a]	1.10	42-3/4 — 32-3/4
1991	1,254,900	136,400	2.57	.90	41-1/2 — 29-1/4
1990	1,224,400	133,700	2.42	.40	34-3/4 — 24-1/2[b]

[a]Includes the cumulative effect of adoption of FAS 106, resulting in a one-time aftertax charge of $39,900,000 ($.77 per share).
[b]Spinoff of Unitrin,Inc., into publicly held company completed April 20, 1990.

Transfer Agent & Registrar:	First Chicago Trust Co. of New York		
General Counsel:	Thomas H. Maloney, Secy.	Auditors:	KPMG Peat Marwick LLP
Investor Relations:	Thomas H. Maloney, Secy.	Traded (Symbol):	NASDAQ (UNIT)
		Stockholders:	11,800
Human Resources:	Ken Oehler	Employees:	7,300
Mgt. Info. Svcs.:	William Whaley	Annual Meeting:	In May

First Chicago Guide

Universal Automotive Industries, Inc.

3350 North Kedzie Avenue, Chicago, Illinois 60618-5722
Telephone: (312) 478-2323

Universal Automotive Industries, Inc., is a distributor of a wide variety of automotive aftermarket replacement parts for domestic and imported cars, vans, and light trucks. The company specializes in the distribution of brake rotors and other brake parts, which it markets under its private label, "UBP Universal Brake Parts." The company manufactures many of the brake rotors it distributes. In December 1994, Universal Automotive Industries completed an initial public offering of 1,300,000 units, consisting of one share of common stock and one redeemable common stock purchase warrant. Subsidiaries include Universal Automotive, Inc. Incorporated in Delaware in 1994.

Directors (In addition to indicated officers)

Sheldon Robinson

Sol Weiner

Officers (Directors*)

*Yehuda Tzur, Chm., Pres. & C.E.O.
*Eric Goodman, Exec. V.P.—Canadian Opers.
*Arvin Scott, Exec. V.P.

*Sami Israel, V.P.
*Reuben Gabay, Secy.
Dan Maeir, C.F.O. & Treas.

Consolidated Balance Sheet As of December 31, 1994 (000 omitted)

Assets		Liabilities & Stockholders' Equity	
Current assets	$19,062	Current liabilities	$ 7,432
Net property, plant & equipment	3,690	Long-term debt	7,710
Other assets	712	Other liabilities	310
		*Stockholders' equity	8,012
Total	$23,464	Total	$23,464

*6,500,000 shares common stock outstanding.

Consolidated Income Statement

Years Ended Dec. 31	Thousands — — — — Net Sales	Net Income	Per Share[a] — — — Earnings	Cash Dividends	Common Stock Price Range[ab] Calendar Year
1994[cd]	$41,824	$ 414	$ .08	$ .00	10-3/4 — 5-1/4
1993[d]	41,809	280	.05		
1992	33,510	1,186			
1991	23,618	40			
1990	18,461	15			

[a]Adjusted to reflect a 1-for-5,200 reverse stock split in December 1994.
[b]Initial public offering in December 1994.
[c]Reflects the results of operations of Aaron Automotive (Ontario), as if the acquisition had occurred on January 1, 1994.
[d]Pro forma.

Transfer Agent & Registrar: Continental Stock Transfer & Trust Co.

General Counsel: Shefsky & Froelich Ltd.

Investor Relations: Dan Maeir, C.F.O.

Human Resources: Dan Maeir, C.F.O.

Mgt. Info. Svcs.:   Dan Maeir, C.F.O.

Auditors: Altshculer, Melvoin and Glasser LLP; BDO Dunwoody

Traded (Symbol):   CSE (UVS); NASDAQ (UVSL)

Stockholders: 1,100

Employees: 100

Annual Meeting: In May

UNR Industries, Inc.

332 South Michigan Avenue, Chicago, Illinois 60604-4385
Telephone: (312) 341-1234

UNR Industries, Inc., conducts its business through two major operating groups: Industrial and Commercial. The Industrial Group manufactures welded steel tubing and computerized warehouse control systems. The Commercial Group manufactures supermarket carts and display equipment for stores; towers and shelters for communication; and stainless steel and Asterite sinks. Major divisions include: UNR-Leavitt Division; UNR-Rohn Division; UNR Home Products Division; Unarco Commercial Products; and Real Time Solutions. Incorporated in Illinois in 1918; reincorporated in Delaware in 1970; and reincorporated in Delaware in 1979 as UNR Industries, Inc.

Directors (In addition to indicated officer)

Gene Locks, Chm.	Thomas F. Meagher
Charles M. Brennan III	Robert B. Steinberg
Darius W. Gaskins, Jr.	William J. Williams
Ruth R. McMullin	

Officers (Director*)

*Thomas A. Gildehaus, Pres. & C.E.O.
Henry Grey, Sr. V.P. & C.F.O.
Victor E. Grimm, V.P., Corp. Secy. & Gen. Coun.

John A. Saladino, Cont. & Asst. Secy.
Michael F. Boyle, Dir. of Taxation & Asst. Secy.

Consolidated Balance Sheet   As of December 31, 1994 (000 omitted)

Assets		Liabilities & Stockholders' Equity	
Current assets	$209,075	Current liabilities	$ 50,042
Net property, plant & equipment	64,339	Long-term debt	23,278
Other assets	26,033	Other liabilities	5,531
		*Stockholders' equity	220,596
Total	$299,447	Total	$299,447

*50,946,000 shares common stock outstanding.

Consolidated Income Statement

Years Ended Dec. 31	Thousands — — — —		Per Share — — —		Common Stock Price Range Calendar Year
	Net Sales[a]	Net Income	Earnings	Cash Dividends	
1994	$372,385	$ 31,325[b]	$ .64	$ .20	7-1/8 — 5-1/8
1993	312,873	18,784	.40	1.20	8-1/2 — 5-7/8
1992	281,776	123,683[c]	2.74[c]	2.20	8-1/4 — 3-5/8
1991	257,978	16,568	.37	1.20	5-7/8 — 3-5/8
1990	264,329	21,827	.48	.20	4-7/8 — 3-3/8

[a]Restated to reflect the 1994 discontinuance of Unarco Material Handling and the 1992 discontinuance of Midwest CATV and Midwest Steel.
[b]Includes a $2,500,000 aftertax charge for the discontinuance of Unarco Material Handling and a $10,000,000 reduction in a tax valuation allowance.
[c]Includes a tax benefit of $90,000,000 ($1.99 per share) as a result of recent tax regulations and $8,100,000 ($.18 per share) as the result of insurance litigation settlement.

Transfer Agent & Registrar:	First Chicago Trust Co. of New York		
General Counsel:	Victor E. Grimm, V.P.	Traded (Symbol):	NASDAQ, CSE (UNRI)
Investor Relations:	Henry Grey, Sr. V.P.	Stockholders:	3,300
Mgt. Info. Svcs.:	John A. Saladino, Cont.	Employees:	2,200
Auditors:	Arthur Andersen LLP	Annual Meeting:	In May

USG Corporation

125 South Franklin Street, Chicago, Illinois 60606-4678
Telephone: (312) 606-4000

USG Corporation is a holding company whose major subsidiaries include United States Gypsum Company, USG Interiors, Inc., L&W Supply Corporation, and CGC Inc. (76 percent-owned). These subsidiaries are diversified manufacturers, marketers and distributors of products used primarily in the building materials industry. USG is a manufacturer of gypsum-based products, including wallboard, joint compound, and industrial gypsum. Other major product lines include ceiling suspension systems, ceiling tile, and cement board. USG's subsidiaries operate 48 plants in the U.S., seven plants in Canada, and nine plants in various other countries. On April 23, 1993, USG's prepackaged plan of reorganization was confirmed by the Delaware bankruptcy court. USG emerged from bankruptcy on May 6, 1993. Incorporated in Delaware in 1984.

Directors (In addition to indicated officers)

Robert L. Barnett
Keith A. Brown
W.H. Clark
James C. Cotting
Lawrence M. Crutcher

David W. Fox
Philip C. Jackson, Jr.
Marvin E. Lesser
John B. Schwemm
Judith A. Sprieser

Officers (Directors*)

*Eugene B. Connolly, Chm. & C.E.O.
*William C. Foote, Pres. & C.O.O.
Richard H. Fleming, Sr. V.P. & C.F.O.
Arthur G. Leisten, Sr. V.P. & Gen. Coun.
P. Jack O'Bryan, Sr. V.P.—Worldwide Mfg./Tech.
Harold E. Pendexter, Jr., Sr. V.P. & C.A.O.
J. Bradford James, Grp. V.P.—Worldwide Ceilings
  & Int'l.
Donald E. Roller, Grp. V.P.—N. Amer. Gypsum

Raymond T. Belz, V.P. & Cont.
Brian W. Burrows, V.P.—R&D
Matthew P. Gonring, V.P.—Corp. Comm.
John E. Malone, V.P. & Treas.
Robert B. Sirgant, V.P.—Corp. Accts.
S. Gary Snodgrass, V.P.—Hum. Res. Oper.
Frank R. Wall, V.P. & Pres./C.E.O.—L&W Supply
Dean H. Goossen, Corp. Secy.
Paul J. Vanderberg, Pres./C.E.O.—CGC, Inc.

Consolidated Balance Sheet   As of December 31, 1994 (000 omitted)

Assets		Liabilities & Stockholders' Equity	
Current assets	$ 644,000	Current liabilities	$ 455,000
Net property, plant & equipment	755,000	Long-term debt	1,077,000
Net excess reorganization value	561,000	Deferred income taxes	179,000
Other assets	164,000	Other liabilities	421,000
		*Stockholders' equity	(8,000)
Total	$2,124,000	Total	$2,124,000

*45,083,211 shares common stock outstanding.

Consolidated Income Statement

Years Ended Dec. 31	Thousands — — — — — Net Sales	Net Income	Per Share[a] — — — Earnings	Cash Dividends	Common Stock Price Range Calendar Year	
1994	$2,290,000	$ (92,000)	$(2.14)	$ .00	36	— 17-1/4
1993[b]	1,325,000	(129,000)	(3.46)	.00	30-1/2 —	9-5/8
1993[c]	591,000	1,434,000[d]				
1992[c]	1,777,000	(191,000)				
1991[c]	1,712,000	(161,000)				

[a]Due to restructuring and fresh start accounting, prior periods per share information is not meaningful.
[b]From May 7-Dec. 31. Per GAAP bankruptcy accounting rules, results for restructured company must be reported
  separately from predecessor company.
[c]Predecessor company from January 1 to May 6, 1993, and prior fiscal years.
[d]Includes restructuring gains.

Transfer Agent & Registrar: Harris Trust and Savings Bank

General Counsel:	Arthur G. Leisten, Sr. V.P.	Auditors:	Arthur Andersen LLP
Investor Relations:	Keith E. Kahl, Mgr.	Traded (Symbol):	CSE, NYSE (USG)
		Stockholders:	6,072
Human Resources:	Harold E. Pendexter, Jr., Sr. V.P.	Employees:	12,400
Mgt. Info. Svcs.:	William H. Duran, Dir.	Annual Meeting:	In May

Varlen Corporation

55 Shuman Blvd., Suite 500, P.O. Box 3089, Naperville, Illinois
60566-7089
Telephone: (708) 420-0400

Varlen Corporation manufactures transportation products and laboratory equipment. The company supplies precision, high volume stampings to automobile manufacturers and their suppliers, and is a primary independent supplier of automatic transmission clutch plates. Varlen is a manufacturer and rebuilder of shock control devices for freight cars and locomotives as well as a supplier of outlet gates for covered hopper cars and locomotive components, including heating, ventilating and air-conditioning systems, valves, toilets, and refrigerators. It is also a producer of rail anchors for track fastening systems. The company provides aluminum castings, hubs, and fuel water separators for the large truck and trailer market in addition to die cast parts and engineered structural foam components. Varlen produces research laboratory equipment, primarily for the life sciences industries, and petroleum analysis equipment for oil refineries worldwide. The company also performs testing services for physical property analysis of petroleum products, and manufactures petroleum reference samples used to calibrate petroleum analysis equipment. Varlen is a market leader in products such as water baths, incubators, and ovens used in the nation's research laboratories and schools. Operating subsidiaries and divisions include Aciéries de Ploermel, Chrome Crankshaft Companies, Alcor Petroleum Instruments, Inc., Consolidated Metco, Inc., Walter Herzog GmbH, Keystone Railway Equipment Company, Means Industries, Inc., Precision Scientific, Inc., Precision Scientific Petroleum Instruments Co., Prime Manufacturing Corporation, Unit Rail Anchor Company, and Varlen Instruments, N.A. Incorporated in Delaware in 1969.

Directors (In addition to indicated officer)

Ernest H. Lorch, Chm.
Rudolph Grua
L. William Miles

Greg A. Rosenbaum
Joseph J. Ross
Theodore A. Ruppert

Officers (Director*)

*Richard L. Wellek, Pres. & C.E.O.
Raymond A. Jean, Exec. V.P. & C.O.O.
George W. Hoffman, Grp. V.P.

Richard A. Nunemaker, V.P.—Fin. & C.F.O.
Stephen A. Magida, Secy.

Consolidated Balance Sheet As of January 31, 1995 (000 omitted)

Assets		Liabilities & Stockholders' Equity	
Current assets	$111,535	Current liabilities	$ 53,822
Net property, plant & equipment	59,636	Convertible subordinated debentures	69,000
Other assets	49,015	Other long-term debt	3,788
		Deferred items	4,838
		Other liabilities	9,707
		*Stockholders' equity	79,031
Total	$220,186	Total	$220,186

*4,865,000 shares common stock outstanding.

Consolidated Income Statement

Years Ended Jan. 31	Thousands — — — — Net Sales	Net Income[a]	Per Share[c] — — — — Earnings[ab]	Cash Dividends	Common Stock Price Range[c] Fiscal Year
1995	$341,521	$14,762	$2.11	$ .36	26-3/8 — 16-3/8
1994	291,908	10,766	1.73	.36	25-1/4 — 16-1/4
1993	266,054	6,317[d]	.86[d]	.36	18-1/4 — 9-5/8
1992	230,517	3,444	.46	.36	10-1/8 — 7-5/8
1991	242,786	5,685	.76	.36	12-1/4 — 6-5/8

[a]Includes FAS 106 and FAS 109.
[b]Fully diluted.
[c]Adjusted for a 10% stock dividend in June 1995 and a 3-for-2 stock split in the form of a stock dividend in October 1993.
[d]Includes cumulative effect of a change in accounting principle of $1,351,000 ($.18 per share) in 1993.

Transfer Agent & Registrar:	Harris Trust and Savings Bank		
Investor Relations:	Richard A. Nunemaker, V.P.	Traded (Symbol):	NASDAQ (VRLN)
Human Resources: Howard Futterman, Corp. Benefits Mgr.		Stockholders:	1,700
Mgt. Info. Svcs.:	Steven E. Obendorf, Corp. Cont.	Employees:	2,500
Auditors:	Deloitte & Touche LLP	Annual Meeting:	In May

The Vigoro Corporation

225 North Michigan Avenue, Suite 2500, Chicago, Illinois 60601
Telephone: (312) 819-2020

The Vigoro Corporation is a leading North American producer and distributor of potash, nitrogen-based fertilizers, and related products serving agricultural, industrial, and consumer markets. Potash and other agricultural fertilizer products are marketed by the company principally in the U.S. and, to a lesser extent, in Canada and overseas. Subsidiaries include KCL Holdings, Inc., Vigoro Industries, Inc., and Phoenix Chemical Company. Sales in the U.S. are made principally to corn and soybean farmers in midwestern and southeastern states. The company also manufactures and markets a complete line of consumer lawn and garden, and professional and institutional products. In January 1995, the company acquired Central Canada Potash. In April 1994, Vigoro acquired Mid-Ohio Chemical Co., a Midwest manufacturer and distributor of agricultural products. In July 1994, the company acquired Koos, Inc., North America's leading provider of potassium-based deicers. Incorporated in Delaware in 1986.

Directors   (In addition to indicated officers)

Rod F. Dammeyer
Ray A. Goldberg, Ph.D.
Arthur A. Greenberg
Harold H. MacKay
Donald F. Mazankowski
John M. Pasquesi

Sheli Z. Rosenberg
Andrew Sarlos
Robert L. Thompson, Ph.D.
Clayton K. Yeutter
Samuel Zell

Officers   (Directors*)

*Joseph P. Sullivan, Chm.
*Robert E. Fowler, Jr., Pres. & C.E.O.
*Jay D. Proops, V. Chm.
 John U. Huber, Exec. V.P.
 Robert M. Van Patten, Exec. V.P.
 Kenneth W. Holbrook, Jr., Sr. V.P.

Kelly P. Jordan, V.P.—Treas.
Carolyn W. Merritt, V.P.—Envir. Affairs
Karen E. Nyman, V.P. & Treas.
James J. Patterson, V.P. & C.F.O.
Rose Marie Williams, Secy.

Consolidated Balance Sheet   As of December 31, 1994 (000 omitted) Unaudited

Assets		Liabilities & Stockholders' Equity	
Current assets	$301,767	Current liabilities	$199,796
Property, plant & equipment	248,115	Long-term debt	122,717
Other assets	52,954	Deferred items	62,150
		Preferred stock	28,200
		*Stockholders' equity	189,973
Total	$602,836	Total	$602,836

*19,715,941 shares common stock outstanding.

Consolidated Income Statement

Years Ended June 30	Thousands — — — — Net Sales	Net Income[b]	Per Share[a] — — — Earnings[b]	Cash Dividends	Common Stock Price Range[a] Calendar Year
1994[c]	$804,091	$51,956	$2.64	$ .78	36-1/2 — 25-1/2
1994	727,402	47,961	2.43	.72	
1993[d]	578,232	40,093	2.00	.66	30-3/4 — 20-3/8
1992[d]	594,053	40,515	2.03	.60	26-3/4 — 17-1/4
1991[e]	592,824	26,533	1.73	.00	22-3/4 — 13-5/8

[a]Adjusted to reflect a 13,581-for-1 stock split in March 1991. Initial public offering on May 28, 1991.
[b]Available to common stockholders.
[c]Unaudited 12 months ending December 31. The company has selected a December 31 yearend.
[d]Restated to reflect FAS 109.
[e]Unaudited.

Transfer Agent & Registrar:	Harris Trust and Savings Bank		
General Counsel:	Altheimer & Gray	Traded (Symbol):	NYSE (VGR)
		Stockholders:	1,980
Investor Relations:	David A. Prichard, V.P.	Employees:	2,100
Auditors:	Arthur Andersen LLP	Annual Meeting:	In May

Vitalink Pharmacy Services, Inc.

1250 East Diehl Road, Suite 208, Naperville, Illinois 60563
Telephone: (708) 505-1320

Vitalink Pharmacy Services, Inc., provides institutional pharmacy services to nursing facilities and other institutions. The company presently operates 18 institutional pharmacies, which specialize in pharmaceutical dispensing of individual medications, pharmacy consulting, and infusion therapy products. The company, through its subsidiary, Vitalink Infusion Services, Inc., also provides parenteral and enteral nutrition products to patients who qualify under Medicare Part B, and bills Medicare directly for these products. Manor Care, Inc., owns approximately 82 percent of the company's common stock. Incorporated in Delaware in 1976.

Directors   (In addition to indicated officers)

Harold Blumenkrantz
Anil K. Gupta

Marvin Wilensky

Officers   (Directors*)

*Donald C. Tomasso, Chm. & C.E.O.
*Stewart Bainum, Jr., V. Chm.
*Donna L. DeNardo, Pres. & C.O.O.
 Vincent C. DiTrapano, Sr. V.P.—Oper.
 Scott T. Macomber, V.P.—Fin. & C.F.O.

*James A. MacCutcheon, Treas.
*James H. Rempe, Secy.
 Gerald F. Hickey, Asst. Treas.
 K. Peter Kemezys, Asst. Secy.

Consolidated Balance Sheet   As of May 31, 1994 (000 omitted)

Assets		Liabilities & Stockholders' Equity	
Current assets	$20,402	Current liabilities	$ 6,299
Net property, plant & equipment	5,303	Other liabilities	2,589
Other assets	43,882	*Stockholders' equity	60,699
Total	$69,587	Total	$69,587

*13,975,000 shares common stock outstanding.

Consolidated Income Statement

Years Ended May 31	Thousands — — — — Total Revenues	Net Income	Per Share — — — Earnings	Cash Dividends	Common Stock Price Range Calendar Year
1994	$98,569	$9,204	$ .66	$ .00	15-1/2 — 8-1/2
1993	65,714	7,341	.53	.00	13-1/4 — 7-1/2
1992	40,164	5,497	.46	.00	18 — 10-1/4[a]
1991	27,260	3,768	.33		
1990	18,408	2,663	.23		

[a]Initial public offering in March 1992.

Transfer Agent & Registrar: Chemical Bank
General Counsel: James H. Rempe, Secy.
Investor Relations: Shaheen Wolff, Mgr.
Human Resources: Steve Thompson, Sr. Dir.
Mgt. Info. Svcs.:   Chip Phillips, Dir.

Auditors: Arthur Andersen LLP
Traded (Symbol):   NASDAQ (VTLK)
Stockholders: 74
Employees: 700
Annual Meeting: In September

Walgreen Co.

200 Wilmot Road, Deerfield, Illinois 60015
Telephone: (708) 940-2500

Walgreen Co. is in the retail drugstore business, selling prescription and proprietary drugs, and also carrying additional product lines such as cosmetics, toiletries, tobacco, and general merchandise. The company operates 2,035 drugstores in 30 states and Puerto Rico. Nearly 70 percent of those stores have been opened or remodeled in the last five years. Walgreen drugstores serve more than two million customers daily and are served by seven distribution centers and five photo-processing studios. Walgreens Healthcare Plus, the company's subsidiary, provides Walgreen prescription programs—including pharmacy mail service and workers' compensation programs to managed care providers and employers. Incorporated in Illinois in 1909.

Directors (In addition to indicated officers)

Theodore Dimitriou
James J. Howard
Charles D. Hunter
Cordell Reed

John B. Schwemm
William H. Springer
Marilou M. von Ferstel

Officers (Directors*)

*Charles R. Walgreen III, Chm. & C.E.O.
*L. Daniel Jorndt, Pres. & C.O.O.
Vernon A. Brunner, Exec. V.P.—Mktg.
Glenn S. Kraiss, Exec. V.P.—Drug Store Oper.
John R. Brown, Sr. V.P.—Distr.
Roger L. Polark, Sr. V.P. & C.F.O.
John A. Rubino, Sr. V.P.—Hum. Res.

William A. Shiel, Sr. V.P.—Facilities Dev.
Robert C. Atlas, V.P.—Drug Store Oper.
David W. Bernauer, V.P. & C.I.O.
W. Lynn Earnest, V.P. & Treas.
Jerome B. Karlin, V.P.—Drug Store Oper.
Julian A. Oettinger, V.P., Gen. Coun. & Secy.
Roger H. Clausen, Cont. & Chf. Acct. Off.
Chester G. Young, Gen. Auditor

Consolidated Balance Sheet As of August 31, 1994 (000 omitted)

Assets		Liabilities & Stockholders' Equity	
Current assets	$1,672,811	Current liabilities	$1,050,689
Net property, plant & equipment	1,085,487	Deferred items	173,649
Other assets	150,451	Other liabilities	110,771
		*Stockholders' equity	1,573,640
Total	$2,908,749	Total	$2,908,749

*123,070,536 shares common stock outstanding.

Consolidated Income Statement

Years Ended Aug. 31	Thousands — — — — Net Sales	Net Income	Per Share[a] — — — Earnings	Cash Dividends[b]	Common Stock Price Range[a] Calendar Year
1994	$9,234,978	$281,929	$2.28	$ .68	45-3/8 — 33-3/4
1993	8,294,840	221,666[c]	1.79[c]	.60	44-5/8 — 35-3/8
1992	7,474,961	220,628	1.78	.52	44-1/2 — 30-3/8
1991	6,733,044	194,965	1.58	.46	38 — 24-3/4
1990	6,047,494	174,577	1.41	.40	26-1/2 — 20-1/4

[a]Adjusted to reflect a 2-for-1 stock split in February 1991.
[b]Cash dividends declared.
[c]Includes a charge to reflect FAS 106 and FAS 109, resulting in a cumulative effect of $23,623,000 ($.19 per share).

Transfer Agent & Registrar: Harris Trust and Savings Bank

General Counsel:	Julian A. Oettinger, V.P.	Auditors:	Arthur Andersen LLP
Investor Relations:	W. Lynn Earnest, V.P.	Traded (Symbol):	NYSE, CSE (WAG)
		Stockholders:	29,910
Human Resources:	John A. Rubino, Sr. V.P.	Employees:	65,000
Mgt. Info. Svcs.:	David W. Bernauer, V.P.	Annual Meeting:	Second Wednesday in January

Wallace Computer Services, Inc.

4600 West Roosevelt Road, Hillside, Illinois 60162-2079
Telephone: (708) 449-8600

Wallace Computer Services, Inc., is one of the nation's largest manufacturers and distributors of information management products, services, and solutions. These include paperwork systems and forms; labeling products and supplies; electronic forms software and services; commercial printing; promotional and direct mail advertising; computer hardware, software, accessories, and supplies; printer ribbons; ATM and POS machine paper rolls; LaserMax paper handling systems for high-speed, non-impact printing; and TOPS®-branded office products and stock forms. Wallace sells primarily through a direct sales force of 700 sales representatives across the U.S.; the Visible direct mail catalog sent to customers; and the office products dealer network for TOPS products. Besides its corporate offices in Hillside, Illinois, the company operates manufacturing and distribution facilities in 12 other states. Incorporated in Illinois in 1908; reincorporated in Delaware in 1963.

Directors (In addition to indicated officers)

Fred F. Canning
Richard F. Doyle
R. Darrell Ewers

William N. Lane III
William E. Olsen
Neele E. Stearns, Jr.

Officers (Directors*)

*Theodore Dimitriou, Chm.
*Robert J. Cronin, Pres. & C.E.O.
Michael O. Duffield, Sr. V.P.—Oper.
Michael T. Leatherman, Sr. V.P. & C.I.O.
Bruce D'Angelo, V.P.—Corp. Sales
Michael R. Finger, V.P. & Gen. Mgr.—Dir. Mail Div.
Douglas W. Fitzgerald, V.P.—Mktg.
Michael J. Halloran, V.P., C.F.O. & Secy.
Donald J. Hoffmann, V.P.—Eng. & Res.
Michael M. Mulcahy, V.P. & Gen. Mgr.—Colorforms Div.
Wayne E. Richter, V.P. & Gen. Mgr.—Label Div.

Michael T. Quane, Treas.
Michael T. Laudizio, Asst. Secy.
Steven F. Arpaia, V.P.—Colorform Sales Div.
Thomas G. Brooker, V.P.—Gen. Mgr., TOPS Div.
Thomas W. Franke, V.P.—Gen. Mgr.—Wallace Press Div.
Joseph J. Juszak, V.P.—Qual. & Tech. Svcs. Div.
Michael D. Keim, V.P.—Mfg., Bus. Forms Div.
James E. Kersten, V.P.—Direct Sales, West
Mark D. Mindrum, V.P.—Direct Sales, Midwest
Edward A. Riguardi, V.P.—Direct Sales, East
Ronald D. Seavey, V.P.—Direct Sales, Southeast

Consolidated Balance Sheet As of July 31, 1994 (000 omitted)

Assets		Liabilities & Stockholders' Equity	
Current assets	$248,226	Current liabilities	$ 64,794
Net property, plant & equipment	232,862	Long-term debt	23,500
Other assets	57,504	Deferred items	40,159
		*Stockholders' equity	410,139
Total	$538,592	Total	$538,592

*22,393,000 shares common stock outstanding.

Consolidated Income Statement

Years Ended July 31	Thousands — — — — Net Sales	Net Income	Per Share — — — Earnings	Cash Dividends	Common Stock Price Range Calendar Year
1994	$588,173	$47,931	$2.16	$ .64	36-1/4 — 25-7/8
1993	545,315	41,170	1.84	.58	33-7/8 — 22-7/8
1992	511,572	39,455	1.76	.54	27-7/8 — 21-3/4
1991	458,840	35,009	1.63	.50	29-1/8 — 19
1990	448,700	39,555	1.86	.46	31-1/2 — 15-7/8

Transfer Agent & Registrar: State Street Bank and Trust Co.

General Counsel:
   Butler, Rubin, Saltarelli & Boyd

Investor Relations: Michael J. Halloran, V.P.

Mgt. Info. Svcs.:
   Michael T. Leatherman, Sr. V.P.

Auditors: Arthur Andersen LLP
Traded (Symbol): NYSE (WCS)
Stockholders: 4,531
Employees: 3,530
Annual Meeting: In November

Washington National Corporation

300 Tower Parkway, Lincolnshire, Illinois 60069-3665
Telephone: (708) 793-3000

Washington National Corporation is the parent company and sole stockholder of Washington National Insurance Company. At the end of 1994, Washington National Corporation had consolidated life insurance in force totaling $21 billion. The company principally engages in marketing and underwriting of life insurance, annuities, and health insurance for individuals and groups. Primary operating subsidiaries are Washington National Insurance Company and United Presidential Life Insurance Company. Incorporated in Delaware in 1968.

Directors (In addition to indicated officer)

Frederick R. Blume
Elaine R. Bond
Ronald L. Bornheutter
W. Francis Brennan
Lee A. Ellis
John R. Haire

Stanley P. Hutchison
George P. Kendall, Jr.
Frank L. Klapperich, Jr.
Lee M. Mitchell
Rex Reade

Officers (Director*)

*Robert W. Patin, Chm., Pres. & C.E.O.
Wade G. Brown, Exec. V.P. & Chf. Info. Off.
Thomas Pontarelli, Exec. V.P.—Law & Admin.
Thomas C. Scott, Exec. V.P. & C.F.O.

Joan K. Cohen, V.P. Treas. & Cont.
Craig R. Edwards, V.P., Corp. Coun. & Secy.
Kathy A. Glynn, V.P.—Internal Audit

Consolidated Balance Sheet As of December 31, 1994 (000 omitted)

Assets		Liabilities & Stockholders' Equity	
Invested assets	$2,284,634	Policy liabilities	$2,354,818
Deferred insurance costs	293,850	General liabilities	149,427
Other assets	232,084	*Stockholders' equity	306,323
Total	$2,810,568	Total	$2,810,568

*12,163,000 shares common stock outstanding.

Consolidated Income Statement

Years Ended Dec. 31	Thousands — — — — Total Revenues[a]	Net Income	Per Share — — — — Earnings	Cash Dividends	Common Stock Price Range Calendar Year
1994	$656,929	$ 31,301	$ 2.53	$1.08	25-1/8 — 18-5/8
1993[b]	628,527	26,666	2.45	1.08	27-7/8 — 22
1992[c]	570,442	(5,967)	(.63)	1.08	23-1/2 — 16
1991	578,044	(2,964)	(.33)	1.08	16 — 9-5/8
1990	709,083	(8,523)	(.84)	1.08	28-3/4 — 10

[a]Restated to reflect FAS 113.
[b]Includes FAS 112.
[c]Includes a charge to reflect FAS 106 and FAS 109, resulting in a cumulative effect of $22,819,000 ($2.28 per share).

Transfer Agent & Registrar: First Chicago Trust Co. of New York

General Counsel:
  Thomas Pontarelli, Exec. V.P.

Investor Relations: Craig A. Simundza, V.P.

Human Resources:
  Thomas Pontarelli, Exec. V.P.

Mgt. Info. Svcs.: Wade G. Brown, Exec. V.P.

Auditors: Ernst & Young LLP

Traded (Symbol): CSE, NYSE, PHSE (WNT)

Stockholders: 9,900

Employees: 976

Annual Meeting: In June

First Chicago Guide

Wells-Gardner Electronics Corporation

2701 North Kildare Avenue, Chicago, Illinois 60639
Telephone: (312) 252-8220

Wells-Gardner Electronics Corporation is a video products company. It designs and manufactures color and monochrome video monitors for sale to the business, industrial, and computer markets. It has a customer base that is growing both domestically and internationally. Included are makers of coin-operated video games, state lottery terminals, video slot machines, automotive diagnostic and test equipment, medical instruments, industrial process control equipment, and computer and word processing terminals. From time to time, the company also engages in the contract manufacturing of electronic products designed and marketed by others. Incorporated in Illinois in 1925.

Directors (In addition to indicated officers)

John R. Blouin
William L. De Nicolo
Allan Gardner

Wayne Harris
James J. Roberts, Jr.
Albert S. Wells, Jr.

Officers (Directors*)

*Anthony Spier, Chm., Pres. & C.E.O.
Randall S. Wells, Exec. V.P. & Gen.
   Mgr.—Prod.
*Richard L. Conquest, V.P.—Fin., C.F.O.,
   Treas. & Secy.

Eugene C. Ahner, Dir.—Hum. Res.
Kathleen E. Hoppe, Dir.—M.I.S.
Mark E. Komorowski, Dir.—Service
Larry Mahl, Dir.—Mat. Control
John S. Pircon, Dir.—Prod. Dev.

Consolidated Balance Sheet   As of December 31, 1994 (000 omitted)

Assets		Liabilities & Stockholders' Equity	
Current assets	$12,813	Current liabilities	$ 5,252
Net property, plant & equipment	2,806	*Stockholders' equity	10,367
Total	$15,619	Total	$15,619

*3,957,736 shares common stock outstanding.

Consolidated Income Statement

Years Ended Dec. 31	Thousands — — — — — Net Sales	Net Income	Per Share — — — — Earnings	Cash Dividends	Common Stock Price Range Calendar Year
1994	$33,435	$(1,735)	$ (.45)	$ .00	4-5/8 — 2-1/2
1993	36,011	(1,779)[a]	(.46)[a]	.00	7-1/8 — 2-7/8
1992	48,949	1,545[b]	.40[b]	.00	9-3/8 — 1-7/8
1991	38,814	(1,464)	(.39)	.00	3-3/8 — 1-1/2
1990	45,099	1,160	.31	.00	4-5/8 — 2-1/2

[a]Includes a gain of $102,000 ($.03 per share), the cumulative effect of a change in an accounting principle.
[b]Includes an extraordinary gain of $528,000 ($.14 per share) relating to tax effect of loss carryforward.

Transfer Agent & Registrar: Harris Trust and Savings Bank

General Counsel:	McDermott, Will & Emery	Auditors:	KPMG Peat Marwick LLP
Investor Relations:	Richard L. Conquest, V.P.	Traded (Symbol):	AMEX (WGA)
		Stockholders:	941
Human Resources:	Eugene C. Ahner, Dir.	Employees:	176
Mgt. Info. Svcs.:	Kathleen E. Hoppe, Dir.	Annual Meeting:	Fourth Tuesday in April

Westco Bancorp, Inc.

2121 South Mannheim Road, Westchester, Illinois 60154-4363
Telephone: (708) 865-1100

Westco Bancorp, Inc., is a savings and loan holding company for First Federal Savings and Loan Association of Westchester. As a community-oriented institution, the Association offers traditional deposit and mortgage loan products to its customers. The Association currently operates out of its home office and a limited service office, both located in Westchester, Illinois, and its deposit gathering area is concentrated in the neighborhoods surrounding its offices. Incorporated in Delaware in 1992.

Directors (In addition to indicated officer)

James E. Dick
Rosalyn M. Lesak
Edward A. Matuga

Edward C. Moticka
Thomas J. Nowicki
Robert E. Vorel, Jr.

Officers (Director*)

*David C. Burba, Chm. & Pres.
Richard A. Brechlin, Exec. V.P. & Treas.
Gregg P. Goossens, Exec. V.P.—Lending

Kenneth J. Kaczmarek, V.P.
Mary S. Suffi, V.P. & Secy.

Consolidated Balance Sheet   As of December 31, 1994 (000 omitted)

Assets		Liabilities & Stockholders' Equity	
Total cash & cash equivalents	$ 6,146	Deposits	$245,323
Investment securities	81,816	Advance payments by borrowers	3,509
Loans receivable	205,115	Other liabilities	4,351
Other assets	6,494	*Stockholders' equity	46,388
Total	$299,571	Total	$299,571

*1,884,625 shares common stock outstanding.

Consolidated Income Statement

Years Ended Dec. 31	Thousands — — — — Total Income	Net Income	Per Share — — — Earnings	Cash Dividends	Common Stock Price Range Calendar Year
1994	$21,651	$3,961	$1.91	$ .00	21 — 16-1/2
1993	22,681	4,109	1.86	.00	20-1/2 — 14-1/2
1992	23,771	2,643[a]	1.14[a]	.00	15 — 11-3/8[b]
1991	23,704	2,366			
1990	22,506	2,114			

[a]Includes a charge to reflect FAS 109, resulting in a cumulative effect of $254,263 ($.11 per share).
[b]Initial public offering in June 1992.

Transfer Agent & Registrar: Harris Trust and Savings Bank

General Counsel:
  Muldoon, Murphy & Faucette, Washington, D.C.

Investor Relations:
  Richard A. Brechlin, Exec. V.P.

Human Resources: Mary S. Suffi, V.P.

Mgt. Info. Svcs.: Kenneth J. Kaczmarek, V.P.

Auditors:
  Cobitz, VandenBerg and Fennessy

Traded (Symbol): NASDAQ (WCBI)

Stockholders: 1,400

Employees: 60

Annual Meeting: In April

First Chicago Guide

Whitman Corporation

3501 Algonquin Road, Rolling Meadows, Illinois 60008
Telephone: (708) 818-5000

Whitman Corporation is a consumer goods and services company which is engaged in three distinct businesses: soft drinks, automotive services, and refrigeration equipment. Pepsi-Cola General Bottlers, Inc., bottles and distributes Pepsi-Cola and other soft drinks in 12 states in the midwest U.S. Midas International Corp. operates more than 2,500 automotive service shops in the U.S. and 13 other countries. Hussmann Corp. produces capital equipment to satisfy needs of supermarket, commercial refrigeration, and convenience and specialty store customers. Incorporated in Delaware in 1962.

Directors   (In addition to indicated officer)

Richard G. Cline
James W. Cozad
Pierre S. du Pont
Archie R. Dykes
Helen Galland

Jarobin Gilbert, Jr.
Victoria B. Jackson
Donald P. Jacobs
Charles S. Locke

Officers   (Director*)

*Bruce S. Chelberg, Chm. & C.E.O.
Thomas L. Bindley, Exec. V.P.
Lawrence J. Pilon, Sr. V.P.—Hum. Res.
Frank T. Westover, Sr. V.P. & Cont.
Charles H. Connolly, V.P.—Corp. Affairs & Inv. Rel.
Louis J. Corna, V.P.—Taxes
Kathleen R. Gannon, V.P. & Treas.

William B. Moore, V.P., Secy. & Gen. Coun.
Raymond B. Werntz, V.P.—Comp. & Benefits
Gerald A. McGuire, Corp. V.P. & Pres/C.E.O.— Pepsi-Cola Gen. Bottlers
John R. Moore, Corp. V.P. & Pres./C.E.O.—Midas Int'l.
J. Larry Vowell, Corp. V.P. & Pres./C.E.O.— Hussmann

Consolidated Balance Sheet   As of December 31, 1994 (000 omitted)

Assets		Liabilities & Stockholders' Equity	
Current assets	$ 707,700	Current liabilities	$ 483,100
Investments	222,600	Long-term debt	723,000
Net property, plant & equipment	613,800	Deferred taxes	15,600
Other assets	591,300	Other liabilities	361,100
		*Stockholders' equity	552,600
Total	$2,135,400	Total	$2,135,400

*105,031,674 shares common stock outstanding.

Consolidated Income Statement

Years Ended Dec. 31	Thousands — — — —		Per Share — — —		Common Stock Price Range Calendar Year	
	Revenues	Net Income[a]	Earnings	Cash Dividends		
1994	$2,658,800	$103,200	$ .97	$ .33	18	— 14-3/4
1993	2,529,700	78,200[b]	.73[b]	.29	17	— 12-3/4
1992	2,388,000	59,800	.56	.26	16-3/8	— 12-1/4
1991	2,393,300	97,600	.92	.45	27	— 11
1990	2,305,000	19,300[c]	(.19)[c]	1.05	29-3/4	— 17

[a]Before preferred dividend requirement of $38,600,000 in 1990.
[b]Includes a charge to reflect FAS 106, resulting in a cumulative effect of $24,000,000 ($.22 per share).
[c]Includes an aftertax charge of $149,400,000 ($1.45 per share) for restructuring.

Transfer Agent & Registrar: First Chicago Trust Co. of New York

General Counsel:	William B. Moore, V.P.	Traded (Symbol):	NYSE, CSE, PSE (WH)
Investor Relations:	Charles H. Connolly, V.P.	Stockholders:	21,607
Human Resources:	Lawrence J. Pilon, Sr. V.P.	Employees:	15,271
Auditors:	KPMG Peat Marwick LLP	Annual Meeting:	In May

First Chicago Guide

Wickes Lumber Company

706 North Deerpath Drive, Vernon Hills, Illinois 60061
Telephone: (708) 367-3400

Wickes Lumber Company is a major retailer and distributor of building materials. The company sells its products and services primarily to building professionals, as well as to serious do-it-yourselfers involved in major home improvement projects. The company operates 130 lumber and building materials centers under the name "Wickes Lumber" in 24 states located in the Midwest (74 building centers), the Northeast (37 building centers), and the South (19 building centers). Wickes Lumber also operates 11 component manufacturing facilities that produce and distribute such value-added products as pre-hung door units, roof and floor trusses, and framed wall panels. Incorporated in Delaware in 1988.

Directors (In addition to indicated officers)

Albert Ernest, Jr.
Jon F. Hanson
Robert E. Mulcahy III

Frederick H. Schultz
Claudia B. Slacik

Officers (Directors*)

*J. Steven Wilson, Chm. & C.E.O.
*Kenneth M. Kirschner, V. Chm., Gen. Coun. & Secy.
Douglas J. Woods, Pres. & C.O.O.
George A. Bajalia, Sr. V.P., C.F.O. & Treas.
Gene L. Curtin, V.P.—MIS

E. Trevor Dignall, V.P.—Hum. Res.
George C. Finkenstaedt, V.P.—Bus. Dev.
Robert W. Rowatt, V.P. & Sr. Mdse. Mgr.
Robert F. Sherlock, V.P.—Mktg. & Sales
John M. Lawrence, Asst. V.P. & Cont.

Consolidated Balance Sheet As of December 31, 1994 (000 omitted)

Assets		Liabilities & Stockholders' Equity	
Current assets	$239,694	Current liabilities	$ 76,183
Net property, plant & equipment	56,847	Long-term debt	213,244
Other assets	23,032	*Stockholders' equity	30,146
Total	$319,573	Total	$319,573

*5,636,387 shares common and 499,768 shares Class B non-voting common stock outstanding.

Consolidated Income Statement

Years Ended Abt. Dec. 31	Thousands		Per Share[a]		Common Stock Price Range[a] Calendar Year
	Net Sales	Net Income	Earnings	Cash Dividends	
1994[b]	$986,872	$ 28,054	$4.59	$ .00	24-3/4 — 10
1993[c]	846,842	8,183[d]	1.34[d]	.00	18-1/4 — 12-1/4
1992[c]	745,365	6,004	.98		
1991[e]	745,842	(23,877)			
1990	847,112	(15,328)			

[a]Adjusted to reflect a 21.73-for-1 stock split in October 1993. Initial public offering in October 1993.
[b]Includes a charge related to headquarters cost reduction program, a gain on the sale of the private label credit card portfolio, and a deferred tax benefit.
[c]Pro forma gives effect to the recapitalization plan completed on October 22, 1993, as if had occurred on December 29, 1991.
[d]Includes an extraordinary gain of $1,241,000 ($.20 per share).
[e]Includes FAS 106, resulting in a one-time non-cash charge of $1,914,000.

Transfer Agent & Registrar: First Interstate Bank of California

General Counsel:
Kirschner, Main, Petrie, Graham, Tanner & Demont

Investor Relations: George A. Bajalia, Sr. V.P.

Human Resources: E. Trevor Dignall, V.P.

Mgt. Info. Svcs.: Gene L. Curtin, V.P.

Auditors: Coopers & Lybrand L.L.P.

Traded (Symbol): NASDAQ (WIKS)

Stockholders: 6,000

Employees: 4,523

Annual Meeting: In May

Wisconsin Central Transportation Corporation

6250 North River Road, Suite 9000, Rosemont, Illinois 60018
Telephone: (708) 318-4600

Wisconsin Central Transportation Corporation (WCTC) operates the largest regional railroad in the U.S. and the largest railroad in the state of Wisconsin. In addition to Wisconsin, the company provides service to the Upper Peninsula of Michigan, northeastern Illinois, eastern Minnesota, and northern Ontario. The company's operations utilize 2,817 route miles of track and trackage rights, 215 locomotives and 10,715 railcars. WCTC provides freight transportation to customers that ship a variety of products. Subsidiaries include Wisconsin Central Ltd. (WCL), WCL Railcars, Inc., Fox Valley & Western Ltd. (FVW), Wisconsin Central International, Inc., Sault Ste. Marie Bridge Co., Algoma Central Railway Inc. (ACRI), and WC Canada Holdings, Inc. In January 1995, the company consummated the acquisition of the railway assets of Algoma Central Corporation through the company's ACRI subsidiary. Incorporated in Delaware in 1987.

Directors   (In addition to indicated officers)

Carl Ferenbach
Michael R. Haverty
Roland V. McPherson

Thomas W. Rissman, Secy.
Robert H. Wheeler

Officers   (Directors*)

*Edward A. Burkhardt, Pres. & C.E.O.
*Thomas F. Power, Jr., Exec. V.P. & C.F.O.
Randy H. Henke, V.P.—Planning
Walter C. Kelly, V.P.—Fin.
Susan H. Norton, Treas.
Glenn J. Kerbs, V.P.—Eng. (WCL, FVW, ACRI)

Robert F. Nadrowski, V.P.—Mechanical (WCL, FVW, ACRI)
William R. Schauer, V.P.—Mktg. (WCL, FVW, ACRI)
J.E. Terbell, V.P. & Gen. Mgr. (WCL, FVW, ACRI)

Consolidated Balance Sheet   As of December 31, 1994 (000 omitted)

Assets		Liabilities & Stockholders' Equity	
Current assets	$ 59,602	Current liabilities	$ 80,789
Net property, plant & equipment	338,854	Long-term debt	102,500
Investment in affiliate	33,612	Deferred income taxes	42,328
Other assets	1,545	Deferred income	13,431
		Other liabilities	4,087
		*Stockholders' equity	190,478
Total	$433,613	Total	$433,613

*16,647,117 shares common stock outstanding.

Consolidated Income Statement

Years Ended Dec. 31	Thousands — — — — Operating Revenues	Net Income	Per Share[a] — — — — Earnings	Cash Dividends	Common Stock Price Range[a] Calendar Year
1994	$211,139	$36,695[b]	$2.21[b]	$ .00	48-1/4 — 29
1993	151,691	15,371[c]	.93[c]	.00	30 — 17-7/8
1992	124,364	10,881	.84	.00	18-5/8 — 10
1991	113,657	8,251[c]	.76[c]	.00	10-3/4 — 8-1/4[d]
1990	113,289	7,546	.94	.00	

[a]Adjusted to reflect a 2-for-1 stock split in July 1994.
[b]Net of an extraordinary charge of $1,587,000, net of income taxes ($.10 per share) associated with debt restructuring.
[c]Net of an extraordinary charge of $1,398,000, net of income taxes ($.08 per share) in 1993 and $341,000, net of income taxes ($.03 per share) in 1991 for the writeoff of deferred financing costs relating to the prepayment of debt; and cumulative effect of FAS 109, amounting to $2,067,000 ($.13 per share) in 1993.
[d]From the date of the company's initial public offering in May 1991 until December 31, 1991.

Transfer Agent & Registrar:	The First National Bank of Boston		
General Counsel:	Oppenheimer Wolff & Donnelly	Auditors:	KPMG Peat Marwick LLP
Investor Relations:		Traded (Symbol):	NASDAQ (WCLX)
Thomas F. Power, Jr., Exec. V.P./C.F.O.		Stockholders:	4,850
Human Resources:	David M. French, Asst. V.P.	Employees:	1,704
Mgt. Info. Svcs.:	Samuel J. Alex, Asst. V.P.	Annual Meeting:	In May

WMS Industries Inc.

3401 North California Ave., Chicago, Illinois 60618
Telephone: (312) 728-2300

WMS Industries Inc. is engaged in several segments of the leisure/amusement industry. The company designs, manufactures and sells coin-operated pinball, video, and shuffle-alley amusement games, video lottery terminals and gaming devices; publishes home video games; and owns and operates several hotels and casinos in Puerto Rico. The company operates through its wholly owned subsidiaries, Williams Electronics Games, Inc., Midway Manufacturing Company, Lenc-Smith Inc., WMS Gaming Inc., Williams Entertainment Inc., and WMS Games Parts & Services Inc. Games are marketed under the "Williams," "Bally" and "Midway" names. Williams Hospitality Group Inc., which is 62 percent-owned, runs the hotel/casino operations. WMS Industries maintains manufacturing plants in Chicago, Gurnee and Cicero, Illinois. Williams Entertainment Inc. operates from facilities in Texas and California. In April 1995, WMS Industries announced it had reached an agreement in principle to buy Bally Gaming International Inc. Incorporated in Delaware in 1974.

Directors (In addition to indicated officers)

Norman J. Menell, V. Chm.
George R. Baker
William C. Bartholomay
Kenneth J. Fedesna

William E. McKenna
Harvey Reich
Ira S. Sheinfeld

Officers (Directors*)

*Louis J. Nicastro, Chm. & Co-C.E.O.
*Neil D. Nicastro, Pres., Co-C.E.O. & C.O.O.

Harold H. Bach, Jr., V.P.—Fin., C.F.O., Chf. Acct. Off. & Treas.
Barbara M. Norman, V.P., Secy. & Gen. Coun.

Consolidated Balance Sheet   As of June 30, 1994 (000 omitted)

Assets		Liabilities & Stockholders' Equity	
Current assets	$191,346	Current liabilities	$ 47,355
Net property, plant & equipment	70,697	Long-term debt	88,256
Other assets	81,098	Deferred items	3,006
		Other liabilities	23,052
		*Stockholders' equity	181,472
Total	$343,141	Total	$343,141

*24,098,300 shares common stock outstanding.

Consolidated Income Statement

Years Ended June 30	Thousands — — — — Total Revenue	Net Income	Per Share[a] — — — — Earnings	Cash Dividends	Common Stock Price Range[a] Calendar Year
1994	$358,213	$ 28,483	$ 1.19	$ .00	29-7/8 — 15-7/8
1993	331,129	30,709	1.31	.00	34 — 17-1/8
1992	227,008	25,015[b]	1.21[b]	.00	25 — 13-3/8
1991	161,188	10,856[c]	.64[c]	.00	14-1/2 — 1-5/8
1990[d]	147,062	(10,293)	(.62)	.00	5-5/8 — 1-3/4

[a]Adjusted to reflect a 2-for-1 stock split in February 1992.
[b]Includes tax benefits of $8,000,000 ($.39 per share).
[c]Includes an extraordinary gain of $1,984,000 ($.12 per share) from early extinguishment of debt.
[d]Includes a charge of $7,023,000 relating to the writeoff of the company's investment in Divi Hotels N.V. and a $2,800,000 expense related to the relocation of corporate headquarters, offset by a $2,033,000 gain on insurance recovery over the book value of fixed assets damaged by Hurricane Hugo.

Transfer Agent & Registrar: The Bank of New York

General Counsel: Shack & Siegel, P.C.

Investor Relations: Harold H. Bach, Jr., V.P.

Auditors: Ernst & Young LLP

Traded (Symbol):   NYSE (WMS)
Stockholders: 2,000
Employees: 4,500
Annual Meeting: In January

WMX Technologies, Inc.

3003 Butterfield Road, Oak Brook, Illinois 60521
Telephone: (708) 572-8800

WMX Technologies, Inc. (formerly Waste Management, Inc.), is a leading international provider of environmental, engineering and construction, industrial and related services. Operations include recycling, collection, transfer, and disposal of solid and hazardous wastes, the management of low-level radioactive wastes, resource-recovery, and related waste reduction programs. The company's subsidiary, Waste Management, Inc., serves about 1,009,000 commercial and industrial customers and approximately 12-million residential customers in the U.S. and Canada. Chemical Waste Management, Inc. (CWM) provides the nation's largest comprehensive hazardous waste management capabilities. Chem-Nuclear Systems, Inc., a CWM subsidiary, provides low-level radioactive waste disposal. Waste Management International plc provides comprehensive waste management and related services in various countries. Wheelabrator Technologies Inc. (WTI) offers leadership in trash-to-energy and independent power systems, clean air technologies, and wastewater treatment systems and operations. Rust International Inc. (Rust), a subsidiary owned 56% by CWM and 40% by WTI, furnishes engineering, construction, environmental and infrastructure consulting, and related services. Incorporated in Delaware in 1968.

Directors (In addition to indicated officers)

H. Jesse Arnelle	James B. Edwards	James R. Peterson
Howard H. Baker, Jr.	Donald F. Flynn	Alexander B. Trowbridge
Pastora San Juan Cafferty	Peter H. Huizenga	
Jerry E. Dempsey	Peer Pedersen	

Officers (Directors*)

*Dean L. Buntrock, Chm. & C.E.O.
*Phillip B. Rooney, Pres. & C.O.O.
Herbert A. Getz, Sr. V.P., Gen. Coun. & Secy.
James E. Koenig, Sr. V.P., C.F.O. & Treas.
D.P. "Pat" Payne, Sr. V.P.—Hum. Res. & Comm.
Rodney C. Gilbert, V.P.—Tech. Dev. & Mgt.
Thomas C. Hau, V.P. & Cont.
H. Vaughn Hooks, V.P.—Tax

Ronald M. Jericho, V.P.—Rept.
Frank B. Moore, V.P.—Govt. Aff.
Susan C. Nustra, V.P.—Treas.
William J. Plunkett, V.P.—Communic.
Bruce D. Tobecksen, V.P.—Fin.
Donald A. Wallgren, V.P.—Chf. Envir. Officer
Thomas A. Witt, V.P. & Assoc. Gen. Coun.
Linda R. Witte, V.P. & Assoc. Gen. Coun.

Consolidated Balance Sheet As of December 31, 1994 (000 omitted)

Assets		Liabilities & Stockholders' Equity	
Current assets	$ 3,088,844	Current liabilities	$ 3,179,731
Net property, plant & equipment	9,285,752	Long-term debt	6,044,411
Other assets	5,164,318	Deferred items	1,985,298
		Other liabilities	1,788,493
		*Stockholders' equity	4,540,981
Total	$17,538,914	Total	$17,538,914

*484,000,129 shares common stock outstanding.

Consolidated Income Statement

Years Ended Dec. 31	Thousands — — — — Revenue	Net Income	Per Share — — — — Earnings	Cash Dividends	Common Stock Price Range Calendar Year
1994	$10,097,318	$784,381[a]	$1.62	$ .60	30-3/4 — 22-5/8
1993	9,135,577	452,776[b]	.93	.58	40-1/4 — 23
1992	8,661,027	850,036[c]	1.72	.50	46-5/8 — 32
1991	7,550,914	606,323[d]	1.23	.42	44-3/8 — 32-5/8
1990	6,034,406	684,762[e]	1.44	.35	45-1/2 — 28-5/8

[a]Includes a charge of $9,200,000 before tax & minority interest recorded by Rust to write-off assets and recognize costs of exiting certain of its service lines and closing offices in a consolidation of engineering/construct. groups.
[b]Includes nontaxable gain of $15,109,000 relating to the issuance of shares by Rust and a special asset revaluation and restructuring charge of $550 million before tax and minority interest, recorded by CWM related primarily to a revaluation of its thermal treatment business and a provision of about $14 million to adjust deferred income taxes resulting from '93 tax law change.
[c]Results include a non-taxable gain of $240 million before minority interest, from the IPO of Waste Management Int'l. plc; special charges of $219.9 million before tax and minority interest; and one-time charges aggregating $71,139,000 related to adoption of FAS 106 and FAS 109.
[d]Results include a special charge of $296 million before tax and minority interest.
[e]Results include an extraordinary charge of $24,547,000.

Transfer Agent & Registrar: Harris Trust and Savings Bank

General Counsel:	Herbert A. Getz, Sr. V.P.	Traded (Symbol):	
Investor Relations:	James E. Koenig, Sr. V.P.	CSE,NYSE,London,Frankfurt,3 Swiss (WMX)	
Human Resources:	D.P. "Pat" Payne, Sr. V.P.		
Mgt. Info. Svcs.:	Bert Young	Stockholders:	65,000
Auditors:	Arthur Andersen LLP	Employees:	74,400
		Annual Meeting:	In May

First Chicago Guide

Woodhead Industries, Inc.

2150 East Lake Cook Road, Suite 400, Buffalo Grove, Illinois 60089
Telephone: (708) 465-8300

Woodhead Industries, Inc., engages primarily in the manufacture and sale of devices for the control and distribution of electrical power for industry. The company serves a broad range of worldwide industries with electrical specialties and mechanical motion control products. The company's products can be classified into three groups: electrical specialties; reels and power systems; and molded rubber products. Electrical specialty products include portable handlamps, low-voltage safety lights, wiring devices, weatherproof receptacles, circuit testers, portable power distribution equipment, pendant pushbutton enclosures, general-purpose power and control connectors, and custom copper and fiber optic cable assemblies. Reels and power systems include such products as electric cord and cable reels, electric cable festooning systems, collector rings, static discharge reels, tool balancers, ergonomic workstations, hose reels, and multiple-cable carrier systems. To identify its electrical specialty products and for safety purposes, Woodhead makes these products, whenever feasible, in a brilliant chrome-yellow color under the name, Safety Yellow®. The company distributes its products, depending on type and market, to original equipment manufacturers, directly to users, or through selected distributors worldwide. Major subsidiaries include Daniel Woodhead Co., Aero-Motive Co., Aero-Motive (U.K.) Ltd., Woodhead Canada Ltd., AI/FOCS, Inc., Woodhead Asia PTE. Ltd., AKAPP Electro Industrie, B.V., and H.F. Vogel GmbH. Incorporated in Illinois in 1922; reincorporated in Delaware in 1977.

Directors (In addition to indicated officer)

Alan Reed, Chm.
Daniel T. Carroll
Charles W. Denny
Dale A. Miller

Robert D. Tuttle
Richard A. Virzi
Ward M. Woodhead

Officers (Director*)

*C. Mark DeWinter, Pres. & C.E.O.
Robert G. Jennings, V.P.—Fin. & C.F.O.
Robert A. Moulton, V.P.—Hum. Res.

Robert J. Tortorello, V.P., Gen. Coun. & Corp. Secy.
Joseph P. Nogal, Treas, Cont. & Asst. Secy.

Consolidated Balance Sheet   As of October 1, 1994 (000 omitted)

Assets		Liabilities & Stockholders' Equity	
Current assets	$32,256	Current liabilities	$17,684
Net property, plant & equipment	21,131	Long-term debt	63
Other assets	8,876	Deferred items	1,569
		*Stockholders' equity	42,947
Total	$62,263	Total	$62,263

*6,894,000 shares common stock outstanding.

Consolidated Income Statement

Years Ended Abt. Sept. 30	Thousands — — — — Net Sales	Net Income	Per Share[a] — — — — Earnings	Cash Dividends	Common Stock Price Range[a] Calendar Year
1994	$105,689	$7,250	$ .68	$ .23	12-1/4 — 8-7/8
1993	89,864	5,803	.55	.23	10-5/8 — 7-5/8
1992	79,518	4,755	.47	.23	8-3/4 — 5-1/8
1991	73,499	2,820	.29	.23	5-7/8 — 4-3/8
1990	72,168	5,020	.52	.21	5-7/8 — 4

[a]Adjusted for a 3-for-2 stock split in the form of a 50% stock dividend in May 1995 and a 2-for-1 stock split declared in January 1993.

Transfer Agent & Registrar:	Harris Trust and Savings Bank		
General Counsel:	Robert J. Tortorello, V.P.	Traded (Symbol):	NASDAQ (WDHD)
Investor Relations:	Robert G. Jennings, V.P.	Stockholders:	598
Human Resources:	Robert A. Moulton, V.P.	Employees:	1,079
Auditors:	Arthur Andersen LLP	Annual Meeting:	In January

First Chicago Guide

Woodward Governor Company

5001 North Second Street, Rockford, Illinois 61125-7001
Telephone: (815) 877-7441

Woodward Governor Company designs, manufactures, and sells prime mover controls and accessories. Prime movers convert heat or hydraulic energy into mechanical or electrical energy. The company provides controls for prime movers including diesel engines, hydraulic turbines, steam engines, aircraft propellers, industrial gas turbines, and aircraft gas turbines. The company is organized into two main groups — Aircraft Controls and Industrial Controls. The Aircraft Controls group consists of Large Aircraft Controls, Small Aircraft Controls, Aircraft Product Service Center, and Test Equipment business units. The Industrial Controls business units are Turbomachinery Controls, Engine Controls, and Hydraulic Turbine Controls. The products control the rotational speed as well as other functions of these machines. The company distributes its products by direct sale to original equipment manufacturers, service providers, and equipment users throughout the world. Plants are located in Illinois, Wisconsin, Colorado, Connecticut and Australia. Subsidiary operations are located in The Netherlands, England, Japan, Germany, Brazil, Canada and Singapore. Incorporated in Illinois in 1902 as successor to a business originally established in 1870; reincorporated in Delaware in 1976.

Directors (In addition to indicated officers)

J. Grant Beadle
Carl J. Dargene
Lawrence E. Gloyd
Thomas W. Heenan

J. Peter Jeffrey
Mark E. Leum
Michael T. Yonker

Officers (Directors*)

*John A. Halbrook, Chm., Pres. & C.E.O.
*Vern H. Cassens, Sr. V.P., C.F.O. & Treas.
Ronald E. Fulkrod, V.P.
Peter A. Gomm, V.P.
Duane L. Miller, V.P.

C. Phillip Turner, V.P.
Gary D. Larrew, Asst. V.P.
Terry A. Shetler, Asst. V.P.
Carol J. Manning, Secy.
Stephen P. Carter, Asst. Treas.

Consolidated Balance Sheet   As of September 30, 1994 (000 omitted)

Assets		Liabilities & Stockholders' Equity	
Current assets	$181,279	Current liabilities	$ 67,528
Net property, plant & equipment	122,911	Long-term debt	32,665
Other assets	19,128	Other liabilities	29,279
		*Stockholders' equity	193,846
Total	$323,318	Total	$323,318

*2,924,089 shares common stock outstanding.

Consolidated Income Statement

Years Ended Sept. 30	Thousands — — — —		Per Share — — —		Common Stock Price Range Fiscal Year	
	Net Sales	Net Income	Earnings	Cash Dividends		
1994	$333,207	$(3,273)	$(1.11)	$3.72	87	— 65
1993	331,156	(4,028)[a]	(1.36)[a]	3.72	80	— 60
1992	374,173	20,212	7.23	3.70	113	— 70
1991	361,924	24,293	8.86	3.70	115	— 84
1990	340,128	29,439	10.74	3.35	135	—100

[a]Includes a charge to reflect FAS 106, FAS 109 and FAS 112, resulting in a cumulative effect of $17,417,000 ($5.86 per share).

Transfer Agent & Registrar: Wachovia Bank and Trust Co., N.A.

Corporate Counsel:	Chapman & Cutler	Auditors:	Coopers & Lybrand L.L.P.
Intern. Counsel:	Baker & McKenzie	Traded (Symbol):	OTC (WGOV)
Investor Relations:	Carol J. Manning, Secy.	Stockholders:	2,256
		Employees:	3,439
Human Resources:	Thomas A. Parlette, Mgr.	Annual Meeting:	In January

First Chicago Guide

Wm. Wrigley Jr. Company
410 North Michigan Avenue, Chicago, Illinois 60611-4287
Telephone: (312) 644-2121

Wm. Wrigley Jr. Company is a producer of chewing gum. Products marketed under the brand names of Wrigley's Spearmint, Doublemint, Juicy Fruit, Extra, Freedent, Winterfresh, and Big Red are sold throughout the U.S. and Canada. All or some of these brands and other brands are sold in the United Kingdom, Europe, Australia, New Zealand, and more than 100 other countries. The company's main U.S. plant is in Chicago; other U.S. plants are located in Santa Cruz, California, and Gainesville, Georgia. Foreign plants are in Australia, Austria, Canada, China, England, France, Kenya, the Philippines, and Taiwan. Two new international plants are under construction in India and Poland. In addition, Wrigley owns four domestic associated companies: Amurol Confections Company, a manufacturer of children's confectionery products; L.A. Dreyfus Company, a manufacturer of chewing gum base; Northwestern Flavors, Inc., which processes flavorings and rectifies mint oil; and Four-Ten Corporation. Incorporated in Delaware in 1927.

Directors (In addition to indicated officers)

Charles F. Allison III
Lee Phillip Bell
Robert P. Billingsley

Gary E. Gardner
Penny Sue Pritzker
Richard K. Smucker

Officers (Directors*)

*William Wrigley, Pres. & C.E.O.
*R. Darrell Ewers, Exec. V.P.
Douglas S. Barrie, Grp. V.P.—Int'l.
Ronald O. Cox, Grp. V.P.—Mktg.
John F. Bard, Sr. V.P.
Martin J. Geraghty, Sr. V.P.—Mfg.
Donald E. Balster, V.P.—Prod.
Gary R. Bebee, V.P.—Cust. Mktg.
David E. Boxell, V.P.—Personnel
J.E. Dy-Liacco, V.P.—Int'l.
Susan S. Fox, V.P.—Cons. Mktg.
Philip G. Hamilton, V.P.—Int'l.

H.J. Kim, V.P.—Eng.
Jon Orving, V.P.—Int'l.
Dushan Petrovich, V.P. & Treas.
Stefan Pfander, V.P.—Int'l.
Wm. M. Piet, V.P.—Corp. Aff. & Corp. Secy.
John A. Schafer, V.P.—Purch.
Philip G. Schnell, V.P.—R&D
Christafor E. Sundstrom, V.P.—Corp. Devel.
*William Wrigley, Jr., V.P.
Dennis J. Yarbrough, Corp. Cont.
John H. Sutton, Gen. Mgr.—Converting Div.

Consolidated Balance Sheet   As of December 31, 1994 (000 omitted)

Assets		Liabilities & Stockholders' Equity	
Current assets	$623,312	Current liabilities	$209,898
Net property, plant & equipment	289,420	Deferred items	15,760
Other assets	66,102	Other liabilities	64,706
		*Stockholders' equity	688,470
Total	$978,834	Total	$978,834

*91,134,000 shares common and 25,075,000 shares Class B common stock outstanding.

Consolidated Income Statement

Years Ended Dec. 31	Thousands — — — — Net Sales	Net Income	Per Share[a] — — — — Earnings	Cash Dividends	Common Stock Price Range[a] Calendar Year
1994	$1,596,551	$230,533	$1.98	$ .90	53-7/8 — 38-1/8
1993	1,428,504	174,891	1.50	.75	46-1/8 — 29-1/2
1992	1,286,921	141,295[b]	1.21[b]	.62	39-7/8 — 22-1/8
1991	1,148,875	128,652	1.09	.55	27　　— 16-3/8
1990	1,110,639	117,362	1.00	.49	19-3/4 — 14-1/2

[a]Adjusted to reflect a 3-for-1 stock split in September 1992.
[b]Includes a charge to reflect FAS 106 and FAS 109, resulting in a cumulative effect of $7,278,000 ($.06 per share).

Transfer Agent & Registrar: First Chicago Trust Co. of New York

General Counsel:		Auditors:	Ernst & Young LLP
Steven C. Houston, Asst. V.P.—Legal		Traded (Symbol):	NYSE, CSE (WWY)
Investor Relations:	Christopher J. Perille, Mgr.	Stockholders:	24,078
Human Resources:	David E. Boxell, V.P.	Employees:	7,000
Mgt. Info. Svcs.:	Dennis R. Mally	Annual Meeting:	In March

First Chicago Guide

Zebra Technologies Corporation

333 Corporate Woods Parkway, Vernon Hills, Illinois 60061-3109
Telephone: (708) 634-6700

Zebra Technologies Corporation provides bar code labeling solutions principally to manufacturing customers, and also to service and governmental entities worldwide for use in automatic identification and data collection systems. The company designs, manufactures, sells, and supports a broad line of computerized label/ticket printing systems and related specialty supplies. The company's equipment is designed to operate at the user's location to produce and dispense high quality bar coded labels in extremely time-sensitive and physically demanding environments. Zebra's solutions approach integrates its applications expertise, computerized printing systems, and specialty supplies. Applications for the company's systems include inventory control, automated warehousing, JIT (Just-In-Time) manufacturing, CIM (Computer Integrated Manufacturing), employee time and attendance records, weighing systems, tool room control, shop floor control, library systems, prescription labeling, and scientific experimentation. Incorporated in Illinois in 1969; reincorporated in Delaware in 1991.

Directors (In addition to indicated officers)

Christopher G. Knowles
David P. Riley

Michael A. Smith

Officers (Directors*)

*Edward L. Kaplan, Chm. & C.E.O.
Jeffrey K. Clements, Pres.
*Gerhard Cless, Exec. V.P. & Secy.
Jack A. LeVan, Sr. V.P.—Mktg.

Thomas C. Beusch, V.P.—Sales
Clive P. Hohberger, Ph.D., V.P.—Tech. Dev.
John H. Kindsvater, Jr., V.P.—Corp. Dev.
Charles R. Whitchurch, C.F.O. & Treas.

Consolidated Balance Sheet As of December 31, 1994 (000 omitted)

Assets		Liabilities & Stockholders' Equity	
Current assets	$88,679	Current liabilities	$12,438
Net property, plant & equipment	5,632	Obligation under capital lease	236
Other assets	732	Deferred rent	337
		*Stockholders' equity	82,032
Total	$95,043	Total	$95,043

*7,678,200 shares Class A common and 4,354,887 shares Class B common stock outstanding.

Consolidated Income Statement

Years Ended Abt. Dec. 31	Thousands — — — —		Per Share[a] — — —		Common Stock Price Range[a][b] Calendar Year
	Net Sales	Net Income	Earnings	Cash Dividends	
1994	$107,103	$21,073	$1.75	$ .00	57-1/4 — 23-1/2
1993	87,456	18,255	1.52	.00	60-3/4 — 20-1/4
1992	58,711	11,843	.99	.00	24-3/4 — 14-1/2
1991	45,623	8,487[c]	.75[c]	.00	19 — 14-1/2[d]
1990[e]	37,982	6,630[c]	.61[c]		

[a]Adjusted to reflect a 93-for-1 stock split in August 1991.
[b]Class A common stock.
[c]Pro forma.
[d]Initial public offering in August 1991.
[e]Includes results of operations, assets and liabilities of Zebra International Corporation, which now is a subsidiary of the company.

Transfer Agent & Registrar: Harris Trust and Savings Bank

General Counsel: Katten Muchin & Zavis

Investor Relations:
  Charles R. Whitchurch, C.F.O.

Human Resources: Bruce Bebee, Dir.

Mgt. Info. Svcs.: Dean Cochran, Dir.

Auditors: KPMG Peat Marwick LLP

Traded (Symbol): NASDAQ (ZBRA)

Stockholders: 2,500

Employees: 500

Annual Meeting: In May

Zeigler Coal Holding Company

50 Jerome Lane, Fairview Heights, Illinois 62208
Telephone: (618) 394-2400

Zeigler Coal Holding Company, through its subsidiaries, is a coal producer operating 13 underground and surface coal mining complexes located in Illinois, Indiana, Kentucky, Ohio, West Virginia, and Wyoming. In addition, Zeigler operates import/export terminals in Virginia and South Carolina, and owns a clean coal technology demonstration plant in Wyoming. Zeigler Coal was formed in connection with a management-led buyout from Houston Natural Gas Corporation in 1985. In September 1994, the company completed an initial public offering of 10,467,564 shares of common stock. Incorporated in Delaware in 1985.

Directors (In addition to indicated officers)

Roland E. Casati
Robert W. Ericson
Jack E. Little

John F. Manley
Philip G. Turberville

Officers (Directors*)

*Michael K. Reilly, Chm.
*Chand B. Vyas, Pres. & C.E.O.
W. Douglas Blackburn, Jr., Sr. V.P.—Oper.
Francis L. Barkofske, V.P.—External Affairs
George J. Holway, V.P. & C.F.O.

Michael R. Loreman, V.P.—Hum. Res.
Brent L. Motchan, V.P., Gen. Coun. & Secy.
Sharad M. Desai, Treas.
Paul D. Femmer, Cont.

Consolidated Balance Sheet   As of December 31, 1994 (000 omitted)

Assets		Liabilities & Stockholders' Equity	
Current assets	$ 191,242	Current liabilities	$ 123,610
Net property, plant & equipment	951,116	Long-term debt	450,058
Other assets	18,709	Accrued postretirement benefit obligations	252,521
		Other liabilities	236,507
		*Stockholders' equity	98,371
Total	$1,161,067	Total	$1,161,067

*28,355,616 shares common stock outstanding.

Consolidated Income Statement

Years Ended Dec. 31	Thousands — — — —		Per Share[a] — — — —		Common Stock Price Range[ab] Calendar Year
	Total Revenues	Net Income	Earnings	Cash Dividends	
1994	$870,890	$ 25,093[c]	$ 1.01[c]	$ .05	15-3/4 — 10-1/2
1993	873,001	(146,182)[d]	(6.29)[d]	.00	
1992	503,006	74,384	3.26		
1991	455,783	37,608	1.61		
1990	273,700	29,500	1.26		

[a]Adjusted to reflect a 32-for-1 stock split in September 1994.
[b]Initial public offering in September 1994.
[c]Includes an extraordinary charge of $8,400,000 ($.34 per share) for extinguishment of debt.
[d]Includes a charge to reflect FAS 106 and FAS 109, resulting in a cumulative effect of $111,946,000 ($4.82 per share).

Transfer Agent & Registrar:	Harris Trust and Savings Bank		
General Counsel:	Brent L. Motchan, V.P.	Auditors:	Deloitte & Touche LLP
Investor Relations:		Traded (Symbol):	NYSE (ZEI)
Francis L. Barkofske, V.P.—External Affairs		Stockholders:	3,257
Human Resources:	Michael R. Loreman, V.P.	Employees:	3,965
Mgt. Info. Svcs.:	Ronald Goss, C.I.O.	Annual Meeting:	In May

Zenith Electronics Corporation

1000 Milwaukee Avenue, Glenview, Illinois 60025-2493
Telephone: (708) 391-7000

Zenith Electronics Corporation, founded in 1918, has been a leader in consumer electronics, first in radio, later in monochrome and color television, and other video products. The company's operations involve a dominant industry segment — the design, development, and manufacture of video products (including color television sets and other consumer products) along with parts and accessories for such products. These products, along with purchased video cassette recorders, are sold principally to major retail dealers and independent and wholly owned regional wholesale distributors in the U.S., Canada, and other foreign countries. The company intends to change over to an entirely direct-to-retail distribution organization during 1995. The company also sells directly to buying groups and private label customers in the lodging, health care, and rent-to-own industries. Zenith's video products also include color picture tubes that are produced for and sold to other manufacturers and Network Systems products such as cable and telecommunication set-top devices, interactive television, and data communication products, which are sold primarily to cable television operators and other commercial users of these products. The company has sold or downsized its non-core business activities. The company has manufacturing, warehousing, engineering, and research, administration, and distribution locations throughout the U.S. It also has locations in Canada, Taiwan, and Mexico. Subsidiaries include: Zenith Electronics Corporation of Texas; Zenith Radio Canada, Ltd.; Zenith Distributing Corp. of New York; Zenco of Chihuahua, S.A. de C.V.; and Partes de Television de Reynosa, S.A. de C.V. Incorporated in Illinois in 1923; reincorporated in Delaware in 1958.

Directors (In addition to indicated officers)

Harry G. Beckner	Ilene S. Gordon	Peter S. Willmott
T. Kimball Brooker	Charles Marshall	
David H. Cohen	Andrew McNally IV	

Officers (Directors*)[a]

* Jerry K. Pearlman, Chm.
* Albin F. Moschner, Pres. & C.E.O.
* Gerald M. McCarthy, Exec. V.P.—Sales/Mktg. & Pres.—Zenith Sales Co.
Kell B. Benson, Sr. V.P.—Fin. & C.F.O.
Philip S. Thompson, Sr. V.P.—Oper.
Richard F. Vitkus, Sr. V.P.—Gen. Coun.
John W. Bowler, V.P.—R&D & Network Systems Eng.
Larry G. Cockrell, V.P.—Cons. Prods. Sales
Terry L. Conner, V.P.—Mfg., West

Cynthia I. Fricas, V.P.—Purch. & Logist.
Michael J. Kaplan, V.P.—Hum. Res.
Richard C. Lueck, V.P.—Cont.
William G. Luehrs, V.P.—Network Systems Oper.
Wayne C. Luplow, V.P.—Cons. Prods. Eng. & HDTV
Willard C. McNitt III, V.P.—Treas.
Philip O. Savoie, V.P.—Mfg., East
John I. Taylor, V.P.—Pub. Aff. & Comm.
David S. Levin, Secy.
Patricia A. Strandberg, Asst. Secy.
Harlan R. May, Pres.—CRT Div.

[a]Pearlman will retire as Chairman on December 31, 1995.

Consolidated Balance Sheet As of December 31, 1994 (000 omitted)

Assets		Liabilities & Stockholders' Equity	
Current assets	$470,900	Current liabilities	$243,300
Net property, plant & equipment	168,100	Long-term debt	182,000
Other assets	14,600	*Stockholders' equity	228,300
Total	$653,600	Total	$653,600

*45,677,372 shares common stock outstanding.

Consolidated Income Statement

Years Ended Dec. 31	Thousands — — — — —		Per Share — — —		Common Stock Price Range Calendar Year
	Net Sales	Net Income	Earnings	Cash Dividends	
1994	$1,469,000	$(14,200)	$ (.34)	$ .00	14-1/8 — 7
1993[a]	1,228,200	(97,000)	(3.01)	.00	10-1/2 — 5-7/8
1992[b]	1,243,500	(105,900)	(3.59)	.00	11-1/8 — 5
1991	1,321,600	(51,600)	(1.79)	.00	9-3/8 — 5-1/8
1990	1,409,900	(65,200)	(2.43)	.00	13-1/2 — 4

[a]Includes $31,000,000 of restructuring and other charges. The company adopted FAS 112, which did not have a material effect on the financial statements.
[b]Includes $48,100,000 of restructuring and other charges. The company adopted FAS 109, which superseded FAS 96. It had no effect on the financial statements.

Transfer Agent & Registrar:	The Bank of New York		
General Counsel:	Richard F. Vitkus, Sr. V.P.	Auditors:	Arthur Andersen LLP
Investor Relations:	Willard C. McNitt III, V.P.—Treas.	Traded (Symbol):	CSE, NYSE, Swiss SE(3) (ZE)
Human Resources:	Michael J. Kaplan, V.P.	Stockholders:	16,544
		Employees:	22,500
Mgt. Info. Svcs.:	James Novosel, Dir.	Annual Meeting:	In April

Banks
And Savings
Institutions

Bank of America Illinois
231 South LaSalle Street, Chicago, Illinois 60697
Telephone: (312) 828-2345

Bank of America Illinois (formerly Continental Bank), a wholly owned subsidiary of BankAmerica Corporation, is a business bank serving corporations, institutional investors, and high net-worth individuals with complex financial needs. The bank offers credit, capital raising, trade finance, cash management, foreign exchange, risk management, investment management, personal trust, estate planning, and fiduciary services to its clients in the Midwest, nationally, and internationally. With assets of $215 billion, offices in key financial centers and 36 foreign countries, BankAmerica, through its subsidiaries, is one of the leading domestic providers of commercial and industrial loans. In August 1994, BankAmerica Corporation acquired Continental Bank Corporation.

Directors   (In addition to indicated officers)

David A. Coulter	Robert B. Goergen	Linda Johnson Rice
Bert A. Getz	Miles L. Marsh	Michael E. Rossi
Thomas A. Gildehaus	Roger H. Morley	Gordon I. Segal

Officers   (Directors*)

* William M. Goodyear, Chm. & C.E.O.
* Michael J. Murray, Grp. Exec. V.P.
* Michael E. O'Neill, Grp. Exec. V.P.
  Marcus W. Acheson IV, Exec. V.P.—
    Commercial Banking
  James D. Miller, Exec. V.P. —Chf.
    Investment Officer

William H. Minihan, Jr., Exec. V.P.—Chf.
  Info. Officer
Roger H. Sherman, Exec. V.P.—Banking
  Services
Wilma J. Smelcer, Exec. V.P.—Private Bank
Evan L. Evans, Chf. Human Res. Officer
John J. Higgins, Chf. Admin. Services Officer

Consolidated Statement of Condition   As of December 31, 1994 (000 omitted)

Assets		Liabilities & Stockholders' Equity	
Cash & due from banks	$ 2,046,000	Deposits	$10,189,000
Short-term investments	1,256,000	Borrowings	2,892,000
Net loans	10,425,000	Other liabilities	2,702,000
Premises & equipment	200,000	Stockholders' Equity	2,217,000
Other assets	4,073,000		
Total	$18,000,000	Total	$18,000,000

Year Ended Dec. 31	Total Deposits	Demand Deposits	Time Deposits	Foreign Office Deposits	Net Loans	Stockholders' Equity
1994	$10,189,000	$2,804,000	$5,943,000	$1,442,000	$10,425,000	$2,217,000
1993	14,084,000	2,907,000	7,376,000	3,801,000	11,371,000	2,015,000
1992	14,739,000	2,927,000	8,339,000	3,473,000	12,058,000	1,696,000
1991	16,389,000	2,546,000	8,622,000	5,221,000	13,463,000	1,560,000
1990	16,493,000	3,000,000	8,596,000	4,897,000	15,033,000	1,696,000

Consolidated Income Statement

Years Ended Dec. 31	Operating Income	Operating Expenses	Net Income
1994	N/A	N/A	N/A
1993	$1,708,000	$1,475,000	$369,000
1992	1,697,000	1,496,000	199,000
1991	2,258,000	2,322,000	(83,000)
1990	3,003,100	2,947,800	36,100

General Counsel:	Mayer, Brown & Platt	Auditors:	Ernst & Young LLP
Human Resources:	Evan L. Evans	Employees:	4,192
Mgt. Info. Svcs.:	William H. Minihan, Jr., Exec. V.P.		
		Member:	FDIC; Federal Reserve System

First Chicago Guide

Bank One, Chicago, NA

800 Davis Street, Evanston, Illinois 60204-0712
Telephone: (708) 866-5500

Bank One, Chicago, NA (formerly Bank One, Evanston, NA), is a national banking association and a wholly owned subsidiary of Banc One Illinois Corporation. As of April 1, 1993, Bank One, Wilmette; Bank One, Elgin; Bank One, LaGrange; and Bank One, Chicago, were merged with and into Bank One, Chicago, NA. The bank offers its customers full commercial banking services, real estate lending, consumer lending, personal banking services, and trust investment services. In addition to its downtown Evanston office, Bank One, Chicago, NA, has 23 branch offices primarily in suburban areas. Bank One, Chicago, NA, was chartered under the National Banking Act in 1933; present name adopted in 1993.

Directors   (In addition to indicated officer)

Paul Adams	Sally A. Jackson
John N. Brincat	Leonard P. Judy
James W. Collins	Bruce I. McPhee
John J. McDonough	Nancy A. Stevenson
Arthur G. Hailand, Jr.	Anthony Tako

Officers   (Director*)

* Stan Calderon, Chm. & C.E.O.	Jeff Struve, Sr. V.P.
Bill Meinen, Sr. V.P.	Robert Thomas, Sr. V.P.
Dennis O'Neill, Sr. V.P.	Harry A. Wilmer, Sr. V.P.
Molly Smith, Sr. V.P. & C.F.O.	

Consolidated Balance Sheet   As of December 31, 1994 (000 omitted)

Assets		Liabilities & Stockholders' Equity	
Cash & due from banks	$ 96,505	Deposits	$1,268,887
Securities & short-term investments	177,761	Funds borrowed	325,473
Net loans	1,437,537	Other liabilities	30,518
Property & equipment	23,946	Stockholders' equity	161,245
Other assets	50,374		
Total	$1,786,123	Total	$1,786,123

Years Ended Dec. 31	Thousands Total Deposits	Demand Deposits	Time Deposits	Net Loans	Capital Accounts
1994	$1,268,887	$257,748	$1,011,139	$1,437,537	$161,245
1993	1,374,286	289,190	1,085,096	1,336,113	151,628

Consolidated Income Statement (Information not publicly available)

Auditors:	Coopers & Lybrand L.L.P.	Employees:	719
Deposits Accounts:	162,000	Member:	FDIC; Federal Reserve System

Bell Federal Savings and Loan Association

79 West Monroe Street, Chicago, Illinois 60603-4988
Telephone: (312) 346-1000

Bell Federal Savings and Loan Association, a wholly owned subsidiary of Bell Bancorp, Inc., operates as a traditional thrift institution with the principal business being the solicitation of deposits from the general public and investing these deposits, together with funds generated from operations, primarily in single-family, owner-occupied adjustable rate mortgages. Bell Federal currently operates out of 14 locations, four in Chicago, five in suburban Cook County, three in Du Page County, one in Lake County, and one in Winnebago County. Bell Federal has one active wholly owned subsidiary, Bell Savings Service Corporation, which offers a full line of insurance products. Bell Federal was founded in 1925 by employees of Illinois Bell Telephone. Member FDIC.

Directors (In addition to indicated officers)

Richard T. Garrigan, Ph.D.
Fred I. Gillick
Richard W. Hanzel

Louis A. Holland
John L. Vitale

Officers (Directors*)

* Edmond M. Shanahan, Chm.
* Robert G. Rowen, Pres. & C.E.O.
  Joseph J. Bauer, Sr. V.P.
  Frank J. Donati, Sr. V.P. & Compt.
  Peter J. Grealish, Sr. V.P.

* John C. Savio, Sr. V.P. & C.F.O.
  Lucille G. Smith, Sr. V.P.
  Nancy J. Trutwin, Sr. V.P.
  Robert E. Ulbricht, Sr. V.P., Secy. & Gen. Coun.

Statement of Condition As of March 31, 1995 (000 omitted)

Assets		Liabilities & Reserves	
Investment securities	$ 43,604	Deposits	$1,519,220
Loans receivable, net	1,338,414	Borrowed Funds	111,393
Mortgage-backed securities, net	453,093	Other Liabilities	15,810
Other assets	36,131	Retained Earnings	224,819
Total	$1,871,242	Total	$1,871,242

Years Ended Mar. 31	Thousands Total Assets	Loans, Net	Deposits	Retained Earnings
1995	$1,871,242	$1,338,414	$1,519,220	$224,819
1994	1,854,040	1,142,010	1,597,368	229,231
1993	1,923,562	1,430,307	1,645,586	256,830
1992	2,016,817	1,484,561	1,759,290	230,851
1991	1,897,343	1,663,853	1,722,169	154,470

Consolidated Income Statement

Years Ended Mar. 31	Thousands Total Income	Operating Expenses[a]	Net Income
1995	$115,188	$97,850	$10,795
1994	120,585	94,025	14,193
1993	140,825	106,986	21,732
1992	167,802	142,234	14,396
1991	172,461	144,172	18,261

[a]Excludes federal and state income taxes.

General Counsel:	Robert E. Ulbricht, Sr. V.P.	Depositors:	110,787
Human Resources:	Kathryn C. Banky, V.P.	Employees:	350
Mgt. Info. Svcs.:	Peter J. Grealish, Sr. V.P.		
Auditors:	KPMG Peat Marwick LLP	Member:	FDIC

Citibank, Federal Savings Bank
500 West Madison St., Chicago, Illinois 60661
Telephone: (312) 263-6660

Citibank, Federal Savings Bank, a wholly owned subsidiary of Citicorp Banking Corporation, operates more than 50 branches throughout the Chicagoland area. Citibank offers a full range of financial products. Twenty-four-hour banking is available at more than 200 automated teller machines within the branch network. Citiphone banking, the 24-hour telephone banking service, is another convenience available to all customers. Citibank is a member of the Cirrus and Cash Station networks. The core customer account offering is the Citibank Money Management Account, which includes checking, money market, overdraft protection, and Bankcard services. Savings products include statement savings and certificates of deposit for periods from six months to five years. Retirement accounts, IRA's, and Keoghs have additional investment options available, including brokerage and stock index accounts. Citibank also has a wide array of credit products available for its customers, including businesses, such as unsecured and secured revolving lines, fixed and variable mortgages, equity products, and traditional second mortgages.

Officers

J. Eric Daniels, Chm. & Regional Pres.—Calif.
Thomas L. Dahl, Regional Pres.—MidAtlantic
Kenneth O. Danilo, Regional Pres.—Connecticut
Carlos Palomares, Regional Pres.—Florida

Thomas W. Sisson, Regional Pres.—Illinois
John T. Davis, V.P.—Treas.
Arthur Law, Jr., V.P.—C.F.O.
Darcy Walker, V.P.—Credit

Consolidated Statement of Condition   As of December 31, 1994 (000 omitted)

Assets		Liabilities & Equity Capital	
Cash, deposits & investment securities	$ 2,565,798	Deposits	$10,302,589
Loans, net	9,526,295	Borrowings	1,040,458
Other assets	1,431,449	Other liabilities	536,353
		Equity Capital	1,644,142
Total	$13,523,542	Total	$13,523,542

Years Ended Dec. 31	Thousands — — — — — — — — — — — — — — — — —			
	Total Assets	Mortgage Loans	Deposits	Equity Capital
1994	$13,523,542	$9,526,295	$10,302,589	$1,644,142
1993	12,227,176	9,005,362	9,776,341	1,662,113
1992	10,704,302	8,832,513	8,613,018	1,504,516
1991	12,254,126	9,326,745	9,654,830	1,530,474
1990	5,425,351	3,209,255	4,393,714	660,817

Consolidated Income Statement[a]

Years Ended Dec. 31	Thousands — — — — — — — — — — — — — — — — — —			
	Net Interest Income After Loan Loss Provision	Other Income	Expenses	Net Income
1994	$493,457	$120,180	$614,205	$(17,627)
1993	445,438	178,183	701,029	(33,811)
1992	317,255	98,870	445,414	(21,166)
1991	386,658	193,030	429,234	89,290

[a]Citibank in Florida merged into Citibank F.S.B. on January 1, 1993; prior years were not restated.

General Counsel:	Wendy S. Kleinbaum, V.P.	Auditors:	KPMG Peat Marwick LLP
Human Resources:	Ian Ostergaard, V.P.	Employees:	4,500
Mgt. Info. Svcs.:	Gerald Waldron, V.P.	Member:	FDIC

Cole Taylor Bank
350 East Dundee Road, Wheeling, Illinois 60090
Telephone: (708) 537-0077

Cole Taylor Bank is a wholly owned subsidiary of Cole Taylor Financial Group, Inc. The bank provides a full range of commercial and consumer banking services both to small to mid-sized businesses, and to individuals in Chicago neighborhoods and suburban Cook and DuPage counties through nine branch offices. Cole Taylor Bank commenced operations more than 60 years ago in Chicago as Main State Bank, which was acquired by Cole Taylor Financial Group's founders, Irwin Cole and Sidney Taylor, in 1969. Member FDIC.

Directors (In addition to indicated officers)

John S. Bubula	Solway F. Firestone	Langdon D. Neal
Wheeler E. Chapman, Jr.	Richard Kaplan	William S. Race
Irwin H. Cole	Edward T. McGowan	Barbara M. Sellstrom
Armand L. Dann	Edward Meyer	Seymour Taxman
Louis R. Duman	Joseph Mario Moreno	Sidney J. Taylor
Ronald D. Emanuel		

Officers (Directors*)

* Jeffrey W. Taylor, Chm.
* Bruce W. Taylor, Pres. & C.E.O.
* Robert F. Corey, Sr. Exec. V.P.—Govt. Rel.
* Richard C. Keneman, Exec. V.P.—Rel. Banking
Richard S. White, Exec. V.P.—Trust & Invest.
Daniel S. Bleil, Grp. Sr. V.P.—Suburb. Banking
D. Fred DeRoode, Grp. Sr. V.P.—City Banking
Alan R. Gunnerson, Grp. Sr. V.P.—Oper.
Thomas J. Hennessy, Grp. Sr. V.P.—Real Est. Banking

Gerald B. Klein, Grp. Sr. V.P.—Consumer Lending
Daniel L. Lueken, Grp. Sr. V.P.—Spec. Banking
Robin J. VanCastle, Grp. Sr. V.P.—Fin. Mgt.
Michael S. Wien, Grp. Sr. V.P.—Mktg.
* Louis R. Joseph, Chf. Adm. Officer
James I. Kaplan, Gen. Coun. & Corp. Secy.
Roy C. Postel, Chf. Credit Officer

Consolidated Balance Sheet As of December 31, 1994 (000 omitted)

Assets		Liabilities & Stockholders' Equity	
Cash & due from banks	$ 69,715	Total deposits	$1,293,411
Federal funds sold	23,600	Short-term borrowing	243,997
Investment securities	464,419	Long-term debt	47,864
Loans, net	1,107,344	Other liabilities	15,781
Property & equipment	13,511	Stockholders' equity	118,997
Other assets	41,461		
Total	$1,720,050	Total	$1,720,050

Years Ended Dec. 31	Thousands Total Deposits	Interest-bearing Deposits	Time Deposits	Net Loans	Stockholders' Equity
1994	$1,293,411	$974,611	$318,800	$1,107,344	$118,997
1993	1,180,845	902,308	402,160	966,644	101,301
1992	1,130,529	869,060	391,996	889,816	94,902
1991	1,014,080	786,312	379,264	808,045	93,440
1990	1,117,984	903,329	528,239	772,804	89,137

Consolidated Income Statement

Years Ended Dec. 31	Thousands Total Income	Operating Expenses	Net Income
1994	$129,362	$99,573[a]	$15,902
1993	117,633	89,452[b]	12,722
1992	113,469	90,034[c]	9,962
1991	118,751	98,517[d]	7,904
1990	126,898	114,241[e]	4,604

[a]Excludes the provision for possible loan losses of $7,374,000.
[b]Excludes the provision for possible loan losses of $10,521,000.
[c]Excludes the provision for possible loan losses of $8,922,000.
[d]Excludes the provision for possible loan losses of $8,816,000.
[e]Excludes the provision for possible loan losses of $7,005,000.

Corporate Counsel:	Katten Muchin & Zavis	Auditors:	KPMG Peat Marwick LLP
Human Resources:	Joseph E. Kuhel, V.P.	Employees:	696
Mgt. Info. Svcs:	Alan R. Gunnerson, Grp. Sr. V.P.		
		Member:	FDIC; Fed. Home Loan Bank

Columbia National Bank of Chicago
5250 North Harlem Avenue, Chicago, Illinois 60656-1888
Telephone: (312) 775-6800

Columbia National Bank of Chicago is an independently owned and operated financial institution offering a full range of consumer and commercial financial services. The bank has six full-service locations serving the needs of communities on the Northwest side of Chicago, in Niles, and in Norridge. The bank is open seven days a week and has five offsite ATM's for 24-hour banking service. The bank is a wholly owned subsidiary of CNBC Bancorp, Inc. Other subsidiaries of the Bancorp include CNBC Leasing Corp., CNBC Investment Corp., and CNBC Development Corp. Member FDIC.

Directors   (In addition to indicated officers)

Miles L. Berger, V. Chm.
Ronald Berger
Herbert Kuehnle

Myron Lieberman
Michael D. Maremont

Officers   (Directors*)

* Burton L. Gordon, Chm. & C.E.O.
* Lester J. Rosenberg, Chm. of the Exec. Comm.
* Donald V. Versen, Sr., Pres.
* George K. Metzger, Exec. V.P.
* Leon D. Xintaris, Exec. V.P. & C.F.O.
  Steve Irvin, Sr. V.P.—Commercial Lending

Darrell A. Wolski, Sr. V.P.—Retail
Robert I. Braun, V.P.—Branches
Myles W. Crane, V.P.—Audit
Diane Zook, Asst. V.P.—Comm. Relations
Michael J. Ruddick, Treas.
Jennifer Wolf, Pres.—CNB Mortgage Corp.

Consolidated Balance Sheet   As of December 31, 1994 (000 omitted)

Assets			Liabilities & Equity Capital	
Cash & due from banks	$	22,858	Deposits	$627,665
Securities		345,149	Funds borrowed	6,000
Net loans		369,496	Securities sold o/a to repurch.	70,556
Premises and fixed assets		12,767	Other liabilities	6,329
Other assets		14,875	* Total equity capital	54,595
Total		$765,145	Total	$765,145

*81,000 shares common stock outstanding.

Years Ended Dec. 31	Thousands Total Assets	Net Loans	Total Deposits	Capital Accounts
1994	$765,145	$369,496	$627,665	$54,595
1993	737,814	340,085	597,160	47,987
1992	690,581	282,390	583,409	40,020
1991	630,226	271,212	558,435	34,632
1990	493,415	231,599	437,700	30,203

Consolidated Income Statement

Years Ended Dec. 31	Thousands Operating Income	Operating Expenses	Net Income
1994	$57,084	$42,665	$9,767
1993	58,497	44,732	9,466
1992	55,378	45,695	6,927
1991	53,045	45,644	5,713
1990	46,203	40,097	5,013

General Counsel:	Altheimer & Gray	Auditors:	KPMG Peat Marwick LLP
Human Resources:	Dennis Johnson, V.P.	Employees:	247
Mgt. Info. Svcs.:	Richard G. Aird, V.P.	Member:	FDIC

First Chicago Guide

Comerica Bank—Illinois

8700 Waukegan Road, Morton Grove, Illinois 60053
Telephone: (708) 202-3333

Comerica Bank—Illinois (formerly Affiliated Bank) is a wholly owned subsidiary of Comerica Incorporated, a $33-billion bank holding company headquartered in Detroit, Michigan. The name change to Comerica Bank—Illinois occurred in October 1992 in conjunction with the merger between Affiliated Bank's parent company, Manufacturers National Corporation, and Comerica Incorporated. Comerica Bank—Illinois has more than 20 branch offices in Chicago and the north and northwest suburbs, and offers a complete range of retail and corporate banking services, private banking for high net-worth individuals, institutional trust and investment management, as well as international finance and trade services.

Directors   (In addition to indicated officers)

Thomas F. Carey	Frank H. Resnik
Robert E. Hughes	Robert J. Zahorik
William C. Mitchell	

Officers   (Directors*)

* David C. White, Pres. & C.E.O.
* Gregory R. Beard, Exec. V.P.—Trust

Mark W. Shobe, Exec. V.P.—Comm.
   Banking & Admin.
Timothy V. Talbert, Sr. V.P.—Credit Admin.

Consolidated Balance Sheet   As of December 31, 1994 (000 omitted)

Assets		Liabilities & Total Equity	
Cash & balances due	$ 65,269	Non-interest bearing deposits	$ 198,337
Securities	237,165	Interest bearing deposits	816,580
Loans, net	1,119,930	Federal funds borrowed	47,131
Premises/fixed assets	38,352	Other borrowed funds	271,456
Other assets	43,216	Other liabilities	11,697
		Total equity capital	158,731
Total	$1,503,932	Total	$1,503,932

Years Ended Dec. 31[a]	Thousands				
	Total Assets	Interest Bearing Deposits	Non-Interest Bearing Deposits	Net Loans	Total Equity
1994	$1,503,932	$816,580	$198,337	$1,119,930	$158,731
1993	1,409,327	833,741	177,226	1,030,882	151,218
1992	1,453,806	1,010,364	184,031	939,703	141,268
1991	1,602,939	1,052,167	158,581	915,881	146,604
1990	1,591,586	1,194,284	170,080	966,386	144,561

[a]Comerica Bank—Illinois merged with Manufacturers Affiliated Trust Company as of October 22, 1992. The 1991 and 1990 financial information has been restated to reflect the merger.

Consolidated Income Statement

Years Ended Dec. 31	Thousands Net Income
1994	$14,207
1993	12,128
1992	8,226

Human Resources:	Kenneth Holstein, First V.P.	Employees:	800
Auditors:	Ernst & Young LLP;		
	David Mroz, Ill. Audit Mgr.	Member:	FDIC

First Bank National Association

400-410 North Michigan Avenue, Chicago, Illinois 60611-4181
Telephone: (312) 836-6500

First Bank National Association (formerly Boulevard Bank National Association), a wholly owned subsidiary of First Bank System Inc., offers a complete line of personal, corporate, and trust banking services. In April 1994, First Bank System Inc. completed its merger with Boulevard Bancorp, Inc. Member FDIC.

Officers

Larry L. Lewton, Pres.
Rick Glau, V.P.—Retail Bank
Jim Houston, V.P.—Business Banking
Ann Kelly, V.P.—Credit Adm.
Timothy McKeon, V.P.—Private Banking
Teresa McLeod, V.P.—Retail Bank

Thomas D. Panos, V.P.—Corp. Banking
Donna Randel, V.P.—Retail Bank
David A. Raub, V.P.—Trust
Mark Schlagel,V.P.—Retail Bank
Greg Warsek, V.P.—Commercial Real
    Estate

Consolidated Balance Sheet   As of December 31, 1994 (000 omitted)

Assets		Liabilities & Stockholders' Equity	
Cash & due from banks	$ 67,610	Deposits	$ 887,269
Securities	513,369	Funds borrowed	187,800
Federal funds sold	20,000	Other liabilities	25,041
Net loans	552,657	Stockholders' equity	283,103
Properties & equipment	19,916		
Other assets	209,661		
Total	$1,383,213	Total	$1,383,213

Years Ended Dec. 31	Thousands Total Deposits	Demand Deposits	Time Deposits	Net Loans	Capital Accounts
1994	$887,269	$188,155	$699,114	$552,657	$283,103

Consolidated Income Statement

Years Ended Dec. 31	Thousands Operating Income	Operating Expenses	Net Income
1994	$76,615	$67,841	$3,288

General Counsel:	Dorsey & Whitney	Employees:	256
Auditors:	Ernst & Young LLP	Member:	FDIC

First Chicago Guide

First Midwest Bank, N.A.

300 Park Boulevard, Suite 400, Itasca, Illinois 60143-2636
Telephone: (708) 875-7450

First Midwest Bank, N.A., is a wholly owned subsidiary of First Midwest Bancorp, Inc., a bank holding company. The bank, which operates 43 offices in northern Illinois, offers full commercial banking services, real estate lending, consumer lending, and personal banking services. Approximately 80 percent of bank assets are situated in Metro Chicago. In May 1995, First Midwest Bancorp merged its four commercial banks — First Midwest Bank/Illinois, N.A., First Midwest Bank, N.A., First Midwest Bank/Danville, N.A., and First Midwest Bank/Western Illinois, N.A. — into one entity, First Midwest Bank, N.A. Member FDIC.

Directors   (In addition to indicated officers)

Brother James Gaffney
Robert P. O'Meara

Frank Waldeck

Officers   (Directors*)

* John M. O'Meara, Chm. & C.E.O.
* James D. Anderson, Pres.—Central Region
* Keith J. Brown, Pres.—South Metro Region
* Marc R. Parise, Pres.—Western Region
* Thomas J. Schwartz, Pres.—North Metro Region
* Kent S. Belasco, Exec. V.P. & Chf. Info. Officer

* Mark M. Dietrich, Exec. V.P. & C.O.O.
* Thomas F. Franklin, Exec. V.P. & Chf. Planning Officer
* James M. Voss, Exec. V.P. & Chf. Credit Officer
* Judith T. Walz, Exec. V.P. & Chf. Mktg. Officer

Consolidated Balance Sheet[a]   As of December 31, 1994 (000 omitted) Unaudited

Assets			Liabilities & Stockholder's Equity	
Cash & due from banks	$	107,135	Deposits	$2,001,840
Funds sold/other short-term inv.		15,694	Short-term borrowings	356,291
Securities		569,421	Accrued interest payable	
Net loans		1,752,248	& other liabilities	15,562
Premises, furniture & equipment		37,700	Stockholder's equity	169,705
Accrued inter. rec./other assets		61,200		
Total		$2,543,398	Total	$2,543,398

[a]Pro forma combined statement of condition of First Midwest Bancorp, Inc.'s four commercial banks as if they had been merged into a single bank effective December 31, 1994.

Years Ended Dec. 31	Thousands				
	Total Deposits	Interest-bearing Deposits	Noninterest-bearing Deposits	Net Loans	Capital Accounts
1994[a]	$2,001,840	$1,654,216	$347,624	$1,752,248[b]	$169,705

[a]Pro forma combined.
[b]Net of reserve for loan losses of $23,083,000.

Consolidated Income Statement

Years Ended Dec. 31	Thousands		
	Operating Income	Operating[a] Expenses	Net Income
1994[b]	$198,174	$170,135	$28,039

[a]Includes income taxes.
[b]Pro forma combined.

General Counsel:	Hinshaw & Culbertson	Auditors:	KPMG Peat Marwick LLP
Human Resources:	Phillip E. Glotfelty, Sr. V.P.	Employees:	1,082
Mgt. Info. Svcs.:	Kent S. Belasco, Exec. V.P.	Member:	FDIC; Federal Reserve System

The First National Bank of Chicago

One First National Plaza, Chicago, Illinois 60670

Telephone: (312) 732-4000

The First National Bank of Chicago is a wholly owned subsidiary of First Chicago Corporation. The bank provides a broad range of banking, fiduciary, financial, and other services on a worldwide basis to individuals, businesses, and governmental units. The bank maintains seven regional offices in Atlanta, Boston, Cleveland, Houston, Los Angeles, New York, and Washington, D.C., to develop new business and to maintain closer contact with corporate and institutional banking customers. Internationally, The First National Bank of Chicago serves customers within Canada, Europe, the Middle East, Africa, and the Asia-Pacific regions.

Directors   (In addition to indicated officers)

John H. Bryan	Earl L. Neal
Dean L. Buntrock	James J. O'Connor
James S. Crown	Jerry K. Pearlman
Donald V. Fites	Jack F. Reichert
Donald P. Jacobs	Patrick G. Ryan
Andrew J. McKenna	Adele Simmons
Richard M. Morrow	Roger W. Stone

Officers   (Directors*)

* Richard L. Thomas, Chm., Pres. & C.E.O.	Thomas H. Hodges, Exec. V.P.
* David J. Vitale, V. Chm.	Donald R. Hollis, Exec. V.P.
Marvin James Alef, Jr., Exec. V.P.	William G. Jurgensen, Exec. V.P.
John W. Ballantine, Exec. V.P.	Scott P. Marks, Jr., Exec. V.P.
Sherman I. Goldberg, Exec. V.P., Gen. Coun. & Cashier	Robert A. Rosholt, Exec. V.P. & C.F.O.

Consolidated Statement of Condition   As of December 31, 1994 (000 omitted)

Assets		Liabilities & Stockholders' Equity	
Cash & due from banks	$ 11,446,783	Deposits	$25,737,503
Securities	697,082	Funds borrowed	11,310,925
Other short-term investments	4,460,586	Other liabilities	2,593,140
Net loans	15,266,427	Stockholders' equity	2,901,364
Other assets	10,672,054		
Total	$42,542,932	Total	$42,542,932

Years Ended Dec. 31	Total Deposits	Domestic Demand Deposits	Domestic Time Deposits	Dep. Overseas Branches & Consol. Sub.	Net Loans	Capital Accounts
1994	$25,737,503	$6,129,078	$8,974,426	$10,633,999	$15,266,427	$2,901,364
1993	23,124,555	7,494,138	8,376,395	7,254,022	12,968,455	2,687,686
1992	21,850,063	6,623,465	7,244,458	7,982,140	13,701,849	2,089,996
1991	23,670,048	6,032,109	8,042,124	9,595,815	14,771,946	1,749,406
1990	25,289,561	6,226,554	8,561,669	10,501,338	18,031,356	1,752,936

Consolidated Income Statement

Years Ended Dec. 31	Operating Income	Operating Expenses	Net Income
1994	$2,327,469	$2,111,296	$151,978
1993	2,512,928	2,057,837	299,336
1992	2,255,284	2,152,881	(357,466)
1991	2,793,295	2,640,788	(6,008)
1990	3,663,027	3,365,426	88,128

General Counsel:
  Sherman I. Goldberg, Exec. V.P.

Human Resources:
  Marvin James Alef, Jr., Exec. V.P.

Auditors: Arthur Andersen LLP

Employees: 12,500

Member: FDIC; Federal Reserve System

First Chicago Guide   293

First National Bank of Evergreen Park

3101 West 95th Street, Evergreen Park, Illinois 60642

Telephone: (708) 422-6700

The First National Bank of Evergreen Park is a wholly owned subsidiary of First Evergreen Corporation. The bank offers a full range of services including: transaction services, time accounts, special check services, depository and transfer services, investment securities, trust services, convenience services, international banking services, commercial loans, personal installment loans, and mortgage loans. Facilities are located in Evergreen Park, Oak Lawn, Chicago, and Orland Park. Chartered in December 1948.

Directors   (In addition to indicated officers)

Davis Boyd
Daniel Butler, Jr.
James R. Cismoski

Jerome J. Cismoski
Ronald W. Ozinga
Thomas Palmisano

Officers   (Directors*)

* Kenneth J. Ozinga, Chm. & Pres.
  Richard H. Brown, Exec. V.P.
* Stephen M. Hallenbeck, Exec. V.P.
* Robert C. Wall, Exec. V.P.
  Roberta Bauer-Micetic, Sr. V.P.
  Joseph C. Fanelli, Sr. V.P. & Trust Off.

Terrence J. Healy, Sr. V.P.
Barbara L. Heidegger, Sr. V.P. & Cashier
Russell J. Hollender, Sr. V.P.
Ronald J. Homa, Sr. V.P.
* Martin F. Ozinga, Sr. V.P.
Roscoe N. Rush, Sr. V.P.—Loan Div.

Statement of Condition   As of December 31, 1994 (000 omitted)

Assets		Liabilities & Stockholders' Equity	
Cash & due from banks	$ 68,712	Deposits	$1,695,417
Investment securities	1,265,021	Other liabilities	19,955
Net loans	474,912	*Stockholders' equity	156,605
Properties & equipment	28,462		
Other assets	34,870		
Total	$1,871,977	Total	$1,871,977

*716,000 shares common stock outstanding.

Years Ended Dec. 31[a]	Thousands Total Deposits	Demand Deposits	Time Deposits	Net Loans	Capital Accounts
1994	$1,695,417	$163,444	$643,775	$474,912	$156,605
1993	1,718,370	146,510	471,530	412,577	146,611
1992	1,653,625	132,448	475,882	384,150	130,541
1991	1,213,563	121,332	575,512	371,005	118,233
1990	1,116,518	116,444	601,852	343,699	106,195

[a]Effective September 16, 1991, Oak Lawn National Bank and Clearing Bank were merged into First National Bank of Evergreen Park. Prior year has been restated.

Consolidated Income Statement[a]

Years Ended Dec. 31	Thousands Operating Income	Operating Expenses	Net Income
1994	$121,539	$93,544	$20,513
1993	126,706	96,299	22,156
1992	126,484	100,877	19,309
1991	115,499	93,250	17,271
1990	108,108	93,494	14,373

[a]Effective September 16, 1991, Oak Lawn National Bank and Clearing Bank were merged into First National Bank of Evergreen Park. Prior year has been restated.

General Counsel:	Barry N. Voorn	Auditors:	Arthur Andersen LLP
Human Resources:	John A. Camphouse, V.P.	Employees:	645
Mgt. Info. Svcs.:			
	Barbara L. Heidegger, Sr. V.P.	Member:	FDIC; Federal Reserve System

First of America Bank—Illinois, N.A.
Chicago Metro Region, 325 North Milwaukee Avenue, Libertyville, Illinois
60048-2200
Telephone: (708) 362-3000

First of America Bank—Illinois, N.A., Chicago Metro Region, is a wholly owned affiliate of First of America Bank Corporation, a Midwest bank holding company with assets of $24.5 billion at December 31, 1994. The bank engages in commercial banking, retail banking, and mortgage banking; and provides trust, financial data processing, and other financial services. The Chicago Metro Region is one of five regions in the State of Illinois and manages 27 branches in the metropolitan Chicago area. There are 130 branches throughout Illinois. Member FDIC.

Directors   (In addition to indicated officer)

Bill Anest	Patrick F. O'Shea
Michael R. Graham	Carl J. Walliser
G. Dwight Nissly	James R. Warren

Officers   (Director*)

* Nancy L. Singer, Pres.	Patrick F. Stallone, Sr. V.P.—Commercial
Carolyn A. Hanes, Sr. V.P.—Branch Admin.	Loan Dept. Mgr.
Thomas J. Romano, Sr. V.P.—Sr. Loan Officer	David C. Cook, V.P. & Cashier
Paul J. Stahr, Sr. V.P.—Oper.	

Consolidated Balance Sheet   As of December 31, 1994 (000 omitted)

Assets		Liabilities & Shareholders' Equity	
Cash & due from banks	$ 49,247	Deposits	$1,129,600
Investments	242,495	Borrowed funds	321,060
Net loans	1,258,569	Other liabilities	7,094
Other assets	91,881	Shareholders' Equity	184,438
Total	$ 1,642,192	Total	$1,642,192

Years Ended Dec. 31	Total Assets	Total Deposits	Demand Deposits	Savings & Time Deps.	Gross Loans	Capital Accounts
1994	$1,642,192	$1,129,600	$172,302	$957,298	$1,278,615	$184,438
1993	1,200,944	930,693	115,287	815,406	845,596	98,829
1992	805,870	717,452	104,079	613,373	473,018	74,250
1991	788,319	698,965	88,034	610,931	453,901	74,516
1990	622,245	536,322	95,157	441,165	427,835	62,194

Consolidated Income Statement

Years Ended Dec. 31	Operating Income	Operating Expense	Net Income
1994	$116,562	$107,281	$9,281
1993	81,189	63,490	10,035
1992	67,248	60,735	6,513[a]
1991	65,620	59,765	5,855
1990	64,606	57,319	7,287

[a]Before accelerated writedown of $6,779,000 for intangibles and FAS 106.

General Counsel:	Howard & Howard	Auditors:	KPMG Peat Marwick LLP
Human Resources:	Judith E. Wooster, V.P.	Employees:	550
Mgt. Info. Svcs.:	Paul J. Stahr, Sr. V.P.	Member:	FDIC

Harris Trust and Savings Bank

111 West Monroe Street, P.O. Box 755, Chicago, Illinois 60690-0755

Telephone: (312) 461-2121

Harris Trust and Savings Bank, an Illinois state-chartered bank, is a wholly owned subsidiary of Harris Bankcorp, Inc. Harris Trust and Savings maintains its principal office, two branch offices, an international banking facility and five automatic banking centers in the Chicago area. Additionally, Harris Trust and Savings has representative offices in Los Angeles, New York, and Tokyo; foreign branch offices in Nassau and London; and an Edge Act subsidiary, Harris Bank International Corporation, in New York. The bank provides a variety of banking and financial services to commercial and industrial companies, financial institutions, governmental units, not-for-profit organizations, and individuals throughout the U.S. and abroad. Services to customers include numerous types of demand and time deposit accounts; negotiable certificates of deposit; various types of loans including term, real estate, and those under lines of credit and revolving credit facilities; sales and purchases of foreign currencies; interest rate management products including swaps, forward rate agreements, and interest rate guarantees; cash management services, including lockbox and controlled disbursement processing; underwriting of municipal bonds; and financial consulting. Incorporated in Illinois in 1907.

Directors   (In addition to indicated officer)

Matthew W. Barrett	James J. Glasser	Charles H. Shaw
F. Anthony Comper	Daryl F. Grisham	Richard E. Terry
Susan T. Congalton	Leo M. Henikoff	James O. Webb
Roxanne J. Decyk	Stanley O. Ikenberry	William J. Weisz
Wilbur H. Gantz	Richard M. Jaffee	

Officers   (Director*)

* Alan G. McNally, Chm. & C.E.O.
Edward W. Lyman, Jr., V. Chm.
Maribeth S. Rahe, V. Chm.
Richard J. Brown, Exec. V.P.—Corp. Svcs.
Charles H. Davis, Exec. V.P.

Louis F. Lanwermeyer, Exec. V.P.
Ben T. Nelson, Exec. V.P.
John A. Sivright, Exec. V.P.
Charles R. Tonge, Exec. V.P.
Peter O. Greffe, C.F.O.

Consolidated Balance Sheet   As of December 31, 1994 (000 omitted)

Assets		Liabilities & Stockholders' Equity	
Cash & due from banks, incl. interest-bearing bal.	$1,958,836	Deposits	$ 7,015,566
Federal funds sold & sec. pur. u/a to resell	384,031	Fed. Funds borrowed & sec. sold u/a to repurchase	2,822,822
Securities	2,514,968	Other borrowings	916,499
Trading account assets	169,830	Trading liabilities	149,363
Loans & lease financing, net of allowance	6,280,547	Other liabilities	310,349
Property & equipment	136,703	* Stockholders' Equity	729,731
Other assets	499,415		
Total	$11,944,330	Total	$11,944,330

*6,667,490 shares of common stock outstanding.

Years Ended Dec. 31	Total Deposits	Domestic Demand Deposits	Domestic Time Deposits	Foreign Office Deposits	Loans Net of Allowance	Capital Accounts
1994	$7,015,566	$2,659,945	$1,869,203	$2,486,418	$6,280,547	$729,731
1993	6,457,354	2,569,574	2,289,219	1,598,561	5,754,791	734,451
1992	6,070,590	2,534,619	2,009,542	1,526,429	5,245,690	695,134
1991	6,842,514	2,478,702	2,537,822	1,825,990	6,212,376	636,273
1990	6,881,758	2,732,298	2,535,048	1,614,412	6,314,170	587,055

Consolidated Income Statement

Years Ended Dec. 31	Operating Income	Expenses Including Income Taxes	Net Income
1994	$899,651	$831,710	$67,941
1993	819,250	739,793	79,457
1992	897,929	800,568	97,361
1991	1,011,348	930,130	81,218
1990	1,017,949	966,976	50,973

General Counsel:	Chapman & Cutler	Auditors:	KPMG Peat Marwick LLP; Coopers & Lybrand L.L.P.
Human Resources:	Calvin L. Stowell, Jr., Sr. V.P.	Employees:	4,179
Mgt. Info. Svcs.:	Lloyd F. Darlington	Member:	FDIC; Federal Reserve System

First Chicago Guide

Heritage Bank

12015 South Western Avenue, Blue Island, Illinois 60406
Telephone: (708) 385-2900

Heritage Bank is a wholly owned subsidiary of Heritage Financial Services, Inc., and has 13 locations in the southwestern suburbs of Chicago. As a commercial banking institution, Heritage Bank serves a number of diverse light manufacturing and service businesses as well as provides a broad range of banking services to retail customers. Member FDIC.

Directors   (In addition to indicated officers)

John J. Gallagher
Lael W. Mathis
Jack Payan
Arthur E. Sieloff

John L. Sterling
Chester Stranczek
Arthur G. Tichenor
Dominick J. Velo

Officers   (Directors*)

* Richard T. Wojcik, Chm. & C.E.O.
* Frederick J. Sampias, Pres.
* Ronald P. Groebe, Sr. Exec. V.P. & Secy.
  Ramesh L. Ajwani, Exec. V.P.
  John E. Barry, Exec. V.P.

Paul A. Eckroth, Exec. V.P.
Susan G. Peterson, Exec. V.P.
Albert A. Stroka, Exec. V.P. & Gen. Coun.
Michael J. Burke, Sr. V.P.
William N. Masterson, Sr. V.P.

Consolidated Balance Sheet   As of December 31, 1994 (000 omitted)

Assets			Liabilities & Stockholders' Equity	
Cash & due from banks	$	36,869	Total deposits	$823,835
Federal funds sold		49,025	Fed. funds purchased & securities	
Securities, held-to-maturity		236,109	sold for repur.	33,726
Securities, available-for-sale		71,478	Other liabilities	6,123
Net loans		516,095	Stockholders' equity	82,024
Net property, plant & equipment		15,509		
Other assets		20,623		
Total	$	945,708	Total	$945,708

Years Ended Dec. 31	Thousands Total Deposits	Non-interest Bearing Deposits	Net Loans	Total Capital
1994	$823,835	$143,623	$516,095	$82,024
1993	727,415	124,584	446,270	67,303
1992	670,793	116,823	425,765	56,242
1991	570,491	90,646	378,587	47,567
1990	541,282	94,432	387,186	42,988

Consolidated Income Statement

Years Ended Dec. 31	Thousands Interest Income	Interest Expense	Net Income
1994	$60,109	$21,943	$13,276
1993	55,640	21,009	11,994
1992	55,868	25,044	10,717
1991	56,404	29,382	9,229
1990	57,015	31,728	7,589

General Counsel:	Albert A. Stroka, Exec. V.P.		
Mgt. Info. Svcs.:	Linda Duggan	Employees:	478
Auditors:	Arthur Andersen LLP	Member:	FDIC

LaSalle Bank Lake View

3201 North Ashland Avenue, Chicago, Illinois 60657
Telephone: (312) 525-2180

LaSalle Bank Lake View offers its customers a full range of commercial, trust, and personal banking services. The bank was acquired by LaSalle National Corporation in June 1988 and now operates as a wholly owned subsidiary. In July 1995, LaSalle Bank Lake View and LaSalle Bank Northbrook announced that they will merge, effective September 5, after which time the merged bank will be known as LaSalle Bank Northern Illinois. Incorporated in Illinois in 1905.

Directors   (In addition to indicated officers)

Robert W. Carter
Herman Siegelaar

James B. Wynsma

Officers   (Directors*)

* Norman R. Bobins, Chm.
* John R. Newman, Pres. & C.E.O.
* Thomas D. Roegner, Exec. V.P.
  Richard L. Bennett, Sr. V.P.
  Ken Born, V.P. & C.F.O.
  William Burda, V.P.
  Jo Ann A. Clay, V.P.
  Angela DePew, V.P.
  Frank L. Dwojacki, V.P.
  F. Anne Foster, V.P.

Michael Gardner, V.P.--Commerc. Real Est.
Frederick Hausmann, Jr., V.P. & Cont.
Jane L. Hoover, V.P.
Michael J. Imrie, V.P.
William M. Lloyd, V.P.
Karen E. Murphy, V.P.
Martin F. Quinn, V.P.
William T. Roberts, V.P.
Catherine M. Schuster, V.P.
Toni Stanek, V.P.

Consolidated Balance Sheet   As of December 31, 1994 (000 omitted)

Assets			Liabilities & Stockholders' Equity		
Current assets	$	961,995	Deposits	$	729,408
Net property, plant & equipment		6,022	Other liabilities		229,197
Other assets		57,728	Stockholders' equity		67,140
Total		$ 1,025,745	Total		$1,025,745

Years Ended Dec. 31	Thousands Total Deposits	Demand Deposits	Time Deposits	Net Loans	Capital Accounts
1994	$729,408	$74,734	$654,674	$536,912	$67,140
1993	633,863	66,229	567,634	570,407	58,285
1992	667,958	62,962	604,996	463,783	54,453
1991	673,587	59,909	613,678	422,393	46,353
1990	551,629	58,921	492,708	406,863	40,596

Consolidated Income Statement (Information not publicly available)

Human Resources:	Martin F. Quinn, V.P.	Employees:	272
Auditors:	Ernst & Young LLP	Member:	FDIC

LaSalle Cragin Bank FSB

5200 West Fullerton Avenue, Chicago, Illinois 60639-1478
Telephone: (312) 889-1000

LaSalle Cragin Bank FSB (formerly Cragin Federal Bank for Savings) has 27 offices in the Chicago metropolitan area. The bank offers a full range of checking, savings and certificate accounts, mortgage loans, and consumer loans. Cragin Service Corp. is a wholly owned subsidiary. Insurance and investment services are offered through LaSalle Financial Services. In June 1994, ABN AMRO North America, the parent of LaSalle National Corporation, acquired the bank.

Directors   (In addition to indicated officers)

Jeffrey L. Conner
Scott K. Heitmann
David R. Papritz
Robert K. Quinn

Cordell Reed
Theodore H. Roberts
Eugene A. Tracy

Officers   (Directors*)

* Henry G. MacMorran, Pres. & C.E.O.
* Albert P. Harker, Exec. V.P.—Retail Banking

Michael McGrogan, Exec. V.P.—Sr. Lending
* Robert Taylor, Sr. V.P. & C.F.O.

Consolidated Statement of Condition   As of December 31, 1994 (000 omitted)

Assets		Liabilities & Equity	
Cash & securities	$1,179,773	Deposits	$2,096,111
Loans receivable, net	1,718,026	Notes payable & other borrowings	618,188
Properties & equipment	22,563	Other liabilities	76,773
Other assets	316,027	Equity	445,317
Total	$3,236,389	Total	$3,236,389

Years Ended Dec. 31	Thousands Total Assets	Mortgage Loans	Total Savings Accts.	Total Equity
1994	$3,236,389	$1,718,026	$2,096,111	$445,317
1993	2,781,542	1,488,608	2,126,826	278,983
1992	2,698,675	1,499,751	2,098,222	265,858
1991	2,626,585	1,592,363	2,115,106	257,453
1990	2,447,854	1,427,163	1,933,621	195,525

Consolidated Income Statement

Years Ended Dec. 31	Thousands Gross Interest Income	Net Income
1994[a]	$58,706	$14,310
1993	203,406	38,357
1992	220,417	35,877
1991	235,580	25,490
1990	225,454	8,879

[a]Represents the period from June 1 through December 31.

Human Resources: Donald Nielsen, V.P.		Individual Depositors:	134,215
Mgt. Info. Svcs.: Michael Oberholtzer		Employees:	475
Auditors: Ernst & Young LLP		Member:	FDIC

LaSalle National Bank
120 South LaSalle Street, Chicago, Illinois 60603
Telephone: (312) 443-2000

LaSalle National Bank is a full-service commercial bank and wholly owned subsidiary of LaSalle National Corporation, which is a subsidiary of ABN AMRO Bank N.V. LaSalle National Bank was chartered under the National Bank Act as The National Builders Bank of Chicago in 1927; present title adopted in 1940. It serves businesses, institutions, and individuals throughout the Chicago area. Member FDIC.

Directors   (In addition to indicated officers)

Jean Allard	Cordell Reed	William L. Smith
Donald H. Haider	Bryan S. Reid, Jr.	Richard A. Stein
Harvey N. Medvin	Theodore H. Roberts	Eugene A. Tracy
John Rau	Herman Siegelaar	Arthur R. Velasquez

Officers   (Directors*)

* Robert K. Wilmouth, Chm.
* Norman R. Bobins, Pres. & C.E.O.
* Thomas C. Heagy, V. Chm.
John H. Collins, Exec. V.P.—Computer & Admin. Svcs. Grp.
M. Hill Hammock, Exec. V.P.—Commercial Banking Admin.
Mark A. Hoppe, Exec. V.P.—Inst. Banking
Walter M. Macur, Exec. V.P.—Asset Based Lending & Chm.—LaSalle Bus. Cred.
John R. Newman, Exec. V.P. & Pres.—LaSalle Bank Lake View
Larry D. Richman, Exec. V.P.—Commerc. Banking
Henry S. Roberts, Exec. V.P.—Systems & Svcs. Grp.

David J. Rudis, Exec. V.P.—Commer. Banking
Michael Sharkey, Exec. V.P. & Pres.— LaSalle Bus. Cred.
Breck F. Hanson, Grp. Sr. V.P.—Real Est. Admin.
Marty Penstein, Grp. Sr. V.P.—Invest. Portfolio & Int. Rate Risk
Erick J. Peterson, Grp. Sr. V.P.—Service Prod. Admin.(Cash Mgt.)
Michael A. Piccato, Grp. Sr. V.P.—Funds Mgt.
Stephen A. Takahashi, Grp. Sr. V.P.—Service Prod. Admin. (Check Proc.)
Richard G. Maier, Sr. V.P. & C.F.O.
Mark A. Nystuen, Sr. V.P. & C.A.O.
John E. Scully, Sr. V.P.—Hum. Res.

Consolidated Balance Sheet   As of December 31, 1994 (000 omitted)

Assets		Liabilities & Total Equity	
Total cash & due from banks	$ 544,343	Total deposits	$ 7,065,919
Money market assets	3,885,771	Purchased funds and notes	2,495,009
Loans, net	5,389,882	Other liabilities	105,211
Other assets	448,691	*Total equity capital accounts	602,548
Total	$10,268,687	Total	$10,268,687

*184,171 shares common stock outstanding.

Years Ended Dec. 31	Total Deposits	Domestic Demand Deposits	Domestic Time Deposits	Foreign Deposits	Loans, Net U/D	Equity Capital Accounts
1994	$7,065,919	$1,328,045	$3,895,501	$1,842,373	$5,490,992	$602,548
1993	6,006,381	1,401,455	3,555,417	1,049,509	4,580,395	484,939
1992	4,916,231	1,131,322	3,256,227	528,682	3,747,967	411,462
1991	4,067,663	869,184	2,833,551	364,843	3,185,050	345,055
1990	3,872,410	765,701	2,832,602	274,107	3,098,075	288,154

Consolidated Income Statement

Years Ended Dec. 31	Gross Income	Gross Expenses	Net Income
1994	$719,968	$630,323	$89,645
1993	547,610	474,134	73,476
1992	527,871	461,473	66,398
1991	505,983	449,070	56,913
1990[a]	462,027	417,237	44,790

[a]Unaudited combined pro forma for LaSalle National Bank and Exchange National Bank of Chicago.

Human Resources: John E. Scully, Sr. V.P.		Employees:	987
Auditors: Ernst & Young LLP		Member:	FDIC; Federal Reserve System

LaSalle Northwest National Bank

4747 West Irving Park Road, Chicago, Illinois 60641
Telephone: (312) 777-7700

LaSalle Northwest National Bank provides complete consumer and commercial deposit and loan services. The bank has full-service branches in the Jefferson Park community and the northwest suburb of Elk Grove Village. These locations are in addition to the bank's main office in Chicago's Portage Park neighborhood. LaSalle Northwest National Bank (formerly Northwest National Bank of Chicago) is a subsidiary of LaSalle Community Bancorporation, Inc. Chartered under the National Bank Act in 1941. Member FDIC.

Directors   (In addition to indicated officers)

Nancy DeSombre
Fred W. Heitmann, Jr.
Michael R. Lutz

Herman Siegelaar
Joseph E. Valenti, Sr.

Officers   (Directors*)

* Scott K. Heitmann, Chm.
* John J. Lynch, Jr., Pres. & C.E.O.
  Michael A. Lariviere, Sr. V.P.—Cons. Lending
  Lawrence G. Ryan, Sr. V.P.—Commercial Lending
  Jerry Smulik, Sr. V.P.—Commercial Real Est.
  Lloyd S. Szkwarko, Sr. V.P. & C.F.O.
  Nicholas Begley, V.P.
  Monika Casey, V.P.
  Timothy Clary, V.P.
  Terry Collins, V.P.
  Richard J. Feller, V.P.
  Nancy Foster, V.P. & Chf. Credit Officer
  Harolds Gaikis, V.P.
  Jonathan Gilfillian, V.P.

Helmut Gottfert, V.P.
Suzanne Grisolia, V.P.
Deborah A. Grudzien, V.P.
Ida C. Hesotian, V.P.
Jeffrey A. Jones, V.P.
Russell G. Lutz, V.P.
John Matthews, V.P.
Robert E. Nowicki, V.P.
Lucy A. Perrotti, V.P.
Steven Schultz, V.P. & Cont.
Randall Slattery, V.P.
Mike Smith, V.P.
Michael Stump, V.P.
Mari C. Uribarri, V.P.

Consolidated Balance Sheet   As of December 31, 1994 (000 omitted)

Assets		Liabilities & Stockholders' Equity	
Current assets	$ 1,440,579	Current liabilities	$1,357,180
Net property, plant & equipment	10,081	Other liabilities	22,449
Other assets	35,437	*Stockholders' equity	106,468
Total	$ 1,486,097	Total	$1,486,097

*300,000 shares common stock outstanding.

Years Ended Dec. 31	Total Deposits	Demand Deposits	Time Deposits	Net Loans	Capital Accounts
1994	$1,207,447	$133,103	$1,074,344	$1,187,792	$106,468
1993	913,223	119,896	793,327	1,085,885	96,320
1992	933,958	105,287	828,671	897,257	86,570
1991	926,994	81,275	845,719	746,083	66,137
1990	792,054	81,960	710,094	718,274	57,063

Consolidated Income Statement

Years Ended Dec. 31	Operating Income	Net Income
1994	$107,989	$13,279
1993	102,960	14,550
1992	102,265	13,433
1991	95,679	11,774
1990	83,499	11,240

Human Resources:	Russell G. Lutz, V.P.	Employees:	437
Mgt. Info. Svcs.:	Steven Schultz, V.P.		
Auditors:	Ernst & Young LLP	Member:	FDIC; Federal Reserve System

First Chicago Guide

LaSalle Talman Bank, FSB

135 South LaSalle Street, Chicago, Illinois 60603
Telephone: (312) 434-3322

LaSalle Talman Bank, FSB (formerly The Talman Home Federal Savings and Loan Association of Illinois), has 59 offices in the Chicago metropolitan area. The bank offers a full range of checking, savings and certificate accounts, mortgage loans, consumer loans, insurance products, and investment brokerage services. Wholly owned subsidiaries include LaSalle Talman Home Mortgage Corporation (mortgage banking) and LaSalle Financial Services, Inc. (insurance agency and mutual fund sales). In November 1994, LaSalle Talman Bank acquired the 26 Illinois retail offices of Home Savings of America FSB. In February 1992, ABN AMRO North America, the parent of LaSalle National Corporation, completed the acquisition of the bank. LaSalle Talman Bank was founded in 1922; present name adopted in 1992.

Directors   (In addition to indicated officers)

Jeffrey L. Conner
David R. Papritz
Robert K. Quinn

Cordell Reed
Eugene A. Tracy

Officers   (Directors*)

* Theodore H. Roberts, Chm.
* Scott K. Heitmann, Pres. & C.E.O.
  Jay T. Fitts, Exec. V.P.—Chf. Credit Off.
* Albert P. Harker, Jr., Exec. V.P.

William E. Long, Exec. V.P. & Pres.—LTHMC
* Henry G. MacMorran, Exec. V.P.
* Robert J. Taylor, Sr. V.P. & C.F.O.

Consolidated Balance Sheet   As of December 31, 1994 (000 omitted)

Assets		Liabilities & Stockholder's Equity	
Cash & securities	$ 2,178,660	Savings accounts	$5,203,756
Mortgage loans	4,226,950	Notes payable and other borrowings	1,018,000
Other loans	150,646	Other liabilities	149,331
Properties & equipment	68,205	*Stockholder's equity	552,357
Other assets	298,983		
Total	$ 6,923,444	Total	$6,923,444

*100 shares common stock outstanding.

Years Ended Dec. 31	Thousands Total Assets	Mortgage Loans	Total Savings Accounts	Stockholder's Equity
1994	$6,923,444	$4,226,950	$5,203,756	$552,357
1993	5,850,553	3,446,351	3,793,434	402,873
1992	5,313,219	3,090,009	3,936,480	409,598

Consolidated Income Statement

Years Ended Dec. 31	Thousands Gross Income	Total Expenses	Provision for Taxes	Net Income
1994	$214,671	$156,786	$23,456	$34,429
1993	183,084	146,708	16,101	20,275

Human Resources:	Donald Nielsen, V.P.	Employees:	1,759	
Mgt. Info. Svcs.:	Michael Oberholtzer	Auditors:	Ernst & Young LLP	
Depositors:	400,000	Member:	FDIC	

Marquette National Bank

6316 S. Western Avenue, Chicago, Illinois 60636
Telephone: (312) 476-5100

Marquette National Bank is a wholly owned subsidiary of Marquette National Corporation. The bank has 10 facilities, which offer a full range of financial services to individuals and small businesses. Member FDIC.

Directors   (In addition to indicated officers)

Theodore J. Cachey	Thomas D. O'Reilly
James F. Capraro	John R. Thompson
Anthony C. Duvall	Harold J. Tolliver, Sr.

Officers   (Directors*)

* Paul M. McCarthy, Chm.	Patrick F. Donovan, V.P. & Pers. Off.
* George S. Moncada, Pres.	John T. Foote, V.P. & Real Estate Loan Off.
* Jerome R. Martin, Sr. V.P.	John P. Mahoney, V.P.—Lending
* David M. Ransford, Sr. V.P.	Frank Mainczyk, V.P.
Alfred Bacharz, V.P.	Daniel F. McKeown, V.P. & Cont.
Donald Bonistalli, V.P.—Trust	Robert J. Wosneski, V.P.—Leasing

Consolidated Balance Sheet   As of December 31, 1994 (000 omitted)

Assets		Liabilities & Stockholders' Equity	
Total cash & cash equivalents	$ 25,004	Total deposits	$647,350
Investment securities	490,041	Repurchase agreement—securities	17,110
Total loans, net	246,501	Other liabilities	51,694
Premises & fixed assets	9,858	Stockholders' equity	69,443
Other assets	14,193		
Total	$785,597	Total	$785,597

Years Ended Dec. 31	Total Deposits	Demand Deposits	Time & Savings Deposits	Net Loans	Stockholders' Equity
1994	$647,350	$63,584	$583,766	$246,501	$69,443
1993	637,029	56,110	580,919	215,191	77,667
1992	649,124	55,499	593,625	164,416	62,411
1991	617,830	47,075	570,755	141,029	51,517
1990	498,883	44,773	454,110	147,922	44,079

Consolidated Income Statement

Years Ended Dec. 31	Gross Income	Gross Expense	Net Income
1994	$52,359	$42,370	$9,629
1993	55,111	42,636	12,475
1992	57,895	47,000	10,895
1991	54,539	47,101	7,438
1990	45,870	39,597	6,273

General Counsel:		Auditors:	Bansley and Kiener
McCarthy, Duffy, Neidhart & Snakard		Depositors:	50,202
Human Resources:	Patrick F. Donovan, V.P.	Employees:	256
Mgt. Info. Svcs.:	Jerome R. Martin, Sr. V.P.	Member:	FDIC

First Chicago Guide   303

Mid America Federal Savings Bank

55th Street and Holmes Avenue, Clarendon Hills, Illinois 60514-1596
Telephone: (708) 325-7300

Mid America Federal Savings Bank (formerly Mid America Federal Savings and Loan Association) operates 13 branches located in Cicero, Riverside, LaGrange Park, Western Springs, Clarendon Hills, Naperville, St. Charles and Wheaton. Mid America Federal provides a full range of savings and financial services, including passbook, certificate, NOW and IRA/KEOGH accounts; mortgage, construction, home improvement, auto, educational, equity line of credit and consumer loans. Investment advice and brokerage services are offered through INVEST centers located in the Cicero, Clarendon Hills, Naperville, St. Charles and Wheaton offices. In addition, the savings bank operates two wholly owned subsidiaries: Mid America Development Services, Inc., which is involved in land acquisition and development; and Mid America Insurance Agency, Inc., which offers a variety of personal and business insurance products. Member of Federal Deposit Insurance Corporation and Federal Home Loan Bank System. Mid America is a wholly owned subsidiary of MAF Bancorp Inc.

Directors   (In addition to indicated officers)

Robert J. Bowles, M.D.
Nicholas J. DiLorenzo, Sr.
Joe F. Hanauer

Richard A. Kallal
F. William Trescott

Officers   (Directors*)

* Allen H. Koranda, Chm. & C.E.O.
* Kenneth Koranda, Pres.
  Jerry A. Weberling, Exec. V.P. & C.F.O.
  Tom Miers, Sr. V.P.
  Kenneth B. Rusdal, Sr. V.P.
* Lois B. Vasto, Sr. V.P.
  Sharon Wheeler, Sr. V.P.
  Gerard J. Buccino, First V.P. & Cont.

Michael J. Janssen, First V.P.
David W. Kohlsaat, First V.P.
Gail Brzostek, V.P.
William Haider, V.P.
Carolyn Pihera, V.P. & Secy.
Alan Schatz, V.P.
Diane Stutte, V.P.

Consolidated Balance Sheet   As of June 30, 1994 (000 omitted)

Assets			Liabilities & Stockholder's Equity	
Cash & securities	$	154,626	Savings accounts	$1,299,374
FHLB stock		9,747	Deposits for payment of taxes	
Loans receivable, net		1,358,894	& insurance	12,318
Properties & equipment		20,416	FHLB advances	110,500
Other assets		29,853	Other borrowed funds	39,356
			Other liabilities	16,252
			Stockholder's equity	95,736
Total	$	1,573,536	Total	$1,573,536

Years Ended June 30	Thousands Total Assets	Loans Receivable	Savings Accts.	Stockholder's Equity
1994	$1,573,536	$1,358,894	$1,299,374	$95,736
1993	1,539,994	1,325,852	1,297,807	92,885
1992	1,513,319	1,267,394	1,274,089	84,800
1991	1,473,033	1,201,681	1,237,464	59,766
1990	1,597,044	1,220,403	1,208,027	54,404

Consolidated Income Statement

Years Ended June 30	Thousands Gross Income	Interest Expense	Operating Expenses	Income To Stockholder's Equity
1994	$122,702	$67,538	$30,406	$14,699
1993	126,843	72,155	27,484	15,647
1992	138,373	87,264	29,707	9,807
1991	143,707	106,109	28,105	4,978
1990	156,404	119,125	29,086	4,968

General Counsel:
  Rock, Fusco, Reynolds & Garvey

Corporate Counsel: Muldoon, Murphy & Faucette
Human Resources: David W. Kohlsaat, First V.P.

Mgt. Info. Svcs.:   Kenneth B. Rusdal, Sr. V.P.
Auditors: KPMG Peat Marwick LLP
Depositors: 150,000
Employees: 500
Member: FDIC

The Mid-City National Bank of Chicago

801 West Madison Street, Chicago, Illinois 60607
Telephone: (312) 421-7600

The Mid-City National Bank of Chicago is a wholly owned subsidiary of Mid-Citco Incorporated. The bank has nine facilities, which offer a full range of financial services to individuals and small businesses. In April 1994, Mid-City National Bank purchased Peoples Federal Savings and Loan Association. Member FDIC.

Directors (In addition to indicated officers)

Stanley R. Banas
Samuel M. Budwig, Jr.
Charles F. Clarke, Jr.

Alan J. Dixon
Patrick Henry
Marshall S. Leaf

Barbara Proctor
Eugene Sawyer
Richard Wolff

Officers (Directors*)

* E.M. Bakwin, Chm.
* Kenneth A. Skopec, V. Chm. & C.E.O.
* Randall J. Yenerich, Pres.
* Ronald D. Santo, Exec. V.P.
John M. Blackburn, Sr. V.P.
S. Frank Formica, Sr. V.P.
Brian J. Griffin, Sr. V.P.
Richard M. Spielmann, Sr. V.P.
Lawrence L. Steinert, Sr. V.P.
William A. Thuma, Sr. V.P. & Trust Off.

Craig M. Woods, Sr. V.P.
Mary Ellen Braun, V.P.
B. Patrick Crowley, V.P.
John W. Gillie, V.P.
Christopher D. Hula, V.P. & Cashier
Walter J. Koehler, Jr., V.P.
Jeffrey W. Kuppler, V.P. & Cont.
Karen Larson, V.P.
Richard M. Pierce, V.P.
Mary Thomas, V.P.

Consolidated Balance Sheet   As of December 31, 1994 (000 omitted)

Assets		Liabilities & Stockholders' Equity	
Cash & due from banks	$ 52,774	Total deposits	$661,390
Investment securities	358,172	Repurchase agreements	3,471
Total loans, net	289,514	Other liabilities	4,530
Premises & fixed assets	13,902	*Stockholders' equity	57,030
Other assets	12,059		
Total	$ 726,421	Total	$726,421

*5,200 shares common stock outstanding.

Years Ended Dec. 31	Thousands Total Deposits	Demand Deposits	Time Deposits	Net Loans	Capital
1994	$661,390	$144,741	$516,649	$289,514	$57,030
1993	653,994	116,266	537,728	248,234	55,484
1992	653,113	99,613	553,500	246,129	53,730
1991	652,528	87,989	564,539	243,622	48,176
1990	312,658	81,645	231,013	191,922	34,401

Consolidated Income Statement

Years Ended Dec. 31	Thousands Gross Income	Gross Expenses[a]	Net Income
1994	$48,035	$39,989	$8,046
1993	48,065	40,811	7,254
1992	53,096	46,543	6,554
1991	46,471	41,695	4,776
1990	32,588	27,891	4,698

[a]Includes income taxes.

General Counsel:	Winston & Strawn	Auditors:	KPMG Peat Marwick LLP
Human Resources:	Maryann Penczak, V.P.	Employees:	254
Mgt. Info. Svcs.:	John M. Blackburn, Sr. V.P.	Member:	FDIC

First Chicago Guide

NBD Bank

211 South Wheaton Avenue, P.O. Box 687, Wheaton, Illinois 60189-0687

Telephone: (708) 665-0300

NBD Bank is a wholly owned subsidiary of Michigan-based NBD Bancorp, Inc., and has 39 branches serving the Chicago metropolitan area. The bank offers a complete line of commercial, trust, and investment services to individuals and corporate customers. In addition, NBD Bank is a full-service bank with a variety of checking, savings, and customer loan plans. Member FDIC.

Officers (Directors*)

* James R. Lancaster, Pres.
* Joseph E. Ernsteen, Sr. V.P./Cashier
* Harold R. Pehlke, Sr. V.P.

Richard R. Ridenour, Sr. V.P.
* John F. Timmer, Sr. V.P.

Consolidated Balance Sheet   As of December 31, 1994 (000 omitted)

Assets		Liabilities & Stockholders' Equity	
Cash & due from banks	$ 310,312	Deposits	$3,583,248
Securities	1,129,964	Funds borrowed	733,194
Funds sold & securities purchased	8,300	Other liabilities	187,860
Net loans	3,292,776	Stockholders' equity	375,425
Premises & equipment	58,705		
Other assets	79,670		
Total	$ 4,879,727	Total	$4,879,727

Years Ended Dec. 31	Thousands Total Deposits	Demand Deposits	Time Deposits	Net Loans	Capital Accounts
1994	$3,583,248	$891,493	$2,691,755	$3,292,776	$375,425
1993	3,595,137	767,212	2,827,925	2,863,595	385,647
1992	3,846,434	793,544	3,052,890	2,658,795	327,757

Consolidated Income Statement

Years Ended Dec. 31	Thousands Operating Income	Operating Expenses	Net Income
1994	$356,679	$292,104	$64,575
1993	348,151	288,499	59,652
1992	355,921	296,083	59,838

Employees: 1,783

Member: FDIC

First Chicago Guide

NBD Skokie Bank, N.A.

8001 Lincoln Avenue, Skokie, Illinois 60077
Telephone: (708) 673-2500

NBD Skokie Bank, N.A., is a wholly owned subsidiary of Michigan-based NBD Bancorp, Inc., and has two branches serving the Chicago metropolitan area. The bank offers a complete line of commercial, trust, and investment services to individual and corporate customers. In addition, NBD Skokie Bank is a full-service bank with a variety of checking, savings, and customer loan plans. Member FDIC.

Directors (In addition to indicated officer)

Joseph E. Ernsteen
James R. Lancaster

Harold R. Pehlke

Officers (Director*)

* James A. Carlson, Pres.
Frederick E. Thompson, V.P.
Ronald J. Walczyk, Asst. V.P. &
 Mgr.—Personal Banking
David S. Hayes, Cashier

Louise C. Karlin, Personal Banking Officer
Dale W. Kregel, Cont.
Norman K. Solomon, Jr., Personal Banking
 Officer

Consolidated Balance Sheet As of December 31, 1994 (000 omitted)

Assets			Liabilities & Stockholders' Equity	
Cash & due from banks	$	28,026	Deposits	$423,591
Securities		144,326	Funds borrowed	281,585
Funds sold		106,600	Other liabilities	19,334
Net loans		469,271	Stockholders' equity	58,451
Other assets		34,738		
Total	$	782,961	Total	$782,961

Years Ended Dec. 31	Thousands Total Deposits	Demand Deposits	Time Deposits	Net Loans	Capital Accounts
1994	$423,591	$56,009	$367,582	$469,271	$58,451
1993	398,966	51,947	347,019	451,760	58,179
1992	400,623	61,131	339,492	294,849	48,416

Consolidated Income Statement

Years Ended Dec. 31	Thousands Operating Income	Operating Expenses	Net Income
1994	$89,414	$72,133	$17,281
1993	63,456	48,307	15,149
1992	44,793	38,031	6,762

Employees: 98   Member: FDIC

Northern Trust Bank/Lake Forest N.A.

Deerpath & Bank Lane, Lake Forest, Illinois 60045
Telephone: (708) 234-5100

Northern Trust Bank/Lake Forest N.A. is a wholly owned subsidiary of Northern Trust Corporation. In addition to its main banking office, the bank has full-service banking facilities located at 959 South Waukegan Road, Lake Forest, and 120 East Scranton Avenue, Lake Bluff. The bank offers a full range of personal banking services, as well as commercial lending and trust services. Chartered in 1907 as First National Bank of Lake Forest; present name adopted in 1988.

Directors   (In addition to indicated officers)

James J. D'Ambrosio, Jr.	David L. Porter	Harold H. Tyler, Jr.

Officers   (Directors*)

* John A. Andersen, Chm., Pres. & C.E.O.	Karen S. Gould, V.P.
* Robert E. Ross, Exec. V.P.	John M. Hakes, V.P.
George T. Drake, Sr. V.P.	Lora-Lee Hall, V.P.
Martha R. Hinchman, Sr. V.P.	Peter J. Klett, V.P.
Robert W. Holt, Sr. V.P.	Nancy L. Krohn, V.P.
John J. Meierhoff, Sr. V.P.	Zachary D. Lazar, Jr., V.P.
Thomas M. Roberts, Sr. V.P. & Cashier	Peter A. Massa, V.P. & Trust Invest. Off.
* Shirley V. Shipp, Sr. V.P.	Anne G. Merriman, V.P.
* Harold J. Wiaduck, Jr., Sr. V.P.	Thomas A. Oehler, V.P.
Shirley T. Antes, V.P.	Kinley T. Reddy, V.P.
Sharon M. Burd, V.P.	Connie J. Snyder, V.P. & Secy.
Stephen H. Butzlaff, V.P.	Michael V. Valdez, V.P.
* Peter M. Croner, V.P. & C.F.O.	Mark E. Vaughan, V.P. & Invest. Off.
Ronald B. Eich, V.P.	Fred W. Vida, V.P.
M. Claire Frye, V.P.	William G. Waller, V.P.
Margaret M. Georgevich, V.P.	Lawrence R. Whitaker, V.P.
Adriana N. Godinez, V.P.	Ellen Young, V.P.

Statement of Condition   As of December 31, 1994 (000 omitted)

Assets			Liabilities & Stockholders' Equity	
Current assets	$	661,448	Current liabilities	$623,564
Net property, plant & equipment		7,517	Other liabilities	6,503
Other assets		7,614	Stockholders' equity	46,512
Total	$	676,579	Total	$676,579

Years Ended Dec. 31	Thousands Total Deposits	Demand Deposits	Time Deposits	Net Loans	Capital Accounts
1994	$509,355	$80,275	$429,080	$428,282	$46,512
1993	520,030	86,903	433,127	422,516	45,735
1992	537,070	82,300	454,770	374,950	45,961
1991	542,912	69,976	472,936	320,569	44,193
1990	480,193	63,645	416,548	308,125	42,874

Consolidated Income Statement

Years Ended Dec. 31	Thousands Operating Income	Operating Expenses	Net Income
1994	$49,877	$40,781	$9,096
1993	50,118	40,094	10,024
1992	52,471	43,578	8,893
1991	55,304	48,611	6,693
1990	57,070	50,561	6,509

Human Resources:	Shirley V. Shipp, Sr. V.P.	Employees:	145
Mgt. Info. Svcs.:	Harold J. Wiaduck, Jr., Sr. V.P.		
Total Accounts:	34,710	Member:	FDIC; Federal Reserve System

Northern Trust Bank/O'Hare N.A.

8501 West Higgins Road, Chicago, Illinois 60631-2801
Telephone: (312) 693-5555

Northern Trust Bank/O'Hare N.A. is a wholly owned subsidiary of Northern Trust Corporation. The bank offers a variety of trust and banking services with emphasis on "Private Banking" and middle market corporations. Two banking facilities are located in Chicago, and one in Schaumburg, near Chicago's O'Hare International Airport. Incorporated in 1958.

Directors   (In addition to indicated officers)

John A. Andersen
James J. D'Ambrosio, Jr.

David L. Porter
Robert E. Ross

Officers   (Directors*)

* Harold H. Tyler, Jr., Pres. & C.E.O.
  Joseph J. Zielinski, Exec. V.P.
  Thomas M. Roberts, Sr. V.P. & Cashier
  Lisa C. Schmeh, Sr. V.P.
  Raymond C. Schmeh, Sr. V.P.

* Shirley V. Shipp, Sr. V.P.
* Harold J. Wiaduck, Jr., Sr. V.P.
  Thomas G. Wischhusen, Sr. V.P.
* Peter M. Croner, V.P. & C.F.O.

Consolidated Balance Sheet   As of December 31, 1994 (000 omitted)

Assets			Liabilities & Stockholders' Equity	
Cash & due from depository			Deposits	$423,129
institutions	$	47,445	Federal funds purchased & securities sold	37,313
Securities		241,178	Demand notes issued to U.S. Treasury	4,496
Loans & leases, net		204,306	Other liabilities	3,551
Premises & fixed assets			*Total equity capital	33,697
(includes Cap. leases)		1,833		
Other assets		7,424		
Total	$	502,186	Total	$502,186

*924,818 shares common stock outstanding.

Years Ended Dec. 31	Total Deposits	Domestic Interest Bearing Deposits	Domestic Non-Interest Bearing Deposits	Loans & Leases, Net	Total Equity Capital
1994	$423,129	$345,392	$77,737	$204,306	$33,697
1993	413,382	326,644	86,738	195,862	34,967
1992	456,551	369,779	86,772	221,162	34,494
1991	433,268	357,726	75,542	220,141	34,394
1990	418,523	332,156	86,367	261,465	33,482

Consolidated Income Statement

Years Ended Dec. 31	Operating Income	Operating Expenses	Net Income
1994	$29,579	$23,515	$5,308
1993	31,133	24,087	6,028
1992	34,106	27,815	5,600
1991	40,013	33,011	5,412
1990	44,722[a]	37,478	5,958

[a]Restated.

General Counsel: David L. Porter
Human Resources: Shirley V. Shipp, Sr. V.P.
Mgt. Info. Svcs.:
    Thomas M. Roberts, Sr. V.P. & Cashier

Auditors: Arthur Andersen LLP
Employees: 164

Member: FDIC; Federal Reserve System

First Chicago Guide

The Northern Trust Company

50 South LaSalle Street, Chicago, Illinois 60675

Telephone: (312) 630-6000

The Northern Trust Company is a wholly owned subsidiary of Northern Trust Corporation. The bank offers commercial, correspondent, cash management, corporate financial, trust, loan, personal banking and international banking services. The Northern Trust International Banking Corporation, The Northern Trust Company, Canada, Northern Global Financial Services Ltd., Hong Kong, and NorLease, Inc., are wholly owned subsidiaries. The Northern Trust Company has branches in London and the Cayman Islands; and a five percent-interest in Banque Rivaud, Paris. Three banking facilities are located in Chicago, one in Winnetka, and one in Highland Park. Incorporated in Illinois in 1889.

Directors   (In addition to indicated officers)

W.H. Clark	Arthur L. Kelly	William G. Mitchell
Dolores E. Cross	Ardis Krainik	Harold B. Smith
Robert S. Hamada	Robert D. Krebs	William D. Smithburg
Robert A. Helman	Frederick A. Krehbiel	Bide L. Thomas

Officers   (Directors*)[a]

* David W. Fox, Chm.
* William A. Osborn, Pres. & C.E.O.
* Barry G. Hastings, V. Chm. & C.O.O.
Perry R. Pero, Sr. Exec. V.P., C.F.O. & Cashier
Gregg D. Behrens, Exec. V.P.
J. David Brock, Exec. V.P.
John V.N. McClure, Exec. V.P.
James J. Mitchell, Exec. V.P.

J. Terrence Murray, Exec. V.P.
Sheila A. Penrose, Exec. V.P.
Peter L. Rossiter, Exec. V.P., Gen. Coun. & Secy.
William S. Trukenbrod, Exec. V.P.
Jeffrey H. Wessel, Exec. V.P.
David L. Eddy, Sr. V.P.
Daniel S. O'Keefe, Sr. V.P. & Gen. Auditor
Harry W. Short, Sr. V.P. & Cont.

[a]Fox will retire on October 3, 1995, at which time Osborn will add the title of Chairman and Hastings will become President and C.O.O.

Consolidated Balance Sheet   As of December 31, 1994 (000 omitted)

Assets		Liabilities & Stockholders' Equity	
Cash & due from banks	$ 1,013,800	Deposits	$ 8,848,300
Securities	4,149,200	Funds borrowed	4,014,500
Money market assets	2,693,800	Senior medium-term notes	545,000
Net loans & lease financing	5,916,800	Notes payable	209,600
Properties & equipment	200,700	Other liabilities	327,400
Other assets	761,200	Stockholders' equity	790,700
Total	$14,735,500	Total	$14,735,500

Years Ended Dec. 31	Total Deposits	Domestic Demand Deposits	Domestic Time Deposits	Foreign Office Deposits	Loans & Leases	Capital Accts.
1994	$8,848,300	$2,183,800	$2,582,700	$4,081,800	$6,030,500	$790,700
1993	7,769,400	2,039,000	2,555,400	3,175,000	5,408,300	723,800
1992	7,195,800	2,281,800	3,019,100	1,894,900	5,061,400	645,300
1991	6,061,600	1,450,600	3,227,700	1,383,300	4,710,600	574,100
1990	5,962,600	1,662,600	2,931,600	1,368,400	4,162,800	508,900

Consolidated Income Statement

Years Ended Dec. 31	Operating Income	Operating Expenses	Net Income
1994	$1,111,400	$924,800	$130,100
1993	932,200	764,700	121,100
1992	920,800	766,900	111,500
1991	997,500	848,800	99,400
1990	1,048,500	934,700	94,200

General Counsel:	Peter L. Rossiter, Exec. V.P.	General Auditor:	Daniel S. O'Keefe, Sr. V.P.
Trust Counsel:	J. Timothy Ritchie	Auditors:	Arthur Andersen LLP
Human Resources:	William L. Setterstrom, Sr. V.P.	Employees:	4,814
Mgt. Info. Svcs.:	John P. Archer, Sr. V.P.	Member:	FDIC; Federal Reserve System

First Chicago Guide

Northwestern Savings Bank

2300 North Western Avenue, Chicago, Illinois 60647-3195
Telephone: (312) 489-2300

Northwestern Savings Bank (formerly Northwestern Savings & Loan Association) is engaged in the business of attracting deposits from the general public and investing those deposits, together with funds generated from operations and borrowings, primarily into one- to four-family mortgage loans. Northwestern Savings operates two wholly owned subsidiaries. N.W. Financial Corp., through its subsidiaries, is engaged primarily in the acquisition, improvement, and development of real estate into residential subdivisions consisting mainly of medium priced single-family residences. It also provides insurance services through a subsidiary. N.W. Acceptance Corp. is a special purpose subsidiary through which Northwestern Savings issued collateralized mortgage obligations in 1986. In January 1995, Northwestern Savings converted from an Illinois-chartered stock savings and loan association to an Illinois-chartered stock savings bank. Northwestern Savings was organized in 1919.

Directors   (In addition to indicated officers)

James L. Busch
Ramona Castillo
Robert E. Chamberlain

Stanley C. Wielgos
Edward J. Zych

Officers   (Directors*)

* Henry R. Smogolski, Chm., Pres. & C.E.O.
* Andrew J. Zych, Exec. V.P.
  Stephen G. Skiba, Sr. V.P., C.F.O. & Treas.
  Gary M. Smogolski, Sr. V.P.—Hum. Res. & Secy.

Maria M. Cordon, V.P.—Savings
Robert F. Kapolnek, V.P.—Mktg.
Marie L. Phillips, V.P.—Data Systems
Trent N. Fotopoulos, Asst. Secy.

Consolidated Balance Sheet   As of December 31, 1994 (000 omitted)

Assets		Liabilities & Stockholders' Equity	
Loans receivable, net	$ 826,041	Deposits	$ 840,012
Mortgage-backed securities	249,608	Borrowed funds	204,138
Investment securities	96,912	Other liabilities	6,790
Real estate	39,953	*Stockholders' equity	185,478
Other assets	23,904		
Total	$1,236,418	Total	$1,236,418

*1,000 shares common stock outstanding.

| Years Ended Dec. 31 | Thousands | | | |
	Total Assets	Loans Receivable, Net	Mortgage-backed Securities	Stockholders' Equity
1994	$1,236,418	$826,041	$249,608	$185,478
1993	1,207,107	739,584	270,452	180,947
1992	1,270,112	682,961	311,354	213,825
1991	1,364,373	794,092	320,311	179,887
1990	1,376,498	919,137	308,941	171,184

Consolidated Income Statement

| Years Ended Dec. 31 | Thousands | | |
	Operating Income	Operating[a] Expense	Net Income
1994	$73,946	$54,886	$11,715
1993	92,599	54,484	25,630
1992	120,439	70,606	32,093
1991	126,724	89,615	22,739
1990	130,651	104,535	10,958

[a]Does not include provision for loan losses and income taxes.

General Counsel:	Stone, Pogrund, Korey & Spagat	Auditors:	Ernst & Young LLP
		Depositors:	76,512
Human Resources:	Gary M. Smogolski, Sr. V.P.	Employees:	314
Mgt. Info. Svcs.:	Marie L. Phillips, V.P.	Member:	FDIC

Oak Brook Bank
1400 Sixteenth Street, Oak Brook, Illinois 60521
Telephone: (708) 571-1050

Oak Brook Bank, a wholly owned subsidiary of First Oak Brook Bancshares, Inc., is engaged in the general retail and commercial banking business. The services offered include demand, savings, and time deposits, corporate cash management services, commercial lending products such as commercial loans, mortgages and letters of credit, and personal lending products such as residential mortgages, home equity lines, auto loans, and credit card products. In addition, related products and services are offered, including discount brokerage, mutual funds and annuity sales, and foreign currency and precious metals sales. Oak Brook Bank has a full-service trust and land trust department. The bank has seven locations in DuPage County and two locations in Cook County.

Directors (In addition to indicated officers)

Anthony De Santis	Andrew T. Heytow	Geoffrey R. Stone
Miriam Lutwak Fitzgerald	Barry S. Kerstein	Bruce Wechsler
Charles J. Gries	Michael Segal	Alton M. Withers
Thomas J. Hartigan		

Officers (Directors*)

* Eugene P. Heytow, Chm. & C.E.O.
* Frank M. Paris, V. Chm.
* Richard M. Rieser, Jr., Pres.
George C. Clam, Sr. Exec. V.P.
Katharine E. Blumenthal, Exec. V.P. & Trust Officer
Rosemarie Burget, Exec. V.P. & C.F.O.
Mary C. Campbell, Exec. V.P. & Chf. Hum. Res. Officer
Melvin H. Gilfillan, Exec. V.P.
Glenn R. Krietsch, Exec. V.P.
Dennis E. O'Hara, Exec. V.P.
Robert T. Bouman, Sr. V.P.

Jeffrey W. Brown, Sr. V.P.
Patrick L. Doland, Sr. V.P.
Brian C. England, Sr. V.P.
Susanne C. Griffith, Sr. V.P. & Auditor
Rod Kuecker, Sr. V.P.
Ann Nicholson, Sr. V.P. & Cashier
Dennis J. Reidy, Sr. V.P.
James D. Leckinger, Treas. & Chf. Trust Officer
William E. Navolio, Gen. Coun.
* Robert M. Wrobel, Asst. to the Chm.

Consolidated Balance Sheet As of December 31, 1994 (000 omitted)

Assets			Liabilities & Stockholder's Equity	
Cash & due from banks	$	33,710	Deposits	$513,729
Securities		259,653	Funds borrowed	74,577
Other short-term investments		2,591	Other liabilities	3,346
Net loans		305,822	Stockholder's equity	38,034
Properties & equipment		18,751		
Other assets		9,159		
Total	$	629,686	Total	$629,686

Years Ended Dec. 31	Thousands Total Deposits	Demand Deposits	Time Deposits	Net Loans	Capital Accounts
1994	$513,729	$109,271	$154,430	$305,822	$38,034
1993	508,248	113,820	129,237	274,946	41,423
1992	436,677	94,190	111,963	262,648	32,457
1991	402,145	82,791	145,243	200,414	29,999

Consolidated Income Statement

Years Ended Dec. 31	Thousands Operating Income	Operating Expenses	Net Income
1994	$45,081	$38,280	$6,801
1993	41,320	35,337	5,983
1992	39,128	34,334	4,794
1991	39,637	35,810	3,827

General Counsel:	William E. Navolio	Auditors:	Ernst & Young LLP
Human Resources:	Mary C. Campbell, Exec. V.P.	Employees:	283
Mgt. Info. Svcs.:	Dennis J. Reidy, Sr. V.P.	Member:	FDIC

First Chicago Guide

Old Kent Bank

105 South York Street, Elmhurst, Illinois 60126
Telephone: (708) 941-5200

Old Kent Bank is a wholly owned subsidiary of Old Kent Financial Corporation, an $11.0 billion regional bank holding company. The bank provides a broad range of trust, retail, and commercial services to individuals and businesses. Old Kent Bank has 22 branches in the western suburbs and three branches in Chicago. The suburban branches are Clarendon Hills, Countryside, Dundee, Elgin (3), Elmhurst, Hampshire, Itasca, Lombard (2), Naperville, Rolling Meadows, Rosemont, St. Charles (3), Westmont, Wheaton (2), Winfield, and Woodridge. Member FDIC.

Directors   (In addition to indicated officers)

James G. Bauer
Gordon D. Bednorz
Stephen J. Bloom
Charles Bruning
Richard C. Hoskins, Jr.
Larry Larkin
Ann P. McDermott

Dennis P. McDonald
Brien J. Nagle
Joan Portillo
Robert E. Soukup
Alice M. Tybout
Thomas R. Walker

Officers   (Directors*)

* B.P. Sherwood III, Chm.
* Michael J. Whalen, Pres. & C.E.O.
George W. Vander Vennet, Exec. V.P. & Trust Off.
Mason G. Coleman, Sr. V.P.—Retail Banking
Larry R. Lettow, Sr. V.P.—Private Banking

William M. Powell, Sr. V.P.—Trading Mgr.
Peter B. Stickler, Sr. V.P., C.F.O. & Cashier
Daryl J. Waszak, Sr. V.P.—Trust
John Starkey, V.P.—Hum. Res.

Consolidated Balance Sheet   As of December 31, 1994 (000 omitted)

Assets		Liabilities & Stockholders' Equity	
Cash & due from banks	$ 47,618	Deposits	$1,515,334
Short-term investments	51,527	Funds borrowed	221,433
Investment securities	823,249	Other liabilities	14,627
Loans, net	891,492	Stockholders' equity	151,530
Prem. & equip., net	25,105		
Other assets	63,933		
Total	$ 1,902,924	Total	$1,902,924

Years Ended Dec. 31	Total Deposits	Demand Deposits	Savings & Time Deposits	Net Loans	Capital Accounts
1994	$1,515,334	$237,697	$1,277,637	$891,492	$151,530
1993	1,181,838	165,700	1,016,138	674,241	111,979
1992	988,790	160,365	828,425	559,451	93,816
1991	1,061,576	180,755	880,801	664,220	89,600

Consolidated Income Statement

Years Ended Dec. 31	Operating Income	Operating Expenses	Net Income
1994	$124,308	$109,183	$15,125
1993	113,753	98,403	15,350
1992	105,030	95,314	9,716
1991	119,983	113,738	6,245

General Counsel:	Warner, Norcross & Judd	Auditors:	Arthur Andersen LLP
Human Resources:	John Starkey, V.P.	Employees:	780
Mgt. Info. Svcs.:	Peter B. Stickler, Sr. V.P.	Member:	FDIC

St. Paul Federal Bank For Savings

6700 West North Avenue, Chicago, Illinois 60635

Telephone: (312) 622-5000

St. Paul Federal Bank For Savings, a wholly owned subsidiary of St. Paul Bancorp, Inc., is primarily engaged in attracting checking, savings, and certificates of deposit accounts from the general public and investing those funds in a variety of mortgage and consumer loan products and high quality investment securities. In addition, St. Paul offers its customers a variety of allied services. Fifty-two branch offices are located in Addison, Arlington Heights, Aurora, Berkeley, Berwyn, Blue Island, Bridgeview, Buffalo Grove, Carol Stream, Chicago, Cicero, Crestwood, Downers Grove, Elgin, Elmhurst, Elmwood Park, Evanston, Evergreen Park, Franklin Park, Glendale Heights, Hanover Park, Harwood Heights, Lombard, McHenry, Melrose Park, Morton Grove, Mount Prospect, Niles, Oak Lawn, Oak Park, Orland Park, Rolling Meadows, Round Lake Beach, Skokie, Villa Park, Waukegan, Westchester, Wood Dale, and Woodridge, Illinois. St. Paul Service, Inc., a wholly owned general insurance agency, provides a wide range of insurance services. Investment Network, Inc., a discount brokerage firm, offers execution and clearance services for stocks, bonds, and mutual funds. St. Paul Financial Development Corp. and Annuity Network, Inc., other wholly owned subsidiaries of St. Paul Bancorp, Inc., engage in single family real estate development in the Chicago metropolitan area and the sale of annuity products, respectively.

Directors   (In addition to indicated officers)

William A. Anderson	Alan J. Fredian	Jean C. Murray, O.P.	John J. Viera
John W. Croghan	Kenneth J. James	Michael R. Notaro	James B. Wood

Officers   (Directors*)

* Joseph C. Scully, Chm. & C.E.O.
* Patrick J. Agnew, Pres. & C.O.O.
  James R. Lutsch, Sr. V.P.—Info. Services
  Robert N. Parke, Sr. V.P.—Fin. & C.F.O.
  Robert N. Pfeiffer, Sr. V.P.—Hum. Res.

Thomas J. Rinella, Sr. V.P.—Community Lend.
Donald G. Ross, Sr. V.P.—Retail Banking
John J. Schukay, Sr. V.P.—Cust. Oper.
Clifford M. Sladnick, Sr. V.P.—Corp. Secy. &
Gen. Coun.

Consolidated Balance Sheet   As of December 31, 1994 (000 omitted)

Assets			Liabilities & Stockholders' Equity	
Cash & cash equivalents	$	142,289	Deposits	$3,237,632
Investments		98,664	FHLB advances	336,959
Mortgage-backed securities		1,126,617	Other borrowed funds	117,676
Loans receivable (net of reserves)		2,562,665	Advanced payments for taxes & insurance	21,842
Properties & equipment		44,003	Other liabilities	30,557
FHLB stock		29,847	*Stockholders' equity	347,470
Other assets		88,051		
Total	$	4,092,136	Total	$4,092,136

*1,500 shares common stock outstanding.

Years[a] Ended Dec. 31	Total Assets	Mortgage Loans & Mortgage-backed Securities	Total Deposits	Stockholders' Equity
1994	$4,092,136	$3,689,282	$3,237,632	$347,470
1993	3,671,882	3,032,758	3,256,319	351,092
1992	3,491,370	2,900,450	2,985,485	280,212
1991	3,657,295	3,134,020	3,005,162	248,209
1990	3,435,458	3,072,987	2,666,173	221,165

[a]Restated.

Consolidated Income Statement

Years[a] Ended Dec. 31	Gross Income	Interest Expenses	Operating Expenses[b]	Net Income
1994	$276,345	$131,997	$84,361	$34,076
1993	285,386	130,385	80,680	41,798
1992	303,915	165,900	69,956	36,561
1991	343,033	222,512	63,714	27,044
1990	337,663	227,681	62,433	8,023

[a]Certain financial data restated.
[b]Excludes federal and state income taxes.

General Counsel:	Clifford M. Sladnick, Sr. V.P.	**Auditors:**	Ernst & Young LLP
Human Resources	Robert N. Pfeiffer, Sr. V.P.	**Employees:**	1,054
Mgt. Info. Svcs.:	James R. Lutsch, Sr. V.P.	**Member:**	FDIC

First Chicago Guide

Standard Federal Bank for savings
4192 South Archer Avenue, Chicago, Illinois 60632-1890
Telephone: (312) 847-1140

Standard Federal Bank for savings has a total of 13 offices serving Chicago's southwest side, Downers Grove, Evergreen Park, Hickory Hills, Lombard, Oak Lawn, Willowbrook, Palos Heights, and Orland Park. A major subsidiary is SFB Insurance Agency, Inc. Standard Federal was founded on February 22, 1909, by Justin Mackiewich, Sr., and a small group of fellow Lithuanian immigrants. The organization was known as the D.K.L. Gedimino Building & Loan until 1934 when a federal charter was received and the name Standard Federal Savings and Loan Association was chosen; present name adopted in May 1990. In January 1994, the bank formed a holding company in preparation for its conversion to a federally chartered stock savings bank, which occurred in July 1994.

Directors   (In addition to indicated officers)

Stasys J. Baras	Simon P. Gary	George Lane
John A. Brdecka	Fred V. Gwyer, M.D.	Chester K. McMillen
Sharon Reese Dalenberg	Tomas A. Kisielius, M.D.	

Officers   (Directors*)

* David H. Mackiewich, Chm. & Pres.	George Cvack, V.P.
Thomas C. Halm, Sr. V.P.	LuAnn Hennessy, V.P.
Kurtis D. Mackiewich, Sr. V.P.	James Kopacz, V.P.
* Thomas M. Ryan, Sr. V.P.	Donald Kowalski, V.P.
Ruta M. Juska Staniulis, Sr. V.P.	Michael Kowalski, V.P.
John Ahearn, V.P.	Jean Krusinski, V.P.
Patricia Barrera, V.P.	Leonard Metheny, V.P.
Michael F. Barrett, V.P.	David Schaefer, V.P.
Susan Carduff, V.P.	Randall R. Schwartz, V.P.
Mark Collins, V.P.	

Consolidated Balance Sheet   As of December 31, 1994 (000 omitted)

Assets		Liabilities & Stockholder's Equity	
Cash	$ 75,990	Total deposits	$1,393,274
Investment securities	177,287	Advances from FHLB	50,000
Mortgage-backed certs.	759,860	Advance payments by borrowers	
Loans receivable	593,047	for taxes & insur.	6,199
FHLB stock	11,932	Other liabilities	25,303
Property & equipment	28,647	Stockholder's Equity	185,261
Other assets	13,274		
Total	$ 1,660,037	Total	$1,660,037

Years Ended Dec. 31	Thousands Total Assets	Mortgage Loans	Total Deposits	General Reserves
1994	$1,660,037	$593,047	$1,393,274	$185,261
1993	1,508,840	523,637	1,371,214	96,069
1992	1,506,132	492,220	1,379,605	92,201
1991	1,418,494	496,123	1,310,150	82,194
1990	1,311,261	571,658	1,228,436	74,190

Consolidated Income Statement

Years Ended Dec. 31	Thousands Interest Income	Interest Expense	Other Income	Other Expense	Net Income
1994	$99,044	$51,879	$4,593	$41,677	$10,081
1993	98,399	52,839	5,557	47,249	3,868
1992	109,098	65,479	5,722	39,334	10,007
1991	125,971	89,681	4,440	32,726	8,004

Human Resources: Patricia Barrera, V.P.		Depositors:	107,367
Mgt. Info. Svcs.: Mark Collins, V.P.		Employees:	575
Auditors: Ernst & Young LLP		Member:	FDIC

First Chicago Guide

Index and Rankings

Index to Operations by Product Classification
Using Standard Industrial Classification Numbers

MAJOR GROUP 01
0100   **AGRICULTURAL PRODUCTION— CROPS**
0115   Corn
DEKALB Genetics Corporation
0116   Soybeans
DEKALB Genetics Corporation
0119   Cash grains, not elsewhere classified
DEKALB Genetics Corporation

MAJOR GROUP 02
0200   **AGRICULTURAL PRODUCTION— LIVESTOCK AND ANIMAL SPECIALTIES**
0213   Hogs
DEKALB Genetics Corporation
0751   Livestock services, except veterinary
DEKALB Genetics Corporation

MAJOR GROUP 10
1000   **METAL MINING**
1041   Gold ores
FMC Corporation

MAJOR GROUP 12
1200   **COAL MINING**
1221   Bituminous coal and lignite mining
Zeigler Coal Holding Company
1222   Bituminous coal underground mining
Zeigler Coal Holding Company

MAJOR GROUP 13
1300   **OIL AND GAS EXTRACTION**
1311   Crude petroleum and natural gas
Amoco Corporation
1321   Natural gas liquids
Amoco Corporation

MAJOR GROUP 14
1400   **MINING AND QUARRYING OF NON-METALLIC MINERALS, EXCEPT FUELS**
1422   Crushed and broken limestone
Continental Materials Corporation
1459   Clay, ceramic, and refractory minerals, not elsewhere classified
AMCOL International Corporation
1474   Potash, soda, and borate minerals
IMC Global Inc.
The Vigoro Corporation
1475   Phosphate rock
IMC Global Inc.
1479   Chemical and fertilizer mineral mining, not elsewhere classified
IMC Global Inc.
Morton International, Inc.
1499   Miscellaneous nonmetallic minerals, not elsewhere classified
Oil•Dri Corporation of America

MAJOR GROUP 15
1500   **BUILDING CONSTRUCTION—**

GENERAL CONTRACTORS AND OPERATIVE BUILDERS
1521   General contractors—single-family houses
Sundance Homes, Inc.
1522   General contractors–residential buildings, other than single-family
Amerihost Properties, Inc.

MAJOR GROUP 16
1600   **HEAVY CONSTRUCTION OTHER THAN BUILDING CONSTRUCTION - CONTRACTORS**
1623   Water, sewer, pipe line, communication and power line construction
The L.E. Myers Co. Group
1629   Heavy construction, not elsewhere classified
CBI Industries, Inc.
The L.E. Myers Co. Group
WMX Technologies, Inc.

MAJOR GROUP 17
1700   **CONSTRUCTION—SPECIAL TRADE CONTRACTORS**
1731   Electrical work
The L.E. Myers Co. Group
1796   Installation or erection of building equipment, not elsewhere classified
The L.E. Myers Co. Group

MAJOR GROUP 20
2000   **FOOD AND KINDRED PRODUCTS**
2011   Meat packing plants
Rymer Foods Inc.
2013   Sausages and other prepared meat products
Rymer Foods Inc.
Sara Lee Corporation
2023   Dry, condensed and evaporated dairy products
Dean Foods Company
2024   Ice cream and frozen desserts
Dean Foods Company
2026   Fluid milk
Dean Foods Company
2033   Canned fruits, vegetables, preserves, jams, and jellies
Dean Foods Company
The Quaker Oats Company
2035   Pickled fruits and vegetables, vegetable sauces and seasonings, and salad dressings
Dean Foods Company
2037   Frozen fruits, fruit juices, and vegetables
Dean Foods Company
2041   Flour and other grain mill products
Archer-Daniels-Midland Company
The Quaker Oats Company
2043   Cereal breakfast foods
The Quaker Oats Company

First Chicago Guide

321

Elco Industries, Inc.
IDEX Corporation
Newell Co.

3431 Enameled iron and metal sanitary ware
UNR Industries, Inc.

3433 Heating equipment, except electric and warm air furnaces
Continental Materials Corporation

3441 Fabricated structural metal
UNR Industries, Inc.

3443 Fabricated plate work (boiler shops)
CBI Industries, Inc.
Fansteel Inc.

3444 Sheet metal work
Great American Management and Investment, Inc.
Quixote Corporation

3446 Architectural and ornamental metal work
Falcon Building Products, Inc.

3449 Miscellaneous structural metal work
Varlen Corporation

3452 Bolts, nuts, screws, rivets and washers
Chicago Rivet & Machine Co.
Elco Industries, Inc.
Illinois Tool Works Inc.

3462 Iron and steel forgings
ABC Rail Products Corporation
Fansteel Inc.
PORTEC, Inc.

3465 Automotive stampings
Acme Metals Incorporated
Allied Products Corporation
Truck Components Inc.
Varlen Corporation

3466 Crowns and closures
AptarGroup, Inc.

3469 Metal stampings, not elsewhere classified
Allied Products Corporation
Elco Industries, Inc.
Newell Co.

3471 Electroplating, plating, polishing, anodizing, and coloring
Material Sciences Corporation

3479 Coating, engraving and allied services, not elsewhere classified
Material Sciences Corporation
Morton International, Inc.

3489 Ordnance and accessories, not elsewhere classified
FMC Corporation

3491 Industrial valves
AptarGroup, Inc.

3492 Fluid power valves and hose fittings
AptarGroup, Inc.
Binks Manufacturing Company

3494 Valves and pipe fittings, not elsewhere classified
AptarGroup, Inc.

3496 Miscellaneous fabricated wire products
Chicago Rivet & Machine Co.
Elco Industries, Inc.
Falcon Building Products, Inc.
Great American Management and Investment, Inc.
Lindberg Corporation

Northwestern Steel and Wire Company
Selfix, Inc.
UNR Industries, Inc.

3499 Fabricated metal products, not elsewhere classified
Acme Metals Incorporated
AptarGroup, Inc.
The Interlake Corporation
WMX Technologies, Inc.

MAJOR GROUP 35

3500 INDUSTRIAL AND COMMERCIAL MACHINERY AND COMPUTER EQUIPMENT

3511 Steam, gas, and hydraulic turbines and turbine generator set units
Caterpillar Inc.
Sundstrand Corporation
Woodward Governor Company

3519 Internal combustion engines, not elsewhere classified
Brunswick Corporation
Caterpillar Inc.
Deere & Company
IDEX Corporation
Outboard Marine Corporation
Woodward Governor Company

3523 Farm machinery and equipment
Allied Products Corporation
Deere & Company
FMC Corporation

3524 Lawn and garden tractors and home lawn and garden equipment
Deere & Company

3531 Construction machinery and equipment
ABC Rail Products Corporation
Caterpillar Inc.
Deere & Company
PORTEC, Inc.

3532 Mining machinery and equipment, except oil and gas field machinery and equipment
Caterpillar Inc.

3535 Conveyors and conveying equipment
The Interlake Corporation
PORTEC, Inc.

3537 Industrial trucks, tractors, trailers, and stackers
AAR CORP.
Caterpillar Inc.
Navistar International Corporation

3541 Machine tools, metal cutting types
Fansteel Inc.
IDEX Corporation

3542 Machine tools, metal forming types
Allied Products Corporation
Chicago Rivet & Machine Co.

3544 Special dies and tools, die sets, jigs and fixtures, and industrial molds
Federal Signal Corporation

3545 Cutting tools, machine tool accessories and machinists' precision measuring devices
Chicago Rivet & Machine Co.
Federal Signal Corporation

First Chicago Guide

3546 Power-driven handtools
IDEX Corporation

3548 Electric and gas welding and soldering equipment
Illinois Tool Works Inc.

3554 Paper industries machinery
AM International, Inc.
Illinois Tool Works Inc.

3555 Printing trades machinery and equipment
AM International, Inc.
Lawter International, Inc.
Zebra Technologies Corporation

3556 Food products machinery
The Middleby Corporation
Premark International, Inc.
Scotsman Industries, Inc.

3559 Special industry machinery, not elsewhere classified
The Interlake Corporation
Nalco Chemical Company
Safety-Kleen Corp.
Varlen Corporation

3561 Pumps and pumping equipment
Binks Manufacturing Company
IDEX Corporation
Sundstrand Corporation

3562 Ball and roller bearings
Binks Manufacturing Company

3563 Air and gas compressors
Great American Management and Investment, Inc.
Newell Co.

3564 Industrial and commercial fans and blowers and air purification equipment
Advance Ross Corporation
Binks Manufacturing Company
MFRI, Inc.

3566 Speed changers, industrial high speed drives, and gears
Illinois Tool Works Inc.
Sundstrand Corporation

3567 Industrial process furnaces and ovens
Binks Manufacturing Company
Continental Materials Corporation

3569 General industrial machinery and equipment, not elsewhere classified
CLARCOR Inc.
IDEX Corporation
MFRI, Inc.
Morton International, Inc.
Woodhead Industries, Inc.

3571 Electronic computers
Motorola, Inc.

3575 Computer terminals
General Instrument Corporation
Molex Incorporated
Wells-Gardner Electronics Corporation

3577 Electronic computing equipment
AM International, Inc.
The Cherry Corporation
Zebra Technologies Corporation

3579 Office machines, not elsewhere classified
AM International, Inc.
Bell & Howell Holdings Company
General Binding Corporation
Quixote Corporation

3585 Air conditioning, warm air heating equipment and commercial and industrial refrigeration equipment
Continental Materials Corporation
Falcon Building Products, Inc.
The Middleby Corporation
Scotsman Industries, Inc.
Whitman Corporation

3589 Service industry machines, not elsewhere classified
AMCOL International Corporation
The Middleby Corporation
Minuteman International, Inc.
Premark International, Inc.
Safety-Kleen Corp.

3592 Carburetors, pistons, piston rings, and valves
Champion Parts, Inc.

3594 Fluid power pumps and motors
Binks Manufacturing Company

MAJOR GROUP 36
3600 **ELECTRONIC AND OTHER ELECTRICAL EQUIPMENT AND COMPONENTS, EXCEPT COMPUTER EQUIPMENT**

3612 Power, distribution, and specialty transformers
Littelfuse, Inc.
UNR Industries, Inc.
Woodhead Industries, Inc.

3613 Switchgear and switchboard apparatus
The Cherry Corporation
Joslyn Corporation
Littelfuse, Inc.
Methode Electronics, Inc.
Molex Incorporated
Tellabs, Inc.

3621 Motors and generators
Brunswick Corporation
Outboard Marine Corporation
Truck Components Inc.

3625 Relays and industrial controls
Joslyn Corporation
Littelfuse, Inc.
Methode Electronics, Inc.
Woodhead Industries, Inc.
Woodward Governor Company

3629 Electrical industrial apparatus, not elsewhere classified
Joslyn Corporation

3634 Electric housewares and fans
Premark International, Inc.
Salton/Maxim Housewares, Inc.

3641 Electric lamp bulbs and tubes
Juno Lighting, Inc.

3643 Current-carrying wiring devices
The Cherry Corporation
Joslyn Corporation
Littelfuse, Inc.
Methode Electronics, Inc.
Molex Incorporated
Woodhead Industries, Inc.

3644 Noncurrent-carrying wiring devices
Allied Products Corporation
Joslyn Corporation

3645 Residential electric lighting fixtures
Juno Lighting, Inc.
3646 Commercial, industrial and institutional
electric lighting fixtures
Juno Lighting, Inc.
3648 Lighting equipment, not elsewhere
classified
First Alert, Inc.
Juno Lighting, Inc.
3651 Household audio and video equipment
and audio recordings
Cobra Electronics Corporation
International Jensen Incorporated
Salton/Maxim Housewares, Inc.
Wells-Gardner Electronics Corporation
Zenith Electronics Corporation
3652 Phonograph records and prerecorded
audio tapes and disks
Quixote Corporation
3661 Telephone and telegraph apparatus
Ameritech Corporation
Anicom, Inc.
Cobra Electronics Corporation
Motorola, Inc.
Tellabs, Inc.
Teltrend Inc.
Telular Corporation
U.S. Robotics Corporation
3663 Radio and television broadcasting and
communications equipment
Andrew Corporation
Anicom, Inc.
ANTEC Corporation
Cobra Electronics Corporation
Corcom, Inc.
General Instrument Corporation
Itel Corporation
M~Wave, Inc.
Motorola, Inc.
Richardson Electronics, Ltd.
Tellabs, Inc.
Telular Corporation
Zenith Electronics Corporation
3669 Communications equipment, not
elsewhere classified
Anicom, Inc.
Federal Signal Corporation
First Alert, Inc.
Pittway Corporation
Tellabs, Inc.
3671 Electron tubes
Richardson Electronics, Ltd.
SigmaTron International, Inc.
Zenith Electronics Corporation
3672 Printed circuit boards
Circuit Systems, Inc.
M~Wave, Inc.
SigmaTron International, Inc.
Telular Corporation
3674 Semiconductors and related devices
The Cherry Corporation
Motorola, Inc.
Richardson Electronics, Ltd.
SigmaTron International, Inc.
Zenith Electronics Corporation

3676 Electronic resistors
Methode Electronics, Inc.
3677 Electronic coils, transformers, and other
inductors
Corcom, Inc.
3678 Electronic connectors
Methode Electronics, Inc.
Molex Incorporated
3679 Electronic components, not elsewhere
classified
Andrew Corporation
The Cherry Corporation
Corcom, Inc.
Federal Signal Corporation
General Instrument Corporation
Juno Lighting, Inc.
Littelfuse, Inc.
M~Wave, Inc.
Methode Electronics, Inc.
Molex Incorporated
Motorola, Inc.
PORTEC, Inc.
SigmaTron International, Inc.
Wells-Gardner Electronics Corporation
Woodhead Industries, Inc.
Zenith Electronics Corporation
3694 Electrical equipment for internal
combustion engines
Borg-Warner Automotive, Inc.
Champion Parts, Inc.
3695 Magnetic and optical recording media
Quixote Corporation
3699 Electrical machinery equipment, and
supplies, not elsewhere classified
Joslyn Corporation

MAJOR GROUP 37
3700 **TRANSPORTATION EQUIPMENT**
3711 Motor vehicles and passenger car bodies
Federal Signal Corporation
Navistar International Corporation
3713 Truck and bus bodies
Navistar International Corporation
3714 Motor vehicle parts and accessories
Borg-Warner Automotive, Inc.
Champion Parts, Inc.
CLARCOR Inc.
Elco Industries, Inc.
Schawk, Inc.
Titan Wheel International, Inc.
Truck Components Inc.
Universal Automotive Industries, Inc.
Whitman Corporation
Woodward Governor Company
3724 Aircraft engines and engine parts
AAR CORP.
The Interlake Corporation
Sundstrand Corporation
3728 Aircraft parts and auxiliary equipment, not
elsewhere classified
AAR CORP.
Fansteel Inc.
Sundstrand Corporation
Woodward Governor Company
3732 Boat building and repairing
Brunswick Corporation

First Chicago Guide

Outboard Marine Corporation

3743 Railroad equipment
ABC Rail Products Corporation
Johnstown America Industries, Inc.
PORTEC, Inc.
Varlen Corporation

3769 Guided missile and space vehicle parts
and auxiliary equipment, not elsewhere
classified
Fansteel Inc.

3795 Tank and tank components
FMC Corporation

3799 Transportation equipment, not elsewhere
classified
Outboard Marine Corporation

MAJOR GROUP 38
**3800 MEASURING, ANALYZING, AND
CONTROLLING INSTRUMENTS;
PHOTOGRAPHIC, MEDICAL AND
OPTICAL GOODS; WATCHES AND
CLOCKS**

3812 Search, detection, navigation, guidance,
aeronautical, and nautical systems
and instruments
AAR CORP.
Andrew Corporation
Sundstrand Corporation

3821 Laboratory apparatus and furniture
Baxter International Inc.
Varlen Corporation

3825 Instruments for measuring and testing of
electricity and electrical signals
Cobra Electronics Corporation
M~Wave, Inc.
Nalco Chemical Company
SigmaTron International, Inc.

3826 Laboratory analytical instruments
Landauer, Inc.

3841 Surgical and medical instruments and
apparatus
Abbott Laboratories
Baxter International Inc.

3842 Orthopedic, prosthetic, and surgical
appliances and supplies
Baxter International Inc.
UNIMED Pharmaceuticals, Inc.

3844 X-ray apparatus and tubes and related
irradiation apparatus
FluoroScan Imaging Systems, Inc.

3845 Electromedical and electrotherapeutic
apparatus
Baxter International Inc.
Bio-logic Systems Corp.

3861 Photographic equipment & supplies
AM International, Inc.
FluoroScan Imaging Systems, Inc.

3873 Watches, clocks, clockwork operated
devices, and parts
Cobra Electronics Corporation

MAJOR GROUP 39
**3900 MISCELLANEOUS MANUFACTURING
INDUSTRIES**

3914 Silverware, plated ware, and stainless
steel ware

Dyna Group International, Inc.

3944 Games, toys and children's vehicles
except dolls and bicycles
WMS Industries Inc.

3949 Sporting and athletic goods, not
elsewhere classified
Brunswick Corporation
ERO, Inc.

3955 Carbon paper and inked ribbons
Zebra Technologies Corporation

3961 Costume jewelry and novelties, not
precious metal
ARTRA GROUP Incorporated
Dyna Group International, Inc.
The Lori Corporation

3993 Signs and advertising specialties
Federal Signal Corporation

3999 Manufacturing industries, not elsewhere
classified
First Alert, Inc.
WMS Industries Inc.

MAJOR GROUP 40
4000 RAILROAD TRANSPORTATION

4011 Railroads, line-haul operating
Illinois Central Corporation
Itel Corporation
Pioneer Railcorp
Santa Fe Pacific Corporation
Wisconsin Central Transportation
Corporation

4013 Railroad switching and terminal
establishments
Illinois Central Corporation

MAJOR GROUP 42
**4200 MOTOR FREIGHT TRANSPORTATION
AND WAREHOUSING**

4212 Local trucking, without storage
TNT Freightways Corporation

4213 Trucking, except local
Aasche Transportation Services, Inc.
AMCOL International Corporation
Ampace Corporation
TNT Freightways Corporation

4225 General warehousing and storage
GATX Corporation

4226 Special warehousing and storage, not
elsewhere classified
GATX Corporation

MAJOR GROUP 44
4400 WATER TRANSPORTATION

4424 Deep sea domestic transportation of
freight
NICOR Inc.

4432 Great Lakes-St. Lawrence Seaway
transportation
GATX Corporation

4489 Water transportation of passengers, not
elsewhere classified
American Classic Voyages Co.

4499 Water transportation services, not
elsewhere classified
American Classic Voyages Co.

MAJOR GROUP 45
  4500   TRANSPORTATION BY AIR
  4512   Air transportation, scheduled
         UAL Corporation
  4581   Airports, flying fields, & services
         AAR CORP.

MAJOR GROUP 46
  4600   PIPE LINES, EXCEPT NATURAL GAS
  4612   Crude petroluem pipelines
         Santa Fe Pacific Corporation
  4613   Refined petroleum pipe lines
         GATX Corporation
         Santa Fe Pacific Corporation

MAJOR GROUP 47
  4700   TRANSPORTATION SERVICES
  4731   Arrangement of transportation of freight
         and cargo
         Illinois Central Corporation
         TNT Freightways Corporation
  4741   Rental of railroad cars
         GATX Corporation
         Itel Corporation

MAJOR GROUP 48
  4800   COMMUNICATIONS
  4812   Radiotelephone communications
         Ameritech Corporation
         Telephone and Data Systems, Inc.
         United States Cellular Corporation
  4813   Telephone communications, except
         radiotelephone
         Ameritech Corporation
         Telephone and Data Systems, Inc.
  4832   Radio broadcasting stations
         Tribune Company
  4833   Television broadcasting stations
         Tribune Company
  4841   Cable and other pay television services
         Playboy Enterprises, Inc.

MAJOR GROUP 49
  **4900   ELECTRIC, GAS, AND SANITARY
         SERVICES**
  4911   Electrical services
         CILCORP Inc.
         CIPSCO Incorporated
         Illinova Corporation
         NIPSCO Industries, Inc.
         Unicom Corporation
  4923   Natural gas transmission and distribution
         Peoples Energy Corporation
  4924   Natural gas distribution
         CILCORP Inc.
         CIPSCO Incorporated
         Illinova Corporation
         NICOR Inc.
         NIPSCO Industries, Inc.
  4925   Mixed, manufactured or liquified
         petroleum gas production and/or
         distribution
         Peoples Energy Corporation
  4931   Electric and other services combined
         CILCORP Inc.
         CIPSCO Incorporated
         Illinova Corporation

  4939   Combination utilities, not elsewhere
         classified
         CIPSCO Incorporated
         NIPSCO Industries, Inc.
  4953   Refuse systems
         Safety-Kleen Corp.
         WMX Technologies, Inc.
  4961   Steam and air-conditioning supply
         Peoples Energy Corporation
         Unicom Corporation

MAJOR GROUP 50
  **5000   WHOLESALE TRADE—DURABLE
         GOODS**
  5013   Automotive parts and supplies
         Champion Parts, Inc.
         Lawson Products, Inc.
         Universal Automotive Industries, Inc.
  5021   Furniture
         Boise Cascade Office Products
         Corporation
         Shelby Williams Industries, Inc.
         United Stationers Inc.
  5033   Roofing, siding, and insulation materials
         USG Corporation
  5043   Photographic equipment and supplies
         AM International, Inc.
  5044   Office equipment
         Boise Cascade Office Products
         Corporation
         United Stationers Inc.
  5045   Computers and computer peripheral
         equipment and software
         Comdisco, Inc.
         ELEK-TEK, Inc.
         United Stationers Inc.
         Wallace Computer Services, Inc.
  5046   Commercial equipment, not elsewhere
         classified
         The Middleby Corporation
  5047   Medical, dental, and hospital equipment
         and supplies
         Baxter International Inc.
         Vitalink Pharmacy Services, Inc.
  5048   Ophthalmic goods
         RLI Corp.
  5051   Metal service centers and offices
         A.M. Castle & Co.
         Central Steel & Wire Company
         Inland Steel Industries, Inc.
  5052   Coal and other minerals and ores
         A.M. Castle & Co.
  5063   Electrical apparatus and equipment,
         wiring supplies and construction material
         Ameritech Corporation
         General Instrument Corporation
         W.W. Grainger, Inc.
         Itel Corporation
         Littelfuse, Inc.
         Molex Incorporated
         Richardson Electronics, Ltd.
  5064   Electrical appliances, television and radio
         sets
         Cobra Electronics Corporation
  5065   Electrical parts and equipment, not
         elsewhere classified

First Chicago Guide

The Cherry Corporation
Itel Corporation
Motorola, Inc.
Richardson Electronics, Ltd.

5072 Hardware
Central Steel & Wire Company
Chicago Rivet & Machine Co.
W.W. Grainger, Inc.
Lawson Products, Inc.

5074 Plumbing and heating equipment and
supplies (hydronics)
W.W. Grainger, Inc.

5075 Warm air heating and air-conditioning
equipment and supplies
W.W. Grainger, Inc.

5078 Refrigeration equipment and supplies
The Middleby Corporation
Scotsman Industries, Inc.

5083 Farm and garden machinery and
equipment
W.W. Grainger, Inc.
Minuteman International, Inc.

5084 Industrial machinery and equipment
W.W. Grainger, Inc.
Lawson Products, Inc.
Nalco Chemical Company
PORTEC, Inc.

5085 Industrial supplies
Lawson Products, Inc.

5087 Service establishment equipment and
supplies
Alberto-Culver Company
Helene Curtis Industries, Inc.
Safety-Kleen Corp.

5088 Transportation equipment and supplies,
except motor vehicles
AAR CORP.
ABC Rail Products Corporation
Johnstown America Industries, Inc.

5091 Sporting and recreational goods and
supplies
Brunswick Corporation
Dyna Group International, Inc.
ERO, Inc.

5092 Toys and hobby goods and supplies
Ben Franklin Retail Stores, Inc.

5093 Scrap and waste materials
CFI Industries, Inc.
Enviropur Waste Refining and
Technology, Inc.

5094 Jewelry, watches, precious stones, and
precious metals
ARTRA GROUP Incorporated
The Lori Corporation

5099 Durable goods, not elsewhere classified
First Alert, Inc.
Stimsonite Corporation

MAJOR GROUP 51
**5100 WHOLESALE TRADE—NONDURABLE
GOODS**

5111 Printing and writing paper
Boise Cascade Office Products
Corporation
United Stationers Inc.

5112 Stationery and office supplies
Boise Cascade Office Products
Corporation
United Stationers Inc.
Wallace Computer Services, Inc.

5122 Drugs, drug proprietaries and druggists'
sundries
Baxter International Inc.
Helene Curtis Industries, Inc.
UNIMED Pharmaceuticals, Inc.
Vitalink Pharmacy Services, Inc.

5136 Men's and boys' clothing and furnishings
Fruit of the Loom, Inc.
Hartmarx Corporation

5137 Women's, children's, and infants' clothing
and accessories
Evans, Inc.
Fruit of the Loom, Inc.
Hartmarx Corporation

5139 Footwear
The Florsheim Shoe Company

5142 Packaged frozen foods
Rymer Foods Inc.

5145 Confectionery
John B. Sanfilippo & Son, Inc.
Tootsie Roll Industries, Inc.
Wm. Wrigley Jr. Company

5146 Fish and seafoods
Rymer Foods Inc.

5147 Meats and meat products
Rymer Foods Inc.

5149 Groceries and related products, not
elsewhere classified
Alberto-Culver Company
The Quaker Oats Company
Sara Lee Corporation

5162 Plastics materials and basic forms and
shapes
CFI Industries, Inc.
Envirodyne Industries, Inc.
McWhorter Technologies, Inc.

5169 Chemicals and allied products, not
elsewhere classified
CBI Industries, Inc.
DeSoto, Inc.
Lawson Products, Inc.
McWhorter Technologies, Inc.
Stepan Company

5191 Farm supplies
The Vigoro Corporation

5199 Nondurable goods, not elsewhere
classified
Circle Fine Art Corporation
HA-LO Industries, Inc.

MAJOR GROUP 52
**5200 BUILDING MATERIALS, HARDWARE,
GARDEN SUPPLY, AND MOBILE
HOME DEALERS**

5211 Lumber and other building materials
dealers
Wickes Lumber Company

MAJOR GROUP 53
5300 GENERAL MERCHANDISE STORES
5311 Department stores

JG Industries, Inc.
Sears, Roebuck and Co.
5331   Variety stores
Ben Franklin Retail Stores, Inc.
5399   Miscellaneous general merchandise
stores
Ben Franklin Retail Stores, Inc.
Walgreen Co.

MAJOR GROUP 54
5400   FOOD STORES
5411   Grocery stores
Eagle Food Centers, Inc.

MAJOR GROUP 55
**5500   AUTOMOTIVE DEALERS AND
GASOLINE SERVICE STATIONS**
5541   Gasoline service stations
Amoco Corporation

MAJOR GROUP 56
5600   APPAREL AND ACCESSORY STORES
5611   Men's and boy's clothing and accessory
stores
Hartmarx Corporation
Spiegel, Inc.
5621   Women's clothing stores
Evans, Inc.
Spiegel, Inc.
5632   Women's accessory and specialty stores
Evans, Inc.
5661   Shoe stores
The Florsheim Shoe Company

MAJOR GROUP 57
**5700   HOME FURNITURE, FURNISHINGS,
AND EQUIPMENT STORES**
5712   Furniture stores
JG Industries, Inc.
Spiegel, Inc.
5734   Computer and software stores
CDW Computer Centers, Inc.
ELEK-TEK, Inc.
Sears, Roebuck and Co.

MAJOR GROUP 58
5800   EATING AND DRINKING PLACES
5812   Eating places
McDonald's Corporation

MAJOR GROUP 59
5900   MISCELLANEOUS RETAIL
5912   Drug and proprietary stores
Walgreen Co.
5921   Liquor stores
Walgreen Co.
5941   Sporting goods and bicycle shops
Sportmart, Inc.
5945   Hobby, toy, and game shops
Ben Franklin Retail Stores, Inc.
5946   Camera and photographic supply stores
Walgreen Co.
5947   Gift, novelty, and souvenir shops
Classics International Entertainment, Inc.
5961   Catalog and mail order houses
CDW Computer Centers, Inc.
CELEX Group, Inc.

ELEK-TEK, Inc.
Playboy Enterprises, Inc.
Spiegel, Inc.
5999   Miscellaneous retail stores, not elsewhere
classified
Advance Ross Corporation
CELEX Group, Inc.
Circle Fine Art Corporation

MAJOR GROUP 60
6000   DEPOSITORY INSTITUTIONS
6021   National commercial banks
AMCORE Financial, Inc.
American National Bank & Trust Company
of Chicago
Bank One, Chicago, NA
Columbia National Bank of Chicago
First Bank National Association
First Bankers Trustshares, Inc.
First Chicago Corporation
First Evergreen Corporation
First Midwest Bancorp, Inc.
First Midwest Bank, N.A.
First National Bancorp, Inc.
The First National Bank of Chicago
First National Bank of Evergreen Park
First of America Bank—Illinois, N.A.
Firstbank of Illinois Co.
LaSalle National Bank
LaSalle Northwest National Bank
Magna Group, Inc.
Marquette National Bank
Merchants Bancorp, Inc.
The Mid-City National Bank of Chicago
NBD Skokie Bank, N.A.
Northern Trust Bank/Lake Forest N.A.
Northern Trust Bank/O'Hare N.A.
Northern Trust Corporation
Premier Financial Services, Inc.
Princeton National Bancorp, Inc.
River Forest Bancorp, Inc.
TODAY'S BANCORP, INC.
6022   State commercial banks
AMCORE Financial, Inc.
Bank of America Illinois
Cole Taylor Bank
Cole Taylor Financial Group, Inc.
Comerica Bank—Illinois
First Busey Corporation
First National Bancorp, Inc.
First Oak Brook Bancshares, Inc.
Firstbank of Illinois Co.
Harris Trust and Savings Bank
Heritage Bank
Heritage Financial Services, Inc.
LaSalle Bank Lake View
Magna Group, Inc.
NBD Bank
Northern States Financial Corporation
The Northern Trust Company
Northern Trust Corporation
Oak Brook Bank
Old Kent Bank
Pinnacle Banc Group, Inc.
Premier Financial Services, Inc.
River Forest Bancorp, Inc.

First Chicago Guide

SPS Transaction Services, Inc.
TODAY'S BANCORP, INC.
6035 Savings institutions, federally chartered
Avondale Financial Corp.
Bell Bancorp, Inc.
Bell Federal Savings and Loan
Association
Calumet Bancorp, Inc.
Citibank, Federal Savings Bank
Deerbank Corporation
Fidelity Bancorp, Inc.
Financial Security Corp.
First Financial Bancorp, Inc.
Hinsdale Financial Corporation
HomeCorp, Inc.
Household International, Inc.
LaSalle Cragin Bank FSB
LaSalle Talman Bank, FSB
Liberty Bancorp, Inc.
MAF Bancorp, Inc.
Mid America Federal Savings Bank
The Mid-City National Bank of Chicago
North Bancshares, Inc.
Northern States Financial Corporation
Pinnacle Banc Group, Inc.
St. Paul Bancorp, Inc.
St. Paul Federal Bank For Savings
Southwest Bancshares, Inc.
Standard Federal Bank for savings
Standard Financial, Inc.
SuburbFed Financial Corp.
Westco Bancorp, Inc.
6036 Savings institutions, not federally
chartered
N.S. Bancorp, Inc.
Northwestern Savings Bank
6099 Functions related to depository banking,
not elsewhere classified
Advance Ross Corporation
AutoFinance Group, Inc.

MAJOR GROUP 61
6100 **NONDEPOSITORY CREDIT
INSTITUTIONS**
6141 Personal credit institutions
AutoFinance Group, Inc.
Eagle Finance Corp.
First Merchants Acceptance Corporation
Household International, Inc.
Mercury Finance Company
Unitrin, Inc.
6159 Miscellaneous business credit institutions
Caterpillar Inc.
Deere & Company
GATX Corporation
Navistar International Corporation
Prime Capital Corporation
Trans Leasing International, Inc.
6162 Mortgage bankers and loan
correspondents
Household International, Inc.

MAJOR GROUP 62
6200 **SECURITY AND COMMODITY
BROKERS, DEALERS, EXCHANGES
AND SERVICES**

6211 Security brokers, dealers and flotation
companies
Duff & Phelps Corporation
Kemper Corporation
The John Nuveen Company
Prime Capital Corporation
Rodman & Renshaw Capital Group, Inc.
6221 Commodity contracts brokers and dealers
Rodman & Renshaw Capital Group, Inc.
6282 Investment advice
CILCORP Inc.
CIPSCO Incorporated
Duff & Phelps Corporation
Kemper Corporation
The John Nuveen Company
Rodman & Renshaw Capital Group, Inc.
6289 Services allied with the exchange of
securities or commodities, not elsewhere
classified
PC Quote, Inc.

MAJOR GROUP 63
6300 **INSURANCE CARRIERS**
6311 Life insurance
The Allstate Corporation
Aon Corporation
Bankers Life Holding Corporation
CNA Financial Corporation
Household International, Inc.
Kemper Corporation
Horace Mann Educators Corporation
Old Republic International Corporation
Pioneer Financial Services, Inc.
Unitrin, Inc.
Washington National Corporation
6321 Accident and health insurance
Aon Corporation
Bankers Life Holding Corporation
CNA Financial Corporation
Horace Mann Educators Corporation
MMI Companies, Inc.
Old Republic International Corporation
Pioneer Financial Services, Inc.
Unitrin, Inc.
Washington National Corporation
6324 Hospital and medical service plans
CNA Financial Corporation
Unitrin, Inc.
6331 Fire, marine, and casualty insurance
The Allstate Corporation
Aon Corporation
Capsure Holdings Corp.
CNA Financial Corporation
Deere & Company
Intercargo Corporation
Horace Mann Educators Corporation
Navistar International Corporation
Old Republic International Corporation
RLI Corp.
Trans Leasing International, Inc.
Unitrin, Inc.
6351 Surety companies
The Allstate Corporation
Capsure Holdings Corp.
CNA Financial Corporation
Eagle Finance Corp.

First Chicago Guide

First Merchants Acceptance Corporation
Intercargo Corporation
Mercury Finance Company
MMI Companies, Inc.
Old Republic International Corporation
RLI Corp.
Washington National Corporation

6361 Title insurance
Old Republic International Corporation

6399 Insurance carriers, not elsewhere classified
Aon Corporation
Intercargo Corporation

MAJOR GROUP 64

6400 INSURANCE AGENTS, BROKERS, AND SERVICE

6411 Insurance agents, brokers, and service
Aon Corporation
Eagle Finance Corp.
Arthur J. Gallagher & Co.
HealthCare COMPARE Corp.
Kemper Corporation
MMI Companies, Inc.
RLI Corp.
Rodman & Renshaw Capital Group, Inc.
Unitrin, Inc.

MAJOR GROUP 65

6500 REAL ESTATE

6517 Lessors of railroad property
Heartland Partners, L.P.

6519 Lessors of real property, not elsewhere classified
Heartland Partners, L.P.

6531 Real estate agents and managers
Amerihost Properties, Inc.
Heartland Partners, L.P.

6552 Land subdividers and developers, except cemeteries
Heartland Partners, L.P.
NIPSCO Industries, Inc.
Pittway Corporation

MAJOR GROUP 67

6700 HOLDING AND OTHER INVESTMENT COMPANIES

6712 Offices of bank holding companies
AMCORE Financial, Inc.
Avondale Financial Corp.
Bell Bancorp, Inc.
Calumet Bancorp, Inc.
Cole Taylor Financial Group, Inc.
Deerbank Corporation
Fidelity Bancorp, Inc.
Financial Security Corp.
First Bankers Trustshares, Inc.
First Busey Corporation
First Chicago Corporation
First Evergreen Corporation
First Financial Bancorp, Inc.
First Midwest Bancorp, Inc.
First National Bancorp, Inc.
First Oak Brook Bancshares, Inc.
Firstbank of Illinois Co.
Heritage Financial Services, Inc.
Hinsdale Financial Corporation

HomeCorp, Inc.
Liberty Bancorp, Inc.
MAF Bancorp, Inc.
Magna Group, Inc.
Merchants Bancorp, Inc.
N.S. Bancorp, Inc.
North Bancshares, Inc.
Northern States Financial Corporation
Northern Trust Corporation
Pinnacle Banc Group, Inc.
Premier Financial Services, Inc.
Princeton National Bancorp, Inc.
River Forest Bancorp, Inc.
St. Paul Bancorp, Inc.
Southwest Bancshares, Inc.
Standard Financial, Inc.
SuburbFed Financial Corp.
TODAY'S BANCORP, INC.
Westco Bancorp, Inc.

6719 Offices of holding companies, not elsewhere classified
Aasche Transportation Services, Inc.
Acme Metals Incorporated
Advance Ross Corporation
The Allstate Corporation
American Classic Voyages Co.
Ameritech Corporation
Ampace Corporation
Aon Corporation
Archer-Daniels-Midland Company
Argosy Gaming Company
Bally Entertainment Corporation
Bankers Life Holding Corporation
Bell & Howell Holdings Company
Bliss & Laughlin Industries Inc.
Borg-Warner Security Corporation
Capsure Holdings Corp.
CBI Industries, Inc.
CELEX Group, Inc.
CILCORP Inc.
CIPSCO Incorporated
CNA Financial Corporation
Continental Materials Corporation
Duff & Phelps Corporation
First Alert, Inc.
General Instrument Corporation
Great American Management and Investment, Inc.
Hartmarx Corporation
Helene Curtis Industries, Inc.
Household International, Inc.
Illinois Central Corporation
Illinova Corporation
Inland Steel Industries, Inc.
Intercargo Corporation
Johnstown America Industries, Inc.
Kemper Corporation
Horace Mann Educators Corporation
Material Sciences Corporation
MFRI, Inc.
The Middleby Corporation
MMI Companies, Inc.
The L.E. Myers Co. Group
Navistar International Corporation
NICOR Inc.
NIPSCO Industries, Inc.

The John Nuveen Company
Old Republic International Corporation
OPTION CARE, Inc.
Peoples Energy Corporation
Pioneer Financial Services, Inc.
Pioneer Railcorp
RLI Corp.
Rodman & Renshaw Capital Group, Inc.
Santa Fe Pacific Corporation
Scotsman Industries, Inc.
Sears, Roebuck and Co.
Tellabs, Inc.
TNT Freightways Corporation
Tootsie Roll Industries, Inc.
TRO Learning, Inc.
U.S. Can Corporation
UAL Corporation
Unicom Corporation
USG Corporation
Walgreen Co.
Washington National Corporation
Wisconsin Central Transportation
Corporation
WMS Industries Inc.
WMX Technologies, Inc.
Zeigler Coal Holding Company

6726   Unit investment trusts, face-amount
certificate offices, and closed-end
management investment office
Baker, Fentress & Company
Duff & Phelps Corporation
Fort Dearborn Income Securities, Inc.
The John Nuveen Company

6794   Patent owners and lessors
Discovery Zone, Inc.
Ben Franklin Retail Stores, Inc.
McDonald's Corporation
OPTION CARE, Inc.
ServiceMaster Limited Partnership

MAJOR GROUP 70
   7000   **HOTELS, ROOMING HOUSES, CAMPS
         AND OTHER LODGING PLACES**
   7011   Hotels and motels
         American Classic Voyages Co.
         Amerihost Properties, Inc.
         Bally Entertainment Corporation
         WMS Industries Inc.

MAJOR GROUP 72
   7200   **PERSONAL SERVICES**
   7217   Carpet and upholstery cleaning
         ServiceMaster Limited Partnership
   7218   Industrial launderers
         ServiceMaster Limited Partnership

MAJOR GROUP 73
   7300   **BUSINESS SERVICES**
   7311   Advertising agencies
         True North Communications Inc.
   7319   Advertising, not elsewhere classified
         Alberto-Culver Company
         HA-LO Industries, Inc.
   7323   Credit reporting services
         Duff & Phelps Credit Rating Co.
   7331   Direct mail advertising services

Duplex Products Inc.
Pittway Corporation
Wallace Computer Services, Inc.
7342   Disinfecting and pest control services
       ServiceMaster Limited Partnership
7352   Medical equipment rental and leasing
       Trans Leasing International, Inc.
7359   Equipment rental and leasing, not
       elsewhere classified
       Trans Leasing International, Inc.
7361   Employment agencies
       Alternative Resources Corporation
       General Employment Enterprises, Inc.
7363   Help supply services
       Alternative Resources Corporation
       Amerihost Properties, Inc.
       General Employment Enterprises, Inc.
7371   Computer programming services
       Bell & Howell Holdings Company
       Bio-logic Systems Corp.
       Delphi Information Systems, Inc.
       Information Resources, Inc.
       Medicus Systems Corporation
       PC Quote, Inc.
       PLATINUM technology, inc.
       RLI Corp.
       SPS Transaction Services, Inc.
       System Software Associates, Inc.
7372   Prepackaged software
       Delphi Information Systems, Inc.
       The Goodheart-Willcox Company, Inc.
       Information Resources, Inc.
       Medicus Systems Corporation
       PLATINUM technology, inc.
       SPSS Inc.
       System Software Associates, Inc.
       Technology Solutions Company
       TRO Learning, Inc.
       U.S. Robotics Corporation
7373   Computer integrated systems design
       Alternative Resources Corporation
       Bio-logic Systems Corp.
       Delphi Information Systems, Inc.
       Itel Corporation
       Medicus Systems Corporation
       PLATINUM technology, inc.
       SigmaTron International, Inc.
       System Software Associates, Inc.
       U.S. Robotics Corporation
7374   Computer processing and data
       preparation and processing services
       CCH Incorporated
       Market Facts, Inc.
       SPS Transaction Services, Inc.
       Telephone and Data Systems, Inc.
7375   Information retrieval services
       Information Resources, Inc.
       PC Quote, Inc.
7376   Computer facilities management services
       Alternative Resources Corporation
7377   Computer rental and leasing
       Comdisco, Inc.
7379   Computer related services, not elsewhere
       classified
       Alternative Resources Corporation

Comdisco, Inc.
R.R. Donnelley & Sons Company
System Software Associates, Inc.
Technology Solutions Company
7381 Detective & armored car services
Borg-Warner Security Corporation
7382 Security systems services
Borg-Warner Security Corporation
Pittway Corporation
7383 News syndicates
Tribune Company
7384 Photofinishing laboratories
Walgreen Co.
7389 Business services, not elsewhere
classified
Bell & Howell Holdings Company
CCH Incorporated
Information Resources, Inc.
Pittway Corporation
Safety-Kleen Corp.
Sears, Roebuck and Co.
SPS Transaction Services, Inc.
Telephone and Data Systems, Inc.
True North Communications Inc.

MAJOR GROUP 75
7500 AUTOMOTIVE REPAIR, SERVICES AND PARKING
7533 Automotive exhaust system repair shops
Whitman Corporation
7539 Automotive repair shops, not elsewhere classified
Whitman Corporation

MAJOR GROUP 76
7600 MISCELLANEOUS REPAIR SERVICES
7699 Repair shops and related services, not elsewhere classified
NICOR Inc.

MAJOR GROUP 78
7800 MOTION PICTURES
7812 Motion picture and video tape production
Playboy Enterprises, Inc.
7822 Motion picture and video tape distribution
Playboy Enterprises, Inc.
7841 Video tape rental
Eagle Food Centers, Inc.

MAJOR GROUP 79
7900 AMUSEMENT AND RECREATION SERVICES, EXCEPT MOTION PICTURES
7933 Bowling centers
Brunswick Corporation
7941 Professional sports clubs and promoters
Tribune Company
7993 Coin-operated amusement devices
Argosy Gaming Company
Bally Entertainment Corporation
WMS Industries Inc.
7999 Amusement and recreation services, not elsewhere classified
Argosy Gaming Company
Bally Entertainment Corporation
Discovery Zone, Inc.
Outboard Marine Corporation

MAJOR GROUP 80
8000 HEALTH SERVICES
8049 Offices and clinics of health practitioners, not elsewhere classified
Caremark International Inc.
OPTION CARE, Inc.
8082 Home health care services
Caremark International Inc.
OPTION CARE, Inc.
8093 Specialty outpatient clinics, not elsewhere classified
Caremark International Inc.
OPTION CARE, Inc.
8099 Health and allied services, not elsewhere classified
Vitalink Pharmacy Services, Inc.

MAJOR GROUP 82
8200 EDUCATIONAL SERVICES
8221 Colleges, universities, and professional schools
DeVRY INC.
8222 Junior colleges and technical institutes
DeVRY INC.
8243 Data processing schools
DeVRY INC.
TRO Learning, Inc.
8244 Business and secretarial schools
DeVRY INC.
8299 Schools and educational services, not elsewhere classified
TRO Learning, Inc.

MAJOR GROUP 87
8700 ENGINEERING, ACCOUNTING, RESEARCH, MANAGEMENT, AND RELATED SERVICES
8711 Engineering services
CBI Industries, Inc.
CILCORP Inc.
Telephone and Data Systems, Inc.
8731 Commercial physical and biological research
DEKALB Genetics Corporation
Growth Environmental, Inc.
8732 Commercial economic, sociological, and educational research
HealthCare COMPARE Corp.
Market Facts, Inc.
8734 Testing laboratories
Growth Environmental, Inc.
Landauer, Inc.
Lindberg Corporation
8741 Management services
Amerihost Properties, Inc.
HealthCare COMPARE Corp.
The L.E. Myers Co. Group
ServiceMaster Limited Partnership
8742 Management consulting services
Amerihost Properties, Inc.
Caremark International Inc.
Delphi Information Systems, Inc.
HealthCare COMPARE Corp.
Market Facts, Inc.
Medicus Systems Corporation
MMI Companies, Inc.

First Chicago Guide

Pioneer Financial Services, Inc.
True North Communications Inc.
8743 Management and public relations services
True North Communications Inc.
8744 Facilities support management services
ServiceMaster Limited Partnership
8748 Business consulting services, not
elsewhere classified
Growth Environmental, Inc.
Information Resources, Inc.

Industrial, Retail, Transportation, Utility, Insurance and Diversified Financial Companies

Company	Rank by Sales or Revenues '94	'93	Sales or Revenues (000 Omitted)	Rank by Assets '94	'93	Assets (000 Omitted)	Year End Figures Used
Sears, Roebuck and Co.	1	1	$54,559,000	1	1	$91,896,000	12/94
Amoco Corporation	2	2	30,362,000	5	5	29,316,000	12/94
Motorola, Inc.	3	4	22,245,000	10	12	17,536,000	12/94
The Allstate Corporation	4	3	21,464,300	2	2	61,369,400	12/94
Sara Lee Corporation	5	5	15,536,000	16	16	11,665,000	6/94
UAL Corporation	6	6	13,950,000	15	13	11,764,000	12/94
Caterpillar Inc.	7	8	13,863,000	11	10	16,250,000	12/94
Ameritech Corporation	8	7	12,569,500	7	7	19,946,800	12/94
Archer-Daniels-Midland Company	9	10	11,374,372	18	18	8,746,853	6/94
CNA Financial Corporation	10	9	10,999,545	3	3	44,320,433	12/94
WMX Technologies, Inc.	11	11	10,097,318	9	9	17,538,914	12/94
Baxter International Inc.	12	12	9,324,000	17	17	10,002,000	12/94
Walgreen Co.	13	14	9,234,978	36	40	2,908,749	8/94
Abbott Laboratories	14	13	9,156,009	19	19	8,523,724	12/94
McDonald's Corporation	15	15	8,321,800	12	14	13,591,900	12/94
Deere & Company	16	16	7,663,143	14	15	12,781,215	10/94 a
Unicom Corporation	17	18	6,277,521	6	6	23,121,488	12/94 b
The Quaker Oats Company	18	17	5,955,000	35	35	3,043,300	6/94
Stone Container Corporation	19	19	5,748,700	20	20	7,004,900	12/94
Navistar International Corporation	20	20	5,337,000	24	24	5,056,000	10/94
R.R. Donnelley & Sons Company	21	21	4,888,786	27	29	4,452,143	12/94
Inland Steel Industries, Inc.	22	22	4,497,000	31	30	3,353,400	12/94
Aon Corporation	23	23	4,157,000	8	8	17,921,900	12/94
FMC Corporation	24	24	4,051,300	32	36	3,351,500	12/94
Illinois Tool Works Inc.	25	26	3,461,315	41	42	2,580,498	12/94
Premark International, Inc.	26	27	3,394,559	45	49	2,357,900	12/94
Household International, Inc.	27	25	3,360,600	4	4	34,338,400	12/94
W.W. Grainger, Inc.	28	30	3,023,076	57	59	1,534,751	12/94
Spiegel, Inc.	29	31	3,015,985	42	46	2,560,287	12/94
ServiceMaster Limited Partnership	30	28	2,985,207	63	66	1,230,839	12/94
Morton International, Inc.	31	33	2,849,600	44	44	2,462,600	6/94
Brunswick Corporation	32	35	2,700,100	49	52	2,122,300	12/94
Santa Fe Pacific Corporation	33	29	2,680,900	23	22	5,572,900	12/94
Whitman Corporation	34	32	2,658,800	47	50	2,135,400	12/94
Dean Foods Company	35	34	2,431,203	67	70	1,109,154	5/94
Caremark International Inc.	36	41	2,426,000	60	71	1,275,200	12/94
Fruit of the Loom, Inc.	37	40	2,297,800	34	37	3,163,500	12/94
USG Corporation	38	57	2,290,000	48	47	2,124,000	12/94
Tribune Company	39	38	2,154,917	39	39	2,785,825	12/94
Comdisco, Inc.	40	36	2,098,000	25	25	4,807,000	9/94
Newell Co.	41	47	2,074,934	43	53	2,488,276	12/94
General Instrument Corporation	42	53	2,036,323	50	55	2,108,951	12/94
CBI Industries, Inc.	43	46	1,890,907	51	54	2,008,712	12/94
Borg-Warner Security Corporation	44	42	1,792,900	76	77	830,300	12/94
Itel Corporation	45	39	1,732,600	66	41	1,110,900	12/94
Old Republic International Corp.	46	43	1,679,000	21	21	6,262,900	12/94
NIPSCO Industries, Inc.	47	44	1,676,401	28	28	3,944,543	12/94
NICOR Inc.	48	45	1,609,400	46	45	2,209,900	12/94
Kemper Corporation	49	49	1,601,821	13	11	13,153,967	12/94

First Chicago Guide 335

Company	Rank by Sales or Revenues '94	'93	Sales or Revenues (000 Omitted)	Rank by Assets '94	'93	Assets (000 Omitted)	Year End Figures Used
Wm. Wrigley Jr. Company	50	52	$1,596,551	72	75	$ 978,834	12/94
Illinova Corporation	51	48	1,589,500	22	23	5,576,700	12/94
United Stationers Inc.	52	50	1,473,024	73	82	975,949	8/94
Zenith Electronics Corporation	53	60	1,469,000	83	85	653,600	12/94
IMC Global Inc.	54	70	1,441,500	40	51	2,778,300	6/94
Bankers Life Holding Corporation	55	51	1,437,900	29	27	3,928,800	12/94
Sundstrand Corporation	56	55	1,372,700	55	58	1,586,900	12/94
Unitrin, Inc.	57	56	1,365,500	26	26	4,569,800	12/94
Nalco Chemical Company	58	54	1,345,600	59	63	1,282,200	12/94
Peoples Energy Corporation	59	59	1,279,488	53	56	1,809,286	9/94
Helene Curtis Industries, Inc.	60	61	1,265,600	84	81	646,832	2/95
Borg-Warner Automotive, Inc.	61	68	1,223,400	61	65	1,240,300	12/94
Alberto-Culver Company	62	63	1,216,119	86	84	610,208	9/94
GATX Corporation	63	64	1,155,000	30	31	3,650,700	12/94
Outboard Marine Corporation	64	67	1,078,400	77	76	817,100	9/94
TNT Freightways Corporation	65	69	1,016,464	94	92	501,002	12/94
Eagle Food Centers, Inc.	66	65	1,015,063	121	103	311,484	2/95
Great American Mgt. & Invest.	67	62	1,010,300	70	60	1,035,000	12/94
Wickes Lumber Company	68	72	986,872	119	124	319,573	12/94
Molex Incorporated	69	71	964,108	65	69	1,138,517	6/94
Boise Cascade Office Products	70	*	962,045	112	*	352,741	12/94 cd
Bally Entertainment Corporation	71	58	942,255	52	38	1,936,161	12/94
Zeigler Coal Holding Company	72	*	870,890	64	*	1,161,067	12/94
CIPSCO Incorporated	73	73	844,615	54	57	1,777,357	12/94
The Vigoro Corporation	74	85	804,091	88	93	602,836	12/94 ef
Safety-Kleen Corp.	75	74	791,267	71	68	1,015,986	12/94
Gaylord Container Corporation	76	75	784,400	75	73	843,100	9/94
Pittway Corporation	77	80	778,026	90	88	563,287	12/94
Pioneer Financial Services, Inc.	78	78	774,155	68	67	1,075,700	12/94
The Interlake Corporation	79	79	752,592	100	90	444,953	12/94
Telephone and Data Systems, Inc.	80	82	730,810	38	43	2,790,127	12/94
Bell & Howell Holdings Company	81	*	720,340	87	*	603,745	12/94 c
Hartmarx Corporation	82	76	717,706	108	98	392,200	11/94
Horace Mann Educators Corp.	83	77	711,916	33	32	3,285,533	12/94
Federal Signal Corporation	84	87	677,228	93	97	521,600	12/94
Washington National Corporation	85	81	656,929	37	34	2,810,568	12/94
CILCORP Inc.	86	84	605,139	62	64	1,238,384	12/94
Northwestern Steel &Wire Co.	87	90	603,609	107	100	394,176	7/94
Envirodyne Industries, Inc.	88	83	599,029	74	72	896,636	12/94
Central Steel & Wire Company	89	92	595,000	129	129	248,200	12/94
Illinois Central Corporation	90	88	593,900	58	61	1,308,700	12/94
Wallace Computer Services, Inc.	91	89	588,173	92	89	538,592	7/94
CCH Incorporated	92	86	578,776	89	83	581,156	12/94
U.S. Can Corporation	93	95	563,153	105	114	400,724	12/94
Andrew Corporation	94	97	558,457	103	102	415,163	9/94
ANTEC Corporation	95	98	553,510	101	125	438,017	12/94
A.M. Castle & Co.	96	93	536,568	139	128	213,127	12/94
Acme Metals Incorporated	97	94	522,880	81	104	682,330	12/94
U.S. Robotics Corporation	98	138	499,075	118	134	323,277	9/94 gh
Tellabs, Inc.	99	111	494,153	109	107	390,067	12/94
AptarGroup, Inc.	100	99	474,266	96	95	465,395	12/94
Johnstown America Industries, Inc.	101	110	468,525	159	160	143,354	12/94
Stepan Company	102	96	443,948	116	116	324,948	12/94
Falcon Building Products, Inc.	103	*	440,657	147	*	187,461	12/94 h
Sportmart, Inc.	104	105	424,189	134	142	226,812	1/95

336

First Chicago Guide

Company	Rank by Sales or Revenues '94	Rank by Sales or Revenues '93	Sales or Revenues (000 Omitted)	Rank by Assets '94	Rank by Assets '93	Assets (000 Omitted)	Year End Figures Used
American Publishing Company	105	140	$ 422,594	85	101	$ 636,120	12/94
AM International, Inc.	106	91	421,625	124	118	295,338	7/94 fi
General Binding Corporation	107	102	420,449	125	122	284,278	12/94
CDW Computer Centers, Inc.	108	117	413,270	177	204	78,029	12/94
AAR CORP.	109	101	407,754	104	96	413,529	5/94 f
Titan Wheel International, Inc.	110	157	407,000	106	120	400,460	12/94
True North Communications Inc.	111	103	403,690	82	80	673,744	12/94
IDEX Corporation	112	113	399,502	110	121	371,096	12/94
Information Resources, Inc.	113	107	376,570	111	108	354,554	12/94
UNR Industries, Inc.	114	104	372,385	123	119	299,447	12/94
WMS Industries Inc.	115	109	358,213	114	113	343,141	6/94
Arthur J. Gallagher & Co.	116	112	356,377	99	91	451,110	12/94
Ben Franklin Retail Stores, Inc.	117	106	354,788	136	143	219,473	3/95
Varlen Corporation	118	114	341,521	135	136	220,186	1/95
The Cherry Corporation	119	116	339,237	127	130	261,193	2/95
System Software Associates, Inc.	120	119	334,400	115	117	333,200	10/94
Woodward Governor Company	121	108	333,207	117	105	323,318	9/94
United States Cellular Corporation	122	122	332,404	56	62	1,534,787	12/94
DEKALB Genetics Corporation	123	115	320,000	120	109	319,000	8/94
Truck Components Inc.	124	*	312,800	126	*	267,307	12/94 c
ELEK-TEK, Inc.	125	125	305,602	174	183	93,044	12/94
The Florsheim Shoe Company	126	*	302,001	137	*	215,270	12/94 h
Tootsie Roll Industries, Inc.	127	120	296,932	122	115	310,083	12/94
McWhorter Technologies, Inc.	128	118	281,340	161	181	138,563	10/94 h
CLARCOR Inc.	129	124	270,123	146	141	188,448	11/94
Scotsman Industries, Inc.	130	147	266,632	130	161	244,791	12/94
Duplex Products Inc.	131	121	265,791	157	146	146,208	10/94
AMCOL International Corporation	132	127	265,443	128	137	261,047	12/94
International Jensen Incorporated	133	126	252,772	160	155	142,548	2/95
First Alert, Inc.	134	152	248,404	152	153	172,305	12/94
SPS Transaction Services, Inc.	135	133	245,802	78	112	768,493	12/94
Binks Manufacturing Company	136	132	243,599	144	138	193,364	11/94
Material Sciences Corporation	137	139	227,658	151	148	172,357	2/95
Elco Industries, Inc.	138	135	225,901	155	149	151,464	6/94
The John Nuveen Company	139	123	220,303	113	94	348,847	12/94
Playboy Enterprises, Inc.	140	131	218,987	163	156	131,921	6/94
Joslyn Corporation	141	129	216,177	149	144	177,504	12/94
Allied Products Corporation	142	128	215,529	156	133	150,555	12/94
Methode Electronics, Inc.	143	144	213,298	150	150	172,468	4/94 f
Lawson Products, Inc.	144	136	213,097	153	139	168,130	12/94
Mercury Finance Company	145	146	211,565	69	74	1,036,403	12/94
DeVRY INC.	146	137	211,437	169	164	106,798	6/94
Wisconsin Central Trans. Corp.	147	156	211,139	102	99	433,613	12/94
John B. Sanfilippo & Son, Inc.	148	134	208,970	140	145	199,714	12/94
Ozite Corporation	149	141	203,575	154	151	160,550	7/94
JG Industries, Inc.	150	142	196,195	179	178	76,007	1/95
American Classic Voyages Co.	151	163	195,197	133	132	227,798	12/94
Littelfuse, Inc.	152	148	194,454	141	131	199,328	12/94
Lawter International, Inc.	153	143	191,056	132	126	231,827	12/94
ABC Rail Products Corporation	154	158	187,176	171	166	95,774	7/94
HealthCare COMPARE Corp.	155	151	186,606	138	135	215,009	12/94
Schawk, Inc.	156	182	186,145	143	179	193,426	12/94 c
Discovery Zone, Inc.	157	192	180,573	95	123	477,386	12/94
MMI Companies, Inc.	158	154	177,205	80	79	693,804	12/94
Quixote Corporation	159	160	176,938	165	159	122,789	6/94

First Chicago Guide

Company	Rank by Sales or Revenues '94	'93	Sales or Revenues (000 Omitted)	Rank by Assets '94	'93	Assets (000 Omitted)	Year End Figures Used	
Richardson Electronics, Ltd.	160	150	$ 172,094	148	127	$ 179,467	5/94	
RLI Corp.	161	153	171,902	79	78	752,301	12/94	
Rymer Foods Inc.	162	159	162,256	189	180	58,492	10/94	
Shelby Williams Industries, Inc.	163	155	159,072	175	169	88,520	12/94	
Argosy Gaming Company	164	185	153,045	131	165	232,831	12/94	
Bliss & Laughlin Industries Inc.	165	161	152,435	185	182	67,739	9/94	
ARTRA GROUP Incorporated	166	149	152,115	173	167	93,429	12/94	
Oil•Dri Corporation of America	167	162	139,809	167	162	112,267	7/94	
The Middleby Corporation	168	164	129,967	178	177	76,622	12/94	
Juno Lighting, Inc.	169	165	126,777	158	157	145,756	11/94	
ERO, Inc.	170	174	126,734	192	193	56,792	12/94	
Sundance Homes, Inc.	171	180	118,659	170	172	98,907	12/94	
Capsure Holdings Corp.	172	167	112,662	91	87	553,370	12/94	
Zebra Technologies Corporation	173	177	107,103	172	174	95,043	12/94	
Woodhead Industries, Inc.	174	175	105,689	187	187	62,263	9/94	
Lindberg Corporation	175	183	99,858	182	195	70,522	12/94	
Vitalink Pharmacy Services, Inc.	176	187	98,569	183	186	69,587	5/94	
PORTEC, Inc.	177	181	96,474	191	197	57,522	12/94	
PLATINUM technology, inc.	178	191	95,749	145	163	190,325	12/94	
Champion Parts, Inc.	179	170	95,337	194	188	53,312	12/94	
Alternative Resources Corporation	180	193	94,478	219	231	26,581	12/94	
Fansteel Inc.	181	176	89,287	180	176	72,881	12/94	
DeSoto, Inc.	182	168	87,182	176	168	83,112	12/94	
The L.E. Myers Co. Group	183	166	86,842	201	199	39,644	12/94	j
Evans, Inc.	184	172	86,817	196	189	48,816	2/95	
Cobra Electronics Corporation	185	171	82,131	200	191	40,342	12/94	
Intercargo Corporation	186	195	80,885	164	158	128,423	12/94	
Rodman & Renshaw Cap. Group	187	178	77,317	98	111	454,331	6/94	
MFRI, Inc.	188	190	75,495	198	201	47,917	1/95	
Continental Materials Corporation	189	188	75,294	197	196	48,162	12/94	
HA-LO Industries, Inc.	190	207	68,603	203	212	36,129	12/94	
Advance Ross Corporation	191	197	66,503	186	190	64,120	12/94	
Duff & Phelps Corporation	192	169	65,893	166	147	121,100	12/94	
Circuit Systems, Inc.	193	194	60,411	208	208	33,101	4/94	
OPTION CARE, Inc.	194	198	59,395	190	185	58,443	12/94	
Stimsonite Corporation	195	201	55,941	195	194	50,936	12/94	
Market Facts, Inc.	196	202	55,483	209	207	31,682	12/94	
Technology Solutions Company	197	189	53,157	184	175	69,340	5/94	
Delphi Information Systems, Inc.	198	*	53,040	214	*	27,546	3/95	
SPSS Inc.	199	203	51,757	210	214	31,430	12/94	
Teltrend Inc.	200	*	49,454	226	*	19,388	7/94	cd
Salton/Maxim Housewares, Inc.	201	196	48,807	202	202	38,635	6/94	
Amerihost Properties, Inc.	202	208	43,347	207	211	34,403	12/94	
Universal Automotive Industries	203	*	41,824	221	*	23,464	12/94	h
Minuteman International, Inc.	204	205	41,518	213	210	28,067	12/94	
Selfix, Inc.	205	204	40,985	211	203	30,761	12/94	
Duff & Phelps Credit Rating Co.	206	*	40,409	199	*	40,974	12/94	
SigmaTron International, Inc.	207	210	36,690	229	225	17,837	4/94	
Medicus Systems Corporation	208	214	34,485	206	217	35,107	5/94	
The Lori Corporation	209	200	34,431	228	198	18,704	12/94	
Wells-Gardner Electronics Corp.	210	206	33,435	230	221	15,619	12/94	
Landauer, Inc.	211	211	31,653	204	206	35,640	9/94	
CELEX Group, Inc.	212	221	29,785	224	215	21,790	4/94	
AutoFinance Group, Inc.	213	220	29,031	168	170	108,496	6/94	
CFI Industries, Inc.	214	209	28,730	227	216	19,214	6/94	

Company	Rank by Sales or Revenues '94	'93	Sales or Revenues (000 Omitted)	Rank by Assets '94	'93	Assets (000 Omitted)	Year End Figures Used	
TRO Learning, Inc.	215	212	$ 28,365	217	213	$ 26,931	10/94	
M~Wave, Inc.	216	219	28,009	222	223	23,258	12/94	
Trans Leasing International, Inc.	217	215	27,088	142	140	193,735	6/94	
Corcom, Inc.	218	213	26,726	231	220	14,816	12/94	
Aasche Transportation Services	219	*	26,319	220	*	25,113	12/94	
Chicago Rivet & Machine Co.	220	218	23,013	225	218	19,923	12/94	
Ampace Corporation	221	*	21,553	223	*	22,490	12/94	g
Growth Environmental, Inc.	222	230	19,920	215	228	27,328	12/94	
Circle Fine Art Corporation	223	217	19,170	218	209	26,588	9/94	f
Anicom, Inc.	224	*	17,866	238	*	6,040	12/94	h
Telular Corporation	225	234	17,734	188	224	61,242	9/94	
Enviropur Waste Refining & Tech.	226	228	17,294	205	219	35,163	9/94	
General Employment Enterprises	227	224	14,212	240	234	4,046	9/94	
Eagle Finance Corp.	228	*	13,711	181	*	71,245	12/94	
PC Quote, Inc.	229	222	12,904	236	232	9,072	12/94	
The Goodheart-Willcox Co.	230	223	12,641	235	230	11,136	4/94	
Bio-logic Systems Corp.	231	225	12,073	232	226	13,500	2/95	
First Merchants Acceptance Corp.	232	*	10,048	193	*	55,451	5/94	h
Dyna Group International, Inc.	233	226	10,025	239	233	6,040	12/94	
Fort Dearborn Income Securities	234	227	9,840	162	152	133,661	9/94	k
FluoroScan Imaging Systems, Inc.	235	*	9,171	237	*	8,173	12/94	
UNIMED Pharmaceuticals, Inc.	236	232	7,992	234	227	11,805	12/94	
Baker, Fentress & Company	237	233	6,933	97	86	462,540	12/94	l
Pioneer Railcorp	238	*	6,367	233	*	12,296	12/94	
Classics Int'l Entertainment, Inc.	239	*	5,387	241	*	3,387	12/94	
Prime Capital Corporation	240	229	4,678	216	229	26,941	12/94	
Heartland Partners, L.P.	241	231	3,498	212	205	30,243	12/94	

Footnotes

*	New listing	g	Pro forma assets
a	Equipment revenues	h	Pro forma sales/revenues
b	Electric operating revenues	i	10-month data
c	Unaudited pro forma sales/revenues	j	Contract revenues
d	Unaudited pro forma assets	k	Net income
e	Unaudited sales/revenues	l	Net investment income
f	Unaudited assets		

Bank and Savings Institution Holding Companies

Company	Rank by Operating Income '94	'93	Operating Income (000 Omitted)	Rank by Assets '94	'93	Assets (000 Omitted)	Year End Figures Used
First Chicago Corporation	1	1	$5,094,600	1	1	$65,900,000	12/94
Northern Trust Corporation	2	3	1,478,500	2	3	18,561,600	12/94
Magna Group, Inc.	3	4	337,064	3	4	4,638,502	12/94
St. Paul Bancorp, Inc.	4	5	283,033	4	5	4,131,537	12/94
First Midwest Bancorp, Inc.	5	6	215,645	5	6	2,875,101	12/94
AMCORE Financial, Inc.	6	7	158,136	6	11	1,984,629	12/94
Cole Taylor Financial Group, Inc.	7	13	143,771	10	10	1,813,614	12/94
River Forest Bancorp, Inc.	8	14	127,776	8	14	1,889,455	12/94
MAF Bancorp, Inc.	9	8	123,426	13	12	1,586,334	6/94
First Evergreen Corporation	10	9	121,539	9	8	1,872,035	12/94
Firstbank of Illinois Co.	11	10	120,029	11	13	1,753,061	12/94
Bell Bancorp, Inc.	12	12	117,961	7	7	1,907,459	3/95
Standard Financial, Inc.	13	*	104,682	12	*	1,739,363	12/94
N.S. Bancorp, Inc.	14	15	78,262	14	16	1,254,011	12/94
Heritage Financial Services, Inc.	15	18	66,645	15	18	952,850	12/94
First Busey Corporation	16	20	55,132	17	21	728,459	12/94
Deerbank Corporation	17	21	50,517	16	19	765,886	9/94
First National Bancorp, Inc.	18	22	45,908	18	22	692,642	12/94
First Oak Brook Bancshares, Inc.	19	23	45,305	21	23	634,705	12/94
Premier Financial Services, Inc.	20	27	43,213	22	24	620,504	12/94
Hinsdale Financial Corporation	21	26	42,110	20	25	643,289	9/94
Merchants Bancorp, Inc.	22	28	39,797	26	28	496,289	12/94
Calumet Bancorp, Inc.	23	24	39,202	25	27	504,026	12/94
Pinnacle Banc Group, Inc.	24	19	38,537	19	20	684,892	12/94
Liberty Bancorp, Inc.	25	25	38,016	23	26	595,444	12/94
TODAY'S BANCORP, INC.	26	29	35,502	27	29	489,366	12/94
Northern States Financial Corp.	27	31	30,139	28	30	411,635	12/94
Princeton National Bancorp, Inc.	28	33	28,902	29	32	400,531	12/94
Avondale Financial Corp.	29	*	27,569	24	*	539,703	3/95 a
Southwest Bancshares, Inc.	30	32	26,125	30	34	350,400	12/94
HomeCorp, Inc.	31	34	23,601	32	33	330,412	12/94
Fidelity Bancorp, Inc.	32	*	22,284	31	*	338,082	9/94
SuburbFed Financial Corp.	33	36	22,064	33	36	323,257	12/94
Westco Bancorp, Inc.	34	35	21,651	34	35	299,571	12/94
Financial Security Corp.	35	37	19,884	35	37	272,362	12/94
First Bankers Trustshares, Inc.	36	38	11,198	36	38	158,404	12/94
North Bancshares, Inc.	37	40	6,060	37	40	106,959	12/94
First Financial Bancorp, Inc.	38	41	5,079	38	41	71,165	12/94

* New listing
a For Avondale Federal Savings Bank

Commercial Banking Companies

Company	Rank by Total Assets '94	Rank by Total Assets '93	Total Assets (000 Omitted)	Rank by Total Deposits '94	Rank by Total Deposits '93	Total Deposits (000 Omitted)	Year End Figures Used
The First National Bank of Chicago	1	1	$42,542,932	1	1	$25,737,503	12/94
Bank of America Illinois	2	2	18,000,000	2	2	10,189,000	12/94
The Northern Trust Company	3	3	14,735,500	3	3	8,848,300	12/94
Harris Trust and Savings Bank	4	4	11,944,330	5	4	7,015,566	12/94
LaSalle National Bank	5	5	10,268,687	4	5	7,065,919	12/94
American National Bank & Trust Co.	6	6	6,236,005	6	6	5,159,046	12/94
NBD Bank	7	7	4,879,727	7	7	3,583,248	12/94
First Midwest Bank, N.A.	8	*	2,543,398	8	*	2,001,840	12/94 a
Old Kent Bank	9	11	1,902,924	10	10	1,515,334	12/94
First National Bank of Evergreen Pk.	10	8	1,871,977	9	8	1,695,417	12/94
Bank One, Chicago, NA	11	9	1,786,123	12	9	1,268,887	12/94
Cole Taylor Bank	12	10	1,720,050	11	11	1,293,411	12/94
First of America Bank—Illinois, N.A.	13	14	1,642,192	14	13	1,129,600	12/94
Comerica Bank—Illinois	14	12	1,503,932	15	12	1,014,917	12/94
LaSalle Northwest National Bank	15	13	1,486,097	13	14	1,207,447	12/94
First Bank National Association	16	19	1,383,213	16	23	887,269	12/94
LaSalle Bank Lake View	17	16	1,025,745	18	20	729,408	12/94
Heritage Bank	18	18	945,708	17	16	823,835	12/94
Marquette National Bank	19	21	785,597	20	19	647,350	12/94
NBD Skokie Bank, N.A.	20	22	782,961	24	25	423,591	12/94
Columbia National Bank of Chicago	21	20	765,145	21	21	627,665	12/94
The Mid-City National Bank of Chgo	22	23	726,421	19	18	661,390	12/94
Northern Trust Bank/Lk Forest N.A.	23	24	676,579	23	22	509,355	12/94
Oak Brook Bank	24	*	629,686	22	*	513,729	12/94
Northern Trust Bank/O'Hare N.A.	25	25	502,186	25	24	423,129	12/94

* New listing
a Unaudited pro forma

Savings Institutions

Company	Rank by Total Assets '94	Rank by Total Assets '93	Total Assets (000 Omitted)	Rank by Total Svgs. Accounts '94	Rank by Total Svgs. Accounts '93	Total Svgs. Accounts (000 Omitted)	Year End Figures Used
Citibank, Federal Savings Bank	1	1	$13,523,542	1	1	$10,302,589	12/94
LaSalle Talman Bank, FSB	2	2	6,923,444	2	2	5,203,756	12/94
St. Paul Federal Bank For Savings	3	3	4,092,136	3	3	3,237,632	12/94
LaSalle Cragin Bank FSB	4	4	3,236,389	4	4	2,096,111	12/94
Bell Federal Savings and Loan Assn.	5	5	1,871,242	5	5	1,519,220	3/95
Standard Federal Bank for savings	6	7	1,660,037	6	6	1,393,274	12/94
Mid America Federal Savings Bank	7	6	1,573,536	7	7	1,299,374	6/94

Company Changes from Last Year's Edition

New Listings in 1995-96 Edition

Aasche Transportation Services, Inc.
Ampace Corporation
Anicom, Inc.
Avondale Financial Corp.
Bell & Howell Holdings Company
Boise Cascade Office Products Corporation
Classics International Entertainment, Inc.
Delphi Information Systems, Inc.
Duff & Phelps Credit Rating Co.
Eagle Finance Corp.
Falcon Building Products, Inc.
Fidelity Bancorp, Inc.

First Merchants Acceptance Corporation
First Midwest Bank, N.A. (new)
The Florsheim Shoe Company
FluoroScan Imaging Systems, Inc.
Oak Brook Bank
Pioneer Railcorp
Standard Financial, Inc.
Teltrend Inc.
Truck Components Inc.
Universal Automotive Industries, Inc.
Zeigler Coal Holding Company

Company Name Changes

American Colloid Company *to* AMCOL International Corporation
Continental Bank *to* Bank of America Illinois
Filtertek, Inc. *to* Schawk, Inc.
First of America Bank—Northeast Illinois, N.A. *to* First of America Bank—Illinois, N.A.
Foote, Cone & Belding Communications, Inc. *to* True North Communications Inc.
IMC Fertilizer Group, Inc. *to* IMC Global Inc.
Northwest Illinois Bancorp, Inc. *to* TODAY'S BANCORP, INC.
Northwestern Savings & Loan Association *to* Northwestern Savings Bank
U.S. Robotics, Inc. *to* U.S. Robotics Corporation

Companies No Longer Listed

AmeriFed Financial Corp.—Acquired by NBD Bancorp, Inc.
Amity Bancshares, Inc.—Acquired by Advantage Bancorp
Bell Sports Corp.—Moved headquarters to Scottsdale, Arizona
Chemical Waste Management, Inc.—Merged into WMX Technologies, Inc.
Chicago and North Western Transportation Company—Acquired by Union Pacific Corp.
Commonwealth Industries Corporation—No established trading market
Continental Bank Corporation—Merged into BankAmerica Corp.
Dauphin Technology, Inc.—Insufficient information
First Colonial Bankshares Corporation—Acquired by Firstar Corporation
First Midwest Bank/Illinois, N.A.—Merged into First Midwest Bank, N.A. (new)
First Midwest Bank, N.A. (old)—Merged into First Midwest Bank, N.A. (new)
FirstRock Bancorp, Inc.—Acquired by First Financial Corp.
Health o meter Products, Inc.—Moved headquarters to Bedford Heights, Ohio
Katy Industries, Inc.—Moved headquarters to Englewood, Colorado
Morgan Products Ltd.—Moved headquarters to Williamsburg, Virginia
Revell-Monogram, Inc.—Acquired by Hallmark Cards Inc.
Suburban Bancorp, Inc.—Acquired by Harris Bankcorp, Inc.
F.A. Tucker Group, Inc.—Insufficient information
Warehouse Club, Inc.—Insufficient information